FAMINE IN WEST CORK

THE MIZEN PENINSULA
LAND AND PEOPLE, 1800–1852

A local study of pre-famine and famine Ireland

The Mizen Peninsula: Parishes; Kilmoe (Goleen),Schull, Kilcoe/Aughadown

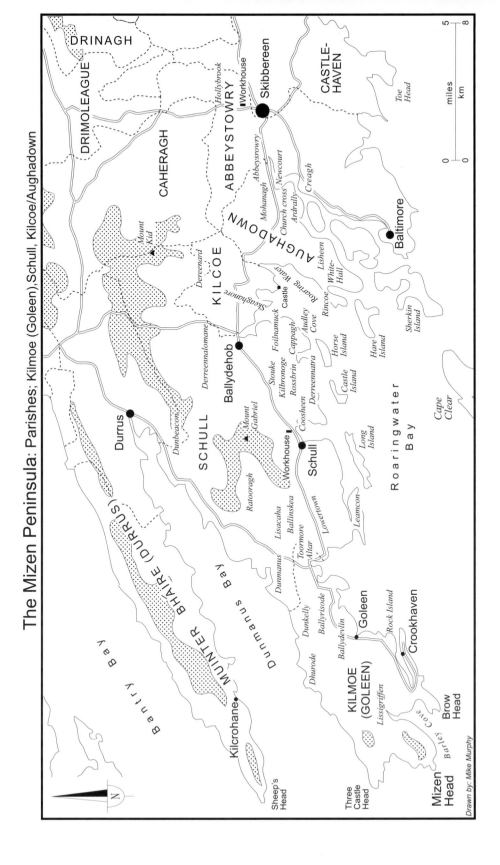

Drawn by: Mike Murphy

FAMINE IN WEST CORK

THE MIZEN PENINSULA
LAND AND PEOPLE, 1800–1852

A local study of pre-famine and famine Ireland

PATRICK HICKEY

ⴰ ERCIER PRESS

MERCIER PRESS
Douglas Village, Cork
and
16 Hume Street, Dublin 2

Trade enquiries to COLUMBA MERCIER DISTRIBUTION,
55a Spruce Avenue, Stillorgan Industrial Park, Blackrock, Dublin

© P. Hickey, 2002

ISBN: 1 85635 388 5

10 9 8 7 6 5 4 3 2 1

TO THE LOCAL HISTORIANS IN EVERY PARISH IN THE COUNTRY

Printed in Ireland by Colour Books Ltd.

CONTENTS

List of Illustrations

LIST OF FIGURES

LIST OF TABLES

ACKNOWLEDGEMENTS

My first thanks are due to John A. Murphy as the supervisor of my MA dissertation (1980). James Coombes, PP, Castlehaven, T. J. Walsh, PP, Blackrock and my sister, Helen Clynch gave me valuable assistance at the time.

As regards the present book, Cormac Ó Gráda, Professor of Economics, University College, Dublin, Vincent Comerford, Professor of History, National University of Ireland, Maynooth, Tim Cadogan, Executive Librarian, Cork County Library, Sr Evelyn Bolster, St Maries of the Isle, Liam Leader, PP, St Patrick's, John Crowley, Department of Geography, UCC and Frank Connolly of Glanmire read earlier drafts. John Shorten, OFM Cap., Gurranabraher, Roibeárd Ó hÚrdail, formerly of the Department of Irish, University College, Cork and James S. Donnelly, Jr, Professor of History, University of Wisconsin-Madison, read recent drafts. Ó hÚrdail also elucidated some words in the Irish language. I have valued both their criticism and their words of encouragement. I have been particularly influenced by Donnelly's *The land and the people of nineteenth-century Cork*. Liz Willows proof-read the manuscript. I received sources from Éamon Lankford, Douglas, Mícheál Ó Mainín, PP, Millstreet and Thomas Davitt, CM, Rome in relation to Chapter XI. Jeremiah Cremin, CC, the Glen, was always available with his skills in word-processing and graphics. Rev. Tom Hayes, Director of Communications, Cork and Ross, and Mercier Press designed the cover. Michael Murphy, Department of Geography, UCC, drew the map. I also wish to thank the staffs of the Cork County Library, Cork City Library, the Boole Library, UCC, the Cork Archives Institute, the National Archives and the National Library.

The Royal Irish Academy granted me permission to publish 'Dr Traill's Potato Pit' and 'Thomas Swanton, *Rabhadh*'. The Geological Survey allowed me to print 'Horse Island, Plan and Elevation, 1857'. Lee Snodgrass, Ballydehob, gave me 'Schull Workhouse, 1978, Aerial view'. 'Captain William Thomas (1807–1890)' is presented courtesy of Charles Thomas, Cornwall, and 'Ellen Harrigan Lucey' comes courtesy of William King, California. I obtained 'Ballinskea, 1826', from *Mizen Journal*, courtesy of J. Coombes. Carcanet Press allowed me to cite from Eavan Boland's 'The Famine Road'. Simon Campbell gave me permission to quote from Joseph Campbell's 'The silence of unlaboured fields' as did the Blackstaff Press to quote John Hewitt's 'The Scar'. The photograph of Dr Traill and his wife, Anne, is courtesy of Thames and Hudson. Fearghal MacAmhlaoibh from Dingle gave me the photograph of James Goodman. Parishes in West Cork, Drinagh Co-operative Society, Drinagh Bowling Committee and some friends provided financial aid towards the publication of this book. My final word of thanks goes to Mary Feehan, editor of Mercier Press, and also to its staff especially Eimear O'Herlihy and Claire McVeigh.

FOREWORD

This book, *Famine in West Cork: the Mizen Peninsula, Land and People, 1800–1852: a local study of pre-famine and famine Ireland,* is based on an earlier work of mine, 'A study of four peninsular parishes in West Cork, 1796–1855', MA, UCC (1980). It was written under the supervision of John A. Murphy, then Professor of History. That dissertation, however, has been completely rewritten and substantially changed to take account of research done by myself and others in the intervening twenty years and particularly in the 1990s when the 150th anniversary of the famine was marked. The parishes being studied are the medieval ones of Kilmoe, Schull, Kilcoe and Aughadown, they roughly covered the Mizen Peninsula. Kilmoe and Schull belonged to the Diocese of Cork while Kilcoe and Aughadown belonged to the Diocese of Ross and had long been amalgamated. In 1838 all of these parishes became part of the Union of Skibbereen. Since Skibbereen now became the union town an eagle eye has been kept on it. This union is situated in the Barony of West Carbery. 'The district' or 'the parishes' refer to the Mizen Peninsula in particular rather than to West Cork in general.

Translations from the Irish are my own. The original spelling is retained. Catholic clergymen are referred to as 'Fr' and Church of Ireland clergymen as 'Rev'. Italics belong to the original texts. Money is expressed in pre-decimal and of course pre-euro terms. There were twenty shillings (20s) in a pound (£), twelve pence (12d) in a shilling, two half pence (1/2d) or four farthings (1/4d) in penny. So there were 240 old pennies (d) in a pound; 2.4d equals one penny (1p) in decimal currency. One pound is equal to 1.27 euro.

As Mícheál Óg Ó Longáin of Carrig na bhFear or Glanmire would conclude, *Oret pro Scriptore Lector*, 'Let the Reader pray for the Writer'.

PATRICK HICKEY
July 2002
Timoleague
(Tigh Molaige)
West Cork

I

FROM THE BRONZE AGE TO 1800:
A BRIEF OUTLINE

Ó Mathghamhna an Iarthair agus Tighearna Cineál mBéice,
Beirt do bhí d'thighearnais 's anois ag iarraidh déirce.

O'Mahony of the West and Lord of the Clan of Bec,
Two who once were lordly and now are begging alms.

BARD OF THE O'MAHONYS

The terror was great.
The moment a redcoat appeared, everybody fled.

GEN. JOHN MOORE, 1798

The Mizen Peninsula was inhabited in the Bronze Age by the people who made the wedge-shaped megalithic tomb at Altar between Schull and Goleen. Copper was mined on the eastern side of Mount Gabriel and at Derrycarhoon near Ballydehob.[1] The next people to arrive were the Celts. The O'Driscolls held sway until they were defeated by the O'Mahonys at the battle of Morrahin in Kilcoe, west of Skibbereen in 747 AD. The O'Mahonys had originally come from a district now known as Templemartin near Bandon and from there expanded into the Mizen Peninsula. The O'Driscolls continued to hold the parishes of Kilcoe and Aughadown; their chief castle was at Baltimore.[2]

The O'Mahonys remained in peaceful possession until the Norman invasion. A Norman, Richard de Carew, seized Long Island near Schull but it was later returned as part of a marriage settlement.[3] The Norman threat prompted the O'Mahonys and the O'Driscolls to build many strong castles. By the middle of the fifteenth century the O'Mahonys had castles at Crookhaven, Dún Locha or Three Castles, Ballydevin, Ardintenant, Leamcon, Rossbrin, Dunmanus and Dunbeacon.[4] The McCarthys who had taken the Kilcoe peninsula from the O'Driscolls built Kilcoe castle. The O'Driscolls also built many castles including Rincolisky in Aughadown and *Dún an Óir* on Cape Clear.[5]

A glimpse at the state of the Church on the eve of the Reformation is obtained from the case of Donogh Coghlan, vicar of Kilmoe. He was reported to Rome in 1458 for having 'neglected the cure of his parishioners on account of his ignorance of letters'.[6]

Disaster befell the O'Mahonys when they joined the Desmond Rebellion in 1579. The lands of Conor O'Mahony of Castlemahon near Bandon were confiscated and granted by Queen Elizabeth to Phane Becher of London. Rossbrin castle was captured by the President of Munster, Sir John Perrott, and granted to a gallowglass or mercenary soldier named McSweeney.[7] The O'Driscolls, however, remained loyal to the crown.

13

When the great Earl of Tyrone, Hugh O'Neill, visited Munster in 1600 to enlist the help of the local septs, the O'Mahonys met him at Inniscarra near Cork and joined the rebellion. The arrival of the Spaniards at Kinsale and Castlehaven encouraged the O'Driscolls to rebel under their chieftain, Sir Fineen O'Driscoll. Therefore both they and the O'Mahonys were first to suffer the consequences of the disaster at Kinsale in 1601. Carew and his army devastated the countryside on their march westwards to Dunboy Castle. They captured the O'Driscoll castles including Rincoe but were in too much haste towards Dunboy to attack Kilcoe, Leamcon or Dunmanus. A party of Carew's soldiers raided Dunmanus Castle and took it while Dunboy was still under siege. After its fall the victors seized Leamcon and Kilcoe. West Cork was 'pacified'.

July 1602 saw an event which could be described as 'The Flight of the Earls of the Mizen Peninsula'. Conor O'Driscoll, eldest son and heir of Sir Fineen, Conor O'Mahony of Leamcon and Dermot McCarthy of Kilcoe sailed for Spain in the company of the Jesuit, Fr Archer, a famous supporter of Hugh O'Neill. This was five years before the Flight of the Earls of Ulster.[8]

Most of the O'Mahony lands were eventually granted to an English planter, William Hull, who like Sir Walter Raleigh came from Devonshire. Hull became Vice Admiral of Munster but that did not prevent him from engaging in some smuggling with pirates. The main merchandise was tobacco, wine and brandy. Nevertheless this gamekeeper turned poacher could suddenly turn back into gamekeeper. In 1625 he captured eight pirates on Long Island and sent them to Cork where they were hanged.[9] Hull was connected by two marriages to Richard Boyle, the Great Earl of Cork. Boyle bought land around Dunbeacon from a bankrupt O'Mahony chieftain and it eventually passed to William Hull. Dún Locha castle and the lands around it fell into the acquisitive hands of the Earl of Cork but he granted certain rights to them to a client of his named Coghlan. By now some members of this family were Protestant.[10] The Earl of Cork also gained possession of the O'Mahony lands in the eastern side of Schull parish on which he founded the town of Ballydehob. He obtained a charter from King James I in 1620.[11]

The Earl of Cork also acquired Church properties. The parishes of Schull and Kilmoe were attached to the College of Youghal founded in 1464 by the Earl of Desmond. This college and all its properties passed from Sir Walter Raleigh to the Earl of Cork by a patent from King James I in 1604. Boyle held them until 1634 when the Lord Deputy, Thomas Wentworth, wrested them from him.[12]

William Hull founded the town of Schull and leased land to another planter, Thomas Roper, on which the latter built the town of Crookhaven. Hull reclaimed the land around Leamcon and established a pilchard fishery in partnership with Boyle, the Earl of Cork.[13]

The lands of the O'Driscolls of Castlehaven and those of the O'Mahonys of Rossbrin were granted to George, Lord Audley, a member of an aristocratic English family. He had been wounded at the Battle of Kinsale and was created

Earl of Castlehaven.[14] Sir Fineen O'Driscoll surrendered so promptly after Kinsale that his castles were restored to him on condition of his paying £500. He had to borrow this and so made a fateful deal with two planters, William Coppinger and Thomas Cook, to whom he mortgaged most of his lands. A complicated legal dispute arose among all three. In the end Sir Fineen lost his lands and died in poverty at Lough Ine near Skibbereen around 1629; he is remembered in song as 'Fineen the Rover'. Walter Coppinger thus gained the castles of Kilcoe and Rincoe and the lands attached to them.[15]

When the 1641 Rebellion broke out the O'Mahonys plundered Crookhaven, Leamcon, Schull and Dunbeacon. The rector of Kilmoe, Dermot Coghlan 'was driven to England by the wars and died in that kingdom'.[16] William Hull and his family barely escaped to Bandon. The rebels whom this planter ironically called 'robbers' destroyed his fish palaces or curing houses and took his cattle. He claimed losses to the value of £15,000.[17] The O'Driscolls also attacked the planters. Another planter, Lord Audley, Earl of Castlehaven, was Commander-in-Chief of the royalist forces in Ireland. At the end of the Cromwellian wars the Irish 'papist rebels' were again defeated and what lands still remained to them were forfeit.[18]

A synoptic view of the Cromwellian Plantation in the Mizen Peninsula can be obtained by a glance across the broad folios of the *Book of Survey and Distribution*. In Aughadown parish the Royalist Coppingers lost their lands, but mostly to other members of the family who had managed to remain in the favour of the Cromwellians. Some Coppinger lands passed to Colonel Richard Townsend. He had been sent to Ireland by the English Parliament and fought under Lord Inchiquin at the Battle of Knocknanoss near Mallow in 1647. He later handed the keys of Cork city to Cromwell. This Cromwellian was the ancestor of the Townsend family that soon spread into the Mizen Peninsula; its principal seat was Castletownshend near Skibbereen. The last McCarthy of Kilcoe was now pushed out into the barren Mannin Island in Roaringwater Bay.

In the parish of Schull, Dunbeacon Castle and lands passed from the O'Mahonys to Richard Townsend. They also lost more lands to William Hull. But the crafty Lord Audley succeeded in holding on to his lands at Rossbrin. Sir William Petty, author of the *Down Survey*, provided himself with 6,479 acres of land in Kilmoe parish. The Earl of Cork also took many acres in this parish.[19]

Thus the Cromwellian Plantation opened the way for many more planters to come to the peninsula. The most important of these was Henry Becher who was in Aughadown by 1659.[20] He was a grandson of Phane Becher who had received Bandon from Queen Elizabeth. It was he who built Aughadown House, a castellated mansion.[21]

When the war broke out between the two kings, James II and William of Orange, the O'Mahonys and the O'Driscolls were Jacobites while the planters for the most part took the Williamite side. The O'Driscolls burned Aughadown House.[22] Colonel Thomas Becher, a son of its owner, was *aide-de-camp* to King William at the Battle of the Boyne, 1690, during which the king gave him his gold watch.[23] The Coppingers, still Jacobite and Catholic, lost their lands to the Townsends. One of the latter, Samuel, a grandson of the Cromwellian colonel, obtained Rincoe castle and the lands around it on which he built a Georgian house at Whitehall.[24] The O'Mahonys and the O'Driscolls lost what lands still remained to them. According to tradition two O'Mahony chieftains met at an assembly. The occasion moved a bard of the sept to compose a lament of which only the first two lines survive and are cited in the epigraph on p. 13.[25]

The Somervilles were the most important planter family after the Bechers and the Townsends. William Somerville was a Church of Scotland minister who fled persecution in Scotland in 1692 and came to Ireland. A son of his, Thomas, became rector of Myross and Castlehaven. Castletownshend and Castlehaven became the principal seats of the family. One of its branches was the Somerville family of 'The Prairie', near Toormore in Kilmoe parish.[26]

Not all of the planters were soldiers, of course; some of them were merchants, for example, the Flemings who came from Glasgow. One of these, Lionel Fleming, came to Skibbereen in the seventeenth century as a merchant and land agent to the Bechers. A son of his, Stephen, married a daughter of Henry Becher of Aughadown. A grandson of Stephen, named Lionel, bought the townland of Ballydevlin near Goleen from William Richard Hull. Lionel also bought New Court near Skibbereen from the Tonsons. He had a son, Lionel John, who in 1819 married Eliza Townsend, daughter of Horace Townsend of Derry near Rosscarbery. The young couple went to live in Ballydevlin until the elder Lionel died in 1837; they then returned to New Court.[27]

The Bernards were English; Francis Bernard received Castlemahon near Bandon from Phane Becher. In 1715 Castlemahon was re-named Castle Bernard. One of the descendants of this Francis Bernard, also called Francis Bernard, became Earl of Bandon in 1800.[28] He bought land from R. H. H. Becher of Hollybrook near Skibbereen. Hollybrook had been bought in 1751 by his grandfather, John Becher, who was a direct descendant of Henry Becher of Aughadown.[29]

The Hungerfords were an aristocratic English family one of whose sons fought at Agincourt in 1415. Captain Thomas Hungerford was a Cromwellian soldier who came to Ireland in 1647. His descendants settled in The Island near Clonakilty. One of them, Richard, married a sister of R. H. H. Becher and they received Becher land at Ballyrisode in Kilmoe parish. They built Ballyrisode House; one of their sons and heir to this property was Richard Becher Hungerford.[30]

The Swantons originally came from Swanton in Norfolk. They arrived in Ireland in the seventeenth century. By the end of the following century they were the leading family in Ballydehob which was then sometimes called Swantonstown.[31]

While most of the planters came from England or Scotland a few came from the continent. The Notters of Crookhaven were a German family that arrived in the middle of the seventeenth century. They may have been refugees from the Thirty Years War (1618–48).[32] Other families were of Huguenot origin, such as Camiers, Dukelows (duClos) and Jermyns (Germains).[33]

THE EIGHTEENTH CENTURY

The seventeenth century had been a period of much violence and destruction. In 1700 the Church of Ireland Bishop of Cork, Cloyne and Ross, Dive Downs, found all the churches of the Mizen Peninsula in ruins. Crookhaven church was built by his successor, Bishop Browne. The rector of Schull, Paul Limrick, constructed the glebe house in Schull in 1727.[34] The parish priest of Kilmoe, Tieghe Coghlan, was virtually banished to Long Island which was in the parish of Schull. The parish priest of Schull, Daniel Carty, was living in the remote townland of Derreennalomane. The pastor of Aughadown and Kilcoe had his abode just outside his own parishes at Coolbawn in the Caheragh parish.[35]

Many priests from the continent were smuggled into Crookhaven.[36] Others were landed at Coosheen near Schull. For example, one day in September 1708 two friars were met by a Cian O'Mahony of the neighbouring parish of Muintir Bháire or Durrus. He and his comrades who carried arms gave hospitality to these illegal immigrants and escorted them to Cork.[37]

In 1714 six O'Mahony brothers who had fought in the Williamite Wars were now 'out' as Rapparees and causing 'disturbances' around Crookhaven. Troops came from Bantry to deal with them but the outlaws escaped to sea.[38] Around 1730 Richard Tonson of New Court, Skibbereen, was appointed collector of revenue for the port of Baltimore which included Bantry Bay. He attempted to prevent some O'Sullivans of Castletownbere from smuggling but one of his men was killed and he himself was lucky to escape the same fate. So he officially proclaimed these smugglers 'to be torys and robbers of the Popish religion out in arms and upon their keeping'.[39] Although the Mizen Peninsula was indeed remote none of its Gaelic chieftains survived into the eighteenth century as a landlord of any standing, unlike the O'Connells of Derrynane or the clan of *Máire Bhuí Ní Laoghaire* of *Uíbh Laoghaire* near Macroom, for instance; the conquests and confiscations had been too thorough. The only hope of the dispossessed now lay in a restoration of the Stuarts. Dermot O'Mahony of Skeaghanore near Ballydehob, 'Irish Papist', had forfeited 1,240 acres of land at the time of the Cromwellian Plantation. In 1731 his son, Kean, left to his children in his will 'the Irish interest I had in this ploughland [of Ardura] if it ever be restored'.[40] He thus bequeathed a hope doomed to disappointment. This must have been keenly felt when Charles Edward Stuart, the Young Pretender, and his clansmen were crushed at Culloden Moor in 1746. In Ireland there was general peace and relief at least from dungeon, fire and sword but not, however, from famine.

In December 1739 it was 'the hard frost' which caused the greatest suffering in the country. According to Francis Tuckey's *Cork Remembrancer*, the river Lee which flows through Cork city was frozen over; tents were fixed on it and amusements carried on. Nevertheless there was great scarcity the following summer and many of the poor perished although they were fed at the 'public mess'. A large pit was dug in Shandon churchyard where several hundreds were buried.[41] The climate of the Mizen Peninsula is relatively mild owing to the Gulf Stream yet its people must have suffered from the Great Frost of 1739–40 and from the resulting famine as they did in other parts of West Cork. In April 1741 Sir Richard Cox of Dunmanway wrote:

> Mortality is now no longer heeded; the instances are so frequent. And burying the dead, which used to be one of the most religious acts among the Irish, is now become a burden: so I am daily forced to make those who remain carry dead bodies to the church-yards, which would otherwise rot in the open air. The dreadfullest civil war or most raging plague never destroyed so many as this season.[42]

West Cork seems to have recovered rather quickly from this calamity. There was, indeed, a certain prosperity as witnessed by Richard Pococke the English clergyman and famous traveller who was appointed Church of Ireland Bishop of Ossory in 1756. He included West Cork in his tour two years later and found 'every spot sown with oats, English barley or potatoes, which they are forced to cultivate for their support'. This is the first reference to the potato and one senses also that the population was increasing. Although Pococke described Crookhaven as a 'poor town' he found that it had a good market for black cattle, wild fowl, fish, lobsters and crayfish because frequent visits from the British Navy 'raised all provisions to an exorbitant price'. 'In the season the people live on fish,' he remarked. Pococke regarded Ballydehob as 'one of the most romantic situations' he had ever seen. At Roaring Water in Kilcoe a mill was working and he watched boats laden with turf six or seven feet above gunwale on their way to markets in Kinsale and Cork. He could see only one serious problem:

> It is a great misfortune that there is no law or justice in this country. For they cannot execute a caption … A Custom Officer can hardly live among them. To the west of Kinsale, they have a term of 'hiding an officer', which is knocking in the head and putting him under a turf: there are many instances of officers never heard of. But they are a most hospitable, generous people in their own houses.[43]

A certain economic well-being was in evidence whatever about political or religious matters. Such prosperity was by no means confined to Protestants; Catholics also began to share in it as the century progressed. The result was the emergence of a Catholic middle class especially in the cities and towns.[44]

In the country however the peasants were deprived of their ancient grazing rights to common land. This was now being enclosed by planters who were becoming landlords in a metamorphosis similar to that in which Rapparees were becoming Whiteboys. In 1761 groups of men assembled at night to level fences which had been erected on commons. They were thus called 'Levellers' or 'Whiteboys' from the white shirts they wore so that they could identify one another more easily in the dark. They resisted the landlords on questions of rent and tenure and took measures – including murder – to prevent people from taking land once held by evicted tenants. George Cornewall Lewis later observed:

> The Whiteboy association may be considered as a vast trades' union for the protection of the Irish peasant; the object being, not to regulate the rate of wages, or the hours of work, but to keep the actual occupant in possession of his land, and in general to regulate the relation of landlord and tenant for the benefit of the latter.[45]

The Whiteboys also wanted to regulate the relationship with priest and parson to their own benefit. The tithes were an ancient tax mainly for the benefit of the Church. In Chaucer's *Canterbury Tales* it was said of a particular priest that the people 'ful loth were him to cursen for his tythes', but this good man seems to have been an exception. In post-Reformation Ireland the Catholic majority was forced to pay tithes to the Church of the small Protestant minority. This made Catholics far less loath to curse the parson for his tithes but there were times too when they were scarcely less loath to curse the priest for his dues.

Unlike the Rapparees who were usually on the run, this new sort of outlaws were organised into oath-bound secret societies within the local community itself. This rendered their suppression a far more difficult task for the government for which they were the cockle among the wheat. In 1765 the Irish Parliament passed an act imposing the death penalty for several Whiteboy activities and some Whiteboys were hanged. In one case a priest, Nicholas Sheehy from County Tipperary, who was accused of being involved in one of their conspiracies, was also hanged. There was another wave of Whiteboy outbreaks in the 1770s. A magistrate who had taken part in the prosecution of Fr Sheehy was murdered and two men convicted for the deed were hanged in Clonmel in 1776.[46] Arthur Young who was travelling in the south of Ireland at the time noted that these and other hangings made the country more tranquil but that the evils connected with the tithe system continued unabated.[47] The Whiteboys hoped for a French invasion because the French fleet was in the English Channel in 1779. But the Capuchin priest, Arthur O'Leary, born near Dunmanway, warned the people not to support the invaders if they should land because 'the common people are never interested in the change of government. They may change their masters; but they will not change their burdens. The rich will be rich. The poor will be poor.'[48]

The next serious wave of Whiteboy violence broke out in Munster towards the end of 1785 and West Cork was no exception. The priests often preached against such incidents. In July 1785 the Whiteboys 'used the priests barbarously' at Drimoleague and Caheragh and drove the parish priest of Caheragh out of his parish. Early one morning they broke into the house of the parish priest of Rath near Baltimore, 'brought him out naked in the midst of the wind and rain' and compelled him to take the Whiteboy oath. *Finn's Leinster Journal* reported that in July 1786 these Whiteboys:

> called on the vicar (Joseph Wright), whom they threatened to destroy … They as-

sembled in the parish of Aughadown and proceeded to the glebe house and pursued the Popish priest (Daniel Burke) who fled for refuge to a neighbour's house, and on not reaching him, broke his windows and doors and almost tore down his house. They demanded him from the person with whom he had taken refuge, and he was forced to flee to some other place for safety.[49]

Early in the century the priests had been on the run from the lawmen but now they had to flee from the outlaws. The Catholic Church was at a low ebb. Henry Grattan declared that 'the influence of the Pope, the priest and the Pretender were at an end'.[50] On the same day as the Whiteboys assembled in Aughadown, the 'delegates of the Munster peasantry' met and protested against the 'avarice of the priesthood, and the intolerable exactions of the tithe-farmers'. Accordingly these 'delegates' swore not to pay priest or proctor any more than certain fixed rates.[51]

The Catholics who had to pay both tithes and dues were not the only ones to resist the payment of tithes; many Protestants did likewise. Even Dr Woodward, the Church of Ireland Bishop of Cloyne, admitted that some Protestant gentlemen 'skilled in law' were instigating the farmers to resist the tithes.[52] The bishop blamed the Catholics to such an extent that he provoked the following retort from Fr Arthur O'Leary:

> Had he as pastor, gone forth among his flock, he would have discovered several of his own sheep among the speckled flock of insurgents and not confine them solely to a *Popish mob*. Were they not Protestants who proposed the oaths to the congregation at Clonakilty? Were they not Protestants who overran the parishes of Aughadown, Skibbereen, etc.? The most respectable criminals, *if a criminal can be respectable*, who were arraigned before the Judges on the Munster circuit were Protestants.[53]

This Whiteboy violence prompted the government to pass two acts, one in 1787 and the other in 1792, which empowered the Grand Juries to appoint constables for each barony.[54]

The Whiteboys and other such societies of the period 1760–90 had their origin mainly in economic grievances and were anti-clerical, against both Catholic and Protestant clergy alike. Nevertheless the ruling classes tended to exploit the religious differences in the various movements. The result was that such agrarian movements were inclined to become sectarian especially in Ulster where the Catholic Defenders and the Protestant Orange Order emerged.

Sporadic outbreaks by Rapparees and Whiteboys did not really disturb the fundamental peace of the country during the eighteenth century. But this old world order or *ancien régime* was now seriously threatened by the French Revolution which broke out in 1789. This threat was all the more serious since the zealous revolutionaries offered to aid other nations to win their liberty from tyrants. Enemies of the revolution in England and Ireland feared that such an offer would be welcomed in Ireland. Accordingly they were on the lookout for agents who might be in league, not any longer with Jacobites but, with Jacobins. This vigilance, not to say nervousness, was illustrated by an incident which occurred in Ballydehob in November 1795. A vessel from Hamburg on a voyage to America was forced to put into Long Island Sound near Schull. Three of its passengers, Germans, paid for refreshments at Ballydehob with a strange coin. The publican showed it to a priest, 'a half starved emigrant', who immediately recognised the features of the guillotined monarch and identified the coin as a *louis d'or*. The priest concluded that the strangers were agents sent by the Convention in Paris 'to disseminate their principles' and reported them to the military. The Germans were arrested but were able to establish their identity. The press reporter admired this clergyman for his 'abhorrence of French principles'. Such ideas or ideals were already influencing the country. For example, in the same newspaper there is an appeal from Henry Sheares,[55] who was later executed for his part in the 1798 Rebellion. He was calling on his supporters as 'Friends of Freedom' to meet him at the hustings in Cork.[56]

The next report about French agents was no false alarm. On 16 December 1796 a fleet of 45 ships with 13,000 troops on board under General Hoche left Brest bound for Bantry Bay. Vice-admiral Morard de Galles was in charge of the fleet. On board the *Indomitable* was Wolfe Tone. He wrote in his diary that they were all in 'high spirits, and the troops as gay as if we were going to a ball'. But the fog was so thick that they could not see a ship's length before them.[57] When they approached the coast of Ireland ten ships were missing owing to the fog and the storm. The *Fraternité* was not to be seen and this carried Hoche and de Galles.[58] Hoche was a dynamic young general, rival of Napoleon himself, but the *Fraternité* had been blown out into the Atlantic. Hoche had just subdued the Vendée in north-western France where, as he himself proclaimed, they had conquered 'the satellites of kings in arms against the Republic'.[59] Lord Longueville of Mallow, then in Bantry, had a different view; the invaders were 'hot and reeking with the murders, rapes and robberies of the Vendée'.[60] The English had given military support to the rebels or *Chouans* so the French government, namely the Directory and especially Carnot, was now determined to turn Ireland into England's *Vendée*.

Early in the morning of 21 December Richard White of Seafield House, now Bantry House, sighted the French fleet and reported it to Admiral Kingsmill at Cork. The admiral was sceptical and thought that it was only 'the Lisbon or Quebec convoy' of merchant ships but he did send a ship to Mizen

Head 'to ascertain the truth'. A Captain Boyle of *H.M.S. Kangaroo* however soon landed dispatches at Crookhaven which left no doubt that these ships were French.[61] Richard White sent a further report on this fleet to General Dalrymple in Cork and added that he had accounts of six English men-of-war being in Crookhaven but that he had warned them of their danger. The ideas of even the English home secretary, the Duke of Portland, about their 'vigilance and superiority' at sea were shaken.[62]

The government at Dublin Castle was similarly caught unprepared. The country's 40,000 troops under Lord Carhampton were scattered all over the land. County Cork's 4,702 soldiers were posted at 14 different locations more for policing than for military duties. At Bantry there were 240, Skibbereen 350, Drimoleague 100, Dunmanway 540, Enniskeane 500, Clonakilty 500 and Bandon 520.[63] These troops would of course be aided by the militia whose officers were mostly Protestant but whose rank and file were often Catholic. Tone assured the French that it was a 'moral certainty' that the latter would desert to them once they had disembarked. There were also 20,000 yeomanry in the country but they were untried and not yet fully equipped. Various sections of these forces now made their way towards Bantry in a rather disorganised manner.[64] The storm and blizzard made matters more difficult and Lord Castlereagh had to shelter in Bandon.[65] General Dalrymple set up general headquarters at Bantry House on St Stephen's Day.[66]

The rector of Kilmoe, Fitzgerald Tisdal, also a Justice of the Peace for the County of Cork, raised a yeomanry corps at Crookhaven.[67] Colonel Hall, father of the writer, S. C. Hall, led a regiment from Killarney to Bantry. S. C. Hall often heard the colonel state that on this march 'his men were cheered by the peasantry, supplied with food and drink by them, and received unequivocal demonstrations of their resolve to fight upon their cabin thresholds against the entrance of a Frenchman'.[68] Richard Edward Hull of Leamcon, however, had another opinion of the people in the cabins. On 23 December he wrote to Richard White: 'I this moment received the enclosed notes, from the purport of them you will see the danger we are in, if you can aid me with arms of any kind, for Godsake do, as the inhabitants of the country are the enemies I fear most'.[69]

Meanwhile out on the bay there was still no sign of Hoche and de Galles. Tone wrote how 'it blew a heavy gale' and there was snow on the mountains. They were near to land 'near enough to toss a biscuit ashore'.[70] Hoche and de Galles being absent, Grouchy and Bouvet on board the *Immortalité* were now in command of the troops and the fleet respectively'.[71] At last Bouvet and Tone persuaded Grouchy to disembark on Christmas Eve but he still delayed action for twenty-four hours. On Christmas Day the storm grew worse making it now impossible to disembark. The ships were dragging their anchors. Bouvet feared that they would all be wrecked or caught in a trap by the English so he ordered his sailors to cut their cables and get out. Grouchy vehemently disagreed but could do nothing.[72]

Tone, Generals Chérin, Humbert and Harty, an Irishman, and Admiral

Bedout, a French Canadian, now decided to proceed to the mouth of the Shannon and await the others there. The wind turned south which was of course favourable but the next day this turned into what Tone called 'a perfect hurricane' which seriously damaged and almost sank his ship.[73] The *Impatient*, 40 guns, was wrecked in Barley Cove near the Mizen Head. Of the 700 persons aboard only seven were rescued; chivalrous attempts by their Irish enemies to save the others were in vain.[74] Tone decided to leave for France and wrote on 26 December: 'England has not had such an escape since the Spanish Armada … Well, let me think no more about it; it is lost and let it go! I am now a Frenchman … I am as eager to get back to France as I was to come to Ireland'.[75]

While the squadrons of Tone, Bouvet and Grouchy were sailing back to France eight ships and 4,000 men under Commodore Durand-Linois arrived at last in Bantry Bay on 31 December and anchored near Whiddy Island. A frigate, the *Surveillante*, was leaking so badly that it had to be scuttled a mile off shore on the Glengarriff side of the bay.[76] The *Fraternité* with Hoche and de Galles on board had gone too far westward both on account of the storm and of having to avoid English ships; now it finally headed towards Bantry Bay and met the damaged *Révolution* which was taking men off the sinking *Scévola*. Only then did these two leaders learn of the fate of their expedition.[77] But they did not know that Linois' ships were still waiting in the bay. So Hoche and de Galles thought that they had no choice but to abandon the whole enterprise and return to France.[78]

There was no insurrection by the United Irishmen in West Cork in support of the French. General Dalrymple however remarked that the people were loyal while 'our Eagles head to the enemy' but that if government forces withdrew the people would turn to the French.[79] The United Irishmen had received instructions not to rise until after a French landing. Thomas Addis Emmet maintained that contradictory reports from France left the United Irishmen completely unprepared.[80] While still in Bantry Bay Tone regretted that the province of Munster was 'the only one of the four which has testified no disposition to revolt'.[81]

The Christmas pastoral letter of Dr Francis Moylan, Bishop of Cork, had undoubtedly some influence on the people. He called his flock to 'loyalty, allegiance and good order'.[82] Dr Jeremiah Collins, a native of Drinagh, educated at Bordeaux, and later vicar general of the diocese, held that this pastoral, the people's first warning of imminent danger, 'inspired them with ardour … to defend their country, their altars and their homes'.[83] That might have been the case, but if the United Irishmen had been well prepared and if the French had disembarked such a pastoral would not have had any great effect.

Although the French invasion had been a total failure Loyalists were under no illusions; they knew full well that they had been saved by 'Loyalist' winds rather than by their much-vaunted army or navy. Dalrymple himself admitted that if the French had landed Ireland could not have been saved.

Lord Beresford was severely critical of both army and navy:

> We had two days after they [the French] were at anchor in Bantry Bay, from Cork to Bantry less than 3,000 men, two pieces of artillery, and no magazine at all. No landing was made. Providence prevented it; if there had, where was a stand to be made? It is clear that Cork was gone; who would answer afterwards for the loyalty of the country, then in possession of the French? Would the northern parts of the country have remained quiet? Not an hour.
>
> The ease with which the French got into Bantry … and the retreat they made into their own ports, without, I may say, molestation … has truly alarmed every thinking man in this nation … and here we may expect them again.[84]

The Irish government and the lord lieutenant, Camden, resolved that the next time they would be better prepared to meet the French and so the supposed 'Falstaffs' would have to be dismissed. Dalrymple was eventually retired. Carhampton was replaced by Ralph Abercromby and in the navy, Admiral Colpoys had to step down in favour of Lord St Vincent. 'The government,' wrote Camden, 'meant to strike terror'.[85] But first it meant to reward loyalty; Richard White was elevated to the peerage as 'Earl of Bantry'.[86]

The terror began in Ulster where General Lake began brutally to disarm the province. Dalrymple was told in Cork that 'the people were greatly enraged by the accounts given of the treatment of their fellow subjects in the North and elsewhere … and this produced inflammatory effects'.[87] Lord Bandon reported that there was disloyalty among his yeomanry and that some woods had been cut down to make pikes.[88]

General Abercromby made a tour of the south of the country. He soon made the controversial judgement that the army was in a 'state of licentiousness which must render it formidable to everyone but the enemy'.[89] One man who agreed with him was his friend, John Moore, a Scot, who on 1 March 1798 was appointed military commander of West Cork with headquarters in Bandon. He himself was under the command of General Stewart.[90] The government now arrested most of the leaders of the Leinster Directory; Lord Edward Fitzgerald was on the run. As the leaders were out of the way it was decided to disarm the country. Camden and General Lake believed in torturing suspects for information, but Abercromby and Moore thought it more humane to use collective punishment in order to force the people to surrender their arms. The first stage of this punishment was dragooning or 'free quarters', according to which soldiers would be freely billeted among the people. The authorities in the castle however were in favour of more severe measures and Abercromby was practically forced to resign. He was suceeded by General Lake. Martial law was proclaimed on 30 March 1798.[91]

Tadhg na Samhna Mac Cárthaigh from Drimoleague and a party of other United Irishmen raided the house of John Gillman in Dunmanway parish, looking for arms. But Tadhg na Samhna was captured and condemned to death in Cork. He was hanged outside Gillman's house on 21 April 1798.[92] John Moore was now ordered to disarm East and West Carbery. He warned the people

Sir John Moore, 1761–1809

that if they did not hand in their arms by 2 May his troops would go into action. He wanted to convince the people that he was serious, he said that he 'marched five companies of light infantry and a detachment of dragoons throughout the country of Schull to be ready to act'. Moore hoped that the mere sight of his troops would frighten the people into handing in their arms but it was having no such effect. He spoke to the priests as well and again reminded the people of the folly of forcing him to resort to violent means.[93] What the priests preached to the people must have been in accordance with the latest pastoral letters from their bishops. Dr Francis Moylan of Cork exhorted his flock 'to renounce all those wicked associations and to obey their local commanders who were known for their benevolent and kind hearts'. He also warned the people not to associate with 'atheistical incendiaries'. 'They [the French] come to you in sheep's clothing,' he warned, 'but inwardly they are ravening wolves'. Dr William Coppinger of Cloyne and Ross, similarly urged his flock to 'call to mind the cries of the fatherless, the widows ... [and] surrender your arms'.[94]

In Aughadown the local landlord, Samuel Townsend of Whitehall, who was also High Sheriff for the county, usually quartered his troops among the people and according to his grandson, Samuel N. Townsend, this tactic 'ate them into subjection'. But Townsend, the High Sheriff, did not want to witness the ruin of the tenants of his own parish. Accordingly he himself together with the parish priest, Timothy O'Sullivan and the vicar, Joseph Wright, agreed to guarantee the peace of the parish. At the priest's request Townsend addressed the people in the chapel yard and told them of this arrangement. The result was that no troops were sent to the parish and there was no disturbance there.[95]

In the other parishes however the situation was different. Neither Moore's threats of ruin nor the priest's threats of damnation succeeded in persuading the people to hand in their arms so he ordered his troops into action. He wrote: 'I directed Major Nugent to march on 2 May into Caheragh which was much disturbed and I placed the five light companies in different divisions from Ballydehob to Ballydevlin [Goleen] with orders to forage the whole country to within seven miles of Skibbereen'. One notices that Aughadown and Kilcoe (seven miles west of Skibbereen) were duly excluded from the district to be foraged. Moore's orders to his men were, 'to treat the people with as much harshness as possible, as far as words and manner went and to supply themselves with whatever provisions were necessary to enable them to live well. My wish was to excite terror and by that means to obtain our end speedily'. People who had hitherto denied having arms were now handing them in. After four days he and his men 'extracted' sixty-five muskets. Major Nugent was obliged to burn some houses in Caheragh before he could get a single weapon. When the troops had one district disarmed, they then moved to another always entreating the people to hand over their arms rather than be ruined. 'Few parishes had the good sense to do so,' wrote Moore, 'such as did escaped. The terror was great. The moment a redcoat appeared, everybody fled.'[96] These redcoats spent three weeks disarming these potential croppies and received 'about 800 pikes and 3,400 stands of arms, the latter very bad'. This was by no means an insignificant haul of weapons and can compare with the 5,462 guns captured by Lake in ten days in Ulster the previous year.[97] The arms found by Moore would probably have been used if the French had landed and could be used should they ever return. Moore found that the 'better sort of people seemed all delighted with the operation, except when it touched their own tenants by whose ruin they themselves must suffer but they were pleased that the people were humbled and would be civil'. He could find only two gentlemen who acted with liberality; the rest seemed to him to have only the most selfish motives. 'The common people have been so ill-treated by them,' he observed, 'and so often deceived, that neither attachment or confidence any longer exists'. He feared that if the government would not introduce some regulations 'for the protection of the lower from the upper order, the pike may appear again very soon'.[98]

As Moore stated the terror was great and everybody fled. One of them was the eight-year-old Ellen Harrigan of Drinane between Schull and Goleen. She emigrated to New Brunswick, Canada and later to Wisconsin, in the United States where she lived to the age of 113. She recalled how her family 'was obliged to hide in a cave'.[99]

A local United Irishman, Robert Swanton, may well have been one of the

Ellen Harrigan Lucey, 1778–1891, in Wisconsin, USA

men sought by Moore. Swanton was a member of the Cork Directory of the United Irishmen.[100] When Lord Edward Fitzgerald and the Sheares brothers were arrested in May 1798, Swanton escaped to America.[101] On 9 June Moore left West Cork and went to Wexford. Ten days later the Westmeath regiment under Sir Hugh O'Reilly was marching from Clonakilty to Bandon when it was ambushed at the Big Cross near Ballinscarty by the rebels. But these attackers were forced to retreat leaving 'a considerable number of dead' according to O'Reilly. There were also some casualties on the loyalist side. Among the rebel dead lay their leader, Tadhg an Asna. His body was thrown into the Croppies' Hole.[102]

Apart from this affray, West Cork remained quiet during 1798 as also did the rest of Munster. Moore's pre-emptive disarming provided the United Irishmen of West Cork with some excuse for not rebelling when faced with the rebuke of the Munstermen by the poet, Mícheál Óg Ó Longáin, from Carraig na bhFear or Glanmire near Cork:

Fiafraigh, créad nach éirig
Is téacht linn sa gleo …
Inis go bhfuil na Laighnigh
Ag adhaint an tine leo.[103]

Ask why they did not rise
And come with us in the fight ...
Tell that the Leinstermen
are kindling the fire.

Some of the gentry concluded that only for the firm but temperate actions of Moore and General Stewart, West Cork would have become a second Wexford.[104] While no doubt it must be granted that West Cork lacked the gory glory of Wexford in 1798, it was not without interest. Rebel activities in West Cork from 1796 to 1798 did involve such great spirits as Hoche, Tone and Moore. No other rebel region could claim such a nationalistic and yet international and tragic trio. Hoche was to die of galloping consumption the following year at the age of twenty-nine and Tone by his own hand in 1798 itself.[105] Moore went on to fight Napoleon in the Peninsular War and was soon killed at Corunna in Spain. There, in the eerie words which the poet, Charles Wolfe, put into the mouth of one of his comrades, 'We buried him darkly at the dead of night, the sods with our bayonets turning'.[106]

II

LAW AND DISORDER; FAMINE AND ROAD-MAKING; CATHOLIC EMANCIPATION: 1800–29

The law doth punish man or woman
That stole the goose from off the common;
But lets the greater felon loose
That stole the common from the goose.

ANON

… sympathetically to address enlightened nations of the world
on Ireland's wrongs and England's intolerance, that enemy of
religious toleration, inimical to the universal law of nations.
ROBERT SWANTON AND 'FRIENDS OF IRELAND IN NEW YORK', 1825

LAW AND DISORDER

The rebellion of 1798 convinced William Pitt, Lord Cornwallis and Viscount Castlereagh that only the union of the two kingdoms would prevent Ireland from being the Achilles' heel of the empire because many of the Irish would welcome invasion and revolution. That was why the government was prepared to use all means of persuasion including bribery and corruption to achieve this union. There was an understanding, though not a condition, that Catholic Emancipation would naturally follow. The hierarchy, for example, Bishop Moylan of Cork, believed that there was little chance of this coming from the Irish Parliament – 'that junta who oppressed them' – but trusted that 'the British Cabinet in its great wisdom and foresight will see the expedience of a liberal arrangement in which his Majesty's loyal subjects of every description without any religious distinction will be equally included'.[1] After all it was this parliament which had passed the Penal Laws. Other Catholics, however, such as the young Daniel O'Connell, opposed the Act of Union. The government also promised that the union would bring economic benefits to Ireland. The national spirit of 1782 was dead and the rebels of 1798 were crushed. All the eloquence of Grattan could not prevent the passing of the act by a majority of forty-six. The members of parliament for Baltimore, John Freke, later Lord Carbery and George Evans voted against the measure. The members for Bandon voted one for and the other against; both the Clonakilty members favoured it. The members for County Cork voted two to one in favour.[2] This act came into force on 1 January 1801.

'You have not forgot Bantry Bay,' General Humbert had urged the rebel men of the West of Ireland in 1798. The government would not forget Hoche either. The defenders of the country had been caught napping; henceforth they were determined to be more vigilant. Hugh Dorian of Donegal wrote: 'Such was their dread while "Bony" conquered that if an extraordinary large sea-gull's wing appeared on the horizon, it was in the hurry of the moment taken for French canvas, and the telescope was adjusted'.[3] If such was the nervous-ness in the north-west it must have been worse in the south-west which was so much nearer to Bony's expanding empire. The lawyer, John Philpott Curran, was warning that the price of liberty is 'eternal vigilance'. The government was quite prepared to pay that price for liberty from 'liberators' and was de-termined not to depend on legislation alone. One loyalist boasted that if the French dared to return they would get plenty of equality but no fraternity. Numerous watchtowers were built on high strategic points all along the coast to provide better vigilance and communications; never again would the govern-ment have to depend on reports from fishermen. Signal towers were placed on the Mizen Peninsula at Leamcon, Brow Head, Mizen Head and also on Cape Clear. Surveys of these sites were made in 1806. The Leamcon tower was on the lands of Mr Hull and there was already a road to it but 210 perches of road had to be made to the Brow Head tower and 437 to the one on Mizen Head.[4]

The coast of England, not to mention that of Ireland, was still badly guarded during the wars with Napoleon. Later, when in exile, he revealed that English smugglers had eagerly accepted money and spied for him. All through the eighteenth century certain families in West Cork and Kerry, Protestant as well as Catholic, were involved in smuggling, including the Deasys, the O'Heas, the Donovan 'Islands' and the Somervilles all of the Clonakilty district, the Gallweys of Skibbereen, the Hutchins of Ballylicky near Bantry, the O'Sulli-vans of Beara and the O'Connells of Derrynane. But it was not all one-way traf-fic in wines, spirits, etc., as potatoes and wool were also exported. Steps were cut into the rock at Brownstown near Clonakilty. Steep, dizzy, 'pirate steps', as they are locally called, were similarly carved out of the bold face of the cliff at Cuasastaighre or 'the Cove of the Stairs' at Canty's Cove in Kilmoe parish facing into Dunmanus Bay and Bantry Bay.[5]

A special service, the 'Coast Blockade', was set up by the Admiralty in 1816 to check the activities of smugglers on the coasts of the British Isles.[6] The foll-owing year the Admiralty obtained a site from Richard Notter for a station at Rock Island near Crookhaven. An officers' house was built with seven rooms; seven cottages of four rooms each were provided for the men. A watch house and boathouse were also constructed.[7] A lighthouse was built on Cape Clear and beamed its first light in May 1818 from *Cnocáinín an tSeabhaic* or the 'Little Hill of the Hawk'.[8] The government had thus resolved to keep a hawk's eye on the coast. Not only would foreign invaders be watched more closely but also the all-too-common smugglers. In 1822 the Admiralty established 'H. M. Coast-guards' to maintain a constant watch on the coasts of both islands.[9] That very year James Gallwey of Skibbereen was sentenced to seven years transportation to Australia for smuggling and he died there. A Michael Long from Roaring

Water in Kilcoe was charged under the Revenue Act at the Cork Assizes with 'running ten bales of tobacco' on to some strand. James O'Sullivan, a miller at Roaring Water, gave evidence on his behalf and he was finally discharged. O'Sullivan actually admitted that he himself had been engaged in smuggling up to 1807.[10]

Towards the end of the eighteenth century an African ship with a cargo of gold, feathers and ivory searching for Crookhaven was lured on to the rocks near Castle Island, Schull, by local people who burned a light on the old castle on the island. The cargo was looted but the crew managed to reach Baltimore.[11] There were also cases of sheer plunder or piracy. In 1794 The *Lady Harriett* of Cork bound for Dublin from Cadiz with a cargo of fruit was forced by an ill-wind to take shelter in Long Island Channel where it was boarded by 'a mob of people who plundered and destroyed the cargo and hull'. It was reported that 'not an atom was left afloat, all cut away with hatchets'. A reward of 125 guineas was offered for the arrest of the ringleaders. The *John and Margaret* of Limerick on a voyage home from Bordeaux went on the rocks off Sherkin Island near Baltimore and was similarly looted.[12]

Returning to political matters, Lord Cornwallis was right when he said that 'the mass of the people of Ireland do not care one farthing about the union'. As J. C. Beckett remarks: 'The enemies they feared were the landlord and the tithe proctor … their only notion of a political programme was to abolish rent and tithe, to put down the Established Church, and to set up their own in place of it.'[13] It was not without reason that the local magistrate, Richard Edward Hull, had exclaimed when the French were in the bay, 'It is the inhabitants of this country I fear most'. The local magistrates' task was often difficult and dangerous, their relations with one another and with Dublin Castle sometimes being ambiguous. They had to deal with all kinds of offences, domestic, agrarian and political. The magistrate was often his own policeman, judge, jury and, one might almost say, hangman. In 1824 Fr Michael Collins, administrator of Skibbereen and the next Bishop of Cloyne and Ross (1827–32), was invited to London to give evidence to select committees of the Houses of Lords and Commons concerning the state of the country. Fr Collins stated that one of the causes of the Whiteboy troubles was 'the partial and corrupt administration of justice' on the part of the magistrates, that the impression on the minds of common people was that there was 'no *fixed law* of the land, except through the interest or favour they may happen to possess with magistrates'. He explained how they enjoyed a good 'trade' by 'receiving presents to a large amount, potatoes dug for them, turf cut … presents of corn and cattle, and presents of money too'. Asked if these matters were notorious, he replied, 'As notorious as the noonday sun'.[14] But Fr Collins granted that this 'evil has been considerably diminished since the introduction of the system of holding petty sessions, whereby the magistrates act in open court and under the constraint of public opinion … and their acts are liable to be scrutinised.' He also said that Catholics had 'an idea that those lower classes of Protestants have the privilege of committing crimes with impunity'. He himself agreed that 'it always happens that the Protestant peasant will have a much better chance of eluding justice than a Catholic'.[15]

Another cause of the disturbances was what Fr Collins called 'the pressure of the tithe system', simply what the English radical, William Cobbett, dubbed 'The Old Corruption'.[16] The Catholic majority looked upon the tax as 'a hardship … on account of its variableness and uncertainty and their inability to pay it'. The priest pointed out that their objection was not that the money was going to the clergy of another Church, and that they would not pay it to their own clergy either. They simply wanted 'to get rid of the burden of it … in common with many Protestants'.[17]

The young reforming Robert Peel arrived in Dublin Castle as the new chief secretary in September 1812. Just a year later he received a petition from a tithe proctor, William Swanton of Ballydehob, or Swantonstown as he himself called it. The tithe proctor complained that he had received 'every possible opposition' from the inhabitants of Aughadown in the collection of the tithes. They assaulted his agents and robbed them of their field books. He had taken legal proceedings against some of the offenders but had failed to execute them on account of the 'lawless state of the parish'. Two of his agents later returned to the same parish this time escorted by a constable. But at Rincoe they were met by 'a mob of 100 at least, armed with guns, pikes, scythes, swords, and bayonets screwed on long poles'. This 'mob' threatened to kill the tithe proctor if he and his policeman remained in the parish and so they departed. The following day Swanton appealed to the local magistrate, Rev. Richard Townsend of Whitehall, who duly called on the military in Skibbereen for reinforcements comprising a corporal and twelve soldiers. The magistrate also succeeded in procuring the services of three sub-constables and together with the tithe proctors they all headed for Rincoe. But the 'mob' had also sent for help so the forces of the law were met not by a mere 'mob' this time but by a 'party of 200 persons armed as before who regularly formed a line of battle and hoisted a flag, continually hurrahing, shouting and throwing stones'. The forces of the law considering, like Falstaff, that discretion was the better part of valour, quickly retreated. Swanton later obtained evidence against certain persons in this 'mob'. He aimed to convict them at the following assizes and accordingly petitioned Peel for assistance.[18] The authority of the magistrate, police and military had been openly flouted by a 'mob' which was virtually a rival army. The whole system of law and order had broken down. Galen Broeker rightly concluded that the primary reason for this breakdown had little to do with corruption; the magistrates were simply afraid to move.[19] This fear was understandable because the military forces available to support them were rather weak as at Rincoe because some regiments had been withdrawn to fight Napoleon.

The magistrate had to deal not only with such agrarian disturbances but also with common crime. In April 1813, another magistrate, William Hull of Leamcon, took the liberty of writing to Peel concerning the murder of a woman by two others. The criminals escaped to Kerry but he had one of them arrested, tried at the Cork Assizes and hanged. The principal evidence had been given by an orphan girl whom Hull had since had to keep under his protection for her own safety.[20] One of Hull's servants was attacked by friends of the executed woman and it looked as if he would not survive. 'I live in a remote and lawless part of the country,' Hull complained, 'in a district thirty miles in circuit without the least military or civil aid, not even a solitary policeman have I to call on for assistance.' This feeling of personal danger and isolation prompted him to appeal to the lord lieutenant for a 'small military detachment' from either Bantry or Skibbereen. He insisted that military aid was necessary because of the lack of co-operation and the 'culpable supineness of the other magistrates'.[21] Peel replied to Hull reassuring him that it was in order for him to seek military aid.[22] But, as Hull would have known only too well, troops were often reluctant to come to the aid of the magistrate because they considered that acting as policemen was beneath their dignity. Indeed the home secretary, Sidmouth, had to remind Peel that the primary purpose of the troops was to defend the country against a possible French invasion and that they were not to be used or misused too frequently as police.[23] Peel was inclined to do precisely that.

If these barony policemen were thin on the ground they were also poor in quality. Sir William Wilde presents us with a pen-picture of such men just as vividly as his famous son, Oscar, might have done:

> The only available forces were the old barony constables – generally superannuated pensioners from the yeomanry or militia; always Protestants, and most of them, *cleevins*, old servants or hangers-on of the magistrate – who dressed in long blue surtout coats, with scarlet breeches, and rusty top-boots. Each of these old men was mounted, and carried a heavy cavalry sword, his only weapon, for he was seldom fit to be trusted with any other. Two or three of these fogies might be seen at fairs, patterns and markets, riding up and down to keep the peace, which, as soon as the superintending magistrate had gone to dinner, they generally broke out by getting gloriously drunk. This the people usually bore, however, with good humour, seldom injuring the constable, but affording themselves much amusement by welting with their blackthorns their crusty nags, which, knowing perfectly what was about to take place, commenced lashing.[24]

William Hull soon had another murder case on his hands. In November 1813 he told Peel that in 1810 a seafaring man having landed at Crookhaven was murdered for his money at Ballydehob. A man informed Hull that he had witnessed the crime. Hull then requested the informant's parish priest to encourage his parishioners to divulge further evidence.[25] The priest acted accordingly and the magistrate duly received the names of the alleged murderers.[26] But it does not seem that any of them was ever arrested in spite of Peel's detailed instructions to Hull.[27]

The year 1814 brought other troubles for Hull. He suspected that arms were being smuggled into the country and he applied to Peel for a warrant to search for them. Peel sent the warrant immediately. Hull told him how 'lower orders' were bartering poultry, eggs, milk and potatoes with sailors for small arms. A government transport ship laden with condemned muskets from Portugal came into the Long Island Channel near Schull and a quantity of arms disappeared from it. Hull could recover only a few of them.[28] The result of this information was that Peel wrote to the Commissioners of Customs quoting Hull and ordered them to give the 'strictest injunctions to their officers on the coast to prevent such traffic in arms'.[29] This must have been the source of many of the arms found by John Moore in 1798.

This year 1814 was one of transition as Europe was trying to return to a state of peace. Napoleon abdicated in April. In May the government in London decided to limit the peacetime military establishment in Ireland to fewer than 30,000 men and the militia was disbanded. Whitworth, the lord lieutenant who had succeeded Richmond in 1813, became alarmed and protested that 'a peace establishment may do in England, but here we are not at peace'.[30] Nevertheless it was a suitable opportunity to try out some sort of police force which Peel had been planning for some time. Hull had no satisfactory police to deal with the various murder cases; neither had the other magistrate, Rev. Richard Townsend, adequate military support to face the Whiteboys at Rincoe. Affrays like this forced Peel to conclude that, 'we have a right to call on country gentlemen for the performance of the ordinary duties of a magistrate, but in the event of a commotion we can scarcely expect of them … that degree of activity and vigilance which is necessary for their suppression'.[31]

Accordingly Peel created the Peace Preservation Force to help the magistrates to do their duty or to do it for them if they were either unable or unwilling to do it themselves. The disturbed districts however would have to pay the expense of the force, i.e., 'pay for the luxury of disturbance … for the rods which are used for their own correction', as Peel expressed it.[32] This was to be a less crude form of free quarters in the manner of 1798. The new force was to be a civilian one organised on military lines, in other words an armed police force. It was to be controlled and paid by Dublin Castle under the command of three castle magistrates namely Wilson, Willcocks and Willis. The castle now had its own stipendiary magistrates and was no longer dependent solely on local magistrates working on a voluntary basis. Peel realised that the day was past for 'part-timers, that putting down disturbances in Ireland was often a full-time job'.[33] The local magistrates could now request the castle to send the Peace Preservation Force but the lord lieutenant could also send it whether the magistrate liked it or not. At the end of the parliamentary session in the summer of 1814 Peel steered through his Peace Preservation Bill which authorised the Peace Preservation Force or police and he also got the Insurrection Act renewed for three years.[34] He had now secured law and lawmen for all seasons.

There were Whiteboy outbreaks in Limerick and Tipperary during the winter of 1814 so the Peace Preservation Force was soon called into action. Some violence also broke out in County Cork. On a Sunday in 1815, Hull received an urgent dispatch from the local parish priest, William Shea of Kilmoe. The latter had just been informed that a 'set of rioters intended to commence hostilities at the chapel'. He appealed to the magistrate to assist him by coming himself or by at least lending him 'some notion of the cost attending the introduction of Mr Peel's law here', so that he could explain it to these 'deluded wretches'.[35] According to the magistrate's report to Peel, 'several hundreds' of men had gathered and were divided into two or more contending factions. Hull was unable to go to the scene himself through 'indisposition' but one suspects also through fear. Neither was he able to send any police because there were very few of them in the district and these were not even worthy of the name. All he could do was to send the alarmed parish priest a copy of the new Peace Preservation Act. According to Hull, Fr Shea made 'proper use' of this act and explained in both English and Irish its force to the 'ignorant and deluded people' with the result that they immediately dispersed. Hull complimented Peel assuring him that this remarkable result was mainly owing to the 'terror of his Peace Preservation Act'. No doubt the would-be rioters feared a visit from the Peace Preservation Force; memories of Moore's redcoats would still have been fresh in their minds.

Fr Shea had other troubles too but of a different sort. Such priests had to oppose tyranny from above as well as anarchy from below. By 1814 the vague promise of Catholic Emancipation which had been given at the time of the union in 1800 had not yet been fulfilled. Nevertheless, a certain measure of emancipation, called 'the Quarantotti Rescript', was now being proposed; this would grant the government some form of control or veto over the appointment of bishops and possibly of parish priests and it would also make some provision for the payment of Catholic clergy. This was vigorously rejected by Daniel O'Connell and by many of the priests including John England of Cork who later became the first bishop of Charleston, Carolina, in the USA. A meeting was held in the new Cathedral of St Mary and St Anne attended by most of the priests of the diocese including William Shea of Kilmoe, Florence Crowley of Schull, David Dore of Caheragh and Michael Doheny, vicar of St Mary's, Shandon, who later became parish priest of Dunmanway. It was presided over by Archdeacon John Murphy who became bishop the following year on the death of Dr Moylan. The meeting called the rescript 'that mischievous document' and declared that:

> Whilst we abjure all temporal or civil control of any foreign jurisdiction within these realms … we, at the same time, look upon any interference of a government of a different religion from ours to be inexpedient, uncalled for and tending manifestly to the serious injury and probable destruction of our religion in this country, and as calculated to withdraw from us the confidence of the people.[36]

That was the end of discussions on any emancipation on any such terms.

This year 1815 was a traumatic one for Europe; it saw the abdication of Napoleon, his escape from Elba and final defeat at Waterloo. It was a time of disturbance in Ireland especially in County Tipperary. Yet the vigilant William Hull endeavoured to prevent disturbances by searching for arms. He applied to Peel for a warrant to search for arms in the parishes of Schull and

Kilmoe as some had been smuggled through Crookhaven. But it seems that the 'lower orders' got wind of his intentions because they handed in some arms voluntarily.[37] In April of the following year, Hull reported to the castle that he had found 12 guns, 1 blunderbuss, 24 swords, 6 bayonets and 7 pistols. His neighbouring magistrate in Skibbereen, Mr Robinson, confiscated 110 guns, 18 pistols, 1 gun barrel and 23 scythes shaped as swords.[38]

It was not only the 'lower orders' who were inclined to break the law by their use of arms because persons of the 'middling orders' or middle classes were sometimes accused of doing so as well. These persons were often Protestants such as Daniel Coghlan of Crookhaven. In 1816, the local revenue officer, Robert O'Neill, reported Coghlan to the castle for attempting to murder him because he had prevented him from smuggling. The under-secretary, Gregory, replied that this accusation was not proven.[39] The irony of the situation was that in this same year Daniel Coghlan was appointed a magistrate. He was soon denounced to the castle by Joseph Baker, tithe proctor to the absentee rector of Schull, Anthony Traill, who was also Archdeacon of the Diocese of Conor in Ulster. This proctor accused the newly-appointed magistrate of aiding the escape to France of a man who was wanted by the law. The proctor insisted that those who recommended Coghlan to the lord chancellor must not have known the character of the man but that he himself would let the chancellor know the facts.[40]

In April 1817 Hull again wrote to Peel on the question of arms. This time however it was not the 'lower orders' who were the offenders but persons of a 'certain class'. He pointed out the anomaly whereby the keeping of arms was 'persecuted and punished' among the 'lower orders' but 'countenanced' among this 'certain class'. Persons of this class were able to obtain arms legally and use them during faction fights. The magistrate was forced to admit that it was 'neither safe nor prudent' for the civil power to try to suppress such 'armed multitudes of sanguinary and generally intoxicated factions'. A weaver had been brought before him for wantonly killing a poor man and even boasting about it. When Hull questioned him on his authority to carry arms he produced a licence to hold several guns and declared that it was in virtue of this that he had acted as he had. Hull therefore urged Peel to introduce some strict legal means of disarming such persons.[41] Peel replied telling him that he felt 'much indebted for his suggestions'.[42] This is a rare reference to the use of firearms rather than of the shillelagh or blackthorn stick in faction fights.

Even after the establishment of the Peace Preservation Force, Peel was still dissatisfied with the magistrates but the old Attorney-General, Saurin, did not want to dismiss the bad ones for fear of insulting the good ones.[43] The young reformer was understandably frustrated. Serious accusations of corruption against magistrates as in the case of the newly-appointed Daniel Coghlan, made Peel exclaim: 'I wish to God, it was possible to revise the magistracy, for half the disorders and disturbances arise from the negligence of some and corruption and party spirit of the others. But what other local authorities can you trust to?'[44] It was the same old question as the Roman satirist,

Juvenal, once asked, *Sed quis custodiet ipsos custodes*? 'But who will police the police?' Peel had ensured that he himself or the government would have direct control over the police at least. It was the first step towards direct state intervention in the field of everyday law and order; hitherto such intervention was confined to times of open rebellion such as 1798.

Peel is usually given credit for being the founder of the first police force in the modern sense of the term. An English historian of police, Sir Charles Jeffries, states that it can perhaps be said that 'modern police history begins not in Britain itself, but in Ireland with the passing of the Irish Peace Preservation Act in 1814'.[45] But the opinion of another writer, G. A. Minto, is less than just to Peel: 'Fortunately, he [Peel] had in a manner of speaking, tried it on the dog. The dog was Ireland.'[46] The judgement of E. H. Glover is fairer, 'He [Peel] was essentially an opportunist … His sojourn in Ireland was timely, although the seed of his apprenticeship was yet to bear fruit in England. He grasped the practicability of a similar police force in England and stored it up in his practical mind for future action'.[47] The fruit in question was the founding of the London Metropolitan Police in 1829 with headquarters in Scotland Yard.

The post-war period from 1817 to 1821 was quiet in the Mizen Peninsula. The number of military stationed in Skibbereen and Bantry was declining. The general situation was one in which rents and tithes remained high while agricultural prices fell drastically after Waterloo 1815. Within a year the prices of oats, barley, beef and pork had fallen sharply and wheat prices were also severely depressed.[48] The historian, G. M. Trevelyan, writes that in England 'farmers were going bankrupt and hanging themselves as the price of corn fell … a vast proportion of the rural labourers became paupers.'[49] In Ireland the population was increasing but employment was scarce and arms were being smuggled. Social conflict was practically inevitable.

The Whiteboy troubles of this period first broke out in County Limerick where a chief constable of the Peace Preservation Force, Major Going, was assassinated. The violence soon spread to North Cork. The magistrates of West Cork were alarmed and called a meeting in Skibbereen in December 1821. The lord lieutenant was requested to send additional military forces to the district to save it from bloodshed. The people were warned not to be seduced into schemes which would lead them only to the gallows and the transport ships. The clergy of both denominations were asked to exhort their flocks to obey the laws.[50] On a night in December 1821 the corn stores of the tithe proctor, Joseph Baker, were set on fire along with his sloop which was moored in Crookhaven. His barley stacks were also destroyed by fire.[51]

These outrages at Crookhaven were some of the many which shocked the country. The government reacted by recalling the lord lieutenant, Earl Talbot and the chief secretary, Charles Grant. The new lord lieutenant was Richard, Marquis of Wellesley and his chief secretary was the able Henry Goulburn; they both took office in December 1821. In January 1822 Robert Peel succeeded Sidmouth as home secretary. Goulburn was a personal friend of Peel's and

Wellesley was a brother of the Duke of Wellington; the Whiteboys were going to have to face stronger government.[52] A local magistrate, Samuel Townsend of Whitehall in Aughadown, applied to Wellesley for permission to re-establish the West Carbery Yeomanry and for arms. He reported that large parties of men were going around to farmers' houses looking for arms. They had 'nightly musterings' in the parish of Schull, sounding horns and firing shots in the air.[53]

Samuel Townsend soon obtained permission to raise the West Carbery Yeomanry Corps but the supply of arms arrived only after a long delay. Townsend did not, as he had in 1798, agree with the rector and the parish priest to guarantee the peace of the parish. That priest was no longer there and his successor, John Daly, found himself in no position to do so even if he wished. All he could do was to curse the Whiteboys who cursed him in return.[54] The chaplain to the West Cork Yeomanry was the Rev. Robert Morritt, rector of Castlehaven and also a magistrate.[55] In January 1822 he informed Wellesley of his night raid by land and sea on the Whiteboys. He sent urgent dispatches to the gentry in Skibbereen and Aughadown to meet him at Ballydehob at midnight. He himself left Baltimore in his rowing boat with fourteen soldiers and duly rendezvoused with the gentry. They failed to encounter any mustering of Whiteboys although they heard them sounding horns in different directions. Morritt's men searched houses and found stolen arms consisting of muskets, pistols and gunpowder probably taken from Lord Audley's copper mines.[56] Three men were arrested and escorted to Cork to be tried under the Whiteboy Acts.[57]

The government thought that these outrages were simply local reactions but were surprised at what happened at Newcestown and Castletown Kinneigh in the Bandon district. One night in January 1822 Adderley Beamish of Palace Anne near Enniskeane, captain of the East Carbery Yeomanry, heard the sound of firearms near Newcestown. He himself, his brother and sixteen yeomen immediately set out for that village and lay in ambush. An advance party of four Whiteboys appeared so the yeomen opened fire on them but they escaped. Captain Beamish later heard that the Whiteboys had been wounded, that two had died and that the wounded were hidden in Castletown Kinneigh north of Enniskeane. He was also informed that six armed Whiteboys were heading from there towards Macroom on horseback. Captain Beamish and his two brothers immediately pursued them and called on them to halt but their only reply was to open fire. The Beamishes returned fire and shot one man dead whereupon the others fled.[58] According to a local historian, Jeremiah O'Mahony, the Beamishes tied the body of the dead man to the tail of his own horse and dragged him to Palace Anne.[59]

At the inquest a woman stated that deceased was her brother, Cornelius Harrington, from Ballydehob. She thought that the bank notes found on him could not have been his own because he had no means of obtaining them honestly because two years previously all he had was then 'canted',[60] i.e., sold to the highest bidder when the lease expired. The next to give evidence was

John Townsend, son of Dr Townsend, who lived near Leap. He said his father's house had been attacked by six armed men who beat him and plundered the house. This witness then identified some of the items found in Harrington's possession. The jury gave its verdict: 'Cornelius Harrington had died from shots fired by Captain Adderley Beamish and Bernard Beamish in discharge of their duty'.[61]

This Harrington case as well as Morritt's raid and the incidents around Crookhaven were duly reported by Wellesley to Peel.[62] The Harrington case particularly worried the magistrates. They insisted to Wellesley that the White-boy disturbances were not simply isolated incidents but the result of a 'concocted system'. They related how Harrington travelled from Ballydehob, a distance of about fifty miles, to where he met his fate. He had been wearing Dr Townsend's breeches robbed only two nights previously about thirty miles away. The magistrates protested that the lives and property of the people were at the mercy of the Whiteboys who 'were growing in strength and confidence, finding no efforts being made to stop their daring and lawless deeds'.[63]

The chief secretary, Henry Goulburn, replied to the magistrates by stating that the lord lieutenant felt 'deeply the painful situation of magistrates in that part of the country'. He also assured them that troops had already been sent to Bandon and that a regiment was on its way south to be distributed among the towns in whose neighbourhoods most outrages were occurring.[64] It is probable that some of this regiment was sent to Skibbereen or Bantry. The Mizen Peninsula continued to be disturbed throughout the month of January 1822, especially the Crookhaven district. The Revenue Department on Rock Island was guarded day and night. The pound at Lissigriffin was demolished and the people were being urged not to pay tithes.[65] Wellesley was also informed that such opposition sometimes extended to the priests' dues as well.[66]

January 1822 was the most violent month for Whiteboy outbreaks in the County of Cork. Even regular troops were attacked at Deshure in the parish of Kilmichael near Macroom.[67] The Whiteboys ambushed Lord Bantry and his yeomanry at the Pass of Keimaneigh, between Bantry and Ballingeary, an incident which became the subject of the poem *Cath Chéim an Fhia*, i.e., 'The Battle of Keimaneigh' by Máire Bhuí Ní Laoghaire. She was married to James Burke, a horse dealer from Skibbereen with whom she had eloped. One of their sons, John, was evicted from his farm near Ballingeary and went with his wife and family to Schull parish. Fr Donnacha Ó Donnchadha, who was curate in Ballingeary, wrote in 1931 that according to local tradition in Uibh Laoghaire he was involved in the Whiteboys and was taken prisoner.[68] Two of his brothers fought at Keimanagh and were captured.[69] County Limerick had now become less turbulent so troops were transferred to County Cork. In February Lord Londonderry had the Insurrection Act introduced on the grounds that 'absolute rebellion' prevailed in the south-west of Ireland. The Special Commission which was to hold sessions in Limerick was now transferred to Cork. On 18 February 1822, many Whiteboy prisoners were tried before this commission, thirty-five of whom were condemned to death and others transported. Five men were hanged at Deshure Cross, Tirelton, in Kilmichael parish and four others at Carriganima also in the Macroom district.[70] Fr Ó Donnchadha wrote that according to local tradition John Burke was also hanged but his name is not to be found among those who were publicly executed in County Cork at this time. His mother, Máire Bhúi Ní Laoghaire, wrote an elegy for him, *Tuaireamh Sheáin de Búrc*, i.e, 'The Lament of John Burke'. Her two captured sons spent nine months in Cork Gaol awaiting trial but were released following their successful defence by Daniel O'Connell. (The services of the eminent counsellor were, no doubt, obtained thanks to the kinship between him and Máire Bhúi; his aunt, Eibhlín Dhubh Ní Chonaill, had been married to Art Ó Laoghaire of Carriginima[71] about whom she wrote the famous *caoineadh*.) The barony of Carbery was placed under the Insurrection Act on 1 March 1822 but Carbery and the County of Cork generally soon became less disturbed.[72] This was due not only to the efforts of the authorities but also to the famine now beginning to be felt because the potato crop had rotted the previous harvest.

FAMINE

There were recurrent famines in Ireland before 1847. As mentioned in the last chapter a great frost in the winter of 1739–40 caused a bad grain and potato harvest which resulted in a terrible famine in 1740–1. The year of 1741 was remembered as *Bliain an Áir*, 'the year of the slaughter'. About 350,000 people died, including at least one-fifth of the population of Munster.[73] The summer and autumn of 1816 were extremely cold and wet. Grain and potato crops suffered severely and there was distress among the poor. A typhus epidemic broke out and the number of deaths from fever was estimated to be at least 65,000. Robert Peel imported seed oats. Two central committees distributed £50,000 to local organisations. Legislation was passed for the setting-up of local boards of health and fever hospitals. In matters of famine relief as well as of law and order Peel was proving himself an innovative administrator.[74] In 1816 soup was distributed in Cork city and more than £2,000 was spent on relief but £20,000 was needed. Bishop John Murphy gave £20.[75] Fr Michael Collins who had come to Skibbereen in 1814 told a select committee that there was a famine 'as great or greater' in 1817 than in 1822 and that 'many perished' in the district. There were also 'a great many fevers' and the effects of famine continued until the summer of 1818. Local subscriptions were raised, potatoes were bought early and later sold at reduced prices to the hungry. This scheme prevented death from starvation but not from fever and dysentery.[76] Among the victims were quite a number of Catholic and Protestant clergymen and also doctors. Dr Richard Townsend, brother of Rev. Horace Townsend of Clonakilty died of a fever 'which proved so fatal to many of his nearest and dearest connections'.[77] The landed gentry with one exception gave very little aid, Fr Collins said. Corn prices were still reasonably high and these enabled farmers to sell their grain and give employment to more of the poor. They 'exercised their usual charity,' he added. Nonetheless the whole country was 'swarming with persons wandering through it, women with shoals of children'. He admitted, however, that in many places they were refused help because the scarcity and the temptation of high prices made the farmers 'more stingy than they used to be in former times'.[78] The exportation of potatoes provoked a riot which was handled by the local magistrate, Mr Robinson, but this transport of food was not of course prevented.[79] Potatoes had always been exported mainly by sea to Cork, Dublin, Waterford, Limerick and even to France and Belgium.[80]

There seem to be no written accounts of this famine of 1817–8 in the parishes of Aughadown, Kilcoe, Schull or Kilmoe but its effects can be seen on the records of baptisms and marriages in the Catholic parish of Schull. There was a decline in both; between 1814 and 1817 the number of baptisms and marriages fell by anything up to one-third as is shown in the following table:

TABLE 1: SCHULL: MARRIAGES AND BAPTISMS, 1811–17

Year	Marriages	Baptisms
1811	84	261
1812	63	296
1813	58	233
1814	71	295
1815	22 (incomp.)	195 (incomp.)
1816	55	195
1817	45	199

In Skibbereen the number of baptisms in 1815 was 393 but by 1817 this had fallen to 280 or by nearly 30%. Records for marriages in Skibbereen at this time do not seem to have survived. The number of marriages in Schull and of births in both Schull and Skibbereen fell just as dramatically as the price of corn.

The high prices farmers got in 1817 were not of course quite so high as those of the years preceding the Battle of Waterloo (1815), but nonetheless they were able to absorb the shock of the potato failure. The potato failure in 1821–22 however had been preceded by years of depressed agricultural prices so this failure was felt more acutely than in 1817. Taking 100 as the price index for the pre-Waterloo years, prices of corn fell in 1817 to about 90 but by 1821 they had fallen as low as 66. The price of beef, bacon and mutton fell rather less, i.e., to 70, but butter fell only to 77.[81] Although prices fell rents remained high. Fr Shea of Kilmoe and Fr Crowley of Schull stated in 1805 that since 1782 rents had trebled and in some places quadrupled.[82] There was also a financial crisis. In June 1820 one-half of the banks failed in the southern half of the country.[83] One of the few to survive the storm was Pike's Bank in Cork.[84]

It was the poor of course who suffered most from the unemployment which resulted from such bad times. In 1820 Bartholomew Murphy, a plasterer from Blarney Street, Cork founded an organisation called the 'Friendly

Brothers' to aid the poor. This soon became 'The Cathedral Sick Poor Society' under the patronage of Bishop John Murphy.[85] The weather was remarkably severe in January 1820. According to Tuckey's *Cork Remembrancer*, the frost equalled that of 1739. The river Lee was again frozen over and was crossed on foot. The thaw was followed by heavy snow, rain and north-east wind. The poor were reduced to 'the greatest poverty and misery.'[86] At the end of 1820 there was heavy snow which caused extensive flooding. The following May and June were dry, cold and frosty. In the autumn and winter the rain poured in torrents and accumulated upon the surface of the ground. It was generally impossible and unprofitable to dig the potato crop so it 'soured and rotted' in the ground. This failure of 1821–2 was thus caused by weather and not by disease.[87] In the *Black Prophet: a tale of Irish famine*, William Carleton described scenes he had witnessed in Ulster in 1817 and 1822:

> Ireland, during the season, or rather year we are describing, might be compared to one vast lazar-house filled with famine, disease and death. The very skies of heaven were hung with the black drapery of the grave ... Hearses, coffins, long funeral processions, and all the dark emblems of mortality were reflected, as it were, in the sky ...[88]

Fortunately, neither Ulster nor Leinster was nearly so badly affected as the counties of the western seaboard from Sligo to Cork.[89] The population of the Mizen Peninsula had been increasing rapidly during the prosperous years of the Napoleonic wars. It recovered from the setback of 1815 and continued to increase. The census of 1821 showed that the population of Aughadown was 5,461, Schull, 12,827 and Kilmoe 5,847.[90] In the spring and summer of 1822, the general situation in the Mizen Peninsula was one of high rents and tithes, depressed agricultural prices, a rising population and rotting potatoes – a quasi-infallible formula for famine.

The first report of distress came from a meeting of the landlords of the County of Cork on 16 April 1822. They informed the lord lieutenant, Wellesley, that if peace were to be maintained the labourers should be employed. The landlords asked the government to spend £100,000 on public works and to give them a loan of £500,000, as it was impossible for them to obtain credit since the failure of the banks. Lord Carbery complained that the state of the landlords and tenants was 'almost calamitous' and that if relief were not given many would be ruined because 'deep and serious distress' was threatening all. Wellesley passed the report on to Henry Goulburn.[91] Famine and fever were reported to be raging in Counties Clare, Limerick, Galway and in Mayo where two people were buried without a coffin early in May. Edward O'Brien, MP for Clare, told parliament of the dreadful state of his own constituency and warned that there were as many as one-and-a-half million people in the country without any means of subsistence.[92] An act for employment of the poor was passed in May. The lord lieutenant was empowered to make advances of money on the security of the county rates for works sanctioned by the Grand Juries and also to subsidise local committees to provide employment. A sum of £650,000 was voted by parliament thanks to the efforts of Robert Peel. A relief commission was also set up which included William Gregory, the under-secretary. A Board of Health had been founded two years previously.[93]

A meeting of gentry and clergy was held in Skibbereen on 27 May to provide relief for that town and its vicinity. The public was informed of 'great distress' caused by the want of employment and the failure of the crops which threatened 'the horror of famine'. A committee was formed consisting of Thomas Clerke,[94] manager of the Provincial Bank, R. B. Townsend, vicar of Abbeystrowry, Rev. Wright, vicar of Aughadown, Fr Michael Collins, administrator, Skibbereen and his brother, Denis, who was curate. Thomas Clerke contributed £100, W. Wrixon Becher, MP, £50 and Dr Coppinger, Catholic Bishop of Cloyne, £11.[95] The response from the English people themselves was generous as some of them had just experienced distress themselves. During their economic crisis of 1812 the famous social reformer, William Wilberforce, founded the 'Association for the relief of the manufacturing and labouring poor'. There were many clergy, merchants and bankers among its members as well as a few of the nobility. That country knew violence too with the Spa Fields Riots and the Peterloo Massacre but by 1822 some peace and prosperity had arrived.

A general meeting was held at the City of London Tavern on 7 May 1822 in response to the reports of famine in Ireland and thus the 'London Tavern Committee' was set up. Merchants, bankers and clergymen took a leading part in this work; among them was Rev. Alexander Dallas who later became involved in missionary work in Ireland.[96] A similar committee was formed in Dublin on 16 May. The Church of Ireland Bishop of Cork, Thomas St Lawrence, John Murphy, the Catholic bishop and Lord Carbery were among the trustees. A sum of £8,000 was soon collected.[97] Another meeting was held in the Mansion House (now the Mercy Hospital) Cork on 22 May attended by the Church of Ireland bishop of Cork, his colleague in Cloyne, Charles Warborton, the Catholic bishops, John Murphy and William Coppinger and clergy of all denominations. They resolved that 'the most beneficial and effectual mode of relief of the existing distress will be to give employment to the labouring poor and thereby to afford them the means of earning themselves their subsistence'. The generosity of the London Committee was fully acknowledged and it was hoped that it would lead to 'a permanent and happy union between the two countries.'[98] The Cathedral Sick Poor Society was already very active. Its membership increased from about half a dozen to twenty-six.[99]

One committee was set up to serve both parishes of Schull and Kilmoe. John Jagoe, Church of Ireland curate of Schull, was secretary; Laurence O'Sullivan, Catholic curate of Kilmoe, Richard Edward Hull of Leamcon, Daniel Coghlan of Crookhaven and William Swanton of Ballydehob were also members.[100] On 18 May John Jagoe gave a general account of his parish to his rector, Anthony Traill in Lisburn, County Antrim. The failure of the potato crop caused a great scarcity of food among its 'wretched inhabitants'. The parish had a population of 12,500 and nearly a third of it was in a 'state of starvation'. There were few resident gentry and the only person who was able to provide relief was a Lieutenant Miggison of the coast-guards who had already subscribed up to £30. John Jagoe hesitated to ask the rector for aid as he knew what little tithes he had received from the parish the previous two years. Jagoe knew more than twenty families that were subsisting on nettles and weeds. A great number of cows had died of starvation and their carcasses were eagerly devoured by the starving people. Dysentery was making its appearance. Miggison and himself had each erected boilers to make soup for the poor of whom sixty were served daily.[101] On 21 May Daniel Coghlan informed the London Tavern Committee of 'the truly calamitous state of the numerous poor of this country, *numbers have already died for want of food'*. He had received £10 from a gentleman and was going to Cork in a vessel for that much worth of oaten meal. He held that nearly 2,000 people were starving out of a population of nearly 6,000. His brother, Captain Jeremiah Coghlan,[102] a famous captain in the Royal Navy, was a member of the London Committee and was instrumental in obtaining £200 for Schull and Kilmoe. Lord Carbery received £100 for Rosscarbery and a similar sum for Schull and its vicinity.[103] At the end of May accounts were sent to the Cork Committee by Rev. Jagoe and Lord Carbery; this committee reported that 'many unfortunate creatures have perished in consequence of the want of food and in Skibbereen 4,500 persons are in a state of starvation'.[104]

Early in June Bishop John Murphy chaired a meeting of the Cork relief committee. Reports were read from many parishes all over the county including Aughadown and Kilcoe. A petition was sent to Wellesley stating that these accounts showed that there were at least 40,000 people in a condition of 'urgent and afflicting distress' and that there were already some deaths from starvation.[105] It was estimated that there were 220,000 distressed persons in the County of Cork or one in every three of the total population.[106] Bishop Murphy told how the poor were bleeding cattle and drinking the blood mixed with a little milk.[107] At this time too a heading in the *Southern Reporter* ran, 'STARVATION IN CROOKHAVEN'. The writer refuted an earlier claim that the distress was no worse than in 1817 and warned that unless immediate aid was sent they would 'hear of deaths by the hundreds'.[108]

Rev. Jagoe reported to the London Committee on 14 June that his poor remote parish contained 13,000 persons of whom 7,500 were destitute of food, with very few resident gentry to aid them. The Schull committee soon presented its accounts thus revealing its diverse sources of income:

Lord Lieutenant,	£60		
Mansion House Committee, Dublin,	£50		
Liverpool (private),	£21	13s	4d
London Committee,	£108	6s	8d
Cork Committee,	£60		
Total	**£300**	**0s**	**0d**

There was now only £108 remaining and this would last only a week. Although there was only one committee for both parishes separate accounts were kept for each. The £60 from Cork was a grant of £5 for every 100 unemployed men showing that the parish had 1,200 such persons.[109]

A great effort was made to employ the poor especially on road-works. John Jagoe was employing 420 men on the road depending on personal and public funds which were almost exhausted. He told how two quarts of meal were given to each of these 'beings more resembling skeletons than living men, the imagination can scarcely conceive more frightening forms of want, misery, famine than are exhibited in those naked and languishing groups which from first dawn of day until night closes surround the Parsonage House of Schull'. Hitherto the Cork Committee had granted £5 or £10 per 100 unemployed men in the hope of securing work for them but in June it offered grants of £15 for every 100 actually employed. Kilmoe got £25 for its 160 at work. Caheragh received £13 for its 87 while Abbeystrowry obtained nearly £30 for its almost 200 men. Cargoes of potatoes, 120 tons, were on their way from England and would be sold at 2d per weight (21 pounds) under their market value.[110] The London Tavern Committee paid bounties on imports of potatoes.[111] The following gives the number of ships and the ports at which they arrived thus indicating the intensity and location of the food shortage; Crookhaven 1; Skibbereen 3; Bantry 1; Berehaven 2; Cork 1; Kenmare 1; Castlemaine 1; Limerick 1; Clare 2; Kilrush 2; Galway 2; Westport 1 and Sligo 2.[112] In addition 300 tons of potatoes were landed at Baltimore out of which 80 tons were sent to Crookhaven and 60 tons to Bantry.[113]

The London Tavern Committee was certainly generous in the summer of 1822. Fr Dore of Caheragh applied for aid as some of his people were fainting from hunger as they tried to sow potatoes. Typhus fever was spreading and had claimed some victims. He was glad that 'not an act of outrage was perpetrated during the late disgraceful disturbances'. The number receiving meal was 1,182. He obtained £100. At Drimoleague Thomas Tucker, the rector and Fr John Ryan, the parish priest, were also granted £100 to help to feed 2,666 people. Fr Michael Collins told how his poor parishioners were being fed with £360 worth of meal and potatoes. Rev. Wright, vicar of Aughadown, obtained £100 and a cargo of potatoes. Kilcoe and Cape Clear were being relieved by Samuel Townsend. A cargo of meal was shipped to Rev. Jagoe for Schull and Durrus. Daniel Coghlan and the Catholic priest, Laurence O'Sullivan, obtained £200 for Crookhaven and a similar sum was sent to Schull. At least 9 tons of meal and 3 tons of biscuit were delivered to the parishes of Abbeystrowry, Cape Clear and Sherkin, Aughadown, Kilcoe and Caheragh during that summer.

The amount of road-work organised by clergymen, both Catholic and Protestant, was significant. Rev. Morritt described how they tried to work in July:

Distress is increasing in ratio most terrific. Their limbs swell at the slightest exertion and fever has begun to spread very widely. Many of those employed can only work part of the day as, in order to give something for their children out of 5d a day, they almost stint themselves and become swollen and faint. My curate and I bid them to stop working.

He was sorry that he had to turn away many fathers of families because they had only four children and he would employ only those who had more than that. In any case he had no money to pay them as 'our incomes have been annihilated by the disturbances and the people naturally look up to our exertions as their sheet anchor'.[114] Fr Dore employed 330 men thanks to money received from the London Committee and also obtained pick-axes free from farmers. The Church of Ireland curate and the Catholic clergy alternated as inspectors and pay-clerks near Baltimore.[115] In County Clare, for instance, Fr Malachy Duggan used these London funds to employ 5,583 men and repair 10 miles of road.[116]

At the end of July the London Committee gave due notice that their weekly aid would soon be coming to an end. So it instructed the parochial committee to 'make a gradual reduction in the numbers of labourers employed by them *as far as the same shall be practicable* as the sudden dismissal of thousands of men may be attested with serious consequences'. There would be no large-scale and sudden dismissals as were to happen in 1847. The Cork Committee recommended the making of a bridge at Baxtersford a few miles west of Bandon and at a place called Aunafulla and granted £2,000 to Richard Griffith who would mark the beginning of a new era in road-making.[117]

As great as the relief effort certainly was not everybody was satisfied. At Crookhaven a union or guild of tradesmen calling themselves 'cordinairers' or shoemakers complained to the London Committee that they had received little or no charity in spite of the 'great failure' of their trade due, no doubt, to the peace following Waterloo. One of them had to pawn his clothes and furniture. Another named Love moaned that his wife had died leaving him four children; she was 'waking when Death and Famine in conjunction came to the door'.[118]

The prevailing feeling was that as the harvest approached conditions were going to improve. Already at the end of June, Lord Carbery announced that another few weeks would put an end to the distress. In August an agent of the London Committee, George Warmington, visited West Cork and was welcomed by Lord Carbery to Castlefreke near Clonakilty. This visitor was told that there was less fever now around Rosscarbery than in ordinary years. Gentlemen at Castlehaven told him that they did not feel justified in applying for any more aid. He found the poor in a healthy state with only a few mild fevers at Bantry. He met the Skibbereen committee which told him that 1,400 heads of families were receiving relief and that all who were capable of working were employed. The system of demanding labour for money had been only recently adopted so that there was little improvement in the roads but 200 men had been wisely directed to cut turf at the expense of the committee. People were suffering from cold as well as hunger. He was informed that in the nearby village of Abbeystrowry two or three persons had died from actual starvation in the early part of the season. It was the first case in all the County of Cork where proof had been given of such deaths.

George Warmington visited Schull 'with special interest, knowing it to have suffered perhaps to a greater extent than any in the county'. He gave the population of Schull as 15,000 of whom nearly 10,000 had been supported by charity for the previous ten weeks. Rev. Jagoe had sufficient money and provisions to supply the poor until the harvest. Their own potatoes were fit for food and selling at only 4d per weight compared to 10d in June. 'A general state of good health prevails,' he concluded, and was glad that Cape Clear and Sherkin had not been neglected either.[119] Several had died of starvation on the islands of Innisbofin and Innisturk off County Galway.[120] Mortality was indeed very low in West Cork unlike Connemara. A similar agent of the London committee found that thirty-two persons had died of starvation in that part of Connaught.[121] The reason why so few died in West Cork was undoubtedly that there was relatively little fever there although 'several families' had fever in Castlehaven as late as October.[122] In Mayo there had been 2,097 cases, Kerry 320 and County Cork 390.[123] Fr Michael Collins of Skibbereen granted that there had indeed been fever and dysentery at this time, but less than in the previous distress thanks to 'ample and timely supplies that came from England'.[124] Dr Daniel Donovan of the Donovan 'Islands', Clonakilty and later of Skibbereen would refer to fevers in 1817 and 1819 but did not mention 1822 at all. Dr Renny of the Board of Health held that famine and fever follow each other as cause and effect.[125] Dr Donovan similarly maintained that the best cure for fever was food and the best prevention, employment.[126] That explains why fever was not allowed to follow famine at this time and get a fatal grip; as it would have been put at the time, fever was fed.

At the end of August the London Tavern Committee announced that its supplies of food and money had come to an end and encouraged the people to depend on their own industry to avert famine in future but they also assured them they had endeared themselves to the English people by their conduct under severe distress.[127] The Dublin Mansion Committee similarly ceased operations in August claiming that 'the more than ordinary pressure of distress had been removed' now that the harvest had come. This committee thanked people in North America and in France who had hastened to relieve their wants. A sum of £5,000 had come from London. The total amount spent was £30,406 of which County Cork contributed £3,180.[128] The London Committee however did continue to provide clothes for the poor as the winter approached. The poet, Mícheál Óg Ó Longáin, who had spent a part of his youth in Caheragh, but was now living in Carraig na bhFear or Glanmire near Cork expressed well the feelings of many people in mind and body during this winter of 1822–3:

Fuacht na scailpe-se, deatach is gaoth gheimridh,
cruas na leapa-sa 's easpa brait lae 's oíche
muarcuid teacsanna, deachmhaithe 's glaoch cíosa
tug buartha cathach mé, easpaitheach éagaointeach.[129]

The cold of this mud cabin, smoke and wintry wind,

the hardness of this bed and the lack of a mantle day or night,
heavy taxes, tithes and rack-rent demands
have made me troubled, in want, and lamenting.

Clothes were gathered or made by Ladies' Associations in England, one of which had Mrs Peel and Mrs Goulburn as patronesses. The Cork Ladies' Society, whose secretary was Ann Marie Lee, also collected clothes as well as donations. Jane, wife of Daniel Coghlan, told the London Committee of the 'naked and pitiable state of at least 1,000 of our poor country women, some near, and others, 100 years … who have not as many rags as would cover an infant. In no part of the County of Cork are there so many naked females'. This is a rare reference to the plight of the very old as well as of the very young in time of famine. Mary Townsend of Aughadown counted 300 naked children in the parish, many of them boys. Some had made clothes from meal bags.[130] Although the Society of Friends was not quite so prominent in this famine as it was to be in 1847 yet it was not absent either. A Quaker lady in Cork sent some clothes from the London Tavern Committee to Bantry; this committee also sent a supply of blankets to Ireland. The County of Cork was allotted 2,700 blankets which were sent to certain ladies to distribute. Kilmoe received 50 blankets which were given out by Jane Coghlan and by Mrs Lionel Fleming of Ballydevlin who was later of New Court, Skibbereen. Schull likewise received 50 blankets which were distributed by Mrs Jagoe, the vicar's wife. Aughadown's share of 35 blankets was handed around by Mary Townsend and by Mrs Wright, the vicar's wife.[131]

The demographic effect of this famine in the parish of Schull is reflected in the baptismal records. In 1820 there were 258 baptisms but this fell to 154 in 1821 and to 119 in 1822 but the next year it rose again to 286 thus reflecting the recovery of the parish in general.[132]

In August 1823 the London Tavern Committee granted £200 for fishing lines and a supply of fishhooks was sent from Bristol. It also gave £5,000 of its remaining funds to the Irish Fishery Board to be given out as loans to distressed fishermen. This board set up a committee from among themselves to administer it which consisted of Lord Carbery, a Colonel Hodder and James Redmond Barry of Seven Heads, Barryroe and later of Glandore, a Catholic middleman, who was also struggling to promote fisheries.[133] The local committee for the district from Roaringwater Bay to Mizen Head consisted of John Jagoe, Lionel Fleming of Ballydevlin and Daniel Coghlan of Crookhaven.[134] It was painfully realised that fishing was not established on a commercial basis and had been of little value during the famine. Rev. Horace Townsend recommended to J. R. Barry that a fish-curing station be established at Baltimore and curing houses in Crookhaven. The fishermen were curing the fish in their own smoky cabins with poor results as regards quality. There were only four boats at Crookhaven whose crews were full-time fishermen and the rest were only fishermen/farmers/labourers.[135]

There can be no doubt about the remarkable benevolence of the English people and of others too in the different parts of the empire in 1822. India, for example, sent £30,000 of which Calcutta gave £19,000.[136] Quite a number of subscribers must have been Irish too in the imperial military or civil service such as Captain Jeremiah Coghlan of Crookhaven. The *Freeman's Journal* commented on 'the generosity of London, the supineness of Dublin and the shaky inhumanity of Cork'.[137] Yet this county gave £12,010 out of the total of £44,177 contributed by the whole country to the London Tavern Committee. There seems however to be little or no account of local subscriptions in West Cork. One Michael Sullivan of Bantry asserted that were it not for the British public 'they could not even buy the coffins for those who would be dead'. Daniel Coghlan was grateful also, 'The humane liberality of the sister kingdom to this unfortunate country,' he declared, 'never can be forgotten by any Irish heart possessing the smallest spark of gratitude'. Richard Deasy of Clonakilty assured the London Tavern Committee that this was going to have profound political results:

> It is quite delightful to us to reflect, that the union of two countries will be, by such acts cemented more completely than it could be by any other; and you have accomplished by your splendid exertions in the cause of suffering humanity, what had been so long unattainable, though so much desired – the making us one people.[138]

Fr Michael Collins when asked by a select committee if there was a growing feeling in that part of the country in favour of England, replied, 'Universally'. He went on to relate that when the agents of the London Tavern Committee came over they 'were hailed as deliverers of the people', that men carried 'pitch barrels on their heads, the upper parts of them on fire … joy and gratitude were testified'. He himself had seen these Englishmen shedding tears of joy 'so much were they affected by the gratitude of the people'. He was convinced that the connection between Ireland and England was growing stronger and that the people 'have latterly attached themselves to England, especially since the year, 1822, they look to England and to England alone for relief'.[139]

Why did some parts of Ireland starve or nearly starve in 1822? The parliamentary inquiry gave the official answer that although the potato had failed:

> There was no want of food of another description for the support of human life; on the contrary, the crops of grain had been far from deficient, and the price of corn and oaten meal were very moderate. The calamity of 1822 may therefore be said to have proceeded less from the want of food itself, than from the want of adequate means of purchasing it or in other words from want of profitable employment.[140]

Fr Collins described in a less official manner how the calamity struck two particular classes at local level:

> First: working men of all descriptions dependent on wages for their subsistence.
> Second: The poorer of small farmers who form a very great portion of the peasantry. Want of employment, joined to the failure of the potato crop, is the cause of the distress felt by the first class. The second is not affected by want of employment but by

want of food caused by the failure of the potatoes and by the necessities of the land-lords whom the low prices of grain compelled to seize the whole of the corn crop for rent, thereby leaving the occupying tenants without food, money or credit.[141]

He also said that when these poor farmers sold their grain it did not even pay all the rent.[142] His own poor list contained 1,505 families or 6,123 individuals out of the 10,000 souls in his care. We have seen how they and others like them were efficiently relieved by food and employment. This explains the fact that while many indeed were hungry very few starved to death.

The relief of the famine of 1822 was carried out in a spirit of ecumenism; 'charity' was still charitable. There were few or none of the religious contro-versies which were soon to mar such works of mercy. In Schull and Kilmoe Rev. John Jagoe and Fr Laurence O'Sullivan worked well together on the same relief committee and possibly on the same road-works. In Kilmeen near Ross-carbery the parish priest praised the 'meritorious conduct' of the rector, Rev. E. H. Kenney, in organising work on the roads, 'in paying the labourers in money or meal, the distribution of soup, etc'.[143] The appeal of John Jagoe to his rector, Anthony Traill, did not go in vain. When a new chapel was being built in the parish at Ballinskea in 1825 Traill gave a generous donation to it and was lauded by the parish priest, Michael Prior, as a 'liberal divine' who had made a 'liberal reduction of his tithe leases and cancelled altogether an arrears of £1,200 for the purpose of alleviating the sufferings of an afflicted people'.[144] This chapel bore a plaque recording the generosity of Catholics and also of Protestants as shall be seen later. 'The Second Reformation' however had al-ready begun in 1822 with Archbishop Magee's famous sermon in St Patrick's cathedral in Dublin, as shall also be seen later.[145] Alexander Dallas was one of the many English Protestant clergymen who preached charity sermons for the Irish in response to the appeal of the London Tavern Committee. He was later to take a leading part in the evangelical movement to convert the Irish to Protestantism and founded the Irish Church Missions in 1849.[146] But in 1822 such evangelicalism had not yet reached many of the parishes in Ireland.

ROAD-MAKING
Wellesley sent Richard Griffith, civil engineer to Munster to make roads at public expense. (He was to carry out his valuation of the country in the 1850s.) Another engineer, Alexander Nimmo, was appointed to the region of Galway, Mayo, Leitrim, Roscommon and Sligo and John Killaly was sent to the Shan-non area. The guiding principle given to Griffith was that he should select re-mote districts where it was unlikely that the Grand Jury would ever make a road.[147] The government had found that such districts had been 'the focus of, and asylum for, Whiteboys, smugglers and robbers', where they could not easily be pursued by troops.[148] A road had been made by labouring soldiers to Sally Gap and Glenmalure, County Wicklow, in the period 1800–5 mainly to facilitate the suppression of Michael Dwyer and his 'mountain rebels'.[149] Yet in 1822 the government was also aware that many remote districts such as the

Mizen Peninsula were now suffering from famine and needed some relief. These roads would be made for reasons both of humanity and of security.

Irish roads were generally better than English roads towards the end of the eighteenth century. Arthur Young wrote: 'For a country so far behind us as Ireland, to have got suddenly so much start of us in the article of roads, is a spectacle that cannot fail to strike the English traveler exceedingly.' Young gave the credit to the Grand Juries for Ireland's 'beautiful roads' but excluded the Turnpike roads from this compliment.[150] At this time, many English roads were 'foundrous', some had even to be ploughed at the end of winter in order to make them level enough for wheeled traffic.[151] Industrialists in general and especially the Board of Agriculture and the Post Office demanded better roads in the nineteenth century. This need was answered by the modern pioneer of road-making, a Scotsman, John MacAdam (1827–1865). Up to this time even the best roads were only rubble-granite causeways but he insisted that a road should be constructed by means of layers of small stones and gravel and be well drained.[152] This method which became known as 'macadamisation' was closely followed by Richard Griffith.

Early in the summer of 1822 some gentlemen and clergy in the Mizen Peninsula sent a petition to Wellesley for the construction of a new road from Skibbereen to Crookhaven. The people were suffering from unprecedented distress. The country was hilly and the roads 'nearly impracticable and not passable to some wheeled carriages to the great hindrance to all improvements in agriculture'. A new road 'would tend much to the civilisation of a very wild district' and would cost only about £600, they estimated. The petition was signed by the following Church of Ireland clergymen, J. Wright, J. Jagoe, R. Morrit and J. Triphook, later to be curate of Ballydehob. J. Daly, parish priest of Aughadown, also signed. Among the gentlemen who added their names were William and Richard Edward Hull of Leamcon, Hugh Lawton of Aughadown and James Sullivan of Roaring Water.[153]

In June 1822 Griffith first visited Kerry where he later made many roads.[154] Early in July he came to Cork and met the relief committee for the county. He learned from it that there were about 40,000 families in want in the county especially in Carbery. He called a meeting of all the overseers of Grand Jury roads in the county. The fund of the County Cork relief committee amounted to £6,000 which had come from the Mansion House Committee, the London Tavern Committee and local sources. To this fund Griffith added the grant of £3,000 from Wellesley. He had now at his disposal £9,000 of a 'charitable fund' and £2,000 Grand Jury money, so he formed 'a systematic plan of relief'.[155] Some roads were paid for by the Grand Jury money and others by the 'charitable fund', but all funds were controlled by Griffith himself.

Griffith soon laid out many roads around Clonakilty, Millstreet and Macroom, districts in which the Whiteboys had been very active. As was recommended to him by the Cork relief committee he duly built a bridge at Baxtersford now Baxtersbridge near Bandon. The bridge at Aunafulla was built at this time too. The road which was of vital importance to the Mizen Peninsula

Sir Richard Griffith, 1784–1878

was the road from Skibbereen to Crookhaven which he laid out in July 1822. He stated that the distance was 27.5 miles and that 23 miles of 'new road' would be required. The old road was so bad that the country west of Skibbereen was 'nearly inaccessible to horsemen except in dry weather'. During the winter communications between Skibbereen and Crookhaven were 'nearly suspended to the great inconvenience of ships which resorted to that harbour for shelter'. Skibbereen was the nearest town in which their crews could post a letter. Since it was difficult or impossible for wheeled carriages to make their way farm produce had to be carried on the backs of horses to the market in Skibbereen. In spite of this, the district sent 6,000 firkins of butter, valued at £10,500 annually, to the Cork market and also had a very large export of oats and barley.

It is clear from Griffith's sketch map that his new road did not begin exactly at Skibbereen but at New Court two miles west of it; neither did this road end exactly at Crookhaven but at Rock Island two miles east of it. For most of the way he did not follow the old coastal road because that route was 'circuitous', steep and went through very rocky terrain. Instead he went further inland; this route was more direct but more boggy. Of course, bogs were more easily cut through than rocks. On the other hand, old chapels at Kilcoe and Stouke near Ballydehob were bypassed.

Work began under Griffith's direction on 29 July 1822. Soon he had 3,000 labourers employed.[156] Griffith found that road-makers like himself had a bad reputation among the labourers who feared injustice and oppression. Labourers wanted to work not by the piece but by the day and they also wanted to do as little as possible. So he divided them into groups of ten or twelve over which he placed a gauger who measured the work and paid the men accordingly. Griffith regarded himself as working among 'a people of wild and turbulent habits', in remote areas, so that 'great caution and firmness, united with good temper' were necessary. Frequently men who could not calculate their earnings would suddenly lose confidence in their foreman and throw up their work. But this engineer also pointed out that: 'They are naturally a fine people: but they have been frequently oppressed by their immediate landlords. They are grossly ignorant and prejudiced; if educated and employed, they would soon become good and peaceful subjects'.[157]

Griffith gave a statement of expenditure from August 1822 to December 1823. We are also given a detailed picture of the work involved. The sum of £4,100 had already been spent on oaten meal given out as part-wages:[158]

TABLE 2: ROADS: COST, 1822–3

Work	£s
Forming, fencing, draining	1,592
Gullies	118
Rock cutting	514
Gravelling	295
Carting	57
Carriage of timber, etc.	397
Overseers	316
James Burke, engineer	250
Upkeep of his horse	85
Total	**3,624**

Griffith reported that some of the bogs he had to drain were so wet that his surveyors had to put planks under their feet to prevent them from sinking. Still the bogs so drained were now producing crops of potatoes and oats. James Barry, parish priest of Schull, confirmed this and added that turf was now becoming accessible to many who had suffered for the want of it. He regretted, however, that there was still a 'great amount of land in the interior that has never been broken up for lack of roads to convey manure to it'.[159] This new road was already helping to reclaim the wastelands and produce more food. Griffith was also in charge of great drainage schemes in many parts of the country. This experience caused him to emphasise the importance of drainage in the making of roads.[160] On other occasions he found it difficult to make a road because rocks, even 'steep precipices' extended out to sea, so he ran the road along the strand. He secured 'firm foundations by building quay walls along the shore and filling the space between the walls and the rocks'.

Since this Skibbereen–Crookhaven road ran through the Mizen Peninsula and crossed over many rivers flowing from various hills and mountains such as Mount Gabriel and Mount Kid towards the sea, it was necessary to build as many as fourteen bridges. Griffith stressed the importance of laying the foundations of the abutments of a bridge and criticised the Grand Jury contractors who, he claimed, often built on loose stones and gravel so that their bridges were virtually built on castors. He himself often instructed his men to dig to a depth of thirteen feet below the level of the bed of a river. Work continued on both roads and bridges until 1826. Griffith gave a list of the bridges built from Skibbereen to Crookhaven and the cost of each.[161]

TABLE 3: BRIDGES: COST, 1822–6

Bridge	Cost £s
Hollyhill (beside Kilcoe chapel)	463
Ballinclare, 'The Crooked Bridge'	164
Ballydehob (repairs; three new arches, etc.)	512
Gloshure	96
Rathcoole	61
Cooridorigan	61
Ballinskea	38
Lowertown	54
Lowertown West	41
Altar	38
Toormore	58
Ballyrisode	41
Goleen	51
Cooradowney	37
Total	**1,715**

The person travelling from Skibbereen to Crookhaven does not realise that he or she has to pass over fourteen bridges because they all are by now flush with the road except Hollyhill, Ballinclare or 'The Crooked Bridge', Ballydehob, Altar and Toormore. The cost of these bridges was £1,715, which was far higher than Griffith's original estimate of only £600. At this period he was also building many bridges in Kerry and Limerick. The most impressive is the five-arch bridge over the Feale at Listowel.[162]

To sum up, the length of the new Skibbereen–Crookhaven road was 23 miles and its breath, i.e., solid or 'macadamised' surface, was 21 feet. The total cost of the road, excluding bridges, was £7,724, a cost of about £335 per mile and almost double Griffith's original estimate of £4,500, or about £196 per mile. The total cost of road plus bridges was £9,439.[163] Although it was a period of deflation he seriously underestimated the difficulty of building roads and bridges in such terrain. The labourers were often hungry too, no doubt. Griffith was sanguine as regards the benefits which his new roads were conferring. The local inhabitants had saved money from their wages which had aided them to buy horses, cattle and implements. They were now able to transport lime and sea-manure to their lands. The old roads had been impassable in wet weather even for horsemen during the Whiteboy disturbances. Districts which had been places of 'lawless outrage', sheltering the equivalent of rebel armies were now 'tranquil and industrious' according to Griffith.[164] He improved and shortened by about 1.3 miles the old road on which Sir John Moore's redcoats had marched. What had been only a 'bridle road' was now an arterial road along which wheeled traffic could easily travel. The improvement was revolutionary as it brought the peninsula out of the eighteenth and into the nineteenth century. The road facilitated the introduction of the manufactured goods of the Industrial Revolution known as 'Manchester goods' and no doubt also the English language. This road naturally facilitated emigration as well. In her study of 'missing friends' in the *Boston Pilot* newspaper, Ruth-Ann Harris has found that a particularly high number of them had come from districts which had been provided with good road-systems. She gives as examples the roads made by Griffith in Cork and Kerry.[165] Griffith's road through the Mizen Peninsula was vital for the development of the villages of Crookhaven, Schull and particularly of Ballydehob as shall be observed later.[166] Griffith's work was significant too in the wider context. It was the first time that the government interfered in road-making, hitherto considered the exclusive domain of the local Grand Juries. This tendency was to continue and culminated in the founding of the Board of Works in 1830. Griffith became its chairman in the period 1850–64.

Road-making to relieve the famine of 1822 thus ended on a happy note. Comparisons between it and the Great Famine of 1845–9 inevitably spring to mind. The potato failure in 1821 was simply caused by severe weather and the crop of 1822 was sound once more. The failure of 1845, however, was caused by a deadly disease and thus the crop of 1846 was even more seriously afflicted again. The famine of 1822 was only a summer famine with the people looking forward to the harvest whereas the famine in 1845 and 1846 was a harvest famine which left them facing into the winter. In addition there were the important matters of duration and extent. The 1822 famine lasted only four months, i.e., April to July, whereas the later famine lasted four years at least, 1845–9. In 1822 only the southern and western regions of the country were affected whereas in 1845 the whole country was stricken. The population was lower and of course less poor in 1822 than in the later starvation. The parish of Schull had 14,000 mouths to feed in 1822 but more than 18,000 in 1847. The famine of 1822 was relieved more effectively. In general, food was offered first and only then work. In those road-works carried out by clergy the labourers were paid in meal as well as in money. Griffith continued this policy, paying at least £4,100 for oaten meal.[167] When he began his works in July 1822 the worst of the famine was over. In 1845–7, however, work was offered first under the Labour Rate Act and only when this failed was food offered in any substantial quantity under the Temporary Relief Act or Soup Kitchen Act. It must be granted, of course, that in this later period the scale of the catastrophe was far greater. In 1822 Free Trade was not yet part of economic thinking; nobody had any inhibitions about putting bounties on potato imports or selling them under market price or even interfering in the corn trade by paying labourers with meal. Griffith, who was to be in charge of road-making with the Board of Works in 1845–7, pointed out that in 1822 road-makers like himself had been allowed more autonomy; they were 'free from relief committees and the encumbrance of Presentment Sessions'.[168] Apart from men who may have been implicated in Whiteboy troubles, it does not seem that that there are any accounts of emigration in 1822 and yet this hunger must have disturbed the people who eventually left in 1830–3. It has been seen that the famine relief in 1822 was ecumenical as regards religion whereas in 1845–52 it was controversial at times. There was a far better spirit of benevolence in England towards the Irish in the 1820s than in the 1840s. The campaigns for Catholic Emancipation and repeal had not yet stirred up latent anti-Catholic and anti-Irish feelings in England. Gratitude for the English aid in 1822 tended to cement the union of the two countries whereas in 1847 disappointment with the British government put further strain on the cracks already appearing in it. In the spring of 1847 Fr Michael Collins' brother, Denis, then parish priest of Mallow, went on a deputation to an unsympathetic Lord John Russell and related that he himself had been involved in famine relief in Skibbereen in 1822 but that now at this late stage a 'radical cure' was necessary because 'the existing evil was not of recent growth'.[169] At both periods, however, courageous men and women struggled to deliver the country from the evils of poverty, famine and fever.

THE WHITEBOYS AGAIN

In the summer of 1822 there was some activity in the Schull district by what William Hull called a 'noted gang of house-robbers'. This gang robbed the house of a Thomas Connell; he recognised two of them as Daniel Carty and Tim Donovan, alias 'Killenuck'. Daniel Carty turned informer and sent Hull a list of outrages with the names of those who took part in them. The list was immediately dispatched by Hull to Gregory in Dublin Castle. The informer revealed that he himself had taken part in the robbery of Thomas Connell's house together with some others by the names of Michael Cotter, John Hegarty and Tim Donovan, alias 'Killenuck'. It was these men who had also robbed Dr Townsend's house but on that occasion they were accompanied by Owen Daly, alias 'Hag' and Cornelius Harrington, alias 'Grerah'. The informer also divulged that these were the men who were riding with Harrington when he was shot by the Beamishs. These Whiteboys also robbed a Mr Freke of Baltimore, John Coghlan of Crookhaven, a widow near Bandon and a man on the boundaries of Cork and Kerry. Hull immediately got some constables, arrested Donovan 'Killenuck' and Michael Cotter and sent them to the County Gaol in Cork. Hull stated that 'Hag' Daly was already in either the Cork or Kerry County Gaol awaiting trial.[170]

Whiteboy activities at this time were permeated by a spirit of millenarianism. This cult often occurs when there is fear of a catastrophe such as famine, plague, or massacre, especially in peasant societies which feel excluded from political power. There is the belief that their enemies will be destroyed by some superhuman power. The Ireland of the early 1820s had experienced famine as we have seen. The brutal suppression of the 1798 Rebellion had caused many to despair of ordinary human methods and all of this was followed by the fall of Napoleon who had been a kind of messianic figure to Whiteboys. According to many peasants, Pastorini foretold the 'slatar' of Protestants. Pastorini was the pen-name of an English bishop who claimed to make out from the Bible that God's wrath would be poured out on the heretics around 1821 or 1825. Lord Carbery lamented that very many Catholics of the lower orders were taken in by these prophecies. 'That diabolical book,' he declared, 'has poisoned the minds of thousands and tens of thousands of those wretched beings'.[171] Fr Micheal Collins told how a man carrying copies of Pastorini's prophesies and pretending to be an agent of the Whiteboys went into the parish of Kilmoe 'to stimulate the people to rebellion'. He was arrested but soon released when it turned out that he was a government agent.[172]

It must be kept in mind that the Whiteboys were themselves victims of injustices which were legal in the form of rents and tithes. Even when the tithe proctors did break the law they were usually able to do so with impunity. The government's and the magistrates' side of the story has been given but we have not heard the Whiteboys' case. Men like Harrington 'Grerah' did not leave us any letters nor was there a Hansard to record the proceedings of their moonlight parliaments. However, we are fortunate that there was one magistrate, Daniel Coghlan of Crookhaven, who gave the Whiteboys' side of the story. In October 1822 he denounced to the castle not only Joseph Baker but also a neighbouring tithe proctor, William Switzer, who worked for the absentee rector of Kilmoe, Francis Langford:

A few years back the Rev. Francis Langford of the County of Limerick was induced into the living of this large parish … Mr Langford does not attend himself to collect his tithes or to officiate in any way … His tithe proctor, William Switzer, is also a native of the County of Limerick, a dangerous, drunken, wicked man. He sets what valuation he pleases on his master's tithes and obliges the people by force of arms to pay the amount of such valuation. Should they dare even to make any observation on the illegality of the act, he presents his gun at them … Complaints are daily made before me against this proctor but the poor people are in such dread and terror of being shot by him and are afraid to prosecute … I also beg to offer it as my humble opinion that many of the nightly depredations that were committed in several parts of this county last winter were occasioned by the severe tyranny and oppression of such petty tyrants.

> Dr Traill is the rector of the parish of Schull. That gentlemen resides in Lisburn in the County of Antrim, he let the tithes of that immense parish ... to Joseph Baker. In oppression in the collection of his tithes he is the equal of Switzer ... About three weeks back some butter of his on its way to market was destroyed. He was personally attacked on the high road by a number of persons unknown and nearly killed.[173]

Coghlan's letter speaks for itself and it vividly illustrates the workings of the tithe system at its worst; the tithe proctor was above the law while the tithe payer was outside the law. A magistrate like Coghlan was in an unenviable position. He was afraid of the tithe proctors and he did not feel sure of effective support from the castle if he moved against them; he would have had some reason to dread the Whiteboys as well. The oppression of the tithe proctors, Baker and Switzer, justifies, or at least, helps to explain the outrages of the local Whiteboys.

The spring of the New Year 1823 was generally quiet all over the country except for the County of Cork. The Grand Jury at the Spring Assizes sent a letter to the lord lieutenant complaining that the spirit of insurrection was rapidly extending. The Grand Jury had before it 100 claims for compensation caused by 'fire, destruction of cattle by houghing, breaking machinery'. It was very difficult to award compensation because of intimidation. Those who came to give evidence often returned home to find their own houses ablaze. Whiteboys threatened a landlord near Macroom, 'Vesuvius or Mount Etna never sent forth such cracking flames as some parts of Aghabullogue will shortly emit, solid mass of fire'.[174] The Grand Jury did award £10,000 in compensation for outrages but it was forced to admit to the lord lieutenant that 'in spite of the exertions of the police, military and armed associations they were yet not able to control those men who defied the law of the land'.[175]

Griffith claimed that the districts became 'perfectly tranquil'[176] once he had begun working in them but this is an exaggeration. The following incident at Lord Audley's copper mines near Ballydehob formed part of the last wave of outrages of this period. Audley informed William Gregory, the under-secretary at Dublin Castle, that he had recently installed a 'mining machine'. Some of the 'unhappy people' of the area had been persuaded that it prevented them being employed so Audley feared that it would be damaged by Whiteboys with Luddite ideas. A mining agent of his had been severely injured by a labourer but the 'terror of the country' was so great that little could be done about it. Audley suggested that 'a few police would be of great help'.[177] Wellesley directed that this letter was to be sent to the magistrate of police for the district. The inspector general of police, Mr Willcocks, was ordered 'to station some police'; Audley was to be informed.[178] These policemen soon headed for their post. Thus, already in 1823, there were Peelers in Ballydehob, six years before they were in London.

The next trouble came from an interesting source – a public house in Ballydehob in 1824. It was St Patrick's Day and also a fair day and the country people were 'indulging freely in honour of the sod'. The police under Major Wynn attempted to clear the house but the revellers called them 'Peelers' and threw stones at them. The police fired over their heads and took nine prisoners who were committed for trial by William Hull.[179] It was an example of co-operation between the old order and the new, the magistrates and the new police, just as Peel had envisaged. But a newspaper protested that the unfortunate members of the peasantry, whether they came together to amuse themselves 'at bowls or with hurls' or whether they were drunk or sober, were construed by some to come within the Insurrection Act.[180]

The next incident however was an example of conflict between these two orders. It was on the subject of religion – a question now becoming particularly sensitive on account of the debate over Catholic Emancipation. At a Petty Sessions court in Skibbereen, a Jeremiah Murphy brought a case against a John McDonald and a P. Caulfield, police constables at Ballydehob, for assault and false imprisonment. On the magistrates' bench were Richard Townsend of Dunbeacon, chairman, Lionel Fleming of Ballydevlin and Alexander O'Driscoll of Crookhaven. Murphy stated that he was going his way along the street in Skibbereen when he observed two constables and an old man, Thomas Swanton, 'aggravating about religion'. They were asking him why he had abandoned the religion of his forefathers to worship the Virgin. Murphy suggested to the policemen that perhaps Swanton was on the right road and that others were going to hell. At this, Murphy alleged that the police beat him, calling him 'Croppy' and landed him in the Bridewell. The chairman of the bench declared that if this were true the policemen were guilty of 'a very violent outrage and a flagrant abuse of their authority'. The police admitted that they had arrested Murphy for saying that Protestants would go to Hell but denied beating him. The chairman warned the policemen that they had no right to provoke religious discussion. One of them replied that it made his blood boil to hear Murphy speak, and that in his own country anybody who said a Protestant might go to Hell would be punished not for religion but for treason. The magistrates warned the Peelers that they did not want 'preaching constables' and that their conduct would probably cause them to be dismissed from the force.[181] These constables were evidently Orangemen. The case illustrates the danger of the Peelers becoming what Daniel O'Connell might have called 'Orange Peelers' after their founder whom he is supposed to have dubbed 'Orange Peel'. Yet it did not become an unduly sectarian force as a substantial number of Catholics joined it especially in the days of Thomas Drummond.[182] By the 1840s two-thirds of Peelers were Catholics.[183]

Unlike the 'Heroes of '98' or 'The Bold Fenian Men', the Whiteboys had little or no romantic ideology. Still they would always be apt pupils for such doctrines because they operated in secret and had an instinctive faith in physical force. They were stigmatised as lawless *banditti* by the government but they would have replied that their ancestors had been legally robbed and that they themselves were being legally robbed too by high rents and tithes. The various outrages and attempts at insurrection by the Whiteboys were of course not a military success. Yet they attracted towards the country some of England's attention which had been so much turned towards the continent by Napoleon. The first reform was that of the magistrates in 1823; some of them were dismissed including Daniel Coghlan.[184] Evidently his denunciation to the castle by Baker, the tithe proctor, and O'Neill, the revenue officer, in 1816 had been heeded.

Another reform was the Tithe Reform Act of 1823 which encouraged the clergymen and parishioners to appoint arbitrators to 'compose' or determine a fixed money payment for a certain number of years. Catholics were hostile to the tithes not only on account of their amount and purpose but also on account of the crude method of their assessment and collection. At least something was being done to check the wanton activities of tithe-tyrants like Morritt, Baker and Switzer. Morritt's high-handed efforts to collect his tithes provoked an affray at Tralagough near Castletownshend where four people were killed including one policeman.[185] According to Fr Michael Collins, when this proctor first arrived he boasted that he would 'screw up' the natives for his tithes.[186] Peel remarked that Morritt was guilty of 'rapacity and oppressiveness'.[187] Morritt resigned his parish in 1824 and returned to England.[188] 'The devil go with him!', the *Freeholder* newspaper cursed.[189]

Clergymen such as Morritt and Jagoe were certainly very active and generous during the famine of 1822, but it must be remembered that this was not only a matter of charity but also of justice or civil duty in that they were in receipt of the tithes originally intended for the relief of the poor as well as the support of the clergy. Although the tithe system was harsh it was sometimes mitigated by personal kindness. We have seen, for example, that Anthony Traill forgave his tithes for 1822 although he had received little of this revenue the previous year. Morrit himself claimed that he was in the same situation.

There was a crude violence permeating society in 1821–3 which was not to be so pronounced in the period 1846–8 for all its revolutions and rumours of revolution. As already stated Harrington 'Grerah' was shot dead and nine men were hanged in the Macroom district which includes Máire Bhuí Ní Laoghaire's district of Uíbh Laoghaire. Donovan 'Killenuck' and Michael Cotter who had been sent to the County Gaol by William Hull were probably transported as well as 'Hag' Daly. The three Whiteboys captured by Morritt near Ballydehob, no doubt, shared the same fate. In the spring of 1822 Peel was asked to supply shipping for 200 convicts as 300 had been held in Cork to appear before the Special Commission. They were to be shipped via Spike Island to Botany Bay.[190] This feeling of sorrow, poverty and oppression comes across in Máire Bhuí's poem, *Tá Gaedhil Bhocht Cráidhte*;[191] the only hope is the slaughter of the enemy which would very soon happen according to Pastorini:

> Tá Gaedhil bhocht cráidhte go céasta cásmhar
> Agus cúirt gach lá orthu mar dhúbailt bróin,
> Clanna sáirfhear dá gcrochadh anáirde
> 'S dá gcur síos láithreach 'sa chroppy-hole;
> Tá loingeas lán díobh dá gcur thar sáile,
> Mo chúmha go bráth sibh faoi iomad yoke …

Is é chuala ó fhláidhibh go ndubhairt Naomh Seán linn
Go raibh deire an cháirde caithe leo
'S go dtiocfaidh slaughter ar gach piarda másach ...

The unfortunate Irish are tormented and pitiable
Appearing in court every day doubling their sorrow,
A race of great men being hanged on high
And thrown down into the Croppy-hole;
Ships full of them being sent abroad,
My constant sorrow that you are excessively under the yoke ...

It's what I heard from the prophets that St John told us
That the day of reckoning has arrived for them
And that slaughter would come on every sturdy fellow ...

In the summer of 1822 there are more references to transportation than to emigration. Yet a Captain Trevor reported to the government that 'great numbers of the lower orders', 5,850 of them, had departed for England to work in the harvest. Some of them too had been involved in the disturbances and were leaving for that reason.[192]

RELIGION

In March 1822 the government put pressure on the magistrates to hold Petty Sessions in which three or four magistrates would all sit in public. This helped to eliminate arbitrary action by one magistrate acting alone as William Hull often did. The new practice was given legal sanction by the Petty Sessions Act of 1827.[193] These reforms in the field of civil liberties prepared both government and people for reform in the domain of religious and political liberty, i.e., Catholic Emancipation. The Penal Laws were by no means a complete failure and had a degrading effect on Catholics, making them – and often keeping them – poor and ignorant. Many of these disabilities had indeed been taken away by 1793, still their effects on the people remained. As the politician and lawyer, Richard Lalor Sheil, put it, 'But the shoulders continued to stoop long after the weight had been removed'. Thomas Davis saw this too and pleaded:

What wonder if our step betrays
The freedman born in penal days![194]

Fr Michael Collins told a select committee how Catholics still felt 'degraded ... and insulted by what they consider the insolence which Protestant peasantry feel on account of the privileges they enjoy'. He gave as an example the fact that a Catholic peasant knows well that although his son can become a lawyer he cannot become a judge, an attorney general or even a sub-sheriff of a county. Fr Collins summed up the effect the Penal Law system still had on the people: 'There is a great moral debasement and degradation arising from it which renders them insincere, crafty, cringing, flattering and disposing them to make professions that they do not feel; and I think they are more or less careless about the improvement of their condition'. Accordingly Daniel O'Connell founded the Catholic Association in 1823 in the aftermath of famine and Whiteboy violence in order to address Catholic grievances and soon to agitate for emancipation itself. The Catholic rent would be a penny a month. But Fr Collins admitted that this rent was not being collected in Skibbereen simply because his people were trying to build a new chapel, but that it was collected in Clonakilty where the farmers and even the labourers were gladly contributing their pennies.[195] It is unlikely that the other parishes to the west were able to afford many pennies either as they were also building chapels as shall be seen later.[196]

Support, however, was already coming from Irish emigrants in the United States. As already stated in Chapter I, Robert Swanton of Ballydehob had escaped to that land in 1798 and was now a counsellor at law in the city of New York. In 1825 he attended a meeting of the 'Friends of Ireland in New York' who described themselves as 'Roman Catholics, warm admirers of civil and religious liberty'. Having been invited to take the chair, Counsellor Robert Swanton called for support for O'Connell and the Catholic Association and regretted that one of his Catholic Relief Bills had been defeated. Swanton demanded to know what true Americans could do for Ireland. The poor in Ireland, he said, swell the capital of the rich proprietors by their labour, digging canals, etc. Another speaker commented that the Catholics and the Orangemen were like the Negroes before their masters who despise and enthral them all. 'Let them copy the American Constitution,' he urged. The meeting passed the following resolution:

> Persons assembled form themselves into a society: proposals; First, rent to help those in Ireland in emancipation of their country. Second, sympathetically to address enlightened nations of the world on Ireland's wrongs and England's intolerance, that enemy of religious toleration, inimical to the universal law of nations.[197]

Here we get a glimpse at the first attempts of Irish exiles and their friends to harness American influence and dollars and to bring pressure to bear on England to right Old Ireland's wrongs.

As the movement for emancipation gathered strength it provoked local Irish as well as English intolerance. The Protestant clergy of Cork and Ross petitioned parliament against 'any concession of further power and privilege' to Catholics. The House was reminded that Catholics were already 'enjoying full liberty of conscience, together with uncontrolled exercise of their religion and now only seek the acquisition of power which history tells us cannot with safety be put in their hands'. These petitioners argued that what Catholics were really seeking was religious and political ascendancy aided by Papal authority 'professing to be founded on infallibility'. Among the petitioners were John Jagoe, now vicar of Kilcoe and John Triphook, now curate of Ballydehob.[198] It was a sign of the times that these petitioners should have considered Catholic Emancipation to be a further privilege rather than a universal right as Robert Swanton and his friends saw it; the weight of history was too much. Nevertheless these clergymen were to be proven right in warning that the Catholics, especially the middle classes, had the ulterior motive of political power and would not allow any emancipation to fix the boundary to their march. Although the movement for emancipation was constitutional and often led by the priests, as James S. Donnelly, Jr, points out, there was a certain cultural continuity between this and the Whiteboy/millenarian movement. No other barrister saved so many Whiteboys from the gibbet as O'Connell, an example being the 'Doneraile conspirators', immortalised in Canon P. Sheehan's *Glenanaar*. O'Connell also successfully defended Whiteboys at the courthouse in Timoleague near Clonakilty in 1822. A marriage connection between a local family, the Goulds of Ardfield, and the O'Connells together with some old smuggling/ trading contacts were undoubtedly used to obtain the services of the eminent Catholic lawyer of the day.[199] As already stated, he defended the sons of Máire Bhuí Ní Laoghaire. Gearóid Ó Tuathaigh shows that O'Connell 'inherited the mantle of deliverer and the winning of emancipation became for many of the peasantry the pursuit of the millennium'. The poet, Raftery, called on all to pay 'the Catholic rent' and cast O'Connell in the role of one who scatters heretics – shades of Pastorini.[200]

III

RELIGION AND EDUCATION, 1825–45

Mock on, mock on, Voltaire, Rousseau:
Mock on, mock on: 'tis all in vain!
You throw the sand against the wind
And the wind blows it back again.

ROBERT BLAKE (1757–1827)

I do not hesitate to assert that the existing generation in this country is half a century
ahead of that which is dying off, and that the generation now at school will be a century
in advance of us.

DR ROBERT KANE, 1844

CHURCH OF IRELAND: METHODISTS

The eighteenth century was generally an age of rationalistic Enlightenment rather than of religious enthusiasm but a gradual reaction took place towards the end of the period. The Evangelical movement was now gathering strength in the Anglican Church and disturbing the old rather rationalistic ways of Latitudinarianism. There had been much pluralism and absenteeism among the rectors of the parishes of Schull and Kilmoe. It has already been noted that Anthony Traill, rector of Schull, was an absentee. In 1791 Fitzgerald Tisdal was appointed rector of Kilmoe. As already stated he raised a yeomanry corps in 1798. In 1809 he exchanged his parish for that of Kenmare, County Kerry, where he was murdered on an Easter Sunday morning. He was succeeded in Kilmoe by Stephen Dunleavy who resigned in 1818. His successor was Francis Langford who, as we have been told, usually resided in his other benefice in County Limerick.[1] There was no glebe house in Kilmoe and this was given as a reason for non-residency.

The most enthusiastic of the evangelicals were the Wesleyans, the followers of the brothers, John and Charles Wesley. Charles preached in Bandon in 1748 and John came the following year. In 1784 Bandon was set up as a separate 'circuit' which was a local administrative unit. A chapel was opened by John Wesley who was paying his nineteenth and last visit to Bandon in 1789.[2] By then the Wesleyans had practically seceded from the Anglican Church and were also called Methodists. They had some doctrinal difference with their parent Church which they criticised for its subservience to government patronage and control. They also accused its clergymen of absenteeism and lack of zeal though living well off the tithes of the people. Methodist preachers found fertile fields in the parishes of the Mizen Peninsula. The first of these itinerant preachers, John Bredin, arrived in Skibbereen in 1779 and held service in the

Town Hall. He then organised the Skibbereen preaching circuit. The first Methodist house in the circuit was that of Captain Evans of Ardralla in Aughadown parish. By 1783 the home of Robert Swanton of Gortnagrough near Ballydehob had become a preacher's 'stopping place'. The first resident preacher in the Skibbereen circuit was John Hamilton who was soon joined by another preacher, Henry Deery. It was they who put the district on the Methodist map.[3] John Hamilton visited Ballydehob, Schull and Lissacaha near Toormore. At Lissacaha he found a large crowd assembled for a pattern. When invited to dance by a buxom damsel he replied that he could not but that he could pray, and kneeling down began to 'plead with God on behalf of the people'.[4]

In 1797 the Methodists in these parishes received a visit from the president of the Methodists in Ireland, Rev. Adam Averell. He told how he found 'serious' congregations at Ardralla and Aughadown. In another place he encountered 'a few dark, ignorant persons buried in superstition and dirt'. At Altar in Kilmoe he discovered a little cabin, 'where assembled upwards of thirty Protestants; but they were piteous objects, clothed in rags, like sheep without a shepherd'. They were as 'benighted as heathens'. He preached in Crookhaven to a large assembly of Protestants who had 'almost gone over to the Church of Rome'. As Averell returned through Ballydehob it happened to be St Patrick's Day and many people had arrived by land and sea 'to drown their shamrocks'. He occupied the hall of the largest house. He described the scene: 'During the sermon, the cry for mercy became so general that we could not have a love-feast, but engaged in a general prayer-meeting. Such were the cries of the people that the ground began to shake under us.' Outside on the street, other preachers exhorted the people in Irish and many of them were 'greatly affected'. 'Oh brother,' the preacher exclaimed, 'never did any now living, I believe, see such a day as this in Ireland'. The age of rationalism or indifference had certainly gone.

These preachers were becoming a cause of schism within the Church of Ireland. One notices that Averell merely attended service in Aughadown church but was not allowed to preach. He afterwards preached to the same congregation in a nearby granary.[5] When the preacher, John Deery, went to preach in Crookhaven he was arrested by the rector, Fitzgerald Tisdal, in his role as magistrate. Another preacher, John Rogers, fared better in 1804; he was not only given permission to preach by the same rector but was also invited to dine. He had got a sick stomach at Roycrofts of Kilpatrick. 'It was nothing there,' he grumbled, 'morning or evening but potatoes'.[6]

As the number of Methodists increased private houses were not large enough for worship so chapels had to be built. Methodist architects did not yet favour the Gothic Revival in architecture and preferred the Classical Revival in the building of their larger churches.[7] The humble style of the chapels in these parishes is best described as vernacular. The earliest Methodist chapel in the Skibbereen circuit was built in Skibbereen itself in 1802. The next chapel was built the following year on Captain Evan's land in Ardralla in Aughadown parish. The preacher, Henry Deery, provided Schull with a chapel in 1825. It cost only £60 as the roof was given free by a man named John Whitley. About the same time another chapel was opened in Ballydehob and yet another in Lissacaha in 1831. The Methodists made an important convert, James H. Swanton of Ballydehob, who was the owner of large flour mills at Rineen near Castletownshend; his ships plied between Cork and his other mills and stores along the coast.[8]

The reaction against rationalism was strong by 1820. The forces of the French Revolution had been defeated at Waterloo. The evangelical wind referred to by Blake in the epigraph began to touch not only the Methodists but also the Church of Ireland as well and produced a spirit of reform. An historian of this Church, D. H. Akenson, has called the period 1800–30 'the era of graceful reform'.[9] Such reform, however, was slow to reach these parishes. No major church building had been done in the parish of Schull for a century since the parish church had been built in 1721 and the glebe house also in 1721.[10] Ballydehob became a centre of population largely owing to Griffith's new road which had been constructed between 1822–6 and also owing to the opening of copper mines which shall be seen later. It had a Methodist chapel, as already stated, and a Catholic chapel as will be seen presently but as yet there was no Church of Ireland church. The new reform however now expressed itself in the opening of a church in 1829. This was built by means of a generous gift of £650 from the Board of First Fruits.[11] Accordingly the architectural style of the church is what is known as First-Fruits Gothic. This has been described by two historians of architecture in a rather uncomplimentary manner as 'overwhelmingly a simplified Gothic, with square towers, crude pinnacles, walls with clumsy battlements, and pointed windows with elementary tracery'.[12] Nevertheless Ballydehob Protestant church has a unique character and must have been a prominent symbol of reform and improvement in a countryside dotted with so many mud cabins.

There was an old church built in Aughadown on the shores of Roaringwater Bay. It was in ruins at the time of the visit of Bishop Downes in 1700; the vicar preached in his own house. The bishop suggested that a new church should be built. This was not done until 1813 and it was called after St Matthew. The old church in Kilcoe had also been beside the sea near Kilcoe castle. A new church was built in 1830 at Corrovolley with the aid of a gift of £630 from the Board of First Fruits.[13] It was beside Griffith's new road. Such new churches were usually located more inland than the old ones, reflecting the movement of the population towards lands or bogs which were only now beginning to be cultivated.

The last of these parishes to be touched by the evangelical reform in the Church of Ireland was the remotest, Kilmoe or Goleen, which most needed revival. No church or glebe house had been built since Crookhaven church was built by Bishop Brown early in the eighteenth century. In the meantime, the population had increased especially in the northern side around Toormore and Ballydevlin but no church had been built to accommodate it. The difficulties encountered by such people in going to church in Crookhaven were described by Horace Townsend Fleming, son of Lionel Fleming of New-court, then living in Ballydevlin near Goleen: 'We had to go about six miles to Rock Island, cross in a boat and walk a mile to church.[14] But not all had such conviction and were inclined to stray away from their own church. William Allen Fisher came to the parish in 1839 as vicar and was appointed rector in 1842. He lamented that 'in evil days, this old church [Crookhaven] was let fall into decay. The congregation belonging to it became Romanists'. He added that 'Many families living near it, whose grandfathers were of the Church of Ire-land, are now bitter Romanists and Protestant Hill was without a Protestant'.[15] The rector of the parish of Kilmoe was appointed on alternate occasions by the crown and by the bishop. Fisher censured the crown for the bad state of the parish alleging that its nominee was usually 'some political character that they wished to provide for in secret … many of them were no ornament to their profession.' Fisher also blamed the bishops themselves for neglecting to visit the parish. They would usually come only as far as Schull, he complain-ed, then give their 'We bless you all out west' and quickly depart. He granted that there were two exceptions, however; Bishop Kyle visited them in 1840 and his successor, John Gregg came on 'a preaching tour' while not yet bishop apparently.[16] The first important work undertaken by Fisher was the building of Goleen church in 1843.[17]

The reform of such lax ways was led by John Magee who had become archbishop of Dublin in 1822. He insulted both Catholics and Nonconfor-mists in one fell blow when he declared from the pulpit of St Patrick's cathe-dral:

We, my reverend brethren, are placed in a station in which we are hemmed in by two opposite descriptions of professing Christians; the one, possessing a church, without what *we* can properly call a religion; and the other, possessing a religion, without what *we* can properly call a church; the one so blindly enslaved to a supposed infallible ecclesiastical authority, as not to seek the word of God a reason for the faith they possess; the other, so confident in the infallibility of their individual judgment … that they deem it their duty to resist all authority in matters of religion.

Archbishop Magee also showed Catholic priests scant recognition by main-taining that the parson should consider himself 'the true *parish priest*, in con-tinual contact with his flock …' According to Desmond Bowen most Catholic critics read this 'like an open declaration of religious war – the beginning of a "Second Reformation"'.[18] And so it was.

The ideas of the 'Second Reformation' were promoted by Rev. Edward Nangle in Connaught. During the minor famine of 1831 he organised a ship-ment of meal to the starving people of Achill Island and soon set up a Pro-testant colony which mainly consisted of converts from among the Catholics. This provoked the opposition of Archbishop John McHale. At Dingle the Rev. Charles Gayer, an Englishman, began to organise a similar colony in 1833 and by 1845 claimed to have won 800 converts. He was supported by the Irish

Society, which had been founded in 1818 to bring the Bible in the Irish language to Irish people.[19]

This spirit of evangelical activity arrived in Kilmoe parish in the person of Rev. Thomas O'Grady (father of Standish James) who was appointed vicar in 1831. He built Altar School in 1833.[20] He was transferred to Castletownbere in 1839 where he was later accused of trying to win converts with the help of soup in 1846 as shall be seen in Chapter XI on souperism.[21] He was praised by William Fisher, his successor, for being 'indefatigable' and labouring single-handed for nearly nine years in Kilmoe until he became almost broken down from 'mental and bodily toil'. But Rev. O'Grady had 'spread the seed of divine truth widely and successfully.' Fisher acknowledged that when he himself arrived in the parish 'not only were the foundations of the great works laid but a considerable part of the spiritual structure already existed, I had nothing more to do than to try to follow the track'.[22] In 1849 Rev. Daniel Foley, an agent of the Irish Society, visited West Cork and gave credit to O'Grady who 'originated the movement in Kilmoe where he is remembered with a freshness of enthusiastic admiration and affection'. According to Daniel Foley there were only five Protestant families in Toormore when O'Grady arrived but by now this number had risen to eighty.[23] This was of course also due to the enthusiasm and hard work of Fisher.

When Fisher came to the parish he found some of the flock in the process of building a Methodist chapel which he persuaded them to abandon although the walls were nearly finished.[24] Henceforth the Church of Ireland was not going to allow itself to be hemmed in by Catholics and Nonconformists, a situation so lamented by Archbishop Magee. While O'Grady's activities do not seem to have attracted any public opposition, Fisher's soon did. He was defended by an Irish-speaking Protestant poet and *bíoblóir*, Séamus Ó Súilleabháin, who wrote a poem in the Irish language and prefaced it as follows: 'The following poem was done by myself in January 1841 on account of some popish fellows speaking evil of a little charity which Rev. William A. Fisher distributed to the poor of his parish,viz, *Cíllmóghladha* in the County of Cork'.[25] There is no reference to Fisher in the poem, which merely compares Catholicism unfavourably with Protestantism and we do not know who these 'popish fellows' were but they probably included the parish priest, Laurence O'Sullivan. What is clear is that well before 1847 Fisher's 'little charity', like that of Nangle and Gayer, was already controversial. Fisher was born of Quaker parents but was left an orphan and was brought up in the Church of Ireland. As a young man at college he was, like John Henry Newman, influenced by the Oxford Movement. Fisher's biographer and son-in-law, R. B. Carson, relates that on one occasion he was reading one of this movement's tracts and was 'on the verge of Rome' when he suddenly realised that he was being 'led away from Christ'. Fisher spoke the Irish language fluently.[26]

The Penal Laws were withering away towards the end of the eighteenth century. As has been seen in Chapter I, the priest who formerly had been on the run from the Protestant lawmen now had to run from the mainly Catholic outlaws, the Whiteboys.[27] This suggests that the state of religion was not much more healthy among the Catholics than among the Protestants of these parishes. In 1773, Jeremiah Harte, a priest of the diocese of Ross, was incardinated into Cork and appointed parish priest of Schull by Bishop John Butler, Lord Dunboyne. The bishop described the parish as 'vacant by the free resignation of Thady Agherin, last peaceful possessor of the same'.[28] In any case Fr Harte did not hold it long. The following year the press reported that 'Jeremiah Harte, PP of Schull and Kilmoe, renounced the Popish communion before the Lord Bishop of Cork and Ross and was … publicly received into the communion of the Church of Ireland in the Cathedral of St Finbarre'. He was soon appointed curate of Killeagh in East Cork.[29] Catholics, however, called him *Diarmuid 'a Casadh* or 'Jeremiah the Turncoat'. In 1786 Catholics were again scandalised by the apostasy of their bishop, John Butler, Lord Dunboyne.[30]

Although Catholics were certainly concerned about emancipation from the Penal Code they were also determined to emancipate themselves from the indignity of the old Penal Law chapels which were now far too small and even a danger to the increasing population. New chapels which could well be called churches had to be built. Their location must be observed. The main difficulty was not so much persecution as poverty. Bishop Francis Moylan of Cork built the cathedral of St Mary and St Anne in 1808, which was seventeen years earlier than the Pro-Cathedral in Dublin. But it may have been too early because in June 1820 it was extensively damaged by a fire which many Catholics at the time believed had been started maliciously by some Protestants who had difficulty in tolerating the Catholic revival.[31] Fr Michael Collins, administrator of Skibbereen, said in 1824 that his old chapel was in danger of falling in on the congregation. This chapel had been built up a lane nowadays called 'Old Chapel Lane' and he was now trying to build the new church in a conspicuous location at the eastern entrance to the town. He told that he had 'no means but a half-penny collection on Sunday, at the chapel, from the poor as they went in; a great number of the people going there have not often the means of paying a half-penny, they are consequently excluded and lose the benefit of religious worship and religious instruction'. The number of priests had indeed increased but not 'in proportion to the population'. He had only one curate, his brother, Denis, and had not the means of supporting any more and they had the care of 10,000 souls. In the Protestant Church the district which corresponded to his large parish had three or four clergymen while there was only one Protestant to every fifteen Catholics. Fr Collins considered that the numbers of persons that attend religious duties 'diminish in consequence of the inability of the priests to attend them all'. Neither were there enough teachers to catechise the children. Regarding confession he feared that 'many are falling off' for the same reasons. 'In a wide district,' he remarked, 'a priest on horseback loses a great deal of time going from place to place.' At the time there were 'Stations of Confession' which included some catechetical instruction and Mass and were held at Christmas and Easter; they were also occasions for the people to pay their dues. Many confessed but paid nothing according to Fr Collins.[32] In brief, he was admitting that the priests were losing contact with some of their flock especially the poor who could not afford a half-penny for Sunday Mass.

The accident which Fr Collins feared would happen in his chapel in Skibbereen actually happened in the parish of Kilmoe near Goleen. On a Sunday morning in April 1825 the roof of a chapel in Ballinskea fell in during Mass and several people were injured. Yet the building was only twenty years old.[33] A correspondent of the *Southern Reporter* told its readers that it would be impossible for the parishioners to replace the chapel without outside aid because they had 'suffered more from the famine than any other people in the south-west of Ireland'. So he appealed for subscriptions to help them.[34] The collapse of the roof of this chapel symbolised the virtual end of the era of the Penal Laws. The parish priest, Michael Prior,[35] also appealed to the general public for aid. He was delighted with the response of people to build a chapel in this 'remote and impoverished district'. The rector, Anthony Traill, gave a 'munificent donation of thirty guineas'. In November of this same year, 1825, Fr Prior also thanked the following subscribers, the Catholic bishop of Cork, Dr John Murphy, who contributed £11 7s 6d; Richard E. Hull of Leamcon, £5 13s 9d; R. Notter of Cork, £3; James O'Sullivan of Roaring Water, £2 5s 6d; other subscriptions brought the total to about £58.[36]

While the new chapel was being built Mass was said in the open air although it was winter. A man calling himself a 'Liberal Protestant' was rather sceptical about Fr Prior's appeal for a new chapel so he rode out from Skib-

Ballinskea Chapel, 1826

bereen to Ballinskea to find out for himself. He saw 'at least 2,000 men and women kneeling on the side of a barren mountain assisting in silence and in apparent reverence at the ceremony of the Mass, literally no canopy over them but the broad expanse of the heavens whilst a heavy winter's shower descended on their uncovered heads'.[37] Mass was said under such conditions for fourteen months before the foundation stone was laid for the 'commodious and slated' new chapel by Richard Edward Hull of Leamcon. He had given the site for the church rent-free, as well as a donation of twenty guineas. His son and heir, William, gave £3. Richard Edward Hull also gave the people permission to quarry stone and raise bog timber on his lands. The *Southern Reporter* pointed out that the case of Ballinskea chapel illustrated the neglect of the rulers of the country to provide for the spiritual needs of the people. The newspaper also congratulated Richard Edward Hull on his good relations with the Catholic peasantry. His position was not based on 'brute force or persecution but the more honourable and permanent foundation of a people's love and esteem'.[38]

Although the building of this chapel brought out generosity and goodwill in some landlords it stirred up only latent bigotry in others. A middleman in this parish, James McCarthy of Goleen, later told the Devon Commission that he had known landlords to 'absolutely refuse slate to be quarried' on their lands for this chapel.[39] In 1825 building began on a Catholic chapel in the village of Ballydehob. The actual location of chapels at different periods was a sensitive barometer as to the level of religious toleration in a parish. The early Penal chapel was in the remote townland of Cooragurteen while the later chapel was at Stouke at the side of the old Ballydehob–Schull road and is marked on the Grand Jury map of 1811. This chapel was now by-passed by Griffith's new road and was probably in a bad state in any case. It was symbolic of the new tolerant spirit of the age that the new chapel should have been built in the middle of the plantation town of Ballydehob. In 1764 a Protestant had complained that formerly Catholics were satisfied to build their chapels in retired places but that now they do so 'in the most conspicuous place they can pitch upon'.[40]

The usual appeals were made on behalf of this chapel. In September 1825, the parish priest, Fr Florence O'Mahony, publicly thanked a Protestant gentleman, a Mr Classon of Dublin, for a donation of £150. He was associated with the Audley Mines which shall be discussed in the next chapter. A miner gave £1. The priest assured his benefactor that the people would show their gratitude by their 'orderly and correct behaviour'. He also thanked Mr Atteridge of Greenmount and other Protestants of that neighbourhood for their donations.[41] The following January, 1826, Fr O'Mahony publicly thanked other subscribers to the chapel many of whom were Protestants. A certain William Swanton gave £4 while six other Swantons gave £8 between them. Other contributors bore names such as Roycroft, Atteridge and Levis. A 'handsome donation' of £10 was received from Gerald Callaghan of Cork, who was a middleman for Lord Audley.[42] The new chapel dedicated to St Brigid was cruciform in shape and had galleries as were necessary in most chapels of this period to accommodate the growing population. Lord Audley attempted to sell his estates in 1833 and had them valued. Since the chapel was built on part of these lands it was described in the survey:

> This chapel is built upon a piece of waste ground … and cost the parishioners £3,000. The building is on a site that was quarried out of the rock. The grounds are planted with trees. The new chapel is not yet furnished, for want of further means, as the parishioners are too poor.[43]

Fr O'Mahony informed the surveyor that he had to pay £6 or £7 a year to the middleman, Gerard Callaghan, for the lease of the site.[44] This contrasts with the generous terms on which the site for Ballinskea chapel was given. The chapel at Schull was also built in 1825–6.[45]

In the neighbouring parish of Kilcoe there was a late Penal chapel beside the old Skibbereen–Ballydehob road not far from Roaring Water. This can be seen on the Grand Jury map. In Aughadown parish there were also two Penal chapels as shown on this map; one was at Mohanagh in the eastern extremity of the parish and the other was in the western side of Lisheen at the western end of the parish. In 1835 a new chapel was built in a more central and conspicuous location at Lisheen Cross. The site was given by the local landlord, Samuel Townsend, to the parish priest, James Mulcahy, for a nominal rent. The lease is dated 4 April 1832 and the bell 1835.[46]

The last chapel to be built in these parishes in this period was in 1836 at Dunbeacon in the northern or Bantry side of Schull parish. The parish priest was no longer Florence O'Mahony as James Barry had come in 1831. He told the public that this chapel was for 'a poor population in a remote district'. It was a 'necessary and long contemplated object' which could not be carried out through want of resources. Dr John Murphy, Bishop of Cork, gave £10 and the Cork Brewery firm of Beamish contributed £2. Smaller subscribers gave a total of £36.[47]

Apart from the Lisheen and Dunbeacon chapels all the others namely Ballinskea, Schull, Ballydehob and Kilcoe, were built in the period just before emancipation. There was a brief spell of generous toleration and indeed of ecumenism. The Penal Laws had been relaxed while the movement for emancipation and the missionary efforts of the 'Second Reformation' had not yet caused real bitterness. Dr Murray, archbishop of Dublin, Dr Doyle, Bishop of Kildare and Leighlin and Fr Arthur O'Leary of Cork were very ecumenically minded.[48] This spirit was reflected in the generosity of men like Rev. Anthony Traill, William Edward Hull and the Swantons. Even though such men exacted high rents and tithes Catholics were extremely grateful for their generosity. The following inscription was engraved on a stone plaque that was placed over the door of Ballinskea chapel:

In the period 1800–43, five Catholic chapels, four Methodist chapels and four Church of Ireland churches were also built in these parishes in the Mizen Peninsula. Thus Schull and Ballydehob became what Kevin Whelan would call 'chapel-villages'.[49] Perhaps they could more accurately be described as 'church/chapel-villages'. All thirteen churches or chapels were symbols of the religious revival. They were also built without any major local dissension although at that time the building of churches was occasionally controversial and even provoked serious schisms. The nearest place where such dissension occurred was Baltimore. The people of Sherkin Island refused to pay a heavy tax for the building of the Church of Ireland church in the village. They had failed to collect money to repair their own old chapel which was 'a mere hovel, partly covered with ragged straw, and without door or window'. An order came from Dublin Castle to send police to the island.[50]

What percentage of the people of each denomination attended these churches? According to the Commissioners of Public Instruction in 1834 there were 7,872 Catholics in Kilmoe parish and 'the average number of persons usually attending Divine Service' in Goleen was 1,400, i.e., 17.8%. The number was given as 'increasing', as it was in all the other parishes except the Church of Ireland parish of Kilcoe. Mass or service was usually held once on Sundays in all churches. In the Church of Ireland church in Ballydehob, however, services were held twice on Sundays and also in Kilcoe and Aughadown during the summer. The numbers attending were increasing in all the parishes except the Church of Ireland parish of Kilcoe. It was reported that there was only one chapel in Kilmoe parish because its second chapel at Ballinskea was in the civil or Church of Ireland parish of Schull. There were 601 members of the Church of Ireland in Kilmoe parish out of whom 180, i.e., 30%, attended service. The Catholic population of Schull was 13,912 which was served by three chapels at Schull, Ballydehob and Ballinskea. The number which attended these Masses was 3,550, i.e., 25.5% of the Catholic population. There were two Church of Ireland churches in this parish, one at Schull and the other in Ballydehob. Service was also held in three school-houses. The Church of Ireland population was 1,898 out of which 530, i.e., 27.9% went to service. There was also one Wesleyan meeting-house in Schull where 70 persons attended a service every Sunday conducted by an itinerant preacher. Kilcoe had a Catholic population of 2,158 out of which 800, i.e., 37.1% went to Mass in the one chapel where Mass was celebrated. This number was 'stationary'. The Church of Ireland population was 218 out of which 90, i.e., 41.2%, went to service in the one church. Attendance was 'diminishing'. The Catholic population of Aughadown was 5,623 out of which 1,300, i.e., 23.1% attended Mass in the one chapel. The commissioners, however, failed to mention the other chapel at Mohanagh. The

Church of Ireland population was 506 out of which 90, i.e., 17.7% went to service. In all Church attendance was 23.8% among the Catholics and 29.7% among the members of the Established Church.[51]

The American historian, David W. Miller, in his 'map of estimated mass attendance as percent of Catholic population, 1834' places the parishes of the Mizen Peninsula in the 20–40% range. However, he places some districts in Connaught in as low a bracket as 0–20% and others in the south-east of the country as high as 80–100%. I would agree with Patrick Corish that these figures for Connaught and the Mizen Peninsula are too low because Miller does not allow sufficiently for those who were not canonically obliged to attend Mass such as children, the sick, the old and others who would be excused on account of weather, distance and lack of clothing, etc. He suggests that Miller's figures should be increased by 25%, which would mean an attendance of from 25% to 50% in the parishes of the Mizen Peninsula. This was still low, and I would agree with Corish that this represents 'a deterioration over the previous fifty years', something which Miller denies. Yet the latter grants that the official Church was finding it difficult to reach the labouring classes which were increasing in numbers and also getting poorer.[52] As already stated, Fr Collins of Skibbereen admitted this regarding his own parish. Nonetheless there is also evidence that the people were remarkably Mass-going. Can the figures presented by the Commissioners of Public Instruction be accepted as being reasonably accurate? While of course it is usually very difficult if not impossible to check them there is some evidence which gives general indications as to their accuracy in a few cases. As already stated, the 'Liberal Protestant' found 2,000 people at Mass in the open beside the collapsed Ballinskea chapel in 1824 while less than ten years later the commissioners stated that only 950 attended the new chapel there. Michael Collins, administrator of Skibbereen, told a select committee in 1824, 'We have two Masses in the [old] chapel, and at each Mass about 2,000 persons, or more, attend'. He admitted that the chapel was 'so small that half of the congregation stayed away – the old, the infirm and the delicate – rather than be in the open air'. Of those who did attend more than half had to remain outside the chapel. 'You may see them in severe weather,' he pointed out, 'and under the pelting of storms, with their hats off, kneeling in the mud'.[53] So according to Fr Collins there was a total of about 4,000 attending two Masses in this chapel whereas less than ten years later the commissioners claimed that there was only one Mass in the new church attended by only 400 people. It must also be remembered that the population was increasing.[54] It does seem that even in the south-west of the country people were somewhat more Mass-going than would appear from the evidence of the Commissioners of Public Instruction, in spite of the difficulties outlined by Fr Collins. In his study of official religious practice all over the country, Desmond Keenan similarly tends to conclude that such practice was remarkably frequent and hence satisfactory to the clergy.[55] Donal Kerr comes to a similar conclusion.[56]

Common interest in the education of priests and especially hostility to the French Revolution prompted the English government and the Irish Catholic bishops to found the Royal College of Maynooth in 1795. In the following century they had a shared interest in popular education and a common fear of violence, ignorance and poverty. A commission reporting between 1809 and 1812 asserted that 'these hedge schools and town schools were under no control, were supported by parents, owned by schoolmasters who were incompetent, antagonistic to constitutional authority and cause much political uneasiness'. It can be sensed that such schoolmasters may have been sympathetic to the Whiteboys and even have had ideas about 'Bony' and Liberty, Equality and Fraternity. The government, gradually becoming more powerful, was bound to become uneasy about schools under no control and to favour a system under State/Church control such as the National System.[57] This was by no means a creation out of nothing; there were already many hedge schools, Bible schools and parish schools. The parish schools were set up in Tudor times and were obliged to spread not only the Protestant religion but also the English language and customs. Early in the nineteenth century the government gave grants to religious societies engaged in education. Among these were the Incorporated Society for the Promotion of Protestant Schools in Ireland and also the Association for Discountenancing Vice and Promoting the Knowledge and Practice of the Christian Religion. The Hibernian Bible Society was founded in London in 1806. The most active society in these parishes was the Irish Society as will be seen in Chapter XI on souperism. The Kildare Place Society was founded in 1811 for the education of the poor of all denominations. Scripture was taught, but 'without note or comment'. This society obtained Catholic support for some time but was later accused of proselytising. A royal commission reported in 1812 that it would be desirable if all the people were educated 'under the one system, without any attempt being made to influence the peculiar tenets of any description of Christians'.[58] This policy was too radical to be put into practice just then because it would have meant the end of the old Protestant monopoly in education.

The Penal Laws discriminated against Catholic schools and so hedge schools were then set up.[59] But when these laws were relaxed the hedge schools could be better described as cabin schools. The teachers were paid mainly by the pupils. Many of these schools however received assistance from the priests and functioned in effect as Catholic parish schools. During the first quarter of the nineteenth century there were ten schools in the parish of Schull; three of these were Protestant. The Protestant parish school was at Gubbeen near Schull. The teacher, Richard Cole, was paid £24 10s 0d a year. The school house was of 'stone and clay mortar, slated, in good repair and cost £112'. It was attended by 48 children of whom only 5 were Catholics. The manner in which the building of this school was financed shows the great variety of resources at the disposal of a Protestant school. The rector, Anthony Traill, contributed £10, as also did the archbishop of Cashel. A Judge Daly gave £5 and Colonel Limrick, a local gentleman, gave £4. The school received a grant of £80 from the lord lieutenant's fund[60] and was generally aided by the Association for Discountenancing Vice. The rector also allowed the master £2 10s 0d in lieu of tithes.

There was another Protestant school in Ballydehob whose teacher was Thomas Crowley, a Protestant. He taught in a new school costing £45 10s 0d of which £32 had been granted by the Kildare Place Society. The school had 45 pupils of whom only 4 were Catholics and it was aided by the Hibernian Society. The rector paid the master £5 per year. There was another Protestant school in Gortnagrough taught by Florence McCarthy, a Protestant, and another school in Lissacaha whose teacher was John McCarthy, a Protestant. Both schools were assisted by the Kildare Place Society. The poorest Protestant schools were better off than the 'richest' Catholic ones. The 'richest' Catholic school was at Stouke in an old chapel. The master was paid about £8 a year for teaching 65 pupils. There were four other schools in the parish all of which were miserable cabins, huts or hovels. The poorest was at Leamcon where the master was paid £2 per year for teaching 17 Catholics and 1 Protestant in a 'miserable hut'. The only school that could be described as mixed as regards religion was in Schull. In this 'miserable' cabin the master, a Catholic, was paid about £10 10s 0d a year for teaching 40 Catholics and 20 Protestants. He was the best-paid teacher in any Catholic school in these parishes. The Bible was read by the Protestants.

In Kilmoe parish there were thirteen schools. The Church of Ireland parish school was at Rock Island where the master was paid £10 per year to teach 45 Protestants and 4 Catholics in a good slated house which cost £50 granted from the lord lieutenant's school fund. The Kildare Place Society made a grant of books and school requisites. This was the only Protestant school in the parish. In all the others the masters were Catholics and did not receive aid from any Protestant Society yet their pupils were mixed as regards religion. In one school in Crookhaven 67 Catholics and 12 Protestants were 'in a comfortable slated house, rented by the master'. In the other school there the master was paid £2 per year to teach 25 Catholics and no Protestant 'in a wretched house'. In Toormore school there were 25 Catholics and 15 Protestants in a 'thatched cottage'. The teacher was Catholic but the Bible was read by the Protestants. In Goleen there were 26 Catholics and 24 Protestants in a 'poor cabin'. The poorest schools were at Lissigriffin, 'a wretched hovel' and at Carrigat 'a miserable hovel in which the master lives'. There was no Protestant in the former and only one in the latter.

In Kilcoe there were only two schools so they can be easily compared. At Correvolley James Baker, a Protestant, taught 56 Protestants and one Catholic for £18 a year in a 'miserable cabin'. He received assistance from the Munster Hibernian Society and the incumbent gave £2 per year. The Authorised Version of the Bible was read. At Ardurabeg Michael Driscoll, a Catholic, was paid between £7 and £9 for teaching 57 Catholics and no Protestant in a 'thatched cabin worth 5 guineas'. He received no other assistance and the Douai or Catholic version of the Bible was 'read occasionally'. There were seven schools in

Aughadown parish where circumstances were similar to the others. In one school however we meet a hedge schoolmistress, something rare. She was Jane Barry, a Catholic, who was paid between 1s 3d and 1s 8d a quarter whereas near-by James Fitzgerald got between 1s 8d and 4s 2d a quarter. This schoolmistress taught in 'a thatched cabin which serves both as a cow house and a school house' and she had 13 Catholic pupils and no Protestant. The Bible was not read. In one school in Skibbereen the master, a Catholic, received a salary of no less than 40 guineas a year and the Bible was read in Greek.[61] This looks like a classical school. Many of the schools in the Mizen Peninsula however must have been something like the 'dark, smoky and smelly' cabin whose patron was the local priest described by the master to a visitor as his *Magnus Apollo*. In 1829 the school in Cape Clear was visited by Rev. Caesar Otway, an Evangelical who had founded the *Christian Examiner*; here he found:

> about twenty children sitting on stones, humming forth their lessons like hornets pre-paring to swarm; every little healthy, ragged, fish-smelling urchin, had a bit of a book in his hand – one had a leaf of *Reading made Easy*, another a scrap of the Church of England catechism, another a torn copy of the *Heart of Jesus* … In the corner by the fire-side was the pedagogue's bed, over which were hanging sundry kinds of fish to dry and cure, along the wall were hanging a number of dead rabbits, and over the game was suspended a bag full of foetid ferrets.[62]

In general, education was in the hands of the Church of Ireland, the Protes-tant Societies and the hedge schoolmasters who were sometimes aided by the Catholic parishes. These Protestant Societies were receiving grants from the government and so was the Kildare Place Society but little of this money found its way to the poor hedge or cabin schools of these parishes. The main reason was that Catholics feared proselytism. Fr Michael Collins said that the bishops considered that the Kildare Place society had a 'latent purpose' in introducing scripture into schools and that it was only 'laying the foundations of prosely-tism'. He made it clear that he had nothing against Protestant schools once no attempt was made to proselytise. 'I myself,' he declared, 'was educated in a school of a Protestant minister'. He was then asked whether the opposition of priests to the establishment of schools had not been with a view to prevent the progress of proselytism; 'certainly,' was his answer, 'we should hail edu-cation most cordially if it were given to us upon fair terms'.[63]

NATIONAL SCHOOLS

The National Schools were an effort to offer education to all the people of Ire-land. For historical reasons those who were most in need of it were Catholics. An attempt was now to be made to provide education on what Fr Collins called 'fair terms'. Catholic Emancipation came in 1829 and it was an age of liberal reform. Emancipation would have to be brought out of the Statute Book and into the schoolbooks as it were; Catholics would also have to be emancipated from ignorance. In 1831 Edward Stanley, the chief secretary, outlined his plan 'to unite in one system children of different creeds'. Nevertheless, he emphasised that the schools of this system should be free from 'even the suspicion of proselytism'. The system was to be neither Protestant nor Catholic and was thus called the 'National System'. The Protestant and Catholic archbishops of Dublin, Doctors Whately and Murray respectively, were members of the National Board. Bishop John Murphy of Cork was a strong supporter of Dr Murray on the question of the National Schools as against Archbishop McHale of Tuam.[64] Daniel O'Connell called National education a 'boon'.[65] The main opposition to these schools, however, came from clergymen of the Church of Ireland. Many of them were hostile; the new system seriously threatened their long established dominance in education and curtailed the role of the Bible as only certain extracts were allowed. There was to be no 'scriptural education' because many Catholics regarded it simply as proselytism.

The Protestants objected vehemently to the National System at many meetings all over the country. The Kildare Place Society in particular felt outraged. It organised a 'Great Scriptural Educational Meeting', in Wesley Chapel, Patrick Street, Cork. The venue showed that there was a united front being made by the Church of Ireland and the Methodists against what they both saw as a 'blasphemous attack on the Word of God'. Fifty clergymen of the Established Church attended as well as many Methodist and Presbyterian ministers. Long indignant speeches were made including one by Dr Robert Traill who had succeeded his father, Anthony, as rector of Schull in 1830. He accused the government of a conspiracy to mutilate and adulterate sacred scripture. 'It is no light thing to trifle with the authority of God,' he warned the Board of Education.[66]

The Catholics were now endeavouring to put a roof over the hedge or cabin schools but had received little aid from landlord or parson to whom they paid so much in rents and tithes. They had hitherto sufficient reason to suspect the aid offered in the field of education by various societies which enjoyed the favour of the government. The Catholic attitude to the National System was, *Timeo Danaos et dona ferentes* or 'I fear the Greeks and they bearing gifts'. Nevertheless, sheer necessity arising out of poverty and also a love of learning and fear of proselytism obliged priests and people to extend a guarded welcome to the new system.

The first National School in these parishes was in Ballydehob. In June 1836 Fr James Barry and his curate and brother, John, applied to the Board of Education for aid. They described their school as 'Ballydehob Parish School established on May 8th 1835' and desired it to become a 'National School'. It had been built in the chapel grounds but enclosed by a wall and therefore was 'totally detached'. If a school were fully attached to any place of worship it could not be taken into connection by the board. Ballydehob school was built with the best possible mortar and was slated. It had two storeys with a classroom on each floor. The remains of its walls can still be seen. It had been built from collections at the chapel and donations from Catholics and Protestants

Dr Robert Traill, rector of Schull, 1830–47, and Mrs Anne Traill

connected with the parish. The ground rent for school and chapel was paid by means of a collection at the chapel. There were no desks in the school but 'temporary substitutes'. The school was receiving no aid except what the parents of the children could give. Concerning the sensitive question of religious instruction, the priests stated that all day Saturday would be devoted to religious instruction and also from 9.00 a.m. to 10.00 a.m. and from 4.30 p.m. to 5.30 p.m. on weekdays, when they would be able to attend to it themselves. They emphasised that they had always followed this arrangement and that parents were at perfect liberty to withdraw their children from any religious instruction of which they did not approve.

The attendance at Ballydehob school was 74 boys and 24 girls but 150 boys and 100 girls were expected in the near future. The applicants agreed to use the books issued by the board. There was no fixed salary for the master and mistress; the pupils were paying from 2s 6d to 3s 6d per quarter but it was hoped to reduce this to a figure ranging from 6d to 10d. In answer to the question as to whether clergymen of other denominations had been asked to sign the application the priests replied that they had in fact been asked but that they refused because the 'unmutilated word' was not a class book. The applicants for this school at Ballydehob next applied for about £20 for windows for the school and furniture. They also applied for text-books for English, Geography and Arithmetic, and a salary of £20 for the master and £15 for the mistress. The application was signed by James Barry and John Barry as Catholics and by James H. Swanton and a William Swanton as Protestants who testified that the priests had truthfully answered all the queries and would conduct the school according to the regulations.[67] Such local Protestant laymen supported the National Schools more often than their clergymen. The application was finally accepted two years later in 1838. The school received a grant of about £12 for repairs and for furniture; the master was paid an annual salary of £8 and the mistress £6. Thus Ballydehob Catholic Parish School became Ballydehob National School while a short distance away stood the Protestant Parish School. Far from being brought under the one system Catholic and Protestant children were usually going to be educated separately.

If there was little mixing as regards religion in these National Schools there was sometimes less mixing as regards gender. Ballydehob Catholic Parish School became Ballydehob Boys' NS and Ballydehob Girls' NS. The boys were on the ground floor and the girls upstairs 'in the loft'. In April 1838, there were 157 boys and 109 girls on rolls.[68] Even allowing for poor attendance, especially in bad weather, the one teacher had to teach at least 100 children in a relatively small room. In September 1838 James Barry applied for aid for Schull Parish School which had just been opened but was still only a 'bare shell'. The other schools within a radius of three miles were a Protestant school in Gubbeen, an infant school in the village and hedge schools in Long Island and Lowertown. The new school was paid for solely out of the contributions of parishioners. It was attended by 70 boys and 30 girls but if separate schools were established for boys and girls they would be attended by 120 boys and 100 girls. The master had been trained at Kildare Place. This is the only reference to any Catholic school in these parishes benefiting from the Kildare Place Society. The priest also applied for grants for desks and for the teachers' salaries.[69] This application was accepted immediately. A salary of £8 per year was granted to the master and £4 to the mistress and a grant of £7 10s 0d was given to the school. In 1838 there were 90 boys and girls going to the school but by 1841 the number had risen to 240.[70]

Fr Barry, anticipating the need for more accommodation, had applied for a girls' school for Schull in 1838. This was the first National School which was originally conceived as such in these parishes (the two other schools at Ballydehob and Schull had already been in existence and were simply connected to the board). The site was 'on chapel ground detached from chapel yard'. He did not set up any committee because he claimed that, 'In this locality a committee would scarcely be practicable'. The parish priest of Creagh, Baltimore, similarly declared that a committee would be 'inconvenient, inefficient and impracticable'. Priests were quite willing to accept state aid but often unwilling to share control; the National Board would not usually insist.[71] Fr Barry's application for Schull NS was signed by one Catholic layman but by no Protestant.[72] This application was accepted and the school was built. It received a grant of £87 for the building and £6 for the furniture. It opened in August 1841.[73]

In September 1838 James Coppinger, parish priest of Aughadown, applied to have the parish school at Lisheen connected with the National System. The application was signed by the local landlord, Samuel Townsend of Whitehall and by nine other Protestants; it was not signed by the local vicar. It was also signed by twelve Catholics.[74] The application was eventually accepted in 1841. In September of that year the school had 171 pupils on roll, all taught by the one teacher.[75] In November 1840 a new National School was opened at Dunbeacon in Schull parish. The site had been obtained rent free from the local landlord, Richard Townsend, who even became one of the trustees of the school together with the priests, James and John Barry.[76]

In October 1842, the parish priest of Kilmoe, Laurence O'Sullivan and his curate, James Hurley, applied to have the parish school at Crookhaven connected to the board. This was done the following year.[77] The parish priest of Aughadown, Robert Troy, applied to have the school on Hare Island connected with the board and stated that it had been built at his own expense. The landlord visited the school and was so delighted with the appearance of the children that he forgave the rent. The school was accepted into the National System late in 1845.[78]

Laurence O'Sullivan also applied to have a school built at Lowertown. A large site was given at a nominal rent by the landlord, Richard Edward Hall. The trustees were the parish priest himself and local farmers. It was the first time in these parishes that farmers were allowed to act as trustees; the inspector emphasised, 'I consider them fit so to act'. Dr Traill refused to sign the application and informed the inspector that he would not join the board 'for all the money they had'. The inspector recommended the application because of 'the zeal and energy of the priest and the poverty of the people'. The inspector also praised the generosity of Richard Edward Hull adding that 'no other gentleman could be induced to grant a few perches of bare rock for the site of a National School'. Hull was 'a kind old Protestant gentleman who had expressed much satisfaction on being this far able to accommodate his Roman Catholic neighbours'.[79] The school was opened in March 1846. It had 190 boys and 117 girls on roll.[80]

In the decade from 1836 to 1846, the priests and people of these parishes had either built or brought into connection with the board eight National Schools – no mean achievement in the circumstances. The Protestant clergymen were hostile to these schools but were in no position to prevent their establishment. Fortunately, some landlords were more liberal and it was they who could give or refuse sites. These early National Schools are described by A. M. Sullivan, a native of Bantry:

> But the first National Schools were useful makeshifts: thatched cabins with earthen floors … deathly in their effects on the health of teacher and pupil. To set up even one of these in a considerable district was at first a great achievement. I have seen myself children from six to sixteen years of age trudging (bare-footed, of course) over bog and moor … to such a school distant four or five miles from their homes.[81]

There was a high degree of continuity between the old parish or hedge schools in these parishes and the National Schools. In the County of Cork, 80 out of 105 National Schools could be said to have existed before 1831 and nearly 70% of the teachers appear to have taught in them. Yet these schools had not received state grants and the 1824 commission gave the reason why: 'Were we to recommend a grant of money in aid of such schools the result would be that they would be eagerly supported by the Roman Catholic Body, their numbers would increase and the masters would be better paid, the schools better supplied and the instruction rendered more effective, but its character would still remain the same'. As Mary Daly rightly observes, 'This is precisely what happened when the parochially-organised hedge schools became National Schools in the 1830s'.[82] It did not escape the critical eye of the novelist, Thackeray, as early as 1842:

> The National System – a noble and liberal one – which might have united the Irish people, and brought peace into this most distracted of all countries – failed unhappily in one of its greatest ends. The Protestant clergy have always treated the plan with bitter hostility; and I do believe, in withdrawing from it, have struck the greatest blow … to their own influence in the country. Look at the National School: throughout the country it is commonly by the chapel-side – it is a Catholic school, directed and fostered by the priest; and as no people are more eager for learning … he gets all the gratitude of the scholars who flock to the school, and all the fuller influence over them, which naturally and justly come to him.[83]

THE SCHOOLS OF THE CHURCH EDUCATION SOCIETY

The rejection of the National System by Protestants led them to found the Church Education Society in 1839. Its purpose was to provide Protestant and Catholic children with 'scriptural education' denied to them in the National Schools.[84] The Protestant clergymen of these parishes were zealous in bringing their schools into connection with this society. Its third annual report for the year 1841 showed that there were already nineteen schools in these parishes under the auspices of the society. On roll were 1,072 pupils.[85] The following year the school at the Audley mines with its twenty-seven children on roll closed when mining ceased.[86] The list of schools and the numbers on roll in 1845 is given in the following table.[87]

TABLE 4: CHURCH EDUCATION SOCIETY SCHOOLS, 1845

Parish	School	No. on Rolls
Kilmoe	Altar	70
	Ballydevlin male	72
	Ballydevlin female	12
	Crookhaven	41
	Rock Island	39
	Three Castle Head	29
Schull	Schull	40
	Lishencreg	50
	Gubeen	106
	Leamcon	72
	Lissacaha male	103
	Lissacaha female	71
	Ballydehob	88
Kilcoe	Kilcoe	61

Aughadown	Aughadown	23
	Roaring Water	40
	Whitehall	52
	Newcourt	77
Total	**18 Schools**	**1,046**

Eighteen schools was quite a large number of schools for this society especially as it began to organise eight years after the National System had been introduced although most of these Protestant schools were already in existence before 1831. The increase in the number of National Schools was far more gradual than that of the Church Education Society schools. The following table shows the number of National Schools in these parishes and the number of pupils on roll in 1845.[88]

TABLE 5: NATIONAL SCHOOLS, 1845

Parish	**School**	**No. on Roll**
Kilmoe	Crookhaven	91
Schull	Schull male	154
	Schull female	76
	Ballydehob male	133
	Ballydehob female	76
	Dunbeacon	135
Aughadown	Lisheen	141
Total	**7 schools**	**806**

When these two tables are compared the great strength of the Church Education Society becomes evident. It had eighteen schools with 1,046 pupils on roll, as compared with the National System's seven schools and 806 pupils. The Church Education Society had more than twice as many schools and 23% more pupils as its rival. In the country in general, the Church Education Society had only about half of the number of schools and one-third of the number of pupils as the National System. Many of the pupils attending these Protestant schools in these parishes must have been Catholics, probably around the one-third which was the average for the whole country.[89] The ideal that Catholic and Protestant children should be educated together was thus frustrated from the very beginning. Between the Church Education Society and National Schools there was a total of twenty-five schools providing primary education in these parishes. They were attended by 1,852 children. There were also some hedge schools which still remained unconnected with any system. Taking into account that National Schools were not opened in England until 1870 it is doubtful if any similar district in Ireland or England was better supplied with schools than these parishes. Interdenominational rivalry was contributing to the struggle against illiteracy.

The National Schools were a blow to the privileged position of the Church of Ireland. The absence of state grants meant that the local contributions would have to be substantial and continually be maintained. In 1845 the local contribution to the Church Education Society schools in these parishes amounted to £162.[90] The National Schools received £91 in aid, which consisted of the teachers' salaries, school requisites and 'free stock' or free supplies of books. Such supplies were granted every four years. Although they would not be sufficient for the whole school they were a successful sales technique which usually succeeded in ousting rival books.[91] For example, Lowertown school in 1846 received £8 8s 6d worth of school requisites at half price, £3 15s 0d worth of 'free stock' and the teacher was paid £8 a year. This pay was low, £12 or £15 being more usual.[92] The amount of aid given to each Church Education Society school is not given in the annual reports. Much space is given over to considerations of fund-raising and long lists of subscriptions. These schools were putting a strain on the financial resources of many Protestants who had been accustomed to centuries of endowment. Moreover they did not have to support in full even their own Church thanks to the tithe system. The failure of the Church Education Society to procure state aid was virtual disendowment – foreshadowing disestablishment.

Schools of whatever kind were a dire necessity. In the education map of the Census of 1841 the Mizen Peninsula is to be found in the darkest shade thus indicating 'the worst state of education' although the commissioners granted that 'in a large portion of the island, there is still considerable darkness'. As many as 79% of the inhabitants of the Mizen Peninsula who were over five years of age could neither read or write. The figure for County Cork was 68.1%; Antrim was at the bottom of the illiteracy league with only 23.7% who could neither read or write while Mayo was at the top with 80.5%.[93] No doubt figures for literacy have an upward bias as people may well have tended to exaggerate the extent of their literacy. The following table gives the state of literacy or perhaps illiteracy in the parish of Schull in 1841:

TABLE 6: PARISH OF SCHULL 1841
NUMBER AND PROPORTION OF LITERATE PERSONS

No. of Persons	1841	Proportion
Read and write	2,466	16.7%
Read only	1,036	7.0%
Total	**3,502**	**23.7%**
Neither read/write	11, 245	76.3%
Grand Total	**14,747**	**100.0%**

The table shows that the proportion of persons who could neither read or write (76.3%) was somewhat higher than the figure for County Cork (68.1%). Although the rates of illiteracy were very high all over the country the situation was gradually improving and morale was by no means low among those responsible for the education of children. In spite of the financial strain the annual reports of the Church Education Society were optimistic and not without cause. The Commissioners of National Education expressed 'high satisfaction' in their report for 1845.[94] Dr Robert Kane was a medical doctor and also a scientist who was soon to become president of the new Queen's College, Cork. He was sanguine about education in 1844 as is clear from his prediction cited in the epigraph on p. 64.[95] Such was his faith in 'improvement' or progress.

The National Schools and the new chapels were solid symbols of the Catholic revival from the poverty, ignorance and degradation of the Penal Law era. Yet this Church was still finding it a struggle to maintain the faith, morals and discipline of its flock. A papal jubilee or special season of prayer and penance was held in 1842. Penitents were offered special indulgences if they would confess their sins and amend their lives. Bishop Murphy of Cork told Dr Paul Cullen in Rome that, 'Sinners who have for years lived in fornication, adultery and incest have recourse to the tribunal of penance' and were coming in droves. He had already a 'melancholy list of sixty-four couples' from the first parish in which the jubilee was held and did not dare to estimate how many would be on his blacklist before the jubilee would be concluded in the whole diocese.[96]

Parish missions were now also being held and in particular by the Vincentian priests, a congregation which had been founded from Maynooth in 1833. Archbishop Murray presented them with St Peter's church in Phibsboro, Dublin, in 1834 and they soon opened a school at Castleknock, County Dublin. Their first famous mission took place in Athy, County Kildare, in 1842, and was attended by very large and fervent crowds. The demand for confession was particularly great.[97] In spite of many difficulties there was a growing confidence within the Catholic Church. This is reflected by Bishop John Murphy in his general report to Pope Gregory XVI in 1845 in which the bishop concluded as follows:

> Generally speaking, the state of religion in the Diocese of Cork is changing for the better. Many rich merchants in this city who for many years did not approach the sacrament of Penance now humbly ask God for pardon; they frequent the sacraments regularly … There is a general return to the bosom of the Church and very few – even those shackled by poverty – fall victims to heresy.[98]

Perhaps those who were falling 'victims to heresy' were not quite so few as the bishop thought or wished to report to Rome especially in the distant parts of his diocese such as Kilmoe or Goleen. Whatever about the number of those who 'fell' when shackled by poverty, it was soon to be seen how many would 'fall' when this poverty suddenly deteriorated into famine.

IV

MINING FOR COPPER AND BARYTES, 1800–45

*With backs bent to nearly right angle, with devious footsteps at no time on dry land …
but often indeed up to our knees in a pool, with a splash which spurted up acherentic mud
into our eyes and mouths … Onward, onward …*

MINER

The Bronze Age mines on Mount Gabriel were significant yet there seems to be little evidence of subsequent activity in the district until the time of Colonel Hall who came to oppose the attempted French invasion in 1796. A native of Devon, he was interested in copper mining in Cornwall and rediscovered copper mines in Kerry and West Cork. When Hall's regiment was disbanded in 1803 he re-opened an ancient copper mine in Killarney and discovered the famous copper mines of Allihies in the Beara peninsula. He later found copper on the lands of Lord Audley at Ballycumisk and Horse Island near Ballydehob and so obtained a mining lease for £50 a year.[1] In 1814 he shipped to Swansea 58 tons of copper ore from the Ballycumisk mine and 5 tons from the mine on Horse Island. Hall then abandoned these mines and opened another at Coolagh on the lands of a William Swanton. This became known as the Ballydehob mine and was opened around 1817. By 1822 some 606 tons of ore had been shipped to Swansea. It made between £6 and £7 per ton.[2] Still this mine was soon abandoned on account of 'an objectionable family alliance'. The mine was worked to a depth of 30 fathoms by means of a horse whim. Lack of capital for machinery may have contributed to the decision to relinquish the venture.[3]

Hall also discovered another mine in Letter near Mount Gabriel. At least one shaft was sunk which became known as 'Hall's shaft'. He procured the mining lease from the landlord, R. H. H. Becher of Hollybrook, Skibbereen.[4] Hall also opened mines at Mizen Head, one mine was quite near where the lighthouse now stands. He raised several tons of ore from this mine but during a storm the sea washed the ore off the rocks. He then abandoned the mine and opened another nearby at Clohane.[5]

Hall suggested to Lord Audley that his mines could be valuable so Audley employed Richard Griffith to survey them in 1819. (Griffith was also a distinguished geologist.) Griffith found that the mine at Cappagh, 'though conducted in a very rude and slovenly manner had produced 239 tons'. The ore was green malachite and the vein was very rich but had been worked only to a depth of 6 fathoms. He suggested that a shaft should be sunk to 15 fathoms to find if the vein would still be rich and he thought that it would. Griffith also reported that the mine at Filenamuck was 'encouraging' and that the vein at Horse Island was perhaps even superior to that of Cappagh. At the Ballycumisk mine nearby he saw some 'sulphate of barytes'. This is the first reference to the mineral which was to be of importance later. He considered that the copper ore in these mines was similar to that of the Allihies mines which were just then beginning to prosper. Griffith concluded that the Audley mines held out 'a fair prospect of success, if worked judiciously and cautiously in the commencement; and should they be found to prove well in depth, there can be little doubt of their ultimately enriching those who undertake to work them.'[6]

Accordingly Lord Audley borrowed £2,500 and began to mine at Cappagh. His chief mining captain was Matthew Luke who had been working in the copper mines of Cornwall. In its first year, 1820, Cappagh produced 30 tons of ore and 57 tons in the next year. At this stage, 1821, Griffith made a second report. He found that the general situation at Cappagh was 'much more favourable' than in his first report because the rich vein had now been traced to a depth of 20 fathoms. He made a plan and section of the mine. The only difficulty was the 'injudicious, though not unusual' way the mine was first opened; an ordinary hole was excavated in the ground which soon filled up with water so that it was impossible to work it without a steam engine. He suggested a way of draining the mine. The vein was up to 2 feet, 6 inches in thickness and appeared to increase in thickness as it descended. The ore varied from 10% to 15% copper.[7]

Although prospects appeared to be very good Audley had no more capital. He applied for a government loan on the security of his estates. His mining captain, Matthew Luke, told a government agent that the ore of the Cappagh mines was richer than any in his native Cornwall. It had fetched £12 a ton so he considered that there was about £150,000 worth of ore in the mine. Luke held a similarly high opinion of the mines at Ballycumisk and Ballydehob. One suspects that the mining captain had been prompted by Audley to give a very optimistic account of the mines. As a result Audley succeeded in obtaining a loan of £6,000 in 1822.[8] Nonetheless this same year he exported only 33 tons of ore and ceased mining altogether.[9] This may have been caused to some extent by Whiteboy activities and famine. Audley mined some manganese near Cappagh. He also quarried slates and paving stones at Filenamuck. Quarrymen were brought from Bangor in Wales and some of the paving stones were exported to London. The quarries were now also abandoned.[10] Why did Audley abandon his mines? According to his detractors it was because he considered that the mines were useless as another geologist named Weaver had reported to him.[11] Audley himself claimed that it was simply that he lacked the necessary capital.[12]

The Mining Company of Ireland, whose principal mines were in Wicklow, soon surveyed Audley's mines, accepted Griffith's favourable report and began to negotiate with Audley. The agreement finally reached between them in 1824 was that he should grant the company a mining lease of 31 years for a royalty-rent of 1.5% of the produce and a loan of £10,000 at 3% interest to enable him to pay mortgages already on the mine.[13] The Mining Company of Ireland began to work the mines with high hopes. In its second half-yearly report of 1824 it informed its shareholders that it had taken leases of mines containing copper ore, manganese, slate and even coal. It also stated that it had found the Cappagh mine in an 'advanced state' as it had been worked under the direction of Richard Griffith. The company concluded that the Audley mines would form the 'most important metalliferous district in Ireland'.[14] The next report was equally optimistic. The work was being conducted under the direction of practical and scientific miners who knew the Cornish system of mining. The engine shaft had been sunk to 20 fathoms and 'several tons of copper ore of remarkably rich quality have been raised and prepared for market'. The company had now also got a lease of the Ballydehob mine from William Swanton and the lease of a mine in Kilbronoge from Lord Bandon.

All this work was expensive. In the first half of 1825 the company spent £2,725 on the Audley mines and more than £1,000 on timber and iron at the Ballydehob mine. Although only 20 tons of ore were raised at Cappagh (the chief Audley mine) it made £20 a ton so hopes were high. The captain of the mine, a Captain Davey from Cornwall, decided to install a steam-engine to work the mine to 80 fathoms. It would cost £1 6s 0d a day but was cheaper than raising the ore by means of horses. There were now almost 100 men working in the mines. They worked in partnerships of between four and eight men and were paid about £5 per ton of ore raised which was sold for £15 a ton at Swansea. The company feared that the lode would fail at lower levels as a Cornish miner had stated would happen in the case of all mines in Ireland. The company, however, was happy to report that even at 24 fathoms the lode was getting larger and remaining as rich as ever. This year 1824 was a good one, £6,419 worth of ore was shipped to Swansea.[15]

The year 1826 was even better. In one day 39 tons of ore were sold in Swansea at £14 per ton. It assayed 17.5% copper while the average from the Cornish mines was only 6.5%. Some stones contained as high as 40% copper. Captain Davey affirmed that this mine was as good a speculation as almost any he had seen in Cornwall. The company however deliberately concealed a contrary opinion from its shareholders. In the previous year, 1825, it had requested Griffith to survey the mine and this time he changed his mind about its prospects. He now decided that the mine would become poorer as it descended and expressed serious doubts about the wisdom of continuing to work it.[16] Still in view of the money already spent he advised the company to take a risk.

In 1826 the main shaft was now sunk to 34 fathoms and the horizontal shaft was driven 140 fathoms in breadth. A house was built for the steam-engine which would soon be in operation to work the mine to 150 fathoms. The produce of the mine paid the cost of these improvements except for the steam-engine.[17] Some 387 tons of ore were exported which was to be a record output for any single year.[18] The company also reported that the Audley property contained slate quarries which were formerly worked but had been abandoned because it was thought that they were of poor quality. Nonetheless the company's agents re-opened one quarry and considered the slate to be as good as the best Westmoreland slate. These quarries were at Filenamuck and Audley Cove.[19] According to Lewis, 500 men were soon employed in them. He states that the slate was of excellent quality and was shipped to London and other English markets where it was in great demand.[20]

The steam-engine rendered the working of the mine less expensive during the year 1827. It hauled up the ore and pumped out the water. The engine shaft was sunk to 50 fathoms and the horizontal shaft was extended to 180 fathoms. The deeper the mine went the richer and more abundant became the ore thus tending to confirm Griffith's first opinion. The total output for the year 1827 was 448 tons. The total expenditure for the year including engine and pumps was £6,901 while the output was worth only £3,051. Nevertheless the company was confident that henceforth expenses would decrease and profits increase.[21] During the first half of the following year, 1828, the engine shaft was sunk further to 54 fathoms and the ore was richer than any mined elsewhere by the company. It was so abundant that the captain was able to reduce rates payable to the miners from £5 to £3 a ton. Suddenly the mine began to fail. Nonetheless they continued to sink the engine shaft to 58 fathoms and another shaft to 61 fathoms; there was a slight improvement. A total of 203 tons of ore was exported and a profit of £1,334 was made.[22]

The first really bad news came in June 1829. The mine was 'unprofitable … so much so as to absorb the profits of the preceding half-year, which amounted to £520'. The engine shaft was sunk to 70 fathoms but no improvement was visible in the lode. The experts however judged that there would be an improvement after another 4 fathoms; this and some horizontal drillings would take three months and cost £200. By December the engine shaft had been sunk to 75 fathoms and there was some improvement. This and other workings had paid cost and were giving a 'trifling profit, but was not commensurate with the high expectations formed at the commencement of the undertaking'. Still the company was confident that the ore would soon become as abundant and rich as ever. In spite of these difficulties, 359 tons of ore were exported in this year, 1829. It was a bad year for the company in general so it postponed paying dividends to its shareholders. There was also a general depression in the mining world and prices in England had fallen. Yet the company was basically confident about its future.[23] It also worked the copper mine discovered on Horse Island by Colonel Hall. The ore was rich near the surface, some samples yielding 55% copper; 230 tons were sold at Swansea for £2,800. But when the shaft was sunk to 40 fathoms and driven 70 fathoms in length, the lode became impoverished and about 1829 the mine was abandoned.[24]

From 1830 onwards not only the mines themselves but their proprietor became a source of trouble for the Mining Company of Ireland. Lord Audley alleged that his mines were of great value but that the company through lack of capital and skills was not working them properly. So he 'remonstrated' against the company's conduct and entered into negotiation with it.[25] The company agreed to surrender the lease. Since the Mining Company of Ireland had begun working the Audley mines in 1824 it had spent £26,027. The ore made only £13,065, so the company lost £12,962. It made a profit in most of its other mines but at Cappagh it maintained that the lode became less rich further down.[26] Mining was a risky business. The prospector, Colonel Hall, was himself ruined financially by all his enterprises and his wife had to go to work in Cork to support their eleven children.[27]

Audley now tried to sell his estates both in Schull and Castlehaven to pay off his numerous debts. He offered to sell for £100,000 with encumbrances or £11,000 without; no buyer could be found.[28] He then met a banker, Joseph Pike, who suggested to him that a new company should be formed to exploit the mineral wealth of his estates. So the West Cork Mining Company was set up in 1834 with Pike himself as managing director.[29] A great number of shares were sold and luxurious offices were acquired in London over which Pike and Audley resided.[30] One of the shareholders who was also a director accused Pike of fraud. This shareholder was supported by most of the others and they began legal proceedings. In 1837 Audley died but had named Pike as his executor and guardian of his son who was still a minor. The shareholders took their case before the Irish Court of Chancery but lost it. They appealed to the House of Lords and lost again.[31]

Eventually in 1843 Pike and the young Audley were obliged by the Irish Court of Chancery to sell the assets of the West Cork Mining Company. The mines were then put up for sale.[32] No buyer could be found this time either. By now the West Cork Company was 'notorious', as S. C. Hall (son of Colonel Hall) described it.[33] The scientist, Robert Kane, condemned the company as a scandal which contributed towards 'bringing into disrepute Irish industrial enterprises'.[34] There was far more litigation than mining done by this company. In the period 1835–37 only 326 tons of ore were exported by the West Cork Mining Company.[35] By 1842 all work had ceased and only one man remained at Cappagh to prevent the mine from being looted.[36]

COOSHEEN COPPER MINE

The vein of copper ore which was discovered at Cappagh extended westwards to Coosheen on the eastern shores of Schull harbour. A mine was opened here in 1840 by two Cork city entrepreneurs, William Connell and Mr McMullen. An adit or horizontal passage was driven just above high water mark for about 25 fathoms. This adit enabled the mine to be drained and the ore to be extracted by means of a railway track along which trucks were drawn by horses. The capital subscribed was only £2,500, but by 1845 £17,000 worth of ore had been shipped to Swansea.[37] The mining captain was William Thomas, of a well-known Cornish mining family. He was a Methodist who is believed to have done some preaching around the district.[38] Fr James Barry told the agents of the Devon Commission that the only labourers who were improving their conditions were those who had the good fortune to be taken on in the mines. He said that the mine was 'flourishing' – a word rarely used in describing the

Capt. William Thomas (1807–1890) and daughter, c. 1857

economy of the Mizen Peninsula at this time.[39] His evidence is borne out by the list of prices for mining shares as £15 shares were now making £150.[40] The labourers were earning a shilling a day while they would receive eight pence or less from a farmer.[41] A government agent visited the mine in 1841 to examine the conditions under which any children might be working. He found that there were none there but eighty men and forty strong young women. He was told that the women were working for four pence a day and that any number of others could be obtained for the same wage.[42]

In the autumn of 1845 the men in charge of the Coosheen mine, William Connell and Mr McMullen, became even more enterprising and formed a company, the Southern and Western Mining Company. Its chairman was Major Ludlow Beamish of Ballincurrig, County Cork. He was a son of William Beamish, the co-founder of the brewing firm of Beamish and Crawford. The secretary of the new mining company was William Connell and its committee consisted mainly of landlords including Lionel Fleming of Newcourt. It sought £200,000 capital. In its prospectus it affirmed that the mines of West Cork were as rich as any in Europe and could be worked very economically because they were so near the sea. The success of those at Coosheen and Berehaven was offered as proof of what could be done with capital, enterprise and labour. It was stated that Robert Kane had corroborated the claims of the prospectus.[43]

Horse Island, Plan and Elevation, 1857

The Southern and Western Mining Company duly continued the mining at Coosheen. Most of the ore raised was purple and consisted of up to 60% copper which was extremely rich and was called peacock ore. The rest of the ore was green and was not quite so rich but some samples of it were specially cut as ornaments. This mine was so highly valued that its £20 shares were making £200 in the international share market.[44]

A new vein of copper was discovered in 1843 at Dhurode on the lands of Lionel Fleming in Kilmoe parish. This discovery was attributed to the miner, Captain Foster and also to Dr Traill. A new company called the Dhurode Mining Company was formed and 1,000 shares were bought at £2 each. Dr Traill was the principal shareholder.[45] There was a horse whim for raising the ore and a wheel with stamp heads for crushing it; the wheel was driven by water from a nearby stream. The mine was 'well studded with neat slated cottages' for the miners and was under the direction of Henry Thomas, a brother of William Thomas of Coosheen.[46] From 1844 to 1846 it exported 229 tons of ore to Swansea.[47] Traces of gold are occasionally found in copper ore and this occurred at Dhurode. One sample of ore weighing 10.5 pounds was assayed and found to contain more than 7 ounces of gold.[48] Other mines were also discovered at Roaring Water,[49] Kilcoe, Derreenatra and at Shronagree near Ballydehob. By 1845, however, the total number of tons of ore exported amounted to only 215 tons so these mines were soon abandoned.[50] In 1846 a mining captain named Pierre Foley discovered copper at Spanish Point near Crookhaven.[51]

BARYTES

Next to copper the most important mineral to be discovered in the Mizen Peninsula district was barytes or barium sulphate, $BaSO_4$, which is a heavy white mineral. The earliest commercial use of barytes was probably in the manufacture of white pottery in Staffordshire by Josiah Wedgewood about 1770.[52] According to local tradition around Ballydehob boulders of barytes were used as ballast in the ship of a local merchant, James Bennett. The ballast attracted the attention of a person in England who identified it. This discovery led to the mineral being mined at its source in Derreennalomane near Ballydehob. As already stated the earliest reference to barytes in the district was by Richard Griffith in his report on the Cappagh mine in 1824. The mineral was discovered in conjunction with copper, as often happens, but it was never raised in commercial quantities there. In 1840 a mine was opened at Derreennalomane by Dr Traill and Captain William Thomas but it was actually copper that they were seeking. The mine proved unprofitable on account of the large quantities of barytes mixed with the copper ore so they turned to mining barytes instead. They ground it in a local corn mill and exported several tons. Still it was not ground finely enough for the English pottery market so the enterprise was abandoned.[53] According to the geologist, Grenville A. J. Cole, Derreennalomane is 'probably the earliest barytes mine in Ireland and, indeed, one of the earliest in the world'.[54]

All the mines in this district except Coosheen were closed by 1845. This was to some extent caused by the general depression which was beginning to affect British mining. The new railways were attracting capital away from the mines which made the miners complain loudly of 'railway mania'. Prices for ore were falling on account of the importation of large quantities of American and African ore raised by slave labour as the English miners alleged. The new spirit of free trade had caused duties on foreign ore to be reduced. This was naturally welcomed by the smelters but opposed by the miners, resulting in angry confrontations between the two interests. These were the first squalls in the storm which was soon to break out concerning Free Trade and the Corn Laws. Nevertheless such troubles over mining would never become any more than squalls because, unlike the landlords, the miners were not a powerful interest. Back at home, October 1845 was an inauspicious hour for launching the Southern and Western Mining Company. The same newspaper which carried its glowing prospectus also contained gloomy reports of some strange potato disease.[55]

The discovery which attracted most attention in 1846 was of more archeological than of commercial interest. Captain William Thomas and his brother, Charles, exposed ancient mines at Derrycarhoon between Ballydehob and Bantry. Thomas Swanton of Ballydehob, a landlord and Gaelic scholar, answered a long query from the antiquarian, John Windele, about artefacts found in these mines. They consisted of a wooden 'crooked tube', 'an 128 foot tree-trunk ladder', 'a few sticks pointed', 'a piece of an Irish harp' and also numerous 'river stones of a very hard quality battered at one end'. William O'Brien concludes that Derrycarhoon seems to be a Bronze Age mine which was also worked in medieval times or later.[56]

One wonders just how much this mining contributed to the social and economic life of the surrounding area. These mines were by no means as important as those of Allihies or Wicklow, but they were not without significance. Ballydehob unlike, for example, Avoca,[57] did not become a 'copper village' and no character emerged such as 'Copper' John Puxley of the Berehaven mines. Yet the population of Ballydehob increased by 75% between 1821 and 1831, the period in which the mines were flourishing. There seems to have been no bad mining accident at a time when mining conditions were generally so dangerous. Conditions at Berehaven were harsher and some miners lost their lives in accidents.[58] Labouring in the dark and wet adits by the light of a tallow candle was even cruel. A miner from another part of the country described it as cited in the epigraph on p. 86.[59] This account could have come out of Émile Zola's *Germinal* where he depicts life in the coal-mines of France later in the century. Apart from some Whiteboy incidents while Lord Audley was working his own mine there were no serious 'combinations' or outrages at the mines. Although the labourers would have been easy victims for exploitation the mining captains seem to have paid fair wages. The Mining Company of Ireland contributed towards the building of Ballydehob chapel as has been seen in the last chapter.

It was the discovery of copper that first brought Richard Griffith into the district. He saw the need for an improved road and seized the opportunity to provide it. This facilitated the arrival of the steam-engine to the Audley mines. The slates from the quarries were put on the new houses at Ballydehob. Slate was a visible sign of the new improved housing just as the steam-engine was the powerful symbol of the industrial revolution. The coming of the mining captains must have increased the spread of the English language which, together with the slate and the steam, contributed towards the modernisation of life in the Mizen Peninsula. Still the demise of the West Cork Mining Company in 1842 meant that the general mining depression was felt more acutely around Ballydehob than elsewhere. In January 1847 the miner, Pierre Foley, told how the closure of the mines had 'melancholy results for the labouring classes of miners and the hundreds employed'.[60] The failure of the potato crop was thus preceded by the failure of the mining.

V

TITHES;
POVERTY; DANIEL O'CONNELL:
1830–45

There was a parson
Who loved 'divarshun'
And ne'er was harsh on
His flock so few ... ;
The tithe was heavy
That he did levy,
And he kept a 'bevy'
Of tithing men ...

FR THOMAS BARRY (attrib.)

My name is Jeremiah Murphy. I have been living and starving at the weaving trade ... I
have not covering for myself or for my family at night and sometimes I find it hard to get
one meal a day for them. There were formerly 2,000 weavers in and about Bandon. There
are now only 20 or 30. The rest are either in the workhouse, America, dead or trying to
get in at something else. England ruined the trade; they get up everything so well there
that we have no chance with them.

BEGGAR TO POOR INQUIRY, BALLYDEHOB, 1832

My father played the violin or the cello. Mr O'Grady, the clergyman, joined in with the
flute and my mother played ... the piano. We ventured on Handel and Mozart very often,
and so we had our music and enjoyed it, and it promoted serenity in that remote place.
[Goleen].

REV. HORACE TOWNSEND FLEMING, C. 1832

As has been seen in Chapter II, the most important reform resulting from the
Whiteboy violence in the period 1820–3 was the Tithe Composition Act of
1823 originated by the lord lieutenant and introduced to parliament by the
chief secretary, Henry Goulburn. Upon application from the incumbent Protestant clergyman or five landowners occupying lands valued at £20 a year,
the lord lieutenant could create a 'special vestry' in each parish. This vestry
and the clergyman would each appoint an arbitrator and these would together determine the amount of tithe to be paid by each occupier of land. Another act passed in the following year, 1824, abolished the exemption of pasture from tithes and gave power to the lord lieutenant to compel the special
vestries and the clergymen to agree on arbitrators. The amount of tithe to be
paid was fixed for twenty-one years though in some cases slight revisions
could be made every three years. The Tithe Composition Acts were condemned
by Churchmen such as Lord John Beresford, archbishop of Armagh, as 'un-

just and unconstitutional' and an attack on the sanctity of property in general and on ecclesiastical property in particular.[1]

Schull was the first of the parishes in the Mizen Peninsula to implement tithe composition in 1826. The chairman of the special vestry was William Edward Hull. It selected Thomas Evans of Aughadown parish while the rector, Anthony Traill, was represented by his curate, John Jagoe. The method of assessing the amount of tithe to be paid in Schull and in the other parishes was as follows. Each tithe payer's land was valued according to the average price of wheat for the seven preceding years. In most parishes throughout the county the tithe was calculated literally as 10% of the value of the payer's property but this was reduced in a small number of cases, Schull being one of them, where the rate was 7%. Fr Mahony, parish priest of Schull, paid 12s 6d for eight acres of land. The arbitrators assessed the tithes of the parish to be worth £850 and declared that this assessment 'shall last for the space of twenty-one years … and shall not be liable to any change or variation in consequence of any change or variation in the price of grain in that period'.[2] The tax was thereby stabilised and no longer depending on market conditions or the will of the proctor. It was the decreasing corn prices after Waterloo which had rendered the tithes an increasing burden.

Kilmoe was the next parish to introduce composition in 1828. Here, unlike Schull, the rate of taxation there was the usual 10%. Schull's tithe proctor, Joseph Baker, was himself assessed for £3 16s 7d tithes; he had hitherto fixed the tithes in an arbitrary manner. This change was genuine reform; the 'outrages' of his Whiteboy enemies such as Harrington 'Grerah' and the protests of the magistrate, Daniel Coghlan, had not been in vain. The tithes of the parish were now officially pronounced to be worth £500 and payable to the absentee rector, Rev. Langford.[3]

Tithe composition was put into effect in Aughadown in 1829. The parish priest, James Mulcahy, paid £3 13s 0d on 36 acres of parish land around his house in Mohanagh. Henry Becher of Aughadown paid £13, as did Samuel Townsend of Whitehall. Such substantial landowners would have been paying less in the days when pasture lands were exempt from tithe. The tithes of the parish were valued at £600 but only half of this amount was payable to the vicar, Robert Wright. The other half was 'impropriate', i.e., assigned to a layman, namely Samuel Levis of Skibbereen.[4] This procedure was common because after the Reformation monastic tithes passed to laymen.

The last of these parishes to accept composition was Kilcoe in 1830. The tithes were worth £215 but only £150 went to the vicar, Henry Steward. The remaining £75 was 'impropriate' and the private property of Lord Audley.[5] Thus tithes were sold, leased or farmed out like any other property. In addition to the tithes, the wealth of the Established Church in these parishes consisted of glebe land of which there was a total of 137 in these parishes.[6] The Catholic clergy was not landless either, holding 44 acres. An example of a farmer paying tithes was Patrick Hickey of Skeaghanore in Kilcoe; he paid £2 6s 0s on his 22 acres of land.[7] By 1832 tithe composition had been put into effect in more than half of the parishes of the dioceses of Cork and Ross which was representative of the rest of the country.[8] The tithe composition of these parishes was very high. Schull's valuation of £850 per year was higher than Bandon's which was £650; Kilmoe paid £500, and Dunmanway £461, while Watergrasshill near Cork paid only £43.[9] Since the tithes were calculated on the price of corn they must have been higher during the Napoleonic wars. In the eyes of Catholics the Established Church was a parasitic body. Their perception of some Protestant clergymen was expressed in a polemical verse which was popular during the anti-tithe agitation of the 1830s. It was attributed to Thomas Barry, parish priest of Bantry and entitled 'The Parson'; it is quoted in the epigraph on p. 86.[10]

The reforms of the Tithe Composition Acts satisfied the people during the period that may be called a period of peace from exhaustion which followed the Whiteboy troubles and famine of 1821–3. Such reforms, however, could not meet the demands of a people that had won Catholic Emancipation in 1829. They now demanded that the certain measure of justice obtained at parliamentary level should seep down to their own parish level and alleviate the tithe burden. Not only Catholics opposed the tithes; so also did the Presbyterians, the Methodists, and indeed some liberal members of the Established Church. One such person was the Earl of Mountcashel from Moorepark near Fermoy. In a letter to the *Cork Constitution*, he attacked the privileges of his own Church citing the particular example of the 'lucrative parish' of Schull. He alleged that it had not been visited for many years by the absentee rector, Anthony Traill, and that the only provision for the one curate, Alleyn Evanson, was the glebe house and land.[11] This curate himself replied that he was satisfied with his income as the glebe house and 63 acres of land were worth £100 a year. He also acknowledged the generosity of his rector and excused his absenteeism on grounds of age and ill-health.[12] The other curate in the parish, John Triphook, also replied to the earl and pointed out to him that there were now two curates, not one, as he himself had been appointed four years previously at a salary of £80 a year. He praised his rector's generous patronage of five schools in the parish and of other charitable causes as well.

The early 1830s were a time of social and political unrest in Europe. The Bourbons were overthrown in France and the Belgians broke free from the Dutch. All of this impressed the politically conscious in Ireland especially the enthusiastic new member of parliament, Daniel O'Connell, who was hoping to win repeal of the union or, at least, justice for Ireland. This was the 'age of Liberal Reform'; liberal reform was precisely what the tithe system sorely needed. The anti-tithe agitation of this period first broke out in Graignamanagh, County Kilkenny in December 1830. A clerical magistrate seized the parish priest's horse in lieu of tithes. The priest, Martin Doyle, was a cousin of Bishop Doyle of Kildare and Leighlin who had told the people that their hatred of tithes should be as lasting as their love of justice.[13] In March 1832 Daniel O'Connell addressed a great anti-tithe and repeal meeting in Cork at which 200,000 people attended.[14] There was another anti-tithe meeting in Bantry in

June. A crowd of 20,000 people gathered not only from Bantry but from the neighbouring parishes of Muintir Bháire (Durrus), Schull and Kilmoe. They were under the leadership of their respective parish priests. The various tradesmen of Bantry marched in procession, each trade with its own banner. On one side of the tailors' banner was a portrait of Bishop Doyle with the inscription, 'May our hatred of tithes be as lasting as our love of justice' and on the other side was a portrait of O'Connell.

Fr Thomas Barry proposed John Hamilton White of Drombrow House near Bantry as chairman of the meeting and he was accepted. The most recent tactic of the people was to refuse to pay the tithes in cash but to allow the proctor to take payment in kind which would sabotage the whole system. Hamilton White accordingly assured the people that they were obeying the spirit and letter of the law because they were prepared to allow the proctor to take away their goods without murmur and thus 'to restore the tithe system to its original purity by paying in kind'. The crowd cheered and laughed. Thomas Barry himself then called for the 'total extinction' of the tithe system. The last to arrive was Fr Begley, curate of Kilmoe, with an 'imposing cavalcade' of tithe payers. He told his hearers that they were only slaves 'forced to pay for a system that reason disapproves of, justice condemns, and religion in self-defence must abhor'. He made it clear that he was not attacking the Protestant creed as such but was appealing to 'pure disinterested Protestant feeling' and was finding that some Protestants were equally anxious 'to crush this monster, tithes'. The meeting then dispersed with three cheers for O'Connell and Old Ireland.[15]

Encouraged by this enthusiastic meeting the tithe payers of Schull, Kilmoe and Muintir Bháire (Durrus) held a meeting of their own a month later at the foot of Mount Gabriel. Many Protestants and Methodists attended; some were descendants of the Huguenots but they 'joined heart and hand with the children of the Gael for the removal of a common grievance'. A procession of boats came in from the islands. The men of Muintir Bháire arrived under the command of Richard O'Donovan of Tullagh and accompanied by the parish priest, Fr Quin and his curate Fr Kelliher. Richard O'Donovan explained the aims of the meeting but emphasised that they were to be achieved by the 'most implicit obedience to the laws'.[16] Yet Quin and Kelliher were soon prosecuted for urging their people not to pay tithes.[17]

Dr Robert Traill, the new rector of Schull, boasted that he 'waged war against Popery and its thousand forms of wickedness'.[18] He wrote in his diary that the outbreak of cholera was God's punishment for the tithe agitation which had been stirred up by 'the iniquity of these wicked priests'. The day after the anti-tithe meeting several died of cholera and he dreaded the 'similar display of ferocity and rebellion' which was soon to be held in Schull in order to deprive him of what was legally his right. But he rejoiced when God showed his hand and drenched 'the mob' with heavy rain. 'The scaffolding, too, broke down,' he wrote, 'when the priest was holding forth, and just as he put his hand on his heart declaring that his conscience was his guide'. Traill feared that he and his curate would be murdered like a Protestant clergyman only thirty miles away, and added that another clergyman would also have lost his life had he not taken refuge in a priest's house.[19] The man who lost his life was Charles Ferguson, rector of Timoleague, who had attempted to collect his tithes by force.[20] The regatta or carnival atmosphere of the meeting and its non-violent resolutions were only one side of the coin; there was also a sinister side to the whole agitation. Throughout the country in 1832 the enforced payment of tithes had resulted in 242 homicides, 1,179 robberies, 401 burglaries, 568 burnings, 290 houghings of cattle, 161 serious assaults, 203 riots and 723 attacks on houses.[21] Unlike the period 1821–2, there seem to have been no serious outrages in the Mizen Peninsula. The only report of trouble came from Dr Traill. He told the Poor Inquiry that in 1832 'priests and demagogues excited the most alarming disturbances which yielded only to military force; tithes were the ostensible motive'. This was however denied by Fr James Barry who stated that 'in tithe agitation even, there were no outrages worth remark, and none that must not be borne with at all times.'[22] The rector was rather alarmist as compared with the more pragmatic parish priest.

The only effort at reform that had so far been made by the government was a bill by the chief secretary, Edward Stanley, which became law in August 1832. This made tithe composition compulsory on all clergymen but it was a very weak measure and so the agitation continued. In 1834 one notices a change in the anti-tithe meetings; they were now becoming repeal meetings as well and even to the extent that repeal was taking priority. This was the case with the two 'Repeal and Anti-Tithe' meetings held in Bantry and Skibbereen in January 1834, where the guest speaker was the fiery Chartist leader, Fergus O'Connor of the Connor family of Manch, Ballineen and member of parliament for County Cork. At Skibbereen he was welcomed by 40,000 people who cheered him all the way to the chapel yard where the meeting was held. The administrator, Fr Power, took the chair and first spoke of the tithe question although he regarded it as 'far inferior' to the issue of repeal. Fergus O'Connor spoke next condemning the tithes by giving local illustrations of their injustices and then went on to 'the question of questions, the magic word – repeal'. He blamed the union for landlord absenteeism, lack of capital for industry, evictions and the general unemployment and poverty.[23]

In December of that year (1834) the country was shocked by a tithe affray at the Widow Ryan's at Gortroe near Rathcormac, County Cork, where twelve people were killed and forty-two wounded, of whom seven later died including the widow's son. The new year, 1835, brought hope to the tithe agitators. Lord Melbourne replaced Earl Grey as Prime Minister. Viscount Morpeth became chief secretary and the following year Thomas Drummond became undersecretary. Daniel O'Connell came to an understanding with Melbourne. It was a sign of the times that it was now the Protestant clergy who had to petition parliament. In April 1838, the bishop and clergy of the United Dioceses of Cork, Cloyne and Ross met in Cork and 'viewed with alarm … the curtailment of the Church revenues, as proposed in parliament, to be an uncalled for infringement on the rights of property.'[24] They looked on the Whigs now in power as the enemies of their Church. Not all the Protestant clergy were as intransigent as it would seem from this petition. By now there were conciliatory meetings held throughout the country, presided over by landlords and attended by Protestant and Catholic clergy and laity. There was a feeling that the tithe question should be settled simply for the sake of peace.

A meeting held in Skibbereen in March 1838 was attended by people of 'all grades and castes and religion and politics' including Lionel Fleming of Newcourt, R. H. H. Becher of Hollybrook, Dr Traill, his curate John Triphook, Fr Fitzpatrick, the new administrator of Skibbereen and Fr James Barry of Schull. The chairman declared that never before had the gentry of the country assembled in similar circumstances and that the peace and prosperity of the country depended on 'an equitable arrangement of tithes'. He was cheered by all. The next speaker, R. H. H. Becher, proposed a petition to parliament. It stated that the law forced the clergyman either to suffer the loss of his income or engage in litigation with his parishioners. The meeting implored parliament to pass 'a law that would remove the evils of the present system and give general satisfaction and consequent peace to the country'. This petition was moderate; there was no question of the extreme 'total extinction' of the tithes.[25]

The spirit of goodwill and compromise which was displayed at the conciliatory tithe meetings eventually resulted in the Tithe Act of 1833. This reduced the tithes by 25% and converted the tax into a rent charge to be collected by the landlord together with his usual rent. Although it could be argued that the same old tithes had only been reduced and renamed yet the tithe proctor became extinct and his tax less visible – less in sight, less in mind.[26] A similar bill was passed for England where there had also been anti-tithe agitation and outrages. As G. M. Trevelyan expressed it, this bill 'put an end to the quarrel that had been renewed in the English village every year since the Conquest and beyond, over the parson's tithe pig and sheaves'.[27]

It can be seen from the events in these parishes that the 1830s were troubled times for the Church of Ireland. In the words of its historian, D. H. Akenson, it was 'knocked about like a shuttlecock from one issue to another'.[28] Its official monopoly in religious and educational matters established for centuries was being undermined by Catholic Emancipation and the National Schools. Its financial resources were curtailed by the tithe settlement. Competition from the Methodists continued to increase. They were making more converts from among Dr Traill's parishioners so he accused them of 'leading the people to Hell' and denounced their chapels as 'synagogues of Satan'.[29] The local preacher, Rev. Ballard, called him a 'raving Calvinist' and challenged him to a public debate which took place in the church in Schull. According to the Methodists many Catholics supported 'the humble Methodist preacher against the aristocratic rector' in a debate which lasted three days. The Methodists claimed that Traill argued in favour of the Calvinist doctrine of predestination and reprobation while Ballard successfully proved to him from the Book of Common Prayer that his own Church believed in 'universal redeeming grace'.[30] Nevertheless Traill maintained that he had 'the best of the argument', and condemned Methodism as 'the Popery of Protestantism' with its 'utter ignorance of scripture, its preachers flattering the people and they in turn extolling them, filling their bellies and pockets'.[31]

POVERTY

The population of the Mizen Peninsula was increasing rapidly during this period 1823–45, but agriculture and fisheries were in a backward state as will be seen in the next chapter. There was little employment for what was called the 'surplus population'. Mining employed only a few hundred and in a precarious manner. There was no institution to relieve the poor; widespread poverty was the inevitable result. The government commission which was set up to inquire into the condition of the poorer classes made thorough and sympathetic reports which were published in 1835 and 1836. The commission was chaired by Richard Whately, Church of Ireland archbishop of Dublin and a leading political economist who had taught at Oxford; Daniel Murray, Catholic archbishop of Dublin, was also on the commission. Agents of this commission held an inquiry into conditions in the parish of Schull and were instructed to record 'as nearly as might be possible in the words of each witness'. This session took place in Ballydehob in 1833. Thomas Gray, the poet, was wrong for once; the annals of the poor are not 'short and simple' but present us with charming word portraits and indeed self-portraits of people many of whom were fated soon to disappear off the face of the earth.

Representatives of every religion and class attended the session and were asked for information on certain subjects. The first was the condition of deserted and orphaned children. There were no foundlings being supported at the expense of the parish because the vestry had refused to levy rates the previous year. One child had been exposed; the churchwarden paid a woman to nurse it for two months and she nursed it gratis for another nine months. The child was then handed over to Dr Traill who had it nursed at the expense of the parish. It was not sent to the Foundling Hospital in Cork, as was usually the case. The final responsibility for the foundling lay with the rector since it was he who received the tithes, one-third of which was originally for the relief of the poor. There were no abandoned children reported from the parish of Aughadown but there were two or three from Kilmoe. Fr James Barry knew of a few who remained with their finders. These people calculated on obtaining the children's labour until they should become of age to look after themselves; no child however died through neglect.[32]

The next subject to be inquired into was that of bastardy or illegitimacy. This was less frequent in Ireland than in England or other European countries. Many foreign visitors described the Irish as 'remarkable for their chastity'.[33] Fr Barry said that for the three preceding years ten illegitimate children had been baptised in the parish but he thought that some infants on account of their mothers' shame were baptised elsewhere or exposed. Baptisms of illegitimate children accounted for about 3.2% of all baptisms, which was rather high as compared to the average for the rest of the country which was only 2.5%. The remark 'bastard' or less harshly, *pater ignotus*, 'father unknown' was usually entered in the register after their names. Barry said that having an illegitimate child in his parish 'was less thought of than elsewhere'. The reason he gave was that the people were all 'too much reduced and in too great a poverty to feel the distinction. There is little feelings of respectability among them.' Illegitimate children were usually neglected by their fathers. He stated that there were five cases of infanticide in the previous five years; the mothers were suspected. Of course such sad events took place in other parishes too; for example in Glanmire there is *Crosaire na mBastardí* or 'The Cross of the Bastards' where such babies were buried.[34] In County Mayo the illegitimate infants of soldiers suffered a similar fate.[35]

The witnesses at Ballydehob gave the case histories of twelve girls who had given birth to a total of thirty illegitimate children. Most of these girls were still in their teens and were servants in farmers' houses; they had become pregnant by the farmers' sons or by fellow servants. The following was a typical case history:

> Nelly Donovan was a servant in a farmer's house; about two years ago she had a child by the farmer's son. He gave her no assistance, 'not a penny,' said Sullivan (quarryman, a witness), 'I heard her say the child died in about three months; while it lived she was getting about a night's lodging and a meal'. Her own friends would not let her in … After that she was employed by a poor man whose wife had died, to nurse his child for 10s 0d a quarter; 'he could not pay a decent nurse'. Being asked was she a good nurse Daniel Sullivan says, 'the like of her would not be taken if it could be helped, a man don't like to give such suck to his child.' He was a poor miner with two children besides the young one; he went away and left her in care of the children.

The mother of illegitimate children usually lived by spinning wool, selling eggs, and jobbing in different ways. She was a 'fallen woman' with little prospect of marriage as no decent man would ever marry her unless she was a gentleman's daughter 'that he might get something with her to support her'. The witness knew of three strong farmers married to illegitimate daughters of gentlemen who gave them good fortunes.

There were about 200 widows in the parish. Four of these widows had lost their husbands, and one a son as well, in the cholera epidemic of the previous year. Some widows lived by trafficking in various goods while others became servants or beggars. Only a few were independent such as the Widow Field whose husband had died of cholera. She had one son 'on board a man-o-war' and another married at home. One of her daughters was in America while another was married locally.

The only institution where the sick poor could get any relief was the dispensary. Fr Barry would not venture to make any collection for these sick poor because the people themselves were already so poor. When a labourer fell sick he went to the neighbours for assistance or sometimes the farmers would send food to the sick-house. Nonetheless one farmer admitted that hundreds would die before the farmers could send them anything, because the farmers were 'too much taxed and strained and troubled themselves'. Several labourers immediately cried out in unison, 'that is the truth you are telling' – more truth than they realised. A labourer told of a man near him who had been so seriously injured that he was unable to work. His children aged eight and five were in great distress but were too ashamed to beg. Although they were 'yellow with hunger' they used to 'be striving to stick potatoes for the neighbours but could not do so; still the neighbours gave them something'. Dr Sweetman said that there were 2,400 persons receiving aid from the Schull dispensary and its branch in Ballydehob but that many of them could be cured much more easily if only they had proper nourishment. He lamented that certain absentee landlords with property valued at hundreds of pounds contributed only £3 to the dispensary although many of their tenants were attending it daily.[36] According to Dr McCormick of Kilmoe a dispensary was set up in that parish in 1829 'when the cholera was threatening'.[37]

Such communities were very vulnerable to disease or plague such as cholera. This struck Cork in April 1832 where the fever hospital held almost a thousand patients, nearly half of whom died.[38] Dr Traill wrote in his diary that it had swept nearly a thousand altogether to their graves and that several had died of it in Skibbereen, 'once so busy, now a desert'. Soon there were some victims in Ballydehob and in Schull where it carried off the wife of Mr O'Neill, one of his curates. 'She was seized in the morning,' Traill lamented, 'and in ten hours was a corpse'. The plague made a return visit in 1834; twenty-four persons died in Castletownshend, several in Skibbereen and some also in Ballydehob and Schull.[39]

Many foreign visitors to Ireland complained of being pestered by beggars. It is not surprising that the witnesses should have been questioned on the subject of vagrancy. Fr Barry calculated that about 336 persons, not counting children, left the parish each summer to go begging and that even more passed through it, as it was 'great potato country'. Some of these were distressed weavers from Bandon. One of them, Jeremiah Murphy, spoke for this class as cited in the epigraph on p. 96.[40]

The small farmers paid their rent by potatoes as often as by cash. John Triphook, the Protestant curate, said that some tenants could procure only 'mountain-ground' at a high price. Since this ground could grow only poor quality potatoes known as 'lumpers', he considered that the tenants were better off begging. A beggar named Hegarty was allowed to tell his own story:

I am nearly 50 years old. I have a wife and five children, the eldest is only nine. I went to beg last summer; I had no employment. She went out every summer since. In the winter I used to gather twigs for making little baskets for gathering potatoes. The neighbours used give us potatoes in the plentiful season. I was obliged to go out myself last May; we had another young child and I went to carry it. I would rather stay at home if I could. I would be willing to go to America, if anyone would take me, or into a workhouse. I pay no rent for the cabin I have; it is built in the corner of an old road. I do not keep a pig; I could not buy one. I have no clothes but these [his clothes were literally a heap of rags]. I did not go to Mass in my own parish those five years, for want of clothes.[41]

A landlord, Mr Swanton, stated that the farmers were very poor but that if the rents were fully exacted they would be paupers. It was on them however and on the labourers that the relief of beggars mainly depended. One labourer said that many a farmer could not let in a beggar as he had his cattle and his family in the same house but that a labourer had no cattle. One labourer complained that there were some 'strong farmers' who did not give as much to the beggars as the labourers did and that the gentry did not give as much as they ought; 'they do not like to let the beggars inside their gates'. One reason was that such travelling people could well be carriers of fever. Nonetheless the witnesses were unanimous in preferring this form of charity to any sort of taxation in support of the workhouse system. The report stated that religion had a 'great influence in producing habits of charity'. One farmer considered that if there were a poor-house, the people would be deprived of good opportunities for giving charity: 'we do it for the good of our soul,' he added. The only beggars that were disliked were the 'buccoughs', able-bodied men, who if refused alms would threaten violence and curse with the special beggars' curse; at times they were accused of theft, debauchery and gambling. These 'buccoughs' (*bacach*, a beggar) were distinguished from the 'the deserving poor' or *bochtáin Dé*, i.e., God's poor.[42]

In the opinion of the witnesses, the beggars and poor labourers would have great objection to going into the poor-house on account of the confinement and separation from family and friends but they could be forced to go by pressure of hunger. Fr Barry insisted that employment should be given by making roads and reclaiming waste lands. A labourer shrewdly concluded that 'it would be better to have both, the poor-house for those that could not work and employment for those who could'.[43] This question about the poor-house was of special relevance because one of the purposes of the whole inquiry was to find out if the English workhouse system should be extended to Ireland. The Poor Inquiry commissioners estimated that if it were, accommodation would have to be provided for as many as two million paupers. Chronic unemployment was one of the fundamental causes of poverty since there was little work available except during the spring and harvest. Half of the labourers of the peninsula were unemployed from May to August and during the winter most of them were idle. One labourer would have preferred to be in jail rather than be unemployed and he knew persons who had committed crimes in order to be put in jail. Some of the labourers went from the district to North Cork, Limerick or Tipperary to reap corn or dig potatoes. One such *spailpín fánach* or migrant labourer named Regan told of his way of life which he called 'spailpeening':

> I was out last year near Doneraile, cutting the harvest, I went out in August and stayed thirteen weeks. I brought home £1 14s 0d. I did not drink a pint of whiskey while I was out. On a Sunday when I was not getting my diet from a farmer, I might take a

pint of porter and a 1d or 2d worth of bread. I did not spend it on myself because it was for my little family that I went out to earn it. I did not go out this season because I expected to get employment at the mine.

Many others had stayed at home for the same reason and must have been similarly disappointed because the Audley mines were closed the previous year, 1832. Wages were not bad for 'spailpeens' in the corn-growing belt at least in the harvest. According to Amhlaoibh Ó Súilleabháin of Callan, Co. Kilkenny, *spailpínighe bochta* or poor migratory labourers could obtain 8d a day and the *lucht coráin* or sickle men as much as 15d.[44] Labourers went to England to work in the harvest. On land they would beg their way but when they arrived at the boat money was needed 'to pay for the steam'.[45] As poor as living conditions were in the Mizen Peninsula none of the witnesses had heard of anybody dying of 'actual starvation'. Still Barry had often seen cases where he felt sure that the 'ordinary necessaries of life would have prolonged the existence of people'.[46] It was disease especially cholera which caused deaths; people did not die of starvation thanks to the potato.

The gentry lived well, of course, such as the Townsends and the Flemings. Eliza, daughter of Horace Townsend of Derry, Rosscarbery, married Lionel Fleming of Newcourt in 1819 but the young couple was sent to live out west on the remote family property at Ballydevlin near Goleen. One of her sons, Rev. Horace Townsend Fleming, gives us a delightful glimpse of the family entertaining itself as cited in the epigraph on p. 96. Occasional visits were made by Eliza to her old home at Derry when the journey was made by chaise and two horses. The common cart was no longer necessary thanks to Griffith's new road. It was not until the elder Lionel died, in 1837, that the younger Lionel, Eliza and family finally moved to Newcourt. A grand-daughter of theirs also described the manner of living of her grandparents:

> The winter menu in those days was incessant salt meat. In the autumn some fat sheep and bullocks were killed and cut up, and the joints put in barrels of brine … The only variety of food for the dinner table was an occasional rabbit or hare or wild duck. At Ballydevlin, failing cabbage, a seaweed was used for vegetable. Mutton fat was melted down and poured into moulds for candles. They had a nasty smell and gave poor light. In the kitchen at Newcourt there was a large open fire and a spit, on which a joint of meat was hung. This was kept turning by an old woman who sat at the side, close to the blazing fire.[47]

According to the commissioners one of the root causes of Irish poverty was drunkenness, arising from the 'extreme use of ardent spirits'. There were at least thirteen public houses in Schull parish and seven in Kilmoe. Dr Traill remarked that there were public houses *ad infinitum* in his parish although illegal distillation was not common. He was glad that the parish was free of the 'nuisance' of pawnbrokers.[48] The district seems to have had the traditional Irish drink problem. An attempt had already been made by a poor nailer to tackle it, Geoffrey Sedwards, who founded Ireland's first temperance in Skibbereen in 1817.[49] A group of benevolent people persuaded the Capuchin priest, Theobald Mathew, to found and lead the Cork Total Abstinence Association on 10 April 1838. One of Fr Mathew's first large temperance meetings was held on a Sunday morning in the following July, at Durrus, between Ballydehob and Bantry in the parish of Muintir Bháire. Great crowds assembled from the neighbouring parishes and the Skibbereen Temperance Band arrived playing 'Rory O'Moore'. The Apostle of Temperance ascended a platform in the churchyard; also on the platform were Fr Quin, the local parish priest, James Doheny, parish priest of Dunmanway, James Barry of Schull and many Catholic and Protestant gentlemen.

The Apostle of Temperance spoke of the great benefit the pledge had already been to five million people who, he claimed, had now taken it in Ireland. He condemned excessive drinking as the root cause of poverty in the country and cited the local parish of Muintir Bháire where as much as £50 a week was being spent on drink. He pointed out that people had no right to blame Providence for not giving sufficient food while it was being perverted into 'maddening liquors' and claimed that temperance had led to a diminution of crime in the country. He finally administered the pledge with great solemnity first in English and then in Irish. The first person enrolled was James Barry to whom he gave the temperance medal from around his own neck.[50] Fr Mathew was by no means exaggerating the problem of drink. The consumption of whiskey had been increasing and in that year, 1838, there were 12,296,342 gallons of whiskey drunk which was to be the record for pre-famine Ireland. Two years later consumption had declined to 7,401,051 in spite of the increase in population; consumption then stabilised.[51]

Faction fighting was no doubt closely associated with drinking. The travellers, Mr and Mrs Hall, asked an 'intelligent countryman' what the cause of the fighting was. 'Whiskey', came the reply; 'No gun will go off unless it is primed, and sure whiskey was the priming. That made more orphans and widows than the fever or starvation'. S. C. Hall himself recalled a faction fight he witnessed at Ballydehob. (His father, Colonel Hall, had been mining there in 1814.) It was a fair day and the rival factions assembled each armed with a stout shillelagh. The leaders parleyed for a while but an old hag rated one of them 'coward'. Soon sticks were crossed and in a moment hundreds had joined in the clash. They fought for more than an hour when one party was beaten off the field.

Traill describes a faction fight which took place during a total eclipse of the moon:

A number of Roman Catholics had collected together, and, after drinking an abundance of whiskey, began to fight, when lo! the moon, shining before in splendour, became obscured. Struck with terror, as if the very heavens were frowning upon them, they instantly sank upon their knees, and began to mutter their prayers. So much for Popery and this most wicked and superstitious country.[52]

Such faction fights must have been among the last in the district. This same 'intelligent countryman' told the Halls that these clashes were 'almost gone

Faction fight at Ballydehob, c. 1814

off the face of the earth.' This countryman's own brother had been a faction fighter mainly due to the influence of whiskey but had given up fighting since he became a 'temperance man'.[53]

The influence of Fr Mathew and, of course, Daniel O'Connell tended to discourage faction fighting but so also did the increasing strength of the Peelers. Up to the time of Thomas Drummond the policemen often felt it was more prudent not to interfere but Drummond instructed them to break up such gatherings and arrest the chief offenders.[54] The resident magistrates appointed under Peel's Peace Preservation Act in 1814 were usually strangers unlike the local magistrates and were therefore in a more favourable position to deal with factions. John Gore Jones was an example of such a magistrate. When he was transferred from Skibbereen to a post in County Tipperary in 1844 he received a complimentary address from many of the leading inhabitants of his district. He was thanked for making 'justice loved and revered as well as dreaded, and winning the confidence of all, without sacrificing to the prejudices of any'. The address was signed by Justices of the Peace, such as Lionel Fleming of Newcourt and J. R. Barry of Glandore. It was also signed by many Catholic and Protestant clergymen of the Mizen Peninsula. Gore Jones replied that he had always borne in mind that 'under no circumstances should the laws be perverted for personal or political motives. I felt I enjoyed the confidence of the peasantry of my extensive district'.[55] The resident magistrates were beginning to win a degree of respect from a people that previously had some reason to view the law with deep suspicion.

During the eighteenth century the problems of poverty and public health were usually left to private charity or philanthropy; governments seldom considered it their place to interfere. The comprehensive and thorough report of the Poor Inquiry commissioners rejecting the workhouse system was dismissed by the government. On the other hand, the hastily written report of George

Nicholls, the English Poor Law commissioner, recommending the workhouse was accepted. The harshness of this institution had just been illustrated by Charles Dickens in *Oliver Twist*. The Irish Poor Law which divided the country into 130 unions, i.e., unions of parishes, was passed in 1838. Each union was to be controlled by a Board of Guardians, the first elected local body in Ireland.[56] The chairman of the Board of Guardians of the Skibbereen Union was Richard Townsend of Castletownshend. Each parish was represented on the board by a person or persons elected by those who held £4 worth of property or over and would therefore be paying the new poor rate.[57]

By the end of 1841 there were thirty-seven workhouses open in the country; the one at Skibbereen was not completed as early as planned. There was no real opposition to these institutions on humanitarian grounds as there had been in England; in Ireland they were accepted as a crude necessity. In the end of January 1842 the Skibbereen Board of Guardians received a deputation complaining that the house was not yet open to receive the poor now suffering so much from both cold and hunger. The deputation pointed out 'the comparative luxury and comfort of the workhouse when contrasted with the filthy, muddy, and wretched hovels of the poor'.[58] Nonetheless the comfort of the workhouses was to be severely restricted. The Poor Law commissioners of England and Wales and now of Ireland gave instructions to the English architect, George Wilkinson, who had designed several of the English poor-houses: 'The style of building is intended to be of the cheapest compatible with durability: and effect was to be obtained through harmony of proportion and simplicity of arrangement, all mere decoration being studiously excluded'.[59] The poor of Skibbereen received their 'luxury' on 19 March 1842. The workhouse was built to hold 800 inmates and cost £8,300.[60]

Thackeray visited the town that very year and drew the following grim word-sketch of the house:

> The tall new poor-house presents itself to the eye of the traveller; of a common model, being a bastard-Gothic edifice, with a profusion of cottage-ornée roofs, and pinnacles and insolent looking stacks of chimneys. It was built for 900 people, but as yet not more than 400 have been induced to live in it, the beggars preferring the freedom of their precarious trade to the dismal certainty within its walls.[61]

The large workhouse system had to be paid for by the poor rate, the latest tax. The landlord had to pay this as well because half of it had to be borne by the owner and half by the occupier of land. The landlord was in addition obliged to pay all the poor rate on holdings under £4 valuation. Some landlords were therefore suspected of secretly opposing the poor rate. In November 1842 an affray broke out at Rath Chapel near Baltimore between the people and the police who were escorting a rate collector; one of the agitators was killed and another wounded.[62] He died later, ironically enough, in the workhouse itself. This stirred up resentment among the people and rumours spread that a mob was assembling 'to raze the workhouse to the ground'. The government soon acted and troops poured in from Bandon, Kinsale and Cork.[63] What was unusual about these troubles was that the magistrates suspected that 'certain landlords' had instigated the people to pay no poor rates, telling them that the government would then be forced to 'do away with the poor-houses and clerks and commissioners and you won't be taxed any longer for the support of every idle vagabond'.[64] The nineteenth century taxpayer was reacting violently against the novel principle of taxation for mere social welfare.

The general opposition to the Poor Law was loudly voiced by Daniel O'Connell, MP for County Cork, who accused the landlords of making the tenants pay more than their just share of tax. He would have preferred to have appealed to the clergy and the religious orders of men and women to create a system on Christian principles. He had, nonetheless, voted for the Poor Law.[65] His opposition may have contributed to making him even more popular in Skibbereen. His 'tribute' amounted to £91 for the year 1842, e.g., double the sum of the previous year.

As has been seen in Chapter II, the cause of Catholic Emancipation had received support from the United States due to the efforts Robert Swanton of Ballydehob, a United Irishman who had escaped to that land in 1798. He returned home in 1836 where he died in 1841. The *New York Evening Post* published his obituary:

> The loss of this inestimable man cannot fail to be severely felt by the poor and oppressed. He was an unswerving and ardent advocate of the rights of man. In the great effort undertaken … by a band of patriots to rescue their native land from the grasp of the oppressor he nearly sacrificed his life, to become a friendless and destitute exile.

The inscription on his grave in the cemetery in the town of Skibbereen describes him as 'Counsellor at Law and One of the Judges of the Marine Court of the City of New York' and declares, '*Do ghrádhaigh sé na Gaedhil agus an Gaeilge*', 'He loved the Irish people and the Irish language'.[66] The tone of patriotism in the early 1840s, however, was not that of Wolfe Tone and the Republic but that of Daniel O'Connell and repeal. The people of Skibbereen through the person of Daniel Welply of Westfield, Aughadown, invited him to attend a Repeal Banquet; he agreed to come on 22 June 1843.[67]

DANIEL O'CONNELL

The appeal to the people of Carbery to welcome the Liberator was signed by many of the priests of West Cork, including James and John Barry and also Laurence O'Sullivan. No Protestant clergyman nor any landlord did so although the Protestant farmers of Aughadown gladly paid the repeal rent.[68] Dr Traill had a short time previously received an anonymous letter calling him a 'bloody Orangeman', demanding 'Repeal or Blood!' and presenting him with a drawing of his own coffin.[69] O'Connell spent the night in the house of Fr Doheny of Dunmanway and then travelled with him by coach and four towards Skibbereen. At a bridge between Drimoleague and Skibbereen the procession was formed made up of carpenters, blacksmiths, shoe-makers, brogue-makers, bakers, weavers and tailors preceded by a band. Next came the Liberator's coach which was followed by the carriages of the gentlemen and clergy. Most of the priests, for example, Laurence O'Sullivan and the two Barrys, were leading their parishioners. All cheered their distinguished visitor and headed to the actual place of the meeting, the Hill of Curragh, north-west of the town.

O'Connell shared the platform with Edmund Burke Roche, Repeal MP for Cork, J. F. Maguire, founder-editor of the *Cork Examiner*, John Shea Lawlor of Bantry and other gentry and some thirty-six priests. The address of welcome was read by Timothy McCarthy Downing, the local Catholic solicitor and champion of Catholic rights. O'Connell began to speak in Irish but soon changed to English. He told the people that he had the honour of being their representative in parliament but that it was a packed parliament as if a jury packed against an innocent man. He said that Robert Peel pretended to be the farmers' friend and asked his hearers if they had received the same price for corn as two years previously; they all shouted 'No!' The next grievance he referred to was the tithes and claimed credit for the settlement of 1838. On the question of emancipation, O'Connell quoted the home secretary, James Graham, as saying that it had been 'conceded'. 'Conceded!' The Liberator exclaimed ironically and asserted that it had been obtained 'in spite of England', whose rulers dared not refuse. Next he asked the great rhetorical question, 'Who was it that obtained emancipation?' A voice cried 'O'Connell!' and the whole meet-

Timothy McCarthy Downing

111

ing gave loud cheers. He granted that he had been at the head but that victory could not have been won if the people had not been behind him; again the crowd roared. The next grievance which O'Connell brought up was the disfranchisement of the forty-shilling freeholders. He promised that after repeal every man with a house would have a vote and every man would have the opportunity to own a house.

The Liberator went on to promise that after repeal taxation would be reduced, the Grand Jury cess for the roads would be abolished and the roads taken over by the expense of the public treasury. The poor rate would also be abolished because the tithes would be used to support the poor – one of their proper functions. The duties on tea and sugar would be reduced. The millions of pounds spent annually by the absentee landlords abroad would be spent at home; the extra capital would 'make Irishmen chirp'. The smith would be busy again and no shoe-maker would go to sleep without an awl in his hand! The people laughed. He went on to describe the stimulation which would be given to manufacturers by a domestic parliament. Then the meeting dispersed having given three monstrous cheers for the queen, O'Connell and repeal. The crowd had just been assisting at a performance of the Liberator who, as the historian, William Lecky, observed, could 'play on a popular Irish audience like a great musician on his instrument, eliciting what tone and what response he pleased'.[70]

O'Connell, the gentry and the clergy then went to the Repeal Banquet in the Skibbereen Temperance Hall. After the meal a toast was drunk not only to the queen but also to 'the People, the true source of all legitimate power', a democratic or rather republican idea. In answer Shea Lawlor of Bantry, a man of Young Ireland sympathies, declared, 'I am now also determined to shed my blood for repeal, no matter where it might be, on the scaffold or elsewhere'. This was greeted with 'tremendous shouts of applause and renewed cheering'. The next toast was to 'O'Connell and repeal' to which he himself replied, expressing his hope that they would all succeed in making

> Ireland what she ought to be, a nation; what nature intended her to be, a nation; what nature's God intended her to be, a nation. I confess, I do not go as far as my excellent friend, Mr Shea Lawlor. I am not determined to die for Ireland, I would rather live for her, [cheering] for one living repealer is worth a churchyard full of dead ones.

Shea Lawlor interrupted him insisting that 'None can live for Ireland but those who would die for her'. O'Connell denied this and added that what his friend probably meant was that they should be prepared to die for Ireland if their enemies violated the constitution. Then he went on to condemn the union in the usual way and finally urged his hosts to support those who had led them to bloodless victories and resumed his seat amidst loud applause. Nevertheless, Shea Lawlor again interrupted asserting that he had been misinterpreted by the Liberator and that he had said nothing inconsistent with repeal. This exchange between O'Connell and Lawlor reveals the ambiguous attitude of many repealers towards physical force. Thus in the conviviality of the banquet this difficult and dangerous question was glossed over but it would soon erupt again and provoke a split between O'Connell and the Young Irelanders. This declaration of his unwillingness to die for Ireland was clearly a toning down of his 'Defiance' speech at Mallow eleven days earlier where he had referred to laying down his life.[71] This had bordered on the seditious.

O'Connell stayed for the night with the administrator, Fr Fitzpatrick. The following morning the honourable guest was presented with nearly £500 repeal rent and headed for Galway.[72] His picture of Ireland after repeal is, of course, rather utopian. He presented repeal as the panacea for the country's ills according to his diagnosis, 'Cause – Union: Cure – Repeal'. This was, of course, an oversimplification. The cause of the decline of Irish manufactures was not so much the union as the Industrial Revolution and the vast production of England's factories. As Jeremiah Murphy, the weaver, told the Poor Inquiry, 'They get up everything so well there we have no chance with them'. It must be granted, however, that an independent Irish Parliament might have adopted protectionist policies. This decline in production was particularly sharp in the case of textiles. In 1829 Bandon had about 1,750 hand-loom weavers but by 1834 there were only 150. Most had emigrated to England while others had gone out begging.[73] The weaver, Jeremiah Murphy, was not exaggerating much to the Poor Inquiry. According to Lewis, Skibbereen 'had formerly a considerable trade arising from the manufacture of woollen cloth, linen and hand-kerchiefs, which has altogether declined'.[74] This explains the great numbers of tradesmen as well as peasants at the monster meeting.

In the following September the repealers of Schull held 'a parochial meeting' in Ballydehob on a Sunday morning after Mass. James Barry told the crowd of about 5,000 to follow the course marked out by the Liberator and to show kindly feelings towards the police and military who had been so unnecessarily brought among them. One speaker granted that O'Connell had no intention of renouncing allegiance to the crown but that, if he did, he and his seven million followers 'could in one fortnight drive the most powerful army in Europe from the country'. Another man condemned the tithes but denied that the repealers were seeking ascendancy for the Catholics but only equal rights for all. The next speaker presented the following argument which was characteristic of repeal reasoning:

> In 1829, Wellington and Peel yielded to the moral power of the people – concentrated and directed by O'Connell; we have now the same or greater power wielded by the same O'Connell, and is there any reason to doubt that the same Wellington and Peel will be found to yield once more to the voice of the millions.

There was every reason to doubt it, but O'Connell and his followers preferred to pay little heed to Peel who had insisted that repeal would mean 'the dismemberment of this great empire' and that he was even prepared to go to war to prevent this.[75] The banning of the Clontarf monster meeting less than a month after this Ballydehob gathering showed the world that Peel meant exactly what he had said. The manner in which the speaker at Ballydehob argued that the strategy which won emancipation would similarly win repeal showed that he must have been listening carefully to O'Connell in Skibbereen. Yet there was a serious fallacy in this argument because repeal, unlike emancipation, was perceived as dismembering not only the 'great empire' but the United Kingdom itself.

The last speaker at the Ballydehob meeting, John Barry, the curate, proposed the setting up of repeal courts in which local arbitrators would settle the differences between people, thus bypassing the ordinary courts. The crowd agreed wholeheartedly. Some of them had cheered O'Connell at Skibbereen when he said that 'justice had been frightened away from the courts'. In folk tradition O'Connell, the Counsellor, is a greater hero than O'Connell, the Liberator.[76] With hindsight the weaknesses or fallacies in the political and economic thinking of these speakers at Ballydehob can easily be seen. Their political consciousness however and their awareness of the power of the people must be recognised. They were sophisticated local leaders compared to the Whiteboys twenty years earlier. These repealers were learning the art of popular politics, which many of them would practice later, not only in Ireland but also in America. Some credit must surely go to their teacher, Counsellor O'Connell. This he did receive, however belatedly, as a dangerously ill man in a hotel in Paris on this way to Rome in 1847. The French liberal Catholic leader, Charles de Montalembert, visited him and paid him the following tribute: 'But you are not only *the Man of one Nation*, you are the Man of all *Christendom* … Wherever Catholics begin anew to practice civic virtues and devote themselves to the conquest of their legislative rights under God, it is your work'.[77] And so indeed it was.

VI

Agriculture, Fisheries, and Population, 1821–45

Early marriages are very common in this parish. Fr Barry, PP, says 'I have married boys of 16 and girls of 14 or 15 and many from 16 to 20; it arises in part from the facility of setting up an establishment, and in part from the wretchedness of their condition. When a poor servant boy is with a farmer he says "I have no one to wash for me … I may as well have a wife to keep house, we will be able to make out life some way or other, and I do no more now"'.

POOR INQUIRY, 1836

AGRICULTURE

The Industrial Revolution in England caused an increase in population which had to be fed. New scientific methods were used in the production of crops and livestock. The 'Black' Industrial Revolution provoked the 'Green' Agricultural Revolution. New breeds of cattle were being developed in the north of England and in Scotland. The Durhams or Shorthorns and the Ayrshires were replacing the old Longhorns and black cattle such as the Kerry cow.[1] A new breed of sheep known as the Leicester was introduced. The round fat Chinese pig was crossed with the native lean and lanky English or Irish hog to produce the black and white Berkshire.[2] A German, Justin Liebig, was a pioneer on the subject of crop fertilisers. The cultivation of turnips was advocated around 1730 by 'Turnip' Townsend; other green crops such as mangolds were also introduced. The Norfolk system of crop rotation was increasingly practiced, i.e., roots followed by barley or oats, next grass and then wheat.[3] The old wooden plough which took four horses and two men to work was being replaced by the Scottish swing plough worked by the one man and a pair of horses.[4] These new ploughs were made in factories rather than in forges. Foreign travellers such as Arthur Young found that Irish farmers were generally backward and slow to adopt the improved methods of their English and Scottish counterparts. He saw that in some places colts were still forced to plough by the tail. Still he praised the efforts of the Royal Dublin Society founded in 1731 and described it as 'the father of all similar societies now existing in Europe'.[5] The Carbery Agricultural Society was founded in Skibbereen in 1836; its secretary and treasurer was Thomas Hungerford, an agent for R. H. H. Becher of Hollybrook.[6]

The system of land tenure did not encourage investment in agriculture. Many of the landlords in the Mizen Peninsula were absentees. James Barry of Schull told the Poor Inquiry in 1833 that land in his parish was let not by the acre but by the 'gneeve', a variable unit which usually meant the grass of one cow or one-twelfth of a ploughland. He considered that one-third of the land in the parish was arable, one-third pasture and one-third bare rocks and bogs. Richard Notter of Rock Island estimated that only half of the land in Kilmoe was arable and the rest mountain and bog. Some farms had a right to turbary and grazing on certain mountains. The rent ranged from 15s 0d to 18s 6d per acre but good land with sea manure available nearby could cost from £1 to £3. These rents were high; land around Bandon for instance could be rented for 14s 0d to 16s 0d. John Kelliher, curate of the neighbouring parish of Muintir Bháire (Durrus) and later parish priest of Schull, summed up the general state of land tenure in a description which would also have been true of Mizen Peninsula: 'In a word, the lands are generally let to the highest bidder; the competition is very great, the tenant holds by no tenure in almost every case, but his landlord's will or caprice and that neither landlord nor tenant look beyond the gain of the hour, the face of the country testifies'. The rent for conacre was very important as it was by this means that the labourer got ground for potatoes. It usually varied from £2 10s 0d to £4 per acre. This was not high as around Bandon it was £3 to £7.

The fact that many of the landlords were absentees and not inclined to be 'improving' had its advantages for the tenants since there was less consolidation of farms and accordingly fewer evictions. As pasture became more profitable than tillage after Waterloo (1815) the landlords changed to pasture, thus rendering the consolidation of holdings desirable. The tenants however favoured subdivision on account of the increased population resulting from wartime prosperity. Two landlords of Kilmoe, Richard Notter and Lionel Fleming, stated that subdivision had taken place and that tenants had been evicted for it. According to Fr Kelliher, however, the more usual reason for evictions was failure to pay the rent or the landlord's desire to make room for a favourite or to replace a Catholic with a Protestant. Those evicted 'fell into the ranks of the labourers', took to the roads as beggars or emigrated to America.[7]

Eviction had been made cheaper and swifter by the Ejection Acts passed in the period after Waterloo. Tenants could now be evicted by Civil Bill for as little as £2 at only two months' notice. It was by Civil Bill that the proprietor, Patience Swanton, proceeded against some of her tenants in the parish of Kilcoe in 1828. One tenant, James John Hickey, owed £14 2s 1d, i.e., one year's rent while another, Owen Hickey, owed £14 2s 0d, also one year's rent. In both cases the bills 'were decreed on consent' so these tenants were evicted but evidently on certain terms. Swanton also brought Civil Bills against nineteen other tenants including Thomas and Patrick Hickey. They owed a total of £140 rent for one year but the bills were all either 'nilled or dismissed' and never issued.[8] Rents remained high although agricultural prices had dropped since Waterloo. The population remained high too and 'improving' proprietors like Patience Swanton were determined to do something about it. Fr Michael Collins told a select committee: 'The landed proprietors have taken up the opinion latterly that the cause of their distress is the over-stocking of land with people; and as the leases fall in, they get rid of the surplus population by turning them out entirely from their lands'. He knew of an estate of 500 acres which had held 40 families of whom 30 were evicted.[9]

There had been trouble between the Hickeys and Swanton for some time. The previous year she had advertised for 'improving tenants' for the lands in Skeaghanore which those tenants were occupying.[10] Apparently the Hickeys were not 'improving tenants' so she had little patience with them. Perhaps it was just as well for all concerned that they were able to hold on to their land by legal means as they probably would have been inclined to resort to other means. Nonetheless serious agrarian crimes such as murder seem to have been few in the Mizen Peninsula or even in West Cork unlike other parts of the country, Tipperary, for instance.[11] An English Radical, Poulett Scrope, however, wrote in 1834:

> But for the salutary dread of the Whiteboy Association ejectment would desolate Ireland and decimate her population, casting forth thousands of families like noxious weeds … Yes, the Whiteboy system is the only check on the ejectment system; and weighing one against the other, horror against horror and crime against crime, it is perhaps the lesser evil of the two.

The disfranchment of the forty shilling freeholders at the time of Catholic Emancipation, 1829, meant that they were no longer an electoral loss to the landlord although they were tending to become less subservient to his wishes in any case. Evictions carried out by Tipperary landlords at this time in the name of improvement prompted the under-secretary, Thomas Drummond, to give them his famous reminder that property had its duties as well as its rights.[12] There were, however, a few landlords who were already aware of this, for example, Edmund Richard Hull. One observer wrote, 'He was a landlord who during his long life never evicted a peasant nor sold a single beast for rent'.[13]

The main crops grown by the people in the Mizen Peninsula were potatoes and corn. The majority of the people were becoming more and more dangerously dependent on the potato to keep the famine at bay. This was known to all but perhaps not fully realised until the strange potato disease struck. The extraordinary role of the potato was explained by the rector of Kilmoe, William Fisher in December 1846: 'Potatoes were the chief crop grown; no turnips or any sort of green crop. The potato fed the family, the cattle, the pigs and the poultry; cargoes of potatoes were taken around by sea to supply the Cork market'.[14] While the potato was not the only food produced by the people it played a literally vital role in their lives.

An excessively gloomy picture of agriculture must not be painted. The general movement for improvement was gradually reaching the district. A clear insight into this is given by the Agricultural Show held by the Skibbereen Agricultural Society in 1843. The landlords were, of course, the chief exhibitors, but there were also 'working farmers' such as Andrew Caverly of Ardintenant, Schull. The traditional black cattle were not as numerous as at the previous shows and there were more of the 'improved class'. W. Wrixton

Becher of Creagh, Baltimore, exhibited a 'very handsome five-year-old Ayrshire bull'. R. H. H. Becher of Hollybrook presented a variety of improved cattle, Shorthorn and Ayrshire. The sheep brought by the 'working farmers' were of an inferior class but there were some handsome Leicester sheep presented by W. W. Becher.

The exhibitors, both landlords and farmers and also the judges, attended the dinner on the night of the show. The judge of the cattle urged the farmers to obtain the assistance of their landlords and not allow price to prevent them from obtaining a good purebred Ayrshire or Shorthorn bull or a good Leicester ram or a good Berkshire boar. The secretary reported that at its first ever ploughing match in 1837 there were ten old wooden ploughs and only one Scotch plough and that not a single farmer could use a long reins. At the second ploughing match, however, there were twenty-five farmers with Scotch ploughs and well-trained horses. The cultivation of turnips had made great progress during the previous three years. He found that the cross-breed between the native cow and the Ayrshire or Shorthorn did not produce more or better milk than the old Irish cow. The improved breeds of pigs were becoming plentiful so that the 'Old Irish long-sided hog' was becoming rare. The quality of sheep kept by the farmers was poor and some sheep were 'kept to starve' but some landlords were giving good rams to their tenants. The chairman proposed a toast to the successful exhibitors mentioning Andrew Caverly. This farmer acknowledged that he owed his success to the kindness of his landlord, Lord Bandon, who gave him the bull and to R. H. H. Becher who gave him the ram. The very fact that a tenant could dine with his landlord and discuss agriculture was certainly genuine improvement.[15]

The growing threat to repeal the Corn Laws was seen by landlords as a new and serious difficulty which the movement for the improvement of agriculture had to face. The landlords and tenants held a meeting in the courthouse in Skibbereen in February 1839. The courthouse was 'thronged almost to suffocation'. Lionel Fleming told the excited meeting that the prosperity of Ireland depended on agriculture unlike that of England where the manufacturing classes were raising the cry for cheap bread so that they could procure the labour of the working classes at a cheaper rate. The motion in favour of the Corn Laws was greeted with shouts of 'yes! yes!' from the galleries but with cries of 'no! no!' from the floor of the meeting. He then reminded the labourers that they got employment from the farmers whose distress would mean their distress as well. One landlord told how they all 'sighed' for the prices during the 'reign of Bonaparte' when wheat was three guineas a bag. It was not half that now, he lamented, and was amazed that there should be people who wanted it even less. His speech was also met with cries of 'no! no!' and a 'big loaf!' Finally, the meeting appealed to the government to oppose the repeal of Corn Laws because it would ruin the country which was struggling to improve its agriculture, employ its large and hungry population, and also carry the burden of the new poor rates.[16]

A more inveterate and fundamental obstacle to progress in agriculture was, no doubt, the system of land tenure. This was receiving more and more critical attention which culminated in the report of the Devon Commission set up by Robert Peel. It is true that agriculture was often backward on farms with leases and that tenants were sometimes unwilling to obtain leases because of the cost of the stamp. Yet, in general, the system tended to discourage progress in farming. One of the evils of the whole system was the role of the middleman or middlemen situated between the landlord and tenant. An excellent illustration of this was the case of the Audley estate. In 1755 James, Lord Audley, leased his lands in Rossbrin in the parish of Schull to William Hull of Leamcon for a term of 99 years at £535 per year. It is interesting to observe how a part of these lands, for example, Horse Island, eventually came to be held. In 1810 Hull's son re-leased the island for a period of 21 years to a Mr Callaghan of Cork, a land agent. This agent rented it to a tenant, a Mr Somerville, who in turn rented to undertenants one of whom was a Patrick Driscoll. The latter yet again rented some of his portion to various labourers.

In the period under review, 1801–1845, the security of middlemen was rapidly diminishing. Indeed the position of some of the landlords themselves was being threatened because they were sinking further and further under encumbrances. In 1850, W. Neilson Hancock, Whately Professor of Political Economy at Trinity College, Dublin, delivered a lecture in Edinburgh entitled 'On the causes of the distress in Schull and Skibbereen … ' making special reference to the Audley estate. Lord Audley inherited the family estate in 1816. As has been seen, he soon increased his annual income of £535 by leasing mines but eventually lost money in mining and even more money in the consequent litigation. The following table sets out his deteriorating financial position:

TABLE 7: ENCUMBRANCES, 1819–1837

Period	Encumbrances Amount	Interest	Law costs	Total
Up to 1819	£3,400	£4,000	£1,000	£8,400
Up to 1824	£16,200	£9,000	£1,700	£26,900
Up to 1829	£25,100	£11,600	£3,200	£39,900
Up to 1834	£43,900	£27,000	£4,000	£74,900
Up to 1837	£89,400	£61,700	£16,200	£167,300

Audley died in 1837 owing the enormous sum of £167,300 on an estate worth only £20,000. His executors tried to sell the estate but there was not a single bidder; prospective buyers were wary of encumbrances. Any buyer would have had to treat with no fewer than eighty creditors so the estate was deposited in the Court of Chancery.

The case also shows that there was no reasonably simple and complete registry of debts and encumbrances on land. This enabled a clever and unscrupulous man like Audley to borrow sums of money far beyond the value of his estate. It took seven years of legal proceedings to sort out these encumbrances and yet by 1849, the estate was still unsold in Chancery. Hancock held that it was this system of land tenure and mortgage which gave rise to the 'wretched agriculture' which in turn became the cause of the famine in Schull, Skibbereen and elsewhere rather than the simple failure of the potato crop.[17]

The absentee Audley was not the only encumbered landlord; another was a resident, R. H. H. Becher. One reason for his financial difficulties was long and expensive litigation. One notorious law-suit was with Lord Bandon over the townland of Ratooragh near Mount Gabriel and other lands in the parish of Schull. The case had already been examined by the lord chancellor who referred it to the County Record Court in Cork in August 1838. The case occupied the court for five days until finally a judgment was given which was but a pyrrhic victory for Becher.[18] This litigation must have cost them both far more than this hilly land was worth. Early in 1844 agents of the Devon Commission visited Skibbereen and interviewed certain people one of whom was R. H. H. Becher. He admitted that when he succeeded to his estates he found them in a neglected state. His tenants were building their houses or cabins in clusters and allowing them to be surrounded by the mud hovels of their labourers which had dung heaps up to every door. This led to endless petty session litigation arising out of trespass committed by men, women, children, cattle and fowl. The lands of each were dispersed and neglected and without clear boundaries.

In 1833 W. W. Becher of Creagh, Baltimore, divided the 649 acres of his Cape Clear lands into holdings of about five acres each or *Ceathrúna*.[19] In 1841 R. H. H. Becher decided to do something similar and ordered his bailiff to go to some of his tenants and get possession of their lands in order to divide them into lots. He got 200 surrenders without one refusal. The landlord then divided these lands into separate lots, agreed with the tenants on rent and tenure and then restored to them the land in the new form of lots. There were however a few tenants for whom he could not find any land; these he compensated more or less according to the tenant right of Ulster. He also employed his tenants to make roads through hilly land so that sea manure could be transported to it. The result was that horses and carts could pass where previously there was only a 'bridle road'. In his 'allotment system' Becher insisted that it was he who should choose the sites for the houses. His policy was to place them near the road and not near one another. Previously the houses had been too close together and the lands too scattered as a result of the rundale system; he hoped that his tenants would then work more and quarrel less. Becher worked this system only on lands that were let from year to year; two-thirds of his estate had been let under long leases since 1794 at low rents. He regretted that most of these tenants had not improved their lands and that some had even wasted them by burning the top-soils.[20] Long leases did not necessarily lead to improvement. Becher was changing the system of land tenure or 'improving' it much like Lord George Hill was attempting to do in Donegal.[21]

Such was the position of tenants under an improving landlord; many others were under middlemen. One such middleman was James McCarthy of Goleen. He said that agriculture had not improved and that 'every bit of arable land' was tilled by the very great population on it. The rent for good land by the sea was 30s per acre while ground which was inland would make 6s or 7s less. Yields were low because the people were too poor to manure the land; potatoes yielded 4 or 5 tons to the acre and wheat 20 stone. He blamed the landlords for this lack of improvement because they refused to give long leases. McCarthy did not think that there was any difference between the condition of tenants under middlemen and those under resident landlords. He even knew of a case of a landlord who, having recovered possession from a middleman, actually raised the rent on his tenants. Fr James Barry however held that tenants directly under the landlord were usually better off. McCarthy pointed out that when a lease expired the landlord formerly re-let to the middleman but that now he invariably let directly to the tenants and the middleman was thrown out; he knew one middleman who went to America. So great was the landlord's reluctance to grant leases, the witness continued, that one refused to grant a lease to the parish priest, Laurence O'Sullivan, for a site for a school although the site was only a bare rock as has been seen in Chapter III. This witness stated that little consolidation took place and that evictions were mainly over non-payment of rent or as a punishment for subletting; such ejections often led to agrarian outrages.

James McCarthy and R. H. H. Becher, present a good picture of the landlords, middlemen and tenant farmers, but they say little or nothing about the labourers. The agent of the Devon Commission interviewed Michael Sullivan, a labourer/spalpeen from the neighbouring parish of Abbeystrowry near Skibbereen:

1. *What quantity of ground do you hold?*
   I hold no ground, I am a poor man, I have nothing but my labour.
2. *Under whom do you hold your house?*
   Under a farmer … just a house and one acre of ground.
3. *Have you the acre of ground always in the same place?*
   Different acres from time to time. The acre I have this year I cannot have it next year; he will have it himself. I must manure another acre, and without friends I could not live.
4. *What do you pay for it?*
   I pay £3; £2 for the acre of ground and £1 for the house.
5. *Have you constant employment?*
   No; but whenever he wishes to call me he gives me 6d a day and my diet; and then at other times I go down the country and earn £1 or 30s.
6. *Where do you generally go?*
   I may go to Limerick or Tipperary.
7. *Is that in harvest time?*
   Yes; I went out in harvest time and digging the potatoes.
8. *What family have you?*
   I have five children.
9. *How do you manage on 6d a day to support the family?*
   My landlord has a road making for the use of the farm and has employed the

tenants there.
10. *What is the general food for the family?*
    Nothing at all but dry potatoes.
11. *What does your wife make by the week from her eggs?*
    She may make 2s 6d or 3s 0d now. The farmer has a corn field convenient and we must keep the fowls off the corn.
12. *Have you fish?*
    Not one, except they may bring a pen'orth home in a month; if my poor wife sells her eggs or makes up a skein of thread in the market, she may take home with her a pen'orth or two pen'orth of something to nourish the children with that night. But in general I do not use 5s of kitchen from one end of the year to the other except what I may get at Christmas.
13. *Have you generally milk with your potatoes?*
    Not a drop; I would be middling happy if the five children … were near a national school, I could give them schooling. A better labouring man than what I am cannot afford his children any schooling and even some of the people called farmers are in the same place.
14. *Have you not a little garden attached to the house?*
    Yes, for 400 cabbages.
15. *Have you a pig?*
    Yes.
16. *Have you a pig-house?*
    No.
17. *Where is he kept?*
    He must be kept in some part of the house, in a corner.
18. *Have you any room for a pigsty outside?*
    No. I might make room for the pig if I was sure of the house for a second year but I do not mean to go to the trouble.
19. *What bedsteads have you or bedding?*
    I have a chaff bed and bed-clothes. There are others who have no beds … and they must lie in the clothes they wear by day.

Sullivan also pointed out that many of the small farmers were very poor too. Most of them could not give milk to their children between Christmas and St Patrick's Day and even then they often had to sell it to pay the rent or even pawn their clothes. Some of them could not manure their land properly and had to burn it which was forbidden by the landlord. Many observers especially foreigners regarded it as typical of the laziness and dirt of the Irish peasant that he would prefer to allow a pig to live with himself and his family for a whole year rather than go to the 'trouble' of building some kind of a sty for him – a few days' work. Daniel McCarthy of Goleen stated that the labourers were a 'separate class' and that their condition was 'wretched'. Yet one notices the importance of the economic role of O'Sullivan's wife; thanks to her eggs and skein or thread she was earning as much as her husband. On the debated question of the importance of leases, McCarthy considered that a short lease was of little advantage and that it should be about three lives. He suggested that if there were some employment for the labourers on the road or in industry or fishing it would take some of their attention off the land and so would improve the country a great deal.[22]

Many of the landlords were clearly anxious to improve agriculture and the general conditions of their tenants. Such development however is often ambiguous and usually has its victims. It was tragic that an improved agriculture should mean eviction for some and that new roads should have been yet another grievance for the tenant. McCarthy protested against 'extermination in the West'. He told of six families who although they owed no rent, were 'set adrift upon the world'. He condemned the 'improvement system' as the 'depopulating system'. Nonetheless he did not want to give the impression that all the landlords were as cruel as that. He also praised William Edward Hull of Leamcon: 'A better landlord does not exist, whose tenants enjoy the blessings of his patronage; he does not send them to draw money from the banks, neither does he impound their cattle'. McCarthy acknowledged Hull's generosity towards the local Catholic chapel and school.[23] Both landlord and tenant wanted improvements but each on his own terms. Insecurity of tenure combined with high rents and low agricultural prices were the main obstacles to improvement. Traditionally it has been thought that insecurity of tenure was the more important factor while Raymond Crotty holds that the crucial matter was market conditions.[24] Perhaps it was a combination of both. However backward these Irish landlords, middlemen, farmers and labourers may have been, their social and economic system ensured that nobody starved – to death, at any rate. It was a system which was propped up, so to speak, by the two pillars of the potato crop and the Corn Laws. If anything should touch either of them – or both – then the whole system would stagger dangerously.

FISHERIES AND SHIPPING

Irish fisheries declined after the union (1801). Compared with their English or Scottish counterparts, Irish fishermen were generally backward and ill-equipped just like many of the farmers. Indeed many of them were mere fishermen/farmers/labourers. Most still had only curraghs which were not as efficient as clinker-built decked vessels.[25] Ireland soon changed from being a fish exporting country to being a fish importing one. Herrings to the value of £58,197 were imported in 1818 and the export trade had fallen to only 5% of its former volume.[26] Pilchard fishing was carried out by William Hull at Leamcon and Crookhaven in the seventeenth century. This continued until the nineteenth century but by then it had declined. There are still remains of fish palaces or curing-houses at Crookhaven, Schull and Dunbeacon.[27] Early in the nineteenth century fishing in West Cork was presumably as backward as anywhere else. As has been seen in Chapter II, one man who made brave efforts to improve this situation was J. R. Barry of Glandore. In 1818 he founded the Southern Fishery Association in Kinsale. He was invited to Dublin and helped to draft the Fisheries Bill which became law the following year. A Fisheries Board was set up and he was appointed Commissioner for Fisheries for the Maritime district from the Suir to the Shannon.[28] The new board provided bounties payable to fishermen according to the tonnage of their ships and the quantity and species of fish landed. A grant of £5,000 a year was given for the building of piers and £500 a year was allotted in small loans to fishermen. This government encouragement stimulated the fisheries causing increased employment and production. Imports of fish almost ceased. In J. R. Barry's district there were soon 48 decked vessels, 127 half-decked vessels, 536 open sailing boats and over 2,000 rowing boats, all manned by 15,000 boys and men. By 1830 this number increased to 25,000. However, these bounties were intended only as a temporary stimulus and were programmed to expire in 1830.[29]

As that date approached there were appeals to the government from all over the country to prevent the expiration of the Fishery Acts. A meeting was held in Skibbereen by all those interested in fisheries in the district such as Samuel Townsend of Whitehall, Aughadown, Lionel Fleming and R. H. H. Becher. A resolution was passed declaring that the Fishery Acts had had 'the most beneficial effect and expressing their deepest regret that the government should intend to allow them to expire'. A second resolution stated that the acts enabled the poor fisherman to feed his family which he could not otherwise have done and also provided food for the poor all over the country and especially along the coast where the 'redundant population' was particularly large. The meeting regretted that the government was more interested in Poor Laws than fishery laws.[30] Nevertheless the bounties were withdrawn and the Fishery Board duly abolished while the Scottish one was allowed to continue and be subsidised by public money. Irishmen alleged that the Scottish interest in parliament worked against Irish fisheries. These fisheries were now transferred to the charge of the Board of Works where, the repealers claimed, more attention was paid to the Inland Fisheries, the property of the landlords.[31] This transfer was a strange *laissez-faire* attitude of a government which was about to interfere so decisively in the fields of education and Poor Law.

The subsequent decline in the Irish fisheries was so painfully obvious to all that in 1835 the government set up a commission to inquire into their state and to suggest ways of improving them; one of the commissioners was J. R. Barry. They found that under the bounty system 'a great increase in the activity of the trade was experienced'. But when the bounties were discontinued, 'the trade began to fall back into languor and exhaustion.' Boats were immediately withdrawn 'and suffered to rot on the beach while the men sought other employment or sunk into mendicancy'. The bounties, the commissioners reported, lasted for far too short a period and were withdrawn too abruptly. They admitted that they were 'an excess of stimulation' and that there were some frauds connected with them. Before the bounties were given in 1819 there were 38,000 fishermen along the Irish coast. By 1830 thanks to the bounties the number of fishermen had risen to nearly 65,000. By 1835, however, it had decreased to about 50,000.

Trawling was an improved method of fishing but like improved methods of agriculture it caused sufferings to poorer people. The trawlers caught greater quantities of fish and depressed the market. Evidence about fishing around Crookhaven was given by local fisherman, James Driscoll. The fish were caught by long lines, hand lines, seine and drift nets. The long lines were used in deep-sea fishing and were mounted with 2,000 to 3,000 hooks on which fish were caught, cod, haddock, conger and turbot. He regretted that there were not more regulations about fishing. The right of shooting seine nets caused 'violent breaches of the peace'. It was usually strangers who came trawling; the local fishermen complained about them but did not attack them as fishermen would in Dingle or Galway. Still other fishermen were hostile to any regulations. A Mr Donovan from Dunmanus held that the object of the fishermen was to catch fish and that they should not be interfered with by the 'opinions of men who endeavour by theory to teach a fisherman his occupation'. The condition of the fishing boats around Crookhaven was bad. Their riggings were old and worn and they were badly tarred and caulked; their oars were pieced and their ropes knotted. A hooker would cost £154, and a smack about £5; nets would cost from £2 to £8. The fisherman had no capital and there were now no loans available to him. James Driscoll said that the loans of the Fishery Board had encouraged many men to take up fishing and improve their condition. In his opinion the fishermen in Long Island and Schull were even worse off than those in Crookhaven. Many of those who had been able to support themselves by means of the bounties from the Fishery Board were now in the 'greatest distress'. They were obliged to let their boats and gear rot for want of repair 'as no credit is now given to poor fishermen'.

Most of the fish was sold to dealers who took it to the towns. Little of it was sold locally because the people either had boats of their own or were too poor to buy it although they needed it. Some Scottish and Newfoundland fish was also for sale. It was cheaper than local fish but more salty. In general, the fishermen's 'moral habits' and general conduct were 'good' but their circumstances 'miserable'. They were not as comfortable as tradesmen and were on the same level as labourers. Almost all of them had a little land. The commissioners declared that the law should be reformed and more power given to the magistrates in maritime affairs. A special department should be set up to give loans and grants for boats, gear and piers. Vessels should be provided for the protection of fishermen and to keep the peace among them. National Schools near the coast should provide practical education on fishing.[32] There was no question of re-introducing the bounties because it would have been against the new *laissez-faire* spirit of the age.

In 1843 a new Board of Fisheries was set up on the principle of 'non-interference by government'. The coast was divided into districts. The Mizen peninsula came within the Skibbereen district which extended from Clonakilty to White Horse Head in Bantry Bay. All vessels were to be registered by the coast-guards. These coast-guards were given a more important role than that; they were to enforce any new fishery regulations which would be sanctioned by the Board of Customs. Accordingly the coast-guards offered 'very important aid in the preservation of order among vessels which had hitherto been subject to no regular control'.[33] The government which was preaching the principle of non-interference on the question of the bounties was now interfering when it considered it expedient. Although the commissioners of the 1837

Fishery Report had recommended that extra powers be entrusted to the magistrates it was not to these but to the coast-guards that these powers were entrusted. The coast-guards were more directly under the control of the government.

The new Board of Fisheries was much more liberal in allowing trawling and other 'improved modes' of fishing. The fact that they would injure the poorer classes could not be admitted as a reason for their suppression. In the Skibbereen district, 1,027 boats were registered with crews of 6,054 men and boys in 1844. The board defined its policy which was, 'to provide facilities for carrying out fisheries and not for providing stimulants',[34] such as the bounties presumably. The beginning of the new *laissez-faire* thinking can be sensed. By 1846 there was a slight improvement in fisheries in the country generally and also in the Mizen Peninsula. In January of that year there were 8,322 boats registered in the entire country as against 6,054 in 1844. However, this was partly due to the fact that some boats which had already been at sea were only now being registered.[35]

Whatever improvement did take place was too slight to be noticeable. Fr James Barry said that labourers should be encouraged to go out fishing as they did so only very little. Fish was abundant but what prevented people from catching them was 'want of apparatus'. Even those who had some means, he said, were scarcely able to hold on to their farms as their rents were so high.[36] *The Times* reporter, T. C. Foster, quoted these words of the priest as a typical Irish excuse – sheer laziness being the real reason. Foster granted that the Irish were good labourers in England or in the mines when they were *'compelled* to work, but left to themselves, they do *nothing'*.[37] Foster was rather harsh. A more sympathetic witness was J. R. Barry from whom we get the following charming picture of the resourcefulness of the poor fisherman:

> He will repair his crazy bark … if he can get his boat once on the stocks and have a few pieces of timber and plank, his ingenuity will suggest a thousand little devices for the supply of materials. If he can give the carpenter subsistence he will get credit for the wages, the smith will afford the same accommodation; the houses of his neighbours are searched for pieces of old timber; so that between a small sum on hand, a little credit, some kindly feeling on the part of his friends, and a great deal of ingenuity and perseverance the boat is afloat once more.[38]

The poor man however was very dependent on his neighbours, let alone weather and season. Just like much of the farming the fishing was often merely subsistence fishing and it was even more precarious.

Such was the depressed state of the fisheries in the country in general and in the Mizen Peninsula in particular. In no other sector of Irish life or of the economy was government neglect so blatant. This was all the more unfortunate since it occurred at a vital time and in a vital area – the years before the famine and along the coast where the population was very dense. As already stated the new Fishery Board was run very much on passive *laissez-faire* principles. The cold winds of this economic thinking were, so to speak, first felt at sea before they ever reached land; they struck the fishery laws before they struck the Corn Laws. Nevertheless there was little real protest; unlike the landlords and like the miners, the fishermen were not a powerful interest.

For all their great beauty Carbery's Hundred Isles and thousand rocks and reefs were often graveyards for ships. The Irish name for Roaringwater Bay is *Loughtrasna*, thought locally to mean the 'Bay of Destruction' and is no misnomer. Dean Swift visited Glandore in 1723 after the death of Vanessa and admired the coast in a Latin poem, *Carberiae Rupes* or the Cliffs of Carbery, but was aware too of the threat to the fishermen of *saxa undique* or 'rocks all around'.[39] The danger of sailing itself as well the great quality and quantity of the cargoes in these ships is revealed by the numerous shipwrecks which took place along the Mizen Peninsula. The *Providence* sailing from Gibraltar was lost with all hands at Mizen Head in 1813. *H.M.S. Confiance*, a sloop of war, left Cobh for Galway in 1822 with 120 men aboard. A storm broke out and distress shots were heard by people on Mizen Head in the night; four bodies along with the ship's gilt figure-head were washed ashore. Four local men were also drowned in a vain attempt to salvage the wreck. The loss of the ship became the subject of a lament by J. J. Callanan, *A Lay of the Mizen Head*. This same year the brig, *Darthula* of Newfoundland, was on a voyage from Liverpool to St John, Newfoundland, but was wrecked on the rocks at the mouth of Crookhaven Harbour. The *Pride of Newry* was *en route* from its home port to New York in 1823 but lost its sails and put into Crookhaven. It attempted to go to Cork to refit but was soon forced back by contrary winds and wrecked at Ballyrisode. Of the thirteen persons on board, the captain and six others were lost. The *John Campbell*, trading regularly between Cork and Quebec, was wrecked near Crookhaven on its return trip with a cargo of timber in 1831. The crew was saved. The brig, *Mary*, was on a voyage from Demerara in the West Indies with sugar and coffee when it was wrecked on the Barrell's Reef in Crookhaven harbour. The *Thomas Worthington* of St John, New Brunswick, Canada was also lost in this harbour in 1836. Its hull and a considerable quantity of its cargo of timber were auctioned. Like the *John Campbell* it was one of the 'timber ships' which usually carried emigrants on their return voyages to Canada.

The brig, *Lady Charlotte*, coming from Callao, Port of Lima, Peru, in 1838 with a valuable cargo mainly consisting of precious metals, was wrecked on the Barrel Rocks in the Long Island Sound. Of its crew of ten only one survived, he was rescued by the coast-guards under Henry Baldwin. Sunk in only twenty-four feet of water most of the cargo was salvaged to the value of £70,000. This was mainly made up of $36,000 in *specie*, seven large silver plates weighing a hundredweight each, gold and silver bullion and seven sacks of silver ore. A fracas broke out at the wreck site during which a small number of the silver coins was stolen and Baldwin was assaulted. A Michael Sullivan was sentenced to eighteen months hard labour for his part in this incident at the Summer Assizes.[40] It was a great change from the time of the visit of Pococke, the traveller, eighty years earlier when the smugglers' treatment of the coast-guard would often have been 'knocking in the head and putting him under a turf'. The boot was now on the other foot. The coast-guard service reported to the Treasury in 1839 that smuggling both in England and Ireland was by now said to be 'at a low ebb'.[41] There was now a coast-guard station even on Long Island.[42] In addition, the coast was being gradually lit up; the lighthouse on Cape Clear was now joined by another at Crookhaven or Rock Island in 1841.[43] The halcyon days of piracy and plunder were gone forever.

Ships however continued to be wrecked. Whatever about the loss of life shore-dwellers anywhere along the coasts of Ireland and the British Isles were seldom sad after such disasters not only owing to the wreck timber but to the other goods which were washed ashore. The people of Cornwall, for example, seem to have been quite happy after the loss of the appropriately named *Good Samaritan*:

> The *Good Samaritan* came ashore
> To feed the hungry and cloth the poor.
> Barrels of beef and bales of linen,
> No poor man shall want a *shilin*.

Neither do these good people seem to have any sad memories of the 'tea-wreck' or the 'coffee wreck'.[44] Similarly Tomás Ó Criomhthain of the Blasket Islands tells that meal from a wreck fed the people during a famine.[45] As shall be seen in Chapter XII the *Stephen Whitney* was wrecked on the Calf Islands off Schull in 1847 and the resulting beams of timber still form part of the roofs of houses on Cape Clear.

POPULATION

It has been noted in Chapter II that the large population growth that took place in the Mizen Peninsula owing to the prosperity resulting from the French wars received a setback from the peace after Waterloo and again from the famine of 1822. Yet this population recovered and generally continued to increase in the period 1821–41.[46] The rural population showed a steady increase of 8% from 1821 to 1831 and of another 8% from 1831 to 1841 but this population change did not necessarily correspond to the change taking place in each of the towns: Ballydehob, Schull and Crookhaven. These were far more sensitive barometers to the economic pressures which were local, national and international. Although the rural population rose in the period 1821–1841 it did not rise quite so rapidly as it did in the two towns, Ballydehob and Schull. In Crookhaven, however, the population actually declined steadily. (See the following tables.)

TABLE 8: POPULATION, 1821–41: RURAL AREA

	Kilmoe	Schull	Kilcoe	Aughadown	Total	Change	%
1821	5,427	12,309	3,110	5,461	26,307		
1831	6,465	14,226	2,616	5,419	28,726	+2,419	+9
1841	6,838	16,226	2,339	5,757	31,160	+2,434	+8

TABLE 9: POPULATION, 1821–41: BALLYDEHOB, SCHULL, CROOKHAVEN

	Ballyd	Change %	Schull	Change %	Crookhvn	Change %
1821	342		176		447	
1831	601	+76	358	+103	424	-5
1841	636	+6	452	+26	396	-7

Between 1821 and 1831 the population of the town of Schull more than doubled, increasing from 176 to 358 or by 103%. The population of Ballydehob also increased rapidly between 1821 and 1831, going from 342 to 601, a rise of 76%. It was a good decade for Ballydehob, although to describe it as a boom may be an exaggeration. The Census of 1821 now called it 'Swantonstown'; this was intended no doubt to reflect its improved status. The new Griffith road must have made a great contribution to social and economic life as such roads did to an even greater extent for towns in County Galway particularly Clifden and Roundstone. As has been seen, the Audley mines were now prospering near Ballydehob, the chapel was built and a police station had been opened.

The populations of Schull and Ballydehob continued to grow from 1831 to 1841, Schull by 26%, Ballydehob by only 6%. The withdrawal of the bounties on fish in 1830 does not seem to have affected Schull too much whereas the abandonment of the Audley mines by the Mining Company of Ireland in 1832 was a serious blow to Ballydehob.

As already stated, the population of Crookhaven not only failed to rise but actually declined slowly but surely. In 1821 it had the largest population of these three towns, i.e., 447 but by 1831 it had decreased by 5% to 424 and by 1841 by a further 7% bringing it down to 395, which was the lowest population of the three towns. This counter trend was mainly owing to the falling off in the provisions trade to the navy after Waterloo. Not even the bounties on fish or Griffith's new road to it could compensate for this loss. There was no longer the general air of prosperity around here as there had been eighty-three years earlier when Pococke visited it. And all for the want of a war.

The number of baptisms in the Catholic parish of Schull recovered quickly after the 1822 famine; that year the number was 119 but the next year it was 286 and it continued to rise steadily. In round figures, in the 1820s the number of baptisms was in the 200s; in the 1830s it was in the 300s and in the 1840 in the 400s almost reaching the 500s. In 1846 the number of baptisms was 496 although the potato blight was already in the land. This figure was fated to remain a record. The birth rate was similar in the Catholic parish of Kilmoe; it recovered quickly after the famine of 1822. In 1828 there were 362 baptisms and by 1845 this figure had risen to 413. It was similarly fated to remain a record.

Although the population thus increased rapidly in Schull and Kilmoe it is surprising to discover that this did not happen in the Catholic parishes of Kilcoe and Aughadown. (These parishes are completely rural.) In Kilcoe the population actually fell by 25% from 3,110 in 1821 to 2,339 in 1841. In Aughadown it rose only marginally or could be said to be stable going from 5,461 to only 5,757. Although the census reports of these periods may not be always accurate this absence of any substantial increase in population is borne out by the records of the Catholic parishes of Kilcoe and Aughadown, amalgamated into the one parish of Kilcoe/Aughadown. In 1824 there were 285 baptisms but the average for the 1830s was only 208. Nevertheless, the number tended to increase again in the 1840s and in 1845 reached 331, which would also remain a record. Kilcoe/Aughadown, like the village of Crookhaven, had made some adjustments to the new economic situation resulting from Waterloo. On the other hand, the populations of the poorer and more western parishes of Schull and Kilmoe continued to increase inexorably. As already observed, the number of baptisms in Schull parish in 1846 was practically 500 which was extremely high. By way of comparison, in the large parish of Glanmire/Carraig na bhFear, north-east of Cork city – 'strong farmer' country containing some industries – the number of baptisms that year was much less, 331.[47]

The number of marriages in Schull corresponded of course with its high number of births. In 1835 James Barry counted 109 marriages which would remain a record. In 1838 he counted 107. He was concerned about such high figures and annotated 'making an average of 91 for the last six years'. The agents of the Poor Inquiry explained why there were so many births in Schull by citing Fr Barry as has been seen in the epigraph on p. 115. Other witnesses at this inquiry gave the names of four couples of which each party was only 17. Barry told how he frequently entreated young persons who came to him to be married, 'to desist, and not to bring upon themselves the weight of a family with so little preparation; but I have scarcely ever been able to prevail'. Another witness made an important distinction: 'It is the man that is worst off marries soonest here, the man that has something is not in such a hurry.'[48]

There is disagreement among historians as to the value of this sort of evidence. Michael Drake dismissed it as 'anecdotal and impressionistic,'[49] as compared with the data of the 1841 census but Joseph Lee rightly disagrees.[50] The latter points out that a *rapprochement* can be made between these two sources by paying more attention to the differences in the marriage patterns between regions and between classes. This is the key to the interpretation of the Poor Inquiry. It must be emphasised that this inquiry reported that early marriages were common 'in this parish', i.e., Schull and not necessarily in others. A witness made a clear class distinction between those who were badly off and who married early and others who 'had something' and were not in such a hurry. In the parish of Schull there would have been many very small farmers, labourers and fishermen who were badly off and who married earlier. On the other hand, those who 'had something' and were not in such a hurry to get married were probably those who were improving their condition in general. They may well have been adopting an improved system of agriculture and similarly an 'improved' system of marrying, i.e., postponing it in the hope of getting a wife who would have, likewise, postponed her marriage until she might have a dowry. Such men and women, however, would not have been so numerous in the Mizen Peninsula at this time as they would for instance in Glanmire or in other parts of the country. Early marriages were not quite so frequent as may be understood from the Poor Inquiry. The authors of *Mapping the Great Irish Famine* conclude from the Census of 1841 that 'Contrary to some stereotypical accounts of life in Ireland on the eve of the Famine, the Irish did not marry at a very young age, recklessly and without forethought. More usually, Irish women married in their mid-twenties while Irish men in their late twenties'.[51]

We have seen that the town of Crookhaven and the parish of Kilcoe/ Aughadown somehow controlled their populations to correspond to the new economic circumstances after Waterloo. Regarding Schull and Kilmoe, however, it was a case of a Malthusian population explosion. According to the principles of Malthus they would sooner or later be struck by a 'gigantic inevitable famine'.[52] Still he was not the only commentator to sound such a warning note. The commissioners of the 1841 Census reminded the country of the principle: 'The prosperity of states ought to consist less in the multiplication than in the preservation of the individuals who compose them.'[53]

Such were the demographic trends among the Catholics in these parishes; but what were the trends were among the Protestants? K. H. Connell dismissed the value of Protestant parish records as 'belonging to a group which differed from the remainder in occupation, custom and wealth'.[54] But Joseph Lee rightly values them as they reveal disparate patterns between different groups which an ordinary census conceals.[55] The only Protestant records that survive for this period are those of the births in the eastern or Ballydehob side of the parish of Schull; even these begin as late as 1830 when 30 Protestants were baptised. The Protestant birth rate increased from 1830 until 1846 but the increase was slower than among the Catholics. Still the highest number of baptisms of Protestants, 43, took place in 1846. That the Protestant population was also rising significantly was borne out by the rector, Dr Traill. As late as January 1846 he appealed to the public for funds to enlarge his two churches which were 'totally inadequate to accommodate the present population'. He was obliged to make the appeal on account of 'a large Church rural population of the humblest class ... while the two churches could not contain more than 500'. He and his curate had been obliged to hold seven or eight services many miles apart every Sunday.[56] This is all the more significant because the Methodists had made many converts among his flock. Although the Protestant population may have differed in ethos from the Catholic one, a substantial part of it was of the 'humblest class' and was therefore subject to the same social and economic pressures.

The main check on increasing population was emigration. According to Cormac Ó Gráda this removed one-half or more of the natural increase as a disproportionate share of young males departed. He rightly disagrees with Malthus who thought that this only leaves a 'vacuum' soon to be filled up.[57] In the eighteenth century it was Catholics rather that Protestants who had been slow to emigrate. Daniel Corkery thus observed the people of West Cork and the west of the country generally:

> … the natives being home-keeping to a fault. They seem not only tied to the country, but almost the parish in which their ancestors lived. Arthur Young wrote of the Catholics who had not learned to emigrate. Among themselves they had a proverb, *Is maith an t-ancoire an t-iarta.* ('The hearth is a good anchor'.)[58]

Yet when peace came after Waterloo many forces tended to drag this anchor. General economic depression, hunger and evictions provoked emigration. Kerby Miller estimates that between 1815 and 1844 nearly a million people left Ireland for America. Many went to Canada until about 1826 and most of these were Protestants. In the period 1823–5 the British government offered free passage and land in Upper Canada. This attracted poorer Catholics especially from North Cork. Passenger Acts which had kept fares artificially high were repealed and replaced by less stringent regulations. While previously fares could be anything up to £10, now they fell to as low as £1 10s. The ticket from Liverpool to New York cost from £2 to £3. Between 1828 and 1837 nearly 400,000 Irish emigrated to North America and about two-thirds of them went to Canada.[59] Kevin Kenny points out that 'By the 1830s, Catholic exceeded Protestants in the transatlantic migration from Ireland for the first time since 1700'.[60] The falling prices of tickets had clearly something to do with it.

The timber trade with Scandinavia had been blockaded during the Napoleonic wars, so Canada and particularly New Brunswick became an important source of this raw material. Thus the famous or notorious timber or lumber ships came into prominence on the Atlantic trade. Arthur Lower maintains that until about 1835 conditions for passengers on the lumber ships were 'abominable' and 'probably worse than the slave trade'. Deaths from fever and dysentery were commonplace. In 1834 thirty-four of these ships foundered.[61] Such ships sailed from Irish ports to Quebec, Miramichi, Halifax and St John in New Brunswick, Canada.[62] William Justin Dealey of Bantry owned the *Dealy Brig*, 400 tons, which was built in 1839 and made thirteen trips across the Atlantic, usually to St John, bringing passengers out and timber back.[63] There were already strong Irish immigrant communities there. Riots broke out in 1822 when unemployed Irish labourers fought with lumbermen, seasonal workers from the neighbouring state of Maine. Troops had to be sent to quell the riots and over fifty 'Paddies' were arrested.[64]

Dr Traill told the Poor Inquiry that 90 persons had departed from his parish in 1831 and 40 in 1832; they were mainly Protestants in comfortable circumstances. Fr Barry described the emigrants of this period as 'tradesmen, hardy labourers and farmers with £20 to £60 capital, though few of the last class.' They went 'almost universally' to Canada. Richard Notter of Goleen claimed that the emigrants were 'of a better description; in fact most of the people here who could afford to emigrate would do so'. Lionel Fleming of the same parish said that 100 had left, 'respectable farmers' mostly Protestants. According to Fr Kelliher of Muintir Bháire or Durrus 300 had left that parish and went mostly to Quebec because the passage was cheaper, but they had the intention of going from there to the United States. They were generally evicted tenants or young men lately married who could not obtain land at home. Others were servants but 'all were persons willing and able to work with little capital, few of them left with as much as £20,' he added. Some had only £2 or £3 while one man emigrated without even shoes. Another departed without a coat, leaving his wife and family after him begging about and hoping to receive a remittance from America. All emigrants promised to send money home but sometimes forgot it. Still the priest added that those who went were persons of good character.[65]

The Sullivans, Fitzgeralds and Harrigans of Drinane and Derryleary townlands in Kilmoe parish were among the people who sold their interest in their lands worth £60 and emigrated at this period to Miramichi in New Brunswick, Canada, on the Gulf of St Lawrence. The first to leave was probably Michael Sullivan who left in 1825 and brother, Patrick, joined him in 1832. William Fitzgerald, his wife, Ann Harrigan and their five children left in 1830. Dennis Harrigan (brother of Ann), his wife, Catherine Driscoll and their nine children soon followed them. By 1835 William Fitzgerald and two of this sons were paying taxes on their three 100-acre lots in the Williamstown Settlement. The land was probably similar to that in another 100-acre lot for which the Fitzgeralds would offer only 2s 6d an acre because it was in 'its natural wilderness state, no improvements having been made thereon'. These settlers were clearly 'improving' farmers in the New World – as they probably had been in the Old World as well. All the Harrigan family emigrated except the eldest daughter, Ellen, who had married William Sauntry, a labourer from Ballydehob.

The Harrigans and the Fitzgeralds soon brought over other relatives and friends, Regans, Kingstons, Sullivans, Briens and Sauntrys. This was typical of the 'chain' emigration which was to continue right through to 1847 and beyond. One of the Fitzgeralds, Mary Ann, lived to be 102 years old and recalled that 'there was a great deal of crying among the women when they left and that the boat was large and that the passage took a great deal of time'. One of Dennis Harrigan's sons, John and also one of the young Fitzgeralds obtained lots of land in Williamstown in 1841 and were described as 'freeholders … by grant of the crown'. John Harrigan lived there as a bachelor for most of his life but came to poverty and was in the Alms House in 1877. Another son of Dennis Harrigan, namely Patrick, married a Catherine Hogan and they later moved to Winconsin in the United States. As late as 1960 a grandson remembered the old man, Dennis Harrigan, who had been brought from Kilmoe in 1831 as one-year-old babe-in-arms: 'Grandpa Harrigan was poor but far from illiterate. He was a tremendous reader and a self-educated man. He imbibed freely, spouted poetry and died at the age of ninety-four'. The only one of Dennis Harrigan's children who was not born in Ireland was Dennis Jr; he first saw the light just a year after his parents' arrival in the New World. (Around 1867 Dennis Jr married a Catherine Ahearn and also moved from Canada to the United States, i.e., to Minnesota and later again to Washington. One of their children, Catherine, became the mother of the singer, Bing Crosby.) The Harrigans, Fitzgeralds and Sullivans became lumberman-farmers, farmer-fishermen and 'sodbusters' in Miramichi on the Gulf of St Lawrence. They lived in log cabins in the Catholic part of the Williamstown Settlement among the 'pine trees so tall that the clouds were torn as they passed over them', as an Indian story put it.[66]

Others who emigrated to America in 1832 were Samuel, Henry and George Ford of Ballinascarty near Clonakilty, who were Protestants. They went 'with the desire and determination to establish homes in which the fullest sense of freedom and independence could be had,' as one of that family explained defiantly. The Fords went farming at Dearborn near Detroit. Mayburys and Mahoneys from Dunmanway also came to that city at this time. So many people from County Cork had settled in one part of it that it was called 'Corktown'.[67] The Fords left another brother, John, at home but they were the links in the chain which would pull him over too in 1847. There was also, no doubt, the push of famine.[68] This family was soon to make the famous motor car. It is often believed that most of the Irish preferred or were forced to settle in the cities because they were gregarious and lacked the skills and capital necessary for farming in the New World. As shall be seen, however, more of them headed out for the country than is sometimes thought.

The general situation regarding emigration ten years later is given by the Census commissioners of 1841:

> It would be fallacious to estimate any common sum or value taken from the county by these migrants so various in circumstances. It has been estimated as high as £10 and even £20 from some parts; but the numbers of such can be but small … still there can be no doubt that immense numbers carry no capital but their manual labour and that the great majority are of agricultural habits, without acquired skill of any kind. It may, however, be doubted whether voluntary emigration will ever prevail among people wholly destitute … It is when man has already begun to move upwards, that he seeks a more advantageous field than his native country affords.[69]

The Fords, the Fitzgeralds, the Harrigans, the Mayburys and the Mahoneys may well be typical examples of people who had already begun to move upwards and who sought in America a more advantageous field that Ballinascarty, Kilmoe or Dunmanway afforded. Others would join them if they had the money but the destitute had neither the mind nor the means required. There would be no 'voluntary emigration' for these; some sort of push would have to be applied. Yet 90,000 people left the country in the following year,

1842; this decreased to 38,000 in 1843. Apparently, many had hoped that it really would be repeal year and that times would be better. But when this did not happen emigration increased again to 54,000 in 1844 and to 75,000 in 1845.[70] This general situation all over the country is seen in clearer focus and *locus* or place in the answers of Fr James Barry to the Devon Commission in 1844:

1. *Do you think that the people would be willing to emigrate, if means were provided?*
   There are many people who do emigrate, who sell off their interest in the land they hold thinking they may do better in America.
2. *What are the accounts received from them?*
   In general they are very good.
3. *If locations were provided for them in the colonies do you think there would be an extensive emigration from this country?*
   Yes, I think there would, for I am in the habit of receiving letters from the parties there. When they write home, the friends come to me to read them. The accounts are very flattering … that there is no tyranny, no oppression from landlords and no taxes. In the village I live in there has been a ship or two freighted every year for the last four or five years and if the ship were larger she would get enough to make up her compliment.[71]

Fr Barry said that the ship left from Ballydehob, 'a small inlet', and if that number departed from such an inlet one must ask how many left from such ports as Castletownbere, Bantry, Baltimore, Crookhaven or Schull. We know that 901 persons left Baltimore in 1845.[72] So by this time emigration was already substantial and the desire to depart even greater. The priest's words are an accurate summary of the forces of push from home and pull to America, e.g., the 'American letter' – forces which were increasingly dragging the anchor which was the hearth.

The houses or cabins which held many of these Irish hearths were miserable. Of course, such housing was not necessarily proof of poverty. Contemporaries warned of people living in apparent squalor who still found money to dower daughters or buy farms for sons. Nevertheless, miserable housing was usually the result of population pressure and chronic poverty.[73] The Census commissioners of 1841 divided all houses into four classes. The fourth-class consisted of single-roomed mud cabins without windows. The third-class was made up of two- to four-roomed mud cabins or houses with windows. Good farm-houses were included in the second class. All better dwellings such as the 'Big Houses' were categorised as first-class. In the rural area of the whole country, 43.5% of families were living in fourth-class houses, 40.0% in second-class, 15.3% in third-class but only 1.2% in first-class houses. Thus more than 80% of houses or cabins fell into the two lowest categories. The basic housing structure and by implication, the social structure, was that of a very broadly based pyramid. Its base, of course, was far broader in some counties than in others. In Down and Wexford, for example, only 24.7% and 29.4% of families, respectively, were living in fourth-class cabins. There was also a correspondingly higher percentage of families living in third-class cabins/houses, i.e., 28.2% and 46.5%, respectively. Accordingly the basic housing or social structure in such counties was not pyramidal at all but rather egg-shaped. In Cork, however, it was distinctly pyramidal since the county was the fourth lowest in the housing league, having as many as 56.7% of families living in fourth-class abodes. Cork was followed by Clare, Mayo and lastly Kerry; these counties had 56.8%, 62.8%, and 66.7% of families, respectively, living in these single-roomed windowless mud cabins. In the Mizen Peninsula as many as 83% of families were occupying these fourth-class houses but it was not much higher than some other poor districts in the west of the country. The commissioners stated that reports of the housing conditions of the working classes 'even in England' were 'frightful' and 'melancholy' so they requested to be excused from describing the abodes of the Irish poor. The following table gives, for example, the number and percentage of families living in each class of house in the rural area of the parish of Schull in 1841:

TABLE 10: RURAL HOUSING, PARISH OF SCHULL:
NUMBER AND PROPORTION OF FAMILIES IN EACH CLASS OF HOUSE, 1841

Class	Number	Proportion
1st	12	0.4%
2nd	71	2.5%
3rd	345	12.2%
4th	2,391	84.9%
Total	**2,819**	**100.0%**

This table shows how extremely broadly based the housing or social pyramid really was. *(See Figure 1 on p. 137.)* At the summit were the few landlords (0.4%) and underneath were some larger farmers (2.5%). Lower again were the small farmers (12.2%) and lowest of all were the vast numbers of labourers (84.9%), the majority of whom lived in fourth-class houses, i.e., hovels. This was almost double the national average.[74] James Barry had no inhibitions in describing such hovels and the conditions within:

> Such buildings are in general of stone and mud and in some instances a chimney and a cross-wall covered with reeds and clods or potato stems and in many cases heath and ferns; very few have straw for bedding, heath or mountain grass the substitute. No bedsteads and only a few have the luxury of a bad blanket.[75]

Such a mass of poverty at the broad base of the pyramid could well be said to be social dynamite; all that was needed was some sort of detonator.

Housing conditions in the cities and large towns of Ireland were not quite so bad; 36.7% of families lived in fourth-class houses, 33.9% in third-class, 22.4% in second-class but only 7% in first-class houses. Nonetheless 70% of houses or cabins fell into the lowest two categories. The basic housing structure was still pyramidal but the base was less broad than in the rural districts owing to the relatively good houses of the commercial or middle classes. In Skibbereen the housing structure was pyramidal but in better off towns such

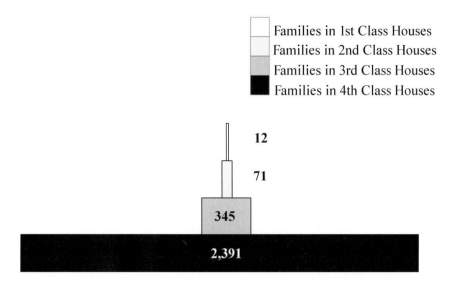

12

71

345

2,391

Figure 1 (based on Table 10): Rural Housing, Parish of Schull:
Number and proportion of families in each class of house, 1841

as Clonakilty or Bandon it was egg-shaped in that there were more families living in the third class-houses than in the fourth-class houses. Small towns such as Ballydehob, Schull and Crookhaven were placed in the rural rather than the civic area of the whole country, but their housing structure resembled that of the larger towns much more closely than it did that of the surrounding countryside. The following table shows the number and percentage of families living in each class of house in the three towns of Ballydehob, Schull and Crookhaven in 1841:

TABLE 11: BALLYDEHOB, SCHULL, CROOKHAVEN: TOTAL NUMBER AND PROPORTION OF FAMILIES LIVING IN EACH CLASS OF HOUSE, 1841

Class	Balydhob	Schull	Crookhvn	Total	%
1st	7	0	2	9	3.0
2nd	58	0	16	74	24.7
3rd	33	52	44	129	43.0
4th	24	44	20	88	29.3
Total	122	96	82	300	100.0

Here the housing or social structure is not pyramidal but egg-shaped: the bulge in the middle is evidence of a growing middle class. Schull was clearly the poorest of the three towns having no good houses at all, yet there were more families living in third-class houses than in fourth-class houses. In Ballydehob there was a large number of families living in good second-class houses, i.e., 58 compared with 16 in the old town of Crookhaven. Looking at the housing structure of these three towns taken together it is clear that it was egg-shaped like Clonakilty or Bandon and not pyramidal like Skibbereen.[76] The houses in Ballydehob were slated, as shall be seen later from the sketch by James Mahoney of the *Illustrated London News* in 1847. The general picture of the small towns which emerges from the census reports, both as regards population and housing, is further developed by Samuel Lewis who described Ballydehob thus in the 1830s:

> It consists of a long and irregular street containing about 100 houses some of which are large and well built; and is rapidly increasing in size and importance, particularly since the formation of the new road [Griffith's] which has made it a considerable thoroughfare, aided by its propinquity to the copper mines of Cappagh and the slate quarries ... which renders it well-adapted for business.

Twelve fairs were held each year for horses, sheep, pigs, and pedlary while only one fair was held in Schull. The decline of Crookhaven after Waterloo was also noted by Lewis:

> It was formerly a place of considerable importance, many foreign vessels having resorted thither for provisions and during the last war was much frequented by ships of the navy. A considerable trade is carried on in the exportation of wheat, oats, pork and butter; timber and coal are occasionally imported.[77]

CONCLUSION

Pre-famine Ireland is often represented as a period in which little progress of any kind was made and as a time of general misery culminating in the famine.[78] At best rather negative conclusions are reached in relation to the efforts at improvement made by government and people during this period.[79] The period deserves a more positive assessment; considerable progress was made all over the country from 1823 to 1845. The assertion of the American historian, Joel Mokyr, is borne out at local level in the Mizen Peninsula: 'By the standards of the time, Ireland enjoyed a fine administration of education, public health and the police force'.[80] A total of thirteen Protestant churches or Catholic or Methodist chapels was built in the parishes of the Mizen Peninsula. The tithe question was settled for some time. Seven National Schools and eighteen Church Education Society schools were either built or brought into connection with these new systems. National Schools were not set up in England until 1870. David Thompson explained that 'the more rapid growth of popular education had been prevented partly by the clash between Church and Dissent, partly by the apathy of the people'.[81] Cork was granted a Queen's College in 1845. In the domain of public health and social welfare three dispensaries were set up which were attended by two doctors. A workhouse was established in Skibbereen. R. B. McDowell pointed out that, 'The Irish poor enjoyed better medical services than their fellows in wealthier and healthier countries'.[82] The poor badly needed such services as malignant fevers were endemic. The chaplain of the Skibbereen Workhouse, P. Mahony, died in March

1845, probably of fever.[83] According to Peter Froggatt, eminent doctors such as Whitley Stokes, William Wilde (father of Oscar) and Robert Graves 'ensured for Irish medicine a primacy in Europe'. The two medical journals, the *Dublin Quarterly Journal of Medical Science* and the *Dublin Medical Press,* were 're-nowned'.[84] Medical men from the district contributed to them as shall be seen. Fr Nicholas Callan, professor of Mathematics and Natural Philosophy at Maynooth College, was making discoveries in the field of electricity.[85] In relation to justice and law and order there were Petty Session Courthouses in Ballydehob and Toormore which were backed up by the police barracks at Aughadown, Ballydehob, Schull and Goleen.[86] We have seen that Ballydehob had Peelers six years before London had. Less tardy communications were made possible by Griffith's new road from Skibbereen to Crookhaven along which mail coaches could travel. Post Offices were established at Ballydehob, Schull and Crookhaven.[87] Safety at sea was enhanced by lighthouses on Cape Clear and Crookhaven; signal towers and coast-guard stations also kept a look out.

The people were made more politically conscious by Daniel O'Connell's agitation for emancipation and repeal. Agriculture was being improved. The Marxist historian, E. Strauss, described the period 1815–45 as Ireland's Thirty Years War against poverty.[88] There was some reason for thinking that the country was on the way towards winning the struggle. To look at the first forty-five years of the nineteenth century through potato blight-tinted glasses is to falsify the picture. In spite of all the problems there was a certain new-found confidence throughout the land as expressed in 1844 by Robert Kane:

> We were reckless, ignorant, improvident, drunken and idle. We were idle because we had nothing to do; we were reckless for we had no hope; we were ignorant for learning was denied to us; we were improvident for we had no future; we were drunken for we sought to forget our misery. That time has passed away forever.[89]

Crookhaven, c. 1840

Nevertheless, for many of the inhabitants of the Mizen Peninsula it was not this prediction which was about to come to pass but that of Malthus, alas. All the improvement had a tragic flaw namely the great mass of poverty which lay at the base of the social structure, as is clearly shown in Figure 1. The potato disease was a natural phenomenon beyond human power, an ecological disaster, or an affliction of Providence; it struck other countries in Europe too. But how and why the blight should have provoked such a terrible catastrophe in Ireland and in the Mizen Peninsula in particular is a question which has to be faced.

VII

ROTTING POTATOES AND ROAD-MAKING
SEPTEMBER 1845–DECEMBER 1846

Else, the public will hear such tales of woe and wickedness as will harrow the feelings and depress the spirits of the most stout-hearted man.

FR LAURENCE O'SULLIVAN

Hunger tames the lion and will more surely tame the heart of a poor Irishman.

DR TRAILL

ROTTING POTATOES

The strange disease that descended on the potato crop in the harvest of 1845 became the general subject of discussion. There were other matters too which were inclined to become extremely controversial, namely, the repeal of the Corn Laws and the question of religion. Soon the topics of potatoes, popery and politics became entangled in one and the same debate. Robert Peel, who had dared to increase the Maynooth grant, now proposed to repeal the Corn Laws to save the people from famine resulting from the failure of the potato crop. He granted that such calamities were indeed caused by 'the dispensations of Providence' but challenged the landed interest to consider whether such dispensations might not have been 'aggravated by the laws of man restricting, in the hour of scarcity, the supply of food'.[1] His conversion to Free Trade appalled his party just as much as John Henry Newman's turning to Roman Catholicism scandalised his Church. The statesman and the theologian were similarly denounced as traitors and apostates.

Agriculturalists all over Ireland and indeed England and the continent made great efforts to diagnose and cure the mysterious potato disease. In Ireland, at least, it was closely associated with warm damp conditions so it was thought that keeping the potatoes cool and dry would arrest the disease. Peel's government set up a scientific commission to examine the whole problem. The commission consisted of Robert Kane and two Englishmen, Dr Lyon Playfair, a physician, and John Lindley, professor of botany at the University of London. They concluded that the disease was caused by dampness and recommended dry, well-ventilated pits which were to be constructed in a most complicated manner. Instructions were published in the press and seventy thousand copies were distributed around the country as well as thirty for each parish priest.[2] There was also a theory that the disease was caused by a fungus but this view was held by only very few. One of them was Garrett Hugh Fitzgerald from County Limerick who was discovering that the rot could be controlled by bluestone.[3]

Among those who were convinced that the disease was caused by wet conditions was Dr Traill. Like many others he was fully convinced that specially constructed pits would keep the potatoes cool and dry and thus preserve them. Traill's often repeated motto was, 'It is in the construction of pits that ruin or safety lies'. He diagnosed the new disease as 'wet rot' and had great faith in his own design of 'ventilated pit'; his instructions for its making were printed in a pamphlet in English and in Irish. He illustrated his plan in the following diagram.[4]

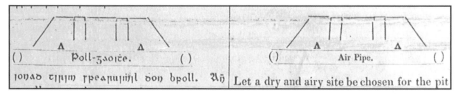

Dr Traill's Potato Pit

Traill was delighted that Lord Bandon had both instructions and diagram published in a pamphlet in English and in Irish under the title 'Extract from the Letter of a Western Rector' or '*Páirt don' litir fhir Seagailse san Iarthar*'. If these instructions were only carried out the resulting pit would, '… *a bhfágáilt na dhiaig na potátaoi tirim agus slán*', i.e., 'leaving the Potato dry and healed beneath it.'[5] Cornelius Buttimer states that the passage has a style which is a mixture of both the literary and vernacular.[6] This pit was of course a rival to that designed by the potato commissioners. Robert Kane claimed that Traill had spent twenty years translating the Jewish historian, Josephus, 'which has cracked his brain' and he ridiculed him as 'a perfect Knucklewrath' who, he enlightens us, was the 'Mad Cameron, main preacher in Sir W. Scott's *Old Mortality*'.[7] Traill spent most of October 1845 riding around his parish exhorting the people to construct their pits according to his plan. He explained that his anxiety was based on the fact that there were more than two thousand Protestants in his parish and very many of them in a state of almost utter destitution. He was also concerned about the thousands of Catholics whom he regarded as having an 'almost equal claim' upon his aid. If the potato crop could not be preserved, he predicted, a 'fearful shriek will yet be heard throughout the land'.[8]

The general state of agriculture in the district on the brink of famine can be seen at the show held in Skibbereen by the Carbery Agricultural Society in October 1845. W. W. Becher of Creagh, Baltimore, exhibited a pedigree Shorthorn bull while R. H. H. Becher's three pedigree Ayrshire bulls were much admired. This exhibitor won a prize for the best three acres of turnips. There were more improved breeds of sheep and pigs at the show than ever before. At the society's dinner that evening John Limrick of Schull said that butter was making as much as £3 a hundredweight at the Ballydehob market which was even better than at Skibbereen. R. H. H. Becher was enthusiastic about the progress that had been made in agriculture. 'No person', he declared, 'could pass through without being struck with the change that had taken place on all sides'. Even 'working farmers' were now buying Scotch ploughs from the society's depot at reduced prices. Six years previously such farmers would not have used these ploughs even if they had got them for nothing, he remarked. Becher then outlined a plan for the importation of seed from England and Scotland to be sold on a co-operative basis through the society.

Such pleasant discussion on improvement was brought to an abrupt end when the inevitable topic of the potato disease raised its ugly head. Mr Somerville of Drishane near Skibbereen felt quite confident that the potato crop could be preserved by the special system of pitting and saw little cause for alarm. Nevertheless the dispensary physician, Daniel Donovan, warned that he had been riding around six parishes and the wail all around was that the potatoes left in their beds were bad, those pitted worse, and those housed worst of all. John Limrick said that he had pitted half of his potatoes according to Traill's plan and they had remained sound. In the opinion of a Mr Levis of Skibbereen, Schull parish was the worst affected part of the country. Henry Marmion of Deelish, west of Skibbereen, asserted that they all had a duty to buy corn to protect the country from the plague of famine. Thereupon Mr Welply of Skibbereen offered no less than £100 and Mr Clerke of the Provincial Bank an equal sum. The discussion ended at 11.00 p.m.;[9] it was also the eleventh hour of this era in Irish history. As these gentlemen headed home that night the sound of their horses' hooves on the stony road rang the death knell of pre-famine Ireland.

At the end of October Alexander O'Driscoll of Crookhaven reported that the people had already stripped their pits and to their horror discovered that half of the potatoes were rotten. 'The poor people are in tears,' he insisted, 'nothing less than a famine is expected.' Scarlet fever soon broke out, two boys who had been infected were found dead in their beds.[10] All during November the potatoes continued to rot in the ordinary pits, 'receptacles of death', Traill dubbed them. At this stage he seems to have suspected that the rot was caused by a fungus as he referred to the disease being 'concealed perhaps in the first green germ of the fungus'. Still he was confident that his own design of pit would save the crop.[11] Fear of famine increased as the winter set in. A meeting of landlords, farmers, labourers and Protestant and Catholic clergymen was held in Skibbereen early in December 1845. The common enemy of famine united people of all creeds and classes. The courthouse was filled with farmers and labourers and the galleries were thronged. Landlords who attended were James H. Swanton, R. H. H. Becher and also the lawyer, Timothy McCarthy Downing. The clergy present were Traill, his curate, Francis Webb, and the administrator of Skibbereen, John Fitzpatrick. It was agreed that one-third of the potato crop was lost. Traill proposed that the government should be appealed to for public works and stated that he had written to the heads of government in both Ireland and England concerning the scarcity. He also wrote to the landlords of his own parish requesting them to allow their tenants to keep their grain so that they would be able to spare potatoes for seed. He still claimed that his own pit was successful while that of the commissioners was 'childish' and 'utterly futile'. One landlord, William Edward Hull and some others agreed to leave the grain with tenants for which they were cheered. The rector hoped that there would be enough grain in the country in case of famine. The meeting was taken aback by a tradesman who stepped forward and, quoting Thomas Drummond, reminded both landlords and farmers that 'property has its duties as well as its rights'. He spoke 'upon the part of the humblest classes' and proposed that the landlords should make a reduction in rents for the farmers who should then pass it on to the 'labouring classes'. He boldly remarked on the absence of a great many landlords and asked if a 'trying crisis' should come whether their granaries would be secure.[12]

Further building at the workhouse at Skibbereen had ceased because the Board of Works had delayed to pay an expected £8,500 due to lack of funds. Dr Donovan reported that there had been one fatal case of smallpox and re-commended that a section of the Fever Hospital should be isolated for the treatment of other cases. Six infected persons were then 'lying in a shed in the graveyard'.[13] Such was the position of the people as they faced the winter. Scar-let fever was spreading from the west, smallpox from the east and the blight was wreaking havoc throughout the land.

One of the last acts of Peel's cabinet before it split on the Corn Law ques-tion was to appoint a Relief Commission for Ireland in November 1845. The chairman was Edward Lucas who had been under-secretary, the secretary was John Pitt Kennedy who had been secretary of the Devon Commission. Other members were: James Dombrain, inspector of the coast-guard service, Colonel Harry Jones, chairman of the Board of Works, Edward Twistleton, the Poor Law commissioner, Colonel McGregor, inspector-general of the consta-bulary and Robert Kane. The leading member of this Relief Commission was Randolph Routh of the Commissariat service of the army, his duty was to buy corn. The Relief Commission was to encourage landlords, the principal clergy-men of both denominations and important residents to form local relief com-mittees. Their duties were to raise subscriptions, purchase food and provide employment. The Relief Commission would give a grant amounting to one-third of the subscriptions. The relief committees were forbidden to distribute free food unless the workhouse was full and then only to persons incapable of working.[14]

Such committees were set up in the distressed parts of the country in the spring and summer of 1846. Traill was chairman of the Schull committee, the secretary was John Limrick, a local landlord, and the treasurer was Traill's new curate, Alexander McCabe. The members of the committee were the other Protestant curate, John Triphook, the parish priest, James Barry and his curate, John Barry. The parish priest of Kilmoe or Goleen, Laurence O'Sullivan, was also a member of this committee because the eastern side of his parish was in the civil parish of Schull. Other members of the committee were: Philip Somer-ville of the Prairie near Goleen, John H. Swanton, W. R. Swanton of Rathruane,

William Connell of the Coosheen mines and Stephen Sweetnam, the Schull dispensary physician. The chairman of the Kilmoe relief committee was Richard Notter of Rock Island, the secretary and treasurer was the rector, William Fisher. The committee consisted of R. H. H. Becher, R. B. Hungerford of Ballyrisode, John Coghlan of Crookhaven, Laurence O'Sullivan, the parish priest, his curate Thomas Barrett, Dr Sweetnam and also Dr James McCormick of the Kilmoe dispensary. In Kilcoe parish the vicar, Rev. James Freke, was chairman of the relief committee; John H. Swanton was secretary and treasurer. Rev. Alexander Stuart, vicar of Aughadown, was the chairman of the committee in his parish. Robert Troy, the parish priest and his curate, Fr Walsh, were members.[15]

The Relief commissioners had established food depots in the west and south by February 1846. The officer in charge of the depot at Skibbereen was Colonel Hughes and the commissariat officer for West Cork was a William Bishop who had been recalled from Jamaica for this work. Private traders were not allowed to purchase food from these stores; only the relief committees could do so and only when prices were rising through scarcity. The purpose of these depots was not to supplant the traders but to prevent them charging exorbitant famine prices.

In the hungry spring and summer of 1846, Traill and his Schull relief committee were much more concerned with obtaining meal and money to pay for it. They had collected subscriptions amounting to £143 by June. Traill, John Limrick and William Connell gave £10 each; James and John Barry and Laurence O'Sullivan gave £5 between them; the Protestant curates, John Triphook and Alexander McCabe and Dr Sweetnam gave £2 each. Many others contributed £1 each, for example, Captain Thomas of the Coosheen mine. A sum of £32 was collected from farmers and shopkeepers, some of whom bore such names as Swanton, Wolfe, Willis and Atteridge. A total of only £13 was obtained from absentee landlords. In the covering letter requesting a grant from the Relief Commission in Dublin, Rev. McCabe stated that he had delayed in applying for this aid as long as there was any hope of subscriptions from absentee landlords. He deplored that the burden of such a scattered and destitute population of nearly 24,000 had been thrown on a few clergymen, farmers and shopkeepers. His relief committee realised that it would have to sell at least two tons of meal per week at a loss of £7 per ton. The Relief Commission's chairman, Randolph Routh, allowed a grant of £100.[16]

The Kilmoe relief committee was similarly active. On 27 May its chairman, William Fisher, sent a list of subscriptions to the Relief Commission. He had subscribed £10 himself as also did the parish priest, Laurence O'Sullivan. Most of the other subscriptions came through Fisher himself or were given by local landlords such as Richard Notter £10, R. B. Hungerford £5 and R. H. H. Becher £10. The Relief commissioner, Edward Twistleton, recommended a grant of £38 and urged Fisher 'not to give any relief except in return for work'. According to the constabulary reports one-third of the potato crop in the parish had been destroyed, half of the labourers were idle and there were 359 vacant places in the workhouse in Skibbereen.[17] In January 1845, Peel's government had passed acts for the construction of roads and piers. One statute laid down that half of the money would be paid by the Consolidated Fund as a free grant and the other half by the local cess. (This fund resulted from crown revenues and was independent of parliament.) According to another statute the money would be advanced by the Treasury purely as a loan and the work could be carried out by the landowners and local contractors.[18]

It was under this act that Presentment Sessions were held in Ballydehob on 26 June and 10 August 1846 under the chairmanship of John Limrick. A pier for Schull and roads to the cost of £39,044 were passed and sent by the secretary, Lionel Fleming, to the lord lieutenant who passed them on to the Board of Works for approval.[19] They were all rejected except the Poulgourm road in the parish of Kilcoe. The county surveyor, Mr Tracy, was almost ready to begin work on this road and employ eighty men recommended by the local relief committee when suddenly he himself rejected the road, the people's 'only hope'. This prompted J. H. Swanton to call a meeting of the Schull and Kilcoe relief committees. The chairman, Lionel Fleming, proposed that a 'strong' petition be sent to the lord lieutenant informing him of the 'awful distress' and requesting the immediate execution of works recommended at the Presentment Sessions. Fr Barry almost despaired of the government doing any good for the people because they had already sent two petitions and there had not yet been a shilling of public money spent in the barony. He saw that the magistrates and cess-payers were ready to do their part but that their good intentions were frustrated by the Board of Works. The meeting now agreed that he and Traill should draw up yet another petition. A cess-payer, Charles Regan, proposed that a list of the landlords who had subscribed should be published in the press and also a list of those who failed to do so. He had in his possession a document showing that the rental of the parish of Schull amounted to £15,000 a year while the subscriptions amounted to only £70. All the remainder had been paid by clergy and 'industrial classes'. Traill would not agree to publishing the list of defaulting landlords although Barry was in favour of it; no such list was published. The meeting recommended roads to the cost of £16,000.[20]

Barry was not the only person who was inclined to despair of the government, this was also the feeling of the miner, Captain Thomas of Coosheen. On 21 August 1846, he wrote to the chairman of his mining company, Major Ludlow Beamish, informing him that the grant paid by the Relief commissioners to the Schull relief committee was 'hopelessly inadequate' to employ 500 men whose families were wholly dependent on public works for their support; what was needed was £1,000. In his opinion the small farmers were now as badly off as the labourers. The relief committees 'in a corner here and there' were utterly inadequate to relieve the sufferings of 'hundreds, thousands, nay, millions of starving people.' The next day, Captain Thomas scribbled a hurried note to Beamish expressing his despair:

I really am … afraid I shall be obliged to look out for another place: for whatever is done by government or public works will be too late, after the people are driven to despair by hunger. The whole country is nothing but a slumbering volcano, it will soon burst.

Major Beamish forwarded these two letters to Charles Trevelyan, assistant secretary to the Treasury, in London; the secretary was Sir Charles Wood. Beamish informed him that West Cork was in a very alarming state and warned that if the government would not intervene soon the people would break out and plunder. He granted that in the city competition among merchants would control prices but in the small towns the poor would be at the 'mercy of the griping and covetous'.[21] Trevelyan replied that it had already been decided to establish a reserve depot of Indian meal at Schull and that he would write that very day to Randolph Routh instructing him to do so without delay. Trevelyan made it clear however that he relied on the merchants of Cork to supply the eastern part of the county as such interference would be confined to the remoter areas. The government was quite strict about this, he pointed out, even Viscount Bernard, MP for Bandon, had been refused a depot for his own town.[22]

It was the second and even worse failure of the potato crop that created the panic and gloom which brought the Catholic and Protestant leaders of the people together at a meeting held in Skibbereen on 17 August 1846. Its purpose was to alleviate the distress among the people and to call on the government 'to avert the impending disaster'. There were farmers there too such as Charles Regan of Ballydehob and Florence McCarthy of Schull. Clergymen who attended were Fr Fitzpatrick, administrator of Skibbereen; R. B. Townsend, vicar of Abbeystrowry; Alexander Stuart, vicar of Aughadown; Laurence O'Sullivan and James and John Barry. The meeting agreed with Fr Fitzpatrick that the potato crop was 'all but destroyed'. The workhouse which usually held only 200 or 300 people at harvest time now held 614; the Fever Hospital built to hold only 40 now held 67, with three patients in some beds. The labourers and even many of the farmers had pawned their clothes. 'Hungry hordes of labourers travelled the streets and the country with poverty depicted on their countenances,' said Fr Fitzpatrick. One of these labourers had died and it was believed to have been of starvation. The priest deplored that many landlords had not subscribed towards relieving the distress and others only 'stingily'. There were some others, however, who deserved the 'encomium and praise of the country', such as the chairman, Mr Somerville. Fr Fitzpatrick asserted that he had always preached law and order but now feared that neither he nor anybody else could any longer maintain it if the people were not relieved because self-preservation was more powerful than any teaching. Lionel Fleming explained the extraordinary chain reaction caused by the failure of the potato crop. Those who were affected were not simply those whose potatoes were destroyed but the 'whole fabric of society was dissolved' on account of the large numbers of persons thrown out of employment. Farmers were discharging their servants and labourers, and since sea

147

manure was no longer in demand those engaged in gathering it were thrown on the relief committees for support. McCarthy Downing, the solicitor, appealed to the landlords to reduce their rents to the farmers who should then pass on the reduction to their labourers. He was sorry to say that the farmers 'dealt more hardy' with those under them than the landlords themselves; there were cheers of agreement from the meeting. McCarthy Downing went on to condemn the landlords who had an annual rental of £20,000 from the Skibbereen Union but yet gave only £200, 'a most niggardly subscription' compared with what they spend at Cheltenham. He added that £70 out of this £200 had been given by one man, R. B. Townsend, and that only for people like him the country would be in a state of anarchy. Dr Donovan found that the people were getting sick from eating rotten potatoes. The meeting agreed to send a deputation to the new lord lieutenant, Lord Bessborough, to inform him of the alarming state of the union and to request relief to save it from anarchy. The deputation was to go on to London, if necessary, to address the new Prime Minister, Lord John Russell. Finally, a vote of thanks was passed to his predecessor, Robert Peel, on account of his 'wise and beneficial measures of precaution in regard to food and of liberality in regard to employment'. It was hoped that Russell would continue this successful policy.[23] The death of the labourer reported by Fr Fitzpatrick may well be regarded as the beginning of famine-related mortality, i.e., August 1846.

On the very same day as this anxious meeting at Skibbereen, Lord John Russell informed parliament that due to the ravages of the potato disease, the House would have to take 'extraordinary measures of relief'. Public works for the employment of the poor were to be undertaken but their total cost had to be borne by the local rates; hence it was called the Labour Rate Act. One half of the cost was no longer to be paid out of the Consolidated Fund as under Peel but the ratepayers would receive a loan at 3% interest to be repaid in ten years. The only free grant given was one of £50,000 for districts too poor to pay the full amount out of the rates. This act also rendered relief measures more centralised and more government-controlled than previously. Presentment Sessions could no longer be called by local landlords but only by the lord lieutenant; neither could works be carried out by local persons but only by the Board of Works. This body was specially re-organised and a relief department established under two very able men, Richard Griffith and Thomas Larcom. The latter had taken part in the Ordnance Survey and had also been a commissioner of the 1841 Census. Since direct, local and personal responsibility had been largely removed, the repayment of the loans was to be made by the ratepayers in general.

The Labour Rate Act was very badly received by the Irish landlords who alleged that it was rushed through parliament in the middle of August 1846 when most of the Irish members had already left London. Lord Palmerston, then foreign secretary and moreover an Irish landlord, declared that the act would eventually make the landlords as well qualified as their cottiers to enter the workhouse.[24] Viscount Bernard attended this parliament and a week later gave a first-hand account of the new act at a meeting in Dunmanway on 25 August. He appealed to his fellow landlords to carry out works under the act. Traill told how he had urged Lord John Russell to make some 'great and mighty effort commensurate with the circumstances'. The rector did not believe that employment alone was adequate, the government should also 'provide sustenance'. He regretted that no road-works had yet begun in his parish. Nonetheless, for the first time ever he had no fears of civil disturbances as 'hunger tames the lion and will more surely tame the heart of a poor Irishman'.[25] The gentry and clergy who had spoken at this meeting immediately set to work by forming the West Carbery Relief Association and collecting subscriptions. The most extensive landlord in Carbery, Lord Carbery of Castlefreke, headed the list with a subscription of £50 out of a yearly rental of £15,000. W. W. Becher, on whose lands the town of Skibbereen stood, gave £58 out of a rental of £10,000. R. H. H. Becher's contribution was £25 out of a rental of £4,000. Others subscribed smaller sums which brought the total amount to £1,004 for which the government gave a grant of £390.[26] The Kilmoe relief committee acknowledged subscriptions of nearly £98. Lord Bandon, William Fisher, Laurence O'Sullivan and R. H. H. Beecher contributed £10 each; Thomas Barrett and McCormick gave £1 each while the policemen at Goleen made up eleven shillings between them.[27]

The condition of the fishermen and labourers of Crookhaven was well expressed in their own petition to the lord lieutenant dated 4 September 1846. They informed him that over 500 of the town's 600 people were in 'actual distress and want' as a result of the failure of the potato crop. Almost all of them lived by piloting, fishing and growing some potatoes. It was only by a 'great struggle' that they endeavored 'to scrape a poor subsistence, not having cattle or any other substance except a few fishing boats which they could not dispose of to meet their present wants'. There was little or no demand for the 'trifle of fish' which they had on their hands. The people had applied to the Board of Works through Fr Barrett for a new line of road between Crookhaven and Rock Island and a pier at Crookhaven which would be of great advantage to local fishermen and ocean-going vessels. They begged the lord lieutenant to approve these works to save them from starvation. The appeal was signed by fifty-four fishermen and labourers, only seven of whom could sign their names; the others placed their marks. Fr Barrett praised the proprietor of Crookhaven as a humane landlord who had given generous subscriptions.[28] This landlord was David Cagney who was an absentee living in Cork. It is sometimes thought that the potato disease should not have struck the livelihood of fishermen as heavily as that of farmers. These fishermen explained why this was not the case. The vast majority of them were not full-time men of the sea equipped with good boats, gear and fish-curing facilities, but rather fishermen/farmers/ labourers who were dependent on their own potato patch. They also had to rely on the local people to buy or barter their fish for potatoes, something which could not be done when the potato failed.

This petition was passed from the lord lieutenant to the Board of Works.

The under-secretary, Thomas Redington, replied to Fr Barrett informing him that the lord lieutenant had decided to call Extraordinary Presentment Sessions to be held under the Labour Rate Act in Ballydehob on 15 September 1846.[29] Four days later, Redington wrote again with the disappointing news that the Board of Works had not received any regular application for a pier at Crookhaven and that in any case there was already fine anchorage and shelter there.[30] The government however did send some officials to inquire into the condition of the people there. The visitors were shown around in a coast-guard boat by Captain Baldwin and accompanied by Fr Barrett and a townsman, John Coghlan. Alexander O'Driscoll suggested that the government should buy meal from the traders and send it around by steamer to the coast-guards who would distribute it to the famishing people.[31] It was precisely this kind of thinking which was rank heresy to believers in the economic doctrine of *laissez-faire* such as John Russell, Charles Wood and Trevelyan.

The only refuge these hungry people had was the Kilmoe relief committee but even this was now in dire straits. It applied to Colonel Hughes of the Skibbereen depot for thirty tons of Indian meal but had received no reply. So on 7 October it appealed to the chairman of the Relief Commission, Randolf Routh, for a special depot in Crookhaven as the labouring classes were now completely dependent on Indian meal and there was not a stone of it to be had nearer than Skibbereen, twenty-six miles away.[32] The committee sought aid from Lord Bandon who had land in the district. Funds were running low on account of the high price of corn and worse still the merchants of Cork city were no longer able to supply Indian meal as they said there was no more on the market. 'What are we to do?' the committee asked helplessly, 'the people are famishing and we do not know where to turn for food for them, every application we have made to the government has been totally disregarded'.[33] Lord Bandon sent this letter to the chief secretary, Henry Labouchere,[34] who forwarded it to Routh. The latter replied to Lord Bandon admitting that sufficient Indian meal had not been imported with the result that it was now more expensive than wheat. Accordingly Routh advised the Kilmoe relief committee to buy wheat instead of meal and enclosed a recipe for making brown bread.[35]

This exasperating lack of response from the government prompted the Kilmoe relief committee to call a special meeting. R. B. Hungerford was determined to give publicity to the 'letter from the castle with a paper on brown bread'. Fr Barrett pointed out that they had no money to buy wheat and that in any case there was neither mill nor bakery nearer than Skibbereen. Lionel Fleming had seen the people reduced to eating salt herrings and seaweed because the last supply of meal had been sold at three shillings a stone although it had an offensive smell. 'Rapine has already commenced and who can wonder?' the meeting asked. It agreed with the proposal of the parish priest, Laurence O'Sullivan and the rector, William Fisher, that its proceedings should be published in the press including *The Times* and that copies of the proceedings should also be sent to Routh and Russell with '*a faint hope* that something might be done without delay'. Fr O'Sullivan warned that if something was not done the public would soon hear 'such tales of woe and of misery that will harrow the feelings and distress the spirits of the most strong-hearted man'. These proceedings were duly published;[36] the power of the press was thus being recruited for famine relief. Russell and Routh merely acknowledged receipt of these resolutions but failed to make the slightest promise of aid. Fisher commented indignantly that 'by these answers the public will be able to judge what the poor famishing creatures of this district have to expect from these honourable gentlemen' – in other words little or nothing. What the result would be was already plain to be read in the same newspaper that day. Dr McCormick reported the death of a man from *'absolute starvation'*, which had taken place on 18 November 1846.[37] He was probably not the first victim in the parish either.

ROAD-MAKING

Presentment Sessions under the Labour Rate Act for the barony of West Carbery East Division were held in Skibbereen on 14 September 1846. R. H. H. Becher's suspicion of this act was characteristic of Irish landlords. He was prepared to grant as many roads as possible without encumbering too heavily the property of the district but would 'strongly object to proceeding rashly which would only end in confiscation'. Nonetheless the meeting passed many roads in the Skibbereen district including the following roads in the parish of Aughadown:

Whitehall to Cunnamore Point	340 perches	£310
A road through Turk Head	600 perches	£570

The total cost of the roads passed at these Presentment Sessions was greater than the valuation of the half barony. The liberal *Southern Reporter* praised the landlords for their courage and sense of responsibility while the conservative *Cork Constitution* hoped that for the sake of the property of the barony most of the roads would be rejected by the Board of Works.[38]

The Presentment Sessions for the barony of West Carbery, West Division were held in Ballydehob on the following day 15 September. The usual venue, the courthouse, was totally inadequate to accommodate the 'vast concourse of people which flowed in from the surrounding countryside', so the meeting had to be held in the Catholic chapel. The Catholic and Protestant clergy also attended including L. O'Sullivan and W. A. Fisher. Many ratepayers attended such as Richard Beamish of Ardura Beg, Kilcoe. Captain Gordon of the Board of Works said that the county surveyor, Mr Tracy, had surveyed the following roads which were now put to the meeting (one perch is equal to five and half yards or five meters; 320 perches are equal to one mile):

Road	Length (perches)	Cost (£s)
Poulgourm to Crooked Bridge (Kilcoe)	330	240
To Reen of Skeaghanore (Ballydehob)	320	240
Laurel Hill to Audley Cove (Ballydehob)	620	510
To Rossbrin Cove (Ballydehob)	456	350
Mount Gabriel Road	1,100	1,250
Meenvane to Ardmanagh (Schull)	510	588
Schull to coast	700	588
Pier at Schull – 900 Glan Road (Schull)	600	659
Toormore to Dunmanus, Cashelean (Kilmoe)	1,280	1,240
Ballydevlin to Canty's Cove (Kilmoe)	490	496
To Kilmoe Churchyard	46	35
Rock Island to Crookhaven	1,280	1,857
To Mizen Head	700	875
Total	**8,432**	**8,928**
Average	**1 perch**	**£1 1s 0d**

Mr Somerville of Skibbereen proposed that all these roads as well as many others should be passed by the meeting but the chairman, Lionel Fleming, said that one of them was obviously unnecessary and asked the county surveyor to reject it. He refused, whereupon Lionel Fleming declared that they were taxing themselves too much. David Dore, parish priest of Caheragh, reminded him that the main object was not to tax the country but to feed the people but he was soon told that he did not pay any rates. The proprietor of Crookhaven, Mr Cagney, offered £100 towards the Rock Island–Crookhaven road but others said that the £100 should simply be donated to the relief committee. The Rock Island–Crookhaven road was duly passed. Other roads in the parish of Kilmoe, listed above and costing £3,549, were also passed. Many other roads must have been accepted as well because the total cost of the roads passed was £6,540 which was above the valuation of the parish, £6,283. (For famine roads see my 'Four Peninsular Parishes', Map 8.)

The roads listed above which were mostly in Schull parish and cost £2,045, plus the pier, £900, were passed by the meeting. Other roads must also have been passed because the total cost was as high as £11,936, exceeding the valuation of the parish, £11,668. In this manner, the landlords and ratepayers of Kilmoe and Schull proposed to tax themselves into debt to the tune of at least £18,476. At the ordinary Presentment Sessions of the previous year they had proposed to spend less than £3,000 but now they had what one man called 'presentment mania'. This was really a sort of gloomy resignation. Lionel Fleming admitted that 'most of the roads were not necessary but were passed through a spirit of charity under the affliction of Providence'. He was extremely disappointed with the aid offered by the 'greatest empire that ever flourished'. J. H. Swanton stated that he was ready to put 100 men to work on one of the roads passed at the meeting and would run the risk of its being rejected by the Board of Works in which case he would lose the wages he had paid his men.[39]

The labourers in Kilmoe were also losing patience with the Board of Works so they 'flocked in their masses' into Goleen and declared they 'were dropping with hunger and that they might die themselves of want sooner than lay hands on their neighbour's substance, but they could not bear to see their little ones craving – crying for food and not a morsel to put into their mouths'. They protested that they been 'living too long on hope, and that the road relief will come too late as they will not be able to work'. The priests, L. O'Sullivan and T. Barrett, who were returning from stations, assured them that the relief committee would strive to get the road-works opened as early as possible. But the labourers received these words 'half grateful, half grumbling'. When they were reminded of 'the objectionable character of such a gathering – however legitimate their demand, however pinching their want – an air of discontent and distress marked every face'.[40] Frustration with the Board of Works was even more serious in Caheragh at the end of September. There were rumours that the works would be closed down and also delays in paying the men. Even when they had money, Colonel Hughes of the Skibbereen depot refused to sell any food as he had orders from Trevelyan not to open the store until December. So these men numbering up to a thousand were determined 'to march into Skibbereen, levy contributions and enforce compliance with their demands'. Dr Donovan related how he saw them marching in, ten deep, with spades and shovels on their shoulders. McCarthy Downing asked them why they came and they replied:

> We are famishing because we have no food of any kind; we could suffer death from hunger ourselves, but we cannot look upon our children and our wives dying of hunger, and we are ready and anxious to work for bread, if we can get as much as would get us one good meal a day? But it is not with 8d a day that we will give our families a meal, and Indian meal 1s 10d a stone.

The labourers were however met by a force of seventy military under a magistrate, Michael Gallwey, who read the Riot Act to them but they shouted back: 'We may as well be shot as starved; we have not eaten a morsel for more than twenty-four hours!' The magistrate gave orders to the soldiers to 'prime and load' but he was also a man of 'kindness and humanity' and then cried out in a loud voice to the labourers, 'Three cheers for the queen and plenty of employment tomorrow!' and they responded as well as they could. Then he turned to Mr Hughes and demanded biscuits from the store which was promptly opened; a quantity of biscuits was given to the labourers and thus 'effusion of blood was avoided'. They then went home discontented, denouncing the government and threatening 'that while a stack of corn remained in the country they would not allow their children to starve'.[41]

There was undoubtedly quite a large stock of provisions in that store. Records show that on 17 October there were 121 tons of meal and 36 tons of biscuit.[42] Nonetheless meal at 1s 10d a stone retail price was an inflated famine price not to mention the 3s 0d for the bad meal at Kilmoe. Was the government hoarding? These starving people did not obtain very much food not because it was not there but because the government maintained that they were not entitled to it – not yet anyway. Amartya Sen wrote of a similar situation in India:

> In fact, in guarding ownership rights against the demands of the hungry, the legal forces upheld entitlements; for example in the Bengali famine of 1943 the people who died in front of well-stocked food shops protected by the state were denied food because of *lack* of entitlement, and not because their entitlements were violated.[43]

Returning to West Cork, J. H. Swanton paid his men every evening and after about two weeks had spent £240 on the road; it was later taken over by the Board of Works. The board delayed paying its men who were forced to eat wild parsnips. A member of the staff of the *Southern Reporter* was sent on a tour of the county to find out the facts about the road-making which was a subject now becoming controversial. He found that the destitution at Bally-dehob, 'equalled if not surpassed that of Skibbereen' and was surrounded by famishing children, running out of cabins on all sides begging for alms. He saw a large crowd gathered in the village and was told that the Board of Works pay clerk had at last arrived. The men had been working for the board for two weeks and had not received any pay until then. They rushed into the shops to buy Indian meal. J. H. Swanton of Ballydehob had imported a cargo of wheat but it was soon devoured. The relief committee had sent carts to Skibbereen for meal but succeeded in buying only twenty bags of wheat. The labourers had no food at all. The farmers had some left but, subtracting what they would need for seed and calculating on not selling any to pay the rent, they still would not have enough for four months. The majority of landlords did not press for rent though a few did seize cattle. Half of the people were not going to Mass as they had pawned their Sunday clothes. There were 100 men employed on the Skeaghanore Road, 200 on the Rossbrin road and 400 on the Shanavagh road, i e., a total of 700 in the Ballydehob district.

The reporter next visited Schull and Kilmoe. No road-works had yet begun near Schull. Some labourers had to be taken home from the Sheep's Head road in Muintir Bháire because they had fainted with hunger. A man and a woman had died in Kilmoe from sheer starvation, it was said. A man came to John Limrick looking for work only to faint of hunger; this prompted the landlord to go to the depot in Skibbereen for food. He was at first refused by Colonel Hughes but afterwards received two tons of biscuit at £12 a ton. The Schull relief committee had 20 bags of wheat but could obtain no more. Employment was far better in Kilmoe. Twenty men were making a road to Kilmoe churchyard, an ominous destination. There were 200 men employed on the Mizen Head road, 200 on the Toormore road and another 200 on the Bally-devlin road, i.e., a total of 620 men. In spite of this employment, the reporter found that the general impression among thinking people was that the Labour

Rate Act was a 'bungle from end to end'. In their opinion the landlords in a liberal spirit recommended many roads but only a few paltry ones had been sanctioned by the Board of Works.[44]

With all its faults it should be noted that the Board of Works had within the space of four weeks employed and eventually paid a total of 1,300 men in the Mizen peninsula. In conditions bordering on famine the delay of the Board of Works in paying its labourers was having serious effects. On 24 October a man named Denis McKennedy died on the road in Caheragh parish, he had been due two weeks' wages. At the inquest Captain Gordon of the Board of Works explained that the money intended for this road had been sent else-where by mistake. He complained that the Board of Works had been the subject of much gossip but was reminded by the Rev. R. B. Townsend of Abbey-strowry that the evidence against it was not now based on gossip but on a dead body. Then the jury gave the verdict that the deceased 'died of starvation, owing to the gross negligence of the Board of Works'.[45] This was a serious indictment of the government's relief measures and indeed of the Treasury itself because Trevelyan had made it clear that the Board of Works was a 'subordinate Board to the Treasury'.[46] Trevelyan demanded an explanation for this death.[47] Jeremiah O'Callaghan, a reporter for the *Cork Examiner*, commented that the deceased was no longer a slave of the Board of Works but its victim.[48]

In justice to the Board of Works it was overwhelmed. By the end of October 1846, it was employing 102,769 men on the roads and 7,482 in drainage schemes at a total of 5,000 different sites all over the country. Its chairman, Colonel Jones, described its offices as resembling a 'great bazaar'.[49] As already stated, some critics of the Board of Works accused it of rejecting most of the roads recommended at the Presentment Sessions in Ballydehob on 15 September but this was simply not true. All the roads in the above list that were passed at the Sessions were sanctioned by Griffith and Larcom on behalf of the Board of Works on 18 December 1846. In addition to the above roads there were others which were passed by the Sessions and sanctioned by the Board of Works though not reported in the press. The following is a list of the roads sanctioned on the same occasion.[50]

Ardintenant to Schull Harbour	£170
Leamcon to Gun Point (Kilmoe)	£340
Road to Ballydehob Bridge	£650
Ballybane Road (Ballydehob)	£500
Footpath at Schull	£60
Road on Horse Island (Ballydehob)	£50

Other roads passed at the same Sessions were sanctioned by the Board of Works on various occasions between 18 December 1846 and 18 February 1847. These roads included the following:[51]

Cooragurteen to Mount Gabriel Wood	£500
Gurteenakilla to Scrahanyleary (Ballydehob)	£300
Gortnagrough to Letterlicky (Ballydehob)	£500
Schull chapel to Cooradarrigan	£650

As Griffith sanctioned these roads he must have remembered working in the district during the famine of 1822–3. No doubt he expected that road-making would again have similarly beneficial effects both regarding the relief of distress and general improvement. What is surprising is not that the Board of Works' labourers had to wait so long for their wages but that they were paid so soon because final sanction had to come from the Treasury in England. Indeed, the Board of Works commenced work sooner than the Grand Jury and R. H. H. Becher who did not begin to work on their Mount Gabriel road until the middle of November 1846. This was about six weeks after the board had begun its works in the locality although the Mount Gabriel road had been passed at the ordinary Presentment Sessions a year previously.[52] Even if the Labour Rate Act had given a greater role to landlords it is doubtful if they would have been any more efficient than the Board of Works or indeed as efficient at all. In the last resort the board was fully supported by the government; the Imperial Treasury was far sounder financially than some encumbered, famine-shaken, Irish landlords. The Skibbereen district soon struck the headlines in the press again. On this occasion it was not the Board of Works so much as the landlords who were criticised. An inquest was held on the body of a man named Jeremiah Hegarty of Caheragh who had been working on the road for eight days before his death and had not been paid. The jury passed the verdict that he had died of actual starvation. He possessed stacks of corn but they had been 'crossed for rent' by the landlord's agent, Curley Buckley.[53] Jeremiah O'Callaghan reported that some of the landlords were hourly impounding cattle while others had forgiven arrears.[54]

Even at this early stage people were asking why there was more destitution around Skibbereen than anywhere else in the country. A local landlord, J. H. Marmion, explained that it was because of the 'superabundance of sea manure' which enabled the inhabitants to grow large quantities of potatoes. The markets of Cork and Waterford were 'principally supplied' with potatoes from this district and he himself had exported two thousand tons of them to England and Wales in one season. According to the *Economist* (20 June 1846) Cork was 'the chief market for potatoes in Ireland'. This crop 'induced a superabundance of population, contrary to the wishes of the proprietors'. However, when the crop failed the labourers went hungry, Marmion added.[55] In spite of this hunger no serious outrage took place but there were some minor incidents. One Saturday night in August 1846 a crowd of hungry-looking persons came into Ballydehob in search of work. When they were promised employment they went home quietly but some returned and 'levied contributions' from the shopkeepers.[56] Another night some 'comfortable farmers' damaged a road being made by the Board of Works on Horse Island because they had been refused employment. In the comparatively well-off area of Ballinspittle near Kinsale a large military force had to be in attendance at the road-works because the men refused to work by task and threatened to get food wherever they found it.[57] Hunger had indeed now tamed the poorer people in the west. It was understandable that some of them should have stolen food, for example, bags of meal were taken from the stores at the Coosheen mines. This was particularly regretted as the food was intended to be distributed at a reduced price to the miners by Captain Thomas who was employing 200 men, women, boys and girls and paying them generously.[58]

Even when men could obtain employment and wages for it, food was scarce. This forced the Schull relief committee to open a depot in Schull and another in Ballydehob. It had received about £100 in subscriptions which included £10 from Lord Bandon and £20 from an Indian fund known as the Calcutta fund which arose from subscriptions given by the British and Irish in India. The chairman of the Relief Commission, Randolph Routh, duly gave the Schull Relief committee a grant of £23.[59] Nevertheless it was very difficult to buy food from the depot in Skibbereen because Colonel Hughes had been strictly ordered not to open it until 27 December. He did however issue two and a half tons to the Skibbereen relief committee and also sent two tons to Baltimore under police escort. The police warned him that if he refused food to the starving people of Leap, near Rosscarbery, who had money to pay for it, he himself would be held responsible for any outbreak so he allowed them six tons. The Schull relief committee sent money to Hughes for twelve tons of Indian meal, otherwise there was no food to be obtained in Schull on any terms.[60] The response of Hughes does not seem to have been recorded. It was a great pity that food should have been so scarce or hoarded towards the end of 1846; corn had been exported but cargoes of Indian meal had not yet arrived. People were already starving but fevers had not yet broken out. Prevention would have been better than cure; a ton in time would have saved nine.

During the autumn of 1846 there was a constant demand for 'reproductive works', i.e., work which unlike road-making would produce the one thing needed – food. Such reproductive works could by no means be carried out under the Labour Rate Act because it would have been regarded as state interference in the normal production of food and therefore anathema to *laissez-faire* thinkers. Finally Russell and Trevelyan begrudgingly allowed drainage to be carried out under this act. The concession was made public in an official letter of the chief secretary, Henry Labouchere, in October 1846. Landowners could now drain their land but they would have to be personally responsible for the repayment of the loan if they should fail to levy it on the barony.[61] This concession gave some hope to the people. A number of new Presentment Sessions were held all over the country one of which was held in Ballydehob in November. No more new roads were recommended but some drainage schemes were recommended by R. H. H. Becher.[62] How cynical some had grown about road-works was shown by one Skibbereen landlord, Thomas

Marmion, who proposed that they should make presentments for coffins. In Aughadown a dead body had remained unburied for a week until the parish priest and curate got a coffin for it and buried it in a corner of a field. The meeting demanded food and no more road-works. Marmion also suggested that they get rid of the Board of Works altogether but J. R. Barry of Glandore pleaded: 'God help the poor Board of Works, for they are acting under a heartless government. It is only fair to do them justice, they are bewildered.' The meeting showed its disillusionment with road-making as a means of relief by opening a subscription for a soup-kitchen.[63]

The applications for drainage made at the Ballydehob sessions were rejected for technical reasons. Accordingly new sessions were held in Ballydehob on 23 December 1846. Becher was bitterly disappointed by the failure of the applications but declared that he had come to advocate the cause of the people who were dying by the hundred and would soon be dying by the thousand if nothing was done for them. In his opinion many of the roads in other baronies were not useful but those made in West Carbery were extremely useful and would, in any case, be made by the Grand Jury in due course. He asserted that the people should be provided for as long as the gentry had food or raiment themselves, so he called for more roads. John Limrick thought that it was just as well that drainage works were rejected because sending healthy men into bog holes in winter was only sending them into their graves.

Part of the difficulty about the roads was that most of the money which had been granted for them had been spent long before the works had been finished. Indeed in a few cases the money had run out completely and perhaps symbolically, e.g., the road to Kilmoe graveyard and the road to Mizen Head. (Samuel Beckett might have called such scenes 'Endgame'.) Further applications for funds had to be made:

TABLE 13: ROADS 1846: ADDITIONAL EXPENSES (£s)

Road	Expended (£s)	Required (£)
Poulgorm Quay to Crooked Bridge	200	200
To Reen, Skeaghanore (Ballydehob)	240	170
Shanavagh Road (Ballydehob)	240	170
To Rossbrin Cove	350	350
To Lissacaha	200	375
Ballydevlin to Canty's Cove	490	230
To Kilmoe graveyard	35	30
To Mizen Head	870	500

These roads which had been estimated to cost about £1 a perch were now going to cost an average of £1 13s 0d at least. Indeed some of the most important roads, namely those leading to Mizen Head and to Rossbrin Cove, were going to cost almost £2 a perch. Becher protested that this was too high.

He objected that nearly £2 a perch should now be charged for narrow roads which could just previously have been made by the Grand Juries for only 12s 0d a perch. He thought it a 'monstrous thing' that the 'infallible Board of Works' should be demanding so much. But a voice shouted out the reason at him, 'Because the people are starved and not able to work as they used'. Hunger was indeed taming the heart and weakening the hand of the poor Irishman. New presentments were next discussed:

Road to Long Island Sound (Schull)	£600
Dunlough to new road at Lackavaun (Kilmoe)	£400
Lissigriffin to Cloghanacullen (Kilmoe)	£400
Lissacaha Bridge to Cashelean (Kilmoe)	£600
Leamcon Hill (Kilmoe)	£135
To Dhurode Mine (Kilmoe)	£100
Derreenatra Road (Ballydehob)	£300
Repairing bridge at Ballyrisode (Kilmoe)	£70
From Skeaghanore to Ballea (Ballydehob)	£220
Dunlough to Millen (Kilmoe)	£796
Lisrobe bridge to Crookhaven	£600
Letter to Ratooragh (Schull)	£1,200

These roads were certainly useful because they were leading from where sand and sea-manure was available, e.g., Lissigriffin (Barley Cove), Derreenatra and Skeaghanore, towards the hilly interior such as Letter and Ratooragh which are just under Mount Gabriel. But the hungry, badly clothed, labourers must have suffered terribly from cold on such an exposed site. John Limrick agreed that these roads were useful but would have preferred to have had power to apply for seed for the people. James Callaghan of Dunmanus wished they could enlarge the workhouse.[64] General disillusionment with road-making as a form of famine relief is obvious. In the ordinary Presentment Sessions of the previous summer of 1845 roads were to be made for 12s 0d a perch. The following September 1846 the same road would cost £1 a perch and by December, almost £2. The rising price of a perch of road was a true indicator of the declining strength of the labourers due to hunger. At 12s 0d per perch the Grand Jury had been making roads for £192 per mile. Now at prices ranging from £1 13s 0d to £2 per perch these famine roads were going to cost from £580 to £640 per mile, at least, while Griffith's superior Skibbereen–Crookhaven road, 1822–6, had been made for only £335 per mile as has been seen.[65] Already at the end of 1846, many feared that road-works as relief measures would turn out to be not only a failure but an expensive one – in both financial and human terms. A little girl was asked why she was out begging near Ballydehob since her father was working on the roads but she replied, 'No, he is not, Daddy is asleep all day; he was asleep yesterday and the day before too'. His dead body was found in a cabin with a younger child gazing into the face.[66]

Part of the reason why sending men to do drainage or to make roads was often only sending them to their graves was that it happened to be a particularly severe winter. Thomas Marmion described the scene near Skibbereen in the middle of December:

> I saw a gang of about 150 composed principally of old men, *women*, and little boys going to work. At that time the ground was covered with snow, and there was also a very severe frost; seeing that they were very miserably clad, I remarked to a bystander that it was a miracle that the cold did not kill them even though they had enough to eat.[67]

Unusually low temperatures were recorded in Dublin. In December 1846 and January 1847 the mean temperature was 2.4 degrees centigrade whereas normally the mean temperatures would have been from 4.4 to 6.0 degrees.[68] While it may not have been exactly a return of the 'arctic Ireland' of 1740 there must have been hours when it felt something like it to the hungry, poorly clad, labourers and beggars on the roads of the Mizen Peninsula.

Owen Hickey, a great-great-grandfather of mine, was a man who travelled along the road being made from the pier at Skeaghanore through his farm and on the main Skibbereen–Ballydehob road. He had a daughter, Johanna, married to Richard Caverley of Coulanuler, Caheragh. Their first child was baptised 'Catherine' in the church at Killenleigh on Christmas Day 1846; one of the sponsors was her grandfather, Owen Hickey. When he returned to our hearth after the christening he must have been able to tell some sad stories of starvation.

VIII

SWIFT FAMINE AND TARDY RELIEF
DECEMBER 1846 – FEBRUARY 1847

I have only a handful of meal, I am going to prepare this for myself and my son to eat, and then we shall die.

(I KINGS 17:12)

AN GORTA DUBH

The poverty and destitution of the Mizen Peninsula had deteriorated into black famine by the middle of December 1846. This was announced by the reporter of the *Cork Constitution* who had attended the Presentment Sessions in Ballydehob on 23 December 1846. Having described the misery and death which he had witnessed in Dunmanway and Skibbereen he declared:

> Greater misery was reserved for me in Ballydehob. Here they are in a deplorable state dying in all directions … The people are living on seaweed and cattle they steal … On Sunday night, they broke into the food-store and stole all that was in it, seven bags of wheat and two barrels of barley. There were thirteen buried in the Schull churchyard yesterday; not one of them had got a coffin, they were taken on doors covered with a little straw. Under such circumstances it is cruel to insist on these wretched skeletons going miles to and from work to earn a few pence: it would be much wiser to give them a little food and permit them to remain within doors.

This report of dire famine coming from an outside observer shows that the local relief committees were by no means exaggerating or being alarmist. Ballydehob was even more wretched than Skibbereen which was already becoming notorious for famine. Yet a fair effort was being made to employ the people. This reporter wrote that the number of labourers on the roads in the parish of Schull was 1,473, Kilcoe, 114, Kilmoe, 375 and Caheragh, 450. But he also remarked 'Several works are run out' – of money, no doubt. He provides more evidence for the shortage of food. John H. Swanton's mills had only ten days work left and were unable to supply many of their orders. The miller had 30,000 tons of Indian corn and wheat 'afloat' on its way from England and America. The reporter was also told that a family of eight persons was found eating a dog in Kilcoe. John Limrick of Schull informed the public that conditions there were just as bad as at Ballydehob. He had received little aid from the absentee landlords but did receive a 'handsome and well-timed donation' from the Society of Friends. These Friends gave him instructions for the erection of a soup-kitchen which he immediately set up but now he called for subscriptions to keep it going. John Limrick, as magistrate, stated that hitherto the killing or stealing of cattle was very rare, but that now famine had 'changed the very face of society'. He believed that only large imports of flour would save the people and accused the government of being unwilling to bring food into the country.[1]

W. A. of Kilmoe, being of Quaker stock, brought the attention of the Society of Friends to the district. The relief committee of the Society of Friends had been formed in Dublin the previous month and Fisher informed it of the famine conditions of his parish.[2] The Cork Auxiliary Committee included Abraham Beale, William Harvey and Abraham Fisher.[3] Two Quakers, William Harvey and Joshua Beale, made a tour of inspection and reported back to their committee. At Aughadown the police told them that the night before they were attracted to a cottage by an unsteady light. When they went to investigate they found a father and son lying dead while the survivors were endeavouring 'to keep up a light with straw pulled from the thatch'. In spite of reports of robberies these Friends were impressed by the peaceful submission of the people. The visitors saw that the farmers would be unable to grow their own food in the spring because they had no seed. They had hoped in vain that the government would grant them some.[4] John Gregg, an Evangelical clergyman who later became bishop of Cork, collected £10 at Trinity College and sent it to Archdeacon Stuart of Aughadown.[5]

Commissary Inglis, who had been sent to Skibbereen in December, observed that 'mortality is confined to a certain class of persons ... such as labouring people and beggars. The country people generally never looked more healthy, and, I am told, will have provisions until about May next. They are eating the produce of their own grain and paying no rents'.[6] The following are examples of how famine-related death first picked off the weakest. An inquest was held by Dr Sweetnam on three bodies – the first case was that of the father of two very young children whose mother had already died of starvation. His death became known only when the two children walked into the village of Schull. They were crying of hunger and complaining that their father would not speak to them for four days and that he was 'as cold as a flag'.[7]

Some time later an inquest was held by both Drs Sweetnam and McCormick, the first case was that of Michael Crowley:

Ellen Driscoll, sworn; knew Michael Crowley to have been exceedingly distressed wandering from house to house in quest of food; he had been at work on the Lowertown road but was put off, a large number of hands besides have been dismissed; on the Wednesday before Christmas Crowley's little boy came into witness, another child was with him and witness gave a few spoons of food to each but the other child said that Crowley wanted it worst as he had not eaten anything for some days. On this, witness inquired of the child why his father was not out looking for food but the boy answered that he was lying on the straw and not sick at all for he was saying nothing and was kicking with his feet. Witness went immediately to the house and found the house built up with loose stones through the crevices of which the other child said he had crept out and that his father had built up the door in that manner before he laid down. On throwing down the stones Crowley was found lying dead inside and his little girl lying beside him quite emaciated and weak. Witness is fully persuaded that Crowley built himself in with his family that they might all die together.

The second case at this inquest was that of Denis Brien, an unemployed labourer. His mother told through an interpreter that her son had worked on the road until dismissed and was buried without a coffin. The third case was that of Mary McCarthy, her husband and one of their two children, a beggar family. Catherine Hunt, witness, told they had pleaded with her to let them into her hut for the love of God as nobody else would. They shared a little food but the man soon became swollen, complained of 'the pain from emptiness' and died. This happened a few days before Christmas. Witness had no more food as she was only depending on begging herself and had received a little money from the priest. Soon the beggar woman began to pine and her child, Timothy, to get very hungry. 'The cries of the child were terrible,' the witness said, 'but at last he died. It was the time of the snow.' Witness told that he had died 'on his mother's bosom and had cut the nipple across trying to draw milk from her'. The next day the mother herself succumbed.

The coroners found that an intestine of Michael Crowley had been blocked by undigested Indian meal which was the immediate cause of his death while absolute starvation was the remote cause. Starvation was given as the simple cause of death of Denis Brien and the child, Timothy. John Limrick reported that the coroners had stated on oath that 'these cases far from being isolated, afford no more than a mere illustration of what is taking place with thousands around us who must also sink into the same calamity unless relief is speedily and extensively administered'. The coroners had recommended soup-kitchens and he was glad to be able to open one the following day thanks to the generosity of the Society of Friends'.[8] This inquest held early in January was a microcosm of famine mortality at its initial stage. Death first struck the most vulnerable, i.e., the beggars and next the unemployed labourers. Two families from these classes were victims. The road-works and Indian meal, 'Peel's brimstone', were already failing as relief measures and were even contributory factors in bringing about death. There is no mention of fever – yet.

People were traditionally hospitable to beggars but when the potatoes rotted it became a question of survival and all this suddenly changed. A verse from a poem of famine times in Ballymacoda in East Cork laments:

Ba maith é an práta, dob fhial is dob fhairsing é
Chun é a roinnt ar bhochtaibh Dé,
Is gach stróire gheobhadh a tslí bhíodh lóistín seachtaine 'ge
'S suí go daingean istigh ón spéir;
Nú gur laghadaigh a gcroí 's is gur dh'iompaigh a gcrathacha
Nuair a chonaiceadar na mílte sínte cois na gclathacha.
'Imigh, bí ar siúl, níl aon tslí leapan againn'
Ar eagla go mblaisfimis an mhin bhuí féin.[9]

The potato was good, generous, and plentiful
To be shared with God's poor,
And every stranger who passed the way had a week's lodging
And sure shelter inside from the sky,
Till their hearts hardened and their affections turned away

When they saw thousands lying dead by the ditches.
'Go away, clear off, we have no room for a bed'
For fear we ourselves may taste the yellow meal.

As shall be seen in Chapter X, the poor were far more vulnerable to famine than the rich and the child more vulnerable again than the adult. Hence the most vulnerable of all was a beggar's child such as Timothy McCarthy.

The British government and the whole empire were bluntly informed of the horrific conditions in Skibbereen and its vicinity by an open letter from Nicholas Marshall Cummins, JP, Ann Mount, Glanmire, which was published in *The Times* of 24 December 1846. He described famine and fever at South Reen in the parish of Myross near Castlehaven which he had visited. He appealed to the Duke of Wellington as an Irishman to save 'the kindred of that gallant Irish blood which you have so often seen lavished to support the honour of your British name'. He also requested the duke to lay these matters 'before our young and gracious queen'.[10] Richard Townsend, chairman of the local relief committee, pointed out that South Reen was part of the estate of the absentee, Lord Audley, where there was a 'miserable system of sub-letting land by con-acre, thus increasing the population beyond the powers of the land to support'.[11] Conditions in that part of the Audley estate which lay south of Bally-dehob were undoubtedly just as bad, as would soon emerge.

By now two soup-kitchens were in operation in Skibbereen, each being guarded by a policeman. Randolf Routh, chairman of the Relief Commission, instructed William Bishop, the commissariat officer for West Cork, to open similar soup-kitchens in Schull, Crookhaven and other towns. Local subscriptions should be raised and the government would now match them with an increased grant of pound for pound.[12] These were the first soup-kitchens which could justly be described as government sponsored and were tantamount to an admission that the road-works were not very successful as relief measures. On 3 December Trevelyan had insisted that the food depots be kept closed in order to 'draw out the resources of the country before we make our own issues'.[13] On 12 December, however, Routh informed him that the Skibbereen depot had been opened three days a week with discretionary power to extend sales if necessary.[14] Still little food was actually sold, no doubt, on account of the exorbitant price. By 2 January 1847 the 121 tons of meal and 36 tons of biscuit which had been in the depot since 17 October had decreased to only 116 tons of meal and 26 tons of biscuit.[15] This surely was more hoarding.

At the end of December 1846 Skibbereen had captured the attention of the government and the public generally but the state of the people in the districts west of Skibbereen was less known. A Major Hugh Parker of the Board of Works made a tour of the west and discovered that in the parish of Schull 16,000 of its 18,000 people were in a state of 'utter destitution'; only 1,150 labourers were employed while 2,000 remained idle. Even if they could be employed it was impossible for him to say where they could obtain food. On the last day of December 1846 Major Parker sent a precise account of the prospects of the people in the west for the New Year 1847 to Colonel Jones, chairman of the Board of Works:

> A great number of people must inevitably be swept off by starvation and by diseases … Food is daily becoming scarcer and much dearer and where are future supplies to come from? Hitherto, Skibbereen … has been the peculiar object of solicitude but Schull and Kilmoe are equally as badly off; they are further removed from assistance, less noticed, have not participated in the benefit of money subscriptions, and there are no gentlemen to relieve them. Dr Traill … is exerting himself to the utmost, he employs about fifty men in his own premises in every way he can; has soup-kitchens constantly at work, sells meal at reduced prices in his own house but all will not do. Individual charity will not go far.[16]

Major Parker found that deaths were just as frequent in Kilmoe in spite of the best efforts of Richard Notter. Parker considered that it was absolutely necessary to establish a large provisions depot at Schull or Crookhaven and concluded that unless something was 'speedily done *by throwing in supplies* at a moderate price, by affording *gratuitous* relief or by affording immediate means of emigration for the most destitute, the bulk of the population must be swept off'.[17] Colonel Jones lost no time in forwarding this letter to Trevelyan. It alarmed him not only because of what was stated but because of who stated it. Here was no local clergyman or landlord who might be suspected of exaggerating local distress to attract aid; Parker was an Englishman from Yorkshire and was known to Trevelyan. Trevelyan immediately sent the letter back to Dublin to Routh together with the following instructions, dated 5 January:

> The accompanying description by Hugh Parker, of the state of the population in the remote districts to the west of Skibbereen, is the most awful I have yet seen, and it makes me as well as you, anxious to hear what progress Mr Bishop is making in his mission in that quarter, for the extension of soup-kitchens. I lament to have to express my opinion that this rude expedient of the public kitchen is the only thing which stands between multitudes of our fellow countrymen and death.[18]

Routh was highly indignant at Parker's contention that there was a shortage of food supplies and that Trevelyan should have given the claim so much credence. So Routh attempted to refute Parker's statements. Routh held that there was plenty of food in the market at Skibbereen which he claimed was only five miles from Schull; it is fourteen miles. Routh further stated that J. H. Swanton's two large mills at Skibbereen were full of meal for sale and that the depot was also open. His explanation for the famine was that 'food is not wanting but rather the money to buy it'. This was a counter attack on Parker's Board of Works which was supposed to provide employment and money. Bishop agreed with Routh and lamented that it was 'a famine in the midst of plenty' and held that there were fewer cheaper or better-supplied markets in the county than Skibbereen. He granted however that Schull received little assistance from 'the Trade' and that poor quality meal was being sold there by a small dealer for 2s 8d a stone and in Kilmoe for 2s 10d. Such was the trade of the 'gombeen man'. Thus began the food debate as to whether it was food which was lacking or the money to buy it. It was impossible for a man to support himself and his family on 8d per day when meal was up to 2s 10d a stone. Mr Hewetson, the deputy commissary general at Cork, informed Trevelyan that the merchants in Cork were said to have made up to £80,000 profit in Indian meal and wished the government would do 'something to check the extortionate prices' but supposed that they were 'according to the spirit of the trade and therefore legitimate'.[19] Relief agents differed and the people died. The Board of Work's wages of 8d per day was not that bad, especially outside of spring and harvest. The sudden increase in food prices hurt all the more because during the previous decade they had been falling at least in Cork and labourers' wages had been high, ranging from one to four shillings depending on their skill.[20] By September 1846 the price of Indian meal in this city had risen from £9 to £10 per ton and was expected soon to reach £11.[21] By the end of January 1847 it was to soar to £19 a ton as shall be seen later.

Routh ultimately blamed the landlords of the Skibbereen district. They had an annual income of £50,000. The wealthiest were Lord Carbery with £15,000, R. H. H. Becher, £4,000, Samuel Townsend of Whitehall, £2,000 and W. W. Becher, on whose lands the town of Skibbereen stood, £10,000. Routh could have added Lord Bandon, £30,000. Lord Audley's estates were, as Routh stated, in the Court of Chancery. 'Ought such destitution prevail with such resources?' he exclaimed, and then complacently assured Trevelyan, 'I dare to say we shall settle the whole of that district very well'. The response of Trevelyan was summed up in the following Treasury minute:

> It is their Lordship's desire that effective relief should be given to the inhabitants of the district in the neighbourhood of Skibbereen ... the local relief committee should be stimulated to the utmost possible exertion; soup-kitchens should be established under the management of these committees ... liberal donations should be made by the government in aid of funds raised by local subscriptions.[22]

Cecil Woodham-Smith rightly described this Treasury minute as a list of 'counsels of perfection'.[23] The word 'should' predominates but the Treasury itself took no emergency measures to deal with the situation. Next to 'should', the most revealing word is 'local'. More should be done by the local people. The lords of the Treasury did not seem to realise that it was precisely these people who were most severely hit by the famine.

There was much recrimination and shifting of responsibility. Parker thought that the government should be doing more while Trevelyan expected that the Relief Commission should be making greater efforts. But the Relief Commission's chairman, Routh, held that the local landlords and local relief committees should be exerting themselves more. In justice, it was these local relief committees which were doing most, but their brave efforts were inadequate to hold back the tide of famine. The only solution was for the government to distribute large quantities of cheap or free food and to do so speedily as Parker and also Traill and Limrick had recommended. New measures and increased effort were called for. On the first day of January 1847 the Schull relief committee was divided into two sections and so the Ballydehob relief committee came into being. Its chairman was Richard Townsend of Dunbeacon but most of the work was done by the acting chairman, Fr James Barry. The secretary and treasurer was Robert Swanton of Gortnagrough which lies between Bally-dehob and Bantry.[24]

The sheer necessity of famine relief brought women into public affairs which was still unusual in Victorian times. At the end of December 1846, a ladies' society calling itself the Cork Ladies' Relief Society was founded in Cork. It was affiliated to the British Ladies' Association from which it received subscriptions. The secretary of the new society was Anna Maria Lee who called on the ladies of each parish to set up their own relief associations and encourage their members to collect subscriptions from absentee landlords and to plant their own gardens not with potatoes but with parsnips and carrots.[25] It was in this spirit that the Ballydehob Ladies' Association was formed on the first of January 1847. Its secretary and treasurer was a local lady, Jane Noble. The new association soon gave relief in food and clothing to 130 families.[26]

With the notable exception of the Society of Friends the most powerful voluntary relief organisation of all was founded in London on the first of January 1847. This was the 'British Relief Association for the relief of extreme distress in the remote parishes of Ireland and Scotland', which became known as the 'British Relief Association'; it had something of the spirit of the London Tavern Committee of 1822. The chairman of the British Relief Association was a prominent corn merchant, Thomas Baring. Other founder members were merchants, such as Baron Lionel de Rothschild, a member of that famous banking family and J. J. Cummins, a banker; Mr Pim, secretary of the relief committee of the Society of Friends, attended meetings and advised. Nicholas Marshal Cummins of Glanmire was involved in the setting up of this association. Another Nicholas Cummins, a cousin, was secretary of the association. The sum of £10,000 was soon contributed from merchant princes and bankers such as Barings, Rothschilds, Lloyds and some others who gave a thousand pounds each as did also the Duke of Devonshire; Lord John Russell added £300.[27] From the very beginning the British Relief Association discovered the right formula for efficient relief; grants would be given in food and not in money and this food would be 'exclusively for gratuitous relief'. This association immediately saw that 'what was wanted was food and more especially CHEAP FOOD and that there was no absolute want of money'. Accordingly the British Relief Association promptly bought corn and shipped it to depots in Ireland. The British Rail Association provided free transport for relief supplies. Admiral Pigot, who commanded the navy around the Irish coast, was instructed by the government to provide every assistance by way of ships, stores, etc.[28] The ships that were made available to the British Relief Association amounted to a virtual fleet of 44 ships, weighing 27,523 tons, with 7,943 horse-power and carrying a crew of 2,660 men. Five other ships were also made available by private shipping companies in England.[29]

The British Association soon collected many subscriptions including £2,000 from Queen Victoria, £1,000 each from the Duke of Devonshire and Charles

Wood. In January 'a speedy shipment' of flour and peas left London for the south-west coast of Ireland on board the *H.M.S. Dragon*, 1,270 tons, but its progress was soon delayed by a violent gale. The ship did not reach Cobh until ten days later but could proceed no further because its engines were in a disabled condition. The British Relief Association's agent for the south-west coast, Captain Harston, delivered some of the cargo to Crookhaven by means of another boat loaned from the coast-guards. A revenue steamer, *H.M.S. Vulcan*, delivered ten tons of meal at Crookhaven directly from London on behalf of the British Relief Association.[30]

The delay caused to the *Dragon* was unfortunate. Dr McCormick reported that there was not a morsel of food in Crookhaven and none could be obtained from Cork or Skibbereen except poor quality meal at an inflated price. 'The further west you go the greater the distress,' the doctor lamented. He complained that the people in the west received little aid because 'Skibbereen absorbs it all'. Deaths were now seven a day while one hundred had already died. The few gentry in the area had received very little in rents so there were no subscriptions for a soup-kitchen. This doctor had often found entire families unable to move with fever, and even 'the dead, the dying and the living in the same bed'. He protested that all that the people of Crookhaven knew of the workhouse in Skibbereen was its taxation.[31] The priests of Kilmoe parish, L. O'Sullivan and T. Barrett, were described by R. Notter of Rock Island as 'indefatigable in their exertions'.[32] All these deaths occurred in spite of the best efforts of the local relief committees which soon began to give out soup. A subscription of £25 came through W. A Fisher. James McMullen of the Southern and Western Mining Company gave £8. Dr McCormick, Fr Barrett and a Richard Hull of Cork subscribed £2 each. Many small subscriptions brought the total to £80 for which a corresponding grant of £8 was paid by the government.[33] Around this time also Dr Murphy, Catholic Bishop of Cork, gave a subscription of £20. The total subscribed on this occasion was £105 for which Routh gave a grant of pound for pound.[34] The next list of subscriptions included £10 from Lord Bandon and another £10 from R. Notter's cousin, Thomas Deane, the famous architect, then building Queen's College, Cork. Although this list totalled only £64, Routh now gave a grant of £100 as he had been just authorised by Trevelyan to grant more than pound for pound in cases of dire necessity.[35] McCormick considered that nothing could 'depict as miserable a condition as the deserted state of our house of worship', i.e., the Protestant church at Crookhaven. A few months earlier the attendance was 400 but it fell to as low as 50 and then further to 21. He cited from the sermon of their clergyman, probably Fisher:

> I do not know but there is one lying dead *now* at my house, the third that was brought in to be a corpse within the last ten days. I was yesterday through the parish; it was shocking to see the infants dying on the breasts of their mothers, as they had no nourishment to afford them. And the children who were fine and plump a few months since, now nothing but sinew and bone, with their eyes larger than their sockets.

McCormick asked a woman why she had not buried her husband but she replied, 'The coffin was buried the other day and I had no one to put him into the earth'.³⁶ She was of course referring to 'a hinged, sliding, or trap coffin' thus called because the base was on hinges like a door which opened and allowed the corpse to drop into the grave so that the coffin could be used again.³⁷

The conditions in Kilmoe were paralleled in Schull as Traill announced to the country. He was concerned not only about the Catholic population but also about the Protestant one which he described as 'one of the largest rural ones in the kingdom and amounting to 2,000 souls and one of the most miserable and impoverished that can be conceived'. Traill was thankful that no Protestant had yet died but lamented that Catholics were dying 'at a rate of twenty-five daily, and hourly increasing'.³⁸ Dr Sweetnam was now finding 'three or four dying almost together in every cabin and dropping on the roads and the ditches'. He was sorry to have to tell J. Limrick that all his great exertions for relief were but 'a drop in the ocean, if some gigantic measure of relief is not immediately carried out by the government'.³⁹ At this stage the middle of January 1847, it was painfully obvious to many that no matter what efforts were made through the relief measures or by private charity they would be inadequate to cope with such a large-scale famine. State intervention on a vast scale was an urgent necessity.

All through this month of January 1847 hungry men tried to work on the roads under harsh weather conditions. This was fatal for some as was reported by Jeremiah O'Callaghan of the Cork Examiner who visited the Ballydehob district:

> A poor man named John Coughlan from Kilbronoge … was on his way to one of these new roads, that lead to nothing save death, when he fell from exhaustion and … was numbered with the other victims of the Board of Works … I enquired of James Wolfe, who is the head overseer on the road, whether he supposed his death was occasioned by starvation and he told me he had no doubt of it, and moreover this was the fifth who met a similar fate on that road since 14 November! So much for the life-saving Board of Works! Death here is multiplying – the total extermination of the labouring classes is inevitable. Lord Russell looks on with folded arms while her Majesty's Irish subjects are dropping in hundreds.⁴⁰

Four men had also died as a result of working on the roads in Kilcoe.⁴¹ A week later O'Callaghan visited Ballydehob again and continued his condemnation of the relief measures of the Board of Works. He blamed the foreign government and declared that Ireland could have 'no salvation without the paternal solicitude of the native government'. Although this repealer was already politicising the famine there can be no doubt that road-making was failing as a means of relief. The Protestant curate of Ballydehob, John Triphook, told of another man who had died of starvation although employed on the roads.⁴² James Barry wrote that a man returning home from the roads was so weak that he collapsed and drowned in a pool of water. Out of 100 such persons, 17 had to be supported on their way home by their fellow labourers.⁴³ On Cape Clear the labourers were so weak that when they met a hill or *leaca* they had to go down on all fours and walk like an animal. The curate, Fr Fenton, regretted that some people had to steal sheep and geese.[44] The frequency of death on the roads gave rise to a new expression 'road sickness'. Indeed a new disease was even suspected since the bodies of two men who had died on the road near Ballydehob were exhumed for inquest. It was no new disease; a doctor diagnosed it simply as dropsy caused by starvation.[45]

From the middle of January 1847 onwards the main hope of the starving people was the soup-kitchen. More men would have died on the road near Ballydehob only for J. H. Swanton's soup-kitchen.[46] It was to set up a soup-kitchen that the Schull relief committee was now gathering subscriptions. Its secretary, J. Limrick, sent a list of subscriptions to Routh which amounted to £92. Nearly half of this had been given by the Quakers, Joshua and Abraham Beale. Routh paid the corresponding grant of £140.[47] Ten days later Limrick sent another list with subscriptions totaling £83, of which £50 came per Traill. Routh awarded a grant of £100.[48] At this stage it was difficult for a relief committee to obtain food and even more difficult to store it safely. This Schull committee succeeded in buying two tons of meal and two tons of biscuit from the depot in Skibbereen but its store in Schull was broken into and most of the biscuit stolen.[49]

In Aughadown parish the vicar, Archdeacon Stuart, chairman of the relief committee, appealed to Anna Maria Lee of the Cork Ladies' Association for money, food and clothing. He had a list of 1,900 persons who needed aid although one-fifth of them were working on the roads. The vicar was glad that deaths from actual starvation were not common but saw that fever was 'hurrying to eternity hundreds'. The soup-kitchen gave out 1,440 pints of soup daily, a quantity which was 'quite insufficient' but subscriptions would not allow any more.[50]

Even when Limrick was able to obtain food in Skibbereen, he found it difficult to transport it to Schull because of the sixteen miles of very bad road. Furthermore the long-continued easterly wind prevented him from sending a ship to Cork.[51] This wind had the deadly double effect of delaying food supplies and of hastening mortality, especially among the men working on the road. J. H. Swanton, received subscriptions from English firms some of which were engaged in the corn trade. This was welcomed by the *Southern Reporter* as 'English mercantile generosity' but, of course, the corn merchants were making enormous profits from the famine. Some of this money was given to the Ballydehob Ladies' Association whose members visited poor widows and women near their confinement. This seems to be the only reference to any special help given to pregnant women although infant mortality was appallingly high.

The main hope of the starving people lay in the workhouse at Skibbereen. Although it had been built to take only 800 inmates, by early January 1847 it held 1,169 of whom 332 were in fever. The fever hospital built for 40 persons now held 80 and patients were pushed out into the stables. From the 10 October 1846 to 7 January 1847, deaths in the workhouse amounted to 266. Several of the staff were down with fever; the nurse and the apothecary had resigned but Dr Donovan persevered in his duty. The house was £1,300 in debt and £1,680 was due in rates which were impossible to collect. Food was so expensive that the guardians had to raise a loan of £1,000 on their own personal security. 'In this awful crisis with a house full to suffocation, surrounded by an atmosphere of pestilence', the guardians informed the lord lieutenant that they were forced to close the doors against further admissions and appealed to him for aid.[52] The inherent weakness, if not contradiction, of the government relief measures was that much of their cost was to be borne locally, i.e., by the very districts which were least able to afford it. This principle may have worked satisfactorily in the case of ordinary poverty but in famine conditions the principle was pushed to a *reductio ad absurdum*. For example Joseph Driscoll, the collector of poor rates, knocked at the door of Patrick Regan of Rossbrin demanding the rates. There being no answer he pushed in the door and found the man, his wife and son apparently dead. He fled the scene and reported the matter to the Board of Guardians. James Barry soon visited the house and discovered that the man was still alive though looking more like a corpse. His wife was on the point of death and died immediately; their son had been dead for five days.[53] It was largely on such people as Patrick Regan that the inmates of the workhouse depended for support.

As dreadful as the workhouse was many like Dr McCormick of Crookhaven envied Skibbereen because of it. Still there was no need for such envy because the house acted only as a 'magnet for misery', as Rev. R. B. Townsend of Abbeystrowry, exclaimed. He pointed out that the 'scum of the destitution of all the surrounding parishes' was thrown upon the unfortunate town. Fever was raging in it and they feared that they would all fall victims. J. H. Swanton, gave a vivid description of these people as they plodded their weary way to the workhouse which was then actually closed; 'I saw some groups of families today crawling towards the workhouse, whose appearance almost broke my heart – fine frames, decent, well-conducted people – but actually starved into the workhouse and out of their own houses. One or two in particular were crying silently, as they moved silently along'.[54]

At the end of January 1847 William Bishop, went on a tour of inspection of West Carbery and reported to Routh. He found that distress was even greater around Ballydehob than around Schull, there being only one soup-kitchen in Ballydehob, that of J. H. Swanton. Mr Bishop gave donations towards this and urged that another be set up. He saw that there were 3,000 distressed people at Dunmanus in Kilmoe parish, and no soup-kitchen at all. He persuaded a local landlord, Mr Callaghan of Rock Cottage, to undertake to superintend one. The two soup-kitchens in Aughadown were at Newcourt under Lionel Fleming and at the glebe house under Archdeacon Stuart. They were supported by private funds and were 'conducted with great care and discrimination'. In Kilcoe a soup-kitchen had been established since September 1846. It was efficiently run by the vicar, Rev. James Freke and by J. H. Swanton. At Ballydehob Bishop found that there was a ladies' association:

doing much good at a great personal sacrifice and upon a very limited fund. These ladies visit the cabins where the worse cases of fever and sickness prevail and by judicious distribution of nourishment and clothing, have doubtless, been instrumental in saving many lives.

There was a total of twenty-six soup-kitchens in West Carbery, of which nine, or over one-third, were in the Mizen Peninsula. Schull, Crookhaven and Aughadown had two each; Skibbereen, Ballydehob, Dunmanus and Kilcoe had one each. New supplies were promised from a ship which was a floating depot. It had just left Castletownbere where it had been weather-bound and arrived in Schull harbour. The *Dragon* had not yet reached Crookhaven as its engines were not repaired. This seriously delayed relief operations because she carried not only food but also soup-boilers. Finally Bishop was forced to admit that 'great and unquestionable as are the benefits which the soup-kitchens bestow, it is but as a drop in the ocean. Hundreds are relieved but thousands still want.'[55]

Bishop was correct in stating that the famine was now at its worst not in Schull, nor in Crookhaven nor even in Skibbereen but in and around Ballydehob. The worst parts of this stricken area were not in the town itself but out in the country, beside the sea in the village of Kilbronoge, for example. This townland of Kilbronoge had a very dense population because extra large quantities of sea-manure made possible the intensive cultivation of the potato with the result that a village or clachan had grown up. The proximity of the Audley mines, now closed, must have helped this development. Little or no relief had yet reached the mountainous areas or isolated headlands like Kilbronoge. James Barry told of a visit to what he called the 'village of Kilbronoge' at the end of January 1847:

> I am sorry to be obliged to state that fever consequent upon starvation is rapidly spreading and widely, so much so that in some clusters of cabins along the sea shore, and in the recesses of the mountains half the wretched population will in a few weeks be swept away. This is no exaggeration … On this day, I attended five adults. Seven corpses lay there four or five days without interment not through any unwillingness about committing them to the earth without coffins but the want of help to move them. There are in this field of death I allude to, sixty-seven houses – rather hovels – surely not three of them are free from disease … I have instanced but one townland, which is the most afflicted for there are several others in nearly as deplorable a state – this will, it seems, be soon at the immediate disposal of the head landlord, Lord Bandon. There will be no need of extermination or of migration to thin the dense swarm of poor people that were crowded into it; this will take place without his lordship's intervention or agency, I hope to a better world.[56]

At this time, the end of January 1847, O'Callaghan of the *Cork Examiner* also visited Kilbronoge and described it as a 'perfect charnel-house' with a corpse in almost every cabin. He concluded that in 'a few weeks all the inhabitants of this graveyard-village will disappear'. He was quite correct. The village itself disappeared; it died in the famine and became its own graveyard. One notes how O'Callaghan accused Lord John Russell and Fr Barry charged Lord

Bandon of conniving at the extermination not so much of the Irish people but of the labouring classes. Conditions were clearly just as bad in the lands of the resident and 'improving' Lord Bandon as on those of the absentee and negligent Audley. Fr Troy of Aughadown found that conditions were similar in some of the cabins of his parish. He took a coffin to one of them to bury a man who had been dead for six days but discovered that his wife and three children were too weak to help him to coffin the putrid corpse so he had to call his curate.[57]

The repealers were not the only people who were being disillusioned with the relief measures of parliament; even the landlords were disappointed. They felt that they had not been properly consulted on the Labour Rate Act although it was they who would have to pay for the resulting road-works. They were being accused of neglecting their duty by the English Whig government that had little love for them as Irish Tory landlords. It was this attitude that rendered them more open to the call by Daniel O'Connell to associate with the repealers on a non-political basis in order to make a stronger demand in parliament for more aid for Ireland. The ailing Liberator pleaded with the landlords that he was not trying 'to involve them in agitation for repeal by any trick … but simply if they can do anything to save the people without repeal, I will go with them'. His plan was to persuade the government to give Ireland a loan of thirty or forty million pounds in order 'to ransack the world for food and buy it at any price'. This was by no means an unreasonable request, he maintained, as twenty million pounds of public money had already been given as free grants for the emancipation of the Negro slaves. He would support neither Whig nor Tory as such, but whoever would grant most aid to Ireland. 'In fact,' he admitted, 'I go to parliament as a food man'. Referring to his own constituency of County Cork, the Protestant clergy of the fourteen parishes of the city deanery informed him that 5,000 had already died of starvation in their parishes, that 10,000 were actually dying and that a quarter of the labourers was already dead. He was also told that 'one-fourth of the inhabitants of a district in the neighbourhood of Skibbereen are in their graves'. 'Why, this is horrible!' he exclaimed; 'I cannot – I cannot go on. My blood freezes – the tears rush to my eyes – I am unmanned.' He burst into tears and was unable to continue for some time.[58] This district in the neighbourhood of Skibbereen may well have been Ballydehob because there were reports later on that a quarter of the people had died there.

O'Connell's call to the landlords did not go completely unheeded. They held an important meeting in Dublin on 14 January 1847 that was attended by many landowners including Lord Bandon. They considered that the famine was not simply a local one but one 'imperial calamity' and therefore the cost of relieving it should not be a local charge but should be borne by the imperial exchequer alone. This meeting, which consisted of as many as eighty-three peers and members of parliament, formed themselves into the 'Irish Party' and pledged themselves to support this policy in parliament. On the previous day the Young Irelanders, now finally broken from O'Connell, had held the first meeting of their new 'Irish Confederation'. O'Shea Lawlor of Bantry, who had crossed words with the Liberator at Skibbereen, was prominent at the meeting. Even John Mitchel showed that he had hope that the landlords would reform and accept repeal.[59]

This was the general climate of social and even political reconciliation that prevailed in the country when a meeting was held in Skibbereen on 15 January 1847 to petition parliament for greater famine relief. Like previous famine meetings it was attended by persons of all creeds and classes; what distinguished it was that now politics was discussed – a subject which usually caused division and was hitherto carefully avoided. There were 1,084 inmates in the workhouse and there had been even more but some were now dead. Rev. R. B. Townsend was convinced that the relief measures were intended for the benefit of the corn merchants of England rather than of the people of Ireland and blamed Lord John Russell for allowing it. He condemned the relief measures as producing famine and repeating it. These measures resulted in only 'blinding the eyes and sealing the ears' of the English public against the Irish people. While in England on a deputation he discovered that the ordinary people there thought that the loans under the Labour Rate Act were free grants of money. They bluntly told him that his people had work but were still begging. Townsend supported the motion that 'the burden arising from the unexpected national calamity should not be placed upon the locally afflicted, but shall be borne by the nation at large'. He stated that making the union of Skibbereen find its own means of relief was like 'telling the paupers to provide for themselves out of their own purse'.

The next speaker, Lionel Fleming, praised the relief measures of Peel as compared to those of Russell. He thought that the Irish people deserved better because they were prepared to shed their blood for the honour of the English nation. The last admission ticket to the workhouse he had issued was to a man from Kilcoe who had endured harsh captivity in Kabul while fighting with the British army in Afghanistan. Lionel Fleming had asked how many fields were being tilled in Kilmoe and was told that the 'only red field in Kilmoe was the graveyard'. Timothy McCarthy Downing regretted that *The Times* should be accusing the Irish landlords of taking advantage of the famine to clear their estates of people. 'We never thought of the like,' Becher interjected. McCarthy Downing was enthused by the formation of the Irish Party and hoped that the 'Glorious Era of 1782' was returning. Francis Webb, rector of Caheragh, was more realistic and down to earth. He remarked that there was now 'an awful mode of emigration – emigration to the next world, without even the expense of a coffin'.

Traill told the meeting how he had taken the liberty to address Lord John Russell. The rector promised Russell that if the government provided seed he would see to it that it was planted and not eaten, but he replied that although the government had thought of providing seed, it was considered 'impolitic' to do so. Traill lamented that if the government did not change its mind there would not be a single seed sown in parts of his parish. The landlords had told him that although their tenants had no seed they still would not give up the land. This implied that some landlords, at least, were putting pressure on their tenants to give up their lands, thus taking advantage of the famine. Traill's motion was that the government should help to supply seed for all and this was seconded by Becher who went on to declare his own willingness to join the 'Irish Party'. The resolutions of the meeting were to be put to parliament by Viscount Bernard of Bandon and by O'Connell.[60] These resolutions as well as the petition to the queen were an accurate expression of the hopes and fears of the people of the peninsula as they turned towards parliament opening at the end of January 1847.

O'Connell left Derrynane to plead in parliament for the people. It has been seen how the various groups and public bodies were blaming one another for the terrible state of the country. Nevertheless the final responsibility had to rest somewhere; it lay in parliament particularly in the hands of Lord John Russell. O'Connell warned the people about what to expect:

> If individual generosity could save a nation British generosity would do it now; but it is impossible without the bountiful hand of parliament and the disposition of bounty of parliament appears to be extremely limited. I am bound to forewarn the people of Ireland, that, in my judgment parliament is not disposed to go far enough – that there will not be sufficient relief given by the parliament – and that it will not be until after the deaths of hundreds of thousands that the regret will arise that more was not done to save the sinking nation. How different would the scene be if we had our own parliament – taking care of our own people – of our own resources. But Alas! Alas![61]

The Liberator's feelings of hopelessness and helplessness were understandable. Any meeting of any 'Irish Party' consisting of Conservatives and/or of repealers would be powerless; it could pass only resolutions and send petitions but not pass acts of parliament. In justice to the parliament which had passed the Labour Rate Act the previous August 1846, it was not easy to foresee that the failure of the potato crop would have quite such terrible consequences. Nonetheless it was now clear to many, even to John Russell, that this act was a failure as a relief measure. Accordingly he presented a new scheme to parliament on 25 January 1847, 'The Temporary Relief of Destitute Persons Act' which became known as the Soup Kitchen Act. This was to aid the people only until September when the harvest would come in and new relief acts take over. The emphasis was as much on 'temporary' as on 'relief'. A loan of £1,724,631 was given and would have to be repaid out of the poor rate. New relief committees were to be formed which would distribute soup gratuitously. Road works were to close down gradually thus giving farmers and labourers a better opportunity to till the soil for the spring. The Treasury now conceded that as soon as the first half of the debt due on the roads was paid it would forgive the remainder.

The Soup Kitchen Act would be financed mainly from the local rates and also from private subscriptions, which would be increased by government donations as previously. Each union was to have a financial committee and an inspecting officer who would act as a means of communication between the union and the Relief Commission in Dublin. A new Relief Commission was now appointed, its chairman was Sir John Burgoyne, Inspector General of Fortifications in Great Britain; Randolph Routh, the former chairman, was demoted and was now an ordinary member. The other members were, Edward Twistleton, the Poor Law commissioner, Colonel Jones, chairman of the Board of Works, Duncan McGregor, chief of the constabulary, and Thomas Redington, the under-secretary.[62]

Those who had hoped to persuade parliament that the famine was an imperial calamity, deserving imperial sources of relief, received an answer from the Radical MP for Bath, Mr Roebuck. The very principle of giving out-door relief to the poor was anathema and it was condemned as 'demoralising'. Roebuck asserted in parliament early in February 1847 that the famine was not an imperial calamity and that therefore it should be borne by the residents of Ireland. He held that, apart from education, the government had done all that a government could do and should do for Ireland. The Irish people had as rich a soil and were as intelligent as the English, he said; all they lacked was 'that single quality of moral courage and self-reliance', which they should acquire and then rival England, instead of being an 'abject spectacle'. The Irish people were defended by Viscount Bernard who deplored that Mr Roebuck should have satisfied himself with economic doctrine while people were dying of famine. Bernard quoted the following from a letter addressed to him by Traill: 'In my opinion no human efforts can keep us alive. Two days ago, three uncoffined bodies were brought in one cart and thrown in a hole.' Bernard warned the House of the inadequacy of the Labour Rate Act and the consequent high mortality among road-workers. As an illustration of this, he quoted from a letter he had received from Crookhaven: 'Every day the relief committee meet they have to fill up vacancies in the lists of those employed on the public road, so insufficient is the rate of pay given to sustain life at the present exorbitant price of food'. Bernard blamed Trevelyan for allowing the corn merchants to charge such prices. He told the government that its 'greatest error' was the breaking up of the food depots established by Robert Peel. Even in the remote areas which the government had promised to supply with relief, it was 'tardy and indeed ... hardly felt until the present time'. He proved this tardiness by citing the example of Schull where a floating depot was so slow to arrive. It had been requested by Bishop on 3 December 1846, granted by Trevelyan on 15 December and he did not know whether it had yet arrived, i.e., by 3 February 1847.[63] (It had just arrived as shall be seen later.) It was thus through Bernard that the cries of the people of the district reached the ears of parliament. As regards communications, however, it was a long way from parish to parliament and as regards famine relief it was going to be long way from parliament to parish. Bernard however was not the only man to protest about the tardiness of the relief measures. Fr Laurence O'Sullivan of Kilmoe informed the public that 'the average mortality caused by famine which is now raging in my parish amounts to nearly 100 *per week* ... and is rapidly on the increase'. He was convinced that 'the tardy relief contemplated by government, will not in all probability come into operation before some weeks, until some additional hundreds have been added to the victims that have been already sacrificed'.[64] So he went on a fund-raising mission to Cork as shall be seen in Chapter XI.

The most passionate appeal of all on behalf of the Irish people must surely have been the dying parliamentary words of the tottering Liberator now reduced to being a mere 'food man': 'Ireland is in your hands … If you do not save her she cannot save herself. And I solemnly call on you to recollect that I predict with the sincerest conviction that a quarter of her people will perish unless you come to her relief'.[65] This parliamentary session was not a successful one for the new Irish Party or for the repealers. They split over the Irish Railway Bill introduced by the Protectionist leader, Lord Bentinck.[66] The Irish members failed utterly to persuade parliament that the famine was an imperial calamity which should be relieved from imperial resources. The only imperial money available was a small loan which would be given to a union to set up a soup-kitchen.

Those involved in the relief effort in the district organised themselves according to the stipulations of the Soup Kitchen Act. The financial officer for the Skibbereen Union was a Thomas Gibbons. New relief committees do not seem to have been established as such but the Ballydehob relief committee did form itself into a 'soup committee'. The officers remained the same; James Barry was acting chairman for the nominal chairman, Richard Townsend of Dunbeacon and the secretary and treasurer was Robert Swanton of Gortnagrough. There was a large and very representative committee however, which included John Triphook, the Protestant curate, John Barry, the Catholic curate and his brother, Richard. Other members were Protestant farmers such as T. Atteridge, P. Willis and W. Shannon, and also Catholic farmers such as Charles Regan and Andrew Caverly. The two miners, William Thomas, his brother Charles and J. H. Swanton were also members. This committee applied to Bishop and to Captain Harston of the British Relief Association for a boiler to contain 400 gallons of soup. The committee received £30 which had been transferred from the Schull committee and also £20 from Bishop John Murphy of Cork via Fr Barry. A donation of £10 from J. H. Swanton and some other contributions brought the total to £81.[67]

J. H. Swanton sent this list of subscriptions to the new Relief Commission together with another list of £146 from the Kilcoe relief committee of which he was treasurer. He ended his letter on a note of despair: 'things are getting worse every day, I don't know what will become of us … I cannot leave my post with a clear conscience'.[68] He had more reason to despair when the Relief Commission replied that his acting on two committees was irregular and refused to pay any grant. This miller indignantly explained that some people were members of both committees because part of Kilcoe parish was being relieved by the Ballydehob relief committee. He added that if he and others had to comply with all the formalities they might as well 'give up'. He then asked Bishop to urge his claim for the grants as he was prepared to do any-thing for the 'dying thousands' and was grateful to him for a boiler he had promptly sent to Ballydehob.[69] Both grants were eventually paid and corre-sponded to the subscriptions pound for pound.[70] Rev. John Triphook had a private fund of £190, to which Lord Bandon had given £5 and Quakers £13 per Rev. James Freke, vicar of Kilcoe. The Relief Commission gave the corres-ponding grant of £190.[71] In the middle of February the funds of the Ballyde-hob Soup Committee consisted of £123, which was considered very low as it had to feed 'a starving population of six or seven thousand'. The committee, therefore, asked Routh to use his influence with the commission to obtain unconditional grants because the people were 'daily perishing with hunger'.[72]

On 1 February the Skibbereen relief committee gave a gloomy report on the state of the union to the Relief commissioners in Dublin. A soup-kitchen had been opened as early as 27 October. The commissariat depot had been 'nominally' open since 10 December but Col Hughes insisted that 5 tons per week was the most that could be issued for the entire district. Richard Notter of Kilmoe had applied for 10 tons but could obtain only 2 tons although 'his district was destitute of food and that 20 people had died the previous day'. The price of meal had been raised from £18 to £19 a ton at the Skibbereen and Berehaven depots. As for the ratepayers, 'Some are in the workhouse – some dead – some have emigrated – others are employed on the public works. On entering the houses of many ratepayers, they found the corpses of the tenants.' Arrears were over £1,400 although for the previous four-and-a-half years (i.e., since the beginning of the workhouse) they had been only £134. Dysentery raged to an even greater extent than fever. The number of cases of these dis-eases was 700 and increasing; 49 new cases were entered in the book for 1 Feb-ruary. This 'famine pestilence in its double form' prevailed in every parish in the union and 'has caused everywhere a mortality in proportion to destitu-tion'. Dr Donovan held that fever could not be checked except by clean cloth-ing and food. The average mortality per day was estimated at 25 for Schull; in Kilmoe 20 died on one day and 18 on another. In the workhouse itself 46 died in one week and on 30 January alone 16 died. So the committee asked, 'Why should the unfed, unclothed, unsheltered and unattended poor outside its walls, be more fortunate?' Numbers of them had sought admission but were refused on account of the crowded state of the house. This committee had no way of ascertaining the mortality in the district but claimed that deaths 'should be numbered in thousands'.[73]

This state of affairs is corroborated by the administrator of Skibbereen, John Fitzpatrick, in one of his many letters to the *Tablet*, the leading English Cat-holic newspaper. He told how 'the aged, the infirm, the blind, the lame, the hun-gry, the starving, the dying creatures are every hour flocking into the town, with a hope of obtaining an asylum in the workhouse, of procuring a little food'. In spite of 'the great mortality' he considered that the population of the town had increased by nearly one thousand. Bodies were not buried at all or coffinless in the next field and 'no regret expressed'. Their only concern was 'bread, bread! food, food!'[74] As parliament deliberated people died. 'My parish,' Traill lamented in biblical language, 'is verily an *Aceldama*, a field of death, if not a field of blood'. Thirty-five people were dying every day.[75] This was February; we have seen that the death rate in the parish for January had been 'only' twenty-five a day.

In the middle of this month of February significant supplies of food arrived in the peninsula from the British Relief Association. It was disappointing that the long-awaited *Dragon* never arrived at Crookhaven because her crew objected and she went on to Castletownbere. The men probably heard that there was dysentery at Crookhaven as this disease had now spread to some of the relief ships. However, Captain Harston of the British Relief Association did call at Crookhaven in a small revenue steamer and delivered 100 tons of rice at various places between that town and Myross, a parish near Rosscarbery. He called at Ballydehob and found that the funds of the relief committee would not allow it to buy the provisions intended for the area; still he gave it the provisions. He met the Ballydehob Ladies' Association and saw that these ladies were 'personally cognisant for miles around of the individual state of the inhabitants in cottages scattered far and wide'. The ladies had £30 with which they wanted to buy food from him but he gave them £50 worth of food *gratis* and suggested that they spend their funds on clothes instead. Indeed it was a combination of starvation and exposure which was weakening the people and rendering them easy victims for the next and greatest enemy, namely fever. People were also asking for soup boilers.[76]

In the midst of all this famine there was still food around but it was stored in the depots. It is strange that Bishop could calmly state: 'Throughout east and west Schull and Kilmoe the average mortality has daily increased since my last visit. Disease has too firm a hold to be checked by food, of which Crookhaven has an abundant store and there is a well-supplied depot for east and west Schull.' A few days later *H.M.S. Zephyr* landed one load of rice at Crookhaven and another at Schull.[77] On 29 January Bishop informed Trevelyan that 'the floating depot for Schull arrived yesterday and has commenced issues; that removes all anxiety for that quarter'.[78] She was a lighter, *H.M.S. Devon*, 50 tons and anchored in Long Island Sound, but there was some unreasonable delay in getting the food into the mouths of the people. Bishop seems to have been the only one who saw no further need for anxiety. John Triphook protested that 'there lies at anchor a government lighter filled to the bends with Indian meal and the people are thus dropping off on all sides with hunger'. He held that such a light ship could have easily landed her cargo directly as there were good harbours nearby.[79]

A similar protest about this sort of delay in actually distributing the food comes from the miner, Captain Thomas. According to him the *H.M.S. Rhadamanthus* landed a cargo of bread-stuffs from the British Relief Association at the coast-guard station in Rock Island but the officer there, Captain Baldwin, was not allowed to distribute it. Only a few bags of flour were sent to Goleen at 2s 3d a stone. Captain Thomas compared the famine around him to that of

Jerusalem while besieged by the Romans in 70 AD. 'But here,' he contrasted, 'in a Christian country – in a time of profound peace, people are perishing like dogs and their bodies allowed to remain the prey to rats – causing pestilence and death to ravage the land.' 'If the people could get food at moderate prices,' he held, 'they will be able to live, but they cannot live by political economy.'[80] The treasurer of the Kilmoe relief committee, Richard Notter of Rock Island, told how the hungry people were now becoming 'a prey to fever, dysentery and other diseases and are dropping like the blasted leaves off an October tree'. Entire families were found together in fever, dead and dying; all that the neighbours would do was to place a jug of water outside the cabins so that the inmates would crawl out and get it. The relief committee had two 'coffins with sliding bottoms' to carry the corpses to the graveyard, some had remained unburied for up to nine days. This task was done by gangs of men who were ordered to leave their work on the road.[81] Dr Sweetnam stated that very many deaths were not directly due to starvation but to fever. The victims had an insatiable thirst. They would tell him that they could drink the river dry.[82] 'We are,' the doctor sighed, 'broken in mind, body and state.'[83]

Rev. Webb, of Caheragh published in the press an account of how the bodies of a woman and six children were left unburied only to be eaten by dogs and asked in disbelief, 'Are we living in a portion of the United Kingdom?' Bishop sent the newspaper cutting of this to Trevelyan but also enclosed with it a letter from the miller, J. H. Swanton, reporting that he had up to 200 tons of Indian meal and other flour but that he had difficulty in disposing of it as the Skibbereen relief committee was selling meal *indiscriminately* for as little as 2s 2d a stone. If the government bought his meal, Swanton bargained, it would save him 'the freight of shipping it to another market'. Bishop pointed out that this meal was within *two* miles of Caheragh and asked indignantly, 'May we not conclude with the rector, "Are we living in a portion of the United Kingdom?"'[84] The answer to that question is that they certainly were and that Swanton was only acting according to the principles of *laissez-faire* and responding to market forces – what Trevelyan himself was calling 'the spirit of the trade'.

At this time, the middle of February 1847, Bishop went on a special tour of inspection of the district and gave his official and yet vivid report to Trevelyan:

At Schull I found the distress or rather the mortality had greatly increased ... between Ballydehob and Crookhaven, the population is so scattered that it is difficult to find out where disease exists. When fever attacks the inhabitants of a cabin, the nearest relative of the party attacked will not assist them – no persuasion will induce them to enter a cabin where fever is, though it may contain a parent or child. Thus many die from positive neglect, and the bodies are allowed to rot upon the straw from dread of contagion. None but strangers hired by the clergy will assist in the burial ... it is very difficult to ascertain correctly the amount of mortality. The clergymen admit that they can give but a very imperfect estimate; many die without their knowledge, the Church rites being now disregarded ... Relations saying 'better times will come when they will be able to get a coffin and Church rites for the bones'. This imperfect interment may lead to alarming results when the hot weather sets in. In the parish of Kilmoe, I found ... that fever, dysentery and consequent death have greatly increased; the poor people have no stamina left to sustain disease; the moment they are attacked, they, without any effort, give themselves up to what they term 'their fate' – they resignedly say, 'tis the will of God' and die. The relief committee at Schull exert themselves greatly to benefit the poor. There is an ample supply of provisions in each place.[85]

Once again we are told of an 'ample' supply of provisions amid such terrible scenes of famine. It is no wonder that the early historian of the famine, Canon John O'Rourke, who had visited the district, asked in 1875, 'How did they manage to die of starvation in Schull? ... yet they did and at Ballydehob too.'[86] What did Bishop mean by 'ample'? It is obvious that it was not 'ample' to feed the people but perhaps it was 'ample' for the little money they and the relief committee had to pay for it. Or was it that there was not enough food in these depots even if the people had the money to buy it? We are fortunate that some light will be thrown on that question and that the whole situation will be illustrated for us, not only in words but in drawings from the hand of a visiting artist, James Mahoney of the *Illustrated London News* which had just been founded in 1842 – the world's first illustrated newspaper.[87]

In the middle of February 1847, Mahoney visited West Cork. At Skibbereen he drew some sketches one of which shows the miserable Old Chapel Lane where a coffin is being shouldered with few mourners around. Mahoney then went on to Ballydehob which he sketched with Mount Gabriel in the background and the pound in the foreground. The water is that of Roaringwater Bay. On the left is the chapel and we just get a glimpse of the National School nearby. On the right is the Church of Ireland church. Most of the houses have two storeys and are covered with slate from the Audley quarries. Nevertheless, at the side of Griffith's new road and beyond the bridge, we must also

Old Chapel Lane, Skibbereen, 1847

Ballydehob, 1847

Schull, 1847

notice the row of single-roomed, windowless, thatched mud cabins the like of which were to be found at the ends of towns and villages. The artist met J. Trip-hook who told him that anybody who could command £5 was abandoning the place and emigrating for fear of fever and the appalling scenes of people dropping dead around them daily. The clergyman added that the village was 'more than five times fuller of people than it had accommodation for'. Such overcrowding must have facilitated the spread of disease.

Dr Traill in Mullins' Hut

Mahoney then continued westwards to Schull where he also sketched the village. Apart from the chapel on the right and the 'Big House' in the background, the village consisted of only two rows of thatched mud cabins or houses. In one cabin he drew 'an almost indescribable in-door horror'. A poor man named Mullins lay dying on a heap of straw while his three children were 'crouched over a few embers of turf'. He had buried their mother five days previously. One observes another child begging at the door. On the street he saw about 400 women with money in their hands who were seeking to buy food while a few government officers doled out Indian meal to them. One of the women told him she had been there since dawn to get food for her family. This food was doled out in 'miserable quantities at famine prices'. It came from 'a stock lately arrived in a sloop with a government steamer to protect its 50 tons, while the population amounts to 27,000; so you can calculate what were the feelings of disappointment,' the artist commented. This was the floating depot about whose long delay Viscount Bernard was protesting in parliament. It is clear from this artist's eye-witness account that in spite of what Bishop was now reporting there was by no means 'ample' provisions for the people even for those who had money, not to mention those who had not; the latter must have been in the majority. On his way out of the village, Mahoney met Traill's daughters returning from their work of charity in the poorest portion of the town. (One of these, Catherine, married a John Synge and became the mother of the playwright, J. M. Synge.)[88]

Boy and girl at Caheragh, 1847

Mahoney then returned to Skibbereen and travelled towards Drimoleague. He drew the forlorn boy and girl at Caheragh searching for potatoes. He next sketched the village of Meenies north of Drimoleague. Meenies no longer exists: it was wiped out in the famine like Kilbronoge near Ballydehob. He hoped that his sketches would make this affliction known to the charitable public'.[89] They contributed greatly towards making Skibbereen and Schull by-words for famine all over the empire and beyond, moving the hearts and hands of many to subscribe. Margaret Crawford considers that these illustrations have been sanitised and points out to 'the anatomical sturdiness' of the individuals and claims that only for the accompanying text the reader might well gain the impression that the Irish crisis was not severe.[90] While it may be true that these sketches do not always depict the full horrors of the word-pictures of Traill, for example, yet the fearfulness of these realities has been only very slightly toned down.

In the Mizen Peninsula the members of the Society of Friends usually delivered supplies of food and went their way. In February 1847 some of them stayed in Ballydehob to distribute it themselves and found that 'the poor people often swell to a great degree when they receive relief and soon after die'. These Quakers also gave out some tea and coffee because such stimulants were regarded as being medicinal. The government loaned two steamers, the *H.M.S. Scourge* and the *H.M.S. Albert*, to the Society of Friends for relief purposes. The *Scourge* was one of the finest ships of the British navy and was under Captain Caffin. Edmund Richards, a Quaker, was also on board to supervise distri-

The village of Meenies, 1847

butions.[91] Its heavy mortars had been put ashore and it was now loaded with food instead – a sign of the times. On 15 February it landed ninety-six tons of meal, biscuit, flour and peas from the Society of Friends in Liverpool. Captain Caffin saw that three-quarters of the inhabitants of Schull had been reduced to mere skeletons, especially the men, 'their physical powers wasted away'. He wanted to see with his own eyes the miseries which were supposed to exist in the area so he accepted Traill's offer to drive him around the parish. Caffin soon saw the 'horrors of famine in its worst features'. He had presumed that accounts had been 'coloured to attract sympathy' but 'the reality is ... no exaggeration for it does not admit of it – famine exists in a frightful degree with all its horrors'. In nearly every cabin they visited they found the sick, the dying and the dead all thrown together. Caffin described what they saw in five cabins as typical of all the rest. What was particularly disturbing was that most of these cabins belonged to Protestants who were now dying like the Catholics. His description of one such cabin is valuable in that it illustrates the gradual but fatal process whereby a once comfortable farmer and his family had been reduced to famine:

> They had been well-to-do in the world with their cow and a few sheep and potato ground: their crops failed and their cattle were stolen: the son had worked on the roads and earned his eight pence a day but could not keep his family and he, from work and insufficiency of food, is laid up and will soon be as bad as his father. They had nothing to eat in the house and I could see no hope for any of them.

Caffin was convinced that it was not possible for human power 'to stay the evil but that it might be possible to alleviate it'. He thought that this could be done by 'good organised systems with the supply of food and medicine mainly gratuitous'. He suggested that a number of naval surgeons and pensioners

185

should be sent to do this in co-operation with the relief committee. He called for the aid of the Board of Health because 'a pestilence will rage when the mass of these bodies decomposes, as they were not properly buried'.

Caffin's letter reached Admiral Pigot who passed it on to Trevelyan.[92] Although it was marked 'private' it was leaked to the press.[93] The *Freeman's Journal* commented 'Dogs may tear people on the highways and in the graveyards … but trade, thank God, runs free at a profit of cent per cent'.[94] The English newspaper, the *Daily News*, condemned the government for 'higgling for pounds while the economy is paid in the lives of starving wretches'.[95] Caffin continued to deliver cargoes of food along the west coast of Ireland. He remarked from Belmullet, County Mayo, that famine scenes 'are all alike, getting worse as you travel south, and at Schull and its neighbourhood the very climax of misery finds its resting place'.[96] The captain continued his voyage northwards and became the subject of a verse, 'Lines composed among the mountains of Donegal on the *Scourge*, Man of War, being placed by the government at the disposal of the Society of Friends'. Its author was delighted to comment that, in the words of the prophet, swords had been turned into ploughshares.[97]

Caffin's letter about Schull shocked Trevelyan out of his complacency for which Bishop must take some responsibility. He had to admit the credibility of Caffin, 'the commander of the *Scourge*, and officer of undoubted honour and veracity'. Trevelyan described this letter as 'awful' and enclosed a covering letter to the new chairman of the Relief Commission, Sir John Burgoyne, informing him that the government was in favour of sending medical aid to Schull. The admiral of the navy, Lord Auckland, had agreed to send two doctors and some male nurses to attend to the sick and bury the dead. Trevelyan admitted that 'this kind of relief could only be carried out to a humble extent', but he was satisfied that it would 'do good as far as it goes, and the calamities of the Irish are so great and pressing that it was only by bringing every available means of relief to bear on them that we can hope to make an impression. Let us save *as many as we can*'. Caffin's letter was a moment of truth for Trevelyan. The next day he wrote again to Burgoyne asking him to provide horses and carts to enable the naval men to distribute the soup to the homes of the sick.

Major General Burgoyne who had served under the Duke of Wellington was not going to be rushed by any Treasury clerk. He replied that the suggestion of horses and carts was a good one 'when practicable', but horses were 'diminishing fast'. He granted that this cart system could be easily organised if the calamity were a local one, but it was 'far too extensive to be essentially mitigated by any such means from available government sources'. He calmly reminded Trevelyan that, 'Terrible as are the accounts from Schull', there were other places in the interior that would have less chance of obtaining supplies. Regarding the burial of the dead, Burgoyne held that it would require new legislation because the famine dead had no right to be buried at public expense since they had not paid vestry dues. He did however consult the Board of Health on the legality of introducing the naval medical persons and found out that it would be legal. Burgoyne thus assured Trevelyan that measures would be taken 'according to the law'. A Treasury minute directed that copies of the letters of Caffin, Bishop, Webb, and Swanton be forwarded to the Relief commissioners in Dublin and that it be stated that they described 'the dreadful state of destitution in the parishes of Schull and Caheragh'. The lords of the Treasury also desired that food should be provided for those who could go out to obtain it and also for those who were confined at home by sickness. These lords stated also that the commissioners should communicate with the Board of Health to provide medical aid for the sick and burial for the dead.[98]

Thus ended the correspondence which had begun with Caffin's letter. No emergency relief measures were taken to aid Schull. In fact, nothing at all resulted. Trevelyan's plan to send the naval medical men was rejected by the Board of Health on the grounds that there were already sufficient doctors in Ireland. Between March and August 1850 the board appointed 473 additional doctors for fever duty.[99] The official procedure which followed Caffin's letter was a repeat of the same process of shifting of responsibility which had followed Parker's letter in December 1846. Both letters were forwarded to Trevelyan who described both with the same word 'awful' and passed them on to the Relief Commission in Dublin. This commission, whether under Routh or Burgoyne, refused do anything extra and informed Trevelyan accordingly. On both occasions Trevelyan and the Treasury replied with a similar rather mild rebuke – more counsels of perfection. One can observe the limitations of Trevelyan's power, great as it was.

The large cargo of food brought by Caffin was hopelessly inadequate to relieve the famine at this stage. On the same day as the commander's visit, Traill pointed out that there were many more cabins even worse than those seen by the captain. He had seen only those on the roadside but further up among the rocks he could have seen others 'hopelessly filled with the dying and the dead'. The rector was afraid to leave his house even on horseback and often had to be rescued by his servants and even by the police from the 'crush and grab of the miserable multitudes'. On the previous Saturday night he had spent £10 on food and medicine but it was 'a mere drop in the ocean'. He had spent from £600 to £700 'without much effect'. He had been educated mainly in England and it was from friends there that he was now receiving many subscriptions. The £50 which came to him through the lord lieutenant was donated by the Bishop of Durham and The Ladies' Association of England sent £30. Still the rector was forced to conclude with 'the lamentful prayer; famine is rising and pestilence rolling in terrific waves around us and who can tell what barque will outlive the storm? Oh, that we may watch and be ready for the hour wherein the Son of Man cometh.'[100]

The only criticism of the Schull relief committee came from the miner, Captain Thomas. It refused to send him two bags of meal and biscuits. It also refused to help a man and his family because they were farmers. They had a cow, a heifer, two sheep and a horse, all half starved, he said. The cow was not milking but they could not sell her in order to buy a bag of seed wheat because there was no buyer. This family of seven was starving, the miner stated.[101] The small farmers were now being hit by the famine just as well as the labourers. On the last night in February the Crookhaven men at the risk of their lives towed into the harbour wreckage consisting of masts and sails but it was confiscated by the coast-guards. Feelings ran high against them. A body of 500 labourers from the roads went to Mr Baldwin, the coast-guard officer, to demand food. They had shovels in their hands and expected to receive some food, H.M.S. Protheroe having just arrived in the harbour with a cargo of 109 tons of bread-stuffs from London on behalf of the British Relief Association.[102] Captain Harston of the British Relief Association ordered the captain of the ship to continue to Schull without unloading any of her cargo; evidently he was afraid it would be looted. The Crookhaven men, however, would not allow him to leave the harbour. The port pilot was unwilling to steer the ship out 'from dread of the consequences with which he was threatened'. The vessel was rescued by another government steamer and towed to Schull where it discharged 364 sacks of food. Some of this was later sent to Ballydehob, Kilcoe and Aughadown. The Ballydehob relief committee received three tons of biscuit, Indian meal and rice. Harston considered that famine conditions were worse in Crookhaven and Bantry than in any town along the south-west coast.[103] The departure of this ship was a sad disappointment for the people of Crookhaven where deaths were twenty-five a day according to Alexander O'Driscoll, a local middleman. There was no bread in the place and the last loaves had cost four pence each. A labourer on the roads could afford to buy only two for a day's pay.[104]

Apart from the roads and the Coosheen mine the only employment in the Mizen Peninsula was drainage at Ratooragh near Mount Gabriel. This was being done by R. H. H. Becher as part of a government scheme. There were twenty men employed there but five were now sick. An inspector, Mr King, observed that between Rosscarbery and Skibbereen the fields were sown with oats and wheat but from Skibbereen westwards there was not a trace of tillage of any sort because the people were famine-stricken.[105] On the last day of February, the Tartarus landed a cargo of food at Ballydehob; there was little danger of the food being looted. One of the sailors described what he saw:

We passed a crowd of 500 people half naked and starving. They were waiting for soup to be distributed among them. They were pointed out to us … my conductor, a medical man said, 'Not a single one of these you see will be alive in three weeks; it is impossible'. The deaths here average 40 to 50 daily; 20 bodies were buried this morning and they were fortunate in getting buried at all. The people build themselves up in their cabins, so that they may die together with their children and not be seen by passers-by. Fever, dysentery and starvation stare you in the face everywhere – children of 10 and 9 years old I have mistaken for decrepit old women, their faces wrinkled, their bodies bent and distorted with pain, the eyes looking like those of a corpse. Babies are found lifeless, lying on their mothers bosoms … a dead woman was found lying on the road with a dead infant on her breast, the child having bitten the nipple of the mother's breast right through … Dogs feed on the half-buried dead, and rats are commonly known to tear people to pieces, who, though still alive, are too weak to cry out … Instead of following us, beggars throw themselves on their knees before us, holding up their dead infants to our sight.[106]

This sailor was seeing the results of hunger oedema, swollen bodies and premature ageing. In Skibbereen the American philanthropist, Elihu Burritt, now also saw a two-year old child whose arms were 'not much larger than pipe-stems, while its body was swollen to the size of a full-grown person'.[107] The sailor's account also shows a terribly high infant and child mortality; baptismal and other records will confirm this. It is no wonder that Fr Barry was almost despairing. He had sometimes thought that at last they had reached the 'climax of wretchedness' when the next hour would bring a tale more horrifying still. 'When will the famine have done its worst?' he asked. He gave the usual sad account of deaths around Kilbronoge and Ballydehob but found that conditions were as bad in the hilly interior of the parish. He had visited Laharn, Shanntolig and Derreennalomane where whole families were wiped out and their cabins tumbled down upon them. When fever struck such small cabins were death-traps which turned into tombs. One woman had asked J. Limrick to bury her husband and children. Fr Barry praised this landlord as 'a good magistrate, it is but little to say of him that his time, his talents and his health are unsparingly devoted to deeds of benevolence'.[108] The spring of 1847 brought little hope; there was scarcely any seed to sow and any warmth in the weather would only facilitate the spread of pestilence. Neither Barry nor Traill could see any sign of abatement in the rising flood of famine and fever. The horror of the famine and disillusionment with government relief measures drove at least one man to question his political beliefs, namely, the Gaelic scholar landlord, Thomas Swanton of Crannliath near Ballydehob. He wrote to the *Nation* newspaper announcing his conversion to repeal:

> My conversion has been brought about by witnessing the neglect of the sufferings of the poor, and the waste of the resources of my country in these calamitous times … But, sir, what I now desire, in the bitterness of my soul, to represent, is the famished, diseased, helpless, perishing state of the people of this, my native district. We have no landlords in fee resident, no medical man resident, no hospital, no refuge, no asylum. The pangs of dysentery and the agonies of death are suffered without shelter … I challenge any district in Ireland to prove its superiority in wretchedness to Ballydehob. I see no laws enacted – no plans proposed by those in authority, calculated to revive prosperity in our peculiarly depressed circumstances. The horrors of famine and pestilence are before us, and the black cloud of despair hangs over us.[109]

Such was the suffering and death of the people of the Mizen Peninsula up to the end of February 1847. They had already endured at least six long months of famine – September, October, November, December, January and February. There were problems both with the supply of food and its distribution. This was severely criticised by such diverse voices as Captain Thomas, Major Parker (both English), John Triphook and James Mahoney. Evidently, there was not sufficient food in the district to compensate for the heavy loss of the potato crop; what food was there was available only at inflated famine prices which those who needed it most could not afford even if they were employed on the roads. Men like Caffin, Harston and Bishop belonged to the navy or to the commissariat service and they were more experienced in the transportation of troops and provisions. Strictly speaking, the distribution of food was not their job especially to a starving and scattered population. What was badly needed was very cheap or free food and this would have to be carefully distributed because the hungry and the sick were less and less able to go out to seek it. As Fr Laurence O'Sullivan granted, 'the tardy relief contemplated by government', i.e., the Temporary Relief Act (Soup Kitchen Act), had indeed the good intentions of doing precisely that, but arrangements for its implementation moved tardily while famine and fever were advancing swiftly.

IX

Bringing the Food and the
People Together
March–September 1847

There is no want of food in any place …

REV. F. F. TRENCH

Further Presentment Sessions about roads for the barony of West Carbery were held in Ballydehob early in March 1847. Some of the proceedings were ominous. Lionel Fleming of Newcourt got the following motion passed: 'To place a layer of earth over a number of burial grounds, to a depth of three feet', and also 'to dig trenches for future interments with a view to preventing contagion'; a sum of £2,600 was granted. The graveyards of Kilmoe and Crookhaven were among those listed.[1] Dr Traill's translation of the works of the Jewish historian, Josephus, was now published.[2] The terrible conditions in his own parish often reminded him of the famine in Jerusalem under siege by the Romans. His letters about the famine, however, received far more attention from the public than his book did. He found sixteen people huddled together in one hovel whose windows were stuffed with straw and all were sick with fever. The sixteen belonged to three different families, the original family having taken in two others that were homeless.[3]

Captain Harston of the British Relief Association gave grants of food to the Ladies' Society at Ballydehob and also to the newly founded one at Schull. Each relief vessel now also carried bundles of clothing. This association landed more food at Ballydehob on 8 March. The captain also met the Skibbereen relief committee and allotted £500 worth of flour in five weekly instalments. He also gave £100 worth of provisions to each of the relief committees of Aughadown and Kilcoe. The people were crying out for seed and asking if the British Relief Association would supply any at cost price. There was yet very little seed sown west of Skibbereen.[4] Another agent of the British Relief Association, Captain Ladd of the *H.M.S. Zephyr*, landed food at Crookhaven. He found that the government boilers which had been landed there were not being used and that the want of food appeared great; it seems that there was nothing to put into the boilers. In Schull John Limrick had the parish divided into four equal parts and placed a boiler in each.[5] He sent a list of subscriptions amounting to £119 to the Relief Commission in Dublin; the Society of Friends gave James Barry £12 and Traill £32; Archbishop Murray of Dublin sent £8 to Barry and a like sum to L. O'Sullivan of Kilmoe. Limrick obtained a grant of a corresponding sum of £119.[6] The Ballydehob relief committee received a second subscription of £20 from Bishop Murphy of Cork and £75 worth of food from the British Relief Association.[7] The Kilcoe relief committee had received a boiler from Mr Bishop but had not any funds to buy soup. The list of subscriptions sent by its secretary and treasurer, J. H. Swanton, contained only three subscriptions, £10 each from himself and Rev. J. Freke, the chairman and £5 from Major Parker of the Board of Works. The only hope of a food supply that the committee had was a promise from the British Relief Association. Randolph Routh gave the corresponding grant of £25.[8] Famine was now even worse in March than it had been in February. R. B. Townsend told that the workhouse in Skibbereen now held 1,449. Deaths in the poorhouse one week numbered 65 and up to 40 others were dying every day in the parish. The institution was still closed to further paupers. The hinged-coffin had taken at least 65 bodies to the grave.[9] Parker reported to Trevelyan that there were 14,000 men working on the roads in Carbery but warned that 'mortality is very high as a result of fever, dysentery and dropsy.'[10] He himself caught fever and died on 8 March and was buried at Creagh near Baltimore. Trevelyan described it as 'melancholy news' and wrote a letter of sympathy to his widow.[11] Parker's death and especially the fact that the roads were still costing the Treasury £40,000 a day caused Trevelyan to put more pressure on Colonel Jones of the Board of Works to speed up their closure. Otherwise the Treasury clerk warned they would be only 'adding national bankruptcy to famine'.[12] Yet road-works were not being phased out quickly enough so an ultimatum was issued in the form of a Treasury minute of 10 March; a reduction of 20% of the men employed was to be made by 20 March and the remainder according as the Soup Kitchen Act was being brought into operation.[13]

The dynamic response which Parker and Caffin had expected from their appeals arrived at last, not from the government, however, but from a Church of Ireland clergyman, Rev. F. F. Trench, curate of Cloughjordan, County Tipperary. He was a son of William Trench of Cangort Park a few miles from Cloughjordan. The Trenches were a substantial landed family of which there were a number of branches in that area. William Trench was chairman of the Cloughjordan relief committee of which his son was a member. By Christmas 1846 F. F. Trench had opened what he called an 'eating-house or soup-kitchen' where 'one meal a day is given to all in distress'. His attention was drawn to Schull by Caffin's letter. He had no connection of family or property with the district but 'volunteered to come out of charity'. 'It was painful to myself and others,' he wrote, 'to think that within two or three days' journey from our homes thousands of our fellow creatures should be dying of absolute starvation'.[14] He noted that all the families visited by Traill and the captain were Protestants and if they were in that state he feared to think about condition of the Catholics. John Triphook visited thirteen Protestant families with dysentery near Ballydehob.[15] Nine persons had died on the lands of Richard Notter in Kilmoe and seven were Protestants.[16] F. F. Trench was struck by the absence of children except for a few sick and dying ones. His cousin, W. Steuart Trench, the famous land agent, related that this visitor, F. F. Trench found that the parish priest, James Barry, was 'utterly paralysed by the magnitude of the desolation around him. He had given all he had to the people and there was no food whatever in his house so he stood really in danger of being starved himself.' Near Ballydehob F. F. Trench saw a house that had been burned down because all its occupants, nine in number, had died of fever. He met Miss Noble of the Ladies' Association, Traill and Dr McCormick. On the following day, Sunday 14 March, Trench met the Ballydehob relief committee. He outlined his plan of establishing 'eating-houses' at various places. He set up a sub-committee consisting of John Barry, John Triphook, the Catholic and Protestant curates respectively and also some others to carry out this plan. Trench went on a visit to Cappagh where he found 'a starving population which had been collected around mines now not worked'; he proposed to establish an eating-house there. He spoke to the coast-guard who told him that he had buried many bodies including that of a man who had died on his way home from the road-works.

On another occasion he was visiting the nearby Kilbronoge when he happened to meet John Barry and Captain Harston; the three together visited nine houses in which they found the dying and the dead. In the first house they found a man, his wife and child, all in fever; four had died. The second house, Patrick Driscoll's, contained three sick and one dead by the fire. When asked if he died of fever, 'No, sir, of starvation,' came the reply. In the third house, Regans', Trench heard the groaning of a dying man; there were eight in the family, 'pictures of death'. Barry said they had been respectable farmers. In the fourth house, Widow Driscoll's, a young man was dying, five in the family all sick and swollen. One of Trench's companions said to him, *'None of them can live'*. Nobody was able to open the door of the fifth house, Mat Sullivan's; two of his children sat by the fire and two others 'lay pale as death'. The sixth house was Widow Cunningham's; she had buried her husband and three of her children. She had been ill and her last boy had just fallen sick. The seventh house had belonged to Philip Regan but he was dead and his widow was dying; she was terribly swollen. Eight people, all sick, were found in the eighth house, Paddy Ryan's. Only three out of eleven still remained in the ninth house, Charles Regan's; the mother said, 'We have no sickness but hunger'. Turning to Barry, Trench asked 'Are the houses I see lower down as bad?' 'They are, in fact, worse,' was the reply 'it is more populous; I have come from a house there in which I saw two were stretched'. These nine houses visited seem to have been farmers, those lower down were probably labourers, the 'dense swarms' already referred to by James Barry. To sum up for the 56 persons who had been living in these houses, 18 were now dead and most of the others were dying or in fever. It was in these extremely poor and densely populated clachans that famine and fever were raging most terribly. Fr James Mulcahy of Castlehaven, formerly of Aughadown, was prepared to swear that out of the 472 persons alive in the fishing hamlet of Carrigilly on 1 January 1847 as many as 87 had been carried away by starvation in less than two months.[17]

This meeting of Barry, Trench and Harston represents a coming together of forces that would make a renewed effort to deal with the famine. Harston was well placed to provide the food and the clergymen and other local people could distribute it. He assured Trench that he would be 'most happy in affording him every assistance' in his power. At Schull Trench met Traill, his curate, Alexander McCabe, Dr Sweetnam and John Limrick. The children in the locality looked so much like skeletons that it was difficult to tell whether they were boys or girls. Dr Sweetnam took up one 'skeleton child' and rattled it saying 'all the legs swing and rock like the legs of a doll'. He held that none of these children could live long because they had fever. The doctor described many of the adults as 'delirious with fever and hunger'. This delirium was a symptom of typhus which affected the brain (*tuphos*, mist). Limrick told Trench that in one day he had employed thirty-five road-workers in gangs of four or five to bury the dead. Trench also saw McCabe giving tickets to two women to work on the road in place of their husbands who had died. This appalled Trench but McCabe informed him that in the previous eight days he had replaced the names of 100 men with those of their widows and that there had been six cases in which he had 'altered the name from the father to the son and from the son to the widow and from the widow to the daughter, all having died'. This calm statement of fact is the most eloquent indictment of the roads as relief works because they were by now only disease and death traps for many. Trench admitted that the Soup Kitchen Act would be 'as complete a remedy as possible' but pointed out 'until it is in full operation, which may not be for a considerable time, the people must die by thousands'. He then outlined his plan to establish 'eating-houses, where a meal of substantial food might be given daily to all who were certified in danger of perishing from hunger', rather than giving just soup which might be only 'thin gruel or greasy water'. This meal was to consist of 'substantial Indian stir-about and porridge' and would cost no more than $1\frac{1}{2}$d a day. His observation on the vital question of the availability of food and of its reaching the mouths of the people should be noted:

> In none of the places where I was did the case appear to be desperate: there is no want of food in any place – delightful consideration – nor want of medicine, but there is a most deplorable want of *available agencies, and a consequent want of suitable measures to bring the food and the medicine within the reach of the people.* Take for example the parish of Schull. What can one physician do among 18,000 in such a state? What can the ordinary number of clergy do in such an extensive district? Can Dr Traill be expected to carry meal to the people in the mountains, as he has done? Can Mr McCabe be expected to push the door and look for a vessel … putting a drink in it for the sick, as he has done?[18]

It must be remembered that by now, March 1847, food was less scarce and less expensive than it had been in November and December because at this stage it was being brought across the Atlantic. Still the new supplies of meal were too late arriving in the Mizen Peninsula as many people now had fever and were unable to procure this food. Typhus causes a bodily stiffness like rheumatism to grip its victims. On this occasion Trench remained in the parish only a week, but he organised four or five 'eating-houses'. He also had a special doctor sent to Schull to treat fever cases. He formally approached John Burgoyne and Thomas Redington, the under secretary, and was assured that no time would be lost in bringing the Soup Kitchen Act into operation. 'But arrangements are complicated,' Trench impatiently asserted, 'and the lives of thousands depend on what is done *now*.' Government agents lacked his dynamism and sense of urgency. Trench's account of his visit received widespread publicity in the press and attracted many subscriptions.[19] One man sent £100 while another sent so much that Trench had to decline to accept any more than half. At this stage, early in April, he had sufficient money, food and medicine. Next he announced: 'I solicit free contributions of personal service from intelligent and devoted men. Money I know will be required but we want men now to make the money which we have work in the most efficient manner.'[20]

Traill was much encouraged by Trench's plan of giving one good meal to those in need. He regarded it as one which 'wears the aspect of practicality unlike other Utopian schemes'. Still he saw that 'the grand difficulty, supposing we had a sufficiency of food, is to reach remote localities to which no roads lead'. It seems clear, however, that in spite of what Trench said there was still a scarcity of food. Both he and Traill agreed that the tragedy was that whatever food was available was out of reach of those who needed it most because they were too sick to come for it and there was no means of taking it to them. Up to now most of the soup-kitchens were in the towns, Crookhaven, Schull and Ballydehob. It was to deal with this difficulty that the 'eating-houses' were situated in the country. Traill calculated that two thousand people in his parish had already died and Doctors Sweetnam and McCormick were prepared to swear 'that thousands were in a dying condition beyond the reach of food and medicine'. By now Traill had spent £1,500 on food and £350 on seed for the people.[21]

Three gentlemen named Kennedy, Pickington and Rochford volunteered to come from Cloughjordan to supervise the eating-houses. Trench also sent James Gavin, his lay assistant and five young men. When they arrived in Schull they found that Rev. McCabe and Mr Kennedy had gone to Dunmanus and were making preparation for setting up a boiler in the ruined castle. On the following day Gavin distributed biscuits to the 'poor creatures naked and covered with filth'. The moment they saw food, they rushed on him, their screams and cries terrified him, Gavin wrote, 'Nonetheless many of them were so weak that the smallest touch of the finger will cause them to fall and soon die.' He found that they were 'well pleased with half we give in Cloughjordan'. Two days later the boiler arrived with eighty gallons of porridge and a bag of meal but this was little enough for a crowd of 800. Even water was scarce and Gavin had to pay as much as 8d to 10d for each 'back load' of turf.

The appeal of Trench to the Board of Health for a doctor was successful and a Dr Lamprey was sent to Ballydehob to work under his direction. The doctor visited the sick, prescribing the necessary food and medicine and sep-

Professor R. C. Trench, later archbishop of Dublin, 1864–84

arated the sick from the healthy. The sick were placed in four army tents provided by the Board of Health and he was even thinking of converting cabins emptied by death into hospitals. Lamprey also visited the Dunmanus 'eating-house' and found Gavin distributing food to over 600 of the 'most wretched people in the world'. Trench lamented to the doctor, 'I do not know, sir, where it will end, nor can I be equal to the work; there will be almost 800 here to be fed.' Lamprey praised the system as 'the only means yet devised to stay the famine.' He complimented Kennedy who was 'working quietly and effectually, sparing neither time nor trouble.' Lamprey also visited the Kilbronoge 'eating-house' and informed its patron, Trench, of its 'great success'. No one, he stated enthusiastically, 'can form an idea of the amount of relief it has afforded hundreds unless they can be eye witnesses of it'.[22]

Another man who answered Trench's call for volunteers was his first cousin, Richard Chevenix Trench, rector of Itchenstoke, Hants and Professor of Divinity at King's College, London and later (1864) to become archbishop of Dublin in succession to Dr Whately. Professor Trench collected £150 and arrived in Dublin on 6 April. He next went to Cloughjordan to consult his cousin on 'eating-houses' and headed for West Cork along with two helpers. It was not until they reached Ballydehob that 'the extremity of the misery became visible'. He considered that 'Skibbereen had the appearance of a flourishing place' compared to Ballydehob and Schull[23] and, finding that F. F. Trench's five eating-houses were not one-tenth of what was necessary, he opened two more in Ballydehob. Professor Trench also supervised the eating-house at Kilbronoge and was gratified at the sight of 200 people eating together. He also took Rossbrin into the system and fed 100 more from a distribution from the Kilbronoge boiler. In spite of its three eating-houses he almost despaired of doing anything for Ballydehob, 'the mass of wild hunger there is unimaginable'. He was spending nearly £100 weekly. Dr Sweetnam praised this system as the 'first efficient plan of feeding the people which has yet been in the parish'. There was now a total of nine eating-houses but new ones were also being opened and 500 people were fed from each on a daily basis. Nevertheless Professor Trench was forced to admit that all this still 'left vast regions yet untouched' in the parishes of Schull and Kilmoe. He examined the returns of five eating-houses and found that he and his helpers had distributed nearly 10,000 meals at an average cost of only one penny farthing thanks to the 'trifling daily cost of food'. He pointed out however that 'the agency which is essentially necessary, and for want of which, more than for the want of food, life was lost, will necessarily cost much'. Yet he felt able to claim that, at least, in the areas attended to, 'the mortality, though it had not ceased … yet it had been arrested'. It was around 12 April.[24] This was for him the first glimmer of hope that the tide of famine and fever was beginning to be turned at last. On 14 April he wrote from Cork to his father stating that when he arrived in Schull the eating-houses organised by F. F. Trench were feeding 15,000 people and that those set up while he was there fed another 3,000. Professor Trench returned to England apparently in good health and visited his friend, the theologian, F. D. Maurice, who with Charles Kingsley led a movement known as 'Christian Socialism'. It was there that Trench was struck down with fever but, as we know, he survived.[25]

There were various reports that Dr Traill was down with fever. Colonel Hughes who was in charge of the Skibbereen depot informed Trevelyan who replied, 'I am greatly concerned to hear of Traill's illness and trust you will be able to give me a more favourable account of him'.[26] His curate, John Triphook, admitted that he was indeed suffering from a 'severe attack of dysentery, accompanied by fever', but was recovering. He had the attentions of Doctors Sweetnam and McCormick, and was fortunate to have the added care of Dr Lamprey and also of a Dr Stephens who had been sent by the Board of Health to report on the sanitary conditions of West Cork, particularly of Bantry.[27] Two weeks later Traill wrote a brief letter, he felt himself 'almost unequal to the exertion of writing … my health having suffered from anxiety and fatigue'. His expenses had reached 'the alarming amount of £60 per week' and he could not see any prospect of its diminution, only the contrary.[28] The following day Triphook announced: 'This moment I have just performed the last sad duty of closing the eyes in death of a dear friend and brother Dr Traill. His end was emphatically PEACE.'[29] Traill was surrounded by his wife and family of three sons and five daughters. The *Cork Constitution* doubted whether it ever made any announcement with more pain and whether there was any person in the country or even in the United Kingdom who had done more work for the starving people than Traill. What he had done for the Protestants and Catholics of the parish of Schull is best summed up in the following inscription over his grave in Schull:

> Sacred to the memory of Rev. Robert Traill D.D. who for a period of 17 years that he presided over the parish of Schull as rector with his Blessed Master 'went about doing good'. 'Till at length in full sacrifice to his superhuman efforts in relieving the prevailing distress in the Famine years of 1846 and 1847'.
> Interred to his rest April 21 1847.

A poet named A. Southern composed a long lament for him and felt sure that 'a grateful nation' would always remember 'the reverend warrior'.[30]

In Skibbereen McCarthy Downing was ill with fever, as also was Dr McCormick of Rock Island, Crookhaven. He left the district for a while and was replaced by a Dr Brady.[31] The fever hospital in the Skibbereen workhouse was built to accommodate 40 patients but it held 159 on 27 March 1847. Lamprey reported that, 'Some of those in fever are expelled from the workhouse when they appear to be ill, and wandering through the country, expire in the fields.'[32] Nonetheless the number of deaths in this workhouse ranged from 80 to 106 a week during March.[33] Mercifully these were to be highest figures for the famine and were greater than in Dunmanway, Bantry or Bandon where the record numbers were 76, 70 and 59 deaths per week respectively.[34] Many of those who perished in the Skibbereen poorhouse were buried in the common pit in Abbeystrowry graveyard. Two visitors from Oxford, Lord Dufferin and G. F. Boyle, were horrified to see corpses being thrown in one on top of the other. Coffins were 'piled in layers' in another part of the pit.[35] A macabre incident which happened there is told by the Fenian, Jeremiah O'Donovan Rossa:

> Rackateen [the workhouse undertaker] took the bodies to the abbey graveyard in a kind of trapdoor wagon. He took Johnnie Collins in it one day, and after dumping him, with others, into the grave-pit, one of his knees protruded up from the heap of corpses. 'Rackateen' gave it a stroke of his shovel to level it down even; the corpse gave a cry of pain, and the boy was raised from the pit. That lame man – whose leg had been broken by the stroke of the shovel – used to come into my shop every week; and we used to speak of him as the man who was raised from the dead.[36]

According to local tradition this man's name was Tom Guerin and he became a travelling man who did odd jobs. Bernard O'Regan of Aughadown, aged almost 100, told me that he remembered him walking the roads with a lame step. Guerin would often recite the following verse:

> *I arose from the dead in the year of '48,*
> *Though a grave in the abbey had near been my fate,*
> *And since for subsistence I've done all my best,*
> *Though one leg points east and one leg points west.*[37]

198

The ravages of fever prompted the government to introduce a new Fever Bill which became law on 27 April 1847. The Central Board of Health was now re-appointed and it went on to open 373 Fever Hospitals and employed 473 additional doctors for fever duty including Dr Brady who was sent to the Caheragh Hospital. This act made fever patients the responsibility of the relief committees rather than of the Board of Guardians. The committees could apply to the Board of Health for a temporary fever hospital. A fever hospital was set up in Schull and another in Ballydehob in May 1847. In June and July other hospitals were opened in Skibbereen, Kilcoe and Kilmoe. At one time in that summer Skibbereen Fever Hospital held 60 patients, Aughadown 80, Ballydehob 50, Schull 50, Kilmoe 30, Caheragh 80 and Drimoleague 100. Two nurses worked in each hospital except Caheragh, Drimoleague and Aughadown where there were four; there were also one or two ward maids in each place.[38] The Board of Health was proving to be efficient and generous. It was under the authority of the lord lieutenant who was nearby, unlike the Board of Works which was under the control of Trevelyan in England; the Board of Health's procedures were therefore more direct. It had an adequate supply of money and medicine but above all it had many doctors or what the Trenches called 'agency'. For example, the board could afford to send two men, Doctors Lamprey and Stephens, to West Cork.

April 1847 was a time of pestilence and gloom in the region. Many who had turned their faces eastwards towards England had been disappointed; some would now turn westwards towards America. This land was not only a source of refuge for emigrants but also a source of food. Unlike the harvest in Europe, the harvest in America had been abundant. An enthusiastic fund and food-raising campaign was run all over the United States. Nicholas Cummins' open letter to the Duke of Wellington was read aloud. The Irish who had emigrated in the previous decades contributed generously as did others such as the Choctaw Indians. Many ships were freighted and loaded for Ireland. One of the first of these was the *Jamestown* under Captain Forbes which arrived at Cobh on 12 April with nearly 600 tons of food from the Irish Relief Society of Boston.[39] A committee called the 'New England Committee' was formed to distribute the cargo; its vice-chairman was N. Ludlow Beamish, chairman of the Southern and Western Mining Company. Many localities around the County of Cork were to obtain four tons of meal and three bales of pork. Richard Notter of Rock Island received the consignment to be distributed for the Crookhaven district and beyond. The following localities duly received their allotments: Crookhaven, Schull, Dunmanus, Ballydehob, Aughadown, Skibbereen, Cape Clear and Sherkin. This aid was not confined to western districts but went all over the county, for example, to Carrigtohill, Lisgould and Whitechurch which are not far from Cork city.[40] There were starving people, no doubt, in these places too. Before Captain Forbes sailed for home he received a deputation from the newly formed Tenant League of Cork.[41] The times, they were changing.

The new relief committees under the Soup Kitchen Act were at last organised by April 1847. John Limrick succeeded Traill as chairman of the Schull relief committee while McCabe succeeded him in turn as secretary. As F. F. Trench and L. O'Sullivan, parish priest of Kilmoe, feared, this act would prove slow in coming into operation. It was bureaucratic, the paper weighed over fourteen tons and took six weeks to print. The Labour Rate Act had been expensive both in terms of finance and in the lives of the road-workers and yet famine mortality continued to increase. The new act was going to be under greater government or Treasury supervision. The key men in its implementation were carefully selected inspecting officers who were highly paid, a guinea a day plus expenses. Each Union was also to have a financial controller.[42] One inspector was appointed for each Union but Skibbereen obtained two. At last it was receiving the extra aid it needed. Perhaps the 'awful' letters of Major Parker and Captain Caffin had not been completely in vain after all. Now under the Temporary Relief Act Trevelyan had more direct control than he had at the time when he was dealing with the likes of Sir Randolf Routh and Major General Sir John Burgoyne. The extra inspector was a medical man, a Dr Prendergast, appointed evidently by Trevelyan himself who explained to the Relief commissioners that, 'the case of Skibbereen is one of more than usual preference – the district being in a state of *frightful want and disease*'. He praised the 'able manner' of the doctor and called for support for his 'plan of putting the whole district into hospital'. The other inspector similarly appointed to the Skibbereen Union was a J. J. Marshall who had been introduced to Trevelyan by Lord Clanricarde because he had 'distinguished himself in the management of Portumna soup-kitchen' in County Galway.[43] By 10 May the new act was in operation in all of the parishes of the Mizen Peninsula except in the most westerly, Kilmoe, which had to wait until 24 May.[44] Yet most of these parishes were more advanced than many others. By 15 May only about 1,250 electoral divisions out of an eventual 2,000 in the whole country were operating the act and the Poor Law commissioners expressed 'considerable disappointment that this progress should have been so slow, seeing no good reason why the measure should not, by this time, be extended all over the country'.[45] This was a rebuke to the relief committees; May 24 was indeed late for government soup-kitchens to be opening in Kilmoe. It had been fully five months since this Soup Kitchen Act had been introduced to parliament. It was indeed a long way from parliament to parish – on the Mizen Head.

As the Soup Kitchen Act was being phased in the road-works were to be phased out. On 20 March at least 20% of the labourers were to be dismissed and 10% on 24 April. All the engineers in the Board of Works were ordered to close down the works on 1 May unless they received specific instructions before then. This appeared reckless even to Trevelyan.[46] When 200 men were dismissed at the end of March, Captain Thomas of Coosheen protested because they were heads of families, which would mean that there were now 800 more people hungry.[47] The Soup Kitchen Act had not yet come into operation in most districts including the Skibbereen Union so there was a certain hungry gap between the two systems of relief. If the road-works had been retained even after the coming into operation of the Soup Kitchen Act the result would have been that combination of employment and food distribution which had been successful during the famine of 1822. In April 1847 Thomas Gibbons, the financial officer for the Skibbereen Union under the new act, wrote an account of the state of agriculture in the Schull district. He discovered that the landlords on the new relief committees were threatening to put their tenants off the road-works unless they would give up their lands. Some tenants were forced to do so because they had no seed. This threat was illegal but very immediate. Gibbons granted that there were some kind-hearted men among the landlords but that most of them were 'harsh – mercenary'. Out of 16,000 acres in the parish of Schull, he could not see as many as 600 acres that were yet sown. On one estate of 900 acres not 10 were sown because the estate was in the Court of Chancery. Not even the landlords had money to buy seed, as their tenants often could not pay the rent. The general tendency among the landlords was 'to take up the land without giving any compensation to the outgoing tenant'. But some tenants were clever enough to hold out and, knowing the expense it would be to the landlord to evict them, would make a bargain with him such as, 'I go out quietly if you give me £2'. This was common so land was falling into the hands of the landlords. The people were still trying to sow potatoes. When advised to sow grain, their answer was 'we have none' or 'the landlord will not give us any'. Gibbons believed that 'the reason why the landlords do not (whether able or not) give seed is the difficulty of getting rid of their tenants next year – death is doing this work'.

This is a revealing letter showing the profound distrust between landlord and tenant and making the serious allegation that the landlords were taking sinister advantage of the famine to get rid of tenants. Gibbons took the precaution to mark his letter 'private' and to stipulate that 'some parts of it should not be published'. Colonel Jones of the Board of Works, however, considered it important enough to forward to Trevelyan.[48] Nonetheless what Gibbons covered up another man would eagerly publish; he was John Francis Maguire, editor of the *Cork Examiner*. His informant was a local clergyman, probably James Barry. Maguire announced that even in the middle of May people were still dying of fever. One reason he gave was the 'reckless dismissals' of labourers from the road-works. He pointed out that the farmers were 'woefully deceived' by the government's promise to supply the country with £50,000 worth of seed.[49] They had depended on this supply and eaten their own seed potatoes. The government broke its promise owing to the protests of the English seed merchants.[50] Finally, Maguire exposed the following evictions to the gaze of the public:

> The destruction of houses is going on steadily. Whenever the landlords have an opportunity of demolishing a human habitation, they raze it to the ground. They look upon the razing of cabins as a famous plan of clearing off human incumbrances from their properties. And, in the ardour of their zeal for this great plan of 'elevating the condition of the people and improving the conditions of the country', they are frequently as deaf as adders to the pleadings of humanity … For instance, the roof of a

cabin in Ballydehob was torn off by the zealous agent of one of those improving and reforming landlords, *while a sick woman lay dying on the floor.*[51]

Just like before the famine it was the 'improving' landlords who were inclined to evict. Not all of them however would take advantage of the famine. Alexander O'Driscoll reported that the land around Crookhaven was now cultivated thanks to seed provided by its absentee landlord, David Cagney of Cork, but added that few landlords followed his example. He also made the serious allegation that the relief food sent to Crookhaven was not distributed in a just manner, that, for example, part of the cargo of peas sent by the British Relief Association was rotting and sprouting in the depot on Rock Island. A cargo of meal from the *Jamestown* had just arrived and was being placed in Notter's stores on Rock Island, he wrote. Although it took the food only fifteen days to cross the Atlantic it took it twenty-six days to go from Cobh to Crookhaven and it still had to go to other places from there. He requested that in future food should be sent either to Fr Barrett, Pierre Foley of the Crookhaven mines, or to himself to ensure fair distribution.[52] O'Driscoll repeated the charge about the food rotting on Rock Island and adduced the further evidence of Dr Brady.[53] A writer informed the public that a similar situation had arisen in Haulbowline but that the Mayor of Cork protested to the British Relief Association and that the result was that £1,000 worth of food was distributed to the famishing crowd. This writer advised O'Driscoll to protest likewise.[54] O'Driscoll also alleged that some of food and clothes which had come from the *Jamestown* had not yet been distributed by Notter while the people were hungry and clothed in rags and old sails.[55]

Captain Thomas made similar allegations against the British Relief Association or its agents in Schull. He complained that he could not feed the men he employed in his newly-established fishery because of the high price of flour at 2s 11d a stone:

> This flour last week was £25 a ton at the depot belonging to the British Association! Since then the price has been lowered £2 a ton! and what is still worse the flour is heating and spoiling in the stores, and several individuals … have actually died but three days since, a few fields only from this place, from starvation. The poor men here were nearly naked, and I employed a tailor to make up the empty meal bags for trousers for them. I suppose those in authority consider it better to allow the meal and bags to rot together than allow the poor to be fed and clothed.

The *Southern Reporter* called this 'a shameful situation'.[56] Such accounts of food rotting in stores have metamorphosed into folklore. A child told the Irish Folklore Commission how such food arrived in Crookhaven but was hoarded by the landlord who would sell it but not give it out for nothing so 'it rotted in the stores and after the famine they sunk it to the bottom of the sea'.[57] Even as late as June 1847 there were reports of people dying of starvation within reach of food-stores. Although the supplies of the British Relief Association were supposed to be 'exclusively for gratuitous distribution',[58] there is evidence that its agents sometimes obtained money for it. Captain Harston referred to 'sales or grants' to people in Ballydehob, Schull and Crookhaven; provisions would be either 'given or sold'. The government was evidently still holding out here for the high prices which had generally fallen by then. In March Fr Mathew had announced, 'The markets are rapidly falling; Indian corn from £16 to £15 a ton due to vast importations'.[59] Such hoarding or delaying the delivery of food did indeed take place. In September a large quantity of provisions belonging to the British Relief Association in Haulbowline was sold by public auction 'to prevent this food from deteriorating by being left too long in stores'. Thirteen sacks were 'more or less damaged'. The lots consisted of a total of 3,332 bags of meal, 883 sacks of peas and 152 bales of pork according to the advertisement.[60]

In Crookhaven in the middle of May there were twenty-one persons with typhus. The warm weather now facilitated the spread of disease. On one day Alexander O'Driscoll counted 120 poor people picking cockles on the strand. He met a woman who declared to him that she was the sole survivor of a family that had died in the famine. She survived only because she killed three dogs and ate them; he mentioned this to Fr Barrett who corroborated it. Conditions would have been far worse in Crookhaven also were it not for the arrival of F. F. Trench. In the beginning of May Trench set up a large boiler to hold 120 gallons of soup. Soup was also distributed to seven neighbouring townlands and this meant that a total of 500 persons were fed daily.[61] The Society of Friends continued to send food. Abraham Beale sent 25 barrels of Indian meal and 5 bags of rice to Fr Barrett[62] and this society also later sent 15 barrels of meal and 5 bags of biscuit to Pierre Foley and in July another 60 bags of Indian meal to Barrett.[63]

During this summer of 1847 the various leaders of the people were anxious for some means of 'reproductive employment' in agriculture and fisheries to produce the one thing necessary – food. An understandable reaction had set in against the unproductive road-works. Captain Thomas had quickly become disillusioned with these road-works and other means of relief as well. He received funds from friends in the mining business and during March and April 1847 kept 200 from starvation while spending as little as £21. Nobody realised better than Captain Thomas that the people could not depend forever on English generosity or even on the Poor Law. One fine day at the end of April instead of going mining he mustered some fishermen newly dismissed from the roads, found a few shattered boats and trammel nets and went out fishing. The catch was good; he sold ten shillings worth of fish. Then Captain Thomas decided to set up a fishery and did not care how 'feeble beginnings may appear'. His men began to build a curing house. He was confident that they could catch 'a sufficient quantity of fish this summer to provide food and employment for all the people of this townland (Coosheen) during the winter'. In his opinion it was a far more legitimate way of employing the poor than 'teaching them to seek after subsistence or existence on the tender mercies of the Poor Law'. The *Southern Reporter* was enthusiastic about this venture into 'reproductive employment' and held that 'if there were a few more like it in the country, there would be no need of relief committees'.[64] This miner evidently knew a great deal about fisheries as might be expected of a native of Cornwall where fishing and mining went hand in hand. The weather even in May 1847 was still boisterous so little fishing was done but the men were busy building the curing house and a store. Stone, slate and flags for the floors were quarried locally.

Fr Barrett told of the general transition which was taking place in Crook-haven. Five hundred men had been suddenly discharged from the roads although the Soup Kitchen Act had not yet come into operation in the Crook-haven district at least. These men and their families were now added to the number of the famishing in a district where between 1,200 and 1,300 had already died. Now however men were organising crews and going out to fish. Barrett himself had supplied six boats with meal from the *Jamestown*. These fishermen did not lack skill, he wrote, but they did need money for provisions so he appealed to benevolent English people through the medium of the *Tablet*.[65] Captain Thomas received four sacks of meal and four sacks of biscuit from the Society of Friends specially for people employed in the fishery.[66] It was characteristic of the Friends to support fisheries.

As already stated, the Soup Kitchen Act finally came into operation in Schull, Kilcoe and Aughadown, on 10 May 1847 but not until two weeks later in Kilmoe.[67] Many had died since Russell first introduced it in parliament back on 25 January. Nevertheless, the act was at least good in principle since, unlike the Labour Rate Act, it did not insist on work to obtain money for food but simply provided food which was free in the vast majority of cases. In May 622,684 people received daily rations nationally while only 107,000 paid for them. In June the number of persons receiving free rations rose to 2,728,684, while in August it reached a peak of over three million. The total amount advanced as a loan from the Treasury to the Relief commissioners was £1,724,631, but only a negligible sum was ever repaid or indeed ever could be.[68]

A far more sinister aspect of the Soup Kitchen Act was the mentality of the Gregory Clause which stipulated that nobody who owned a quarter acre of land could obtain relief. Not only the occupation of land but the ownership of a horse or even a donkey excluded persons in some areas from the relief lists.[69] With all its faults and late though it was, the Soup Kitchen Act was welcomed by contemporaries, e.g., James Barry. The new and relatively hopeful situation became evident on 20 June 1847 at a meeting of the Ballydehob relief committee. A resolution was passed and forwarded to F. F. Trench expressing gratitude to him and to his agency for their great efforts to relieve the people. Barry's covering letter summed up the latest state of affairs:

> The face of the country is changed for the better – the people look healthy, sickness is
> less prevalent and deaths so few that the burial staff and slide-bottomed coffins are
> no longer in requisition … The daily ration is, evidently, the principal cause. Many
> noble-minded and charitable Christians had contributed largely to the alleviation of
> our sufferings, and much had been dispensed; yet, there was a want of combined and

systematic action – the administration of relief did not embrace all the afflicted community. Some were pretty well supported through the eventful visitation – others only for a time, and then left with the greatest number to struggle out as they best could or perish. The mode providentially adopted by you, Rev. Sir, of giving one substantial meal of cooked food in the day to each poor person within the district, to be used at the soup-house, opened the first prospect of escape from the dreadful scourges of sickness and death from starvation under which numbers of the people were daily disappearing. Next, the government measure, so ably conducted as it is, and likely to be, under the guidance of a wise and indefatigable inspector, J. J. Marshall, Esq., affords a hope, if not of plenty, at least of few or no deaths from dire want. There is also hospital treatment with the aid of a second medical officer for fever patients. Some efforts to incite the occupiers of land to sow turnips, cut turf, etc. have been attended with success beyond the most sanguine expectations of the promoters of the good work. The rules laid down by the commissioners regarding the exclusion of all persons from the relief lists, who have one or more cows, are too stringent. Fresh orders and the most imperative instructions, to this effect, are daily poured down before us, and this is the only reason I have to fear that the pleasing hope I have indulged may not be realised.[70]

Although Barry felt relatively satisfied at this stage, one can notice his anxiety about the rule excluding from the relief list owners of even a cow. It was the local landlords, rather than the commissioners, who were 'pouring down the most imperative instructions in this matter'. In fact the commissioners had already relaxed this rule and decided that owners of animals need not be excluded if there was a prospect of their being able to support themselves by means of the animals later on. In this letter one meets the first reference to the new effort to grow turnips rather than just potatoes. The new emphasis on turf-cutting is significant also; people had suffered enormously from the cold as their clothes became ever more ragged. Worse still, some of the dysentery was caused not simply by bad food such as seaweed but by yellow meal which was half-raw owing to the shortage of fuel to cook it.

The Soup Kitchen Act was now certainly working well – at last. On 19 June 1847 the number of free rations issued in these parishes is shown in the following table:[71]

TABLE 14: NUMBER OF PERSONS ON RATIONS, 19 JUNE 1847

Parish	Rations	Pop. 1841	%
Kilmoe	4,924	7,234	68
Schull	4,918	8,604	57
Ballydehob	4,612	8,710	53
Kilcoe	1,074	2,339	46
Total	**15,528**	**26,887**	**58**

The percentage of the population receiving rations appears high, (58%) but it is not quite as high as in the neighbouring parish of Muintir Bháire (60% to 70%) or in Connaught (70% to 100%).[72] Sometimes the conclusion is drawn that since the number receiving soup rations was lower in the Skibbereen

Union than in Connaught therefore the famine was not quite as severe here as in the west, but this conclusion is invalid. The reason a relatively low percentage of people was on soup rations in the district was not that many had already enough to eat but simply that they had already died or had emigrated but mainly that they had died. Christine Kineally analysed the 'variability in the take-up of soup rations in the Poor Law Unions of Ireland' and used it as 'an indicator of the geographical distribution of distress'.[73] Unions which had a percentage of their 1841 population on rations ranging from 68.5% to 79% or over are classed as suffering from 'high distress' or 'very high distress'. Unions having from 57% to 68.5% on rations are classed as being in 'fairly high distress'. These comprise most of the Unions in Connaught and west Munster including Bantry but excluding Skibbereen. As shown in the above table, the parishes of the Mizen Peninsula had 58% on rations but as shall be shown in the next chapter they had a mortality rate varying from 9.7% to 18.8% with most of the parishes being in the upper ranges; most of the deaths had taken place even before the Soup Kitchen Act was implemented. Surely this cannot be described as 'fairly high distress'? Yet even within the Mizen Peninsula there was a correlation between the take-up of soup rations and mortality. Kilmoe had the highest soup take-up rate (68%) and also the highest mortality (18.8%) while Kilcoe had the lowest soup take-up rate (46%) and also the lowest mortality rate (9.7%). Nevertheless in the last analysis the mortality rate must always remain the best indicator or acid test of the impact of the famine.

The Poor Law commissioners, however, were highly pleased with the results of this soup-kitchen scheme. In June they reported thus:

> The absolute starvation that was … spread over the land has been greatly arrested, as has also the progress of the particular diseases engendered by the great destitution prevailing extensively. As an instance we may give the Union of Skibbereen, the sufferings of which district were so notorious. Although much wretchedness is still to be found in them there is now a provision made in every part of the union, the population is gradually amending from their former emaciated state and the people are beginning to turn their attention to future occupation and improvements that may tend to their permanent employment and subsistence.[74]

The commissioners and people such as James Barry breathed a sigh of relief but there was indeed still much wretchedness around. The summer and autumn of 1847 was a period of transition. Daniel O'Connell died in Genoa on 15 May 1847. The following day the lord lieutenant, Bessborough, died and was succeeded by William Villiers, Earl of Clarendon. The Poor Law Extension Bill became law on 8 June 1847. The Soup Kitchen Act had been only temporary but this new act transferred the destitute permanently to the Irish Poor Law and legalised outdoor relief. In August a separate Irish Poor Law Commission was set up in Dublin. Hitherto the Irish Poor Law had been supervised from London and had been in the charge of Edward Twistleton; he was now appointed Chief Poor Law commissioner. The soup rations were to be phased out during August and September and were to terminate on 1 October.[75] The government was determined to close its purse and wash its hands of Irish relief.

Political excitement was provided by the by-election to fill the seat left vacant by the death of Daniel O'Connell. The repeal candidate was Dr Maurice Power who was born in Deelish near Skibbereen. He had been at the monster meeting at Skibbereen in 1843. Two of his brothers were friends of Robert Swanton, the 1798 rebel.[76] Power pledged to support repeal and Tenant Right. After the hunger, political thinking was now coming literally down to earth. He was proposed by a repealer from Kinsale and seconded by James Doheny, parish priest of Dunmanway. The opposing candidate was Nicholas Leader of Dromagh Castle near Banteer in north Cork. He was an improving landlord but could not support repeal or Tenant Right. He argued that it was not the union or the landlords that caused the famine but the repealers themselves who had neglected practical issues such as agriculture. Leader's policy was that landlord and tenant should co-operate to improve agriculture. When he declared that he favoured emigration he was met by a wave of booing from the crowd that considered this policy as a form of transportation.[77]

The election, held in Cork in July 1847, lasted four days. Power led from the beginning and was declared elected. McCarthy Downing was delighted with the result especially as Lord Bandon failed to muster the 600 voters among his tenants as he had promised Leader. Bandon would have to bring them 'with a hook by the nose', a heckler shouted. McCarthy Downing declared that the devotion of the freeholders of the country was exemplified by the men who came all the way from Schull 'where every field is a graveyard'.[78] The famine was already being used as a motivating force by nationalists. In the following month, August 1847, there was a general election and it was feared that Power might lose his seat. At last news arrived that he had been re-elected so 'tremendous cheering … rent the air and houses were decked with green banners'. Lighted tar barrels were carried through Ballydehob followed by 5,000 people. They halted at the home of J. H. Swanton 'for the purpose of cheering that worthy and patriotic gentleman'; he was a repealer, apparently. The people then moved to the open ground in front of the chapel where they were addressed by the curate, John Barry. He reminded the people not to celebrate too extravagantly lest their enemies should accuse them of 'forgetting the thousands of dear friends whom they had lost in the late famine'. The crowd then dispersed 'first giving three cheers for repeal, Tenant Right and the newly elected representatives and nine for O'Connell and Old Ireland'.[79] The cause of Tenant Right had an increasing urgency; the politics of romantic 'Old Ireland' had now to be firmly rooted in her soil.

The Commissariat operation was now to be quickly wound up. On 9 August 1847, Trevelyan ordered its agents 'to ship all off, close your depots and come away'. He wanted to leave the people to their own 'independent exertion'.[80] According to Alexander O'Driscoll, a government steamer shipped 90 bags of bread and 17 bags of peas from Notter's stores on Rock Island. Many distressed people assembled on the quay expecting to obtain some of the food but were bitterly disappointed. O'Driscoll protested that the food belonged to the British Relief Association and at least should have been sold. The Society of Friends, however, still continued to send food.[81] Pierre Foley of the Kilmoe relief committee stated that between May and October it sent more than eight tons of foodstuffs. Rev. Fisher also received five tons of Indian meal in August from these same people.[82]

The final rations under the Soup Kitchen Act were distributed on 12 September 1847. There were still 3,766 persons on rations but this was only 12% of the total population; it had been around 53% during the summer, as has been seen.[83] This 12% must have been among the poorest of the people. Nonetheless the relief committees of the Mizen Peninsula were grateful to the act as shall be seen in the next chapter. David Dore, parish priest of Caheragh, publicly praised the efforts of Marshall. Similar expressions of gratitude to other inspectors were also published by relief committees because these officials had relieved the destitute while being 'careful of the interests of the rate-payers'.[84] In their final report the commissioners themselves declared, 'that the Temporary Relief Act [Soup Kitchen] had succeeded in its object there cannot be the slightest doubt'. They referred to Tuosist in the Union of Kenmare where before the coming into operation of the act there had been a mortality of 20% which would have been similar to our study area in West Cork. The commissioners reported an interesting admission: 'Many committees regret on the score of economy that the Temporary Relief Act was not originally introduced in lieu of the Labour Rate Act, while it reached the helpless destitute, whether capable or incapable of labour, it cost only one-third of the expenditure'.[85] On the score of humanity alone it was the simple and fundamental fault in the whole relief system that hungry men had been expected to work whereas in 1822 the men had already been fed before Richard Griffith arrived to make roads as has been seen in Chapter II. In addition, meal was at that time distributed as wages or part wages and not placed in depots. Such direct dealing in meal in 1847–8, however, would of course have been seen as unduly interfering in the free trade of the corn merchants and anathema to *laissez-faire* thinking. By September 1847 the tide of famine and fever had at last been turned. Trevelyan boasted that 'the famine was stayed … upwards of three millions of persons were fed every day'.[86] Nevertheless, the famine had not been stayed – at least not to the extent that he would have liked the world to believe – because it already had taken a heavy toll. For whom and for how many did the bell toll?

VOYAGE TO THE NEXT WORLD OR TO THE NEW WORLD
MORTALITY AND EMIGRATION, 1846–7

By the memory of Schull and Skibbereen, oppose them! [the Whigs]
By the souls of the two million dead, oppose them!

NATION, 1847

Excess mortality in the period 1846–51 has been a sensitive and emotive issue ever since the autumn of 1846. Government officials usually preferred not even to mention that word 'famine' but spoke rather of 'distress', 'calamity' or 'crisis'. Thus Trevelyan called his own prompt account of this event, *The Irish Crisis*. Similarly, the Great Bengali Famine, India, 1942–4, was never officially declared a famine. The governor of Bengal explained: 'The Famine Code has not been applied as we simply have not the food to give the prescribed ration'. Estimates of excess mortality in that country vary between 1.5 million and 3 millions and according to Amartya Sen the famine became 'a focal point of nationalist criticism of British imperial policy'.[1] In Ireland the government tended to minimise if not cover up 'distress' or famine-related mortality while others especially those with nationalistic sympathies were determined to emphasise or even exaggerate it. The Tories, then in opposition, were less inclined to conceal this mortality than was the Whig government. The speech of George Bentinck, leader of the Tories, in the House of Commons in 1847 was extraordinarily outspoken:

> They [the Whigs] know the people have been dying by thousands, and I dare them to inquire what has been the number of those who have died through their mismanagement, their principles of free-trade (oh, oh). Yes, free trade; free trade in the lives of the Irish people (laughter, cries of 'oh, oh, oh', and great confusion) … Never before was there an instance of a Christian government allowing so many people to perish – (oh, oh) – without interfering (great confusion and cries of 'oh, oh'). The time will come when we shall know what the amount of the mortality has been and though you may groan and keep the truth down, it shall be known, and the time will come when the public and the world at large will be able to estimate, at its proper worth, your management of the affairs of Ireland.[2]

Bentinck also declared publicly in July 1847 that in 'the last sad nine months' of 1846–7 six million pounds had been expended and that at least one million people 'perished from famine'[3] – a devastating summary of the human and financial cost of the worst period of the catastrophe. Dr Donovan of Skibbereen found that this epidemic had 'swallowed up the memory of its predecessors, and compared with which the pestilence of 1741 proverbially known as the "year of slaughter", scarcely deserves notice'; he concluded that one mil-

Dr Daniel Donovan, 1808–77

lion had died of fever and starvation in 1847.[4] The land agent, W. Steuart Trench, wrote that it was 'generally admitted' that about 200,000 persons died in the famine'.[5] This was among the lowest contemporary estimates; others were ten times that figure. The *Nation* in July 1847 claimed that two million people had died in the previous two years and was already politicising the disaster by calling for support against the Whigs: 'By the memory of Schull and Skibbereen, oppose them!' 'By the souls of the two million dead, oppose them!' Its editor, Gavan Duffy, had condemned the famine as 'a fearful murder committed on the masses of the Irish people'.[6] John Mitchel bitterly held that 'British policy, with the famine to aid, would succeed in killing fully two millions'.[7] (Hereinafter 'mortality' connotes 'excess mortality'.)

Estimates of famine mortality have varied widely among historians also. Canon O'Rourke (1874) calculated that 1,039,552 died.[8] S. H. Cousens estimated that 860,000 perished.[9] Mary Daly puts it at half a million.[10] Joel Mokyr considers this far too low and at least doubles it to a figure ranging from 1,082,128 to 1,491,599.[11] Cormac Ó Gráda and P. P. Boyle have together arrived at the figure of about one million.[12] The Census commissioners of 1851 (among whom was William Wilde, father of Oscar) took the 1841 population figures as a base and calculated that mortality was 5.6% of the total population in 1844, 6.4% in 1845, 9.1% in 1846, 18.5% in 1847, 15.4% in 1848, 17.9% in 1849 and 12.2% in 1850. This would amount to 1,314,790 deaths. Unfortunately these figures included normal mortality and excluded cases of death where whole families had been wiped out or had emigrated. Yet the commissioners claimed that their figures 'notwithstanding the *unreturned* deaths, show very forcibly the intensity of the calamities which befell Ireland, arising from the famine and pestilence of 1846 and following years'. The commissioners gave the simple reason why many deaths had not been reported:

> No pen has ever recorded the numbers of the forlorn and starving who perished by the wayside or in the ditches, or of the mournful groups, sometimes of whole families who lay down and died, one after another, upon the floor of their miserable cabins and so remained uncoffined and unburied till chance unveiled the appalling scene.[13]

Many others, including whole families, arose and emigrated and neither has any pen ever recorded their numbers. Various attempts however were made to count the famine dead. The *Nation* published an occasional 'death census' for some parishes. A few death censuses from North Tipperary did not count the number of children that perished.[14] There were also various *ad hoc* estimates of mortality by people on the spot. Few if any, however, are as authoritative and comprehensive in relation to the mortality and emigration as a census entitled *A Return of Deaths and Emigrations in the western divisions of the Skibbereen Union, from the 1 September 1846 to 12 September 1847*. At the end of September 1847 the relief committees of Schull and Ballydehob held a joint and last meeting late in September 1847 at which both chairmen attended, namely, John Limrick and James Barry. The meeting thanked J. J. Marshall for 'the zeal and untiring perseverance with which he laboured to overcome the difficulties' of introducing the Soup Kitchen Act and for 'his benevolent sympathy for the poor'. Richard Notter said 'many lives were saved by his exertions in bringing the act into speedy operation'. The meeting declared that the act had done 'great good' in its own district and therefore as 'a criterion by which the public may judge the good results of that act generally' they presented the above *Return of Deaths and Emigrations*, describing it as follows:

> A copy of the statistical return made out with scrupulous exactness under the directions of J. J. Marshall, inspecting officer for the district, showing at one view the very great mortality which preceded, and the equally great decrease of such mortality which followed, the introduction of that measure.[15]

This return provides the numbers of those who died in each parish whether men, women, or children, almost on a month-to-month basis, and also the causes of death. It is exactly what the Census commissioners such as William Wilde regretted not having for the whole country. Figures for emigrants as well as their destination are also given. *(See following tables.)* It is an authoritative document, bearing the signatures of John Limrick, James Barry and J. J. Marshall. The return was published by Dr Donovan in the *Medical Journal* (edited by William Wilde) as the work of 'the most intelligent and zealous public officer, Mr Marshall' and was adduced by him as evidence to support his medical opinions as shall be seen later.[16] The fact that this return was accepted by landlord, parish priest, medical man and Poor Law inspector shows that it can be considered to be apolitical and objective. Marshall's figures were not the result of guesswork or impressions; he had instructed the relieving officers to

TABLE 15: MORTALITY IN THE SIX PARISHES (SEPT. 1846 – SEPT. 1847)

(M. Men; W. Women; C. Children)

PARISH	SEPT. 46 – JAN. 47			FEBRUARY			MARCH			APRIL			MAY			JUNE			JULY			AUG. - SEPT.			TOTAL	1841 POP.	% OF POP. DEAD
	M	W	C	M	W	C	M	W	C	M	W	C	M	W	C	M	W	C	M	W	C	M	W	C			
Kilmoe	77	69	90	70	58	83	114	84	129	82	76	145	54	68	73	21	17	15	8	7	15	4	2	2	1363	7234	18.8
Schull &	63	44	86	76	53	90	139	106	191	109	98	170	50	54	107	16	14	11	11	14	15	4	3	1	1525	8604	17.7
Ballydehob	67	36	53	75	44	111	155	121	233	112	72	166	60	52	124	12	12	31	8	6	9	3	5	2	1569	8710	18.0
Kilcoe	14	6	6	7	7	8	29	30	41	14	12	11	7	6	15	2	2	3	1	1	3	2	1	0	228	2339	9.7
Caheragh	113	60	117	46	25	36	57	36	60	120	77	178	87	51	162	7	21	41	5	7	10	3	2	0	1321	8375	15.7
Drimoleague	43	36	44	40	37	42	69	58	100	76	44	69	65	23	49	17	10	15	11	6	4	2	3	2	865	5501	15.7
Drinagh	47	32	22	31	15	8	25	13	48	21	28	30	27	25	35	13	8	19	1	2	4	4	1	2	461	2503	18.4
Totals	424	283	418	345	239	378	588	448	802	534	407	769	350	279	565	88	84	135	45	43	60	22	17	9	7332	43266	17.0
Grand Totals	1125			962			1838			1710			1194			307			148			48			7332		
% of Total Mortality	15.3			13.1			25.1			23.3			16.3			4.2			2.0			0.7			100		

'keep a registry of deaths in each electoral division showing the names and ages and deaths from what cause'.[17] In addition there had already been a continual effort to enumerate the dead. It has already been seen in Chapter VIII how attempts were being made by Fr L. O'Sullivan of Kilmoe, Drs Sweetnam, McCormick and Traill and others to estimate mortality. J. F. Maguire of the *Cork Examiner*, citing as his informant a clergyman (no doubt, James Barry), claimed that it had been 'computed from accurate data, that from the end of October 1846 to the beginning of May 1847 – a period of six months – ONE-FOURTH *of the entire population of East Schull [Ballydehob] has been swept away by disease and famine'*. This did not surprise him because he had also been told that in the month from 17 March 1847 to 17 April 200 bodies had been buried by the relief committee with sliding coffins and that 100 more had received a decent burial. This same clergyman had also informed him that mortality would perhaps have doubled were it not for 'the noble and God-like exertions and benevolence of F. F. Trench' who, however, 'had not made the least attempt to interfere with the religious faith' of the people.[18] In the middle of March Traill announced that it had been 'computed' that 2,000 of his parishioners had already fallen victim.[19]

This *Return of Deaths and Emigrations* (hereinafter cited as 'Marshall's Return') refers to all this inspector's district which comprised the six civil parishes of Kilmoe, Schull/Ballydehob, Kilcoe, Caheragh, Drimoleague and the western part of Drinagh.[20] On this occasion the latter three neighbouring parishes (Caheragh, Drimoleague and Drinagh) will come within our remit for the purposes of analysis and comparison. Although they are not, of course, in the Mizen Peninsula they were in the Skibbereen Union. (See Map p. 2.)

According to the 1841 census the six parishes had a total population of 43,266, but Marshall's Return states that in the period from 1 September 1846 to 12 September 1847 the number of deaths from starvation and disease was 7,332 or 17.0%. (See Table 15.) Is this percentage inflated? The population had certainly increased since 1841 when, for example, the population of the parish of Schull was given as 17,314, but Traill and many others put it at 18,000 in 1846.[21] Joseph Lee maintains that the census suffers from an adult undernumeration of at least 1%.[22] But as has already been seen in Chapter VI emigration was substantial in the early 1840s. However, while we keep in mind that the population had risen significantly between 1841 and 1845, the census must remain the basis from which all calculations are made. Are the mortality figures exaggerated by these relief workers to gain extra credit for implementing the Soup Kitchen Act? We can check them against some *ad hoc* estimates.

The Skibbereen Soup Committee reported that deaths in the parish of Schull in January numbered 25 daily.[23] On 2 January Traill also wrote that the average mortality in this parish was 25 daily. William Bishop reported the same figure.[24] This would yield 775 for January alone, but Marshall gives 'only' 349 for that parish for the whole period from September 1846 to January 1847. As has been seen in Chapter VIII, Dr McCormick wrote that deaths in Kilmoe in the middle of January numbered 7 a day. Mr Bishop similarly reported deaths in the parish to be 8 per day which would be 248 deaths for that month alone. These figures are low but Marshall's would be even lower since he gives 'only' 236 for the whole period September 1846–January 1847. However the figures submitted by the Skibbereen Soup Committee would seem to be higher, this held that 20 had died in Kilmoe in one day in January and 18 in another but an average figure is not given. On 5 February Fr L. O'Sullivan of Kilmoe lamented that 1,000 of his flock had already fallen.[25] Marshall's Return shows 'only' 236 deaths in that parish for this whole September–January period; this is only about a quarter of Fr O'Sullivan's estimate even allowing for the fact that the Catholic parish was a little larger than the civil parish. Thus the data of Dr McCormick, Mr Bishop, O'Sullivan and the Skibbereen Soup Committee indicate that Marshall's figure for January is on the low side.

Traill and Sweetnam agreed that the mortality in Schull parish was 35 daily in early February;[26] this would yield 980 casualties for the whole month whereas Marshall gives 'only' 449. Traill reported on 20 March that 2,000 of his people had died;[27] Marshall however shows a figure of 'only' about 1,407 up to that date. As already stated, J. F. Maguire published that 2,000 or 25% of the people of Ballydehob had already perished but Marshall gives 'only' 1,245 or 14.3%. The figures given by people such as Traill, Sweetnam and O'Sullivan are averages, and, of course, impressionistic yet they all indicate that Marshall's Return is a conservative statistic as would be expected from its official provenance. The dead may well have been undercounted.

Nevertheless, this overall mortality rate of 17.0% given by Marshall for these six parishes still remains very high for a single year. S. H. Cousens calculated that mortality in the County of Cork in 1847 ranged from 5.0% to

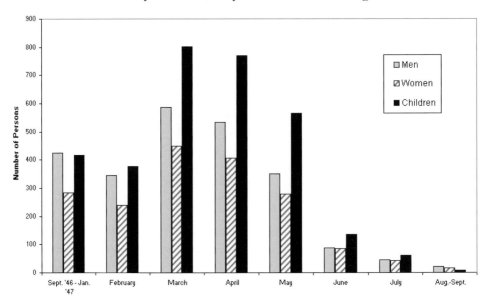

Figure 2 (based on Table 15): Mortality in the six parishes, September 1846–September 1847

5.9%, which with County Leitrim's 3.0% to 3.9%, was the highest in the country.[28] This estimate is probably too low as also is his figure of 860,000 for the whole country. According to Joel Mokyr,[29] the annual average excess death rate for the years 1846–51 lies between 3.2% and 4.2%. But since there was such a wide variation in the death rates for each of these years this overall figure is not very meaningful.

Let us now examine Marshall's Return in relation to the timing of these deaths during the first five months, September 1846–January 1847. (See Table 15, p. 212.) Unfortunately figures have been conflated and show a total of 1,125 deaths, i.e., 15.3% of the total mortality for the whole period September 1846–January 1847. Yet this was not much higher than the figure for the one short but hard month of February when 962 died, i.e.,13.1% of total mortality. The number of deaths rose still further in March to 1,838 or 25.0%, mercifully coming to a peak which in fact was little more than a plateau because in April mortality fell only slightly to 1,710 or 23.3%. The district had to wait until May when a significant but not dramatic decline took place; 'only' 1,194 or 16.3% perished. As has been seen in the last chapter, the Soup Kitchen Act had come into operation on 10 May in all parishes except Kilmoe where it was implemented two weeks later, i.e., on 24 May. Fever had already too much of a grip on the people. Indeed, the average number of deaths per day was higher in May than in February, 39 compared with 34.

A dramatic decline in mortality did not occur until June when it fell from 1,194 to 307. It then decreased further to 148 in July and finally to 48 in August–September as the act expired. As already stated, 25.1% of deaths took place in March; if the April toll of 23.3% is added to this it means that 48.4% or nearly half of the casualties occurred in March/April. If February's figure of 13.1% is now added to that of March/April's 48.4%, we find that 61.5% of all victims fell in the spring. People were, of course, physically and mentally run down and therefore vulnerable after the long, hungry and cold winter. The dramatic decline in mortality which occurred in June is corroborated by James Barry who, as has been seen in the last chapter, felt confident that, thanks to F. F. Trench and also to the Soup Kitchen Act under the supervision of J. J. Marshall, the slide-bottomed coffins were no longer in use and there was hope that there would now be 'few deaths from dire want'.[30] Only 4.2% died in June.

There are significant differences in mortality as between the men, women and children under 15. In the first period, September 1846–January 1847 there were 1,125 persons dead. Male mortality was very high at 424, which is not only higher than the female mortality, 283, but even higher than the child mortality itself, 418. This very high male mortality must be partly due to casualties among the road-workers whose numbers were very high at this time. In February, however, there was an important change; male mortality, 345, was overtaken by child mortality, which was to continue until August/September when child mortality finally returns to being the lowest of the three categories. The road-works had all been closed down by May but more men than women still continued to die. The total figures for mortality among men, women and children in all six parishes (peninsular and inland) from September 1846 to September 1847 are as follows:

TABLE 16: MORTALITY: GENDER, 1846–7

Gender	Number	% Dead
Men	2,396	32.68
Women	1,800	24.55
Children	3,136	42.77
Total	**7,332**	**100.00**

Almost twice as many children as women perished. Mortality among men, women and children is in the ratio of 3:2:4. To sum up in simple figures; out of every 9 persons who died, 3 were men, 2 were women and 4 were children.

It is interesting to notice that child mortality was also extremely high in France where there was famine in some poor districts mainly on account of the failure of the *pomme de terre* or potato. The parish of Corps near Grenoble in the south-east had a population of only 1,300, but in 1845 the number of children who died of famine-related causes was 13. In 1846 it rose to 24 and in 1847 still further to 63 while only 36 adults died that year. This represents a mortality of less than 8% of the population of that parish; nearly two-thirds of the victims were children.[31]

Returning to our own country, the Census commissioners observed that fewer women died than men.[32] David Fitzpatrick concluded from the census that in the rural areas of Ireland 44.0% of deaths occurred among the women, a figure which is almost double that of the six parishes of the Mizen Peninsula (24.5%).[33] Boyle and Ó Gráda have estimated that for the whole country there were 'slightly more excess deaths among males than females', i.e., 511,000 males as compared with 474,000 females', i.e., for every 100 women who died there were 108 men who succumbed.[34] As already stated, in the Mizen Peninsula, 2,396 men died as compared with 1,800 women, i.e., for every 100 women who died there were 133 men who succumbed. Men seemed to be more vulnerable to disease. In the fever hospitals in the peninsula 196 men died compared to 193 women but in all West Cork 674 men and 604 women died.[35] In at least some present day famines, however, more women are inclined to die than men. Fr Jack Finucane of the relief agency, *Concern*, writes that in the famines in Sudan and Ethiopia the highest mortality was among children followed by women, both of whom were more vulnerable than men. In the Bangladeshi famine more women than men are reported to have died.[36] Yet Mary Daly points out that in certain famine conditions men can be more vulnerable than women since they need more calories. In the famine in West Holland in 1944 male mortality rose by 16% but female by only 7%.[37] There is, besides, the physiological fact that women tend to store more fat in their bodies than men and are usually smaller.

We find that the old were just as vulnerable as the young if not even more so. Traill was one of the few to note this:

Frightful and fearful is the havoc around me. Dr Sweetnam informed me yesterday that … the children in particular … were disappearing with awful rapidity, and to this I add the aged – who, with the young – neglected perhaps amidst the widespread destitution – are almost all swollen and ripening for the grave.[38]

The findings of Boyle and Ó Gráda corroborate Traill's observation concerning the vulnerability of the old as well as the young. These scholars estimate that 12% of the people who died were over 60 years of age while they numbered only 6% of the population. The best survivors were the young and middle-aged, i.e, those aged between 10 and 59, who accounted for only 40% of the deaths although they numbered 68% of the total population.

This high rate of mortality among the old was recorded by Dr Kidd, a Limerick-born homoeopath, who came from London to treat the sick in Bantry from April to June 1847, and who was later to treat Disraeli. Kidd reported as follows on 81 patients suffering from dysentery:

Table 17: Mortality: Age, Bantry 1847

Age	Patients Treated	Deaths	%
1 – 16	34	6	17.6
16 – 50	27	2	7.4
50 – 70	11	3	27.2

Allowing for the fact that the numbers treated in each age group were not equal in this sample Kidd was justified in concluding 'mortality to have been highest in old people (27.2%), next in the young (17.6%) and far less in adults (7.4%)'.[39] Incidentally, mortality among the fever patients admitted to the North Infirmary in Cork was similar. Of those from birth to 10 years, 10% died; of those from 10 years to 50 years, 7.4% died; and of those from 50 upwards, 33.3% ended their days extra quickly.[40] As a matter of interest, famine-related death in our own day often selects its victims in a similar fashion. Jack Finucane has seen that 'the children and the weakest, including the elderly, usually die when famine strikes'.[41]

Marshall knew only too well that there was a relation or nexus between mortality and property or lack of it, i.e., poverty, because he also presented the Poor Law Valuation in his return. Property or poverty was a vital or mortal factor. The parishes of Kilmoe, Schull and Ballydehob were in the poorest category in the whole country while Kilcoe, Caheragh, Drimoleague and Drinagh were in the second poorest. It has been seen in Chapter V how the Poor Inquiry had warned that the sheer poverty of much of the population especially the labourers rendered them very vulnerable to famine. Nobody had known of anybody dying of 'actual starvation' in Ballydehob, but James Barry had often seen cases where the 'ordinary necessaries of life would have prolonged the existence of people'. When the ordinary potato suddenly rotted the existence of some was fated not to be unduly prolonged. The following table presents the percentage mortality in each parish together with the value of its property:

Parish	Mortality %	Poor Law Valuation (per person)		
		£	s	d
Kilmoe	18.8	0	11	10
Schull	17.7	0	12	7
Ballydehob	18.0	0	14	7
Kilcoe	9.7	1	0	7
Caheragh	15.7	0	19	2
Drimoleague	15.7	0	18	5
Drinagh	18.4	1	4	0

Examining the above table we see that the highest rate of mortality, 18.8%, and the least amount of property per person, 11s 10d, were to be found in the most westerly parish, Kilmoe. As has been already noted this was also the last place where the Soup Kitchen Act was put into operation. Schull and Bally-dehob similarly show very high mortality rates, 17.7% and 18.0% respectively, and a very low valuation rates, 12s 7d and 14s 7d. Kilcoe shows the lowest mortality rate, 9.7%, combined a high valuation £1 0s 7d, the second highest. Caher-agh and Drimoleague reveal a moderately high mortality rate, 15.7% each, together with a moderately low valuation, 19s 2d and 18s 5d respectively. Drinagh, however, is an apparent anomaly. It has a very high mortality rate, 18.4%, but this is combined with a very high valuation, in fact, the highest of all, £1 4s 0d. With the exception of Drinagh, therefore, mortality varied inversely with valuation – the higher the mortality the lower the valuation. It cannot be maintained, however, that the further west the worse the famine because Kilcoe (near Ballydehob) was much further west than Drinagh or Drimoleague. The two highest rates of mortality occurred at the two extremities of the Union namely in Kilmoe, the most westerly, on Mizen Head, and in Drinagh, the most north-easterly and inland district, towards Dunmanway. Both Kilmoe and Drinagh were remote from the union town, Skibbereen, and of course Drinagh was far from the harbours through which much aid arrived. Location was an important factor as Dr McCormick and Fr L. O'Sullivan pointed out in the case of Kilmoe.

Mere location, however, does not explain the fact that Drinagh, which had a very high valuation, still had such a very high mortality rate, 18.4%, practically equalling the highest, Kilmoe's 18.8%. But George Robinson, treasurer of the Drimoleague relief committee, gave the reason why. He pointed out that Drinagh had no resident gentry or rector and that it was 'the most neglected part of West Carbery'. Robinson had set up a soup-kitchen in Drimoleague but by the middle of February he still had not the funds to set up one in Drinagh. There were 5,000 labourers in the parishes of Drimoleague and Drinagh. He described the Drinagh labourers, 'This class in this district have always been miserably poor'. Now they were thrown on the public works or on charity, the large farmers with rarely an exception *'not having retained in their employment a single labourer'*. There were about 150 small farmers, he wrote, but they were reduced by the potato failure to 'abject misery'. He added that five-sixths of the population, i.e., 'the labouring class … felt the gnawing of intense hunger every day'. He maintained that the parishes of Drimoleague and Drinagh contained a higher proportion of poor than the parishes in which Skibbereen was situated'.[42] This situation may have contributed towards provoking 'the barbarous outrage' which took place in Drinagh one night in April 1847. 'A range of thatched offices' belonging to a farmer named James Calnan was set on fire and four cows were burned to death although a horse and some sheep escaped. The neighbours' thatched cabins were only barely saved. The motive was thought to be that the farmer 'was rather too active in enforcing his rents from his undertenants', namely the labourers.[43] He may also have been one of those farmers who had dismissed their labourers.

In brief, there was a very high proportion of poor labourers and also many small farmers in 'abject misery' in Drinagh, which explains why mortality was very high there in spite of the very high valuation. Accordingly, the case of Drinagh serves only to reinforce the general rule; mortality varied inversely with property, the lesser the property the greater the mortality. As the Skibbereen Soup Committee put it more simply, the calamity was causing 'a mortality proportioned to destitution'. There was a definite mortality/poverty nexus.

Marshall next presents the causes of death. Fever had been endemic in the country for centuries. The Census commissioners such as William Wilde pointed out that it was 'lurking in hovels and corners … but ever ready like an evil spirit to break out at the slightest provocation'.[44] And *phytophthora infestans* or the potato blight was no slight provocation. Marshall categorised the causes of death under the headings of 'fever', 'dysentery' and 'destitution and other causes'. As regards what exactly 'destitution and other causes' mean the commissioners were in no doubt, asserting that they are 'synonyms', that is 'want, destitution, cold and exposure, neglect; in Irish it is *gorta*, starvation'.[45] The following table gives the causes of death in the wider study area, i.e., the six parishes:

TABLE 19: POST-MORTEM RESULTS, 1846–7

Cause	No. of deaths	%
Fever	3,191	43.6
Dysentery	1,626	22.1
Starvation	2,515	34.3
Total	**7,332**	**100.0**

Dr Donovan held that the effect of food in actually curing fever was 'clearly proven' by the table drawn up by Marshall. The doctor further observed:

This document shows the dreadful waste of life that occurred in this neighbourhood in the early part of 1847, exhibits the sudden falling off in mortality, even from fever, that took place on the introduction of the Temporary Relief Act [Soup Kitchen Act] that came into operation on 10 May, and establishes the fact that food is the best cure for Irish fever; and there is no doubt but that employment would be the best preventative.[46]

At this time, of course, the existence of microscopic organisms, *rickettsia*, causing typhus and *spirochaetes* giving rise to relapsing fever, and the role of the louse in their transmission, had not yet been discovered. Neither had anybody heard of bacilli which cause dysentery. (The world had to wait for Louis Pasteur and Robert Koch.) Some of Ireland's leading doctors such as Dr Corrigan believed famine and fever were simply cause and effect, and that therefore fever could simply be cured by food. Dr Donovan was of the same opinion although he admitted that it was a *questio vexata*. He stated that the people who died in 1847 perished from '*fever, dysentery and starvation*'. He granted that at times large numbers of the poor and labouring classes suffered from malnutrition but pointed out that until the previous year few had seen human beings die from 'absolute want of food'. He observed that the majority of those who had perished of starvation were able to provide some food which preserved life for a while but that exposure to cold or some accident 'extinguished the faint spark'. Then diarrhoea or asphyxia often preceded the fatal attack so that many attributed the resulting death to disease whereas in reality it was the result of sheer hunger. Dr McCormick similarly found that 'that there were many cases which bore the name of 'the fever' which were in fact … that state of febrile excitement which forms one of the last symptoms of starvation'.[47] Thus both doctors agreed that more people died of actual starvation than was thought. Donovan had made 'particular inquiry' of those who had suffered from starvation; they described 'the pain of hunger as at first very acute but said that after twenty-four hours had passed without food the pain subsided and was succeeded by a feeling of weakness and sinking, accompanied with insatiable thirst and a distressing feeling of coldness'. He went on to point out that starvation 'induces dysentery' and caused 'immense mortality'. From September to October 1846 dysentery prevailed but only to a trifling degree although the poor were existing on diseased potatoes. But as soon as the crop was all eaten and the poor had practically nothing to eat except Indian meal, then 'dysentery broke out generally and raged to a frightful extent until the spring of 1847, when the virulence of the disease began to decline in proportion as the supply of milk increased'. Farmers had turnips and vegetables which lasted up to December but from then on they were obliged to eat maize and they likewise fell victims to dysentery. He remarked that diarrhoea was aggravated by the 'soups (or rather slops) with which the poor were drenched'. As we know nowadays milk and vegetables provide essential vitamins. Dr Donovan reported that scurvy resulted from eating meal without vegetables. A nutritionist, Margaret Crawford, concludes that this deficiency in vitamins combined with exertion caused scurvy and sudden death due to cardiac arrest.

The death of McKennedy of Caheragh would be a typical case.[48] William Bishop pointed out that soup-kitchens had their 'attendant evils', for instance, poor small farmers were selling their cows to supply them thus leaving their children without milk.[49]

Writing in the *Dublin Quarterly Journal of Medical Science* Dr Lamprey discussed the diseases he had treated in Schull. He found that 'dysentery was far more prevalent' there than any other illness. Dysentery was caused by people eating seaweed, shellfish or half-raw Indian meal because they often lacked the firing to cook them properly, he wrote. The victims complained of excessive abdominal pain and great thirst; their stools consisted of 'pure mucus'. It was easy to know if the inmates of a cabin were suffering from dysentery as 'the ground around it was usually marked with clots of blood'.[50] This disease was also called 'bloody flux' or in Irish *rith fola*.[51] Dr Donovan also described the symptoms of dysentery: 'The discharges continue unabated; the body wastes to a skeleton; the face assumes a haggard and ghost-like appearance … blotches sometimes appear on the body'. He noted that there was also another sort of dysentery which developed from diarrhoea, the patient was able to walk about but suddenly dropped dead. Weak sickly children who had already suffered from hunger were the most frequent victims.

Donovan also described cases of typhus where the skin had 'a dusky hue', in Irish, *fiabhras dubh* or 'black fever'.[52] According to Dr Lamprey the next most common disease after dysentery was 'a typhoid or typhus fever'. He observed that among the upper classes typhus assumed a new form, a gastric or 'jaundice fever'. This was known as 'yellow fever' or *fiabhras buí* in Irish. He stated that Traill had died of this disease, i.e., relapsing fever. William P. MacArthur wrote that some doctors thought that relapsing fever and typhus were no more than symptomatic variations of the same disease and made no attempt to distinguish them. This seems to be the case with Lamprey. Old people at home around Ballydehob used to tell that some hungry people attempted to survive on seaweed and shellfish gathered on the strands of Skeaghanore but were found dead and were buried in the *cill* or graveyard in the Reen. The findings of Lamprey indicate that such people probably died of dysentery as they would have no means of cooking the sea-food properly or would not have had sufficient other food to eat with it and make up a balanced diet.

The Census commissioners however did have official evidence that 11,304 died of starvation, 57,095 of fever and 35,474 of dysentery but as we have seen them admit, their figures are far too low. Yet their proportions may well have a certain validity as Cousens suggested, i.e., 11% died of starvation, 54% died of fever and 35% died of dysentery.[53] When this information is compared with our West Cork data the main difference is that the census figure for starvation, 11%, is only half that of Marshall's figure, 22.1%. Since the census information tended to come from institutions rather than from hovels or ditches its figures for starvation are probably too low because people were less likely to die of starvation than of disease in institutions. Thus the West Cork data are probably more representative of the famine-stricken regions of the country in general. To sum up for the study area of the six parishes: 43.6% died of fever, 22.1% of dysentery and 34.3% of starvation. If fever and dysentery taken together designate famine fever, then 65.7% died of famine fever and 34.3% of starvation.

A death census was compiled by Fr Thomas Synnott who was involved in the distribution of the funds which came to Archbishop Murray of Dublin. Returns for the numbers of 'deaths from starvation' and 'deaths from disease produced by starvation' were made for certain districts throughout the country up to the 25 September 1847. These deaths numbered 22,241 or 30% from starvation and 51,884 or 70% from disease.[54] These percentages are remarkably close to those of Marshall's Return for the region. Therefore it may be concluded from both counts that approximately two-thirds of the people died of famine fever and one-third of starvation. Donovan finally declared that a physician was forced to admit that his art can by itself do little about diseases which owe their origin to 'squalor, misery and starvation'.

EMIGRATION

It has been seen in Chapter VI that emigration had been substantial since the early 1830s and right up to 1845 a year in which 901 persons emigrated from Baltimore alone. But when the potato failed the next year for a second time the number of emigrants more than doubled to 2,122.[55] 'Respectable', planned emigration was now becoming panic emigration and at times even pauper emigration. In October 1847 John H. Swanton announced that he had a ship going empty to Newport in Wales for corn and that he would give 100 free passages. Dr Donovan soon had eighty applicants. They had no food or clothes for the voyage but the doctor obtained two shillings for each from the relief committee for 'sea-stock'.[56] On landing they were accused of bringing 'pestilence on their backs and hunger in their stomachs'. The colonial officer complained to Trevelyan who asked Routh to investigate the matter. The latter was informed that Donovan and Swanton were applying funds intended for the relief of the poor 'to shipping the wretched creatures to England and Wales' and that the Mayor of Newport had detained one of Swanton's ships on the charge of landing paupers.[57] Donovan lamented that the overcrowding on ships was a 'pre-eminently pest-generating agent'. He related how he embarked 100 healthy persons on board a collier bound for Newport but it was detained by contrary winds. Fever broke out, some passengers died and many others became infected.[58] He was accused of 'shovelling paupers' into England. A woman and her son were brought before a London magistrate for begging. She said she had come from Skibbereen and that Donovan had paid her passage; the indignant magistrate wished he could punish that doctor.[59]

Already early in the spring of 1847 people were preparing to emigrate – if they only had the money 'to pay for the steam'. As John Triphook told Mahoney of the *Illustrated London News*, anybody in Ballydehob 'who could command £5 was emigrating for dread of fever'.[60] As has been seen already fares to the United States could be anything up to £5 while tickets to Canada could be as low as £1 10s. Hence Canada-bound ships tended to be overcrowded, fever-filled, and even unseaworthy – coffin-ships – but for some it was a stark choice between the coffin-ship and the hinged-coffin. Vessels such as the *Dealy Brig* of Bantry were going to be even busier than ever on the usual Canada route. The following advertisement appeared in the *Cork Constitution* of 9 February 1847:

> The 'Dealy' of Bantry, 400 tons, is now fitted out in a very comfortable manner for the reception of passengers and, wind and weather permitting, she will sail from Bantry for St John, New Brunswick, about 25 March.

Cornelius Harrington of Castletownbere similarly advertised the following sailing on the same route in the same newspaper of 8 March:

> To set sail from Berehaven, Bantry Bay, convenient to Skibbereen, Ballydehob, Dunmanway, for St John, New Brunswick, convenient to Boston, on or about 1 April next, the well known fast sailing bark, 'GOVERNOR DOUGLAS' 1,000 tons burden; the splendid clipper ship, 'OCEAN', 400 tons. The above ships will be fitted up in a superior manner for the accommodation of passengers.
>
> N.B. Passengers by these ships will be supplied with one pound of biscuit daily during the voyage according to Act of Parliament.

As mentioned in Chapter VI, the *Dealy* was well known as a 'timber ship', i.e., engaged in the lumber trade, and it seems that the *Governor Douglas* and the *Ocean* were timber ships as well because they also needed to be 'fitted up' for the accommodation of passengers. We shall now follow the *Dealy*, the *Governor Douglas* and the *Ocean* to see how they fared. On 23 May an emigrant agent reported that they were in quarantine in Partridge Island in the port of St John. The passenger list for the *Dealy* showed 169 persons of whom 22 or 13% had died at sea, 40 or 24% were sick on landing and 3 had since died 'like fish out of the water'. The number of passage days was somehow not given. It was something of a coffin-ship and was wrecked the following year off the coast of Cornwall although no loss of life was reported.[61] The *Governor Douglas* carried 261 passengers in 32 passage days which was normal and the *Ocean* had 89 on board for 31 days. Nobody from either ship had died at sea or since landing – as yet. The *Ocean* was among the ships whose passengers were satisfied with food, water and general conditions although she had only temporary decks of uncaulked planks.[62] The medical officer for the quarantine station reported that she had been discharged. Oliver MacDonagh found that the mortality on two government transports which sailed from Cork in the spring of 1847 was much higher than on many of the timber ships.[63]

Unlike the *Ocean*, however, the *Dealy* and the *Governor Douglas* were still detained:

> These cases have been severe, the fever having returned, and the greater number of passengers have suffered from disease after landing the sick; many of the others on board in a day or two would be attacked, and it was impossible to land all the pas-

sengers from the fever vessels for purification for want of accommodation, as the tents would only contain the sick.

Of those who had been aboard the *Governor Douglas*, 26 were now ill and 5 of the crew. There were 450 sick on the island at the time. Nevertheless, the medical officer stated that the *Governor Douglas* and the *Dealy* were undergoing purification and would shortly be released.[64] It must have been a welcome release for the survivors. By now it was June; they had left Bantry on or about 1 April.

It should be noted that the advertisement for the *Governor Douglas* and the *Ocean* claims that St John is 'convenient to Boston'. The United States rather than Canada was always the 'promised land' for many of these emigrants. Nonetheless there were serious difficulties; not only were fares greater but the welcome was less since many Americans wanted to know nothing of Irish fever-ridden 'Papist' paupers. In February and March Congress had passed strict legislation stipulating better conditions for passengers and higher taxes on arrival and ports were allowed to adopt similar regulations. By the laws of the state of New York ship-owners in the passenger trade had to enter into bonds for sick passengers, bonds which were forfeit when any of them became a charge on the public. In Boston the bond was a thousand dollars and this placed a virtual ban on many Irish emigrants. A British brig, the *Seraph*, from Cork was turned away from Boston and her passengers were in such a state of starvation that the British Consul had to supply them with food. She was then ordered off to 'St John, New Brunswick, or some other British port'. When her passengers tried to rush ashore they were brutally beaten back on to the ship.[65] On arrival at St John three of her 120 passengers had died and 45 were in fever.[66] These immigrants would no doubt have taken Yankee boasts about 'Democracy' and 'Liberty' *cum grano salis* from the briny ocean. At this time at least there was little of the spirit of the famous inscription later to be read from the Statue of Liberty – little welcome for the 'huddled masses' and the 'wretched refuse' from the 'teeming shore' of West Cork, for instance. The Irish Canadian, Nicholas Davin, told Irishmen always to remember that 'when the doors of the United States were closed against the sick and the miserable of their countrymen, Canada's gates were open'.[67] That explains why some of these emigrants from West Cork would have had to go through these gates and then into the United States by the back door, as it were. About one-half of the 9,000 emigrants to New Brunswick that year crossed the border into the United States.[68] One such immigrant grumbled, 'we left miserable St Johns it is allmost as Bad as Ireland we are getting on very well since we came to the state of Maine' (US).[69] Yet those who remained in New Brunswick obtained good employment in the boom in shipbuilding and the public works.[70] Many of the emigrants who left Bantry Bay must have joined kinsfolk in the lumber trade such as the Harrigans and the Fitzgeralds away north on the banks of the Miramichi river which flows into the Gulf of St Lawrence.

As summer approached more and more emigrants rushed towards the ports, indicating almost panic emigration as the press reported: 'Their only anxiety seemed to be to leave Ireland … the United States, or the British colonies – they cared not which … a convenient ship was their only object – hence ships calling at Baltimore, Crookhaven and Bantry took off large numbers who had not the means of proceeding to Cork'.[71] There was an element of hysteria in it also. In Roscommon some parishes lost up to 17% of their populations and in Galway some villages lost almost one-third.[72] They seemed more like refugees than emigrants, yet others had made reasonable preparations. Fr John Fitzpatrick of Skibbereen remarked that a good many 'substantial farmers' were leaving.[73] Thomas Swanton of Ballydehob, landlord and Gaelic scholar, complained that 'some of the best tenants were going off with three years' rent'.[74] Thomas Gibbons, the Poor Law financial officer, also reported that tenants were using the rent as passage money, leaving 'the dregs' behind, as he put it.[75] There must also have been many labourers among the emigrants as David Fitzpatrick has shown for the rest of the country.[76] These emigrants must have been similar to those of the 1830s whom James Barry had described as mostly tradesmen, hardy labourers and some farmers with capital rather than 'the dregs'.

The emigrants from the Mizen Peninsula who left from Cork for New York must have been among the thousands whose names are on the ship lists of passengers.[77] One vessel leaving Baltimore was the *Malvina*. On board were 183 passengers and she arrived in St John on 9 May 1847, only one man dying on board. The *Ocean* also sailed from Baltimore with 80 passengers and arrived in St John on 28 May. The *Leviathan* also departed from Baltimore on 6 July with 131 passengers and arrived with only two persons having died at sea.[78] Mortality on these ships was by no means excessive. The *Margaret Hughes* of Sherkin Island took passengers to Liverpool. On 7 May she sailed back to Sherkin and then westward to St John with a complement of emigrants.[79] By August the *Dealy* had returned from New Brunswick with cargo and would soon sail again for St John.[80] Some likely passengers on board were Ellen Harrigan, her husband Tim Lucey and family who emigrated to New Brunswick in 1847 but later moved on to Wisconsin in the United States. (It was she who hid in a cave from Moore's redcoats in 1798.)[81] The annual report of the emigration officer at St John – where most landed – gives the following figures for New Brunswick in 1847. Ninety-nine vessels had sailed from Irish ports and seven from Liverpool but the passengers were practically all Irish:[82]

TABLE 20: COFFIN-SHIP MORTALITY: CANADA ROUTE, 1847

		%
Total Embarked	17,074	
Died at Sea	823	4.8
Died in quarantine on Partridge Island	601	3.6
Died after landing, mostly in St John	1,292	7.6
Total Mortality	**2,716**	**16.0**

One notices that almost as many immigrants died soon after landing as had died at sea and on Partridge Island taken together. Many of those who had survived the horrors of the coffin-ships and the quarantine stations were fated to find but a grave in their 'promised land'. The total mortality among them, 16.0%, was often higher than among those who had remained in the old land. The archbishop of Quebec warned the Irish bishops that 'Many of the more fortunate emigrants who escape from Grosse Île in good health pay tribute to the prevailing diseases either at Quebec or Montreal … where temporary buildings are erected for the reception of the greater number, without still affording sufficient accommodation.'[83] The extremely high mortality rate among the newly arrived has been noticed by Oliver MacDonagh who calculated that 'At least 20,000 immigrants, some 30% of the entire Irish emigration, had perished by the close of 1847'.[84] This was even worse than at home in Schull or Skibbereen. Apart from those who died in St John, there were those who were lost elsewhere in New Brunswick, for example, at Middle Island in the Miramichi River where 96 deaths are recorded, all from the notorious coffin-ship, the *Looshtauk*, in which one-third of the passengers died.[85] Dr Donovan condemned the overcrowding as a 'pernicious evil' which had generated the 'frightful sickness and mortality in the Canadian emigrant ships'.[86] The holds were infested with lice, carriers of fever.

The number of immigrants that died in quarantine on Partridge Island for July was 131, including 6 from the *Governor Douglas* and 1 each from the *Dealy*, the *Malvina* and the *Ocean*. In August there was another death from the *Malvina* and 5 from the *Leviathan* including the five-month-old Bridget Burke.[87] The quarantine island, Grosse Île below Quebec, quickly became even more notorious than Partridge Island. It was almost exclusively ships from Irish ports or from Liverpool which were detained there. The *Sir Henry Pottinger* left Cork with 399 passengers; on arrival at Grosse Île 98 had already died and 112 were sick.[88] In September 1847 the names were published of 300 persons who had left from Cork and died on Grosse Île between 8 May and 3 July.[89] Ships sailing out of Cork were among the worst. On ships bound for Canada from Liverpool and Sligo, 1 passenger in 14 died while on ships out of Cork the rate was 1 in 9.[90] The percentage mortality at St John and Partridge Island was not very different from that of Canada in general; 5% died at sea, 3.4% in quarantine at Grosse Île and 8% in hospitals. The number buried on Grosse Île was 5,424 and on Partridge Island was 601, as already stated.[91] The figure for Grosse Île is taken from the monument; the true figure may well have been much higher.

Many children died or were left orphans. Lord Elgin, the Governor General, wrote, 'Although the mortality among children has been very great nearly 1,000 immigrant orphans have been left during the season at Montreal, Grosse Île, Quebec, Toronto.' An orphanage which was run by Quebec ladies under the title *La Société Charitable des Dames Catholiques de Quebec* took in 619 Irish orphans. One of them was Thomas Sullivan (13) from Schull who soon 'went into service'. Mathew Carroll (7) from Clonakilty was 'sent to his uncle by the Bishop of Pittsburg'. Many were similarly adopted by relatives, fellow country people, or Canadian families.[92]

Marshall's Return not only provides figures for emigration from each parish for the period September 1846 to September 1847 but also gives the destinations, either England or North America:

TABEL 21: NUMBER AND DESTINATIONS OF EMIGRANTS, 1846–7

Parish	N. America	England	Total
Kilmoe	22	45	67
Schull	225	155	380
Ballydehob	105	96	201
Kilcoe	78	17	95
Caheragh	38	85	123
Drimoleague	54	12	66
Drinagh	13	52	65
Total	**535**	**462**	**997**
%	**53.7**	**46.3**	**100**

Out of a total population of 43,266 in the above six parishes in 1841, only 997 persons emigrated in 1846–7, of whom 535, i.e., 53.7% went to America and 462, i.e., 46.3% went to England. As regards destination there is a certain difference between the peninsular parishes (Kilmoe, Schull, and Kilcoe) and the inland ones (Caheragh, Drimoleague and Drinagh). In the peninsular district, more emigrants went to America than to England, 430 compared with 313. In the inland district, however, more went to England than to America, 149 compared with 105. The reason why more people from the peninsular district went to America undoubtedly was that they were nearer to the harbours facing the New World while people in the inland district around Drimoleague found it less difficult to make their way to Cork and go by steam to England. Many of those who went to England via Cork must have been among the people from the western districts who, according to a local doctor, brought fever with them to the cheap lodging-houses from where it spread everywhere.[93]

The Canadian press, for example, the *Quebec Mercury*, reveals the attitude of the people towards the Irish immigrants. The Catholic archbishop of Quebec announced a special collection for Ireland and the Scottish Highlands. In Montreal people of Irish and Scottish origin came together to raise funds, three-quarters of which were to go to Ireland and a quarter to Scotland. Those of English extraction worked independently.[94] It was reported that 50,000 people were starving in the Highlands and that 'deaths from dysentery and cholera were increasing with frightful rapidity among the cottier class and small crofters'. Letters from Ireland describing famine scenes were published. The account by the American visitor, Elihu Burrit, was given special prominence.[95] James Barry was cited as wishing that 'he himself and all his poorer parishioners were transported to the west of America. Would to God that were possible, there at any rate they would not die of hunger'.[96] Excerpts were published from letters by Fr Troy of Aughadown and also by a member of the crew of the *Tartarus* which had delivered food to Ballydehob.[97] By the end of March the sum of £3,260 had been collected.[98] An account was published concerning the money and effects left by the emigrants who had died at Grosse Île from 16 May to 21 October 1847. A fair number had less than £1, most had between £2 and £5 while three possessed over £100; another had only two-pence farthing. A John Regan from Bantry had carried £3. There were 204 boxes and trunks now without owners.[99]

The relationship between mortality and emigration is worthy of note. Kerby Miller and J. S. Donnelly, Jr, found that this relationship is usually inverse; the higher the mortality the lower the emigration and *vice versa*. Donnelly writes:

> This pattern was perhaps clearest in the mid-west and the south-west. In Galway, Clare and West Cork, where excess deaths were high, emigration was relatively low. Conversely, in Donegal and Limerick, where excess mortality was quite low, emigration was either very heavy (Donegal) or moderately high (Limerick).

He admits however that one region did not conform to this pattern, namely South Ulster and North Connaught. Here rates of mortality and emigration were both high at the same time. He considers that the likeliest explanation for this apparent anomaly is that pre-famine emigration had already been high there and that emigrants' remittances enabled many of the poor to escape abroad.[100] Our study of this West Cork district conforms to the general pattern all over the country. The relationship between mortality and emigration was usually inverse but there was similarly one apparent anomaly, namely, Schull. Here also mortality and emigration rates were both high at the same time.

The mortality rate of 17% in our larger study area of six parishes was high compared with the rest of the county or country, and accordingly its emigration rate of 2.3% was correspondingly low. Cousens estimated that emigration from County Cork in 1847 was from 10% to 12% and in north Connaught, south Ulster and Leinster around 20%.[101] The following are the percentage rates of mortality and emigration for the six parishes in our study area:

TABLE 22: PERCENTAGE MORTALITY AND EMIGRATION IN THE SIX PARISHES, 1846–7

Parish	Mortality %	Emigration %
Kilmoe	18.8	0.9
Schull	17.7	4.4
Ballydehob	18.0	2.3
Kilcoe	9.7	4.1
Caheragh	15.7	1.5
Drimoleague	15.7	1.2
Drinagh	18.4	2.6
Average	**17.0%**	**2.3%**

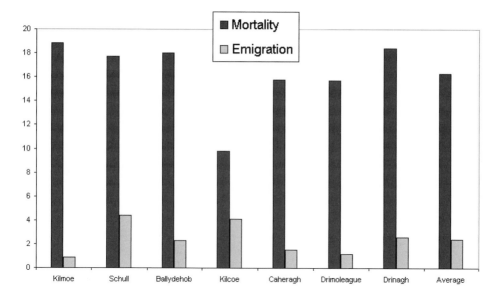

Figure 3 (based on Table 22): Percentage Mortality and Emigration in the six parishes, Sept. 1846 – Sept. 1847

Kilmoe furthest west has the highest mortality rate, 18.8% and the lowest emigration rate, 0.9%. Kilcoe (between Ballydehob and Skibbereen) shows the lowest mortality rate, 9.7% and the second highest emigration rate, 4.1%. These two parishes are the two most extreme examples; the others show correspondingly high or moderately high mortality rates combined with low or moderately low emigration rates, with the exception of Schull as already stated. As in the case of South Ulster and North Connaught the explanation for Schull's high rate of both mortality and emigration rate may be that pre-famine emigration had been already high here as we have seen Fr James Barry state in Chapter VI.

Marshall's figures for mortality and emigration are reliable and revealing. Out of an 1841 population of 43,266 persons, as many as 7,332 died while only 997 emigrated. Those who died amounted to as many as 17.0% of the population while those who emigrated came to only 2.3%. In simple figures, out of every 43 persons, 7 died and only 1 emigrated. As Rev. Francis Webb of Caheragh ruefully remarked, the destitute had no choice but to emigrate to the next world. Farmers such as James Calnan of Drinagh would be in a position to take a ship to the New World but his labourer could only take a coffin to the next world and might even have to voyage without that much. Accordingly, a clear correlation emerges between the four variables, i.e., mortality, emigration, poverty and location. Kilcoe records the lowest mortality rate, the second highest emigration rate, the second highest valuation and the most central location in the union. On the other hand, the highest mortality rate, the lowest emigration rate, the lowest valuation and the most western or remotest location are all to be found together in the one and the same unfortunate parish,

Kilmoe, where lies Mizen Head. This parish had a port of its own, Crookhaven, and Bantry was only ten miles from its other extremity, Dunmanus. If so few of the inhabitants of Kilmoe emigrated it was not for the want of harbours. These people got caught in the poverty/famine trap and many were forced to take the hinged-coffin rather than the coffin-ship.

XI

POT OF SOUP OR THE WORD OF GOD?
RELIGIOUS CONTROVERSY, 1847–52

The time has come to try to break the great enchantment which
for too long has made myth so much more congenial than reality.[1]

F. S. L. LYONS

THE 'SECOND REFORMATION'

Controversy concerning religion and famine relief had begun some time before 1847. Rev. Edmund Nangle on Achill Island and Rev. Charles Gayer in
Dingle were involved in such difficulties in the early 1830s.[2] As already stated
in Chapter III, Rev. Thomas O'Grady arrived in Kilmoe from County Limerick in 1831 as vicar to the absentee rector, Francis Langford, and remained
there until he was transferred to Castletownbere in 1839. He was succeeded
in Kilmoe by William Fisher who gave him great credit in that he had 'spread
the Word of God widely and successfully' and thus had made some converts
from the Catholic Church. Yet there seems to have been no controversy about
it. Fisher himself, however, soon became the subject of a debate with 'some
Popish fellows', probably including the parish priest, Laurence O'Sullivan,
over his 'little charity' to the poor in 1840. Nevertheless, when the potato disease struck we have seen that there did not seem to have been any difficulties
but co-operation between himself and O'Sullivan, a member of the relief committee of which Fisher was chairman. At the end of 1846 both proposed a resolution condemning the government's lack of response to their appeal for aid,
as has been seen in Chapter VII.

Thomas O'Grady became involved in controversy in Castletownbere
also. In the summer of 1846 he distributed soup to hungry people and conversions to Protestantism followed – somehow. One of the converts was made
overseer on the local road-works but as the men refused to work under him
he was dismissed. The overseer brought his case to court where he was supported by Rev. O'Grady but opposed by the parish priest, Fr Healy. The priest
shouted at the minister, ''Tis you that are the cause of all this, purchasing a few
wretches with your Soup! Soup!' The minister replied that it was the Word of
God that was the cause of the conversions and declared that there was no justice for poor Protestants. Whereupon the priest retorted that they were not
really Protestants only 'soupers'. The magistrates dismissed the case. Henceforth a distinction would be made between 'genuine Protestants' and 'soupers'.
This is an early usage of the epithet 'souper' in West Cork. 'Poor Protestants'
was how people such as O'Grady would usually designate such converts.[3]

The word 'souper' had been used earlier by another priest in Dingle which

Rev. W. A. Fisher, 1808–80

is the *locus classicus* for such religious controversy in Munster at this time.[4] A well-know definition of a 'souper' comes from another priest, Patrick Lavelle of Partry, County Mayo, and is as follows: 'a person who traffics in religion by inducing starving creatures to abandon a creed which they believe for one which in their hearts they reprobate, and this for some temporal consideration, be that meal, or money or soup, possession of a house and land.'[5] But in West Cork and Kerry, 'souper' usually designates the recipient of such relief rather than the giver. The argument between Rev. O'Grady and Fr Healy as to whether these conversions were caused by the Word of God or by soup is the kernel of the whole controversy about souperism. Evangelicals like O'Grady and Fisher seldom made any secret of their intention to wean or win the Catholics from the 'superstition of Popery'; indeed they boasted of their successes in order to attract funds. Neither did the Catholics usually deny such successes because they also sought donations. Protestants did not see why they should have anything to hide; on the contrary, this was the mission of their Church ever since the Reformation, a mission which had recently been renewed by Archbishop Magee of Dublin speaking in St Patrick's cathedral in 1822. They did indeed place great emphasis on the Word of God, in Irish too, and abandoned the mentality of the Penal Laws which they saw as having failed in any case. Catholics such as Fr Healy maintained that it was not the Word of God which inspired these conversions but soup, money, employment, or land. In sum, one side put forward reasons of conscience and the other side reasons of hunger or soup, so to speak.

As has been seen in Chapter VII, Fisher, O'Sullivan and Barrett worked together on the one relief committee to try to save the people from starvation. This united front, however, did not last. On 7 February 1847 William Bishop, the commissariat officer, reported to Randolph Routh that 'At Crookhaven and Goleen the Soup Committee is exerting itself to afford relief … An unfortunate dissension between the clergymen of the respective Churches acts injuriously upon the efforts of the committee in carrying out the benevolent instructions under which funds have been constituted'.[6] The priests withdrew from the committee. As stated in Chapter VIII, O'Sullivan went on a fundraising mission to Cork and gave his reasons in a letter written from St Vincent's Seminary (now St Finbarr's)[7] to the *Cork Examiner,* the *Nation* and the *Tablet.*[8] He informed the public that the average mortality from famine was now nearly 100 a week and rapidly rising in a population of 12,000 souls. He was convinced that the Temporary Relief Act (Soup Kitchen Act) would be too little and especially too late as it would be some weeks before it would be put into operation. We have seen that it was to be three months. His parish was remote 'across from Cape Clear' and had few resident gentry, he continued:

> *With greater destitution I have received less aid than has been afforded to other districts* and I am therefore compelled to leave the death-bed which has been the scene of my incessant labours during the last three months – in order to beg food for that portion of my flock who still drag out a miserable existence. As by far the greater portion of the soil under cultivation in this district was occupied by the potato crop, its fatal failure caused us to feel the visitation of Famine as early as the middle of October. No public employment was given until the strength of the majority of labourers was exhausted – and at present no less than one-fourth of the employed are suffering from actual disease – dropsy, dysentery, etc. Of the hundreds that are borne to the grave-yard, not more than one-half are enclosed in coffins … The people have neither seed nor the means to purchase it – and the answer made by a poor fisherman of mine to a gentleman who inquired about the quantity of soil now under cultivation in this district, is almost literally true, 'that there is no red ground in Kilmoe but the grave-yard'.

He asked that subscriptions be sent to Fr Michael O'Sullivan, founder-president of the seminary and a native of Bantry. It could appear that since the priests left the committee that they might have forfeited the grants corresponding to their subscriptions but they sent their applications through the Schull committee. For example, they acknowledged a donation of £8 from Archbishop Murray of Dublin. He sent a like sum to James Barry.[9]

Peter Somerville-Large states that the success of Fisher in gaining converts was partly due to the absence of the parish priest.[10] Desmond Bowen goes further and writes that while Fisher was ill with famine fever 'the people were completely demoralised; they had quarrelled with their priest [Laurence O'Sullivan] who fled the community, leaving them without the paternalistic direction he had once given them'.[11] But he gives no source for this allegation.

Souper Sullivan is a play by Eoghan Harris about the famine in Kilmoe and was first staged in the Abbey in 1985. This character, Sullivan, is a 'souper' or convert. Fisher is quite rightly represented as being very active in the relief of the starving people. However I hold that Laurence O'Sullivan is portrayed as deserting them. This is also the understanding of many critics such as Fintan

O'Toole who stated that the play is based on 'the story of the soupers of Toor-more … abandoned by their Catholic pastor'.[12] Irene Whelan later wrote that it may well have been that the 'priest fled the district during the height of the famine'.[13] Nonetheless, the following points must be noted. The diocesan seminary would have been an unlikely hide-out for a priest abandoning his parish. Furthermore Laurence O'Sullivan cannot have been away for very long in any case; his letter is dated 6 February and he was back in Schull by 15 February at the latest. Traill wrote on that date: 'It was stated in the committee room this morning by the Rev. L. O'Sullivan of Kilmoe that every second person in the Roman Catholic population is in fever and that it was computed that *one thousand* had already fallen'.[14] O'Sullivan would have been at this committee meeting because part of his parish was in the civil parish of Schull. On 15 February Richard Notter complained that 'besides the rector, the curate, the Roman Catholic clergymen, the physician and the coast-guards, there were only five persons who could afford the slightest aid to the multitudes.'[15] If O'Sullivan, a fellow member of the relief committee, had abandoned the parish would Notter not have referred to it? The longest O'Sullivan can have been away is nine days although it was probably much less. Moreover, his parish was up to 100 miles from Cork. The reasons he gave in his letter justify his temporary absence; he decided it was more Christian to leave the souls of his people to the mercy of God rather than leave their bodies to the mercy of famine.

It should also be noted that O'Sullivan already had a certain experience of famine and fever since he had been involved in the relief of the 1822 famine together with the Protestant curate at the time, John Jagoe. O'Sullivan had also seen the cholera in 1832. We find him now in 1847 co-operating with Traill in an attempt to save the people. Why could he not likewise work with Fisher? O'Sullivan had written about his difficulties to a Fr Thomas of St George's church, Southwark, London, who published an extract in the *Tablet*:

> What the sword of the persecutor vainly attempted, viz., the spiritual ruin of our people, this new mode of assault accomplishes. By the instrumentality of funds forwarded by fanatics at your side of the water, the Protestant clergymen of this parish have got three private soup boilers in their schoolhouse, and the starving Catholics are enticed to barter their faith for a mess of pottage. The people do not hesitate to tell their deeply afflicted pastor that they will become the members of that Church that gives them food.

These are the words of a faithful pastor and not of a deserter and they had the desired effect of winning moral support and funds.

The Protestant clergymen may well have been giving large amounts of food to the schools, which they certainly were by September as the accounts of a John Courcey will soon show. Fr Thomas of St George's asked the editor, Frederick Lucas, urgently to send £5, with more soon to follow, to O'Sullivan because 'These fiends in human shape are availing themselves of the poor Catholic's state of bodily and mental prostration to lead him into apostasy by the smell of their soup pots'. He pleaded, 'Give to Rev. Laurence O'Sullivan the means of establishing soup boilers, and face these miscreants with their own weapons'. Fr Thomas also sent £5 from 'some poor working men at Vaux-hall'.[16] Many subscriptions came from various parts of England. The vicar apostolic or Catholic archbishop of York, Dr Briggs, sent £15 to Bishop John Murphy of Cork for Laurence O'Sullivan and thanked their 'liberal benefactor in England'. Another such benefactor was Fr Jeremiah Cotter, a native of Bantry, who worked in St George's, Southwark, London, where there had already been a large Irish immigrant population. (In 1852 he was to celebrate the marriage of Michael Reagan, labourer and a Catherine Mulcahy, grandparents of President Ronald Reagan.)[17] Fr Cotter sent Fr Michael O'Sullivan of St Vincent's Seminary £10 for the 'afflicted pastor', Laurence O'Sullivan; this had been given by some parishioners who had formed themselves into a committee to aid Kilmoe. Michael O'Sullivan wrote:

> I am sorry to inform you that mortality is daily on the increase in this parish. But the calamity of famine is aggravated by the fact that attempts are being made, and I am sorry to state with success, to pervert the poor, and in their misery tempt them to barter their heaven-born right for a morsel of bread.

It must be noted that neither of the O'Sullivan priests attempts to cover up the success of the Protestants in winning converts from their flocks.

Kilmoe received £9 while Skibbereen got £80 from London. One donor was glad to pull out yet another sovereign from his pocket for Laurence O'Sullivan 'in aid of the now grievously afflicted co-parishioners among whom I was born' and felt sure that when the scourge of famine would be over, his people 'will pitch the religion, soup, etc., as well as the said vulpine imps in sheep's clothing to their prompter, promoter and father – the Old Gentleman'. Quite a number of such donors were Irish immigrants and Fr Thomas rebuked the 'Irish tap-room man' who spent 'a shameful portion' of his money on drink while his 'brethren are dying in the fields for want of food'.[18] James Barry also wrote to the *Tablet* for subscriptions and acknowledged the following donations, including some from the president and staff of the Royal College of Maynooth. (It was their wish that £10 of this be sent to Laurence O' Sullivan.)[19] Dr Briggs of York, £10; Dr Murphy of Cork (from England), £50; Dr Renehan, President, Maynooth, £12; Dr Callan, £3; Dr O'Reilly, £5; Dr Dixon, £5; other professors, £13. Nicholas Callan was a distinguished scientist. Dr O'Reilly soon joined the Jesuits and founded the Jesuit House of Studies in Milltown Park, Dublin. Joseph Dixon became archbishop of Armagh, 1852, in succession to Dr Cullen.[20] A subscription of £30 came from William Crolly, archbishop of Armagh. John Hogan, the sculptor, gave £20 for the relief of West Cork (his mother was a Cox from Dunmanway). £5 of this was for Kilmoe.[21] Laurence O'Sullivan acknowledged many subscriptions in May including £10 from Fr Cotter of St George's London through Michael O'Sullivan and other donations from England through the *Tablet*. Laurence O'Sullivan regretted that he was not able to do this sooner because he had been 'confined by fever for nearly the last two months'.[22] The general famine conditions, of course, rendered fever more fatal and recovery more difficult. Count Strzelecki reported: 'In some instances where priests were confined with fever, I found in their cabins nothing available beyond stirabout … there was no tea, no sugar, no provisions whatever; in some of their huts, the wind blew, the snow came in and the rain dripped'.[23] In September Laurence O'Sullivan acknowledged £13 from the new bishop, William Delany, and £10 from the United States per Michael O'Sullivan.[24]

Even at the height of the famine the Catholics were able to win back some converts. In February a John and Ellen King are entered in the parish records as 'reformed soupers' and one Hegarty is described as 'a souper's child rebaptised'. In June Fr Barrett complained to the readers of the *Tablet* that the funds contributed to the relief committee were 'withheld on the grounds that they were given for one side only [Protestant], and thus numbers beyond belief die of starvation'. He wrote that Fisher's 'zeal leads him to confine his bounty to those of his creed, and to famine-constrained proselytes'. He also alleged that Captain Harston of the British Relief Association picked five Protestants from the relief committee and excluded himself and all other Catholics from any share in the distribution of its bounty. When he complained to Fisher 'who in reality is this committee', he was told by him 'that had English contributors known that a Popish priest sat on the same seat with himself, sooner would they have cast it away than give a single shilling to relieve those whose religion he himself had sworn to be idolatrous, etc., and which he, in common with English contributors, believed to be the sole cause of blight, disease, death, etc'. Barrett added, with some irony, that the reason why he had to withdraw from such a committee was that 'a "Romanist", idolatrous, damnable population of seven thousand was being placed at the mercy of our relief rector'.[25] Have we not here the reasons from the Catholic side for the dissension which had broken out in February? No doubt it was for the same reasons that Laurence O'Sullivan also left this committee and went to Cork instead to raise funds.

Fisher's son-in-law and biographer, R. B. Carson, later gave a different version of events, claiming that the motivation of the converts was far more spiritual. One day Fisher was in his vestry room:

> He was surprised by the entrance of a Roman Catholic man who … began a confession. Mr Fisher vainly endeavoured … to stop it, but he was unable to do so; This man was followed by others and week after week they came to him in crowds … He never precisely traced the cause of all this but the result was that his Church was filled with converts.[26]

Fortunately we have an account of what happened from Fisher himself rather than having to depend on what his son-in-law wrote more than thirty years later. Fisher tells how the generous aid sent from England gave rise to the 'difficulty of giving relief without injuring the recipients'. But the solution came from the Holy Book (2 Th. 3:10) where Paul said 'If any man will not work, neither let him eat'. Therefore it was decided to build a school at Toormore 'inhabited chiefly by Protestants'. Funds were soon obtained for timber and slate and the means of employing the poor. Before the site was even decided on, however, so much money had been given for the employment of the poor that it would pay for a far greater building; therefore it was resolved to build a church instead. Fisher himself now takes up the story:

> Everything – quarrying, drawing stones, getting gravel for mortar, was done by contract, so as to employ the able-bodied that were in want. But there was great difficulty experienced in getting funds to buy materials, as all that was given was for the employment of the destitute. While the minds of the projectors were perplexed on this point, the post brought in an anonymous letter enclosing £30, stating it was given to help the erection of the church, on this condition, that the seats should be all free; and that should stand in a conspicuous place (the second, third and fourth verses of the second chapter of St James). For this reason and because it was built by alms for the poor it was called 'Teampall-na-mBocht' or 'the church of the poor'. It is built after the pattern of the old Irish churches. The vestry and southern porch giving it a cruciform appearance … Its gable is an equilateral triangle. Like all old Irish churches, it has a recess in the north wall of the chancel which serves for a credence table.
>
> One fact I think worthy to be noted, that during the famine scarcely any persons perished in the hamlets near the church, who were made to work for what they got; Whilst in other portions of this district, where a larger amount of alms was bestowed, *gratuitously* given, many died.[27]

The reference to St James concerns respect for the poor in church; at the time both Protestant and Catholic churches had special seats which were reserved

Teampall na mBocht or the Church of the Poor, Toormore, 1847

for those who could pay for them. The text from St James was duly painted over the side door and the church's official name became *Teampall na mBocht*, i.e., 'The Church of the Poor', also called the 'Altar Church' from the townland of Altar where it is situated. According to W. M. Brady, an historian of the Church of Ireland, 'No horses were employed in it, all the work was done by hand'. This was to reserve employment for labourers and not farmers. Brady also states that 'The money sent to Mr Fisher for the relief of the destitute, instead of being distributed gratuitously, was employed in giving labour, and procuring materials to erect the church.'[28] We have seen however that Fisher makes it clear that the donation for the building materials was specifically given for that purpose. This church was Celtic Romanesque in style rather than any variety of Gothic. The choice of style underlined the fact that many members of the Church of Ireland especially the Irish speaking people of the Irish Society regarded their church as more authentically Irish than the Catholic church which they looked on as excessively Roman. Fisher had his own printing press from which he published appeals for his church. Lord George John Beresford, archbishop of Armagh, was among the subscribers.[29]

A certain John Courcey, later a national teacher in the parish, left an account of some donations he had given on behalf of Rev. Fisher in Kilmoe, from May 1847 to April 1848. He states: 'This act was written … from tickets which I issued to give the persons mentioned to get paid'.[30] He gave rations to the Church Education Society schools at Gortduv, Gortnacarriga, Rock Island, Ballydevlin, Crookhaven, Balteen and Cloughankilla. A typical entry reads: 'To rations for 180 for 7 days = 1,260 rations or 68 stone at ls 4d a stone, £4 7s 3d'. The school at Altar was given 8 stone and its teacher 14 stone. Individuals were given from 4 stone to 12 stone each but one, Bat Downey, obtained 37 stone. A Robin Love received a half stone of flour, a pound of sugar and half an ounce of tea. Widows and orphans were also helped and some seed potatoes were given to the poor. Other donations were granted to encourage fishing, e.g., 'William King and crew, 2 weeks fishing, £1 4s 0d. In one week in July the crews of six boats received £5 14s 0d in wages.[31] Many donations were given for work done, e.g., 'James Goggin and gang', £7 7s 11d. A man got 10s 6d for tending masons at Ballydevlin school. An Eliza Lee was paid for 'tending at Ballydevlin school, turf, salt, etc.' A smith received wages and another man also received money 'for work at Glebe'. Nowhere however is any mention made of the building of the church. But John Courcey does refer to a quarry and, as already stated, Fisher tells that stones were quarried for it. Courcey's supplies of food to the schools, no doubt, help to explain why the number of children attending them increased dramatically in 1847. In 1845 Altar school had 70 pupils but by 1847 this had increased to 289 and declined to 180 in 1848. By 1852 it had drastically fallen to 64.[32] Whatever about the conditions of aid, implicit or explicit, Fisher organised the distribution of large supplies of food and thus saved many lives. The Society of St Vincent de Paul was soon to do similar work among the Catholics there as shall be seen later.

Although Kilmoe and especially Toormore was the centre of Protestant missionary activity in these parishes it was not confined to that district; it also took place in Aughadown parish, for instance, on Hare Island. This was a small island consisting of only 380 acres but in 1841 it had a large population of 358 persons.[33] In 1848 the island's National School had 75 pupils on the rolls.[34] This did not forestall the establishment of a Church Education Society school on the island that year with 73 pupils on roll.[35] The islanders were visited by Rev. Daniel Foley of the Irish Society in 1849. He found 50 children in the school which he described as Edward Spring's. He also reported an increase in the number of converts in spite of the priests who had told the people not to speak to one convert, Daniel Carty.[36] Edward Spring, a graduate of Trinity College, came from Castlemaine, County Kerry. He was curate at Tullagh, Baltimore, but was also involved with a society, the Irish Islands and Coast Society, which was quite similar to the Irish Society. Cape Clear, Sherkin and Hare Island were regarded as 'missionary stations' of this society. Spring made converts in Baltimore. One of them, a Catherine O'Brien, later returned to the Catholic Church and made the following recantation in the church at Rath near Baltimore:

> I solemnly declare in presence of the Almighty and this congregation that it was hunger and hunger alone made me go to church for I expected that Mr Spring would support me as he supported others who turned with him. He was good to me since I commenced going there … I was always a Catholic in my heart, but I pretended to be a Protestant for the support I was getting from Mr Spring … My mind was very uneasy for I was going against my conscience … I am now very sorry I ever went to church and I will never go there again.

Spring denied that he used famine relief in this manner and asserted that he had actually turned one prospective convert away from his Church warning him of the sin of professing one religion on his lips while he had another in his heart.[37]

Early in 1849 Spring became resident curate of Cape Clear at a salary of £100 a year from the Islands Society. The missions on these islands received grants each quarter from the society. The following amounts would be typical; Cape Clear, £29 10s 6d, Sherkin, £6 3s 0d and Hare Island, £9 15s 0d. Revs Spring and James Freke of Kilcoe and Thomas O'Grady of Castletownbere were official 'visitors' or inspectors of the society. Rev. William Crosthwaite, vicar of Durrus, also received some financial aid. There is an interesting entry in relation to Thomas O'Grady, 'O'Grady gets [to] enable him to hold out against the priest a farm worth £5 per annum … for school master'. Here we see land as well as food being used to support such missions.[38] This farm would consist of at least twenty acres of land. Can this be called ordinary remuneration or is it to be viewed as bribery or souperism?

In October 1849 Spring opened a new church on Cape Clear. The ceremony was attended by James Freke of Kilcoe, Charles Caulfield of Creagh, Baltimore, William Crosthwaite of Durrus and Charles Donovan of Ballydehob. Spring spoke in Irish and the special preacher was Rev. Thomas Moriarty from Dingle who spoke both in Irish and in English. He was a convert who had been ordained a clergyman of the Church of Ireland and was called *Tomás an Éithigh* or 'Tom the Liar' by the Catholics.[39] Upwards of 100 people were reported to be present in the church and they 'joined in most fervently in their own language'.[40]

The 'Second Reformation' had won many converts in the Mizen Peninsula parishes by 1848. Its agents openly admitted that they had taken advantage of the famine but only in a very indirect and sophisticated manner. They strongly denied that they simply bribed the people with food; rather they maintained that the great catastrophe somehow gave the people a liberating shock. It was supposed to be the 'arm of God smiting' them. A member of the Irish Society explained: 'The effects of the famine have been two-fold; on the one hand, it has softened the hearts of the Irish people generally – humbled and broken them; on the other hand it has exposed the deceit of the priests.'[41] The famine was supposed to have freed the people from 'the chains by which they were bound in slavery to the priests'. The Irish Society was determined 'to rend the tottering wall of Romanism … rush into the breach and plant the standards of the Gospel on the ruins'.[42] George Hingston, curate of Ballycotton in East Cork, who had started a fishery as a relief measure, wrote a pamphlet entitled 'The Blessing of the Blight'.[43] Such was the vocabulary of the Church of Ireland militant, for the zeal of these leaders of the 'Second Reformation' was great. It was no wonder that it should provoke an equally vigorous Catholic reaction or 'Second Counter-Reformation'.

THE 'SECOND COUNTER-REFORMATION'

Bishop John Murphy died in April 1847 and was succeeded in July by William Delany, parish priest of Bandon, already mentioned. Michael O'Sullivan of St Vincent's Seminary preached at his consecration and was soon appointed vicar general of the diocese. The new bishop stayed with O'Sullivan at the seminary in Cork until the arrival of the Vincentian Fathers in December; he then went to his future permanent residence in Blackrock. He appointed Dominic Murphy, his theological adviser, to succeed himself in Bandon. It was only to be expected that the new bishop should promptly face the problem that significant numbers of his flock were abandoning their faith whether for reasons of conscience or reasons of hunger. In January 1848 he asked Dominic Murphy to tell the priests of the conference to distribute to the children in the schools some Indian meal he had received in the hope that it might 'in some measure counteract the efforts of corrupt proselytism'. He asked Murphy to inform him if such things were happening because 'anything of that sort should be communicated to Rome'. He had also promised Murphy that he would send an assistant priest to him if he could afford to support him.[44]

This assistant turned out to be the remarkable Fr John Murphy who was a nephew of the late Bishop John Murphy and a son of a wealthy Cork merchant. The young John Murphy went on a voyage to China as a midshipman

Fr John Murphy, 1793–1883

and then worked with the Hudson Bay Company in the Canadian fur trade. He was said to have become an Indian chief called the 'Black Eagle of the North', a sobriquet which remained with him all his life. He next engaged in commercial pursuits in Liverpool where he became wealthy, albeit generous to the poor. Still he abandoned it all to study theology in Rome where he was ordained in 1845. He returned to a newly formed parish in Liverpool where many newly arrived famine stricken immigrants were living or squatting. In 1848 he was recalled by Bishop Delany and appointed chaplain to the convent and to the workhouse in Bandon. We are told that he soon requested to be sent on a mission to Kilmoe to win back those who had been converted or 'perverted' by Rev. Fisher.[45] According to Murphy's biographer, A. J. Reilly, 'the Black Eagle' rode into Goleen on a spirited black horse, wearing a tall black hat and a flowing black cloak. The people were said to gaze upon him as if he were the warrior archangel, Michael. On the following Sunday morning he proceeded to the new Protestant church or *Teampall na mBocht*, mounted the wall and exhorted the converts to return to their former faith. This dramatic gesture was of course a tremendous success. Those who returned were obliged to go to Fisher's own gates and there publicly recant their heresy.[46] This account however must be treated with caution. There seems to be no contemporary source for any such one-man warrior mission and neither was it the practice of his Church at the time. Fr Murphy however did take part in a different manner of mission as shall be seen later.

Fr Michael O'Sullivan of St Vincent's Seminary was a friend of Paul Cullen, president of the Irish College in Rome, where he stayed on a visit to that city in 1841. For some time he had hoped to join the Vincentian Congregation but was unable to do so. If he could not join the Vincentians he thought that perhaps they would join him. In September 1847 Philip Dowley, President of the Vincentian college of Castleknock, County Dublin, held a meeting with his council whose minutes record the following:

> An application on the part of Very Rev. Michael O'Sullivan ... sanctioned and approved by Bishop Delany, to solicit and obtain with as little delay as may be, a branch house of 'The Mission' for that diocese to take charge of the said St Vincent's Seminary, and conduct missions as usual in that quarter.

This application was accepted unanimously and Dowley informed O'Sullivan accordingly. Dowley sought permission from the Superior General in Rome, Jean-Baptiste Etienne. He pleaded that Cork was the second city of Ireland and that they could easily send down two or three of their *confrères* at Christmas to take charge of the school. 'A few months later,' he added, 'we can send some others to give missions in that diocese, where there is a special need for the little works of our missions.' Etienne gave his consent. Fr O'Sullivan and Bishop Delany went to Castleknock and all was arranged expeditiously. In October Roger Kickham was appointed superior of the Cork foundation with Laurence Gilhooly and Philip Burton on his staff. O'Sullivan himself joined the congregation in February 1848 and was the first to be admitted into the new Irish Province with Philip Dowley as Provincial.[47]

On 17 June 1848 Philip Dowley's provincial council instructed that 'the mission at West Schull (Kilmoe) be opened on 23 July; that Messrs Kickham, Burton, O'Grady, Dowling and Martin be named to conduct it'.[48] (Roger Kickham, an uncle of the Fenian, Charles J. Kickam, was one of the founders of the Irish Vincentians.)[49] Roger Kickham preached in the first Vincentian mission of this kind in Athy in 1842 and he as well as O'Grady and Martin had been preaching on the Dingle mission in 1846 in order to win back Rev. Gayer's converts. O'Grady had preached there in Irish as presumably he did also in Kilmoe. These early missions stirred up great excitement; every day the streets of a town would be as full as for a fair or market. One missioner described how the people were inclined to create 'tumult and strife' in their 'holy ardour' to receive the sacrament of confession'.[50] The mission duly opened in Kilmoe on 23 July, Kickham and Burton coming from Cork and O'Grady, Dowling and Martin from Castleknock. On 9 August Fr James Lynch of Castleknock sent the following news to a friend in their *Maison Mère* or Mother House in Paris:

> Our mission in West Schull (Kilmoe) you will be glad to hear is doing much good. A great number of the poor who were perverted in the time of the famine by relief given for that purpose by the Protestants, have returned already. The chapels, even in weekdays, are not able to contain the congregation and the confessional is crowded far beyond the power of our *confrères* to accomplish its work.[51]

These missioners had been encouraged by their council to found the 'Society of St Vincent de Paul and to consolidate the confraternities of Christian Doctrine with a promise of pecuniary aid from the conference here in Dublin'.[52] The conference of St Vincent de Paul was founded on 23 August and it was called after St Charles Borromeo, a leading figure in the sixteenth-century Counter-Reformation. A conference had also been founded in Dingle. Since the conference of Charles Borromeo was founded on 23 August the mission must have lasted for a month at least. The report of the Society of St Vincent de Paul acknowledged funds received from France through the Council of Ireland and then reported on the mission as follows (the original is in French):

> The holy missioners of St Vincent de Paul came, God blessed their work with much success as one would expect from their zeal. The greater part of those who perverted gave in to the exhortations of the missioners. The regrets that they publicly gave and their promises in the future give reason to hope that their conversion is as durable as it is sincere. In order to strengthen the faith of these penitents, the missioners before leaving founded a conference.[53]

In September Fr Dowley of Castleknock made his first canonical visitation to the new foundation in Cork. He reported to the Superior General, J.-B. Etienne, in Paris that the bishop and clergy were, *singulièrement touchés*, 'particularly touched' by the blessings which God had bestowed on the recent mission. 'The famine,' he continued, 'aided by the severity of the proselytisers who had recourse to all sorts of intrigues made apostates in great number *(en grande nombre)* but the abundance of divine graces poured from heaven during the work of our poor missioners brought back these unfortunate people on the right road reconciling them to the Church'.[54]

Such is the Catholic account of the mission in Kilmoe. The Protestant account is given in a statement published in the press and signed by Fisher himself, John Triphook, now rector of Schull in succession to Traill, the curate, Charles Donovan and Rev. Crosthwaite of Durrus. They accused John Murphy, the Vincentians and the Society of Vincent de Paul of failing to come during the horrors of famine and arriving only now in the harvest 'to propagate Romanism'. When Crosthwaite was visiting Fisher, Murphy came and told them that the reason the Vincentians had come was to bring back members of their faith who had abandoned it. According to the statement these missioners also brought with them 'Roman Catholic controversial books', and a number of 'wonder-working medals ... inculcating the worship of the Virgin Mary, who is stated in these medals to have been conceived without sin' and also some crucifixes. The people who came to listen to these missionaries would fall on their knees and make the Sign of the Cross whenever they met a Protestant. This was only following the example of missionaries themselves who did so 'to show their horror of heretics'.[55] The medals to which Fisher referred are known as 'miraculous medals'. (According to the Catholic Church, the Virgin Mary asked Catherine Labouré, a Daughter of Charity of Vincent de Paul, to have these medals struck when she appeared to her in Paris in 1830.) The arrival of such objects of piety in Kilmoe could be seen as an early example of the new devotions which Emmet Larkin called the 'Devotional

Revolution'.[56]

The conference of St Charles Borromeo had twenty-two members and was extremely active for the remainder of 1848. The Council of Ireland told of a 'glorious' case of a girl from Kilmoe parish. Although she was dying of hunger she was said to have cried, 'Mother, when I am too weak to speak, remember never to accept any money from the Protestant minister to prolong my life'.[57] The number of families relieved was 68 comprising 252 individuals. The number of visits made to the poor was 210. The quantity of the relief distributed was 540 pounds of biscuits, 20 stone of meal, 53 pounds of rice meal, and 161 stone of potatoes. This food was all given gratuitously and does not appear in the tables below. The only cash which was spent was £1 10s 9d on tea, sugar and cocoa.[58] These may appear to be luxuries or bribes but such stimulants were regarded as medicinal and had also been distributed by the Society of Friends in Ballydehob in 1847 as has been seen in Chapter VIII.

Charles Donovan of Ballydehob was deeply involved in the work of conversion and indeed was co-ordinator of the West Carbery Branch of the Irish Society. In 1848 this branch had 134 scripture readers, 334 spellers, 124 translators of the Bible and 810 pupils in 25 different schools. Donovan claimed a large number of converts and gives the reasons for his success:

> The prestige of priestcraft is fast dissolving … In the parish of ___, numbers have and are joining our church; in fact, in many places there is a gradual dislocation of the mystery of iniquity and indifference to ecclesiastical terrorism … Many Romanists have solicited my attendance at their dying beds. I have just reckoned up thirty-four who within the past year in this parish alone have renounced Romanism.[59]

This was typical of the vocabulary of the agents of the Irish Society. The Catholics claimed that the converts turned for soup while people like Donovan maintained that it was to be able to read the Word of God and to escape from what they called the terrorism and iniquity of the priests. The Society of St Vincent de Paul soon extended its activities into the parish of Schull; its full title now became 'The conference of St Charles Borromeo, Kilmoe and West Schull'. It met in the National School in Schull on Sunday afternoons. Expenditure was £285 and nearly 1,000 families were visited and relieved, mainly with food, though £14 was handed out in cash. The food was improved not only in quantity but in quality; it included some 590 pounds of bread, 120 quarts of new milk, 63 pounds of tea, 370 pounds of coffee and 283 pounds of sugar.[60] Food was now being used by the Catholic Church in order to hold on to its flock and win back the lost sheep. Did hunger tempt them to stray in the first instance? Were they now coming back because they were simply going to the church which would give them the most food as some of them had bluntly told Fr Laurence O'Sullivan?

What is most surprising is the extraordinary number of converts that this conference claimed to have won back by its influence on the 'morality and religion of the people'. The following list was given:

Number of Protestants in 1841	600
Number of persons who prevaricated in 1847 ... 'Soupers'	1,500
Number of Protestants in 1849	300
Number of 'Soupers'	60

The conference therefore claimed that as many as 1,440 soupers had been won back and that as many as 300 persons who had always been Protestants were also converted.[61] This confidential report fell into the hands of a Protestant in Schull who published it in the *Cork Constitution*.[62] He asserted that these figures were 'pure imagination' and that even if they were true, it was obvious that the conference was a 'proselytising society that labours to convert Protestants'. He gave one example of a Protestant who was converted. This was a Richard Talbot who received a stone of meal and a shilling a week. Others similarly converted were six hungry children who were either orphans or abandoned. Therefore, 'Onlooker' concluded that only eight Protestants were converted and not 300. In all likelihood the claims made by the conference were grossly exaggerated. Probably not quite as many as 1,500 persons turned soupers in 1847; certainly not as low a number as 60 remained two years later. It is difficult to determine precise numbers at this stage but an attempt will be made here later. Did both Catholic and Protestant propagandists exaggerate their victories in order to boost morale and attract funds? The *Cork Constitution* reported in October 1848 that there were 400 Protestant children confirmed in Schull church and 160 in Bantry.[63] It is likely that the children from Kilmoe came to Schull too. This very high figure of 400 indicated that there was indeed a great number of conversions made in this district and that they were not returning to their former religion now that the worst of the famine was over.

We read on the records of Lowertown NS for 21 July 1848 that 'the inspector reports the resignation of Rev. L. O'Sullivan through ill-health, present manager is Rev. John Barry'. Fr O'Sullivan did leave the parish towards the end of 1848 and was succeeded by John Foley who had been curate in Kilmurry in mid-Cork. O'Sullivan was evidently seriously ill since he does not seem to have taken up any official appointment for another year, that is until he became parish priest of Douglas in 1849. He had spent nearly thirty years in Kilmoe both as curate and parish priest.[64] We have seen that in this time that he had helped to relieve the people during the famine of 1822, to build the chapel at Ballinskea, to survive the cholera plague of 1832 and finally to face the famine, fever and religious troubles of this period, 1845–8. He said that he had also been stricken by fever himself.

Although the Protestants did not hold parish missions in the manner of the Vincentians they had visiting preachers who occasionally stirred up the new faith of the people. One such preacher was Rev. Daniel Foley who visited West Cork early in 1849 as already mentioned. He found on Cape Clear 95 persons assembled in prayer of whom all but 8 had originally been Catholics. At Ballydehob he addressed a large congregation in Irish, half of which consisted of Catholics. Donovan exhorted his parishioners to bring one Catholic each to the service. Three of these Catholics attended service again the following Sunday. 'The work of conversion among Romanists there, already prosperous, has been stimulated,' Daniel Foley was pleased to relate. He preached mainly to Protestants and tried 'to enforce the responsibility and duty to the Romanists as taught and practised with zeal and success by their rector, Mr Triphook'. It must be noted that such evangelists passionately believed that it was their 'duty and responsibility' to rescue Catholics from their own religion or superstition. What Daniel Foley had already heard about Fisher led him to have high expectations as he headed for Kilmoe. But his expectations were even surpassed at 'the sight of 250 to 300 people assembled in their own building for it was called *Teampall na mBocht*'. He was impressed by the inscription over the door citing St James' condemnation of snobbery in church. He found them a warm-hearted people who responded to his preaching with sighs and sobs; they complimented his preaching as *blasta*, i.e., savoury. He had spoken in Irish and stated that it was the first time the Irish service was read. Later on he heard it had been used regularly since then. He was informed that when Rev. Thomas O'Grady arrived in the parish there had been only 5 Protestant families in Toormore but that now there were 80. At an average of 5 persons per family that would come to at least 400. That was not counting the 300 Protestants who according to Foley had emigrated. Nonetheless this mission was less than one-third the size of Rev. Gayer's mission in Dingle which had won 255 families or 1,100 persons between 1833 and 1847. Even the curate of the neighbouring parish of Ballyferriter, Denis Brasbie, became a convert.[65]

Foley attacked the Society of St Vincent de Paul and the Vincentian priests: 'The Society of St Vincent de Paul sent an array of proselytising monks with medals for sale or gratuitous distribution and also with money which is daily offered to converts if they would return, while the people of the Romish religion were left to die of want'. He condemned the Kilmoe conference of St Vincent de Paul as 'fraudulent'. We have seen how Fr Barrett accused the Protestants of keeping relief supplies to themselves and their proselytes with the result that others died. Now the Catholics faced counter charges of proselytism and souperism and of even leaving their own die of starvation. Daniel Foley visited the Church Education Society school at Three Castle Head north of Mizen Head. He assured the pupils of the 'folly of the Romish priests in supposing that their medals and gods of brass and copper could stop the progress of Christ's Gospel in their own tongue'. In a dramatic gesture he showed the children 'a bunch of these lying vanities and let them drop on the still undried mud floor'. One convert remarked 'Queer gods!' Foley was then accompanied by Fisher on the journey to Durrus to Rev. Crosthwaite's parish. From there the itinerant preacher intended to travel on to Castletownbere to encourage Rev. Thomas O'Grady's converts there.[66]

Rev. J. D'Arcy Sirr, a member of the Royal Irish Academy and biographer of the most Rev. Power le Poer Trench, archbishop of Tuam, also visited the Toormore mission and spoke to Widow Jack Donovan whose husband and four sons had died in the famine. She had been accustomed to repeating rosaries to the Virgin, 'I have no desire for them now,' she said, 'I have no provider but Jesus'. He alleged that a member of the confraternity of Vincent de Paul was lending a pound or two to farmers but then 'takes it out by living off them' for a period to see that they said the rosary and kept to their duty.[67] It is evident from these accounts that the efforts of the Vincentians, Fr John Murphy and the local clergy were not quite as successful as they themselves would have us believe.

In the autumn of 1849 Fisher received a visit from another itinerant preacher, an Englishman, who signed himself 'J. E.'. He saw the cottages of about eighty families of converts, some of whom were being addressed in Irish by Rev. Crosthwaite. The visitor was impressed by the manner in which one of them argued with a Catholic that sinners were cleansed by the Blood of Christ alone and not by the 'merits of the Virgin or the holy fires of purgatory'.[68] Fisher tells that Rev. John Gregg came on 'a preaching tour' as mentioned in Chapter III.[69] He was a fluent Irish speaker from County Clare who came preaching to Dingle as early as 1829 where he converted the young Thomas Moriarty.[70] (Gregg became bishop of Cork, Cloyne and Ross in 1862 and built the cathedral of St Finbarre.)[71]

Fisher received aid from the Irish Society so it was only natural that he should have given it an account of his mission. He told the society how opposition to his converts followed them even beyond the grave. Fables were told of how converts were seen after their deaths. They were always 'full of misery either scorched up like a cinder or with their teeth chattering with the cold and without a stitch of clothing'. The apparition usually asked that a friend should wear a penitential garment at Mass on so many Sundays for the repose of his or her soul, Fisher related. He himself knew of one dying convert; vain efforts had been made to persuade him to send for the priest and to 'deny his sole trust in Christ and mix up the grace of the sacrament of extreme unction with faith in His precious blood'. On another occasion, however, Fisher visited the home of a man who had been nearly drowned and deplored the fact that 'the people's thoughts were chiefly busied about crosses and beads and the lifting up of the hands of the priest'.[72]

What the Council of Trent did to oppose the Reformation in the sixteenth century, the Synod of Thurles 1850 did to oppose the 'Second Reformation' in Ireland. Seven of its decrees were entitled *De Fidei Periculis Evitandis*, i.e., 'On the necessity of avoiding dangers to the Faith'. It was admitted that 'some famine-afflicted Catholics had been seduced from the faith by means of money, food, and all kinds of corruption'. Missions were to be preached by the Vincentians and others in parishes where the proselytisers had gained converts. Pious sodalities were to be established and Catholic books and medals were to be circulated in place of the Protestant bibles and tracts.[73] This, of course, is what had already been happening in Kilmoe.

Although famine was under some kind of control at this stage fever still remained lurking in many places, for example, the workhouse in Skibbereen. Here it struck the vicar, R. B. Townsend and swept him off. The Protestant clergy at his funeral were joined by the priests wearing crape and black hat-bands as a sigh of mourning.[74] As has been seen in Chapter II, he had also helped to relieve the famine of 1822. He was never accused of souperism.

A dispute, however, broke out in 1851 between Robert Troy, parish priest of Aughadown, and his curate, Edmund Mulcahy, on the one hand, and James Freke, vicar of Kilcoe, and Donovan of Ballydehob, on the other. Freke had an embroidery school near Ballydehob. The teacher was a Catholic; no religious instruction or book was used in order to avoid the very suspicion of proselytism and thus promote the temporal good of the poor girls. In any case this was what Freke claimed. He reported Mulcahy to his parish priest for denouncing the school and threatening all who attended it and of having 'absolutely forced his stick with such violence into the mouth of one of the girls that she has since been in medical care'. The priest was also accused of going to the house of another girl and cursing her mother and family to the seventh generation. Troy failed to reply to this letter of complaint and so Freke published it in the *Cork Constitution*.[75] This drew a sharp reply from Mulcahy. He denied that he had hurt the girl but did reveal his attitude to the school in no uncertain terms:

> I denounced it before it was opened and since and will, while a single Catholic child attends it. The mistress is a Catholic … No books are used. Perhaps so. But the bigoted fanatical evangelical puritans of Ballydehob whose touch is contagion to the un-educated, starving Catholic females, to their faith and morals, these – some of the apostates – are the frequent visitors of this industrial school.

Mulcahy pointed out that if Freke was so interested in the temporal welfare of the children he would have supported the National School where there was an embroidery class, but, that of course he was an enemy of the National System. Mulcahy went on to accuse Freke of forcing Catholic labourers to work at drainage on a Church holiday for which they had to do public penance. He also accused him of ceasing to distribute relief for three weeks during the famine with the result that 400 people died of starvation. The priest concluded by advising the vicar to mind his own flock, small as it was, and to leave the spiritual and temporal welfare of the Catholics to the priests.[76] In his reply to this letter Freke denied that he ever made any man work on a Church holiday and asserted that the mortality in the parish during the famine was not half of 400. He also denied stopping relief for any reason whatsoever. He remarked that it was ridiculous that the priest should have objected to a man working on a Church holiday since he outraged the Sabbath by 'pouring out of the altar denunciation and virulent invective' against himself.[77] Mulcahy was pro-bably exaggerating famine mortality. According to Marshall's Return the per-centage of people who had died in the famine was the lowest of all the six parishes in the larger study area so it is unlikely that relief had been stopped for three weeks. In any case Freke was chairman of the relief committee at the time while Mulcahy did not arrive from Aghabullogue, i.e., Coachford until January or February 1848.[78]

Whatever about the truth of the mutual accusations in the dispute between these Catholic and Protestant clergymen there can be no doubt about the vigour of their efforts to bring children into their respective schools. The importance of education as a means of promoting or countering proselytism was recognised by all. It gradually emerges however that the ownership of land was important too, since a landlord could influence the choice of religion of a tenant. Rev. Donovan who was also a landlord and magistrate summoned one of his tenants, Michael Hegarty, to court on a trifling charge of trespass. It appears that both sides were well aware that the real issue was not trespass but religion. Donovan, the clerical magistrate, reminded his tenant/defendant that if he had conducted himself 'respectfully and with courtesy' he would never have been summoned. The tenant/defendant replied frankly: 'I see I might take the rough with the smooth; I never showed you any disrespect, but by taking my children from your school when Fr Barry desired me'. The defendant was fined.[79]

There was also controversy over a school in Kilmoe. Fisher obtained a grant of some land through the kindness of Lionel Fleming. A dispute arose between Fisher and the Poor Law guardians over the question of paying rates for it. The clergyman alleged that if the land were attached to a National School or other 'Romanising school' it would be exempt from rates. According to him this had actually been the case when it had been previously occupied by 'Rev. Mr Barry, the Roman Catholic missionary, in the district, commonly called the parish priest'.[80] We learn from this reference that James Barry took part in the general mission against Fisher. The Poor Law guardians denied that the land had ever been exempt from rates. Fisher lamented the dilemma of a Protestant clergyman: 'If he gives only a little charity he is accused of living off the fat of the land, but if he denies himself and his family to relieve the poor he is publicly reprobated as one taking advantage of the misery of the poor in order to bribe them into a hypocritical profession of a religion that they do not believe'.[81] J. F. Maguire of the *Cork Examiner*, was quite convinced that the explanation of the whole dispute was that Fisher refused to have any relief given without the 'bible test'.[82]

The latest threat however to the 'Second Reformation' in these parishes came not from Rome but from Encumbered Estates Court. The large estate of R. H. H. Becher would be for sale in October 1851.[83] Fisher had extra reason to be concerned because his new church, rectory and schools had been built on a part of the estate which had now become 'Lot no. 14, Altar and Toormore, 897 acres'. The clergyman was determined to purchase this property. He told how in April 1851 he sent out an urgent appeal for funds 'to a few persons … who would feel an interest in our cause' in Ireland and England. The appeal was private because he did not want the Catholics to know of his purpose. The church had not been consecrated for worship, 'for want of legal provision'. Its position was outlined by Fisher as follows:

Therefore it has no legal existence and consequently may, most probably will, ere long be closed unless the present appeal saves it. If not, the congregation will suffer the same fate as that which, in the beginning of the century, used to crowd the old Protestant church, near Protestant Hill [Crookhaven] and whose descendants are now through a similar process, among the bitterest of Romanists. If this appeal goes unheeded, I feel assured that all the noble efforts at present being made for Irish Reformation will prove a failure, if where substantial work had manifestly been done, it is suffered to depend for its continuance on societies, whose funds are great or small in proportion to the degree of public interest expressed on their behalf.

Fisher thanked the Irish Society but feared that its aid would soon be withdrawn from him because of the decline of the use of the Irish language in his parish. He assured prospective benefactors that if there were any local means 'to rescue his church from many threatening dangers' he would gladly have used them. The rents from these lands would endow the church and 'their inhabitants would be saved from extermination which surely awaits them if an enemy became the purchaser'. These inhabitants numbered 400 and most of them were once 'Romanist', Fisher pointed out. The appeal was strengthened by the fact that some prominent persons had allowed reference to be made to them with respect to the truth of the statement. Among them were Dr Kyle, bishop of Cork, Cloyne and Ross, Viscount Bernard of Bandon, Archdeacon Stuart of Aughadown and Rev. Dr Carson, a fellow of Trinity College. The response to the appeal was good. An Englishman sent £125 and Archbishop Beresford of Armagh gave £10. Miss Burdett Coutts sent £15; she was a well-known philanthropist in England and a friend and co-worker of the novelist, Charles Dickens. Other subscriptions brought the total to £687 19s 0d. It was obvious that this would not be sufficient to purchase the land, but just before the sale two gentlemen 'who knew the circumstances' gave Fisher a loan of £926, so he now had a total of £1,614 at his disposal.

McCarthy Downing, a Catholic solicitor, was suspected of having been instructed to buy the land in trust for Foley, the parish priest. The auctioneer declared that he had been informed by the commissioners of Encumbered Estates Court 'that in all cases of churches, chapels and school houses they would confirm the original lettings and would not allow possession to be disturbed'. When the lot containing the church came under the hammer, the first bid came from McCarthy Downing, £700, but it was finally sold for £1,210 to a representative of Fisher's. A press reporter noticed that 'no small interest was occasioned during the sale of this lot, as it was understood the Protestant clergyman and the Roman Catholic priest were opposed to each other in the purchase. It was said that the place had become a Protestant colony'. Now that the lands had been securely purchased on his behalf Fisher could afford to reveal the fact to the general public. Between November 1851 and May 1852, £324 was collected, leaving £605 to be repaid on the loan. Only then did he publish his original appeal in the *Cork Constitution*.[84] He repeated that the purchase had already meant 'the preservation from certain extermination of over 400 Protestants and converts which certainly awaited them if the purchaser were an enemy of the Truth'. Contributions could be sent to either of his curates, Edward Hopley of Ballyrisode or J. P. Myles of Goleen Glebe. Money could also be sent to Triphook, rector of Schull or to his curate, Donovan.

Fisher held that the 'biddings for this lot far exceed those of any other portions similarly situated in this large estate. This shows the animus of our opponents'. But these townlands of Altar and Toormore did not fetch an unusually high price; in fact, they were bought cheaply. The bleak townland of Ratouragh under Mount Gabriel made £2 per acre which was expensive when compared with the £1 6s 5d per acre paid by Fisher for land beside the main road and the sea with its valuable manure. The animus of Fisher's enemies and their desire to exterminate his converts were not quite as strong as he imagined or wanted his benefactors to believe. It was highly unlikely that the parish priest, Foley, would have been willing or able to buy nearly 900 acres of land at an extremity of his parish. He must have had a different sort of project in mind since his parish church was only 'a crazy and miserable shed' as shall be seen later.

This purchase by Fisher certainly did consolidate his mission making it something similar to Gayer's colony in Dingle, or Nangle's on Achill Island. If any of the converts wished to return to the Catholic religion it would be more difficult now that he had a rector/landlord. According to local Catholic tradition, Fisher evicted people who refused to become converts and some 'turned' to save their lands. Professor B. G. McCarthy of UCC wrote that 'in his dual role of landlord cum parson, he bore down on the starving people who 'verted in great numbers'.[85] In the absence of any contemporary evidence such allegations cannot be accepted. We shall see that some tenants were evicted from the lands of his predecessor, Thomas O'Grady, in Kilmoe but there was no report of religion being the cause. According to Mícheál Ó Mainín the local landlord in Ventry, David Peter Thompson, evicted Catholics to make way for Protestant colonies, but he himself denied it.[86] Catholics claimed that Rev. Spring did likewise in Cape Clear.[87] It does seem that Donovan was able to exert some pressure on Hegarty as to what school he should send his children. Isaac Notter, a Protestant historian who lived in the Toormore/Goleen locality, told me that some people 'turned' for land rather than soup. Land also enters into the definition of 'souper' given by Fr Lavelle above. These colonies always possessed a fair amount of land. Evidently land is a matter which must not be excluded from souperism. Perhaps the sixteenth-century Reformation principle, *cuius regio eius religio*, 'whoever owns the territory determines the religion' had a certain subtle validity in the 'Second Reformation' also, especially when the *rex* or ruler was a rector who desired to make or to keep converts.

The schools of the Church Education Society were well attended from 1839 to 1845 as has been seen in Chapter III. How they fared during the famine and afterwards can be seen from the following table:

Parish	School	1845	1847	1848	1849	1850	1851	1852
Augha-	Aughadown	23	80	84	36	42	40	38
down	Roaring Water	40	90	97	84	closed	–	–
	Whitehall	52	80	90	48	48	62	15
	Newcourt	77	120	124	100	73	21	48
	Hare Island	–	69	73	39	26	55	16
Kilcoe	Kilcoe	61	70	76	73	62	60	57
Schull	Schull	40	76	83	52	69	61	81
	Schull (infant)	–	–	–	–	54	31	closed
	Lisheenacreagh	50	130	130	92	65	65	72
	Gubeen	106	200	94	73	73	70	72
	Leamcon	72	141	129	57	48	42	44
	Lissacaha	174	115	108	96	83	81	42
	Ballydehob	88	158	160	111	109	78	99
	Dunmanus	–	–	–	38	36	30	35
	Rossbrin	–	–	72	48	closed	–	–
	Cashelane	–	138	145	37	closed	–	–
Kilmoe	Altar	70	289	180	113	99	82	64
	Ballydevlin	84	130	177	148	96	81	120
	Crookhaven	41	42	29	21	10	10	closed
	Rock Island	39	70	85	31	28	20	17
	Gortduv	–	–	116	closed	–	–	–
	Three Castle Head	29	78	71	17	20	18	21
	TOTAL	1046	2076	2123	1314	1041	907	841
Local Contribution		£162	£100	£145	£89	£65	£95	£124

It is clear from the table that attendance at these schools increased and decreased in direct proportion to the pressure of famine. The number on rolls nearly doubled between 1845 and 1847 while attendance at the National Schools fell catastrophically, as will be seen in Chapter XIII. This lends credence to the claim of Frs Laurence O'Sullivan and John Foley that extra food and clothing were distributed to the children of the Church Education Society's schools. The high number on their rolls was maintained during 1848 partly owing to the rations of food from the British Relief Association. In 1849, however, the numbers dropped seriously as happened all over the country. According to the Church Education Society, this was caused by emigration, the withdrawal of rations by the British Relief Association, and the more than usual degree of fierce opposition on the part of the Catholic priests.[89]

The years 1849 and 1850 were crucial. The society closed four schools. It now had to admit that the 'violent opposition' of the priests had reduced some schools to 'mere skeletons'. Several National Schools were built during 1849 as shall also be seen in Chapter XIII. The Church Education Society claimed that in other schools 'the tide had turned in their favour'. It had not;

in fact, it was generally turning against them, as has been shown in the above table. There was also a serious decline in the society's financial receipts which it attempted to explain away by pointing out that it received money from certain English sources only every second year. It reassured its members that there was 'no just cause for alarm'. Regret was expressed that the government still refused to subsidise its schools unlike the National Schools.[90] As also shown in the table there was also a serious decline in the local contribution to each school. This dropped to its lowest point in 1850 when it amounted to only £65, mainly because the schools in Kilmoe parish paid nothing at all. Although the schools of these parishes made a reasonably good recovery in 1851 and 1852, it is clear that they were under financial strain. Their existence rested on the sandy foundations of voluntary subscriptions. This explains Fisher's concern to build on the rock, so to speak, and seek land as a more secure source of revenue for his colony than the sand of voluntary contributions. The poorer schools all over the country eventually broke under the financial strain. In 1860 John Beresford, archbishop of Armagh, realistically advised such schools to join the National System, for which he was publicly denounced as a Judas Iscariot by the zealots of the Church Education Society.[91]

The fundamental difficulties of the Church Education Society, however, were not primarily financial. As a system of scriptural education it was failing to attract the majority of the children of Ireland who were flocking instead to the National Schools. This partly explains why the number on the rolls in the Church Education Society schools in these parishes dropped drastically from 2,076 in 1847 to 841 in 1852. On the other hand the numbers of children going to the National Schools soared from 447 in 1847 to 1,865 in 1852 as will be shown in Chapter XIII. The heaviest losses of all for the Church Education Society schools were suffered in Fisher's own stronghold, Altar, which plummeted from 289 to 64. Two National Schools, a boys' and a girls', were opened nearby at Toormore and Kilthomane. Six out of twenty-two Church Education Society schools had to be closed. This dramatic fall in attendance was a true indication that the 'Second Reformation' was now beginning to lose momentum and to be pushed back to some extent by the 'Second Counter-Reformation'.

As late as January 1851 Fisher founded a society 'to rescue from inevitable death many poor Protestants who, through successive failure of their crops, have been reduced to absolute want'. These 'poor Protestants' must have been mostly converts. Thanks to this society, £76 had been collected, 232 individuals had been 'kept from the Poorhouse', 219 had planted potato gardens who otherwise could not have planted any and 273 more had sown considerably more. In June he still appealed for '280 starving individuals'.[92] The famine died hard in the west.

The Protestant missionary movement still had vast resources. The Preachers' Book at Kilcoe church records the efforts of its clergymen during the Lent of 1852. Archdeacon Stuart of Aughadown, Freke, the local vicar, Charles Caulfield, rector of Creagh, and Donovan 'preached controversial'.[93]

In this summer a man of extraordinary talent, Rev. James Goodman, was sent as a missionary to Creagh, Baltimore, by the Irish Society but his district comprised all of West Carbery. He had been a brilliant student at Trinity College winning prizes in Hebrew and in Irish of which he was a native speaker – ó dhúchas. He was a son of Thomas Chute Goodman, curate of Dingle, to whom Rev. Robert Gayer had been sent as assistant in 1833. Thomas Chute Goodman does not seem to have been too enthusiastic about the mission to Catholics. In 1844 Lord Ventry received a note threatening him with a bullet if he would not send Gayer out of the country but conceding that 'Parson Goodman is a good man, he interferes with no man's religion. I lave him to you'.[94] Nonetheless, Thomas Chute Goodman's son, James, was clearly more interested in other men's religion than was his father. In July 1852 James Goodman reported to the Irish Society that in Kilmoe parish he had conducted one meeting attended by 24 Protestants and also by 2 'Romanists' who were anxious for instruction. At another meeting, 18 were Protestants and 4 were 'Romanists'. At Schull he met 45 Protestants, 3 'Romanists' and 8 converts from 'Popery'. He had a congregation of over 80 in a school-house at Ballydehob; more than 20 of these were labourers (presumably Catholic mostly) brought along by Protestant farmers who promised to continue to do so. It seems that these services were conducted in English as he stated that he had an Irish service in Caheragh. He also had 30 converts in Castletownshend. He signed himself 'James Goodman, Missionary'.[95]

Goodman was deeply interested in the Irish language, traditions and music. He was present at the inaugural meeting of the Ossianic Society in Dublin on St Patrick's Day 1853 and soon became a member of its council. This was a great honour because among its members were the leading Irish scholars of the day, John O'Donovan, John Windele and Standish Hayes O'Grady[96] (not to be confused with Standish James O'Grady, son of Thomas O'Grady of Kilmoe and Castletownbere). Shortly after the meeting of the Ossianic Society in Dublin we find Goodman at meeting of clergymen in Kilcoe church on 30 March 1853. The subject was: 'How far the clergy of this district ought or ought not identify themselves with the difference at present existing between the committees of the Irish Society (Dublin) and the Irish Society (London) respecting work, territory, jurisdiction and finance?' Others present at the meeting were Edward Spring, now rector of Kilcoe and Cape Clear, Joseph Lamphier, his curate, an Englishman, Alexander Stuart of Aughadown, Charles Caulfield and William Fisher. Goodman as usual signed himself 'Irish Missionary'.[97] A decision on the above question was postponed.

Goodman used his poetic talent in his work. He soon wrote a long poem entitled *Agallamh Bhriain agus Airt* or 'Dialogue of Bryan and Art' in which Bryan defends the Catholic faith while Art, a convert, denounces it. Its first line runs *Is mairg, a Art, do thréig an t-aon chreidimh cóir* or 'Woe unto the person, Art, who abandoned the one true faith'. A *spéirbhean* literally a 'sky woman' appears in an *Aisling* or vision poem. She is not *Éire* or *Banba*, the personification of Ireland suffering under English rule, but the personification of the

254

Rev. James Goodman, 1826–96

Bible. She is weeping because Rome and the priests had banished her from Ireland by putting the *púicín* or blindfold on the people who now were *go dorcha dall ag siúl san oiche*; 'dark blind walking in the night'. Catholic devotions are condemned:

> *An scaipléir crón agus an éide,*
> *Coinnle céarach agus Ola Dhéanach,*
> *Aithrí, troscadh agus ceirteacha beannaithe,*
> *Tobair, turais, agus Laidean dá stealladh libh.*

> *The brown scapular and the habit,*
> *Wax candles and Last Anointing,*
> *Penance, fasting and holy rags,*
> *Wells, pilgrimages, and Latin spouted at you.*

On the other hand, when the people become Protestant, there will be plenty of milk and potatoes and barns will be full; there will be a sort of *Tír na nÓg* or heaven on earth.

> *Beidh síocháin ghrámhar againn le chéile,*
> *Beidh againn cuigeann is cruach is maothal,*
> *An Bíobla naofa líofa á léamh linn,*
> *Fairsinge, flúirse is beannacht Dé againn.*

We will have love and peace with one another,
We will have churn and reek and new milk,
Reading the holy Bible fluently,
We will have generosity and plenty and the blessing of God.[98]

The spring of 1852 was one of change in Church and State. Lord John Russell's Whig government fell and was replaced by Lord Stanley, Earl of Derby, and the Tories. Clarendon, the lord lieutenant, was succeeded by Lord Eglington. Archbishop Murray of Dublin died at the age of eighty-two; he had been a link with the later Penal Law period, the rebellion of 1798 and the Veto controversy. His successor was Paul Cullen who was to introduce his Ultramontane policies and extend his authority over the Irish Church.[99]

Just as the building of the church, *Teampall na mBocht*, had provided a focus for the 'Second Reformation' it was probably thought that the building of a new Catholic chapel would consolidate the gains of the 'Second Counter-Reformation'. So a new parish chapel was begun in Goleen in the spring of 1852. Fr Foley had to make an appeal to the public on account of the following 'distressing circumstances':

> There are in his parish two chapels, eight miles asunder. Of these, one can scarcely contain 800 out of a congregation of 2,500; it was badly built … its roof is falling in. Besides, since the famine began, bribes were offered, schools where children got food and clothing were opened and other inducements held out to the people to abjure their faith … Newspapers circulated calumnies against the present parish priest with the avowed object of raising subscriptions to relieve the perverts; and huge sums are now being expended in this demoralising work … He therefore calls on the good and charitable, to give him the means of employing poor people whose faith is thus endangered and putting an end *among them*, to that vile traffic of religion – of which he is falsely charged by the Derry papers of encouraging among Protestants.

This is a good summary of the controversy over souperism from the Catholic viewpoint. The employment which would be given by the church building was emphasised. Employment of course had also been provided in the building of the church, *Teampall na mBocht*; perhaps some came merely to work or even scoff but remained to pray. Foley also quoted a letter from Bishop Delany encouraging the building of the chapel. The bishop declared that there was no spot in the Christian world in which a chapel was so badly needed because of the danger that the Atlantic storms would reduce the old one, 'a crazy and miserable shed', to a heap of ruins. He called on Catholics to support the people of Kilmoe. They well deserved it because of 'their noble fortitude in resisting the insidious attempts made to corrupt their Faith by the base and demoralising means of bribery'. Foley thanked those who had subscribed already; the bishop himself gave £20. Thomas Barry, parish priest of St Finbarr's and formerly of Bantry, gave £3. James Barry of Bantry, former parish priest of Schull, gave a like sum. John Murphy, the 'Black Eagle', now administrator of the parish of SS Peter and Paul, contributed £5, as also did the former parish priest of Kilmoe parish, Laurence O'Sullivan. Other subscriptions nearly all from priests brought the total to £69. The only lay subscriber mentioned was a Protestant, Mr Notter of Lissacaha House near Goleen.[100]

Special attention was drawn to Foley's appeal by J. F. Maguire. He was glad that the 'extraordinary efforts' made to 'pervert' the people through the medium of soup had 'proved abortive' in what had been the 'stronghold of proselytism'. He was giving the same sort of publicity to Foley as the *Cork Constitution* was affording Fisher and he published lists of subscriptions.[101] This appeal was also printed in handbills and sent to England and America.[102] The chapel was opened two years later on 11 October 1854 and dedicated to 'Mary, Star of the Sea and St Patrick'.[103] It is a handsome building, clearly Gothic in style, and contrasting favourably with the more humble pre-famine, barn-style, chapels in Schull, Ballydehob. Just as the church, *Teampall na mBocht*, is a symbol of the spirit of the Protestants, especially of the converts during the 'Second Reformation', the new Goleen chapel, worthy of being called a church, is a symbol of the faith and growing confidence of Catholics during the 'Second Counter-Reformation'.

CONCLUSION

An attempt must now be made to discover approximately how many Catholics turned Protestant in Kilmoe between 1831, the year of Rev. Thomas O'Grady's arrival, and 1852. Unfortunately, the census of 1851 does not include religious statistics. The claims made by both Protestant and Catholic propagandists must naturally be treated with caution. As already mentioned Rev. Daniel Foley of the Irish Society claimed in 1849 that there were 75 families of converts in Toormore which would amount to about 375 persons. This presumedly excludes the 300 who he claimed had already emigrated. In 1851 Fisher informed the Irish Society that there were 400 Protestants in Toormore and that they had been 'mostly Romanist'.[104] This is the figure which he also gave in his appeal for funds to buy land as has been seen. Brady (the authoritative Church of Ireland source) stated that in 1860 there were 509 Protestants in the Toormore side of Kilmoe parish.[105] This is a significant number and reveals that Fisher and Foley were not much exaggerating when they claimed that there were upwards of 400 converts at Toormore. What was the maximum number of converts then? How many did the Catholic Counter-Reformation win back? The claim by St Vincent de Paul that 1,500 Catholics 'perverted' is probably a gross exaggeration as certainly is their claim that only sixty 'soupers' remained after the Vincentian mission.

Brady states that in 1860 there were 1,022 Protestants in all of Kilmoe parish which was an increase of 392 since 1830 when there had been only 630 Protestants in the whole parish. This increase took place mainly at Toormore and it tallies nicely with the estimate of Fisher and Foley that upwards of 400 converts had been made since Rev. O'Grady began the missionary work in 1831. The total population was then 6,889, so Protestants numbered only 9% of the population. By 1861 the total population had decreased to 3,779, but the Protestant population had risen to 1,022 so now it numbered 27% of total population. One was obliged to depend on Brady for figures for the Protestant population up to 1860, but the 1861 census gave the numbers for each denomination and records 826 Protestants for Kilmoe;[106] this is 196 lower than Brady's figure, which must be noted. Nevertheless, even according to the census, Protestants still made up 22% of the population of that parish.

In the parish of Schull, however, the Protestant population fell from 1,898 in 1830 to 1,240 in 1860 according to Brady, a decrease of 35%. According to the census it fell to only 1,435, a decrease of 24%. In Aughadown the Protestant population fell from 506 in 1834 to 316 in 1860, a fall of 34%. No figure is given in the census for Aughadown. In Kilcoe there was a marginal increase in the Protestant population from 1830 to 1860, i.e., from 218 to 220, according to Brady, but according to the census it decreased to 169, i.e., by 22%. This was in line with the rest of the country where from 1834 to 1861 the Protestant population decreased by 158,707 persons but was still 12% of the population as compared with 11% in 1834.[107] The fact that the Protestant population of Kilmoe increased by at least 22% (census) confirms that Fisher made great and successful efforts to win converts while the decline of at least 24% (census) in Schull similarly confirms that Traill or even Triphook had made no such efforts.

The number of Protestants in Kilmoe, 826 (census), was of course remarkably high. By now the number of Protestants in Dingle/Ventry had declined to 478 (census). As already stated the number of families that converted in that district was over three times as large as at Toormore. The founder of that Dingle/Ventry mission, Rev. Gayer, died of fever in 1848. Cholera swept off his opponent, Fr Devine, the following year.[108] The outbreak of the Crimean war in 1854 distracted English attention and charitable funds from Ireland. The work of Florence Nightingale quickly became the more fashionable and patriotic charity. Houses in the colony in Ventry were being advertised for leasing for holidays. A correspondent of the *Dingle and Ventry Mission* for 1855 saw Ireland 'reverting to the obscurity of the dark ages'.[109]

Edward Nangle was transferred from Achill to be rector of Skreen, County Sligo in 1852. Irene Whelan observes that the colony 'did not prosper greatly after his passing'; converts either emigrated or returned to their former faith.[110] Spring's mission in Cape Clear did not prosper either.[111] On the other hand, Fisher even consolidated his position in 1855 by arguing that the price of corn had increased since the tithe composition of 1827 and thus secured an increase in the tithes of 3s 2d in the pound amounting to an increase from £500 to £580 per annum in a parish where the tithes were already extremely high.[112] This unjust and anachronistic tax would before very long be abolished with the Disestablishment of the Church of Ireland in 1869. Nevertheless, considering the relative positions of Gayer in Dingle, Nangle in Achill and Spring in Cape Clear at the end of the 1850s, it was Fisher who was holding out best of all against the undoubted vigour of the Catholic 'Counter-Reformation'.

Clergymen such as Gayer and Fisher would not have been so successful had it not been for the active or at least tacit support of the gentry such as Lord Ventry, Viscount Bernard, R. B. Hungerford and Lionel Fleming. Bernard assured a meeting of the Irish Society in London that the Irish were indeed grateful for the famine relief, that the Catholic Church was 'shaken to the foundations' and that every effort was now needed 'to complete its downfall'.[113] Rev. J. R. Cotter, rector of Donoughmore in Mid-Cork, was a rare exception as he was rebuked by the local Protestant landlords and the Justices of the Peace, W. Crook and S. T. W. French, at a large meeting held in March 1847. The following resolution was passed 'by 10,000 to 1':

> At this time of unexampled privations, when the exertions of all parties, lay and clerical, are necessary to alleviate the misery of the poor, we emphatically condemn as mischievous and fraught with danger, any attempt, in any way, to take advantage of the wretched condition of a famine-stricken people to force on them any peculiar notions of religion, contrary to their present belief or that of their ancestors.

Rev. Cotter denied seeking to promote conversion by bribery and was determined to continue his missionary work. But Mr French retorted that he deplored 'all attempts to shake the faith of the ignorant and the uninformed, whether it is done by meal or milk, by soup or tracts'. Cotter resigned as secretary of the relief committee.[114] In Kilmoe, however, it was the priests, Laurence O'Sullivan and Thomas Barrett, who felt obliged to leave the committee.

At this stage the question must be posed: 'Were the numerous successes of the Protestant missionary movement in these parishes the result of pastoral neglect by the Catholic Church?' Dr Paul Cullen lamented the 'continued absence' of the parish priest in Oughterard, County Galway, the 'inability' of the two curates and the 'lack of energy' of the bishop'.[115] So there were indeed some examples of pastoral neglect even allowing for the fact that Paul Cullen could at times be a rather harsh and unfair critic of fellow clergymen. There was no absenteeism, however, among the priests in the parishes of the Mizen Peninsula; indeed they were very active in providing churches and schools for their people in pre-famine times.[116] It is often held that the Evangelical missions had their greatest successes in John MacHale's own archdiocese of Tuam because of his opposition to the National Schools.[117] But in Kilmoe parish there was a National School in Crookhaven and another at Lowertown only three miles from Toormore. The National School set up on Hare Island by Fr Troy in 1845 did not forestall the establishment of a Church Education Society school and a congregation of converts in 1849.

Although the priests were certainly concerned for the welfare of their people, it is clear that some of these pastors were beginning to lose some contact with their flocks, since they had been rapidly increasing in numbers before the famine. We have seen in Chapter III that Fr Michael Collins of Skibbereen admitted it. There were not enough priests and particularly there were not enough chapels which were sufficiently large to accommodate the people. In 1841 there were as many as 4,583 Catholics for each priest in these parishes. Since communications in general and educational facilities such as chapels and schools were so inadequate, it was physically impossible for a pastor to tend his flock properly. On the other hand each Protestant clergyman had an average of only 705 persons to care for.[118] It was only to be expected that he should have been tempted to increase his flock especially if he had an 'evangelical' conscience. Catholics who were hungry spiritually and temporally must have felt attracted to the Protestant clergyman especially in hard times if he were found to be 'charitable'.

Between 1841 and 1861, the number of Catholics for each priest in the parishes fell by 48%, from 4,583 to 2,400. The national average in 1861 was one priest to every 1,500 Catholics.[119] The fall in the ratio of laity to clergy was even more dramatic among the Protestants in these parishes. The number of laity decreased from 3,512 to 2,285 while the number of clergy increased from five to seven.[120] Therefore the number of Protestants per clergyman dropped from 705 to 326, i.e., by 54%. The practice of religion undoubtedly increased steadily among Catholics and Protestants; there was consequently less straying from one fold to the other.

If there had been any pastoral neglect earlier in the century perhaps it was the Church of Ireland which was guilty. As already stated, Fisher himself criticised his own Church for being indifferent to his poor and remote parish with the result that it lost members to the Methodists and the Catholics.[121] For example in the early part of the century there had been only one curate representing the absentee rector, Francis Langford. Now in 1852 there was a resident rector, Fisher, and two curates, J. P. Myles and E. H. Hopley, to care for about 1,022 laity (including converts). In the Catholic parish, on the other hand, there were two priests for 2,500 laity. The Protestant effort of the period 1831–52 was not a case of a zealous Protestant Church winning converts at the expense of a lax Catholic Church. It was rather a case of converts being won or lost as a result of a bitter struggle between two rival and zealous Churches for the allegiance of people in this parish of Kilmoe and to a lesser extent in the other parishes, the Protestants tending to be Evangelical and the Catholics to be Ultramontane. The efforts made to convert Catholics all over the country were described by a Catholic historian, E. J. Quigley, as 'a form of persecution and proselytism and fraud … of such ferocity, of such venom, of such magnitude, that even great priests feared for the faith.'[122] This has been the traditional Catholic assessment and is rather severe. Nevertheless, when taking into account the certain reserve which Protestants have adopted since Disestablishment in 1869, the daring and persistence of the evangelicals is amazing; their own term for it was 'aggressiveness'. By 1856, this approach was generally seen to be counter-productive and was gradually abandoned. A controversial preacher admitted that he had been given good advice by a convert: 'If your riverence was going to catch birds, would you begin by throwin' stones at them'.[123] It had indeed been a bitter struggle. As James Goodman's fictional character, Bryan, warned, *Is mairg, Art, do thréig an t-aon chreideamh cóir*, 'Woe unto the person, Art, who abandoned the one true faith'. No matter who it was, John Henry Newman of the Oxford Movement or Widow Jack Donovan of Toormore, changing religion was often a traumatic and costly experience.

There is a further question to be asked: To what extent did the general body of the clergy of the Church of Ireland support the proselytising drive of some of their brethren, clerical and lay? Desmond Bowen states that the clergy-men of the dioceses of Killala and Achonry were not guilty of proselytism or souperism during 1847. He holds that there is no evidence to indicate that these clergymen were 'any different from the rest of their Established Church clergy-men when they showed great reluctance to support missions to the Catholics'.[124] It is obvious however that several of the parsons of these West Cork parishes did enthusiastically support the Irish Society and made no secret of, or apo-logy for, trying to win converts. We have seen how Fisher even published it in the press. Between 1831 and 1852, at least thirteen Protestant clergymen minis-tered in these parishes at various times. Eleven of them, Thomas O'Grady, his successor, Fisher, his two curates, Myles and Hopley, also Triphook and Dono-van of Schull, Stuart of Aughadown, Freke and Lamphier of Kilcoe, Spring of Kilcoe and Cape Clear, and Goodman all gained converts. The only exceptions were Traill and his curate, Alexander McCabe. The Trench clergymen did not attempt to make converts either. Thus, of the resident clergymen, eleven out of thirteen made varying degrees of effort to increase their flocks during the famine or to fulfil 'their duty and responsibility to the Romanists' as one of themselves put it.

It must always be recognised, of course, that it was extremely difficult for a Protestant clergyman to be genuinely charitable without leaving himself open to charges of trying to make converts as Fisher himself pointed out. It was in-deed difficult but by no means impossible. It has been already noted that a Catholic clergyman, undoubtedly James Barry, publicly acknowledged the great success of F. F. Trench in saving the lives of the people but pointed out that he 'had not made the least attempt to interfere in the religion of the people'. It must be admitted, however, that there was not always a clear line to deter-mine precisely where charity ended and attempts to convert began. Any charity given by a clergyman of one denomination can never be absolutely undenom-inational or neutral. Professor R. C. Trench outlined his own guiding principle on this question:

> The lives of the people of that district [the Mizen Peninsula] seem to be marvellously given into our hands, and who can tell what a blessed influence our charity may have on their spiritual welfare! Yes ... while loathing from my innermost soul the iniquity of holding out an inducement to the miserable to do that which their poverty and not their will might consent, still I say, who can tell the extent to which in this very district the Saviour's words may not ultimately be fulfilled – 'Let your light shine before men that they may see your good works and give glory to your Father which is in heaven.'[125]

There ought to be little objection to this approach. The primary purpose of Professor Trench and of F. F. Trench was to give charity and save the lives of the people without interfering in their religion. This is implicit in Barry's vote of thanks to F. F. Trench published in the press.[126] Trench never made any direct attempt to interfere with the religion of the recipients of his genuinely Chris-tian, though necessarily Protestant, charity. The members of the Society of Friends were excellent examples of persons who gave charity without any question of attempting to win converts. This was explicitly and publicly acknowledged at a meeting held in Ballydehob chapel in September 1848 as shall be seen in the next chapter.[127]

Some Church of Ireland clergymen did not agree with the close association between famine relief and attempts to make conversions. Dr Whately, Church of Ireland archbishop of Dublin, thus addressed his clergy in 1847:

> There cannot be a more emphatically unsuitable occasion for urging anyone to change his religion and adopt ours, than when we are proposing to relieve his physical distress; because the grace of a charitable action is in this way destroyed, and we present ourselves to his mind as seeking to take an ungenerous advantage of his misery, and as converting our benefactions into a bribe to induce him to do violence to his conscience.[128]

Whately himself later admitted that 'attempts were made … in some instances to induce persons to carry on a system of covert proselytism by holding out relief to bodily wants and suffering as a kind of bribe for conversion'.[129] Fisher and most of his fellow clergymen did indeed win converts in hungry or famine times. The vital question is whether they were guilty of souperism; in other words, did they directly or indirectly take undue advantage of the famine to influence these people to change their religion? Let us consider the case of Fisher since, according to Desmond Bowen, he was regarded as being 'a paradigm souper'.[130] Why did so many Catholics at Toormore turn Protestant? The fact that they changed religion in time of famine implies reasons of hunger. The fact however that some of them refused to return to the fold, in spite of the Vincentian mission and the improvement in the times, implies reasons of conscience. Similarly, the fact that other converts did return to the fold after the mission and the improvement in the times implies reasons of hunger. It could also be held that they returned partly on account of the relief offered by the Society of St Vincent de Paul. We have seen that the Catholics accused the Protestants of souperism and the Protestants made counter accusations of souperism against them. There seems to be little documentary evidence which can prove or disprove these allegations. I sense, however, that both souperism and counter-souperism occurred at Toormore. Yet in justice it must be pointed out that it was the Protestants who began this abuse of famine relief. They could have relieved the hungry people without getting excessively involved in religious matters as recommended by Dr Whately and as actually practised by other clergymen such as Traill, the Trenches, Webb of Caheragh, R. B. Townsend of Abbeystrowry. On the other hand, Fisher and his fellow clergymen who made converts associated relief and religion too closely which must be part of the reason too for their undeniable success. It must be fully acknowledged, however, that they did in fact save many lives. The endeavours of Protestants to make converts was greatest from 1830 to 1850 which must be the period in Irish history in which the people suffered most from hunger. These efforts were most intense in the poorer parts of the country. The manner in which such efforts and poverty coincided both in time and in place must be observed. There seems to have been some sort of correlation between such conversions and poverty. A Quaker, Alfred Webb, wrote after the famine:

> A network of well-intentioned Protestant associations spread over the poor parts of the country, which in return for soup and other help endeavoured to gather the people into their churches and schools, really believing that masses of our people wished to abandon Catholicism. The movement left seeds of bitterness that have not yet died out, and Protestants, not altogether excluding Friends, sacrificed much of the influence for good they would have had if they had been satisfied to leave the belief of the people alone.

As Donal Kerr affirms, 'there is much truth in this assertion'.[131] Although souperism was a reality around Toormore, one story of it taking place in another part of these parishes seems mythical. I was told by a local inhabitant at Kilbronoge (where the Trench cousins had an 'eating-house') that during the famine soup was given out by the Protestants in order to convert the Catholics. 'But not even the dogs would take the soup,' he declared defiantly. This man was named Regan. F. F. Trench relates how he visited several families of that name and fed them, for which they expressed their gratitude.[132] Regan admitted, however, that many people at Toormore 'took the soup and turned'. It is regrettable that the genuine and, indeed, heroic charity of men like the Trenches or Dr Traill should have been preserved in folk memory in this distorted fashion as a result of the questionable charity of people like Fisher. According to the myth the hungry people who 'took the soup' nearly all 'turned'. But more than three millions were on soup rations in the summer of 1847 and of course they did not 'turn' nor was any pressure put on them to do so; it was simply government or state relief. So to Desmond Bowen's question 'Souperism: myth or reality?' my answer is 'both myth and reality, but far more myth than reality'.

However, one must not be too delicate about these matters. Christianity is a religion of incarnation; there cannot be any absolute dichotomy between the spiritual and the material. When a people accept the faith of any denomination it sometimes results in some kind of material gain also such as schools and hospitals. An economist might wryly remark that increased competition in the market for souls at Toormore attracted greater supplies of food for the body; if there had been less controversy there might have been more mortality. Surely the most important matter in time of famine is that people survive it. If the government had made an effort similar to that of the Churches – even for the selfish political motive of killing repeal with kindness – not so many lives would have been lost. If there had been more of the spirit of the London Tavern Committee of 1822 and less of *laissez-faire*, the union might have been cemented rather than strained. Mary Daly states that lack of co-operation between Catholic and Protestant clergy 'probably cost lives'.[133] As has been seen, Fr Barrett accused the Protestants of holding on to the funds for themselves while others died. They in turn accused the Catholics of lavishing food on converts trying to win them back while others of their own flocks starved to death. If there had been greater co-operation between clergymen there would indeed have been a more equitable distribution of food in some places. Yet, as already stated, religious controversy meant that much larger supplies of food arrived. Other districts suffered as much and in silence. We have seen that in Drinagh, for example, mortality in 1847–8 was practically as high as in Kilmoe (18.4% compared with 18.8%). We have seen too that according to the local magistrate, George Robinson, one of the reasons for this was that Drinagh had no resident rector. It could be argued that if there had been a man like Fisher there, so many would not have died in a place which had the highest Poor Law Valuation in all six parishes while Kilmoe had the lowest.

Fisher's biographer, R. B. Carson, informs us of this pastor's dismay when later he saw some of his converts abandon him. Carson realised, as probably did Fisher as well, that the peasants possessed a 'shrewdness that they term "crabbidness"'.[134] If they were independent enough to desert the priest one day they would similarly abandon the minister another day – if they so wished. Fr Daniel O'Sullivan, parish priest of Enniskeane at this period, expressed what he called this *'duplex* attitude' in a verse he put in the mouth of a 'convert':

> But, Mother, wait awhile, we'll try to treat them civil,
> Nuair a fhásfaidh na prátaí nua, we'll pitch them to the devil.[135]

Yes, when the new potatoes would grow they were prepared to get rid of such givers of relief. A proverb went, *An uair a thigeas na Lumpers / Imtheochuid na Jumpers.* 'When the Lumpers [potatoes] will come / The Jumpers [soupers] will go.' Such 'crabbid' soupers survived the famine whether they took food from the likes of Fisher or the likes of the Society of St Vincent de Paul or indeed from both. *Laissez-faire* and indifference were far more fatal than religious controversy. Political economy allowed far more people to die than did the Bible or the rosary bead – far more perished of philosophy than of theology.

XII

Towards Local 'Pauper Home Rule', 1847–52

Every civilised, aye or savage nation, is familiar with the name of Skull … 'the place of the Skulls'.

SOUTHERN REPORTER, 1847

No words of mine can give adequate expression to the degradation of a people who when they might rely on themselves alone yet are beggars at every door and calculate on the benevolence and sympathy of foreigners to stay the steps of famine in their own fertile but shamefully neglected land.

JOHN KELLIHER, PP, SCHULL, 1848

PAUPER RIGHT AND TENANT RIGHT

The lord lieutenant, Bessborough, died in May 1847 and was succeeded by William Villiers, Earl of Clarendon. An important change took place in the Irish Poor Law system when the Irish Poor Law Extension Act was passed in June 1847. Hitherto, the supervision of the Irish Poor Law was carried out by the British Poor Law commissioners who delegated their authority. In August a separate commission was set up in Dublin and Edward Twistleton was appointed chief commissioner. He was an Englishman who had two year's experience in Irish relief as a commissioner. Lord John Russell commented that 'an abler man … cannot be found'. A Dublin newspaper dubbed him 'the Cockney Poor Law King'; indeed, he was to be a sort of viceroy of Irish poverty. Other members of this commission were the chief secretary, William Somerville, the under-secretary, Thomas Redington, and the assistant commissioner, Alfred Power. This board met in Dublin Castle and was still under the Treasury, namely, Trevelyan. Local control over the Poor Law was exercised by Boards of Guardians some of whose members would be elected by the ratepayers while Justices of the Peace were *ex officio* members. It was only to be expected that such boards would be controlled by the landlord interest. Temporary Poor Law inspectors were appointed in each union who, as Trevelyan put it, would exercise 'special and powerful controls'; in the Skibbereen Union this inspector was J. J. Marshall. Each union was therefore responsible for its own poverty through the poor rates. The only exceptions were thirty-two unions in the west of the country which were officially described as 'distressed'; they included Bantry but not Skibbereen. These would receive some government aid for another year.

The transfer from the Soup Kitchen Act to the Poor Law was partly made possible by the Poor Law Amendment Act of 1847 which allowed outdoor relief to the 'impotent' poor, i.e., those who were infirm or elderly, orphans and destitute widows with children. Able-bodied men with dependent families were sometimes included. Still the general rule was that able-bodied persons who were destitute could not receive any relief except when the workhouse was full. This act contained the notorious 'Quarter Acre Clause' which stipulated that anybody who occupied more than a quarter acre of land could not be deemed 'destitute' and therefore entitled to relief inside or outside the workhouse.[1] It was also called the 'Gregory Clause' after the man who had proposed it, namely, Sir William Gregory of Coole Park, County Galway.[2] This measure was a harsh one but it was passed by 117 votes to 7. Most of the Irish members of parliament, donning their landowners' top hats, voted for the clause. Canon O'Rourke, named and shamed them and they included John O'Connell, brother of the Liberator. William Sharman Crawford, a County Down landlord but a member for Rochdale, voted against it as also did the English radical, Poulett Scrope.[3] Thus it was only in dealing with their own poverty that the Irish were to obtain some sort of repeal or Home Rule with Twistleton as viceroy, the new 'King of the Beggars' after Daniel O'Connell. There were changes too at parish level in the district. James Barry became parish priest of Bantry and was replaced in Schull by John Kelliher. He had been curate in the Cathedral parish in Cork, where he only barely survived famine fever. His first appointment was in Muintir Bháire or Durrus where we have already met him.[4]

At the end of 1847 the board made its official reply in a special 'final report' on its relief works signed by its chairman, Colonel Jones, and also by Richard Griffith. They admitted that when the potato failed, the 'utility of the work was lost sight of in the struggle for life'. They were no longer commissioners of Public Works but 'administrators of outdoor relief for nearly a million families'. 'A reverse of the natural conditions of labour' took place, they maintained, because 'the work was chosen for the people, not the people for the work.' The Presentment Sessions which should have been 'deliberative bodies ... were in all respects the reverse'. Jones and Griffith went on to assert that it was the board which should have originated the road-works and not the Presentment Sessions. These officials accused the local relief committees of 'constituting themselves into courts of grievance for supporting complaints of every description'. Jones and Griffith reminded the country that in the distress of 1822 those who were in charge of the relief works were 'free from relief committees ... and the encumbrance of Presentment Sessions'. Yet the report endeavoured to be fair:

> It was indeed obvious that all parties were placed in a false position towards each other and that all suffered equally from it. The Presentment Sessions undertook to repay sums beyond their utmost means, the [relief] committees were unable to work with satisfaction to themselves; and this board was saddled with unheard-of and increasing responsibilities but not invested with the powers to meet that responsibility.

This was an impartial description of the spiral of famine in which all were caught. The Board of Works hoped that 'labour will not in future be lowered to the purpose of relief, nor relief deprived of its character of benevolence'. It was admitted that the change from road-works to soup-kitchens meant that some roads were unfinished and remained 'a constant and unsightly monument of a disastrous period'.[5]

The activities of the Board of Works during the famine must be assessed more positively than has been done hitherto. One writer, A. R. G. Griffiths, even claims that in 1846–7 its 'efforts were a daring and ambitious experiment in social and administrative reform'.[6] It was indeed easier for the board's detractors to point out deaths it was supposed to have caused rather than for the board to count the number of lives it had helped to save. The board could also lament that some of its own officials died too, for example, Major Parker in Skibbereen and Captain Gordon in Kinsale. Although the board admitted that the unfinished roads remained a grim monument to its famine relief efforts many of them were actually completed. Still there is at least one unfinished road at Leamcon Hill that would have been useful had it been completed. There is a *Boithrín Glas* or 'Green Road' in Rossbrin near Ballydehob so called because the grass grew over it. Much more grass however has grown over or beside the far more prestigious railways and canals. One man who would remember the men who died working on the famine roads was Richard Hodnett already mentioned. He was arrested following the large public meeting addressed by Anna Parnell (sister of Charles S. Parnell) in Ballydehob in 1881, at the time of the Land League. Hodnett wrote from Limerick Gaol, 'I was an overseer on this road [near Ballydehob] in 1847 and witnessed the first poor man's death by the famine'.[7] Another victim was Jeremiah O'Donovan Rossa's father who 'took sick' while working on a road near Rosscarbery and died; the son took his father's place.[8] As mentioned in Chapter VIII, James Wolfe, an overseer on a road near Ballydehob, told Jeremiah O'Callaghan of the *Cork Examiner* that John Coughlan of Kilbronoge was the fifth man to have died of starvation on one line of road between 14 November and the end of December 1846. This ran from the main Skibbereen–Crookhaven road towards the sea so it could not have been any longer than two-and-a-half miles. It would have had at least one tombstone for every half-mile. Such monuments would have been just as frequent in other parts of the parish of Schull. As stated in Chapter IX, Rev. McCabe, as secretary of the relief committee, told F. F. Trench that 'he had altered in the course of the last eight days in one hundred instances the names of the men who had died to the names of their wives, and that in that space of time there had been six cases in which he had altered the name from the father to the son and from the son to the widow and from the widow to the daughter, all having died'. As mentioned in Chapter XIII, at least four men died on the roads in Kilcoe. This is by far the smallest parish of them all so there cannot have been much more than five or six miles of famine roads in it. Tombstones here would not have been quite so frequent, perhaps 'only' one for every mile.

It is often thought that these famine roads were for the most part useless or just a pretext to employ the people. The poet, Eavan Boland, thus imagines a scene:

Trevelyan's
seal blooded the deal table. The Relief
Committee deliberated: 'Might it be safe, Colonel, to give them roads, roads to force
from nowhere, going nowhere of course?'

In the Mizen Peninsula, at least, it must be held that the famine roads were useful simply because they continued the traditional Grand Jury policy of making communications possible between the sea-coast and the waste or bog-lands of the interior in order that these could be reclaimed with the help of sea-manure. Taking this peninsula as a herring bone, Griffith's road of 1822–6 was the backbone while the famine roads were the ribs reaching towards the sea on one side and towards the hilly interior on the other. These roads were not going from nowhere to nowhere of course.

The surveyors who carried out the Griffith Valuation in 1850 valued such new roads highly and had little regard for places with no roads. For example a part of the townland of Boleagh in the hilly interior a few miles above Bally-dehob is described as 'quite inaccessible to wheeled carriages and scarcely available for horses with top loads', i.e., with baskets across their backs. On the other hand the road from Poulgorm quay leading to the main Skibbereen–Crookhaven road through the townland of Ardura Beg in Kilcoe parish caused this townland to be described as 'well conditioned with roads and sea-manure of all kinds is landed at the eastern extremity'. Skeaghanore West is similarly highly valued on account of the sea-manure made available by the new road to the pier there. Skeaghanore East is valued highly also because 'a new line of road has also been constructed by the Board of Works running the whole way north and south through the centre from the sea to the main road from Bally-dehob to Skibbereen'. This road is of special interest to me as it happens to be the road which goes through our family farm. As a boy I helped to draw sea-manure along it from the pier. If you seek a monument to the famine road-makers walk around.[9] At times the purpose of these roads as relief measures is still remembered. One such road near Drimoleague is still called *Boithrín na Déirce* or the 'Little road of the alms'.

Since the famine relief had been stopped the people had to depend on their own resources which meant the harvest of 1847. What kind of harvest was it? Apart from the potato crop of course it was a good harvest. The parishes of Kilmoe, Schull, Kilcoe and Aughadown produced 2,053 acres of wheat, 1,253 acres of oats, 1,159 acres of barley, 1,176 acres of potatoes, 510 acres of turnips, 22 acres of mangolds, 62 acres of other green crops and 755 acres of meadow and clover.[10] At first glance, this total acreage of 7,058 under crops seems im-pressive. It must have taken a reasonable amount of seed to sow these crops. The landlords and farmers who held the seed while people died of starvation must have judged that giving seed away would only extend the famine to themselves the following winter. For these farmers the famine had not been so much an opportunity for heroic charity as a struggle for survival.

Throughout the country the harvest of 1847 was at least as good as it would be in the following years 1848 and 1849; the potato crop was better.[11] Yet considering what the people had suffered the previous spring and winter they were naturally apprehensive as winter approached again. So the landed proprietors and principal householders of Ballydehob held a meeting early in September 1847. It must have been the last public meeting for the chairman, James Barry, in the parish. He told of all the 'remonstrances' which had been laid before the Relief Commission and other government bodies 'setting forth the peculiarly afflicting circumstances that aggravated the disastrous famine in the locality'. It appeared to him that the government had ignored these representations and was 'determined to let the poor take their chance under the new Poor Law'. In an O'Connellite manner the priest called on those present 'to challenge the attention of the government respectfully but firmly' and to proclaim to the world that they themselves were prepared to give their time, health, strength and even sacrifice their lives, as many of their friends had already done, in an effort to save the people'. Still he admitted that this could not save the people without the aid of the government. He feared that another 'sweep from famine and pestilence would leave few to upbraid cold-hearted officials with unfeeling neglect and inhuman apathy'. Robert Swanton of Gortnagrough near Ballydehob proposed the sending of a petition to the new lord lieutenant, Lord Clarendon, appealing for relief or employment and representing 'the fearful condition of the people since the cessation of relief', i.e., the Soup Kitchen Act. Richard Barry, who seems to have been a brother of the priest, pointed out the 'most awkward predicament' in which they were placed because they were forced to call on the Poor Law guardians to strike a rate 'which would ruin three-quarters of the proprietors who had hitherto withstood the shock'. He calculated that before the famine there were 8,000 people in the Ballydehob side of the parish but that now there were only 6,000. He considered that of those, 4,000 were paupers and the remaining 2,000 could scarcely support themselves but no more. In his opinion a rate of even 10s 0d in the pound would not support all the paupers. The rate was then as high as 2s 0s in the pound.[12] Thomas Swanton, the landlord and Gaelic scholar, said that that 'the intelligent and the independent' should meet and thus come 'between the poor and harm'. He gave his reasons:

> If the sufferers themselves meet, however orderly their conduct may be, all that may be put forward by them will be disregarded and it will be attributed to self-interest. But if you agitate for the poor as the primary consideration and as the thing to be first attended to no matter what rates or ruin, you will be respected in distant places and sympathy will excite such an interest in high places that assistance will come much sooner than by a harsh and selfish policy … We deceive ourselves if we think that adequate relief can come from any earthly source except the government of the country.

So Swanton called for a full meeting of landowners and householders. We can see the dilemma faced by relief workers at this stage. The payment of the rates was localised as much as possible, i.e., according to electoral division. The rate was then struck in relation to the number of paupers from that area who received relief. The poorer an area the more likely were paupers to come from it so the higher its rates were. That is why the rates in the comparatively fertile parish of Aughadown were only 1s 6d in the pound while they were also 2s 0d in the poorer parish of Kilmoe further west. The reason why taxation was so localised was to oblige the landlords or ratepayers to employ the poor or even 'emigrate' them as some landlords did. If paupers died it was convenient of course not only for the landlord but for the ordinary ratepayer as well.

The full meeting of landowners and householders duly took place in the middle of September under the chairmanship of Charles Donovan, the Protestant curate. It declared that the property of the electoral division was not able to support the paupers for even half a year and that if they were to depend solely on the rates 'thousands of lives must be lost'. The people were hungry even in the harvest and would be starving in the winter. The harvest was bad in West Cork because famine had prevented the cultivation of the soil. The feeling of the meeting was expressed in a resolution which was circulated to members of parliament:

> That the owners and occupiers of land in East Schull [Ballydehob] do demand of the members of parliament for the County, City and Boroughs of Cork to explain to the legislature the peculiarly grievous pressure of the famine on the sea coast of Ireland – the impolity as well as injustice of throwing the support of the poor, in the maritime districts, exclusively on the property of the place, and, finally, the impossibility of effecting by means of the Poor Law as it is now, the relief of the destitute of these localities.[13]

The new MP for Youghal, Chisholm Anstey, a repealer, forwarded a copy of the resolution to Lord John Russell. Anstey bluntly told him that he hoped that these 'simple but eloquent statements of Irish distress and ministerial criminality' would not fail to move Her Majesty's advisers. Anstey even dared to remind the prime minister of the 'criminal and impeachable neglects and acts … with which you and your present colleagues are so justly chargeable'. The MP concluded with a long list of wrongs which repealers alleged were done to Ireland under the union. These consisted of the usual grievances but now they were seasoned with the bitter herbs of resentment over the famine dead. Russell's reply was characteristically cold, curt, but crystal clear and also included a hint of a new bitterness:

> I am deeply concerned at the prospect of distress in East Schull [Ballydehob] in the County of Cork. It appears to me that the owners of property in Ireland ought to feel the obligations of supporting the poor, who have been born on their estates, and have hitherto contributed to their yearly incomes. It is not just to expect that the working classes of Great Britain should permanently support the burden of Irish pauperism.[14]

Thus Swanton and the others soon learned what sympathy and interest were to be found in high and distant places. In an angry reply Anstey accused Russell of contemplating the wholesale confiscation of the land of Ireland as the only alternative to the starvation and extermination of the Irish peasantry. He also told Russell that the principle that the Irish people had no right to expect support from the English working classes was a denial of the union and a very substantial new argument for repeal. This correspondence was published in the *Nation* under the heading 'THE CONFISCATION OF IRELAND'. The editor, Gavan Duffy, thought that there would be some compensation if the ruin of the landlords would elevate the tenant farmers into independent proprietors but the 'infernal scheme' would parcel out the land of Ireland to 'London Jews and Manchester capitalists'. To prevent this he called on the landlords to declare for Tenant Right and repeal. The *Cork Examiner* also published this correspondence 'for the comfort of landlords who swear by England, so that they would know what to expect'. The country was thus receiving the message which Trevelyan sent to John Burgoyne of the Relief Commission; he had heard that reports from Ireland were gloomy but he assured Burgoyne 'that nothing but local self-government and self support hold out any hope of improving Ireland'. The widespread interest of the press, including the *Tablet*, was justified because Ballydehob was indeed a test case for Ireland. Russell had already stated that his attitude to Irish landlords and tenants was 'a plague on both your houses'. He warned Clarendon that henceforth there would be very little Treasury money available for Irish relief but only for permanent improvements such as railways and land reclamation. In justice to the government it had forgiven half of the money due under the Soup Kitchen Act, which, together with what had been waived for the road-works, amounted to £4,500,000. In the autumn of 1847, there was a financial crisis and a decrease of one million pounds in revenue to the Treasury in two months. The attitude of the government and many others in England towards the poverty of the Irish was best described by Archbishop Whately of Dublin, himself an Englishman:

> The feeling of the English was a mixture of revenge, compassion, and self-love. They pitied the suffering poor of Ireland; they had a fierce resentment against the landlords, whom they hastily judged to be the sole authors of those sufferings; and they dreaded calls upon their own purse.[15]

A collection on Sunday 17 October 1847 provoked the bitterest elements of this cocktail of feelings. The day was set aside in Ireland as a day of thanksgiving for the good harvest. A letter from the queen was to be read in every church in England appealing for aid for the Irish and a collection was to be made. Several clergymen refused to collect at all and Charles Wood's own preacher at Whitehall took the opportunity to point out the 'ingratitude of the Irish'.[16] Donor or famine fatigue, if not resistance, was quickly setting in. *The Times* exclaimed, 'No more alms for Ireland!' But the *Nation* indignantly retorted, 'Keep your alms, ye canting robbers … We spit upon the benevolence that robs us of a pound and flings back a penny in charity!' The *Nation* claimed that twenty steamers left Ireland every day with choicest food for the 'alms-giving English'. This newspaper insisted that Ireland had a just claim to more money from the Treasury because it was part of a supposedly United Kingdom. John Mitchel wholeheartedly agreed with the *Nation* and added:

In this year [1847] it was that the Irish famine began to be a world's wonder; and men's hearts were moved in the uttermost ends of the earth by the recital of its horrors. The *Illustrated London News* began to be adorned with engravings of tottering windowless hovels, in Skibbereen and elsewhere; and the constant language of English ministers and members of parliament created the impression abroad that Ireland was in need of alms, and nothing but alms; whereas Irishmen protested that what they required was repeal of the union, so that the English might cease to devour their substance.[17]

Fr Kelliher of Schull was certainly thankful for British aid. Still, as cited in the epigraph on p. 265, he protested that his people should be beggars around the world.[18] He would have agreed with Archbishop Slattery of Cashel that the relief system had demoralised the people and 'created … a nation of beggars'.[19] National pride was being stung. This can happen nowadays too especially when relief provided is of foreign origin. The Cork and Ross mission in Peru provided an example – the Irish received a death threat.[20]

The reaction to Russell's letter showed that many Irish people had not yet fully realised the implications of the Poor Law Extension Act. This insisted that Irish property was going to pay for Irish poverty irrespective of the country's status as an integral part of the United Kingdom. The establishment of the Poor Law Commission implied the virtual repeal of any obligation that the rest of the United Kingdom might have in relation to Irish pauperism. Russell's letter was a declaration of virtual pauper 'Home Rule' or in Trevelyan's own words, 'local self government and self-support'. As the *Nation* and *The Times* paradoxically agreed, the age of large-scale famine begging had passed. Henceforth the emphasis would be on rights and particularly rights to land or Tenant Right. Tenant Right had become an urgent issue that spring. 'A meeting of the Tenant Farmers of the County of Cork' was held in Cork at the end of January 1847. These were very large farmers from around Cork city especially the Glanmire/Blarney district. One of them cited the call to unity which Fr John Falvey, parish priest of Glanmire, had issued. Another, Joseph Nash of Monard, pointed out that since the potato disease had destroyed the crop the labourers could not pay for con-acre. This meant that many farmers were not able to pay the rent so he demanded a reduction from the landlords. The following proposition summed up the new situation:

> The present rents were generally assumed when agriculture was protected from foreign competition when there was no Poor Law and when the potato yielded a large return. That now land is largely over-rented generally in this country and heavily taxed and the peace and prosperity of the country require that Tenant Farmers should not be borne down by unreasonable pressure.

J. F. Maguire called for 'sure tenure' for all tenant farmers, compensation in case of ejectment and the extension of the Ulster tenant right to the whole country.[21] As early as March 1847 Fr Barrett of Kilmoe had called for Tenant Right.[22] These Cork farmers were less radical than James Fintan Lalor, who issued the clarion call to tenant farmers to assemble at Holy Cross, County Tipperary, on Sunday 19 September 1847, to demand Tenant Right. He was radical enough to proclaim that 'The land of Ireland belongs to the people of Ireland' and called for nothing short of agrarian revolution. He cried, 'Unmuzzle the wolf dog. There is one at this moment in every cabin throughout the land, nearly fit to be untied – and he will be savager by and by.'[23] Still for many cabins that was not quite true. Dr Traill had remarked hunger tames the lion and would tame the heart of the poor Irishman too. However romantic Irish nationalism may have been up to then, it would now have to be 'racy of the soil', according to the motto of the *Nation*.[24]

Other Tenant Right meetings were held throughout the country but aims were usually less radical. Tenant Right could also mean the terms of a bill which Sharman Crawford had on several occasions brought before parliament but the bill was rejected. Crawford sought adequate legislative protection for the tenant's claim for compensation for improvements before he could be deprived of a holding by the landlord. Tenant Right symbolised the hope of some security from the perils of eviction.[25] A Tenant Right meeting was held in Skibbereen on 24 November 1847. Its purpose was to 'call on the two Houses of Parliament to take into their consideration the relation between landlord and tenant with a view that they might legislate on this question as to give satisfaction to the country'. The chairman was none other than R. H. H. Becher of Hollybrook, Skibbereen. Fr Troy of Aughadown and his curate Fr Walsh were among the clergy that attended. Becher had just returned from a visit to Sharman Crawford at his residence in County Down. Discussions with Sharman Crawford had convinced Becher that a 'sincere union of landlord and tenant' in the spirit of Sharman Crawford's idea of Tenant Right would make Carbery as prosperous as Ulster. Fr Fitzpatrick of Skibbereen appealed to landlords, tenant farmers and labourers to co-operate.

McCarthy Downing called for three cheers for Becher on account of his support for Tenant Right and the response was loud. The solicitor lamented that a client was being threatened with eviction although he had paid the rent for twenty-three years, improved the land and built a slated house on it. Fr Sheehan of Kilmacabea near Rosscarbery related that the previous spring fifty-seven families had been evicted from one townland in his parish.[26] He was attending the sick when he witnessed the scene and said 'that the fumes of the sooty burning thatch of the cabins was to him far more insufferable than the contagious fever which the wretched creatures were labouring under, induced by their exposure to cold and rain'.[27] Rev. Francis Webb of Caheragh, admitted that two years previously he would have regarded Tenant Right as 'flat burglary', but that now he was convinced that a 'juster principle could not exist'. This is illustrative of how the famine changed the attitudes of people. It was felt that with Tenant Right much more land would be reclaimed and employment given. Dr Donovan was applauded when he made this appeal: 'Give the people employment at home and they would exhibit the same amount of industry as they did on the other side of the Atlantic and then no more would be raised such mounds of dead as there had been at Grosse Île or the Pottersfield at New York'.[28]

At this time (November 1847) an eviction took place in Kilmoe in the townlands of Carrigeengour, Oughminnee, Toor and Gortnacashel where the landlord was the former rector, Thomas O'Grady, now rector of Castletownbere. The following were ejected: Charley Regan, 7 in family; John Coughlan, 5 in family; John Mehegan, 3 in family; Michael Regan, 3 in family; Widow Mahony, 5 in family; Widow Leary, 1 person; Poll Supple, 5 in family; Curley Harrington, 11 in family.[29] A year and a half later the *Tipperary Vindicator* reported that the Rev. F. F. Trench of Cloughjordan 'ejected forty families, comprising about 250 souls, from the property called Forty Acres; the houses are removed, a fence wall has been built around the property by the stones that were taken from those houses!'[30] His work in organising famine relief in 1847 has already been praised but now he is observed in the role of an 'improving' landlord.

The new lord lieutenant, Clarendon, attempted to wean the people from the potato by teaching them to grow alternative or green crops. His scheme was to send agricultural instructors around the country. Charles Wood, mocked the idea as Clarendon's 'hobby'.[31] In November 1847, a Mr Moore, an agricultural instructor or 'Clarendon lecturer' as he was called, visited Ballydehob 'to lecture the inhabitants … on the improved system of agriculture pursued in the north of England'. A large number of farmers attended the meeting which was chaired by John Limrick. Moore told the farmers that their destitute condition was caused by their indolence, want of skills and excessive cultivation of the potato. He contrasted their condition with that of the farmers of the north of Ireland and asked to what the north's prosperity should be attributed. A voice shouted 'to Tenant Right' but Moore declared that it was 'skill and persevering industry'. He then outlined the rotation of crops practised in the north. The first crop sown was oats followed by potatoes, turnips and mangolds. Next wheat with grass-seed was put in and this would finally result in the much desired pasture. He concluded by urging the farmers towards 'self-reliance' and appealing to them to relinquish their indolent habits. J. J. Marshall, the Poor Law inspector, supported this appeal by reminding them that those who held a quarter acre could no longer obtain rations. Suddenly a man stepped forward declaring that he was a 'working farmer' and would express the sentiments of his brother farmers. They themselves had already read the works of agriculturists such as Blacker[32] and were therefore familiar with Moore's system. Still they were not able to put it into practice because their resources were exhausted by the famine and the 'high rents and rapacity of the landlord'. This farmer protested that it was therefore 'unjust and unfeeling to ascribe to our indolence our present destitution'. He promised Moore that they would all become faithful followers of his farming doctrine if only the government would supply them with a little seed and the landlords remit arrears of rent. Moore and Marshall both assured the meeting that the government could not and would not supply any seed and recommended the 'principle of self-reliance'. This farmer next alluded to a seizure for rent carried out by John Limrick himself;[33] the tenant farmer was becoming 'bould'.

Politicians and economists of all schools agreed that the resources of the country should be developed after the famine. In a maritime district like this where the soil was often poor the resources of the sea had to be exploited. As already noted the Ballydehob meeting held early in September 1847 passed a resolution stressing the impossibility of supporting the destitute from the rates. In response to this, William Fagan, MP for County Cork, urged the government to set up fisheries because the country imported £200,000 worth of fish each year. The *Southern Reporter* called the attention of its readers to this same resolution by remarking that 'Every civilised aye, or savage nation, is familiar with the name of Skull … "the place of Skulls"'.[34] This village shared in Skibbereen's famine notoriety. One writer called them 'the two famine-slain Sisters of the South'.[35] Dr Donovan maintained that 'cultivating the waste lands of the country and exploring the "circling wastes of the seas" would be found to be more efficient sanitary measures than even placing hospitals in every townland and doctors in every hamlet'.[36]

A splendid example of 'reproductive' or food-producing employment was now to be found at Coosheen near Schull where Captain Thomas and his men had turned from mining to fishing in April 1847, as has been seen in Chapter IX. North Ludlow Beamish, the chairman of the Southern and Western Mining Company, visited Coosheen in August. He praised what the practical miner was achieving while 'senators and orators were deliberating and haranguing'. In Beamish's opinion, if the fishery were properly managed it could prove to be the 'nucleus of one of the most important branches of industrial employment that has ever been organised in the south of Ireland'. At the mine he heard the busy hum of those who were preparing the ore for shipping. There was a heap of ore ready worth £500. At the nearby fishery he visited the various curing houses which were well supplied with salt, bins and racks. A stream had been diverted into a stone tank where three men and a widow were washing fish. Beamish who had heard much about the indolence of the peasantry now saw these fishermen covered only with meal bag clothing going out to sea for a long night up to ten miles from the coast. Captain Thomas gave the following statement of accounts of the fishery since its establishment. As regards income Beamish calculated that £20 worth of fish had been cured since the fishing began three months earlier. The previous week the two boats had caught 600 hake, of which one-twelfth was given to the crew. The account for the week was as follows:

Catch (minus one-twelfth)	£7 10s 0d
Curing and Labour	£4 11s 6d
Profit	£2 18s 6d

The fishery was confident that it could make a profit of £12 a week or £600 a year. This seems rather optimistic but the reason soon became apparent when Captain Thomas hinted to Beamish that £1,000 more capital would place the fishery on a sound commercial basis.[37] The *Dublin Evening Packet* called on all men of enterprise and capital in the country to take a 'hint from the Coosheen fishery' and follow the noble example of Captain Thomas.[38]

The Coosheen Fishery Association was now formed as a limited company with Beamish as chairman. Captain Thomas was managing director and the secretary was William Connell who was also the secretary of the Southern and Western Mining Company. The Coosheen fishery was thus a subsidiary of the mining company. He described the prospects of the company as 'most cheering', a word rarely used in the district in this year of 1847.[39] The new company received an order for 100 tons of ling from a Dublin firm which stated that it was 'strongly disposed to favour our own produce'. The *Southern Reporter* commented that if other firms had such patriotic sentiments there would be no need to import fish from Scotland and Newfoundland.[40] The *Cork Constitution* congratulated the Coosheen Fishery Association as 'a truly national and practical society' which was worth all the political confederations that 'patriots' could devise.[41] It was typical of Conservatives to accuse the repealers of distracting the country from the real problems which were not political but economic. Beamish requested Trevelyan to assist Captain Thomas with stores from the naval yard. Trevelyan did not do this but he instructed Randolph Routh to grant the fishermen £50.[42] During this autumn fishing resumed along the coast. Alexander O'Driscoll complained that six yawls belonging to strangers began to shoot trammel nets too close to the small boats of the line fishermen.[43] For the first time in twelve months the subject of his letters was not famine.

The whole country was horrified by the wreck of an American ship, the *Stephen Whitney*, on the Western Calf Island in November 1847; she had left New York bound for Liverpool. The captain saw the lighthouse at Rock Island or Crookhaven but thought it was that of the Old Head of Kinsale since the light from the Cape Clear lighthouse was not visible through the fog. Accordingly he steered his ship straight for the English Channel – as he thought – but the vessel soon crashed into a cliff; of the 110 persons on board 92 perished. Many of the passengers had emigrated from Ireland and England in the panic emigration of that spring and summer but were disappointed and were returning home.[44] Five weeks later another vessel, a splendid sailing ship, narrowly escaped being wrecked almost in the same place and for the same reason. Fortunately it was daytime and it was rescued by the Coosheen fishermen. Captain Thomas maintained that they were 'equal to the hardy and intrepid seamen of St Ives in Cornwall', but that they would have perished from starvation the previous spring only for 'the infant fishery'. He also asked how many more lives would have to be sacrificed before the authorities could be convinced that the 'Cape Clear and Crookhaven lights are useless and that the Fastnet rock is the only eligible spot for a *real* lighthouse'.[45]

Surprise is often expressed at the fact that the famine should have been so severe along the coast near rich fishing grounds. In their report on fisheries for 1847 the commissioners for Public Works provided the following explanation for this paradoxical situation:

This anomaly is the more remarkable where their great capability of productiveness was so well known, and where in the natural order of things a people curtailed in the supply of the fruits of the land might have been expected to avail themselves of the bountiful supplies of good food which the surrounding sea afforded. Yet it is a fact that in the autumn of 1846 when the impending famine was certain and when deaths from starvation had already occurred ... large quantities of fish were allowed to rot on the shore or were spread on the adjacent fields for manure. This extraordinary state of things resulted partly from a prejudice against the use of fish as a dietary without potatoes, partly from the utter prostration and distress which the want of food produced (and which compelled the coast population to part with their boats, tackles etc ...) but mainly from the fact that the fisheries of this country ... were not fixed on the solid basis of an established trade ... or maintained as a real commercial under-taking ...[46]

Donnachadh Shéamais Ó Drisceoil of Cape Clear told me that according to local tradition the potato blight did not strike the island directly and that therefore the famine was not quite as severe there as on the mainland. Never-theless, there are contemporary accounts of famine deaths from the island.[47] The Aran Islands also escaped the worst of the famine but not quite to the ex-tent that local tradition would have us believe.[48] Still it is likely that islanders would have tended to be more full-time fishermen than many of those on the mainland. It was the subsistence fisherman/farmer/labourer who was at the mercy of the elements on both land and sea. Once again we are reminded that he had neither good boats nor gear nor any way of curing fish. The first famine victims to become notorious were found in South Reen on the shores of Castle-haven harbour by N. M. Cummins and vividly described by him in his famous letter to the Duke of Wellington. It is indeed good fishing ground – I often caught fish there – but in summer and not in winter or spring the very seasons in which the famine was raging. Although there would have been a greater number of full-time fishermen on Cape Clear than along the coast they soon suffered too because the famine deprived them of their market. This was il-lustrated by the case of Kieran Cotter of Cape Clear who caught about 180 cod and ling in four successive nights in January 1849. Such a catch should have fetched £6 15s but he was unable to sell it so he hauled up his boat on the strand and applied for work on the roads.[49] The importance of the work of Captain Thomas and of Rev. Fisher was that they provided markets for the fish.

The government established six fish-curing stations around the coast in 1847 in order to develop subsistence fishing into commercial fishing; one of these was at Baltimore and another at Castletownbere. They were under the supervision of officials sent by the Board of Fisheries in Scotland and the Trea-sury gave a grant of £5,000 towards all six stations. The curing station at Balti-more was in difficulties because, strangely, there was no market for the fish. The commissioners of Public Works were threatening to close it but J. R. Barry of Glandore pleaded that it should be afforded a further trial. He visited the Coosheen Fishery and gave great credit to such 'a benevolent and useful person as Captain Thomas who readily acknowledged his obligation to the government agent and curer in Baltimore'. The captain had just finished a smoking-house for the fish. Barry went on to point out that it was the purpose of the fish curing station at Baltimore to encourage private enterprises such as the Coosheen fishery.[50]

Fishing in the maritime district of Skibbereen which included the Mizen Peninsula was described as 'depressed' in 1847. Fish was abundant but little of it was caught. This depression is borne out by the following statistics of the numbers of boats, men and boys employed in the industry (first- and second-class boats were decked or half-decked, with sails):[51]

TABLE 24: FISHING: BOATS AND CREWS, 1845–7

Boats and Crews	31 Dec. 1845	31 Dec. 1847	Change	%
1st and 2nd Class Boats	1,629	1,757	+128	+8
Men and Boys	8,322	5,566	–2756	–33

The post-famine change in fisheries was analogous to that in agriculture. There was an increase in the number of fairly large boats which corresponded to the increase in the number of fairly large farms. But there was a drastic decrease in the number of men and boys employed on these boats, similar to the decrease which took place among those employed on the fairly large farms because of the change from tillage to pasture. The above table takes into account only the fairly large boats which were registered but many smaller boats were not registered at all. It is impossible to calculate the number of fishermen who were forced to abandon their livelihood because of the famine. Similarly nobody knows how many labourers or very small farmers were removed from the land and their cabins demolished or decayed. The percentage decrease of those employed or partly employed in fishing was probably even greater than the corresponding decrease of those employed in agriculture.

In the winter and spring of 1848 some landlords became interested in fisheries. At the suggestion of Lord Bandon, the Board of Works sent the two most important fishery inspectors, J. R. Barry of Glandore and a W. J. Ffennell to a public meeting in Clonakilty with a view to establishing a fish-curing station in the area. J. R. Barry read a letter to the meeting in which Captain Thomas had informed him of the origin and progress of his fishery. The following is a list of its little fleet: 1 Hooker, 26 Tons; 2 Smacks, 1 ton each; 2 Yawls and 2 Seine Boats. Its gear consisted of 28 hake trammel nets, 1,120 fathoms of hake line, 12 mackerel nets, 8 herring nets, 4 plaice trammels, 2 seine nets, 800 fathoms of small seine nets, 4 plaice trammels, 12 lobster pots and an oyster dredge. There was a good supply of oil casks and 25 tons of salt. Fleet and gear were worth £300. During the previous year the fishery had supported up to 100 souls, men, women and children. The women worked making nets from hemp and the fishermen were paid a shilling a day and shared one-twelfth of the catch. Captain Thomas reported that capital and provisions were gathered which enabled him to start the fishery. He was one of the shareholders himself as well as William Connell and the Mayor of Cork.[52]

TABLE 25: COOSHEEN FISHERY: CAPITAL, 1847–8

Contributions	Amount, £
10 Shares of £50	500
Provisions from Brit. Relief Assoc.	60
Trevelyan	50
Provisions from Society of Friends	50
Society of Friends	20
Lord Bandon	15
Viscount Bernard	10
Lady Middleton	10
Donations from England	30
Total	**745**

Captain Thomas granted that the fishery had been more of a benevolent institution than a commercial enterprise but pointed out that it was still successful on both counts. The prominence of the Society of Friends among its supporters is worth noting. The Friends encouraged such fisheries along the south and west coast as for example at Ring, County Waterford and Castletownbere where they had a fishing-station and a curing house.[53]

Charles Bushe, rector of Castlehaven, was involved in a fish-curing station there and he asked the government to provide a large fishing vessel which would assist smaller fishing boats in heavy weather. The government passed on the request to the Society of Friends who hired a Dublin trawler, the *Erne*, at £45 per month. This left for Castlehaven in December 1847 only to find on arrival that Charles Bushe had been obliged to close down the fishery. The *Erne* however did aid the fishery at Laurence's Cove on Bere Island. The trawler then fished off the coast of West Cork that winter and the following spring and summer. The fishing was good on occasions but was often difficult and much gear was lost on account of the 'foulness of the ground'. Some fish was sold in Skibbereen at a price the fishermen considered low. The trawler then headed for Galway where it took on board William Todhunter, a member of the Central Committee of the Society of Friends. They fished along the west coast of the country for some months, calling at Schull and Crookhaven. Todhunter concluded that the fish banks were not as rich as many people had thought and that the coast was rocky, foul and uncharted.[54] All those interested in the fisheries must have been disappointed when in August 1848 the government closed down the curing stations at Baltimore and Castletownbere – the last victims of *laissez-faire*.[55] It has been seen in Chapter VI that even before the famine fishermen had accused the government of being more interested in Poor Laws than in Fishery Laws.

The Poor Law was the only refuge for those unfortunate persons who could not procure a living from either land or sea. As already stated, outdoor relief would be given by the relieving officer to the 'impotent poor' and to a few other categories. Most of the able-bodied could obtain relief only within the walls of the workhouse. If they were unwilling to undergo this indignity they were considered to have failed the 'workhouse test' and received neither relief nor sympathy. An embarrassment for the Poor Law arose when some able-bodied persons were willing to go to the workhouse but there was no room for them. This occurred in Skibbereen in November 1847. Accordingly J. J. Marshall ordered the removal from the workhouse of the 'impotent poor', so that there would be as much room as possible for 'testing the able-bodied paupers' and thus prevent the 'ruinous alternative' of their being given outdoor relief. Many of those who were then 'evicted' from the workhouse were women and children who had little clothing with which to face the winter. Marshall instructed the relieving officers not to send any more 'impotent poor' to the workhouse only the able-bodied.[56] This was a sad *reductio ad absurdum* of the principles of the Poor Law.

The inspector next put pressure on the rate collectors to pursue the ratepayers. Lists were made of the landlords who were in arrears. The greatest arrears were due from the parish of Schull on lands which were inchancery and on which existed 'the most miserable description of tenants'. The Audley estates must have been among the worst examples. The Poor Law commissioners advised Marshall to make an order for the recovery of these rates through the court of chancery.[57] It was precisely this situation which Clarendon had tried to explain to Charles Wood in an effort to make him understand the difficulty of collecting rates in Ireland: 'He [the landlord] is in chancery … What is to be done with these hordes? Improve them off the face of the earth, you will say, let them die … *but there is a certain responsibility attaching to it*'. Charles Wood, however, wanted to wash his hands of this responsibility. Rather than pay any more money from the Treasury he urged Clarendon: 'send horse, foot and dragoons, all the world will applaud you, and I should not be at all squeamish as to what I did, to the verge of the law and beyond'. Trevelyan similarly lectured Twistleton: 'The principle of the Poor Law is as you know that rate after rate should be levied for the purpose of preserving life until the landlord and farmer either enable the people to support themselves by honest labour or dispose of their estates to those who can perform this indispensable duty'.[58] The spirit of the Gregory or Quarter Acre Clause is not absent from this either: if a person occupying more than a quarter acre could not support himself or herself or the family and if a person with more than a £4 valuation could not contribute towards supporting others as well then neither ought possess this land at all. The Encumbered Estates Act would apply. Those who had concluded that the government intended to confiscate Irish estates had now more reason than ever to fear. It was under this sort of pressure that the Poor Law guardians of Skibbereen struck a new rate of three shillings in the pound and warned their rate collectors to press for arrears.[59]

The operation of the workhouse under the new Poor Law was illustrated by the case of a man from Kilmoe parish, Curly Coughlan. His case was brought before the Board of Guardians by Fr Fitzpatrick of Skibbereen. In November 1847 Curly Coughlan, an able-bodied man, decided that he himself, his mother, wife and five children would have to go to the workhouse which was twenty-seven miles away in Skibbereen. He went to Skibbereen with his family taking a child on his back. He there applied to the relieving officer for the necessary ticket. The relieving officer told him that he could not give him the ticket until he should first visit his house in Kilmoe. The man went home and the following day the relieving officer duly visited him in his house. That was understandable as the officer might have needed to question the man's brothers on the ownership of the house and land and to ascertain that the applicant was not the owner which would disqualify him under the Gregory Clause. The relieving officer still refused the pauper a ticket because his family was not at the house as well. Accordingly he journeyed back to Skibbereen for them and brought them home again with him. At last he got the necessary ticket and they all trudged back to Skibbereen again to the workhouse only to be told that it was full. Eventually, they did succeed in getting into the workhouse but only on the 'insistence' of Fr Fitzpatrick. It may not be clear how exactly the mileage adds up but the priest held that the pauper travelled 135 miles, out of which he had walked 105 miles with his family, carrying a child on his back.[60] Paupers living at the extremities of other peninsulas had similar difficulties. Some Dingle paupers, for example, tramped 30 miles to their workhouse in Tralee only to be told, *Imigh an bóthar agus ná tair arís!* – 'Go for road and don't come back!'[61]

Since outdoor relief for able-bodied paupers was anathema to landlords, to other ratepayers and to the Poor Law commissioners, increased accommodation had to be provided for the able-bodied paupers who were willing to go to the workhouse now that the winter of 1847–8 was approaching. Throughout the country various sorts of buildings were rented as auxiliary workhouses. There were as many as six auxiliary workhouses in the Skibbereen Union. One was in old corn stores at Lowertown between Schull and Goleen and another was in a building at the abandoned Audley mines near Ballydehob. Paupers like Curly Coughlan would not have to walk so far anymore. Marshall intended Lowertown Auxiliary Workhouse to hold some children and 600 adults, mainly women, who would be transferred from the workhouse in Skibbereen. The increased room was 'to test' the able-bodied paupers who were seeking admission to the Skibbereen institution.[62]

Substantial assistance was still being given by the British Relief Association. It was allowed to spend its balance of £160,000 in giving 'outdoor relief to Unions in which distress might arise from the rate payers not being able to meet their liabilities'.[63] The form this relief usually took was through the distribution of food to the children in the schools. This was regarded by Marshall as a 'great boon that should be hailed by all classes'. It was a convenient compromise on the delicate question of outdoor relief. An able-bodied person could still not obtain outdoor relief but his or her children could. There were 96 schools in the Skibbereen Union attended by 5,568 children, but 10,000 were expected to come specially for the food. By the beginning of December 1847, about 15,000 children were daily receiving rations.[64] These consisted of rye bread, warm broth and porridge. The weekly cost of feeding each child was only four pence.[65] The man in charge of this scheme to feed the children was a leading agent of the British Relief Association, Count Strzelecki. Marshall was pleased to report to him that the people were now in much better spirits because, hitherto, a man though willing to work was 'cast down' by being unable to feed his hungry children. This gratuitous relief therefore far from being a 'check on industry' was actually stimulating the parents to exertion. The general state of health of the people in the Skibbereen Union was now good according to Marshall. There were some cases of dysentery but none of fever; the fever hospitals were now able to take care of the dysentery patients.[66]

It was inevitable that the winter should have put extra pressure on people to enter the workhouse. In January 1848 two large stores were rented in Skibbereen as auxiliary workhouses. These two plus the parent workhouse held 1,880 inmates which was about 600 more than at the height of the famine. There were also 900 paupers wandering around the town who refused to go to any workhouse but would not object to being committed to the Cork Gaol under the Vagrancy Act.[67] To ease the pressure on the parent workhouse 400 male paupers were sent to the auxiliary workhouse at Lowertown in the middle of February 1848. O'Callaghan of the *Cork Examiner* saw cart-loads of them leaving; over 100 had refused to go west and took their discharge in preference.[68] Marshall had arranged that those from the eastern side of the union should be sent west to Lowertown thereby making the workhouse test too difficult for them as they would have had to travel further from their homes. An assistant master and matron had been appointed for Lowertown and two sheds were to be used as day rooms and could also be used as schoolrooms; the old corn stores were used as wards.[69] This expansion in workhouse accommodation took place all over the country. The previous year (1847) these institutions held 83,283 inmates all over the country but now they took in as many as 128,020.[70] In March 1848 an application was made to the Board of Works for tools in order to keep the able-bodied paupers in the Skibbereen and Lowertown workhouses employed.[71] This is the first reference to any attempt to provide work for the paupers in the workhouses. In fact little work was done by inmates of these places whose popular appellation as 'poorhouses' was more apt.

Various commentators have referred to the sinister operation of the Gregory Clause. The case of Peter Driscoll and his wife provide an opportunity to observe this at close quarters. Peter Driscoll applied to the relieving officer, William Williamson, for outdoor relief. He was told that if he gave up the land to his landlord, Robert Swanton of Gortnagrough, Ballydehob, he would obtain outdoor relief because he was an old and infirm man. He promised to give up his land but instead of going to the landlord he went to a relative's house where he died eight days later. Soon afterwards his widow and son approached the relieving officer seeking outdoor relief for the widow. They were similarly informed that she could not obtain it unless the land was handed up. They went to the landlord and obtained his 'certificate of surrender'. She spent the night in a nearby house. Two days later her son found her being taken to the fever hospital in Schull where she soon died. Dr Sweetnam stated at the inquest that the woman had not died from actual starvation but from a combination of old age, exposure to cold and exhaustion. The Gregory Clause was certainly harsh, forcing peasants to make a decision between land and life – people for whom land was life. The lord lieutenant had been informed of the case by the constabulary and demanded an explanation from the commissioners who in turn sought information from Marshall. The commissioners were able to point out that Peter Driscoll had died while still occupying land and that his wife had not died from actual starvation.[72] The fact that such cases received so much official attention was a sign that times were not now quite as bad as they had been.

In this hungry spring of 1848 the thoughts of many turned towards the land and naturally towards the landlords. Fr Kelliher addressed an open letter to them in the press challenging them to ask what anybody could think of estates with 'roofless cottages, desolated hearths, uncultivated lands and … starving human beings who are as thoroughly imbued with the spirit of industry as any in history'. 'Landlords of Schull,' he declared, 'the disgrace and the criminality are yours but for two or three exceptions.' 'Are there not among you several who have evinced during this protracted suffering no practical sympathy with the afflicted people of this parish?' he asked bitterly. Nevertheless he lauded Captain Thomas of Coosheen and quoted the labourers as saying that he was 'almost the only good man in the parish' for the employment of people. The priest however conceded that these landlords could still forgive arrears of rent and listen to the voices of their tenants. These were pleading that they had the land, labour and manure but had no seed, and that if the landlord provided this they would soon repay him with fields of crops.[73]

Even in the winter and spring of 1847–8, there were still some deaths from starvation and disease but they were gradually being brought under some kind of control by the workhouses, fever hospitals and outdoor relief. There were temporary fever hospitals in Kilmoe, West Schull, Ballydehob and in Aughadown. By May 1848 these were closed and Lowertown auxiliary workhouse was converted into a fever hospital containing up to 300 beds.[74] This was closed in February 1850. The number of deaths which had taken place in them since their establishment is shown in the following table:[75]

Hospital	Deaths	Opened	Closed
Kilmoe	45	June 1847	May 1848
Schull	235	May 1847	February 1850
Ballydehob	51	May 1847	May 1848
Kilcoe/Aughadown	44	July 1847	April 1848
Skibbereen	603	June 1847	August 1850
TOTAL	**978**		

The mortality in the Skibbereen Temporary Fever Hospital was by far the highest in the County of Cork. The number of deaths in the Schull hospital, 235, was about equal to that of the hospital in Bandon. Nevertheless this mortality was not unduly high compared with the rest of the country.

Most of the rates were being paid in the Union of Skibbereen and there was £3,200 in the hands of the treasurer. Only one rate collector failed to attend with his books and money. The fact that the British Relief Association was giving food to 22,000 children in March 1848 meant that extra potatoes could be saved for seed. Marshall claimed that the lives of hundreds of children were thus saved and that only for this aid the horrible scenes of the previous spring would again have been witnessed.[76] Others were not so sanguine. Dr McCormick claimed that the children around Kilmoe were not receiving any clothes although they were 'absolutely naked' and were given rations of only 'the coarsest and most unsound material'.[77]

The Poor Law was still struggling to cope with the persistence of famine and disease in the summer of 1848. Accommodation in workhouses, auxiliary workhouses or stores and fever hospitals was greatly increased. There were thousands on outdoor relief. It would seem that mortality was now confined mainly to institutions although Marshall does admit some deaths from dysentery in the community. Alexander O'Driscoll reported in May 1848 that 'deaths are occurring in every part of Kilmoe, almost hourly, from dysentery and exhaustion. As to deaths in the hospitals, they are really frightful.' He mentioned the names of two men who had died of starvation and there were also some others, he claimed. He was glad however that the grants of food from the Society of Friends were still saving hundreds of lives.[78] The relieving officer, Mr Williamson, denied that these deaths were caused by starvation and held that it was only ordinary mortality and declared that nobody who was eligible for outdoor relief had died for the previous nine months.[79] Who was right, O'Driscoll or Williamson? Dr McCormick told of what he had seen himself:

> Mr Williamson asserts that since October 1847 no person that was eligible for relief died of starvation. To say the least of it that is an extraordinary assertion. When on Fridays he visits this parish does he not see them dead and dying from starvation? Do they not die before his face at the meal-house? Does he not see the children dead and dying on the backs of their houseless parents? Are not those persons ... now com-

pelled by famine to take a morsel of food in the hope of being sent to jail? Has not famine alone filled the graves, jails, and hulks. He also states that not more than the average deaths have taken place, I will prove to him that four times the average number are dying. He speaks of the number receiving outdoor aid. I do not credit this statement. In all events the feeding of an adult consists of *six pence* worth of uncooked Indian meal. The consequence is that numbers get dropsical … Mr Williamson is placed between two fires, a starving, dying, rotting population on one side, and an over-taxed, over-burdened, industrious, pauper ratepayer. If the commissions do not immediately interfere, between emigration, starvation and transportation, a population will cease to exist in Kilmoe.[80]

This report given in June 1848 comes rather as a surprise and is reminiscent of the terrible accounts of the previous year. It is an important statement in that it covers the crucial transitional period from the end of the operation of the Soup Kitchen Act in September/October 1847 until this summer of 1848 when the Poor Law was taking its first faltering steps. Marshall naturally supported Williamson against McCormick, reporting to the Relief commissioners that the relieving officer had done his duty.[81] Evidently, the poor had received their scant entitlements under the Poor Law Extension Act and especially under the Gregory Clause. At this stage suffering and even death was caused more by lack of entitlement rather than lack of food. Yet in general the condition of the people was not now quite so horrific. The scenes of the previous winter and spring were repeated in parts of Connaught where burials without coffins were again common.[82] Mercifully this does not seem to have happened in West Cork.

The pressure on the rate payers in the Mizen Peninsula was severe. At the end of 1846 rates ranged from 1s 3d to as low as $2^1/_2$d, but a year later they had risen to 3s 0d for nearly every electoral division. At this time in Glanmire, for example, they were only 1s 0d in the pound.[83] In Limerick rate payers whose property had been seized actually died of starvation and in Fermanagh a rate collector was murdered.[84] The pressure of rates must have been heavy in the Skibbereen Union where there were 7,500 paupers on outdoor relief as well as the 4,500 in the workhouses, making a total of 12,000.[85] The following year (1849) was to be even worse in the country in general when the total number of paupers in the workhouses was as high as 227,329 and the number of paupers on outdoor relief reached its maximum at 784,370. This meant that in the summer of 1849 over one million persons were receiving some sort of relief.[86] Yet it was some improvement or decrease since the summer of 1847 when the number being fed both under the Soup Kitchen Act and in the workhouses was something over three million. Now under the Poor Law two important personages emerge on the Irish scene, namely, the rate collector and the relieving officer – two grim faces of the same coin of poverty.

McCormick had emphasised how the starving people were driven to commit petty crimes for which they ended up in the jails and transportation hulks. O'Callaghan of the *Cork Examiner* attended the court sessions in Skibbereen; the dock was crowded with prisoners who were too weak to stand up and who received sentences of transportation as 'a relaxation of their suffering'. But one woman screamed when her husband was sentenced to seven years of transportation for stealing a small quantity of potatoes.[87] A farmer, his three sons and a neighbour, were caught by the Peelers with stolen cattle in Glan up near Mount Gabriel. The neighbour turning informer admitted that they had been killing and eating them for some time. These people were said to be 'in comfortable circumstances'.[88] Three men robbed a car-man's horse and cart, and meal near Ballydehob but were caught by the Peelers and condemned to seven years of transportation, as also was another man for stealing nine sheep.[89] Citing a newspaper account John Mitchel wrote in his *Jail Journal* of a Timothy and Mary Leary who were indicted at Bantry 'for that they … did feloniously steal *twenty turnips and fifty parsnips* … Sentence, transportation for seven years'.[90] A more serious case of theft came before the Skibbereen magistrates. A farmer named Crowley caught a hungry man stealing potatoes from his pit and fired on him with a shotgun. The victim lay dangerously ill in hospital; Crowley was arrested and brought before the magistrates, Lionel Fleming and Thomas Somerville. McCarthy Downing appeared on behalf of defendant who did not really need him because Somerville declared that the defendant '*did quite right, the fellow deserves to be rewarded*'. There was a 'great sensation' in the court and he was duly rewarded by being set at liberty.[91] Another farmer at Courtmacsherry near Clonakilty shot and killed a turnip thief in March 1847.[92] The number of sentences of transportation meted out in the period 1843–6 for the whole country was 485 but from 1848 to 1849 it rose to 1,853 and the number of hangings rose from 6 to 17.[93] Property was dear and life was cheap. Yet the Census commissioners of 1851 commented that in spite of the hunger 'the slight amount of crime of a serious nature … was remarkable'. They reported that at times magistrates allowed the accused to go free when it was obvious that their 'crimes' had been committed to save themselves or their children from starvation. But the commissioners admitted that there were occasions too when people were sent to prison for petty crimes and died of fever contracted in the over-crowded conditions. An example was a John Sexton who had been condemned at the Cork assizes of 1847 for stealing turf and died in prison.[94]

Other crimes however were not so petty. Two women who were bringing home meal were robbed and murdered in Kilmoe and their bodies thrown into a lake, probably Lissigriffin near Mizen Head. Two children tried to prevent a thief from stealing a little Indian meal near Leap, Rosscarbery, and were found by their mother with their throats cut.[95] The murderer was a boy of fourteen and his victims were not much younger. He frankly admitted the crime to Dr Donovan who diagnosed it as a case of 'mental imbecility caused by starvation'. There were cases of people deranged by hunger attempting suicide and one such deranged woman ate the leg of her dead child.[96] Then Donovan went on to describe the insensitivity of starving persons to the sufferings of others. 'I have seen mothers,' he wrote, 'snatch food from the hands of their starving children; known a son to engage in a fatal struggle with a father for a potato; and have seen parents look on the putrid bodies of their offspring without evincing a symptom of sorrow'.[97] The Census commissioners pointed out that as a result of starvation 'not only does the body become blackened but the mind likewise becomes darkened, the feelings callous, blunted, apathetic'.[98] This increase in hunger-related crime reflects the general situation throughout the country. In 1845 the number of crimes and outrages reported to the constabulary was 24,791 while now in 1848 it had more than doubled to 53,502 and was to peak at 56,897 in 1849.[99] The incidence of killing and stealing livestock was so high that the police were permitted to perform 'expedited investigations'.[100] There was indeed a nexus between starvation and crime.

The commissariat continued to supply food to Skibbereen and Schull for outdoor relief and school rations during the winter and spring of 1847–8. William Bishop sent Marshall food and clothing via *H.M.S. Rhadandus* which landed the cargo at Baltimore. In February Bishop sent a ship carrying 20 tons of meal on behalf of the British Relief Association for school rations; this had been ordered by Count Strzelecki. In March, another government steamer, *H.M.S. Zephyr*, landed 50 tons of meal at Baltimore and another 20 tons at Schull. There was a revolution in Paris in this spring of 1848 and there were rumours of a revolution in Ireland especially in Limerick and Tipperary. Bishop now had to inform Marshall that no vessels could be spared because they were urgently needed to transport provisions from Haulbowline in Cork Harbour to Limerick for the troops. Bishop, however, promised to send more food whenever a ship happened to be free. He landed 350 sacks of meal at Baltimore in the middle of April, for example. At other times he ordered ships bound for Limerick with supplies for the troops to transport relief supplies to Baltimore also.[101] Bishop, a faithful commissariat officer, never seems to have made any reference to the incongruity of supplying the troops with one hand and with the other hand supplying people who could be said to be in rebellion against the government. The commissariat service which had been adapted for relief work was, no doubt, ideally suited also to deal with any rebellion that might break out. For example, *H.M.S. Scourge* which had brought a large cargo of food into Schull during the famine now transported the convict, John Mitchel, from Spike Island in Cork harbour to Bermuda and he described her as 'a long low rakish-looking steamer'. He saw too that the heavy mortars which had been removed to facilitate the handling of sacks of meal were now put back on board;[102] the ploughshares had been hammered back into swords.

The great enthusiasm caused by the success of the relatively bloodless revolution in Paris in 1848 reached Skibbereen too. Congratulations were sent in an 'Address of the inhabitants of Skibbereen to the citizens of France' – the *Skibbereen Eagle* was already keeping an eye on foreign powers! McCarthy Downing proposed three cheers for the Provisional Government and Ledru Rollin, the radical Socialist, and also three cheers for the memory of O'Connell.[103] Edmund Mulcahy, curate of Aughadown, was also at this meeting; he had similar political ideas to Fr Kenyon, the 'patriot priest' in Tipperary who was also a Young Ireland leader. O'Donovan Rossa told later of a conversation he had with Mulcahy: 'He told me that he had had his parishioners ready to start into the field with him in '48, if there had been any fighting going on anywhere. He was a good Irish priest.'[104] What sort of success could he and his famishing parishioners in Kilcoe and Aughadown have had? It would have had the same chance as the Young Ireland 'rising' had elsewhere and Gavan Duffy summed that up as follows:

> I believe it had not the slightest chance of success. His [Mitchel's] angry peasants straining to break their chains were creatures of the imagination. The actual peasants had endured the pangs of famine with scarcely a spurt of resistance. They had been taught by O'Connell that armed resistance to authority was justifiable under no circumstances; ... and they submitted and died.[105]

After the skirmish at Ballingarry in County Tipperary, Michael Doheny and James Stephens were on the run. They made their way to Kenmare, County Kerry to the kinsfolk of McCarthy Downing where they 'met friendly hearts and hands' according to the nationalist writer, A. M. Sullivan.[106] He believed that McCarthy Downing himself was 'most directly responsible in arranging their escape'.[107] This seems likely from what O'Donovan Rossa wrote:

> McCarthy Downing ... told me what a strong '48 man he was – how affectionately he cherished the possession of a green cap the '48 men gave him when they were 'on the run', and how he himself would be the first man to handle a pike – *if he thought 'twould be any use*. But with England's army and navy, it was nothing but folly for us.[108]

When Smith O'Brien and Thomas Francis Meagher were freed from prison in May 1848, there were 'seditious' celebrations in Skibbereen. A tricolour flag with the inscription, 'Liberty, Equality and Fraternity' hung from a window. A crowd of Catholics and Protestants gathered; men carrying blazing tar barrels formed a procession which was led by a band playing national tunes. When the procession halted it was addressed by McCarthy Downing.[109] Others, such as those described by McCormick, would have been less inclined to be inspired by Lamartine's revolutionaries hoisting the tricolour on the barricades of Paris in that year of '48, and were more likely to be in sympathy with the mob of labourers who, not being among the 'impotent poor', were obliged to break into the workhouse in Tralee and march into the yard carrying a black flag marked 'Flag of Distress'.[110]

One immediate result of the 1848 Insurrection was to give English people with anti-Irish feelings apparently good grounds for accusing the Irish of ingratitude for relief given to them during the famine. The Irish were generally grateful, but with serious reservations and distinctions as emerged, for example, at a meeting held in the Catholic chapel at Ballydehob on a Sunday in August. The purpose of the meeting was to give public expression of the gratitude of the people towards the English who had aided them during the disaster. Fr Kelliher pointed out that a 'great distinction' had to be made between 'the crimes and cruelties of England's statesmen whose misgovernment of Ireland is the obvious cause of its social miseries and those generous hearted Britons who have made sacrifices to stay the steps of famine in this unhappy land'. The meeting responded to these sentiments with great cheering. Kelliher complimented Marshall as well as Count Strzelecki and the British Relief Association. Finally the priest acknowledged 'the disinterested charity ... of those truly benevolent men the Society of Friends'. Again the meeting cheered. Charles Regan, a farmer, called on the people to thank their beloved pastor himself for his 'untiring energy and great success' in obtaining relief which saved many lives. Regan held that in no part of Ireland were priest and people more united. 'The very affliction ... is the means of drawing more closely the bond of affection which binds us to our pastor,' he said. The next speaker, Richard Barry, read a special address of appreciation to the British Relief Association. He acknowledged that the people had received great favours from others as well but lamented that 'these favours were sometimes of a doubtful character – they were tainted with the poison of proselytism – the stream of charity, which had been probably pure at source, was polluted by the channel which conveyed it to us'. That was not the case, however, with the British Relief Association, he pointed out.[111] Among the 'polluting channels' which he must have had in mind were no doubt William Fisher and Charles Donovan. Rev. Webb was also grateful to English private generosity, exclaiming, 'Thank God, England is not *The Times!'*[112]

English statesmen such as Russell and Trevelyan would have been horrified to find themselves being accused of 'crimes and cruelties'. They considered that England had been very generous towards Ireland and had fed more than three million of its people with rations in the summer of 1847 alone, so they expected gratitude. Their point of view was well put by Clarendon:

> From the queen down to the private soldier and the lowest and most suffering operative, every class contributed cheerfully and unsolicited – it was felt to be a labour of love ... Why is all this love turned into bitterness? The manner in which it has been received, and the attempts to shake off English rule. The great body of the Catholic clergy promoting all this.[113]

It was indeed true that nationalists, especially those of the *Nation*, would tend to forget about the three million saved and concentrate on the million dead and exaggerate it to two millions; hence their slogans already mentioned, 'By the souls of the two millions dead!' and 'By the memory of Schull and Skibbereen!'[114] Nationalists were soon raise the cry 'Revenge for Skibbereen!' and would, no doubt, be scandalised that anybody should expect them politely to say 'Thanks for Skibbereen!'

One of the great causes of nationalist bitterness was the export of food during the famine. John Mitchel claimed that every government ship arriving with Indian corn was sure to meet half a dozen going out with wheat and cattle.[115] T. P. O'Neill however has shown that 'imports of wheat and flour were five times greater than exports and about three times as much barley entered the country as left it. Exports of oats were undoubtedly substantial but at least four times as much Indian meal entered the country'. So he concluded that while 'there was undoubtedly a shortage of food and there is no truth in the assertion [Mitchel's] that the country produced sufficient to feed double the population'.[116] P. A. Bourke similarly calculated that in 1847 and 1848 imports of corn exceeded exports by 868,000 tons.[117] The following table gives the amount of corn exported from West Cork ports in the years, 1844, 1845 and 1846 (Baltimore was the port of Skibbereen):

TABLE 27: EXPORTS OF CORN FROM WEST CORK PORTS:
NUMBER OF TONS, 1844–6

Port	1844	1845	1846
Baltimore	4,000	4,969	
Castletownshend	154	154	
Glandore	160	240	
Crookhaven	20	–	
Bantry	1,600	–	
Total	**5,934**	**5,363**	**2,214**

Potatoes were leaving these ports also; 40,000 tons in 1844, 30,000 tons in 1845 and 983 tons in 1846. The correspondent of the *Southern Reporter* stated that whatever corn was grown was either eaten by a few families in the towns or exported. Farmers grew large quantities of potatoes both to eat and export. He was writing in May of 1847. He estimated that only one-sixth of the land that used to be under potatoes was now planted but that one-half more of corn had been sown than hitherto. He maintained that if both crops were thrown into a granary it would not be sufficient to support the population for the following six months even if it were allowed to remain in the country which was not going to be the case 'as the landlords, who have a great portion of it in their hands, must export a large quantity of the crops'.[118] In short, the correspondent held that even if the exported food had been kept at home there still would not have been enough food for the second half of 1847 in this West Cork district – so drastic was the loss of the potato crop as is shown above. This observer is in broad agreement with Peter Solar who estimated that in spite of imports there was 'an absolute deficiency of food in Ireland in the 1840s' and that this was worse in 1846–7. Nevertheless he grants that matters of entitlement to food may well have contributed to the severity of the famine.[119] While it must be conceded that the quantity of food exported from these West Cork ports between 1844 and 1846 had fallen considerably yet the amount exported in the harvest of 1846 is worthy of note, i.e., 2,214 tons of corn and 983 tons of potatoes. Even Randolph Routh complained to Trevelyan that the exportation of large quantities of oats was 'a most serious evil' and pointed out that the people deprived of this food 'call out on the government for Indian corn, which requires time for its importation'. Nonetheless Trevelyan told him 'not to countenance in any way the idea of prohibiting exportation'. The Treasury official was being doctrinaire rather than practical in his *laissez-faire* thinking. (This was the time Routh had no Indian meal to send the people of Kilmoe but sent a recipe for making brown bread instead.) P. A. Bourke has summed up the situation judiciously:

> It is here that the nationalist, stripped of gross exaggeration, still retains a small hard kernel of truth. The grain crop of 1846, if entirely retained in Ireland, could have made an appreciable contribution to bridging of the starvation gap between the destruction of the potato crop in August and the arrival of the first maize cargoes in the following winter.[120]

According to J. S. Donnelly, Jr, most scholars would agree that the refusal to prohibit exports even for a limited time was one of Trevelyan's worst mistakes and provided 'at least some substance to the later nationalist charge that the British government had been prepared to see a large proportion of the Irish people starve'.[121]

Such exports increased again in 1848 while there was still so much famine in the land. Many cattle, sheep and pigs were so much better fed than many human beings in the same country – for example, those described by McCormick. The following is the official list of food exports and imports from Cork for a particular day after the harvest of 1848:

> IMPORTS: 90 sacks of flour, 2,103 hundredweight of fish, 970 quarters of maize, 335 sacks of oatenmeal.

> EXPORTS: 1,199 quarters of oats, 1,635 firkins of butter, 464 sacks of barley, 235 sacks of oats, 9 barrels of barley, 92 boxes of fish, 60 boxes of eggs, 80 head of cattle, 40 lambs, 80 pigs, 100 sheep, 1,170 firkins of butter, 62 kegs of bacon, 150 kegs of lard, 2,109 barrels of oats, 20 lambs, 542 boxes of eggs and 9,398 firkins of butter.[122]

Although the overall statistics may show that much more corn was imported than exported in 1847–8,[123] still this long list is disturbing. John Mitchel's famous allegation about the food-ships has indeed some basis in reality. Not only were the landlords gaining from these exports but the 'strong' farmers were too. When Dufferin and Boyle, both landlords, visited Skibbereen in February 1847 they reported that 'many of the larger farmers, the men who make the exports which astonish every one, have alone flourished in the midst of the general calamity and are hoarding up their money in the Savings' Banks, witholding his due from the impoverished landlord, in order that they may on the first opportunity escape to America.'[124] In defence of the farmers it could be said that they had to pay high rents and high Poor Rates. But can these exporting farmers and dealers be completely guiltless of the charge of extermination which is levelled at the landlords and the government? The answer must be 'no'. There was little public demand for the closure of the ports to exports even from O'Connell since he hoped that the people would receive far more than they would send.[125] Some, however, did call on the government to close the ports. Indeed an embargo had been put on the export of food by the then Irish government during the distress of 1782–4 and this immediately reduced food prices.[126] Certain continental governments did close their ports in this time of food shortages for example the Pope as ruler of the Papal States as Paul Cullen pointed out.[127] There do not seem to be any accounts of ships exporting provisions being attacked in West Cork unlike in County Clare where a large cargo was plundered with the result that a naval steamer was sent to patrol the Shannon and the Fergus.[128] In this county also, some fifty horses that drew corn to markets were shot dead in October 1846.[129]

This export of so much food in time of such terrible famine worried more that Mitchel. The eminent physician, Robert Graves, gave the following diagnosis of the political and social ills of this country in a lecture to his students:

> To account for a scarcity of provisions in a country whose ports are crowded with shipping employed in carrying away corn and cattle – to investigate the sources of that pollution which has demoralised a people naturally open, frank, and generous, and has rendered intemperance and improvidence the most venial parts of the national character – belongs not to statistical medicine; but he [the physician] owes it to society – he owes it to his country – to proclaim aloud the existence of the evil.[130]

Incidentally, Graves chose as his epitaph the words 'He fed fever'.[131]

The famine was more severe in 1849 than is often realised. In Glanmire with all its mills, for instance, the scribe, Seosamh Ó Longáin (son of Mícheál Óg) had to solicit a loan of five shillings from John Windele to buy Indian meal 'which would enable myself and my family to weather out the bad year until we would have enough of our own corn'.[132] Woodham-Smith claims that the suffering of the people was as much, if not more, than in 1847 owing to the cumulative effect of the disaster.[133] Nevertheless this is not true for the country in general and West Cork in particular. Mortality in the workhouses was indeed quite as high as it had been in 1847 but then the number of inmates was more than double and there was far less mortality in the community.[134] The hand of charity had indeed grown weary and the rebellion of 1848 was no encouragement to English generosity to say the least. It must be granted however that in West Clare the famine and the resulting clearances were even worse in 1849 than in 1847. Ignatius Murphy remarked that what happened there between 1848 and 1851 made 1845–7 look like the good times of the past.[135] Nonetheless the severity of 1849 in the Mizen Peninsula will be truly reflected in school attendance, as shall be seen in the next chapter.

The unfortunate country was struck by the return of yet another disease, Asiatic cholera. Little or no special aid came from England for reasons already stated and in any case that country was hit itself. On 2 February 1849 the plague swept off J. J. Marshall to join the victims of famine and fever whom he had so comprehensively enumerated. The *Cork Examiner* reported that he had been an inspector for nearly two years and that his zeal, efficiency and impartiality had won him the praises of the clergy of both persuasions. Fifteen other Poor Law inspectors also fell victims including a Captain Lang in Bantry.[136] By 17 May as many as 1,014 patients were treated in Cork city hospitals and 444 died.[137] The Quarterly Sessions of the courts were being held in Skibbereen when this plague broke out.[138] It soon 'commenced its ravages' in Schull in spite of the 'humane and efficient' Dr Sweetnam, and it was also 'sweeping off' people around Crookhaven where there were 100 cases of which 31 proved fatal. Alexander O'Driscoll admitted that he had to flee Crookhaven to save his life but the epidemic began to wane.[139] In Skibbereen there were 112 persons stricken of whom 48 died; fatalities usually numbered about half of those afflicted. In Bantry 82 died and in Cork city the number was 1,329. Dunmanway and Clonakilty escaped the plague altogether as also did Fermoy and Millsteet but they were the only towns in the county to be so lucky.[140]

The government set up a commission to examine the advisability of more, and therefore smaller, unions, Irish unions being often larger than English ones. One member of this commission was Thomas Larcom who with Richard Griffith had been responsible for famine relief roads; the other two were a Charles Sharman Crawford and a William Broughton. There was even a little generosity in their report – a hint that poverty had its rights as well as its burdens. They declared that they had to consider:

> the right of the destitute to facile relief, as well as the economy with which relief could be administered, and when we found unions so large that a pauper might travel thirty miles to the workhouse, with a chance of refusal, there could be no hesitating on distance so prohibiting. In one case a man walked 150 miles before he was ultimately admitted to the house.

This was undoubtedly Curly Coughlan of Kilmoe. The commissioners pointed out that larger Unions had led to larger workhouses and auxiliary houses which tended to be over-crowded, resulting in high mortality. They maintained that smaller Unions and workhouses were necessary because the loss of the potato led to the breaking up of smallholdings 'while the relief-receiving classes became much increased'. The commissioners recommended that there should be fifty new Unions 'arranged in order of their urgency'. The first was Belmullet and the second was Killala, both in County Mayo. Dromore West in County Sligo was placed third. Castletownbere came fourth and Clonakilty came fifth which was followed by Schull, coming only sixth on this black/grey list. The new Union of Schull would comprise of the parishes of Kilmoe, Schull and Kilcoe but not Aughadown which remained with Skibbereen.[141] By now (1849) north-west Connaught had surpassed Schull and Skibbereen in famine notoriety.

In November 1849 some members of the Skibbereen Board of Guardians considered setting up yet another auxiliary workhouse because there were as many as 2,664 inmates in the original building. The chairman, however, then placed before the meeting the proposition of the commissioners concerning the new Union of Schull. J. R. Barry of Glandore thought that it would be too poor to support itself and called for special aid for that district which had gained 'unhappy notoriety'. Lionel Fleming of New Court, Skibbereen, who had land in Kilmoe, was likewise opposed to severing the Union because the Skibbereen gentlemen wanted only to be 'rescued from the paupers of Schull'. He reminded these gentlemen that there were more Schull paupers in Cork than in Skibbereen. He did not see any reason for an expensive house in Schull as he had never heard that these paupers had any difficulty in finding the one in Skibbereen. What he did hear was that the fairs were thronged with the cattle of those who were preparing to emigrate on account of the pressure of Poor Rates. Daniel McCarthy of Skibbereen was in favour of the new Union as he knew only too well of paupers who had died on the road from Schull to Skibbereen, and he added that if the landlords had done their duty there would have been less pauperism in the first place. McCarthy Downing said that the reason tenants were emigrating was not high rates but high rents. He declared that 'a system of extermination had been carried out to a most frightening extent', and that 370 persons had been ejected from one property at Gubeen near Schull and their houses levelled to the ground. They had to come to the Skibbereen workhouse; therefore he was in favour of a new workhouse 'in mercy to the people of Schull'. The three most important landlords with property in the west, R. H. H. Becher, John Limrick and Lionel Fleming all voted against any new Union while R. B. Hungerford of Ballyrisode, Goleen, was for it. The majority of the Board of Guardians was in favour of a new union and thus the Union of Schull was grudgingly given birth.[142] The new Unions of Belmullet, Killala, Dromore West and Castletownbere were officially 'declared' on 29 September 1850 and the Union of Schull on 3 October.[143]

The government carried out a special census of this new Union in September 1849 and the results are as follows:[144]

TABLE 28: UNION OF SCHULL: CENSUS REPORTS, 1841, 1849

Parish	1841	1849	Decrease	%
Kilmoe	7,234	4,778	–2,456	–34
Schull	17,314	10,659	–6,655	–38
Kilcoe	2,339	1,212	–1,127	–48
Total	**26,887**	**16,649**	**–10,238**	**–38**

This is a rare and valuable census, coming at the end of the worst period of famine, 1849, making it unnecessary to wait until the census of 1851. The decrease of 38% in the population of these parishes does not come as any surprise considering the terrible mortality and emigration. One may not expect that the most easterly and least poor parish, Kilcoe, would have had a greater loss in population than the most westerly and poorest Kilmoe but that is indeed what happened. Marshall's Return showed that mortality was lowest and emigration highest in Kilcoe, so this loss in population now was probably due more to emigration than to death. In fact, the further east one goes the better the land generally gets and the greater was the loss in population; emigrants of course needed the means and the money to travel.

The building of the Schull workhouse began immediately. The architect of the Irish workhouses, George Wilkinson, found that the greatest difficulty was to refuse offers from 'needy contractors' who would tender at so low a price that they would inevitably do unsatisfactory work. On 24 May 1850 he reported on Schull 'Tender received and contract perfected'. On 24 April 1851 he announced that the 'Schull works are in a forward state and will be almost all finished by midsummer'. His last word on Schull came on 1 May 1852 when the house was 'occupied' and the boundary wall was being built.[145] The workhouse was designed to hold 600 inmates. The building cost £6,000, the fittings £1,115, and it stood on a site of about eleven acres just east of the town. Yet the official date for the opening of the Schull workhouse was as early as 19 January 1850. This is probably what local people called 'the Old Work-house' which had been a fever hospital and was used as a workhouse until the new one was built.[146] Records were lost when the house was burned in 1921. The workhouses at Skibbereen and Schull were among the 160 major build-ings whose construction Wilkinson had supervised since 1838, no mean achieve-ment in the circumstances for this Englishman and his small staff. His office was closed in 1854 and he was transferred to other work.[147]

To sum up, the creation of this new Union of Schull meant that inhabitants would henceforth carry the burden of their own pauperism. The people of the relatively better off Union of Skibbereen would no longer have to share it, not to mention the working classes of Great Britain as Lord John Russell had warned the people of Ballydehob in September 1847. This was of course the policy of Trevelyan who insisted: 'There is only one way in which relief of the destitute ever has been or ever will be conducted consistently with the general welfare, and that is by making it a local charge'.[148] In his manner the Mizen Peninsula was granted what may be described as local 'pauper Home Rule'.

XIII

The Emergence of a Post-Famine Society, 1847–52

> … the great transition period … that social revolution
> brought about by the failure of the potato crop.
>
> CENSUS COMMISSIONERS, 1856

> … that famine … a salutary revolution in the habits of the nation.
>
> TREVELYAN, 1848

EDUCATION

'Society stands dissolved', thus proclaimed the radical nationalist, Fintan Lalor, 'and another requires to be constituted'.[1] The National Schools were seen by many as a means towards forming the new post-famine society in their own image and likeness. These schools, together with those of the Church Education Society, are human barometers which were as sensitive to famine circumstances as were the children who attended or failed to attend them. The table on the next page shows the number of pupils on roll on 31 March, for each year from 1845 to 1852 in the schools of the parishes of the Mizen Peninsula.[2]

The shock of the potato disease did not seem to affect these schools very much from 1845 to 1846. The numbers on roll decreased from 806 to 758 but the number of schools themselves rose from 7 to 8. By the terrible March of 1847, however, the total number of children in these 8 schools had fallen drastically from 758 to 477, i.e., by 37%. Crookhaven had only 8 pupils instead of 91, Schull male 14 instead of 123 and Schull female 11 instead of 80. The master of the boys' school said that half of the children were dead, the other half had no clothes or food to attend, and that he himself was obliged to go working on the roads.[3] The average decline for the country generally was 14%. This was caused not only by death but by the fact that some children were sent to work on the roads.[4] The following year, 1848, the number of children attending these schools suddenly soared from 477 to 1,584 simply because Count Strzelecki was distributing free rations on behalf of the British Relief Association. So many flocked into Ballydehob National School that one class had to be transferred to the chapel in December 1847. The commissioners of National Education declared that this was a violation of their rules and withdrew the teacher's salary until such time as the pupils should be removed from this place of worship.[5] The increase was even greater in Crookhaven where the number of children rose from 8 to 216 and in Dunbeacon from 93 to as high as 355.

School	1845	1846	1847	1848	1849	1850	1851	1852
Crookhaven	91	91	8	216	42	66	69	64
Schull male	154	123	14	134	68	80	109	80
Schull female	76	80	11	106	30	47	45	88
Ballydehob male	133	131	24	184	61	64	75	80
Ballydehob female	76	94	22	180	50	64	58	69
Dunbeacon	135	106	93	355	45	146	106	126
Lisheen	141	72	62	112	42	84	71	87
Hare Island		61	50	73	50	42	49	72
Lowertown			193	224	75	74	81	38
Long Island					35	57	52	48
Goleen male					71	59	41	85
Goleen female					82	67	45	66
Toormore male					56	42	32	60
Toormore female					54	37	35	41
Kilthomane						42	41	70
Kilcoe male						69	53	60
Kilcoe female						72	57	84
Cappagh Workhouse						350	closed	—
Lissigriffin						78	38	60
Dunkelly						82	42	34
Derreenard						67	34	52
Derreennalomane							63	59
Rossbrin							67	63
Schull Workhouse							605	379
Total on Rolls	806	758	477	1,584	761	1,689	1,868	1,865
Total no. of schools	7	8	9	9	14	21	23	23

Attendance at schools in the Mizen Peninsula dropped sharply when the British Relief Association stopped its rations at the end of 1848. The total number on the rolls fell from 1,584 in 1848 to 761 in 1849 although the number of schools had increased from 9 to 14. The 355 children at Dunbeacon dwindled to 45 which was far fewer than in 1847 itself when they numbered 93. Similarly the 216 children attending Crookhaven were reduced to 42. From 1848 to 1849 National School attendance in these parishes declined by 52%, which was much higher than the average for the rest of the country (10%). The commissioners attributed this not only to the withdrawal of rations but to cholera, poverty and extensive emigration.[6] The severity of 1849 is truly reflected. As seen in Table 23, attendance at the Church Education Society's schools in these parishes fell from 2,123 to 1,314, i.e., by 38%, between 1848 and 1849. The society asserted that this decrease had taken place all over the country but that it was due not only to famine conditions but also to the 'violent opposition and persecution of the priests'.[7]

However violent this opposition may have been it certainly was constructive. Many priests had a sense of urgency in providing alternative schooling with the aid of the Board of National Education. For example in Kilmoe the parish priest, John Foley, opened as many as seven National Schools in a single year, 1849. These were Goleen male and female, Lissigriffin, Dunkelly, Kiltho- mane and Toormore male and female,[8] the last three being in the Protestant stronghold itself. The number going to the nearby Protestant school at Altar fell from 289 in 1847 to 64 in 1852. In 1850 we find as many as 350 children attending National School at the auxiliary workhouse in Cappagh in one of the buildings of the abandoned Audley mines. On the closure of that house the foll- owing year they were transferred to the new workhouse in Schull bringing the total number there to 605, which was nearly one-third of all those attend- ing National School in these parishes. In the parish of Schull between 1847 and 1851 six National Schools were opened, namely, Long Island, Derreenard,[9] Dereennalomane, Rossbrin and the two workhouse schools, Schull and Cap- pagh.[10] In Kilcoe parish Fr Edmund Mulcahy set up a National School at Kilcoe itself near the chapel. Regarding Derreenard school John Triphook issued his 'solemn protest against the establishment in my parish of any schools in which the Word of God is not the basis of all education'.[11]

The use of the National Schools as a means of rehabilitating the famine- shattered people is best seen in the case of Lissigriffin hedge school. In apply- ing to the board for aid Foley stated that poverty had prevented the people from paying their own master and attributed their miseries to their lack of education. He rated the hedge schoolmaster, Hodnett, as 'not by any means inadequate'. The board's inspector visited the hedge school in 1849 and recom- mended the priest's application because the people were so destitute. The in- spector described the situation:

> The people here are semi barbarous … The old teacher, Hodnett, would not be al- lowed among the Eskimos, yet nothing but the application will disturb his reign. If ever the full tide of prosperity flows upon this unhappy island, it will never rise from the degradation without a national school, for to any other they will not go, unless to get bread, even if it were conducted by a Pestalozzi [a Swiss educationalist].

The reference to bread is interesting. Hodnett was replaced by a younger man who had experience in a National School and was recommended by the in- spector. Fr Foley was thus obliged to dismiss the old hedge schoolmaster.

Foley also applied for two National Schools for Goleen, one for boys and the other for girls. The inspector reported that 'the poor females of this neigh- bourhood never have got any education'. Yet they would not go to a Church Education Society school which was only one mile distant, 'being conducted on principles of which they conscientiously disapprove'. The man recom- mended by the inspector for the job as the master of the boys' school was John Courcey who distributed relief to Fisher's schools. Still Fisher wrote a formal protest against the new school. Foley, however, asserted that there was no means by which 'this people can arise from the abyss of wretchedness unless the light of education be imparted to them'. The part that the National Schools played in the post-famine struggle against Protestant attempts to win over some of this priest's flock is best observed at Toormore. Foley applied to the National Board for aid for the local hedge school in December 1848. The Church Education Society school at Altar was only a quarter of a mile away so Fisher opposed the application. Still the opposition of the landlords was more effective. The inspector stated how Foley had £60 collected to build a new school, 'if he could get a site – no landlord would give him even a rock for a site as I know'.[12] He finally obtained a site. The hedge schoolmaster, 'an old man named Burke', was dismissed and replaced by Daniel Shea, who had had previous experience in National Schools.[13] The commissioners however were later dissatisfied with Master Shea, withdrew his salary and instructed Foley to dismiss him and appoint another. Foley replied that the master had been examined by Head Inspector Kavanagh who reinstated him.[14] (Kavanagh was one of the few Catholics employed by the Board as inspectors. He resigned in 1855, accusing the commissioners of proselytising in schools under Protestant control.)[15] Master Shea was no sooner restored than two neighbours of his school denounced him 'for neglecting public duties to attend to his private affairs, of allowing persons to come into the school during school hours and make it a common tap-room'. In the subsequent investigation by an inspector the accusers failed even to appear. Foley explained that their real motive was a dispute with the teacher over land.[16]

Toormore was not the only school to have its troubles. The teacher of Derreennalomane was sacked in 1852 for being 'drunk and disorderly and injuring Ballydehob police barracks'.[17] Kilcoe's schoolmaster was dismissed for being 'under the influence of drink four or five times in charge of school and that he was not a moral man'.[18] The steady progress of the National System in these parishes in spite of opposition and harsh conditions is truly remarkable. While there were only 477 children on roll in these schools on 31 March 1847 five famine or hungry years later there were 1,865. Meanwhile the number of schools had risen from 9 to 23. In the same period the number of Church Education Schools had declined from 18 to 16 and the numbers on rolls dropped from 2,076 to 841.[19]

In 1845 the number of children attending the National Schools was 806, while 1,046 went to the Church Education Society schools.[20] In 1847, however, the number of pupils at the Church Education Society schools increased dramatically while the number attending the National Schools decreased correspondingly. The rations given out by the British Relief Association to both systems of schools in 1848 caused children to flock to the National Schools in greater numbers than at any time since the system began. In 1849 the stoppage of these rations caused attendance at both types of school to fall in the same proportion. The major turning point came in 1849/50 with the result that in 1850 the attendance at the National Schools easily overtook that at the Church Education Society schools for the first time ever, 1,689 pupils on roll as against 1,041. This swing continued so that by 1852 there were more than twice as many children at the National Schools as at the Church Education

Society schools, 1,865 as against 841. Once the hungriest days of the famine were over it was clear that most of the people of these parishes had little interest in scriptural education but in National education which was becoming Catholic in ethos. Learning was eagerly desired by many poor people who followed a National Schools' inspector around these parishes. They badly needed education, he remarked, because they were 'a rude people whose minds were as fallow as their fields'.

The priests set up the National Schools with a sense of urgency because they saw them as the only alternative to the Church Education Society schools which they accused of trying to seduce Catholic children from their faith. We have seen in the Chapter XI that Rev. Fisher condemned the National Schools as 'Romanising' but others such as Archbishop Whately, a member of the Board of National Education, had other ideas. Although he disagreed with any use or rather abuse of famine relief as an enticement to conversion he favoured the more sophisticated method of conversion through education. Whately confided as follows to his life-long friend William Nassau Senior, the political economist, who recorded the archbishop's words in his diary:

> The education supplied by the National Board is gradually undermining the vast fabric of the Irish Catholic Church … I believe that mixed education is gradually enlightening the mass of the people and that if we give it up we give up the only hope of weaning the Irish from the abuses of popery. But I cannot venture openly to profess this opinion. I cannot openly support the National Board as an instrument of conversion. I have to fight its battle with one hand, and that my best, tied behind my back.[21]

Whately duly freed his hand the following year by retiring from the board.[22] Fisher and Thackeray (cited in Chapter III) were to be proven more correct than he was; the National Schools tended in Fisher's words more to 'Romanise', and even to become interwoven in the fabric of the Catholic Church rather than to wean the people from 'popery'. The experience of the Mizen Peninsula, at least, indicates that D. H. Akenson is correct in stating that 'Stanley's goal of integrating children of different faiths was unrealistic'.

Such was the situation in the National Schools concerning the 'R' of religion. What was the state of the 'Rs' of reading and writing? Akenson grants that 'although the national system failed to heal Ireland's sectarian wounds, it deserves credit for making Ireland a country of literates'.[23] The number of illiterates fell from being 53% of the total population in 1841 to being 47% in 1851. Fair credit, however, must also go to the Church Education Society schools for whom reading the Bible was so important. What progress had been made in dealing with illiteracy since 1841 in the district? The following table puts some results from the Census of 1851 on the blackboard, so to speak, for the parish of Schull:

No. of Adults	1841	Propr.	1851	Propr.	Change '41–'51	%
Read & write	2,466	16.7%	2,262	22.8%	–204	–8.2
Read only	1,036	7.0%	904	9.1%	–132	–12.7
Total	3,502	23.7%	3,166	31.9%	–336	–9.5
Neither read/write	11,245	76.3%	6,756	68.2%	–4,489	–40.0
Grand Total	**14,747**	**100.0%**	**9,922**	**100.0%**	**–4,825**	**–32.7**

Between 1841 and 1851, adults, who could read and write or read only, increased from being 23.7% to being 31.9% of the total population. Illiterates decreased from 76.3% to 68.1%. This proportional decrease in illiteracy was, no doubt, a reasonable achievement in a decade so marked by hunger. The great difference in the decrease, however, of the absolute numbers of both the literate and the illiterate is revealing. After the ravages of the great hunger there remained only 336 fewer literates, 9.5%, whereas as many 4,489, i.e., 40% of the illiterates had simply disappeared. The famine even more than the schools had gone a long way towards solving the illiteracy problem with one fell blow. Just as the disaster hit most severely those who were not inclined to go to school it must have similarly hit those who were not inclined to go to Mass either – often the same people, no doubt. Thus the famine solved in a similar brutal fashion the problem which priests such as Fr Michael Collins of Skibbereen had in reaching out to a population that was increasing and becoming poorer.

LAND, SEA, POLITICS, SOCIETY, AND LANGUAGE: CHANGE
Towards the end of 1849 there was speculation among Conservatives that Lord John Russell's government would fall and be replaced by the Anti-Peel Protectionist Tories. This gave rise to a short but vigorous campaign for Protection among Irish landlords. On 18 December Lord Bandon came to preside at a meeting in Ballydehob to found an agricultural society for the newly formed Union of Schull but 'his reception was very cold'.[24] A few 'ground-down' farmers attended more in the hope of obtaining a reduction of rents or a supply of seed. An agricultural society, however, was duly formed and an agricultural instructor gave a lecture on green crops, particularly turnips and carrots. The subject soon changed to the question of Protection. Lionel Fleming declared that with Free Trade it was impossible for the farming class to support itself because of the weight of taxation such as grand jury cess, labour rate and poor rate. Lord Bandon also spoke on what he considered to be the evils of Free Trade and urged electors to return only Protectionists to parliament. A reporter for the *Cork Examiner* remarked that no mention was made of rack rents. The farmers remained silent and refused to raise a single cheer for Lord Bandon.[25]

Early in January 1850 Bandon presided at another Protectionist meeting in Dunmanway. He stated that the people of Schull who had suffered so much during the famine were in favour of Protection. Nonetheless a resolution condemning Protection was proposed by Fr Kelliher, now parish priest of Dunmanway in succession to Fr James Doheny. Kelliher called the Protectionist movement 'a most mischievous agitation' because Protection was a 'monster evil'. He stated that he had been parish priest of Schull and knew well that the people there were against Protection because under it 'high rents had picked them to the bones'. Then the priest bluntly declared that 'in the three months after the failure of the potato crop 120 human beings died of starvation on Lord Bandon's estate' in the parish. The landlords tried to drown the priest's voice but he went on to accuse them of raising hopes of Protection in order to save themselves from reducing their rents. Finally the meeting ended with the people shouting for 'Repeal! Free Trade! and a Cheap Loaf!' The *Cork Examiner* congratulated Fr Kelliher and the people of Dunmanway as the Protectionists had been 'fairly beaten on'. The cry of the country should be 'Reduced Rents and not artificial Protection'.[26]

As has been seen in Chapter XII, Lord John Russell had warned the ratepayers of Ballydehob that Irish property would have to bear the burden of Irish poverty. If the property owners were either unable or unwilling to do so they were supposed to sell out to others who would be better able to do their duty. The acts which were specially designed to facilitate this kind of sale were the Encumbered Estates Acts of 1848–9.[27] The spirit of the age denied further protection to bankrupt landlords; there would have to be Free Trade not only in corn but even in the semi-sacred commodity of land itself. Estates such as that of Lord Audley which had been for years in the limbo of the Court of Chancery could now be transferred to the more efficient Court of Encumbered Estates. Creditors could legally petition to have an estate sold in this court. What the Gregory Clause was doing to the tenant the Encumbered Estates Act would now do to the landlord. The government expected that vast tracts of land going at bargain prices would attract English capital in order to improve Irish agriculture.[28] As J. S. Donnelly, Jr, put it: 'Although the fateful events of 1845–9 pushed the encumbered landlords of Cork over the brink of disaster, it was as clear as their best-polished silver by the early 1840s that the long awaited day of reckoning with their creditors was close at hand'. He points out that the Audley estate 'illustrates these conditions most perfectly'.[29] It was similarly as clear as the waters of Audley Cove in Roaringwater Bay that such a day was nigh for others too.

The first indication that R. H. H. Becher of Hollybrook, Skibbereen, was in serious financial difficulties emerges at a Petty Sessions court in Ballydehob around the end of 1848. Two labourers Tom Hodnett and Patrick Healy, dressed in rags, complained that Becher owed them sixteen weeks' wages 'earned in cold and wet with empty bellies' making a road from Dunbeacon through Mount Gabriel Gap towards Schull. The magistrates, among whom was Rev. Charles Donovan, gave some legalistic reasons and dismissed the case. Hodnett however protested:

> There is no law for the poor anywhere. Be the book my childer is living on cabbage this month. If a poor man had the contract of the road Misther Treacy [County engineer] would take the trouble to have it finished and the min paid too but Misther Becher is a Justice o'Pace and he need not finish the road or pay the min's wages and for all he will be paid himself – that's the law to be shure! God be good to O'Connell's soul! What will my seven childer do for supper to-night? Ochoon! Ochoon![30]

O'Connell was missed more as a counsellor than as a Liberator. Unfortunately for Becher he had more powerful creditors who had him imprisoned for debt. While he was able to regain his personal liberty the incident prompted him to sell his large and heavily encumbered estate under the Encumbered Estates Act. He explained that it was an hereditary debt which was now impossible for him to pay owing to the failure of the potato. Nevertheless he would do his duty to his country, to his creditors and to himself.[31] In the following May 1849 the auction of stock was held. A *Cork Examiner* reporter thought it was a 'melancholy spectacle, a landlord being evicted like a tenant'. Pedigree Shorthorns and Ayrshire cows were sold one after another for £4 or £5 when they should have fetched more than double that price. It was a striking proof of the depressed state of agriculture.[32]

The estate itself was sold in October 1851. The particulars of sale showed that the estate was 17,000 acres in size, consisting of 42 townlands, in 8 different parishes, along the coast of West Cork. The yearly rental was £4,500.[33] Becher would not sell the estate as one single unit to prevent its being bought by some large English capitalist;[34] instead he divided it into 52 lots. Some were relatively small so as 'to afford tenants an opportunity of becoming owners in fee … or give small capitalists an opportunity of purchasing land, which they could themselves occupy and cultivate'.[35] Turbary rights and opportunities for fishing enhanced the value of the land. Mining rights at Clohane near Mizen Head and on Mount Gabriel were to be sold together. It was understood that the debts on the estate amounted to £52,275. The encumbrances were fifty-two in number. The estate realised a total of £52,080 which was considered cheap.[36]

Next to be sold under the Encumbered Estates Act was the notorious Audley property in November 1852. The owner was George Edward Audley, son of the Lord Audley of the mining scandal.[37] The estate consisted of 5,676 acres in 26 townlands in East and West Carbery. No buyer could be found for it in 1840 so it was deposited in the Court of Chancery. A prospective purchaser would have to deal with eighty creditors; the estate was in debt to the tune of £167,000 as Professor W. N. Hancock stated in his lecture delivered in Edinburgh.[38]

The Audley estate had been valued at various times as follows:[39]

Valuation of D. Smith of London, 1842	£3,406 per annum
Poor Law Valuation, 1845	£2,688 per annum

Poor Law Valuation, 1849	£2,092 per annum
Valuation by Encumb. Est. Court, 1850	£1,965 per annum

This is a good indicator of the falling price of land in the 1840s and in particular from 1845 to 1850, when the value of this estate fell by 27%. Audley was also lay owner of tithes worth £414 a year of which £104 was raised in Aughadown and Kilcoe. This tithe or rent-charge was now for sale like any other property. The Audley mines were for sale a second time. The Audley lands at Castlehaven were also for sale but the greater portion of the estate, 3,707 acres, was in Schull parish.[39] The townlands of Rossbrin, Cappagh, Filenamuck, Horse Island, Ballycumisk, Stouke, all south of Ballydehob consisting of 3,133 acres were bought by Thomas S. Cave, a mining capitalist from England. Raheenroe, 242 acres, was sold to J. H. Swanton, the miller, for £800. All the Audley mines and minerals were, at last, sold for £7,600 to Cave also.[40] The Audley lands near Ballydehob made a total of £17,538 for 3,700 acres or £4 15s 0d an acre. This was roughly the same sort of land as was sold by Becher little more than a year previously, at the first sale, for only £2 6s 8d an acre, i.e., about half the price. The increased price of land was a clear indication that agricultural prices were rising and pauperism declining. P. J. Lane found a similar trend in Galway: 'That the land market proved very resilient in coping with the amount of land on it can not be questioned, if we are to judge by the rate at which prices developed. The economy which was already picking up, and changing to a livestock land use, created a demand for property.'[41] The entire Audley estate realised £45,490, but it was encumbered to the tune of £167,000. It was only the earlier debtors who were repaid, for example, the Mining Company of Ireland. In December 1852 it announced to its shareholders that it had received £12,000 of the £14,874 owed by Lord Audley and the balance was soon to follow.[42] Thus ended the saga of the Audley mines.

Yet another large estate was sold in the district under the Encumbered Estates Act, namely that of Edward Baldwin Becher. It consisted of 2,974 acres in Kilcoe and Aughadown. The order of sale bore the date 12 February 1851 but the property was not sold until May 1854.[43] The total number of acres sold in our study area under the Encumbered Estates Act was as follows:

R. H. H. Becher,	(remainder is outside study area)	9,264
E. Becher,		2,974
Audley,		4,269
Total		16,507

This total of 16,507 acres amounted to 25% of all the land in the study area in the Mizen Peninsula.[44] This was a large proportion compared with the country in general where only about 17% of the land was sold under the Encumbered Estates Act by 1860.[45] Yet the figure of 25% is in accordance with the high percentage of land which was sold in some counties; 33% in Cork, Kerry, Tipperary, Limerick and Waterford and 23% in Clare, Galway and Mayo.[46]

What was the significance of the Encumbered Estates Act? The good bargains in land failed to attract any great flow of English capital or 'improved' methods of farming as the Whig framers of the act had expected it would. Apart from T. S. Cave only one other Englishman bought any of the Becher or Audley estates and both were more interested in mines than in land. As A. M. Sullivan of Bantry remarked, English speculators preferred 'Turkish bonds and Honduras loans'.[47] The sheer scarcity of Englishmen prepared to invest in the Mizen Peninsula was in keeping with the general trend in land sales all over the country. Up to 1857 only 4% of purchasers were of English, Scottish or foreign origin although they did buy nearly 14% of all the property.[48] The Encumbered Estates Act did not immediately usher in peasant proprietorship; the tenants could not afford to buy as R. H. H. Becher had hoped they would. He was also disappointed that few 'small capitalists' of the mercantile classes could afford to invest. J. H. Swanton was too large a proprietor to be said to come from this category. Those who could and did buy were mainly neighbouring landlords. It was a kinsman, a John Becher, who bought Hollybrook House and demesne itself and another relation Richard Becher Hungerford of Ballyrisode purchased some land around his own residence. John Limrick of Schull bought the mines. Others who obtained bargains were from the professional classes, clergymen like William Fisher or solicitors such as McCarthy Downing. The latter had no land in Skibbereen when he arrived in 1842 but by 1878 he had become a landlord, owning 3,466 acres with a valuation of £1,375.[49] The peasants did not yet become owners of the soil. Formerly, the Bechers and the Audleys wrested the O'Mahony and the O'Driscoll lands which were forfeited after the Desmond Rebellion, 1579, and the Battle of Kinsale, 1601. The Encumbered Estates Act did drive the thin edge of the wedge into the monolithic land structure which arose after the confiscations but no more than that. Cormac Ó Gráda observes that the landlords who sold under this act were atypical, and that the 'majority who had been living within their means before 1845 survived the famine a little bruised, but that is all'.[50]

The general change from tillage to pasture that took place all over the country undoubtedly took place in the Mizen Peninsula as well. Livestock was now more profitable to the landlord and farmer than human beings who therefore ran a higher risk of eviction. Yet there was growing criticism of such harsh measures even in England. Lord John Russell saw that the House of Commons was 'much moved' by accounts of clearances on the Blake estate in Galway which had resulted in many deaths. Even *The Times* declared that such incidents should be dealt with by 'a government which should inflict upon violence and injustice a penalty at once speedy, stringent and commensurate with the wrong done'. Russell decided that there should be some legislation in favour of tenants and told Clarendon, 'Of course Irish proprietors would dislike such measures very much; but the murders of poor cottier tenants are too horrible to bear, and if we put down assassins we ought to put down the Lynch Law of the landlord'. Thus the Evicted Destitute Bill was passed in 1848 'for the protection and relief of the destitute poor, evicted from their dwellings'.[51] It was a rather mild measure. The landlord was to give twenty-four hours notice of the eviction to the relieving officer who was supposed to ensure that there were places available to the evicted in the workhouse before they could be legally ejected.

Henry Sweetman evicted 61 persons from Gubbeen near Schull. He was bailiff to John Hickson, an absentee landlord. Another bailiff, Pat Connolly, evicted 13 persons from Derryfunshion near Dunbeacon. Philip Somerville, who was a receiver under the Court of Chancery for W. H. Hull, a minor, turned out 10 persons from the Hull estate at Lowertown. Another bailiff did likewise to 12 persons at Dunkelly in Kilmoe parish.[52] In the period 1847–9 T. H. Marmion, agent for the Rev. F. Townsend of Skibbereen, an absentee living in England, cleared out 154 families or nearly 850 persons from his landlord's estate in what J. S. Donnelly, Jr, describes as 'the largest recorded clearance of a Cork estate during the famine'.[53] Fr Fitzpatrick of Skibbereen told the traveller, Archibald Stark, about these and other evictions. In the property of W. W. Becher of Creagh near Baltimore, an absentee living in Mallow, 'the clearance system has been carried on to an alarming extent', Stark reported. A James Murragh from Montenotte in Cork city ejected nearly all his tenants from a townland in Aughadown.[54] Yet such clearances in West Cork were not on quite as large a scale as in the Union of Kilrush, County Clare.[55] There does not seem to have been any organised resistance to these evictions in the Mizen Peninsula. On one occasion, however, an agent made a hasty retreat from an eviction scene when the woman of the house 'laid a tongs to his head'.[56] Although the landlords were of course mainly responsible for such evictions they might not always have been able to carry them out were it not for the collaboration of farmers and also of bailiffs such as Pat Connolly. In 1945 an old man explained that in his young days:

> The people ... were never tired of discussing how some of those, taking advantage of the poverty of their neighbours, used to offer the rent of their farms to the landlord, the rent which the owners could not pay and grab their farm. Several people would be glad if the Famine times were altogether forgotten so that the cruel doings of their forebears would not be again renewed and talked about by the neighbours.[57]

This story from an oral source rings true. Special court sessions were held in Skibbereen for two weeks in May 1849. Over 4,000 cases of serious burglaries and church robberies were dealt with. A great number of persons were sentenced to transportation. Over 1,000 civil bills came before the court resulting in fifty ejections.[58] It is thanks to the act for the protection of the ejected that we know of the above evictions and of many others around the country. In 1849 there were 16,686 evictions; this peaked in 1850 at 19,949 and fell to 13,197 in 1851 and to 8,591 in 1852.[59] This was the situation which led to the formation of the Callan Tenant Protection Society by two Kilkenny priests, Tom O'Shea and Matthew O'Keeffe in 1849. The Tenant League was then founded in Dublin in 1850; among its founders were Frederick Lucas and J. F. Maguire. The League hoped to persuade parliament to implement Sharman Crawford's bill which would give tenants some security of tenure. The people of West Cork were naturally very interested in Tenant Right. Dr Keane, the new bishop of Ross, now independent of Cloyne, like many of the clergy, gave strong support to the Tenant League. He held that insecurity of tenure was the 'true cause of Ireland's misery'.[60]

A by-election which took place in the Cork County constituency in March 1852, provided people with an opportunity to express their feelings on the political, religious and agrarian questions of the day. Dr Power, Repeal MP for Cork, who had been elected with so much hope during the famine in 1847, had resigned on accepting a government post. The repeal and liberal candidate for the seat was Vincent Scully, a Tipperary landlord, who was opposed by a Mr Frewen, a Conservative. During his election campaign Scully visited Dunmanway but was coldly received by the parish priest, Fr Kelliher. There was some dissension in the repeal or liberal camp. Nonetheless the candidate was welcomed by Fr Foley of Kilmoe and McCarthy Downing, members of his election committee, who escorted him to Skibbereen for the hustings.

The opposing candidate, Mr Frewen, was leading the poll so the local priests quickly mustered their parishioners. Foley and John Barry, now parish priest of Schull, brought eighty-four electors all on horseback. They were greeted with a banner, 'Welcome men of the Far West! *Céad Míle Fáilte!* To the poll for God and your country'. The men of Caheragh next arrived under their parish priest, David Dore and carrying a banner, 'The Men of Caheragh of Milesian blood, owners of the soil on which they were once serfs'. The sacred causes of religion, blood and soil were harmoniously blended into one dynamic motivating force.[61] A Catholic who voted for Frewen was denounced as voting for 'dear bread, injustice to the tenant and chains for religion'. The 'dear bread' was a reference to Tory protectionism and 'chains for religion' an allusion to the support of Edward Stanley, Lord Derby and the Tories for the Ecclesiastical Titles Bill.[62] The excitement was even more intense the following and final day of the hustings. (It must be remembered that voting was still held in public.) The 'Landlord Brigade' arrived in to support Frewen but Scully's canvassers were determined to meet it 'hand to hand and foot to foot'. Many Protestant clergymen were present too including Triphook, rector of Schull, and his curate, Donovan, as were Freke and Stuart, vicars of Kilcoe and Aughadown respectively. Minor scuffles broke out between the rival supporters and the police intervened. Foley and a Protestant clergyman were involved in one incident.

In the evening the votes at Skibbereen were counted and Frewen won by a majority of ten.[63] But when the votes from all over the county came in it was Scully who was declared elected by 3,956 votes to 3,105. At this final count Scully was accompanied by John Sadleir, MP, who, with John Keogh, MP, was one of the leaders of the Irish Party in parliament known as the 'Irish Brigade'.[64] In his victory speech, Scully assured his electors that their independence would not be sacrificed to 'the intrigues of Whigs or Tories or to the base influence of English gold'. He promised that his position as MP would never be used 'as a stepping stone to personal advancement' and that 'neither place nor power' would ever induce him to abandon the principles of 'an Independent Irish Party, liberty of conscience and religion and the rights of tenants'.[65] This was a concise expression of the new political creed now developing. Nonetheless the Skibbereen liberals or repealers were deeply disappointed with the result of the election at local level. They were inclined to blame landlord intimidation. Scully's election committee thanked the few Protestant landlords, such as J. H. Swanton, who allowed their tenants to vote according to their feelings.[66]

The Liberal Club was founded at a dinner held in Skibbereen on 12 April 1852. John Barry presided at the meeting at which he was elected the first chairman of the club. Foley of Kilmoe and Troy of Aughadown and some other priests and laymen became members of the committee. It was resolved that it was 'indispensably necessary to teach the people their rights as well as the wrongs from which they suffer'. This was to be done not only in the English but also in the Irish language. After the meal Irish jigs and reels were danced. A new nationalistic feeling can be sensed at this gathering, a certain foreshadowing of *Conradh na Gaeilge* or the Gaelic League which was to be founded in 1893. Also on the committee of the Liberal Club were, McCarthy Downing, Morty Downing, Daniel McCarthy and Jeremiah Cullinane.[67] Four years later in 1856, these men together with Jeremiah O'Donovan Rossa were among the founders of the Phoenix National and Literary Society in Skibbereen, a sort of precursor of Fenianism.[68] The newly elected Vincent Scully retained his seat at the general election, held in July 1852; J. F. Maguire became MP for Dungarvan, and Frederick Lucas MP for County Meath.[69] The members of the Skibbereen Liberal Club must have been bitterly disillusioned by the 'defection' of Scully's patron, John Sadleir and also of John Keogh, both of whom soon accepted high government offices contrary to their pledges. Nevertheless such disillusionment was the ashes from which the Phoenix would arise. The leading part played by the Catholic clergy in this election is remarkable; it seemed like a return of the times of O'Connell and Old Ireland but this was to mark the zenith of their political influence.[70] Dr Paul Cullen and the Fenians would soon curtail the power of 'the priest-in-politics'.

Whatever about Faith and Fatherland the question of land simply, its ownership and value, was seldom far away. The agents of Richard Griffith surveyed Mizen Peninsula between 1849 and 1851. They were keen eye-witnesses of the famine-scarred face of the land. We have seen in Chapter XII that they recorded that roads made during the famine had enhanced the value of land particularly when sea manure could now be drawn to it. At Lissydonnell near Mount Kid they did not consider it worthwhile to mark the positions of whole villages because they were abandoned and decayed. They must have looked like the village of Meenies near Drimoleague as sketched by Mahoney of the *Illustrated London News*. Only nettles and weeds were growing around the Audley mines. At the time, 1849, an auxiliary workhouse was being opened there. The engine room, stores and miners' houses were undergoing repair in order to accommodate paupers.[71]

There was hope, nevertheless, for all was not doom and gloom. In spite of famine and emigration, many peasants were still deeply rooted in their native soil no matter who may have had the legal ownership of it. One such person was Owen Hickey of Skeaghanore East who occupied twelve and a half acres of land which was described as 'light, kind, arable, of medium depth on white clay subsoil'. He also had 'superior pasture'.[72] He was evidently an 'improving' tenant. He probably kept cows, thus availing himself of the rising price of butter on the Cork market and no doubt also at the Ballydehob market.[73] Owen Hickey may also have improved his land by drainage. In 1847, his landlord, J. H. Swanton, obtained a loan of £12,000 for drainage under the Land Improvement Act passed by Robert Peel in 1846. This work was done mainly in Skeaghanore East.[74]

Although the consolidation of farms after the famine may not have taken place quite as suddenly or as dramatically as historians once believed yet it happened swiftly enough. Between 1847 and 1851, the number of holdings in the country fell from 803,025 to 608,066. The decrease was greatest by far in the number of holdings of 1 acre which dropped from 73,016 to 37,728, and in farms of from 1 acre to 5 acres which declined from 139,041 to 88,083. Nevertheless the number of farms of from 15 to 30 acres decreased from 164,337 to only 141,311; similarly, the number of farms above 30 acres decreased from 157,097 to only 149,090.[75] Farms of anything from above 5 acres survived the calamity remarkably well but holdings of less than that were swallowed up. The survival or the disappearance of holding is reflected at local level in the Union of Schull. The following table gives the size of holdings, their number, and the percentage of holdings in each category of holding in 1851:

TABLE 31: UNION OF SCHULL, 1851:
NUMBER OF HOLDINGS, SIZE, PERCENTAGE IN EACH CATEGORY

Size of Holding (acres)	1851	%
Under 1	50	3.1
1–5	118	7.3
5–15	390	24.2
15–30	441	27.4
30–50	277	17.2
50–100	249	15.4
100–200	75	4.6
200–500	13	0.8
Total	**1,613**	**100.0**

By 1851 holdings of under 1 acre were almost wiped out and made up only 3.1% of the total number of holdings. Of the 50 survivors, 45 were in Kilmoe parish. The survival rate among holding of from 1 to 5 acres was also low, at 118, and they now made up only 7.3% of all holdings. Nevertheless, farms of from 5 to 50 acres showed a remarkable resilience and amounted to more than two-thirds (68.8%) of all holdings.[76] In the townland of Skeaghanore, for example, there were 34 holdings of this size assessed for tithes in 1831.[77] In 1850, Griffith's surveyors found the same number of holdings although 13 of them had different occupiers. These were often new branches of neighbouring families. For instance in 1831 there were five holdings held under the name Hickey but by 1851 there were eight holdings under that name.[78] Nevertheless, the population of this townland, Skeaghanore, fell from 361 in 1841 to 217 in 1851.[79] This decrease of 40% must be largely due to the disappearance of labourers who had no land at all. No trace of them can be found either in the field books or house books of the Griffith valuation. Although they did not own a patch of soil large enough to have names on any book perhaps their names still survive in the names of tiny fields and gardens which now form part of present day farms; for example there is a *Cúilín Uí Néill*, i.e., 'O'Neill's Little Nook' and a 'Caverley's Garden' in our family farm. There is no record or local family memory of any people of those names in Skeaghanore. Who were they? Perhaps they were labourers who disappeared in the famine either to the new or to the next world.

The same sort of recovery which took place in agriculture in the years immediately following the famine failed to occur in fisheries. In 1850 the commissioners for Fisheries found the 'total derangement in the social condition of the great mass of the coast population' rendered it impossible to obtain accurate returns of the number of men and boats engaged in the industry. This was because boats lay abandoned 'mouldering to decay' on the beaches. Ownership of the boats was often denied lest it would be applied as a test to debar the people concerned from gratuitous relief. The commissioners reported that between 1845 and 1849 the number of fishermen on the Irish coast decreased from 93,073 to 68,380, a drop of 24,693 or 27%. An even greater decrease, however, had been feared.[80]

The only prosperous spot in the fisheries in the Mizen Peninsula was Coosheen on the eastern shores of Schull harbour but on a windy morning in December 1848 disaster struck. The Coosheen fishermen tried to capture a floating wreck but were wrecked themselves and five were drowned. Captain Thomas claimed that the Long Islanders could easily have rescued the drowning men but they were 'so eager after the wreck which they kept lugging at while their fellow creatures were perishing within an arm's length of them'. The islanders also eventually failed to recover the wreck.[81] It is disappointing to read in the press that the shareholders of the Coosheen Mining Company decided 'to wind up the affairs of the company, dispose of plant and materials, and to surrender the lease of the mine'. The auction was to be held on 15 March.[82] No reason was given; it must have been a severe blow to the miners that hungry spring.

This loss of life prompted the Coosheen fishermen to request the Admiralty to build a pier at Coosheen. The people of Schull also sought a pier but at the western side of the harbour, i.e., at the village. It was hoped that a pier could be built at both places.[83] The Board of Works was in favour of Schull and offered to give a grant of £1,800 towards building the pier there provided the local ratepayers contributed £600.[84] In April 1849 a meeting of 500 rate-payers was held in Schull. All voted in favour of Schull except Captain Thomas of Coosheen. The Board of Works duly granted £2,400 for this project and also £460 for a pier in Cape Clear.[85] The refusal of the board to build a pier at Coosheen was a bitter disappointment to the local fishermen. They held that their way of life was too dangerous without a pier so it was decided to close down the fishery.[86] Nonetheless the closure of the mine must have had something to do with it since the fishery was a subsidiary of the Mining Company.

All was not gloom at sea either. It has been already stated in Chapter IX that following the wreck of the *Stephen Whitney* in 1847 Captain Thomas and others demanded that a lighthouse should be built on the Fastnet Rock. The lighthouse was duly granted and was designed by George Halpin, an engineer of the Port of Dublin. It was a 63-foot structure of cast iron topped by a 27-foot light lantern and was soon pointed out as an example of what Irish industry could achieve.[87] The new spirit of enterprise also found expression in the First National Exhibition held in Cork in 1852.[88] This was no doubt inspired by the Great Exhibition at the Crystal Palace in London the previous year, an event which showed the growing confidence and optimism of Mid-Victorian England. The first light beamed from the Fastnet Rock on 1 January 1854 and that on Cape Clear was extinguished forever.[89] Thus the Fastnet became all the more visible not only to sea-faring men but also to emigrants who called it *Deoir Éireann* or 'Ireland's Tear' as it was the last bit of Ireland most of them would ever see again.

The emerging post-famine society did not attach much importance to the Irish language. The census of 1851 showed that only 23% of the people of the country could speak it although the percentage in County Cork was much higher, 53%.[90] It was probably higher than that in the Mizen Peninsula yet it is surprising to find so few references to the language. Thomas Swanton, however, is aptly described by Breandán Ó Conchúir as a *réamhchonraitheoir*, i.e., a 'precursor of the Gaelic League'. He was a member of learned societies in Dublin such as the Celtic Society and urged the people as follows:

> The writer, as a sincere friend to the peasantry, says do not give up the easy, the congenial, language of your race, transmit it to your children what distinguishes you from other people, and teach them not to despise anything that is peculiar to Ireland. Learn English by all means; it is the language of profit, it is the language of the law, it is the language of emigration; but do not for the sake of it lose the voice of the Celtic Tribes.

Still he had great difficulty trying to make his own daughters speak the language and there was little or no support for it in the community either. At the end of 1847 he regretted to John Windele that 'The Revd. James Barry, the only Gaelic acquaintance I had, is now parish priest of Bantry'.[91] Swanton considered that 'though the people here seem desirous to give it up it will be a long time before they can express themselves with much comfort in English'.

He himself endeavoured to make use of the language in public; this was how he advertised a new fair in Ballydehob in 1848:

RABHADH.

Margaidhe Muc, Caorach, Pràtaidhe, Ime, agus Eisg, saor o chustam, a m-Bèal-adàhab gach Dèardaoin s-a m-bliadhain, a tosnughadh leis a g-cèad Dèardaoin a mi na Bealthine, 1848. Buanughadh don Bhainrio-ghain. Sèan d' Eirin.

RABHADH
Margaidhe Muc, Caorach, Prátaidhe, Ime agus Éisc, saor ó chustam
I m-Béaladáhab gach Déardaoin
s-a mBliadhain, a tesnughadh leis a g-céad Déardaoin a mí na Bealthine, 1848.
Buanughadh don Bhainríoghain. Séan d'Éirin.[92]

NOTICE
A market for pigs, sheep, potatoes, butter and fish, free from customs in Ballydehob every Thursday of the year beginning with the first Thursday of May 1848.
Long live the Queen. Prosperity to Ireland.

The Irish language, of course, had been declining long before the famine. In 1815 Horace Townsend had observed that in West Cork: 'Irish is the language in which the common people usually converse, several of them being unacquainted with any other. English is the most spoken in towns and villages where almost every inhabitant understands it, as also the better order of farmers in general. The use of it seems to be rather increasing'.[93] The decline in the use of Irish was accelerated by the fact it was the 'common people' rather than the 'better order' of farmers or others who had suffered most in the famine. English was of course the language of the increasing number of government officials many of whom could not speak very much Irish. Thomas Swanton lamented in 1844 that these officials 'who do not speak the language of the people cannot know the people's hearts'.[94] The use of English must have been quite widespread in the Mizen Peninsula even in the first half of the nineteenth century. When Richard Griffith was making roads there in 1822 he found that 'more than half the men spoke English but a great number of the women did not'.[95] There seems to be no reference to any visitor having much difficulty with language in this district, unlike in the Dingle peninsula, for example, at Ballyferriter. There James Kavanagh, head-inspector of the National Schools, found that in 1850 nobody young or old could speak English and when asked a question their universal reply was *Na Sasenach* ('no English').[96] The National Schools were certainly another factor in the decline of the Irish language but, as Brian Ó Cúiv points out, the effectiveness of the hedge schools in the teaching of Irish does not seem to have been very great. Out of an estimated 1,500,000 whose household language was Irish in 1806 only 20,000 were said to be able to read it.[97]

As regards the levels of Irish speaking in the country, Garrett Fitzgerald has found that one of the regions in which the language 'was still effectively holding its own' by 1841 was 'South Cork, from Mizen Head to beyond Kinsale and as far north as Macroom but excluding Kinsale itself'. He estimates that of those born 1801–11 at least 90% spoke Irish in West Carbery. Among those born 1831–41 the number speaking Irish was still 77%, but among those born 1841–51 this number decreased to 60%. This was low compared to 82% in East Carbery or 90% in Beara. The decrease in West Carbery was only partly due to the impact of the famine because the percentage of people speaking Irish had always been slightly lower here than in these other districts.[98] The Mizen Peninsula held an unusually high proportion of Anglo-Irish. In 1853 Windele invited Thomas Swanton to become a member of the newly founded Ossianic Society but he declined, considering that he had 'done enough in the way of supporting such ancient Irish societies'. Seven years later, however, he joined it together with Richard Hodnett of Ballydehob who had been a foreman on the famine roads. Swanton now attempted to found an Irish language journal at some financial cost to himself but Windele bluntly told him that 'you might as well have flung the same into Roaring Water Bay, for any useful result.'[99] At the end of the century a Gaelic League organiser, Thomas Concannon, was surprised to find that Ballydehob was 'more under Anglicising influences than any yet visited in Cork; in fact the further west one goes here the greater those influences seem to be'. Very few of the pupils in the National Schools could speak any Irish, he found.[100]

The relief system all over Ireland was badly in need of improvement. Even according to the official figures, 431 persons died of actual starvation between January and May 1849.[101] An inquest held in Skibbereen on the bodies of two women gave the verdict that they had died from want of food. Similar cases of starvation were reported from Schull.[102] Sir Charles Wood and Trevelyan were becoming more reluctant than ever to grant any more money to Ireland. Instead, a rate-in-aid of 6d in the pound was to be levied on the more prosperous unions in Ireland for the benefit of the distressed areas. This levy would last only until 31 December 1850 and the Treasury would give a supplement of £100,000. Still the rate-in-aid met vehement opposition. It was claimed that since Ireland was part of the United Kingdom it was the Imperial Treasury alone which ought to rescue the distressed Unions. The relief commissioner himself, Twistleton, resigned protesting that the administration was now 'tolerably complete' and that all that was needed was 'a comparatively trifling sum with which it is possible for this country to spare itself the deep disgrace of permitting any of our miserable fellow subjects in the distressed Unions to die of starvation'. Clarendon told Lord John Russell that he had resigned because he considered that 'the destitution here [in Ireland] is so horrible, the indifference of the House of Commons to it so manifest, that he is an unfit agent of a policy which must be one of extermination'.[103] The use of the word 'extermination' must be noted, especially coming from a man who had just been a relief commissioner.

One of the very few Irish landlords to support the Rate-in-Aid bill was the young Lord Audley. 'With deepest pain and reluctance', he confessed to the House of Lords, that he was nominally the proprietor of extensive lands in the notorious district of Skibbereen, 'the most wretched part of miserable Ireland'. As a result of the report of 'The Times commissioner', T. C. Foster[104] in 1845 Audley had received many offers from prospectors who were eager to work his mines but he was obliged to reject them because his property was involved in a 'web of difficulties' which he had tried in vain to disentangle. He hoped that the Encumbered Estates Act would finally succeed in doing so.[105] We have just seen it cut the Gordian Knot. Much of the hostility to the rate-in-aid came from the north of the country where it was seen as 'keeping up an army of beggars fed out of the industry of Ulster' but opposition came from nearer home too.[106] At Dunmanway Fr John Kelliher argued that the country could indeed afford the rate-in-aid but the local Poor Law guardians took a different view and refused to help their neighbouring Union of Bantry. As already stated, this had been officially declared 'distressed' although Skibbereen itself had not. The Bantry guardians were condemned as 'extravagant' and Dunmanway was being penalised for Bantry's 'mismanagement and wastefulness', the Dunmanway guardians maintained.[107] These Dunmanway men were sounding rather like Trevelyan or Charles Wood.

In January 1850, 150 female paupers were transferred from the auxiliary workhouse at Lowertown to the workhouse at Schull, i.e., the 'Old Workhouse'.[108] Fevers were proving very resistant to treatment and the Census of 1851 was to report that there were still three auxiliary hospitals nearby at Cooradarrigan, Coosheen and Meenvane.[109] But Schull was not the only place where this was happening since the commissioners were obliged to report:

Even in 1850 the mortality from fever had not lessened to the extent that might have been anticipated, the pestilence continued to prevail and the people, tottering under the depressing effect of the recent calamity, were unable to resist the influence of disease for which years of privation had pre-disposed them ... In the first quarter of 1851 as many as 4,385 died of fever.[110]

In districts where such deaths were still taking place the calamity was not yet really over; the famine lingered long in certain places.

The poor rates in Schull still remained very high at 3s 0d in the pound.[111] The following was the situation in the Schull workhouse on the week ending 27 April 1850:[112]

TABLE 32: SCHULL WORKHOUSE, 1850: NUMBER OF INMATES AND COST

Inmates remaining on previous Saturday	1,411
Admitted during the week	79
Discharged during the week	63
Died	9
Cost of provisions for week	£56 8s 8d
Average cost of inmate for week	10d
Average cost in infirmary	11d
Cost of outdoor relief	£25 12s 5d
Rates collected during week	£60 15s 9d
Remaining uncollected	£569 10s 7d
Balance in hands of Treasurer	£317 14s 2d

By 8 June the number of inmates had slightly increased to 1,443 and six had died. The number on outdoor relief had fallen to 1,028. Neither the Skibbereen nor Schull Unions had yet received any money as a result of the Rate-in-Aid Act. Indeed, the tax was actually levied on these unions but a portion of it, £100, was reimbursed to the Schull Union as a grant. The Schull Board of Guardians appealed to the commissioners for assistance as funds were running low. The guardians feared that they would be forced 'to turn out to perish near 3,000 paupers'.[113] Still by 2 August the number of inmates in the workhouse had fallen to 844. Mortality had decreased from nine persons to one person a week.

The guardians now thought that the general situation of the union was improving, but in the month of August 1850, they received a letter from the commissioners ordering that an additional rate of 1s 6d in the pound be levied on the Union. This was to continue for forty years to repay the loan given by the Treasury for the building of the workhouse. An increased rate had to be struck; the new rate ranged from 3s 6d to 4s 10d in the pound. The guardians protested that this would cause the Union to founder altogether. They were convinced that this 'enormous rate' would paralyse the industry of the Union and drive the farmers from the country, leaving the soil desolate.[114] This protest was heeded by the commissioners because they undertook to pay such of the outstanding debts of the Union as were incurred before 17 May of the previous year, 1849. This money would come from the funds raised by the

Rate-in-Aid Act.[115] The rates were certainly very high. In the comparatively well off Kinsale Union, for example, the highest rate was 1s 6d while most rates were under a shilling and some were as low as 3d.[116] Such were the principles of 'local responsibility' of the Poor Law. Now that the inmates of the Schull workhouse had been provided with food and the bare necessities of life, efforts were made to give them some employment. In May 1851, tenders were invited to supply large quantities of scissors, needles, flax, wool and six weavers' looms.[117] The institution was trying to become a genuine workhouse rather than just a poorhouse. By 1852 the general improvement in conditions is reflected in the decrease in the rates to 2s or under.[118]

There was little landlord-sponsored emigration in West Cork compared with Connaught. Mr Newman of Skibbereen did assist some families to go to America at a cost of £7 10s 0d per person. Nonetheless McCarthy Downing held that the money would have been better spent paying the labourers to reclaim the waste lands of their own country for example around Schull.[119] There was also some government-assisted emigration from the workhouses. In 1847 the Governor of South Australia suggested that a portion of the South Australian Land Fund should be used to assist emigration of orphans from English workhouses to the colony. Since sufficient orphans were not available the offer was extended to Irish workhouses. It was welcomed by the Poor Law commissioners because over half of the inmates were children, including many orphans. But it was condemned by the *Nation* which described it as 'one of the most diabolical proposals ever made or conceived since Cromwell's time' and the *Tipperary Vindicator* accused the government of exporting girls as white slaves to pander to the vices of the rich settlers.[120] The cost of the voyage was to be borne by the colony but the Poor Law guardians were to supply the appropriate outfit for the orphans. The majority of those selected were female as women were badly needed.[121] In April 1849 seventy-five 'well looking' young women arrived in Cork from the Skibbereen workhouse, *en route* to Australia. Almost 200 others had already departed from other parts of the country for the same destination.[122] The total number of female orphans who went there from Skibbereen was 110 which was greater than from any union outside of Dublin. Among them was a Mary Colgan who married a James Walton, a man 'addicted to liquor and using violence to his wife'. Although she was innocent he involved her in a murder at a gold digging site and later beat her to death.[123] Over 4,000 Irish women took part in the scheme but it was soon brought to a close by the colonial authorities in 1850. Many of the women were accused of being filthy, lacking in domestic skills, and of being 'workhouse sweepings' and prostitutes. There were still 104,000 children in Irish workhouses.[124] Nevertheless, the usual sort of emigration to that continent continued. One child went from the Schull workhouse, 'A girl, nine years old, who received permission to accompany her mother, a convict'.[125]

Assisted emigration to North America continued, however, especially to Canada. For example the Governor of Quebec sought hardworking single Irish women as servants and men as carpenters and bricklayers. An amendment to the Poor Law in 1849 permitted Boards of Guardians to support emigration from workhouses. Accordingly 253 paupers went to Quebec and 80 to Montreal from the Cork workhouse in 1850. They were among the 1,721 who departed from the workhouses of the country that year; these comprised 360 men, 844 women and 517 children.[126] Bishop Lynch of Toronto wrote that the parish priest of Montreal complained that 'the city had been comparatively chaste until 1852–3, when numerous bands of girls were brought from the poorhouses of Ireland and distributed through the cities. They were exposed in public places to be hired as slaves in many parts of the south'.[127]

A good general picture of the 'poor struggling people' back home in Ireland is given in a report by a 'practical instructor' in agriculture, James Simpson, August 1850:

> From every information I could collect during the last seven months, the number of inhabitants in this Union [Schull] are decreased by nearly one-half; in the remote portions of this district where misery, starvation and death carried off the greater number, there more especially, the exertions made by these poor struggling people in raising a crop of potatoes and turnips were greater than could be anticipated.[128]

It must be noted how he states that it was death rather than emigration which carried off the greater number. Seed was supplied to the farmers at cost price. The 18 hundredweight of turnip seed which he had distributed planted 800 acres of that crop but he had difficulty in convincing the farmers of the necessity of the 'timely thinning and cleaning of turnips'. The seed for carrots, mangolds, cabbage, beans and rape was also sold and the crops were good. Half of the potatoes had gone black but he found that the old varieties although degenerate and not prolific were still the soundest. He stated that 'All appear delighted at the prospect of again rearing and fattening pigs' but regretted that the breed was inferior. He recommended that farm tools should be sold to the farmers as their shovels were only like trowels with long handles which rendered labour on the land and in the bog very difficult.[129] In the following spring of 1851 Simpson found that the farmers were now copying landlords such as R. B. Hungerford by growing turnips, beans and carrots. Indeed both landlords and farmers were complaining about the difficulty of obtaining able-bodied labourers because 'nearly all that class are leaving for America, leaving the rubbish behind'. Yet the instructor was glad that the Union was 'recovering from poverty slowly but steadily'.[130] Here we see once again the effort to modernise and break the fatal monoculture of the potato by growing some green crops. An agricultural adviser who was doing similar work in Wexford at this time often noted that potatoes were 'a total failure' but nowhere was there a reference to famine. One district in particular was 'beautiful and fertile'.[131]

How successful were these efforts to break the monoculture of the potato and to diversify into green crops? As has been seen in Chapter XII, 1847 provided a bumper harvest except, of course, for the potato crop. Indeed there was now a greater area under turnips than under potatoes in the whole country, 370,344 acres as against 284,116. The man responsible for these agricultural statistics, Thomas Larcom, reported that turnips 'were sown in despair, as the food of man, not of cattle'. We shall now compare the harvest of 1847 with that of 1851 in the Union of Schull (by 'other green crops' is meant parsnips, carrots, cabbage and also vetches and rape for cattle):

TABLE 33: UNION OF SCHULL, 1847–51: CROPS

Crop (acres)	1847	1851	Change
Wheat	1,533	2,133	+39.1%
Oats	921	780	−15.3%
Barley	853	438	−48.7%
Potatoes	863	2,774	+221.4%
Turnips	383	876	+128.7%
Mangolds	13	16	+23.1%
Other green crops	56	118	+110.7%
Flax	23	36	+56.5%
Meadow/clover	589	928	+57.6%
Total	**5,234**	**8,099**	**+54.7%**

The increase of 39% in the acreage under wheat was substantial but it was partly because some had been sown instead of potatoes. Yet this increase of 600 acres was almost cancelled out by the decrease of 556 in the acreage under oats and barley. The 'corn era' protected by legislation had gone forever. The increase of 221.4% in the acreage under potatoes looks impressive but that is only in comparison with the disastrous crop of 1847, of course. Thomas Larcom could find no accurate way of measuring the extent of the potato crop in previous years since 1847 was the first year in which such agricultural data were gathered. The total area under turnips, mangolds, other green crops and meadow/clover increased from 1,041 to 1,974, i.e., by just over 89%. The 'grass era' encouraged by market forces was arriving; these forces were soon to be strengthened by a foreign event in 1853. As J. S. Donnelly, Jr, concludes, 'Although the worst was nearly over by the end of 1851, there was no real recovery in prices until the outbreak of the Crimean War'.[132]

Let us see how many animals there were to feed in the district in 1851. Unfortunately livestock was enumerated not by the parish but by the barony. The Mizen Peninsula forms part of the barony of West Carbery, West Division, which also includes the parishes of Muintir Bháire (Durrus) and Caheragh but not Aughadown.

Livestock	1847	1851	Change
Horses/Mules	2,528	2,449	–3.1%
Cattle	8,608	16,802	+95.2%
Sheep	7,726	9,197	+19.0%
Pigs	662	6,274	+847.7%
Poultry	15,103	24,925	+65.0%
Total	**34,627**	**59,647**	**+72.3%**

Between 1847 and 1851, the number of horses and mules in this district declined from 2,528 to 2,449, i.e., by only 3.1%. This corresponded to what happened all over the country where the number of horses and mules decreased from 557,917 to 543,312, i.e., by only 2.6%. The decline was minimal; moreover these figures were quite near the 1841 figure, i.e., 567,115. These animals seem to have been untouched by the famine, their number holding out at something over half a million all throughout the hungry decade.

Between 1847 and 1851, the number of cattle in this West Carbery district increased from 8,608 to 16,802, i.e., by 95.2% – it almost doubled. This too is in line with the increase which had taken place throughout the country. In 1841 their number was 2,220,000 but by 1847 it had increased to 2,591,415 and by 1851 it had further risen to 2,967,461, i.e., by 14.5%, to nearly three million. Even since 1841 the number of cattle had increased by 747,461, i.e., by 33.7%. The Census commissioners rightly commented that there had been a 'considerable augmentation' in the number of cattle.

Between 1847 and 1851, the number of sheep in the West Carbery district increased from 7,726 to 9,197, i.e., by 19%. In the country in general, however, their number had decreased slightly, i.e., from 2,186,177 to 2,122,128. This, however, was still a little above the 1841 figure, i.e., 2,106,189. The number of pigs in the district in 1847 fell to as low as 662 but it recovered by 1851 to reach 6,274. This reflected what happened all over the country. In 1847 only 622,459 pigs were still left but by 1851 their number had increased to 1,084,857. Nonetheless this was still a far cry from the 1841 figure, i.e., 1,412,813. Moreover this figure was regarded as lower than usual in that a scarcity of potatoes led many small-holders to part with their pigs before census day. In 1847 the number of poultry still surviving in the district was only 15,103 but by 1851 it had increased to 24,925. This was in accordance with the general trend throughout the country where numbers had increased from 5,691,055 to 7,470,694. It was still well below the 1841 figure of 8,458,517. In brief, between 1841 and 1847, the numbers of pigs and poultry suffered much more from the famine than did the numbers of horses, mules, cattle and sheep which held their own or even increased significantly. The commissioners called attention to the fact that the pigs and poultry were 'almost extinguished in many districts'. No doubt these were often the same districts in which many of their owners were also extinguished rather than were the owners of the horses, cattle and sheep.[133]

To sum up, between 1847 and 1851 the acreage under crops increased by 54.7% and the numbers of livestock, pigs and poultry increased by 72.3%; such substantial changes in such a short time – four years – were nothing short of revolutionary. The failure of the potato crop provoked not only a social revolution but an agricultural or green revolution as well. Both events were inextricably entwined just like the industrial and social revolutions in other countries.

The shipping trade was also picking up at Crookhaven, a barometer always sensitive to what was happening at sea in time of war or peace. The following were among the ships which called in there during April 1851:

The Austrian Brig, *Porciah*, from Constantinople to Queenstown for orders: corn
The Schooner, *Warfinder*, from Limerick to London: butter
Brig *Lindney*, from Alexandria: wheat, for orders
Tenebrae from Greenock to Liverpool: general
American ship, *Areatus*, Calcutta to Boston, with damaged rudder and bowspit off Cape of Good Hope
The barque, *Mingsteen*, from China to London: general
Ellen Jenkinson of Liverpool from West Coast Africa: oil, wood, to Liverpool.[134]

The ports of departure and of arrival of these ships were far distant and their cargoes had an interesting variety. We are getting a glimpse at the growing foreign trade which Britain was beginning to enjoy in this Mid-Victorian Era.[135] As Vincent Comerford points out, 'Post-famine Ireland is also mid-Victorian Ireland'.[136] The Crimean War must also have provided a boost to the provisions trade at Crookhaven, a trade which, as has been seen, had languished ever since the peace which followed Waterloo – and all for the want of a war.

The census of 1851 provides an authoritative indication of the extent of the catastrophe in general. The population of Ireland had fallen from 8.2 million in 1841 to 6.6 million in 1851.[137] In simpler figures the number of people fell by two million whereas the number of cattle rose by three-quarters of a million. The poet Joseph Campbell (1879–1944) was later ruefully to ask:

Where are the lowland people gone? …
The strength that held the heavy plough?
Grasslands and lowing herds are good,
But better far is human flesh and blood.

This was a drastic drop in the number of people especially when one takes into account that the population must have been even greater in 1846 than in 1841. The severity of the change in population varied in the different regions of the country. The population actually increased in the large towns and cities, Dublin, Belfast and Cork, while it fell by up to at least 80% in some rural districts. We have seen that villages or clachans such as Kilbronoge near Ballydehob or Meenies near Drimoleague simply disappeared. Other villages, however, suffered a similar fate in districts where it might not be expected, e.g., Glanmire, just east of Cork city. The village of Sallybrook was 'wiped from the book of being' as Dr Traill might have said. In 1841 it contained 76 houses but in 1851 it did not contain even 20 and so was included in the townland of Knock-nahorgan on which it stood. The fact that five men died in the fever hospital in Rathcooney in 1847 also implies that the Glanmire area did not escape the famine quite as lightly as local tradition claims. There was also an active relief committee in Rathcooney.[138] The Census commissioners would not let the country forget that not only were districts depopulated but also 'whole villages were effaced from off the land'.[139] As O'Callaghan of the *Cork Examiner* had witnessed in West Cork they became 'graveyard villages'.[140]

As well as missing villages the census revealed that there were many children missing from its roll-call all over the country. Between 1841 and 1851 the number of one year old children declined by 34%; those between one and five years by 38%; those between five and ten by 25%; whereas bigger children and young adults between ten and twenty declined by only 10%. The following is an example of how the famine had struck very young children in the parish of Schull: in 1841 there were 2,567 children under the age of five in the parish but by 1851 there were only 1,078, i.e., an appalling drop of 58%. The number of persons over five years of age declined from 14,747 to 9,922, i.e., by 'only' 32.7%. The commissioners regarded the number of children and very young persons attacked by fever as 'another peculiarity' of this famine; such attacks took place 'to an extent far greater than any previous records of fever have elicited'. Some of the most fatal cases of fever 'followed the reaction after starvation'.[141]

Some families, however, showed remarkable resilience. An American historian, Patricia Trainor O'Malley, has done a micro-study of twelve families – including some of her own ancestors and also some of mine – in the townland of Derreennalomane near Ballydehob during the famine. According to the census reports, the population of the townland decreased by 44% from 1841 to 1851. In these families, however, the survival rate of parents and of the children born during and after the disaster was at the very least 83% as there are further accounts of them such as records of children who had received the sacrament of Confirmation. Women continued to bear children throughout the worst years. In only one family, that of John Field and Mary Driscoll, was there a gap, between 1845 and 1850, in the births of their eight children. Three were born before 1845 and five more after 1850; the youngest of these, Kate (born 1864), was my paternal grandmother.[142] As has been seen in Chapter X, Joel Mokyr referred to 'averted births' due to the famine; the case of Kate Field may perhaps be described as a 'postponed birth'. There must have been many others all over the country. The Fields had sixteen acres of land valued at £7 10s 0d; they were typical of the small farmers who survived the disaster but who were profoundly marked by it nonetheless. Moreover, they were not in that townland for long since they had been evicted from nearby Dunbeacon.[143] Patricia O'Malley asks whether this high survival rate of more than 83% may be partly thanks to Lord Bandon who may have been kinder on his tenants than others. This can hardly have been the case since we have seen that Frs Barry and Kelliher condemned him for the many deaths on his lands near Ballyde-hob. She also asks whether the hilly terrain around Derreennalomane might not have pushed its inhabitants to vary their farming and rear more cattle and sheep, as her great-grandfather is supposed to have done. It may well be that such people were somewhat less dependent on the potato than were the inhabitants of the clachans along the sea-shore near Ballydehob. Yet this must not be exaggerated. Between 1841 and 1851 the population of Derreenna-lomane fell from 309 to 172, i.e., by 44% and the number of houses from 53 to 29, i.e., 45%. As has been seen Chapter VIII, James Barry visited the hilly town-lands of Derreennalomane, Laharn and Shantulig and found that conditions were just as bad as in the Ballydehob district; whole families had been wiped out by famine and fever and their hovels tumbled in upon them.

EMIGRATION

The bereavement, uprooting and scattering of families caused by famine and emigration is well illustrated in the case of Jeremiah O'Donovan Rossa. As already mentioned, his father had died on the road-works during the famine in 1847 and the family was soon evicted. In 1848 an uncle who had emigrated to Philadelphia in 1841 sent the tickets for the passage to Rossa's mother, brot-her and sister, who then all emigrated, leaving him alone in Ireland. He de-scribed their departure in poignant terms:

> At Renascrena Cross we parted … Five or six other families were going away and there were five or six cars to carry them … to the Cove of Cork. The cry of weeping and wailing of that day rings in my ears still. That time, it was a cry heard every day, at every cross-road in Ireland.[144]

Only one of Rossa's eighteen children, Florence Stephen, was to be buried in Ireland; the others chose to live beneath 'the freedom of the Stars and Stripes' as one of them proudly put it.[145]

We have seen in Chapter VI that there was a significant amount of emi-gration in pre-famine times when people such as the Fitzgeralds and the Har-rigans of Kilmoe parish went to Canada. Ellen, the eldest daughter of Dennis and Catherine Harrigan, had remained at home at that time. She was married to William Sauntry, a labourer from near Ballydehob. He died in 1848 of fever, it was said, and then his widow and their eight children emigrated to New Brunswick in Canada about the year 1851 to join her relatives there.[146] We can trace other emigrants who went to Canada at this time; they included Henry Field, his wife, Mary Driscoll, and their five children who left Dunbeacon near Ballydehob. They probably landed at Quebec. By 1850 their names had appeared in Church and Civil records; they were clearing 'stony farm-wood lots' high in the Gatineau Valley, thirty-five miles north-west of Ottawa. Their settlement, now a village, is called Fieldville.[147] 'Big' Flurry Driscoll, born on Long Island off Schull in 1836, went to Kansas in the United States where he farmed on the prairies. His son relates that his first ambition had been to get away from the 'burdensome poverty of his people'.[148] Another emigrant was a Margaret Field born near Rosscarbery in 1835.[149] Around the time of the famine she went to Boston where she married a James Hickey who had also come from Ireland; it is thought to be Clonakilty. A daughter of theirs, Mary Augusta, married a Patrick J. Kennedy; their son, Patrick Joseph, married a Rose Fitzgerald. She was a granddaughter of Katherine Cadogan and James Fitzgerald who had come from Skibbereen. Patrick Joseph Kennedy and Rose Fitzgerald had a son named John Fitzgerald Kennedy who became President of the United States.[150]

Malcolm Cambell questions the idea that Irish immigrants usually lacked the skills and capital necessary for farming in the New World, that they felt a psychological aversion to land resulting from famine and that they were too gregarious to move away from the cities. The following is his conclusion from his study of Irish rural settlements in Minnesota (US) and in New South Wales (Australia):

> In both societies Irish settlers took advantage of the favourable economic opportunities that arose from the time of their arrival in frontier communities and as a result of their pragmatic desire to acquire readily available land, they fared well in farming. By virtue of their strong presence in the regions they enjoyed generally harmonious and supportive relationships with their fellow settlers, a condition which made for stability and prosperity.[151]

Evidently, the same can be said about Irish settlers in Canada such as the Fitzgeralds and the Harrigans, and my relations the Driscolls and the Fields of Fieldville.

It is no surprise that in the circumstances of emigration at this period that there should have been many missing persons. Relatives placed advertisements in the *Boston Pilot* seeking them; some revealing and touching notices have been collected by Ruth-Ann Harris, Donald Jacobs and Emer O'Keeffe. Several such immigrants had arrived in the coffin-ships. The following advertisement appeared in the above newspaper in 1848:

> Denis and Timothy Harrington, sons of Patrick Harrington, who sailed from Castletownbere, Co. Cork, 1 May 1847 in the ship, *Governor Douglas*, and arrived in St John, New Brunswick, in the latter part of June. The father having left both boys in the house of John Buckley, Dowry Lane, St John, came to Vermont for the purpose of seeing his brother. The last heard of them was when they moved out to the country.[152]

And in 1849, the following notice appeared:

> Of Daniel Magrath, formerly of Mount Gabriel, parish of Schull, Co. Cork. He came to America about 2 years since. When last heard from he was in Boston and is supposed to be at present in New Hampshire. Any information respecting him will be thankfully received by his wife, Catherine (who arrived with her child in Boston 3 weeks ago). Direct to her in care of Cornelius O'Driscoll, 141 Broad St, Boston.[153]

Catherine was one of the seventy-two wives from County Cork trying to locate their husbands at this time. According to Cormac Ó Gráda Irish emigration was more female than any other major outflow from nineteenth century Europe'.[154] This is usually regarded as an indication of the poor prospects that lay ahead of them at home. Sons were, of course, far more likely to inherit farms while daughters might not always be able to obtain a dowry. Efforts to find 'missing friends' through the *Boston Pilot* were reasonably successful in the circumstances. Out of the 252 parishes in this County of Cork 110 had at least one such person found. These immigrants were apparently more tightly knit than one might have thought.

Many children however were still missing by 1850, for example:

> John O'Brien, a native of Knocknachagh, parish of Kilmacbea, Co. Cork, who landed in Quebec, 20 May 1847. He was 8 years old leaving Ireland and his father died in the passage. His brother and sister, Jane and Patrick, now in West Machics, Me., are anxious to hear from him.[155]

Others sought relatives who had emigrated in the early 1830s; Florence Donovan for example was looking for his brother who left Abbeystrowry in 1834.[156] Quite a number, such as the above Patrick Harrington, already had relatives in the country. As has been seen in Chapter X, many of those who landed in Canada used it only as a back door to enter the United States. Among them were these Harringtons and also John Collins of Kilmoe; he landed at Quebec in 1848 but a few years later we find him in Buffalo, New York State. His brothers were in Massachusetts.

Some emigrants did not of course go directly to America but via England and Wales. Mary, Ann and Julia Driscoll of Schull sailed from London in 1849 and were being sought by Cornelius Driscoll in New York. A Denis Sullivan also from Schull left Wales and landed in New York.[157] Several of these immigrants went working on the railroads such as John Driscoll of Cape Clear.[158] Harris and Jacobs found that these immigrants were quite 'geographically mobile' and often tended to head out for the country, for example:

> Patrick Murry from parish of Schull, Ballydehob, left New York city about 12 months ago [1850]; when last heard of he was in Cleveland. It is supposed he is in Kentucky. Timothy Murry, his brother ... will be pleased to receive any information on him, care of Patrick Hickey, Kivington St, New York.[159]

This geographical mobility implied a certain upward social mobility. 'The pith and marrow of Ireland,' commented the *Irish American* in 1849, 'averaging between 100 and 5,000 dollars do not stop in cities to spend their money and fool away their time. They go directly into the interior to seek out the best location as farmers, traders and so forth'.[160] David Fitzpatrick points out that it is a myth that the vast majority of the Irish invariably settled in the major cities, if only for the fact that America was still overwhelmingly rural.[161] No doubt some who had skills and capital chose to remain in the cities; but there were many who were still haunted by the same lack of resources as in Ireland, and so lived as labourers or domestic servants in districts which could at times be called slums.[162] J. F. Maguire visited a young couple from Skibbereen, who now lived in New York, 'stuffed into a little room in a tenement house, with four helpless children … A month's idleness or a fortnight's sickness and what misery!' The father was a day labourer.[163] All did not get on as well as the Kennedy family from Dunganstown, County Wexford (ancestors of President Kennedy). Bishop Lynch of Toronto warned the Irish bishops in 1864 that many Irish immigrants lost their faith and ended up in crime, poverty and prostitution. Charles Kickham described Lynch's criticism of emigration as contributing to the 'principles of Fenianism'.[164]

If the young were often physically lost the old were socially lost. In 1863 O'Donovan Rossa visited his mother, brother and sister who had emigrated. But he and his mother failed to recognise each other. 'The most melancholy looking picture' he saw in America was an old father or mother brought over by their children. 'See them coming from Mass of a Sunday morning,' he wrote, 'looking sad and lonely; no one to speak to, no one around they know; strangers in a strange land'.[165]

By the early 1850s emigration was a serious haemorrhage, depriving the country of mostly young enterprising people. Priests lamented it.[166] There was the notorious boast of *The Times* that a Celtic Irishman on the Shannon would be as rare as a Red Indian on the shores of Manhattan. Better would have been expected of a lord lieutenant such as Clarendon but he was as unsympathetic as any Pharaoh: 'Priests and patriots howl over the "Exodus",' he reported, 'but the departure of thousands of Celtic Papists must be a blessing to the country they quit'. 'I would sweep Connaught clean,' he declared, 'and turn in upon it new men and English money just as one would to Australia or any freshly discovered colony – the nearer one can get to that the more probable will be the solution of the "Irish Problem".'[167] No doubt he would sweep the Mizen Peninsula clean too.

According to Kerby Miller 1.2 million departed from the whole country between 1845 and 1851.[168] Cormac Ó Gráda asserts that the story that a million of these crossed over in coffin-ships is a myth; the great majority of them made the voyage safely to the other side – at least as well as other nationalities did. He grants that mortality on the Canadian routes was extremely high in 1847, about 20%, but he shows that mortality among the Irish on New York bound ships during the period 1847–51 was lower than among the Germans, for example, 1.8% as against 2.8%. The figure for mortality among the French, however, was the lowest, at 1.0%. It must also be noted that the death rate among the Irish on the New York route was higher in 1849 than in 1847, i.e., 3.4% compared with 1.3%.[169]

At the end of 1851 John Kelliher, PP of Dunmanway and formerly of Schull stated to *The Times* that 'the attention given in its columns to what is called "Celtic Exodus"' prompted him to offer the newspaper an emigrant's letter. He described it as 'a fair specimen of the epistolary encouragement afforded to Irish emigration by every transatlantic post'. The letter – a struggle with literacy – was written by James Cullinane who with his wife was in Detroit in the United States and it was sent to their daughter, Mary, and many other relatives, friends and neighbours in Dunmanway:

My deer friend Cornelius Farrel and Mrs Coffee and family, I am happy to inform you that we arrived Safe being only 6 weeks from the day I left home until I landed in Detroit where I met my own friends, which was not a place of hunger nor Starvation thanks be to the lord … To tell the truth about my friends here and of the country I See that Every thing is to be preased. By giving everyone his own du, the friends are doing well and in good health and the country cannot be beat in the whole world unless by a man's own faught by drinking or otherwise to leasy to work where a man can earn 7 shillings per day here now … My deer daughter Mairy, I want to inform you that timothy coffee and me met his sister mrs Dinan in New York and Coffee got work there the day he landed … he maid up his mind to Stay there untill he will have mains to Sind for you, this is the best of my opinion. If he did not rite to you direct your letter to John Dinan … Dan Donovan wishes that Cornelius Ferrel would sind him all the information he can about his Brothersinlaw he might try to sind for them. This is the place for any man let him be rich or poor, the more money a man bring here the sooner he can Settle down here is the obgect, whin a man starts poor it will teak double the time to put the foolish thought of home out of his mind. I would advise the best farmer from Cork to Bantry to leav that land of starvation. What signify is the term of their lease on land at home where they could have maid property here that no man could dare say leav my land? James Collins wishes you to show this letter to Charly Collins. I would like to hear from my brothers John and Timothy Cullinane, Charly Collins will find it out and sind us all accounts. I hope to do something for them next spring with the help of god. Michael is here and Denis is about 12 miles out in the country to work and in good health. Dan and his family is well and doing well. James Collins and his family is in good health and doing well. Cornelius died in the city of Detroit, had the sicknes after the voige and died 2 months after he landed. James Driscole is very much obliged to me for all the information I gave him about his mother and Brother, he rote 3 letters and got no answer. Big Leary, John Driscole, John Mahoney and his family is doing well, the Mayburys is doing well. Tell widow Carty that this is a Better place than Boston. You, Jerry Donovan, would do well here, this is as good a times we had in America this last 20 years for Earning money. The first people in this part of the city was the Mayburys and John Mahoney and 3 more families from the county cork, it got the name of corks town.[170]

As Fr Kelliher remarked, this letter needs little comment but it does confirm what we have already found out about these emigrants/immigrants. We observe the 'pull' of the American epistle together with the 'push' of famine leading to chain emigration. Some of these Dunmanway people had arrived in Detroit long before the famine just like members of the family of Henry Ford of Ballinascarty near Clonakilty as has been seen. Family, friends and neighbours were closely knit, mobile, and generally 'doing well and in good health' in spite of the hardships of the 'voige', poverty, and 'the foolish thought of home'. For many of these immigrants sensible thoughts of home would rather have been to 'sind' for some of their people and 'do something for them with the help of god'.

Some of the results of the 'Celtic Exodus' (1841–51) from the 'Pharaoh of famine' in the 'Egypt' of Union of Schull can be seen in the following table:

TABLE 35: UNION OF SCHULL: CENSUS REPORTS, 1841, 1849, 1851

Parish	1841	1849	Change	%	1851	Change since '49	%	Change since '41	%
Kilmoe	7,234	4,778	−2,456	−34	4,189	−589	−12	−3,045	−42
Schull	17,314	10,659	−6,655	−38	11,000	+341	+3	−6,314	−36
Kilcoe	2,339	1,212	−1,127	−48	1,238	+26	+2	−1,101	−47
Total	**26,887**	**16,649**	**−10,238**	**−38**	**16,427**	**−222**	**−1**	**−10,460**	**−39**

As has already been shown in Chapter XII, the main decrease in population had already taken place between 1841 and 1849. Kilmoe did indeed lose 589 persons from 1849 to 1851; this may have been partly due to the cholera. The workhouse had opened in Schull in January 1850 and this must have drawn some paupers from Kilmoe. The opening of this workhouse helps to explain the slight rise of 3% in the population of Schull. There was also a very small increase of 2% in Kilcoe. However, on average there is only a slight decrease of 1% in the three parishes of Kilmoe, Schull and Kilcoe from 1849 to 1851. In Aughadown parish (which remained in Skibbereen Union) the population declined from 5,757 in 1841 to 3,329 in 1851 that is by 42%. Taking the three parishes of the new Schull Union together (Kilmoe, Schull and Kilcoe) there was an average decline of 39% between 1841 and 1849. Still the period in which the greatest decline took place was actually much shorter than this since famine mortality and emigration had not really begun until the autumn of 1846. This means that in the next three years the district was to lose up to 40% of its population – a brutal shock certainly.

Yet this loss is not the full measure of the shock. The Census commissioners pointed out that the decrease of 1,622,739 persons or 20% of the population of the whole country 'conveys but inadequately the effect of the visitation of famine and pestilence' because there should have been a natural increase. If there had been no famine what would the population of these four parishes have been? Between 1831 and 1841 it had increased by 8% so if it had continued increasing at that rate, instead of being only 19,756 in 1851 it would have reached 35,255. Yet it must be considered very doubtful if it could ever have reached that figure because, as we have seen, the rate of increase in these parishes, apart from Schull and Kilmoe, was slowing down and emigration was increasing in all four parishes. It can be maintained, however, that the population of the district, instead of decreasing by 40%, should have increased by from about 5% to 8%. The sudden and violent reversal of a tendency which had been in motion for more than a century was revolutionary in the literal sense; it turned things around and rapidly. This reversal was destined to be permanent too as the population has ever since been on the decline. In parts of Scotland, for example, the clearances were even more sweeping than in parts of Ireland yet some districts recovered. John Macleod comments: 'It is a tribute to the vacuity of the Clearance logic ... that Barra and Lewis [Hebrides] harboured more people in 1900 than they did in 1840, notwithstanding the famine and evictions of mid-century'.[171] It is difficult to imagine that happening in Cape Clear or Sherkin or anywhere in West Cork although it is true that parts of Donegal had a higher population in 1891 than in 1841 thanks to seasonal migration to Scotland. The income from migrants and their part-time labour kept small farms viable. People continued to marry young and the proportion of those who never married remained low.[172]

It might have been expected that population loss between 1841 and 1851 should have been greater in the poorer and most westerly Kilmoe rather than in the better off and more easterly Kilcoe, but that is not the case. In fact this latter parish lost more, i.e., 47% compared to Kilmoe's 42%. Marshall's Return showed that Kilcoe had the lowest mortality rate and the second highest emigration rate so this loss must be largely due to emigration. This pattern emerged in other parts of the country as well. In the well-off parish of Enniskeane there was a decrease of 46% which was greater that in the poorer neighbouring parish of Kilmichael, 35%.[173] It has been observed also in County Mayo that the peripheral and poorest regions suffered less depopulation than did the more prosperous central lowlands. One poor and remote parish actually experienced an increase in population.[174] The reason there was a greater decrease where the land was better was that the landlords had a greater motivation to consolidate holdings and the tenants had more money to emigrate.

Population decline was less among the islanders than among their neighbours on the mainland. The Hare Islanders decreased by 19% and the Long Islanders by only 9%. The people of Cape Clear and Sherkin were reduced by 19%. The population of the towns, Ballydehob, Schull and Crookhaven maintained itself better than that of the rural areas and than that of the town of Skibbereen, as can be seen from the following table:

TABLE 36: BALLYDEHOB, SCHULL, CROOKHAVEN: POPULATION, 1841–51:

Towns	1841	1851	Change
Ballydehob	636	589	–7.4%
Schull	452	535	+18.4%
Crookhaven	395	381	–3.5%
Total	**1,483**	**1,505**	**+1.5%**
Skibbereen	4,715	3,834	–18.7%

The commissioners believed that there was 'a natural law' governing the movement of populations in calamity; if there is famine in the country they flee to the city and if there is plague in the city they head for the country and if there is both famine and plague everywhere they emigrate. The people of the Mizen Peninsula followed that rule; there was migration as well as emigration. The decline in the population of Crookhaven is only a continuation of the trend which began after Waterloo while decline in the population of Ballydehob is more noteworthy in that it had been increasing ever since the building of Griffith's new road and the opening of the copper mines in the 1820s. The increase in the population of Schull must also be pointed out. The new workhouse brought its own trade and employment. Schull obtained the doubtful honour of becoming a Union town. The workhouse contained as many as 1,075 people and the auxiliary workhouse 236 making a total of 1,311. Indeed there had been 1,411 paupers in the workhouse itself the previous year, 1850. On census night 1851 there were nearly as many people in these two workhouses (1,311) as inhabitants in the three towns, Crookhaven, Schull and Ballydehob (1,505). The population of Skibbereen decreased to 3,834, i.e., by almost 19%. This was severe for a town. Moreover, the people in the town's workhouse and three auxiliary workhouses amounted to as many as 2,981, or 44% of all the inhabitants of the town. This reflects the general institutionalisation of pauperism and of other social problems such as that of orphans and abandoned children all over the country. In the Skibbereen Union the proportion of workhouse inmates to the general population was 1:14 and in the Schull Union 1:13. In other Unions it was even worse such as Kenmare and Dingle, County Kerry, 1:7. In Scarriff, County Clare, it was 1:8, but in Ballymena, County Antrim it was as favourable as 1:200. In the whole country, it was 1:26.[175] This sad proportion must have been a cause of concern to the commissioners as it was they who worked out the figures. The number of inmates reached its maximum of 267,170 in June 1851, which was well over a quarter of a million.[176]

While the commissioners made no claims to have been able to count the numbers of those who died in the cabins and ditches, they did give figures for those who died in institutions. The Skibbereen workhouse was opened in 1842; between that and 1851 the number of persons who died there is 4,346. The Schull workhouse was opened in January 1850 and in little over a year 189 persons died there.[177] These figures included normal mortality.

Such a huge population of paupers living and dying in the poorhouses was rightly seen as the final degradation of the Gael. The scholar, John O'Donovan, was presented with a dismal picture of the O'Driscolls by Rickard Donovan, clerk of the crown for the County of Cork. He deplored their downfall in tones reminiscent of Aogán Ó Rathaille's lament for the McCarthys:

> Most of this [O'Driscoll] ancient sept may now be discovered in bitter contests with the over-seers of the workhouses of Skibbereen and Schull, who are more keenly anxious as to the minimum rate of food to keep alive the animal man, than the oldest and most calculating political economist of the day. From these paupers who submissively exclaim that their present abject condition is wholly to be attributed to the will of God, no information can be obtained except a vague tradition about Sir Fineen O'Driscoll having entertained the officers of Queen Elizabeth's fleet at his castle in Baltimore.[178]

The Census commissioners of 1851 called attention to 'the extraordinary decrease in *rural* population'. They also found that 'the population removed from
us by death and emigration belonged principally to the lower classes'.[179] It was
among these that famine had made 'the greatest ravages'. The rural poor or
labouring classes were clearly the most frequent victims which explains the
great loss of nearly 40% in the mainly rural district. The combined decrease
in the towns of Crookhaven, Schull and Ballydehob was only 22 persons. Yet
this average percentage figure conceals the fact that some townlands suffered
more severe losses than others. Kilbronoge lost 66% and nearby Foilnamuck
as many as 87% in spite of the best efforts of the Trench cousins and their agency.
Fisher's stronghold of Altar and Toormore lost only 6%; he himself claimed
that the reason so few died around there was that the people had to work at
the building of the new church while in other places where relief was given
out gratuitously far more died.

What the commissioners called 'the extraordinary decrease in the *rural*
population' prompts one to examine how this population was housed. As
noted earlier, 83% of the people of the Mizen Peninsula lived in fourth-class
houses, i.e., single-roomed, windowless, mud cabins. The commissioners reported that 355,689 such mud cabins had 'disappeared' in the country since
1841 and that this 'was equal to so much as 75% of all houses in the country'.
Only relatively tiny increases took place in the number of other classes of
houses.[180] Tim Harrington's hut which was sketched in Aughadown by Mahoney of the *Illustrated London News* was typical of these mud cabins. He
found that four people 'had lain dead' in it; the sole survivor collapsed mori-
bund begging for fire or water.[181] Such victims were not of course counted in
the Census of 1851 and their cabins must have been nothing less than incu-
bators of fever. The commissioners of 1851 adopted the same categorisation
of houses as those of 1841. (Single-roomed, windowless, mud cabins were re-

Harrington's Hut

garded as fourth-class; 2–4 roomed mud cabins/houses as third-class; good farm or town houses as second-class, and anything better as first-class.) In the rural parts of Ireland in 1841 there were 43.5% of the families living in fourth-class houses but by 1851 this had fallen to less than half, i.e., 21.8%. The number of families living in third-class houses rose from 40.0% to 52.1%; the number living in second-class houses increased from 15.3% to 24% and the number in first-class houses more than doubled going from 1.0% to 2.0%. This marked a fundamental change in the housing or social structure of the country; it changed from being pyramidal to being egg-shaped. The base consisting of fourth-class houses became narrower and the next stratum of third-class houses became wider thus causing the bulge, so to speak. We will now see what change took place at local level in the parish of Kilmoe, for example. The following table presents a synoptic view of the number and the percentage of families that occupied each class of house in 1841 and in 1851 and the percentage change which took place in each class of house in the meantime:

TABLE 37: RURAL HOUSING, PARISH OF KILMOE:
NUMBER AND PROPORTION OF FAMILIES IN EACH CLASS OF HOUSE,
1841 AND 1851: PERCENTAGE CHANGE, 1841–51

Class	1841	Proportion	1851	Proportion	Change '41–'51	%
1st	10	0.85%	17	2.2%	+7	+70.0
2nd	33	2.75%	64	8.6%	+31	+93.9
3rd	76	6.30%	291	38.9%	+215	+282.9
4th	1,088	90.10%	376	50.3%	–712	–65.4
Total	1,207	100.00%	748	100.0%	–459	–38.0

The greatest change took place among the families living in fourth- and third-class houses. In 1841 there were 1,088 families living in fourth-class or labourers' houses but by 1851 this number had dropped to 376, i.e., by 65.4%. However, there was a dramatic increase in the number of families living in third-class or small farmers' houses, the number of such families soared from 76 to 291, i.e., by 282.9%; it almost quadrupled. Some labourers seem to have become small farmers. The number of families living in second-class or 'strong' farmer's houses increased from 33 to 64, i.e. by 93.9%; it almost doubled. Some small farmers seem to have become 'strong' farmers. The number of families living in first-class houses increased 10 to 17, i.e, by 70%; it was significant. Some 'strong' farmers seem to have become 'stronger'. There was evidently a certain amount of social climbing done among all classes not excluding the labourers. The houses and farms of people of all classes who had died or emigrated suddenly became available. Nevertheless there were 712 families who had been living in fourth-class or labourers' houses and who are now simply missing. Those who may have moved up to occupy third-class or small farmers' houses would account for only 215 of these at the most. (215 was the increase in families living in these third-class houses.) But even that leaves about 500 labourer families still missing. The least change took place in the highest strata of society, i.e., among the landlords and the 'strong' farmers whereas the greatest change occurred among the two lowest strata, i.e., the labourers and small farmers. Nonetheless in 1851 the social structure still remained pyramidal although it was now much more narrowly based than in 1841. Its base consisting of fourth-class or labourers' houses had been severely cut back by the famine, i.e., by no less than 65.4% or almost two-thirds.

We shall now examine the housing of families in the rural area of the parish of Schull. The following table presents a similar synoptic view of the number and proportion of families in each class of house in 1841 and in 1851 and also the percentage change which took place in each class of house in the meantime:

TABLE 38: RURAL HOUSING, PARISH OF SCHULL:
NUMBER AND PROPORTION OF FAMILIES IN EACH CLASS OF HOUSE,
1841 AND 1851: PERCENTAGE CHANGE, 1841–51

Class	1841	Proportion	1851	Proportion	Change '41–'51	%
1st	12	0.4%	20	1.3%	+8	+66.7
2nd	71	2.5%	157	10.2%	+86	+121.1
3rd	345	12.2%	914	59.3%	+569	+164.9
4th	2,391	84.9%	451	29.2%	–1,940	–81.1
Total	2,819	100.0%	1,542	100.0%	–1,277	–45.3

Just as in the case of Kilmoe to the west, the greatest change took place in both the numbers and the proportion of families living in fourth- and third-class houses. In 1841 there were 2,391 families living in fourth-class or labourer's houses but by 1851 this number had dropped to 451, i.e., by 81.1%, which was even sharper that Kilmoe's 65.4% decrease. Just as in Kilmoe also, the numbers of families living in third-class or small farmers' houses increased dramatically, soaring from 345 to 914, i.e., by 164.9%; it almost tripled. The number of families living in second-class or 'strong' farmers' houses also increased dramatically, soaring from 71 to 157, i.e., by 121.1%; it well more than doubled. Just as in Kilmoe again, the least change took place in the highest strata of society, i.e., among those occupying first- and second- class houses namely the landlords and the 'strong' farmers whereas the greatest change occurred among those occupying third- and fourth-class houses, namely the small farmers and the labourers. There were 1,940 labourer families missing. Those who may have moved up to occupy third-class, small farmers' houses would account for only 569 of these at the most. (569 was the increase in families living in these third-class houses.) But even that leaves 1,371 labourer families still missing. As has been seen earlier in this chapter there were also 4,489 illiterate adults missing from the parish.

In Schull, however, an even more fundamental change had taken place in the structure of society than in Kilmoe. Schull's base consisting of fourth-

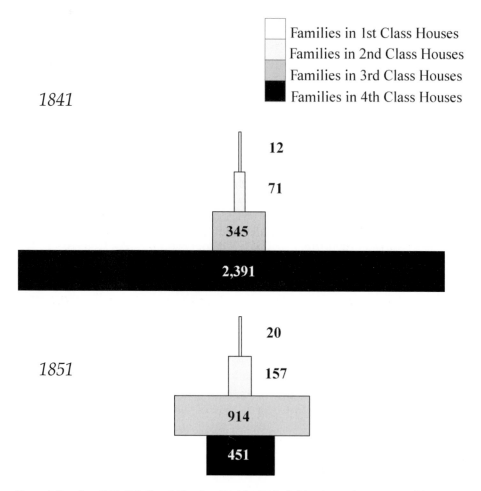

Figure 4 (based on Table 38): Rural Housing, Parish of Schull: Number and proportion of families in each class of house, 1841 and 1851

class, labourers' houses, was not just severely reduced by 65.4% (as in Kilmoe) but brutally cut back by 81.1% with the result that the whole structure now changed from being pyramidal to being egg-shaped, thus reflecting the change which had taken place all over the country. There were twice as many families living in third-class houses in Schull as were in fourth-class houses, i.e., 914 as compared with 451. The trend was similar regarding the housing of families in Aughadown and Kilcoe. In Aughadown there were only 172 families out of 712 that were still occupying fourth-class houses by 1851 and in Kilcoe only 60 families out of 322 were still trying to live in these windowless, single-roomed, mud cabins. The change in the housing situation which took place in the rural area of Schull between 1841 and 1851 is illustrated in Figure 4 which is based on Table 38.

What sort of change took place in the cities and larger towns of Ireland? In 1841 36.7% of families lived in fourth-class houses but by 1851 this had decreased to 30.9%. The number living in third-class houses rose from 33.9% to 35.9%, those in second-class houses increased from 22.4% to 25.3% and those in first-class houses increased from 7.1% to 7.9%. Just as in the rural areas the basic housing or social structure thus changed from being pyramidal to being egg-shaped. What was the housing situation among families in the towns of Ballydehob, Schull and Crookhaven? The following table is revealing as regards the total number and proportion of families living in each class of house in 1841 and in 1851 in all three towns, and also the average percentage change which took place in each class in the meantime:

TABLE 39: BALLYDEHOB, SCHULL, CROOKHAVEN:
TOTAL NUMBER AND PERCENTAGE OF FAMILIES LIVING IN EACH CLASS OF HOUSE,
1841 AND 1851; AVERAGE PERCENTAGE CHANGE, 1841–51

Class	1841	Proportion	1851	Proportion	Av. Change	%
1st	9	3.0%	26	8.7%	+17	+188.9
2nd	74	24.7%	185	61.7%	+111	+150.0
3rd	129	43.0%	78	26.0%	–51	–39.5
4th	88	29.3%	11	3.6%	–71	–86.5
Total	300	100.0%	300	100.0%	–	–

Even in 1841 the housing situation was much better in these three towns than in the surrounding countryside. The town social structure was already egg-shaped rather than pyramidal. In 1841 there were more families living in third-class houses than fourth-class houses, i.e., 129 as against 88; indeed there are almost as many families living in the second-class houses as in the fourth-class houses, i.e., 74 as compared to 88. This is evidence of a growing middle class. By 1851 only 11 families were still living in fourth-class houses in these three towns where there had been 88. In Crookhaven only a single fourth-class house still remained. Unlike in the rural areas, there was a decrease in the number of even the third-class houses, i.e., from 129 to 78 or by 39.5%. The most remarkable improvement in housing conditions took place in the town of Schull. In 1841 there had been not even a single family living a first- or second-class house but by 1851 there were 13 families living in first-class houses and 88 families living in second-class houses. The Schull's new status as the union town was clearly reflected not only in its increased population but by the improvement in the standard of its houses.[182] Unlike in the rural areas, there was more change in the two upper strata of society than in the two lower strata. The number of families living in first- and second-class houses increased by as much as 154% whereas the number of families living in third- and fourth-classes houses decreased by 57.87%. The middle classes especially the shopkeepers seem to have been gathering a little wealth. Thus both in towns and in rural areas there was a considerable improvement in housing conditions in spite of or perhaps because of the famine. The commissioners were not exaggerating when they pointed to 'that social revolution caused by the failure of the potato crop'.[183] The social changes brought about by the famine were more radical and rapid in country, village and town than were the political ones.

Where had all the missing persons gone? The commissioners answered as follows: 'The great mass of the emigrants is comprised of the poorer classes, who, being illiterate, of persons occupying fourth-class house accommodation, and of those dependent on their own manual labour for their support'.[184] As already stated commissioners commented that the famine dead also 'belonged principally to the lower classes'. Thus it has been shown that most of the people missing from the Mizen Peninsula were both illiterate and living in fourth-class houses, namely the labourers. So, of course, they must have either died or emigrated.

Fr Troy of Aughadown annotated on the parish records, 'a frightful famine and fever year, alas! hundreds dying, no marriages or baptisms.' The commissioners pointed out 'a great decrease in the population from non-births owing to the diminution of marriages'.[185] This is clearly to be seen in the parishes of the Mizen Peninsula. The following tables show the numbers of marriages and births in these parishes from 1845 to 1852.[186] The decline which took place from 1845 to 1847 illustrates the first shock of the catastrophe. In the early 1850s there was a definite recovery but this must be measured against the 'good old times' before the famine. The figures for 1845 and 1852 show the contrast between the 'good old times' and the first signs of recovery.

TABLE 40: CATHOLIC MARRIAGES, 1845–52

Year	Kilmoe	Schull	Kilcoe/ Aughdn
1845	95	78	60
1846	23	97	29
1847	7	12	7
1848	6	26	9
1849	15	24	6
1850	20	26	24
1851	33	25	19
1852	39	25	13

TABLE 41: CATHOLIC BAPTISMS, 1845–52

Year	Kilmoe	Schull	Kilcoe/ Aughdn
1845	413	466	331
1846	196	494	301
1847	62	194	119
1848	78	193	105
1849	94	184	100
1850	106	141	87
1851	142	149	65
1852	127	139	88

While the number of marriages in Kilmoe decreased sharply (from 95 to 23) and in Kilcoe/Aughadown also (from 60 to 29) between 1845 and 1846 yet the number of marriages in Schull continued to increase (from 78 to 97) although the potato blight was already let loose on the land. It has already been noted that the number of baptisms in Kilmoe and Schull was extremely high, Kilmoe 413 in 1845 and Schull 494 in 1846. In 1847 however the numbers of both marriages and baptisms were to fall drastically. What was the cause of such a sharp drop in the number of baptisms? Dr Popham of the North Infirmary, Cork, reporting on his fever patients, found that 'in females who were pregnant, abortion commonly took place'.[187] Dr Donovan of Skibbereen observed that 'starvation provoked abortion and asthenic sterility',[188] nowadays known as famine amenorrhoea or malnutrition–induced sterility as women cease to menstruate. This also occurred in the Hunger Winter in Holland in 1944–5.[189] Famine, of course, diminished normal sexual attraction or desire. A woman from Dingle, probably Baile na gGall, lamented

> *Nár fhan dúil i gcéilíocht ag fear ná ag maoi …*
> *Ní miste spéirbhean bheith amuigh go déanach,*
> *Níor fhan aon tréine ins na fir a bhí.*
>
> No desire for courtship remained in either man or woman …
> A fair lady wouldn't mind being out late,
> No strength was left in the men like there used to be.[190]

The numbers of marriages and births in some of the Church of Ireland parishes are also available. They are incomplete because records were lost in the fire at Four Courts in Dublin in 1922. Yet they show that the famine was a catastrophe for Protestants too. In Schull, for example, from 1846 to 1847 the number of marriages fell from 7 to 3 but in 1852 there were 11 marriages. In Aughadown there were 3 marriages in 1846 and 3 also in 1852. Just as there were averted births there were also averted or postponed marriages. In Ballydehob between 1845 and 1847, the number of baptisms fell from 40 to 16, i.e., 60%. This was about the same percentage as in the Catholic parish, 58%, or as in the Catholic parish of Aughadown, 64%. It was not without reason that Traill was worried about his own parishioners whom he described as being of the humblest class.

Class mattered more than religion in this famine. There is more evidence for this in the burial records of the Church of Ireland parish of Drimoleague where there were 3 burials in 1845, 6 in 1846 and 23 in 1847. One family of labourers, the Stouts, seems to have been completely wiped out beginning with the children. In the Church of Ireland parish of Bandon there were 196 burials in 1843–5 but as many as 312 in the period 1846–8. Mortality among Protestants was also significant in parts of Ulster, for example, in Lurgan, County Armagh and even in County Offaly.[191] In the Church of Ireland parish of Caheragh there were 3, 4 and 5 baptisms for 1843, 1844 and 1845 respectively but in 1846 and 1847 none at all; this may well have meant a zero birth rate.[192] While the impact of the famine may have been less severe on Protestants than on Catholics in these West Cork parishes, it was a serious blow for both and they were all obliged to make corresponding adjustments in relation to marriages and births. Joseph's Lee's comment is apt: 'Priests and parsons, products and prisoners of the same society … were in any case powerless to challenge the primacy of economic man over the Irish countryside'.[193] The influence of Catholicism in such demographic change must not be exaggerated as K. H. Connell tended to do.[194]

TABLE 42: CHURCH OF IRELAND MARRIAGES, 1846–52

Year	Schull	Aughadown
1846	7	3
1847	3	1
1848	14	1
1849	6	4
1850	12	0
1851	4	3
1852	11	3

TABLE 43: CHURCH OF IRELAND BAPTISMS, 1845–52

Year	Schull E. (Ballydehob)
1845	40
1846	43
1847	16
1848	32
1849	30
1850	29
1851	22
1852	22

In the parish of Kilmoe the numbers of baptisms, both Catholic and Protestant, fell drastically in 1847 and then slowly began to recover. In Skibbereen the number of baptisms in 1845 was 500, which decreased to 460 in 1846, fell sharply to 271 in 1847 but recovered slightly to 323 in 1848. This number fell yet again to 260 in 1849, which was even lower than the 1847 figure and continued to fall in 1850 to 203. It is impossible to know when it reached its minimum as a result of changes in parish boundaries.[195] The parish where the lowest number of baptisms took place in 1847 was Kilmoe. In Kilcoe/Aughawown it was in 1851 and in Schull in 1852. By way of compasison, in some mainly mid-Cork parishes the trend was similar. In Murragh/Templemartin the lowest number of baptisms occurred in 1852, in Kilmichael it was in 1853, in Enniskeane in 1854, and in Kilmurray as late as 1855.

Concerning marriage it has been seen that in the parishes of Kilmoe, Schull and Kilcoe / Aughadown the number of marriages fell drastically in 1847, and then slowly began to recover. In Skibbereen the number of marriages in 1846 was 113 which plummeted to 28 in 1847. Still it recovered again to 40 in 1848 and then increased slowly as in the other parishes to the west. In the mid-Cork parishes, with only one exception, the number of marriages dropped to a minimum not in 1847 but a little later, in Kilmurry in 1849, Kilmichael, 1853 and Murargh / Templemartin in 1852. The exception to this trend was Enniskeane but even there the number of marriages was very nearly as low in 1849 as in 1847.[196] The overall pattern was that in the poorer western parishes the marriage rates suddenly collapsed under the shock of famine whereas in the less poor mid-Cork districts they were able to absorb this shock somewhat better. Even there, however, the impact of the disaster was slowly but surely going to tell. By way of comparison, South Tipperary resembled mid-Cork rather than the Mizen Peninsula in this matter. [197]

While the number of both Catholic and Protestant baptisms fell drastically during the famine in the Mizen Peninsula and did not recover, the number of Protestant marriages quickly recovered whereas the number of Catholic marriages never did. The pattern was similar in County Offaly, for instance.[198]

Nevertheless, in spite of the famine and emigration – or rather because of them – conditions and living standards improved all over the country for many of those who still remained at home. It must be admitted that the famine did solve some inveterate problems with a brutal efficiency, cutting a few Gordian Knots. The Census commissioners (writing in 1856) were quite pleased to report this in the following summary which is the nearest we have to an 'official history' of the famine, giving the last word to its 'official historian' if not also its theologian, Trevelyan, writing in his *Irish Crisis*. The commissioners concluded:

> Notwithstanding the fearful ordeal through which Ireland has passed … we have good reason to believe that the country has improved in health, increased in wealth … since the recent calamity that seemed to threaten its very existence. The great surplus mass of the population … has been reduced. The system of minute subdivision of land … has been happily got rid of; … it increased the mass of pauper holdings, now rapidly giving place to large-sized grazing farms, which from time immemorial have produced cattle exports … The Acts for the Sale of Encumbered Estates … have relieved the country from expensive and almost endless litigation, and placed the land within the power of a comparatively solvent proprietary, though in some cases it may have produced temporary and individual hardship. In conclusion, we may say that, in the language of Sir Charles Trevelyan, that … 'posterity will trace up to that famine the commencement of a salutary revolution in the habits of a nation; … and will acknowledge that in this, as in many other occasions, Supreme Wisdom, has educed permanent good from transient evil'.[199]

There is a certain triumphant note here which seems unwarranted. Such a note was indeed justified in France, for example, where the period 1815–51 has been described as *une victoire sur la disette*, 'a victory over food shortage' of which 1845–7 was also the worst period.[200] Nevertheless, a small amount of this late Irish prosperity did at last reach the Mizen Peninsula in the Skibbereen Union itself. The new landlords who had bought land under the Encumbered Estates Act were not usually a rack-renting crew as myths would have us believe.[201] In many instances, these landlords were actually in a better position than the former owners to develop their acquisitions. T. S. Cave who bought the Audley estate immediately set about working the mines.[202] One shipment of rich ore in 1857 fetched £150 at Swansea.[203] Work continued in the other mines of the Mizen Peninsula. By 1913 they were listed among the top twenty in the country according to the tonnage of ore delivered to Swansea yet they lagged far behind the great mines in Berehaven or Wicklow.[204]

J. S. Donnelly, Jr, has pointed out that the recovery of Cork farmers from the effects of the famine was 'remarkably rapid'. It was mainly thanks to steep increases in the prices of butter and cattle. Between 1851 and 1859, the price of butter on the Cork market rose by 45% and that of store cattle by 50%.[205] This recovery in agriculture can be closely observed at local level in the Audley estate. T. S. Cave's agent, Thomas Scott, an Englishman, visited the property in 1853. He found that the tenants on the Schull portion of it were far too numerous. He frankly told them that many of their holdings were too small to maintain a family and carry livestock. He regarded the 'higgledy-piggledy mixture of fields' belonging to the different farms as another drawback. Scott suggested to the tenants that he would re-arrange the land and re-let it to them again provided they would pay all rents and arrears; the offer was accepted. Accordingly, the tenants voluntarily surrendered their land and houses on 1 November 1854. For the next two months, Scott 'consolidated, separated and re-adjusted' the small and scattered holdings. There was no land left over for some tenants but he resettled them in other parts of the estate, presumably around Castlehaven. He carried out his adventurous policy of surrender and re-grant so judiciously that it won the unanimous approval of the tenants. They even agreed to pay an increase of 50% in their rent. The landlord, T. S. Cave, was so pleased that he provided a resident agricultural instructor for these tenants. Cave then sent a ton of Italian rye grass seed, mangold, turnip and other seeds to be bought by his tenants at first cost. Ten tons of Peruvian guano and some superphosphate of lime were also dispatched on the same terms. The soil was considered to have been deficient in phosphate from being cropped excessively with potatoes. Hence Scott abolished or 'improved' the old rundale or clachan field system just as R. H. H. Becher of Hollybrook had done on a part of his estate[206] and as Lord George Hill was doing in Donegal.[207] Nonetheless as Kevin Hourihane observes for the Bantry region, 'Rundale also survived'.[208] I was reared on a farm which still comprises some remnants of rundale. However much scholars such as Kevin Whelan may praise 'the cohesive quality of rundale life',[209] the sheer fragmentation of this system of land-holding rendered more difficult the very kind of mixed farming which was emerging after the famine. According to E. Estyn Evans, 'The word used to describe the confusion of innumerable scattered plots and tortuous access ways in the infield was 'throughother', a word which was often applied to other aspects of Irish life'.[210]

The Audley estate was of course only one example of this new relative prosperity and feeling of confidence, Cormac Ó Gráda sums up the general situation at home and abroad and, just like the commissioners and Trevelyan, points out that good as well as evil had resulted from the famine:

> Most of those who survived the famine ended up being materially better off than they would have been had Ireland been spared *Phytophthora infestans*. Labourers operated on a tighter labour market, and the rise in the land-labour ratio benefited farmers. Most of those who emigrated during the famine or immediately in its wake earned more than they would have in an imaginary blight free Ireland in the 1850s. Traders benefited from rising demand. Even landlords, buoyed by the rising demand for meat and dairy products and brutally freed of thousands of nonviable tenants, soon saw their rents recover and their tax bill decline.[211]

Laurence Geary similarly concludes that: 'It was one of the ironies of the Great Famine that the virtual extirpation of the underclass which harboured illness and infection rendered the future safer for the survivors and their children'.[212]

When Thomas Scott revisited the Audley estate in April 1855 the tenants, headed by their priests, opened a subscription to make a presentation to him. So much money was promptly given that some had to be returned. A gold watch costing £50 was purchased in London. The following was engraved on the gift 'Presented To Thomas Scott, Esq., London, Agent for the Audley Estate, County of Cork. As a mark of respect and confidence by The Tenantry, April 17th 1855'. Nearly 100 tenants assembled to make the presentation which was done on their behalf by Fr John Barry. Having thanked and complimented the tenants Scott urged them to keep more cattle and grow crops to feed them. 'Cattle signify manure, manure signifies crops and crops signify income,' he lectured. He told them that they would be able to keep one cow for every two acres, if the animals were properly fed with Italian rye-grass or hay, oats, mangolds, turnips and bruised furze. The whole purpose was to produce 'more and better butter'. Having thus advised the tenants about their farms, he concluded by exhorting them in relation to their families in the following terms: 'You ought also send out your sons and daughters into the world and retain your farms unbroken, instead of trying, as you do now, on how small a spot of earth you can contrive to exist'.[213]

Although the old ways died hard one can perceive the new post-famine way of life gradually but inevitably taking over. The family could be broken or scattered but not the farm. If a son or daughter did not 'go out into the world', he or she could, of course, remain at home; but only the person who would inherit the farm could get married on it. It could not be divided to facilitate the marriage of other members of the family as in the more carefree days before the famine. The farm was taking a certain priority over the family. As Joseph Lee comments, 'the integrity of the family was ruthlessly sacrificed … to the priority of economic man'.[214] Such practises or customs, however, existed in rural life in other parts of Europe too. A French sociologist holds that the rule 'one farm, one household, one family' has played a crucial role in stemming population growth.[215] Nevertheless, in Ireland the decrease in the number of marriages and baptisms after the famine was particularly severe. Marriages tended to take place later in life too or perhaps not at all. In 1841 only 10.2% of males and 12.5% of females were still not married in the age bracket 45–54 whereas by 1911 these figures were 27.3 % for males and 24.9% for females.[216] This social situation is illustrated by the case of Paddy Maguire in Patrick Kavanagh's poem, 'The Great Hunger'. Was there a connection between one Great Hunger and the other?

Epilogue

There is much truth in Kerby Miller's analysis of the emerging society:

> In the 'New Ireland' of the post-Famine period there were three dominant social insti-
> tutions – the strong farmer of the rural family ... the Catholic Church of the 'de-
> votional revolution' and Irish nationalism, especially in its constitutional or quasi-
> legal form.[1]

The Catholic Church and nationalism would soon come together in the Land
League; the call of Faith, Fatherland and simply land seemed to be in harmony. Fr John Murphy, parish priest of Schull, was a great supporter of the
Land League as also was John Crowley, Curate of Kilmoe, who was later imprisoned in that cause.[2] As mentioned in Chapter XII, Anna Parnell attended
a meeting in Ballydehob in 1881. Although banned, it was chaired by Richard
Hodnett, had been a foreman on the famine roads. Anna Parnell urged the
people to take part in the 'honourable fight of farmers to put an end to hunger
and misery in Ireland forever'.[3] When T. H. Marmion cleared 154 families out
of the Townsend estate in 1847–9 he met no resistance but when his son, another T. H. Marmion, evicted some tenants from Castle Island near Schull in
1890 he had to face the fury of the Plan of Campaign.[4]

The figures quoted in the last chapter show the severe fall in the marriage
and baptism or birth rates from 1847 to 1852. This change was destined to become permanent and to shape the pattern of family life throughout the 1850s
and beyond. On the farm itself the potato had to yield primacy to the cow and
to the crops to feed her. In brief, social and market conditions together with
the peasants' perennial struggle for survival ensured that the family and the
potato would relinquish a certain pride of place to the farm and the cow. This
post-famine Ireland persisted and was in many ways the country in which I
grew up in the 1950s. The cow and butter were important and so therefore
were hay, mangolds and turnips. Farms would not be divided to facilitate the
formation of a second family; if a second boy stayed on in a farm he usually
remained unmarried.

The Catholic Church which emerged from the famine was confident or
even, some would say, dominant; but it must be granted that it had suffered
centuries of deprivation to say the least. The emerging post-famine society
was also nationalistic; we have seen, for example, that the members of the Skibbereen Liberal Club were in favour of using not only the English but also the
Irish language in the political life of the country. We have also seen that the
meeting was attended by men who would soon form a Phoenix Club leading
to Fenianism. It has been noted too that the thinking of the Land League and
the Parnells found a ready response in the Mizen Peninsula. A local historian,
Joe Kelly, also told me that he had listened in awe and reverence to a speech

given by O'Donovan Rossa in Skibbereen. The Rossa interpretation of the famine was acceptable to him, for example, and it became widespread. In sum, post-famine Ireland was the rock from which I and others of my generation were hewn – and we are the last such generation.

While the workhouse in Skibbereen had been built before the famine, the one at Schull opening in January 1850 owed its origins to the calamity itself. Its ivy-clad ruins are a very symbol of these 'bad times', *an droch-shaol*. J. M. Synge wrote that the old people would stop and talk for hours 'alluding to three shadowy countries that are never forgotten in Wicklow – America (their El Dorado), the union [workhouse] and the Madhouse'.[5] Nowhere was this more true perhaps than in Schull where, as has been seen, Synge's grandfather, Robert Traill, died of fever and his mother, Catherine, as a young girl, had distributed food to the poor. Some years ago a sick old man, who was leaving his home for the last time to go to Schull hospital in an ambulance, lamented to me, 'The workhouse van is for me now'. James Joyce's reflections in *Ulysses* about the workhouse in Loughlinstown, County Dublin, could also be applied to the one in Schull: 'All those moving scenes are still there for us today rendered more beautiful still by the waters of sorrow which have passed over them and by the rich incrustations of time'.[6] A local historian, Mary Mackey, finds that the ruins of the Schull workhouse are an awesome reminder of the famine but feels that their 'original grimness is softened by ivy'[7] – the ivy of time. As is seen in the aerial photography by Lee Snodgrass, however, these

Aerial view of Schull Union Workhouse [Photo: *Lee Snodgrass*]

ruins still cast long shadows in the setting sun – shadows as long as those cast by the institution itself.

That other shadowy land, America, was also alluded to in song and story. 'Dear Old Skibbereen' was sung and so also was 'The Emigrant's Farewell', better known by its first lines 'I am sitting on the stile, Mary' written by Lady Dufferin whose son Lord Dufferin had visited Skibbereen during the famine.[8] The song told of the simple attraction of the American *El Dorado*, 'They say there's bread and work for all'. All of my father's seven paternal uncles headed for this *El Dorado* as did also many of their neighbours. Four of his maternal uncles and aunts (Fields) emigrated to New Zealand and went digging for gold in Coromandel, North Island; he never again set eyes on most of these eleven men and women.

Did this traumatic experience change the character of the people? 'Verily, the mirth of the land is gone,' Dr Traill lamented. Did much of it ever return? One must be aware of the logical fallacy, *post famem ergo propter famem* or 'after the famine therefore on account of the famine'. A farmer from the Dublin end of the Wicklow mountains said that it made the 'people so sad in themselves. And that it made many a hard one too.'[9] A. M. Sullivan of Bantry witnessed that *'sauve qui peut* resounded throughout the land … Human nature had become contracted in its sympathies'.[10] The annals record a famine in the summer of 1433 which was called 'a greedy summer', *samhradh na mearaithne* or the 'summer of the slight acquaintance' as few would recognise friend or relative.[11] This new cold hardness is expressed in a chilling manner by Edith Martin of Somerville and Ross: 'The Famine yielded like the snow of the northern seas; it ran like melted snow into the veins of Ireland for many years afterwards'.[12] Anna Parnell sensed that, 'Even to persons who were not in existence when they occurred, the horrors of those years had a vividness almost as great as actual experience of them could produce'. To these horrors she attributed 'the sudden and harsh element as a substratum in Irish life and character'.[13] This same sort of harshness is regretted by Mary O'Brien in *The Farm by Lough Gur* written by Mary Carbery, wife of Lord Carbery of Castlefreke near Clonakilty:

> It did not matter who was related to you, your friend was whoever would give you a bit to put in your mouth. Sport and pastimes disappeared. Poetry, music and dancing stopped. They lost and forgot them all and when the times improved in other respects, these things never returned as they had been. The famine killed everything.[14]

Who was responsible for the million or more deaths and all the suffering of the famine? The event can be played down as an act of Providence or an ecological disaster. William Wilde maintained that 'The most strenuous efforts which human sagacity, ingenuity and forethought could at the time devise were put into requisition'.[15] As already stated Trevelyan boasted that three million were fed on soup rations in the summer of 1847. Mary Daly pleads that 'it remains difficult to conclusively argue that greater sympathy with the Irish case would have automatically guaranteed a dramatically reduced mortality'.[16] But surely any such sympathy would have taken the form of food. Her thinking contrasts sharply with the feelings of nationalists like O'Dovovan Rossa who was appalled at the sight of Irishmen joining the British army to fight in the Crimean War which was soon to break out:

> And it sickened the heart of myself who had seen
> the starved and the murdered of Schull and Skibbereen.[17]

John Mitchel had similar feelings and so had Gavan Duffy who condemned the famine as 'murder'.[18] The British government is sometimes accused of genocide against the Irish people similar to that committed by the Nazis against the Jews. The English historian, A. J. P. Taylor, has even claimed that all Ireland was a Belsen but J. S. Donnelly, Jr, asserts that this is 'a gross exaggeration'. Skibbereen was indeed no Auschwitz. Yet Donnelly maintains that 'while genocide was not in fact committed what happened during and after the clearances had the look of genocide to a great many Irish contemporaries.' He similarly holds that the official government responses 'to extreme occasions were murderous in their consequences, though not in their intentions.[19] However, it was never a question of genocide in any case for the existence of the Irish race in Ireland was never seriously threatened; indeed the famine of 1740–1 went closer to doing that. David Dickson maintains that 'in terms of *relative* casualties the older crisis was undoubtedly the more severe' with an excess mortality of 13–20% of the population. George Berkeley, Church of Ireland bishop of Cloyne, wrote that in May 1741 he had heard Sir Richard Cox of Dunmanway say 'that 500 were dead in the parish, though in a county I believe not very populous.'[20] Cox himself found that 'the distempers and famine increase that it is no vain fear that there will not be hands to save the harvest'. And so he prayed, 'God protect them that are yet untouched … The Papists, though they are bad members of this society, are yet better than none'.[21] In 1846–9 nobody feared that there would not be enough feet to dig the potatoes, that is, if only there had been any crop to dig.

While there was no question of the destruction of the Irish race in 1847–9, there certainly was a question of the destruction or extermination of the labouring or cottier class, which was the greatest victim of the catastrophe. Karl Marx claimed that the famine 'killed the poor devils only'[22] but it would be more accurate to state that it killed the poor devils mostly – for we should not forget the people who died trying to aid such poor creatures. While the catastrophe certainly looked like genocide to some contemporaries there were still many others to whom it appeared more like the destruction of a class rather than of a race. We have seen that the Census Commisioners of 1851 pointed out that, 'The population removed from us by death and emigration belonged principally to the lower classes'. As regards the parish of Schull this is clear from a glance at Figure 4. O'Callaghan of the *Cork Examiner* referred specifically to the extermination of the labouring classes and James Barry to the extermination of the 'dense swarms', i.e., the rural proletariat consisting of labourers and some very small farmers whose holdings were under five acres. David Fitzpatrick refers to the 'the disappearance of the Irish labourer' and calculates that the number of male agricultural labourers dropped from about 1.2 million in 1845 to 0.9 million in 1851.[23] This decline must have been even more severe in the Mizen Peninsula. As shall be seen Lionel Fleming complained that England left Ireland to 'fend for itself'. R. B. Townsend, vicar of Abbeystrowry, protested that the principles of political economy had 'been carried out to a murderous extent'.[24] As already stated William Fisher and Laurence O'Sullivan appealed to Lord John Russell and Randolph Routh at the end of 1846 for special aid for their parish but were refused, provoking Fisher's indignant retort: 'By these answers the public will be able to judge what the poor famishing creatures of this district have to expect from these honourable gentlemen'– in other words little or nothing. Referring to famine deaths in his own parish of Carriga-drohid near Macroom, the rector, J. T. Kyle, cited the poet, Coleridge, 'They die so slowly that none call it murder'.[25] The Gaelic scholar landlord, Thomas Swanton, protested that 'murder' was going on for the sake of the profits of English merchants.[26] A repealer on the Cork Town Council, Mr Brady, told that body amid groans and hisses: 'Yes, a million and a half Irish people were smitten and offered up as a holocaust, whose blood ascended to the throne of God for redress but the pity was that the minister [Russell] was permitted to act with impunity'.[27]

Contemporaries such as Brady and O'Callaghan thus blamed Russell rather than Trevelyan for the calamity. As P. A. Bourke points out, Trevelyan was only a faithful and hardworking civil servant who in fairness had been less parsimonious under Peel.[28] It has been seen that Captain Thomas of Coo-sheen, the Cornish miner, was scandalised that in a Christian country at a time of profound peace people should be left to live or die on political economy. He would, clearly, have agreed with John Mitchel that Ireland was 'a nation perishing of political economy'.[29] As already stated, Twistleton, the British civil servant, resigned because he refused to be an agent of extermination. We have noted Clarendon remark to Sir Charles Wood, 'Improve them [the hordes] off the face of the earth, you will say, let them die.' It has been already noted too that Lord George Bentinck charged the Whigs with allowing so many Irish to perish without intervening and that Lord John Russell accused the Irish land-lords of exterminating their tenants as also did the lawyer, McCarthy Down-ing. A jury gave its verdict that Denis McKennedy of Caheragh died 'owing to the gross neglect of the Board of Works'. Nationalists such as Brady, O'Dono-van Rossa, Gavan Duffy and Mitchel can always be suspected of exploiting the famine for their own political purposes however justifiable. But when the press reporter, two landlords, two rectors, the vicar, the parish priest, the Cor-nish miner, the lawyer, the jury, the British civil servant, the lord lieutenant, the leader of the Tories and even the prime minister all similarly use the vocabulary of wilful neglect, murder, extermination and holocaust, there must have been some truth in it – if not, indeed, the whole truth. Briefly, the famine was more a case of the extermination of a class or of classes rather than of the extermination of a race or a people, i.e., genocide. The classes which were the chief victims were the beggars, and next the labourers particularly those who were unemployed, and then the very small farmers particularly those who were evicted.

Apart altogether from England, to what extent, if any, were the Irish people themselves responsible for the famine? After all, they had been warned by recurrent potato failures particularly that of 1822. As shall be seen presently, John Limrick of Schull bluntly told the people that they should lay the blame for the disaster at their own doors owing to their 'indolence'. A. M. Sullivan observed that after the famine 'Providence, forethought and economy are studied and valued as they never were before. There is a graver sense of responsibility'.[30] K. H. Connell concluded that the people had learned a lesson – the hard way; 'No peasant survived the famine unchastened by it', he held, 'nor can we believe, however venomously he imputed blame elsewhere, that he shook off the nagging guilt that drove him to question his own fecklessness'.[31] A French demographer, Jacques Dupâquier, maintained that the teacher of this lesson had been Malthus and that Irish people behaved as if they kept a copy of his *Essay* at their bedsides.[32] Whatever about 'Revenge for Skibbereen' or about the possibility of any such ecological disaster happening ever again, they ensured that by means of emigration, late marriages or none at all, that there would in future be fewer mouths to feed in any case.

Captain Thomas was right in pointing out that the famine happened at a time of profound peace. War is usually the concomitant of famine and plague – three weird sisters that go hand in hand. If for example *phytophthora infestans* had waited until the Crimean War or if that conflict had broken out in 1847, the commissariat would have been engaged in its first duty, i.e., to supply the troops. Men like Caffin, Bishop, Hughes and Parker might well have been sent to Sebastopol or Balaclava rather than to Schull or Ballydehob. As already stated, in the period August 1846 to January 1847 no fewer than 45 ships with crews of 3,134 men were transporting food to Ireland.[33] In the *Oxford Companion to the Second World War* we read about the famine in India mainly in Bengal:

> It was only with great difficulty that General Wavell who became viceroy in October 1943 was able to extort even the most minimum help in terms of grain from the Allies. Helping to feed Indians meant taking urgent shipping space away from the direct war effort; and in Whitehall's calculations starving Indians came second in priority.[34]

Similarly, if England had been at war in 1847–9 starving Irish would similarly have come second in priority. We have received a gentle hint of this from William Bishop in 1848 when he told J. J. Marshall that he could no longer transport food for him with the usual promptness since ships were required to supply troops around Limerick and Tipperary where there were rumours of a rising. As much as £70 million was soon to be spent in the Crimean war compared with the £10 million spent on relieving the famine. War, however, is an exceptionally terrible and expensive reality; comparisons made with other times of peace may be less odious. As has been seen in Chapter VIII, Daniel O'Connell appealed to the government at the end of 1846 for a loan of £20 million or £30 million in order 'to ransack the world for food and buy it at any price'. He also referred to the £20 million which was granted to the slave-owners to compensate them for the emancipation of their slaves. Likewise R. B. Townsend asked if it were right that for the sake of 'a few paltry millions' so many of her Majesty's subjects for whom Christ died should 'be allowed to die of starvation'.[35] Lionel Fleming of Newcourt, Skibbereen, was disillusioned too, declaring that although they were part of 'the greatest empire that ever flourished yet the poorest portion of it was left fend for itself though struck with an affliction of Providence'. He contrasted this with the 'beneficence' of England in the famine of 1822.[36] It was not only the modest amount of money spent during the Great Famine which rankled but the way much of it was spent on expensive road-works which were often a failure as relief measures. We have seen that George Bentinck, leader of the Tories, gave parliament a brutally simple statement of the financial and human cost of that fatal nine month period, October 1846 to June 1847: six million pounds were spent and yet one million people 'perished from famine'.[37]

What would these famine victims who perished have to say? A French writer imagines two corpses, a French and a German, in a trench around Verdun asking each other who was responsible for the war and they conclude *la bêtise humaine*, 'human folly'. Still a fellow countryman, Antoine de Saint-Exupéry, is not so indulgent, *Être homme, c'est précisément être responsable*, 'To be a human being is precisely to be responsible,' he insists. The poet, Speranza, or Lady Wilde (mother of Oscar Wilde) writing in the *Nation* represents the famine dead as rising up in accusation against their murderers:

> From the cabins and the ditches in their charr'd uncoffined masses,
> For the Angel of the Trumpet will know them as he passes.
> A ghastly spectre army before the great God we'll stand,
> And arraign ye as our murderers, the spoilers of our land.[38]

God would then 'take vengeance for the souls for whom Christ died'. In the eyes of the *Nation*, the main murderers were the members of the Whig government and we have already heard its call to the people of Ireland: 'By the memory of Schull and Skibbereen, oppose them, By the souls of the two millions dead oppose them'.[39] One notes too that famine mortality was doubled from one to two millions. It was this appalling loss of life – real or perceived – which was to haunt people for many a year. An old woman lamented to those collecting folklore on the famine, *Mo chás, is mó rud a dheineann an bás*, 'My sorrow, death does many a thing'. One or two million deaths were bound to do many a thing especially when quite a number of people considered that most of them were indeed needless deaths after all, for all that was done and said. Some, however, like O'Donovan Rossa, were too angry to leave vengeance to the Lord; the memory of Schull and Skibbereen was soon to raise the cry, 'Revenge for Skibbereen!'[40]

Fossey Tackaberry, the Methodist preacher who had been on the Skibbereen circuit, told about two orphan boys one of whom had died in the famine and the other was following him closely but was just rescued by the clergy-man. The boy's first remark was, 'Ah! if anybody had done this for my poor brother, he would not have died'.[41] If there had been greater generosity among the well-off generally fewer would have died which is of course true of all the famines of the world. Why did the eastern half of the county not do more for the western half? Why for example were there not a few more people like the Trench clergymen? The Rev. J. Lee, Church of Ireland curate of Aughadown, wrote how an English friend complained to him that while people over there denied themselves butter and sugar to aid the starving Irish they heard all about 'Cork's balls and gaieties'. Indeed glowing accounts of them were to be read in the press.[42] We have seen that the response to the Rate-in-Aid was less than generous and that Dunmanway was unwilling to help Bantry. As already stated, the rate in Schull was three shillings in the pound while it was only three (old) pence in some electoral divisions in Kinsale. Government officials or landlords had no monopoly of cruelty; the murders of two children and also of two women over a little food can be cited. 'Strong' farmers collaborated with landlords to clear lands of cottiers. A Limerick priest, Michael Fitzgerald, saw the result; 'There are now beautiful fields and pastures there, but these beauti-ful fields are the sepulchres of the poor'.[43] Farmers as well as landlords gained from the export of corn and cattle. Some land-grabbing also took place. As al-ready stated an old person related that some people would prefer if the famine were forgotten altogether so that the cruel doings of their forebears might not be known. Yes, some had reason to fear to speak of the famine and to blush at the name; there was a certain conspiracy of silence. The folk-memory of Schull and Skibbereen, like personal memory, can be selective.

What about the landlords? A. M. Sullivan considered 'the censure visited on them … too sweeping and in some aspects cruelly unjust'.[44] Fr Kelliher's condemnation of them was indeed sweeping although he did make two or three exceptions, perhaps R. H. H. Becher, John Limrick and Richard Edmund Hull of Leamcon. There must have been much substance to the frequent com-plaints from relief committees that the response of landlords, particularly ab-sentees, to their appeals for subscriptions was poor. The following judgement on Lionel Fleming by O'Donovan Rossa is representative of the attitude of many Irish nationalists towards the landlords:

> Lioney Fleming was a pretty fair specimen of the English planter in Ireland, who con-siders that Ireland was made for England, and that all the people to whose fathers Ireland belonged, are better out of it than in it. Sheep and oxen were tenants more wel-come to Lioney's estate than men, women and children; and the faster the men, women and children in the poorhouse would die, the oftener would Lioney thank the Lord.[45]

A great-grandson of Lionel's, Lionel S. Fleming, rightly regarded this state-ment as a 'grotesque accusation', although he admitted that his ancestor could be cold and harsh.[46] At the agricultural meeting which was held in Ballydehob at the end of November 1847, John Limrick declared that 'no part of the present destitution could be laid at the doors of the landlords but 'twas owing to the indolence of the people'. There was a loud cry of disapprobation from the floor of the meeting which 'was getting warm on both sides', so Limrick appealed to John Barry to state whether he and his fellow landlords had not done their duty during the famine. The priest replied that he could not justify the conduct of the landlords in general but that there would be another time and place for discussing that subject.[47] His brother, James, then parish priest, had praised Limrick in particular. Both Fr John Barry and Fr Kelliher maintained that the majority of landlords did not do their duty but that a small minority did. Perhaps that is as much as can be said; it is difficult to generalise. Regarding responsibility Limrick was to some extent right; surely the people themselves must share some of the blame for the disaster. As already stated, the drastic manner in which they controlled both marriages and births and favoured emigration after the famine meant that they were going to make sure that never again could there be such a great famine. John Barry's prudence in refraining from publicly condemning the landlords at such a meeting was understandable. Priests were in an unenviable position, as Fr James Maher, uncle of Dr Paul Cullen, pointed out: 'How could they save the Hecatomb sacrificed at Bantry? If they raise their voice against oppression they run the risk of being accused of exciting to murder'. This was exactly what had just happened in the case of Fr McDermott who was charged with abetting the murder of Major Mahon of Strokestown House, County Roscommon, earlier in this November of 1847.[48]

The question of blame for the famine dead often arises. Mortality, however, would have been far in excess of one million were it not for the courageous efforts of certain people. Canon O'Rourke referred to the 'bright and copious fountains of living charity which gushed forth'.[49] A. M. Sullivan wrote, 'No pen, nor tongue, can trace nor relate the countless deeds of heroism and self-sacrifice which the dreadful visitation called forth on the part, pre-eminently of two classes in the community, the Catholic clergy and the dispensary doctors'. He also added the Protestant clergy and some landlords of every creed.[50] In the film version of John B. Keane's play, *The Field*, Bull McCabe declares 'No priest died at the time of the famine'. This is not true. At least ten priests died of fever in the diocese of Cork and three in Ross; they were Archdeacon Thomas O' Keeffe, PP, St Finbarr's, vicar general (former PP of Glanmire and a patron of Mícheál Óg Ó Longáin);[51] Charles McLeod, Cathedral; Michael Prior, PP, Ballinora, Ballincollig and formerly parish priest of Kilmoe;[52] Denis O'Donoghue of Bandon; Michael Denny of Dunmanway;[53] David Cahill of Innishannon;[54] Daniel O'Sullivan and Thomas Haynes of Enniskeane;[55] Patrick Coffey, of St Patrick's,[56] and Alexander O'Mahony, Blackrock (cholera).[57] P. Duggan, OFM Cap., of Cork city also died. The Cloyne and Ross priests who fell victims, in West Cork alone, were Jeremiah Clancy of Skibbereen and Kilworth, Michael Ross of Castlehaven and Patrick Walsh of Sherkin Island.[58] James Noonan of Cape Clear died in January 1847 a short time after leaving the island but the cause is not given.[59] Daniel Donovan, a native of Clonakilty and curate of Aghabullogue or Coachford, died of fever. Of course fever did not suddenly appear with the potato blight or disappear in 1851. As far back as 1810 Florence McCarthy, coadjutor bishop to Dr Moylan, died of typhus in Cork city. Dr McSweeny, parish priest of Bandon and Patrick Mahony, chaplain to the Skibbereen Workhouse, died early in 1845. Augustine Hickey, aged 26, curate at Bantry, perished as late as 1853 from a fever brought on by 'the trying scars of sickness and distress'.[60] A corresponding number of priests died of fever in the dioceses of Cloyne, Kerry, Cashel and Killaloe.[61] The *Catholic Directory* for 1848 gives the names of 36 priests who died of fever during the previous year in Ireland but the list is by no means complete. Names are also given of the 25 who succumbed in England including ten in Liverpool alone. One priest's housekeeper died and cholera took the priest in 1849.[62] Nuns were actively involved in famine relief too. In Killarney they set up a fever hospital in the unfinished cathedral and at least 5 died of fever in the diocese of Kerry.[63] Two Sisters of Mercy died in Cork, one of whom, Gertrude, was a sister of John Hogan, the sculptor.[64] Three members of the Society of St Vincent de Paul also died of fever in the city.[65]

Six priests, two Anglican ministers and 4 doctors died of fever on Grosse Île in Canada. There were 34 other deaths among stewards, nurses, cooks, policemen, carters and gravediggers. The mayor of Montreal died of fever as did the vicar general and 8 other priests. Michael Power, the first bishop of Toronto, also fell victim.[66] Forty Church of Ireland clergymen are reported to have died of fever in 1847.[67] We have noted the deaths from fever of Traill, J. R. Cotter, rector of Innishannon (uncle of the rector of Donaghmore)[68] and R. B. Townsend.[69] Fossey Tackaberry fell a victim to fever in Sligo.[70] Joseph Bewley, joint secretary of the central relief committee of the Society of Friends with Jonathan Pim, soon died in 1851 from the effects of his famine labours.[71] Abraham Beale of the Cork Committee of the Society of Friends died of fever in 1847.[72] His signature is to be found on delivery dockets of food donations to the parishes of the Mizen Peninsula.[73] William Todhunter, a Quaker who had fished around these coasts on the *Erne*, was swept away by fever as also was the New York Friend, Jacob Harvey, who had contracted the disease from Irish emigrants.[74] The number of doctors and students who died in the period 1846–7 was 153.[75] Among them were Dr Brady of Caheragh, Dr Corbett of Innishannon, and also his wife.[76] Some members of the ruling classes died too, such as Richard White, nephew of Lord Bantry,[77] John Lovell, Poor Law guardian in Bandon, and also Maskelyne Alcock from the same district.[78] It has been seen that government officials such as Captains Parker and Gordon of the Board of Works and J. J. Marshall and 15 other Poor Law inspectors were themselves swept off by fever as were also many workhouse staff. In the first four months of 1847 these houses lost 54 of their staff including 9 masters, 7 clerks, 7 medical men and 6 chaplains.[79] Casualties were surprisingly high too in some districts not notorious for famine. In South Tipperary, for example, the toll was 5 Poor Law guardians, 4 doctors, 2 priests, 1 apothecary, 1 MP, 1 Poor Law inspector, 1 policeman and one other person.[80] According to W. J. Lowe, 'The three years

1847, 1848 and 1849 accounted for the highest death tolls of constables on active duty prior to 1919–21 – respectively 224, 150 and 221'. This was about twice as high as the annual average for the entire period 1841– 1914.[81] Richard Butler, Church of Ireland Dean of Clonmacnoise, spoke out on behalf of all such victims: 'The graves of many a magistrate and physician and Poor Law guardian, and clergyman, both Protestant and Roman Catholic, will tell to future times how boldly and how truly the resident gentry of Ireland did their duty in the past year of famine and of fever'. P. A. Bourke pleads that we 'excise from our history books the corroding canker of hatred, and extend the roll of honour to those who died for Ireland to include not only those who fell in armed combat, but also those – English and Irish; Catholic, Protestant, Presbyterian, Quaker – who gave their lives for their fellowmen in peaceful service'.[82] I agree wholeheartedly. The Mizen Peninsula has provided us with individual examples of nearly all of such courageous people.

The controversy about souperism, harking back to the sixteenth century, was quickly to become rather anachronistic. Protestants were soon to find that German rationalist scholarship and Darwinian evolutionism would be a more fundamental enemy of the Bible that the Catholic Church ever was or could be. Charles Bloomfield, bishop of London, observed, 'We have more to fear from the theology of Germany than from Rome'.[83] Whatever about controversy the clergymen involved in the relief of the famine were always to be held in high esteem by their own respective flocks and remembered with *pietas*. The following inscription can be read on a plaque put up to Fisher in his own church, *Teampall na mBocht*:

> Sacred to the memory of
> Rev. William Allen Fisher A.B.
> Born 14th November 1808. Died 7th April 1880
> For 38 years rector of Kilmoe, his zeal for
> the spiritual and temporal good of his people
> never abated. Faithfulness to his Divine Master
> and benevolence to the poor of his flock
> ever marked his course.
> To his untiring energy are due the erection
> and endowment of this church.

Standish James O'Grady, son of Fisher's predecessor, Thomas O'Grady, and son-in-law of Fisher himself,[84] paid another glowing tribute to him in 1911:

> William Allen Fisher: his memory will be preserved by tradition, like that of the saintly founders of the Church of Ireland, in the fifth and succeeding centuries. I knew him well in my boyhood and early manhood and, if ever a saintly man walked the earth, he was one. I never saw in any countenance an expression, so benignant or which so told of a life so pure and unworthy and a self so obliterated. He took a great interest in the secular welfare of his flock and was trusted by Roman Catholic and Protestant alike.[85]

Fisher, however, was stamped on Catholic folk memory in quite a contrary manner. He was regarded as the arch souper, who forced Catholics to 'pervert' their faith, in order to save themselves from starvation. *Teampall na mBocht* was called *Teampall na Muc* or the 'Church of the Pigs' – an allusion to those who 'took the soup'. As already stated, Fisher complained that horrifying fables were told about his converts after their deaths. The same was to happen in his own case.[86]

James Goodman was transferred from Creagh, Baltimore to Ardgroom in the Beara Peninsula in 1858 but returned to the district as vicar of Abbeystrowry or Skibbereen in 1867. He was appointed Professor of Irish in Trinity College in 1884 and died in 1896. Fr Laurence O'Sullivan died in Douglas in 1857. This is the inscription over his grave in Ballyheda then part of that parish; it bears witness to the high regard his people had for him too:

> Sacred to the memory of
> Rev. Laurence O'Sullivan,
> who died on 20 August 1857.
> This monument was erected to
> perpetuate the memory of a
> faithful and zealous pastor,
> his fond and sorrowing flock revered him
> whilst living and now whilst his remains
> rest beneath this slab they lovingly recall upon
> its surface their unbiased testimony to
> his affability of Manner,
> Generosity of Heart
> and blameless and edifying life.

He, as has already been shown, was a 'faithful and zealous pastor' who did not abandon his flock when the wolf of famine came whether in 1822 or 1846–8. His successor, Fr Foley, was transferred from Kilmoe to Kilmurry in mid-Cork in 1867, where he died in 1893. His obituary related that his early missionary life brought him into 'the full sweep of famine misery'. 'Sickness, plague, nothing had terror for him', we read. 'In Schull and Goleen the hand of death was often stayed by his heroic charity and the worse plague of proselytism was met and overcome by his apostolic fidelity'.[87] The plaque in Cloughduv church is somewhat less panegyrical:

> To the memory of
> The Very Reverend John Canon Foley
> Pastor of Kilmurry for a period of twenty-six years
> In the trying years that followed the Famine
> as parish priest of Kilmoe
> his energies were daily taxed in attending to the material
> as well as the spiritual interests of his flock.
> Of his solicitude for the beauty of God's house,
> This church as well as the churches erected at
> Canovee and Goleen,
> are an enduring monument.

John Barry remained parish priest of Schull until he died in 1863 and was buried in Stuake. He had been in the parish for about thirty years and is still remembered as 'a famine priest'. Other victims were at times remembered too. A Dr Willis in Bantry made three crosses out of boards from a hinged-coffin. One was given to Canon O'Rourke and is in the Presentation Convent in Maynooth.[88]

Fr John Murphy, 'the Black Eagle', built the church of SS Peter and Paul in Cork, the architect being E.W. Pugin. The Mercy Hospital was founded in 1857 by Murphy and it contains a plaque in his honour.[89] The tributes paid to these pastors, Fisher, O'Sullivan, Foley, Barry and Murphy by their respective flocks are well deserved. All were great pastors in extremely bad or famine times. Each was zealous for the Gospel as he himself understood it. Perhaps Fisher may be counted among those who in the words of the Quaker, Mr Webb, 'sacrificed much of the influence for good they would have had if they had been satisfied to leave the belief of the people alone'. Perhaps it can also be said that James Goodman similarly sacrificed much of the influence for good he would have had if he had been more like his father, Thomas Chute Goodman, who 'interferes with no man's religion', as it was put. The controversy at Toormore 'left seeds of bitterness'. The unfortunate result was that the great work of clergymen who made no attempt to gain converts came under suspicion and received little or no recognition. This is all the more tragic in that some of them paid for their heroic charity with the sacrifice of their own lives such as Robert Traill and R. B. Townsend. As has already been remarked in Chapter XI, whatever about the serious distraction of religious controversy, it attracted extra funds and food into districts. Far more died of *laissez-faire* philosophy and indifference than of theology and zeal.

The poet, Seán Dunne, visited the common famine grave at Carrigastyra near Macroom whose story is recounted by an t-Athair Peadar Ó Laoghaire in *Mo Scéal Féin*. Dunne reflected:

> And I thought of how history, heritage and memory are selective things, and how despite all the old guff about preserving the past, we really only want to keep those parts of it that raise few questions. We let the grass and weeds grow over the rest, as it grows over the famine grave at Carrigastyra.[90]

The graves of those who died in the relief of the famine are often overgrown with grass as, for example, those of Traill, the Ulsterman, and Major Parker, the Englishman – the grass of oblivion. It must be remembered too that there were more than clergymen, physicians and officials, who sacrificed their lives; there were ordinary people as well. Some were servants in the Big Houses, for example, two maid servants in R. B. Townsend's rectory; their names are not recorded. Ordinary charitable neighbours caught fever too while burying the dead. Just as the coffin-ship became the horror-symbol of famine emigration the hinged-coffin and the famine-pit are rightly regarded as the horror-symbols of the famine mortality but they prevented worse evils such as Rwanda-like scenes of bodies floating down Skibbereen's river Ilen or around

Roaringwater Bay. Charitable persons helped their neighbours to their own cost, of course. Seán Ó hAo (Seán Hayes), a fisherman from Glandore, said of his own people: *Do brishemh iad so Dro-Shaol mar daoine muarchríocha a b'ea iad,* 'They got broke in the Bad Times because they were big-hearted people'.[91] There were times too when generosity cost even more. The Ulster poet, John Hewitt, tells of the fate of his great-grandmother who gave food to a beggar:

> There's not a chance now that I might recover
> one syllable of what that sick man said,
> tapping upon my great-grandmother's shutter
> and begging, I was told, a piece of bread;
> for on his tainted breath there hung infection
> rank from the cabins of the stricken west ... ,
> but she who, by her nature, quickly answered,
> accepted in return the famine-fever;
> and that chance meeting, that brief confrontation,
> conscribed me of the Irishry forever.
>
> Though much I cherish lies outside their vision,
> and much they prize I have no claim to share,
> yet in that woman's death I found my nation;
> the old wound aches and shews its fellow scar.[92]

Whether it is a case of a beggar-man or a clergyman, or whether the place is Ulster or Skibbereen, sickness and distress left their own scars. The British Prime Minister, Tony Blair, struck a similar chord in a message to a conference on the famine held in Cork in 1997. He regretted the 'deep scars' which resulted when the government 'stood by while a crop failure turned into a massive human tragedy'. The east window of the Church of Ireland church in Goleen provides a representation in stained glass of Dr McCormick as the Good Samaritan, with the following inscription:

> To the Glory of God
> and in memory of the late James McCormick M. D.
> the kind and efficient medical officer, 1840–84.
>
> He poured oil and wine into his wounds – Luke 8:12

For many Irish people the famine is an old wound which still aches. Seán Dunne felt that 'the grass grows at Carrigastyra like plaster over a wound'.[93] It is time to pour oil and wine into it but first we must try to find out the nature of that old wound and how and why it occurred. Such has been the quest of much of this book at least in relation to the three parishes of Aughadown/Kilcoe, Schull and Kilmoe on the Mizen Peninsula in the Union of Skibbereen in West Cork.

ABBREVIATIONS

CC *Cork Constitution*
CE *Cork Examiner*
DNB
FJ *Freeman's Journal*
HC House of Commons
HO Home Office
IHS *Irish Historical Studies*
JCHAS *Journal of the Cork Historical and Archaeological Society*
MJ *Mining Journal*
BL British Library
NA National Archives
NLI National Library of Ireland
RIA Royal Irish Academy
SR *Southern Reporter*

CHAPTER I: FROM THE BRONZE AGE TO 1800

1 O'Brien, W., *Mount Gabriel; Bronze Age Mining in Ireland*, Cork, 1994; O'Brien, W., 'A Primitive Mining Complex at Derrycarhoon, Co. Cork', *Journal of the Cork Historical and Archaeological Society*, xciv, no. 253, 1989, p. 1–18.

2 O'Mahony, J., *West Cork and its story*, Cork, 1975, p. 48–50; 'The genealogy of Corca Laidhe', in *Miscellany of the Celtic Society* edited by O'Donovan, J., Dublin, 1849, pp. 142–139, 385–401.

3 O'Mahony, *West Cork*, 99.

4 Notter, I., 'The O'Mahony castles of Ivagha', *The O'Mahony Journal*, ii, June 1972, p. 7–10.

5 Coleman, J. 'The Old Castles of south-west Cork'; *JCHAS*, xxviii, 1927, p. 62–71.

6 Bolster, E., *A history of the Diocese of Cork from the earliest times to the Reformation*, Shannon, 1972, p. 489.

7 O'Mahony, *West Cork*, pp. 165–6.

8 Stafford, Thomas, *Pacata Hibernia: Ireland appeased and reduced ... especially within the province of Munster under the government of Sir George Carew*, London, 1633; 2 vols edited by O'Grady, S. H., London, 1896, ii, pp. 588–593.

9 MacCarthy Morrogh, M., *The Munster Plantation: English Migration to Southern Ireland 1583–1641*, Oxford, 1986, p. 220.

10 O'Mahony, J., 'The O'Mahonys of Kinelmeky and Ivagha', *JCHAS*, xvi, 1910, pp. 9, 24; for Hulls see Appleby, J. C., 'Settlers and pirates in early seventeen century Ireland', *Studia Hibernica*, no. 25, 1989–90, pp. 12–17; O'Donovan, M. R., 'Notes on Sir W. Hull and Leamcon', *Mizen Journal*, no. 1, 1993, pp. 30–6.

11 *Irish patent rolls of James I: facsimile of the Irish Record Commissioners' Calendar prior to 1830*, with foreword by Griffith, M. G., Irish Manuscripts Commission, Dublin, 1966, pat. no. 18, pp. 479.

12 Townshend, D., *The life and letters of the Great Earl of Cork*, London, 1904, p. 263.

13 Went, A. E. J., 'Sir William Hull's losses in 1641', *JCHAS*, iii, 1947, pp. 55–68. Pilchards resemble herrings. Oil was extracted from pilchards in houses called 'palaces'.

14 Townsend, P. (ed.), *Burke's genealogical and heraldic history of the peerage, baronetage and knightage*, London, 1970, p. 136.

15 Copinger, W. A., *History of the Copingers or Coppingers etc.*, Manchester and London, 1814, pp. 46–54.

16 Brady, W. M., *Clerical records of Cork, Cloyne and Ross*, 3 vols, Dublin, 1863, i, p. 168.

17 Went, *Hull's Losses*, pp. 67–68.

18 O'Mahony, *West Cork*, pp. 212–15.

19 *Book of Survey and Distribution*, County of Cork, Barony of Carbery, pp. 239–70.

20 Pender, S. (ed.), *A Census of Ireland circa 1659*, Dublin, 1939, p. 61.

21 Burke, J. & J. B., *A genealogical and heraldic dictionary of the landed gentry of Great Britain and Ireland*, 3 vols, London, 1843–9, p. 72.

22 Brady, *Clerical records*, i, p. 170.

23 This watch has since been treasured in the Becher family. Bernard O'Regan of Aughadown told me that it was shown to him by a Brigadier Becher of Pertshire, Scotland.

24 Townshend, R. & D. (eds.), *An Officer of the Long Parliament and his descendants*, London, 1892, pp. 229–30.

25 O'Mahony, J. 'A history of the O'Mahony Septs of Kinelmeky and Ivagha', *JCHAS*, xvi 1910, p. 23.

26 Burke, *Landed Gentry*, p. 645: see also, Somerville, E. O. E., *Somerville family records*, Cork, 1948.

27 ffolliott, R., *The Pooles of Mayfield*, Dublin, 1958, pp. 227–28, 251–54.

28 O'Donoghue, D. J., *History of Bandon*, Cork, 1970, p. 20.

29 Burke, *Landed Gentry*, pp. 72–3.

30 *ibid.*, pp. 380–1.

31 Coombes, J. 'The Swantons of Ballydehob', *The Southern Star*, 12 Feb. 1977.

32 Notter family papers in the possession of I. Notter of Goleen.

33 Lee, G. L., *The Huguenot settlements in Ireland*, London, 1936, p. 75.

34 Brady, *Clerical Records*, i, pp. 162–172.

35 Buckley, J., 'The parish priests of Counties Cork and Kerry in 1704', *JCHAS*, vi, 1900, pp. 55–7.

36 Report on the state of Popery in Ireland, 1731: information of Paul Limrick, *Archivum Hibernicum* ii, 1913, pp. 140–1.

37 'Examination of Thomas Morgan of Crookhaven, taken before William Hull, 9 January 1710', cited by Burke, W. P., *The Irish priests in the Penal Times (1660–1760)*, Waterford, 1914, p. 177.

38 A letter to Capt. Lermond, March 1714, Marsh's Library, MS 23 1.1, or National Library of Ireland, microfilm, n. 2836, 1946.

39 Fetherstonhaugh, A. J., 'The true story of the two chiefs of Dunboy: an episode in Irish history', *The Journal of the Royal Society of Antiquaries of Ireland*, xxiv, 1894, pp. 35–9: for poems in Irish on John Puxley and Mortí Óg Ó Súilleabháin see R. Ó hÚrdail, '*An Pleantéir agus an Gael Díshealbhaithe*: Seán Pocslí agus Mortí Óg Ó Súilleabháin, etc', *Saoi na hÉigse: Aistí in ómós do Sheán Ó Tuama, Féilscríbhinn Sheáin Ui Thuama*, 2000, pp. 105–151.

40 O'Mahony, 'O'Mahony septs', 1910, p. 23.

41 Tuckey, F., *Cork Remembrancer*, Cork, 1837, p. 130.

42 Dickson, D., *Arctic Ireland*, Belfast, 1997, p. 50.

43 Ó Maidín, P., 'Pococke's tour of the south and south-east Ireland in 1758', *JCHAS*, lxviii, 1958, p. 73; McVeigh, J. (ed.), *Richard Pococke's Irish tours*, Dublin, 1995, pp. 154–6.

44 Wall, M., 'Rise of a Catholic middle class in eighteenth century Ireland', *IHS*, xi, no. 42, Sept. 1958, pp . 91–115.

45 Cornewall, Lewis, G., *On local disturbances in Ireland, and on the Irish Church question* London, 1936, p. 1.

46 Wall, M., 'The Whiteboys' in *Secret societies in Ireland*, edited by Williams, T. D., Dublin and New York, 1973, pp. 13–21.

47 Young, A., *Arthur Young's tour in Ireland (1776–1779)*, edited by Hutton, A. W., London and New York, 1892 edition, p. 84.

48 O'Leary, A., *An address to the common people of Ireland, etc., Miscellaneous Tracts*, London,

1786, p. 83; see also England, T., *The life of the Rev. A. O'Leary etc.*, London, 1822.

49 *Finn's Leinster Journal*, 19 July 1886; Burns, R. E., 'Parsons, priests, and the people: the rise of Irish anti-clericalism 1785–1789', in *Church History*, xxxi, June 1962, p. 157.

50 Rafferty, O., 'Church and Union', *Irish Catholic*, 8 June 2000, p. 13.

51 *Dublin Evening Post*, 1 Aug. 1786, cited in Brady, John, *Catholics and Catholicism in the Eighteenth-century press*, Maynooth, 1965, p. 239.

52 Cornewall Lewis, *Local disturbances*, p. 18.

53 O'Leary, A., *A defence of the conduct and writings of the Rev. Arthur O'Leary during the late disturbances in Munster with a full justification of the Irish Catholics and an account of the risings of the Whiteboys in answer to the ill-grounded insinuations of the Rt. Rev. Dr. Woodward, Lord Bishop of Cloyne*, London, 1786, pp. 40–1.

54 27 Geo. III, c. 40; 32 Geo. III, c. 16.

55 Madden, R. R., *The United Irishmen, their lives and times*, 4 vols, Dublin, 1857–60, iv, pp. 227–247.

56 *Cork Gazette*, 14 Nov. 1795.

57 Tone, T. W., *Memoirs of Wolfe Tone written by himself, etc*, 2 vols, London, 1827, ii, pp. 128–30.

58 Gough, Hugh, 'Anatomy of a failure' in *The French are in the bay; the expedition to Bantry 1796*, edited by Murphy, J. A., Cork, 1997, p. 15 (hereinafter cited as Murphy, *French in Bay*).

59 E. Morgan, *A Journal of the movements of the French fleet in Bantry Bay*, edited by Lee, P. G., *JCHAS*, xxi, 1915, pp. 121–2.

60 Lord Longueville was married to an aunt of Richard White; Lunham, T. A. 'The French in Bantry Bay', *JCHAS*, xxvi, 1920, pp. 62–63.

61 Tyrell, J., 'The weather and political destiny' in Murphy, *French in Bay*, pp. 33–6.

62 Bartlett, T., 'The invasion that never was', Murphy, *ibid.*, pp. 66, 52–3.

63 Whelan, K. 'Bantry Bay – the wider context', Murphy, *ibid.*, p. 109.

64 Bartlett, 'Invasion', p. 59.

65 Packenham, T., *The Year of Liberty*, London, 1972, p. 195.

66 Hickey, P., '"Invasion" and "Rebellion": Mizen Peninsula, 1796–98', in *Mizen Journal*, no. 6, 1998, pp. 21–35.

67 Brady, *Clerical records*, i, p. 195.

68 Hall, S. C. & A. M., *Ireland: its scenery and character*, 2 vols, London, 1842, i, p. 147.

69 Stuart Jones, E., *An invasion that failed: the French expedition to Ireland, 1796*, Oxford, 1950, p. 174.

70 Elliot, M., *Wolf Tone, prophet of Irish Independence*, London, 1989, p. 136.

71 *ibid.*

72 Jones, *Invasion*, pp. 144–45.

73 Elliot, *Tone*, pp. 153–5.

74 Lunham, *op. cit*, p. 60.

75 Elliot, *Tone*, pp. 151–2.

76 Gough, 'Anatomy', p. 18.

77 Tyrrell, 'Weather', p. 43

78 Elliot, *Tone*, pp. 332, 328.

79 Bartlett, 'Invasion', p. 60.

80 Ó Coindealbháin, S., 'The United Irishmen in Cork County', *JCHAS*, lvi, no. 183, 1951, pp. 18–19.

81 Elliot, *Tone*, pp. 129, 153.

82 Moylan was a friend of the Abbe Edgeworth, confessor of the guillotined Louis; Walsh, T. J., *The Irish Continental College Movement*, Dublin and Cork, 1973, p. 120.

83 Bolster, E., *A history of the diocese of Cork: from the Penal era to the Famine*, Cork, 1989, p.158.

84 Ó Coindealbháin, S., 'The United Irishmen in County Cork', *JCHAS*, liii, 1945, p. 119; Elliot, M., *Partners in Revolution: the United Irishmen and France*, London, 1989, pp.

122–3.

85 Bartlett, 'Invasion', pp. 60–1.

86 Jones, *Invasion*, p. 170.

87 Elliot, *Partners*, p. 129.

88 Ó Coindealbháin, 'United Irishmen', 1945, p. 21.

89 Packenham, *Liberty*, p. 63.

90 Moore, Sir John, (1761–1809), *DNB*, xi, 1813–19.

91 Packenham, *Liberty*, p. 71–6.

92 Ó Dálaigh, M., 'Tadhg na Samhna Mac Cáraigh', *Seanchas Chairbre*, Dec. 1982, p. 1.

93 Maurice, J. F., (ed.) *Sir John Moore, Diary*, London, 1904, i, pp. 288–290.

94 Ó Coindealbháin, 'United Irishmen', 1945, p. 26; Bolster, *Cork, penal era to famine*, p. 163.

95 Townshend, R. & D. (eds.), *An Officer of the Long Parliament*, p. 234.

96 Moore, *Diary*, i, p. 290.

97 Elliot, *Partners*, p.1 27.

98 Moore, *Diary*, i, p. 292.

99 Fitzgerald, M. E. & King, J. A., *The uncounted Irish in Canada and the United States*, Toronto, 1990, p. 47.

100 Robert Swanton (1759–1840) may have been influenced by revolutionary ideas because the family had a connection with France. A Colonel Swanton fought under Napoleon. A daughter of the colonel married a Frenchman, Hilaire Belloc; one of their grandsons was Hilaire Belloc, the Catholic apologist. Coombes, J., 'The Swantons of Ballydehob', *The Southern Star*, 6 Feb. 1977.

101 Ó Coindealbháin, S., 'The United Irishmen in Cork County', i, *JCHAS*, liii, 1948, p. 126.

102 Kingston, D., 'Tadhg an Asna and the Battle of the Big Cross', *Mizen Journal*, no. 7, 1999, p. 89.

103 Ó Murchú, T., *Faiche na bhFilí* (n.d., n.p.), p. 91.

104 Dickson, D., 'The South Munster region in the 1790s', in Murphy, *French in Bay*, p. 91.

105 Elliot, *Tone*, p. 400.

106 Kennelly, B., (ed.) 'The burial of Sir John Moore', in *The Penguin book of Irish verse*, London, 1970, p. 133.

CHAPTER II: LAW AND DISORDER

1 Bolster, *Cork, penal era to famine*, p. 169.

2 Barrington, J., *Historic memoirs of Ireland comprising secret records of the National Convention, the Rebellion and the Union*, 2 vols, London, 1833, ii, pp. 370–383.

3 Whelan, K., 'Bantry Bay: the wider context', in Murphy, *French in Bay*, p. 119.

4 Mss 15B 13 (34–6), NLI.

5 Coombes, J., 'Smuggling in the eighteenth century', in *Ardfield/Rathbarry Journal*, no. 2, 1999–2000, p. 64; A. J. Fetherstonhaugh, 'Two Chiefs of Dunboy', p. 40; McCarthy, P. & Hawkes, R., *Northside of Mizen*, Dublin, 1999, p. 102.

6 Webb, W., *An official history of H.M. Coast-guard*, London, 1976, p. 16.

7 Office of Public Works Records, NA, Office of Public Works, 8954/88.

8 Lankford, E., *Cape Clear Island: its people and landscape*, Cape Clear, 1999, p. 87.

9 Webb, *Coast-guard*, p. 33.

10 Cadogan, T., 'James O'Sullivan of Roaring Water', *Seanchas Chairbre*, no. 3, 1993, p. 20.

11 Kingston, W. J., *The story of West Carbery*, Waterford, 1985, p. 94.

12 Cadogan, T. & O'Mahony, C., 'Shipwrecks on the south-west coast of County Cork to 1840', *Mizen Journal*, no. 7, 1999, p. 80.

13 Beckett, J. C., *The making of modern Ireland*, London, 1966, p. 273.

14 *Evidence taken before the select committee of the Lords and commons, appointed in the sessions of 1824 and 1825 to inquire into the state of Ireland*, London, 1825, pp. 48–50 (hereinafter cited as Collins, *Evidence*, 1825).

15 *ibid.*, pp. 49–50.

16 Connolly, S., 'Union government, 1812–23' in *A New History of Ireland*, v, *Ireland under the Union*, i, *1801–70*, edited by Vaughan, W. E., Oxford, 1989, p. 65 (hereinafter cited as Vaughan, *New Hist. Ire.*, v).

17 Collins, *Evidence*, 1825, p. 80.

18 Swanton to Richmond, 20 Sept. 1812; Private and Official Correspondence, 1812–15, Magistrates, 6 (CSO), NA.

19 Broeker, G., *Rural disorder and police reform in Ireland 1812–36*, London, 1970, p. 45.

20 Hull to Peel, 15 April 1813; State of Country Papers, 1534/11 (CSO), N.A. (State of Country Papers hereinafter cited as SOC). Note by Peel on above letter: Hull to Gregory, 7 May 1813; SOC. 1534/12: Hull to Gregory, 25 May 1813, SOC, 1534/13.

21 Hull to Gregory, 10 June 1813; SOC, 1534/15.

22 Note by Peel on above letter.

23 Sidmouth to Peel, 19 Jan. 1814; HO.100/176.

24 Wilde, W., *Irish popular superstitions*, Dublin, 1842, pp. 82–3.

25 Hull to Peel, 6 Nov. 1813; SOC, 1514/24.

26 Hull to Gregory, 23 Nov. 1813, SOC, 1534/26.

27 Note by Peel on Hull to Peel, SOC, 1514/24.

28 Hull to Peel, 7 Feb.; SOC, 1567/5.

29 Note by Peel on above letter.

30 Whitworth to Peel, 8 May 1814; Peel Papers, British Library, London, Add. MS 40188.

31 Peel to Desart, 24 Feb. 1814; Peel Papers, Add. MS 40285.

32 Cited, Broeker, *Rural disorder*, p. 56.

33 Peel, R., *The speeches of the late right honourable Sir Robert Peel, Bart*, London, 1853, i, pp. 29–30.

34 Broeker, *Rural disorder*, pp. 68–79. The police act was Geo. III, c. 131, 25 July 1814.

35 Shea to Hull, 22 Jan. 1815, enclosed in Hull to Peel, 23 Nov. 1815; SOC, 1715/40.

36 Bolster, *Cork, penal era to famine*, p. 224.

37 Hull to Peel, 23 Nov. 1815; SOC, 1715/40: Hull to Gregory, 9 Dec. 1815; SOC, 1715/44.

38 Synopses of this correspondence were copied by Gregory into Private and Official Correspondence, 1815–18, Magistrates, pp. 81, 128.

39 O'Neill to Gregory, 6 May 1816; Note by Gregory on above letter. SOC, 1769/35.

40 Baker to Gregory, 30 Mar. 1816; SOC, 1775/1.

41 Hull to Peel, 6 Apr. 1817, Peel Papers, Add. MS 40264 or NLI, Microfilm Positive 714.

42 Peel to Hull, 17 Apr. 1817; NLI, MS 4210.

43 Saurin to Peel, 4 Apr. 1816; Peel Papers, Add. MS 40211.

44 Peel to Saurin, 8 Apr. 1816; Peel Papers, Add. MS 40324.

45 Jeffries, C., *The Colonial police*, London, 1952, p. 13.

46 Minto, A., *The thin blue line*, London, 1965, p. 1.

47 Glover, E. H., *The English police*, London, 1934, p .53.

48 Connolly, 'Government', p. 57.

49 Trevelyan, G. M., *British history in the nineteenth century: 1782–1919* (1965 ed.), p. 192.

50 *SR*, 20 Dec. 1821.

51 *SR*, 5 Jan. 1822.

52 Bryan, E., *Crown and Castle* (Dublin, 1978), pp. 32–3.

53 Townsend to Wellesley, 10 Jan. 1822; SOC 2392/12.

54 Townshend, R. & D. (eds) *An Officer of the Long Parliament*, pp. 236–7.

55 Brady, *Clerical records*, pp. ii, 429.

56 See Chapter IV.

57 Morrit to Wellesley, 9 Jan. 1822; SOC 2342/12.

58 A. Beamish to Gen. Lambert, 10 Jan. 1822: SOC 2342/26.

59 O'Mahony, *West Cork*, p. 266.

60 i.e., auctioned, cf. the Irish *ceant* or auction.

61 *SR*, 15 Jan., 1822.

62 Wellesley to Peel, 25 Jan. 1822; HO 203/407055.

63 Carbery to Goulburn, 20 Jan. 1822; HO 100/703.

64 Goulburn to Carbery, 19 Jan. 1822: Wellesley's Private Correspondence, i, p. 20.

65 *SR*, 26 Jan. 1822.

66 *SR*, 1, 14 Jan. 1822.

67 O'Mahony, *West Cork*, pp. 264–5.

68 Ó Donnchadha, D., *Filíocht Mháire Bhuidhe Ní Loaghaire*, Dublin, 1931, pp. 16–17, 74; He was a brother of Éamonn and Tadhg (Tórna) of UCC.

69 Brennan, B., *Maire Bhuí Ní Laoire: a poet of her people*, Cork, 2000, p. 44.

70 Ó Coindealbháin, S., *The story of Iveleary*, Dundalk, n.d., pp. 48–50.

71 Brennan, *op. cit.*, pp. 44, 80, 123.

72 O'Mahony, *op. cit.*, p. 237.

73 Dickson, D., 'The other great famine' in *The Great Irish Famine*, edited by Póirtéir, C., Cork, 1995, pp. 55, 62 (hereinafter cited as Póirtéir, *Famine*).

74 Connolly, S. J., 'Union Goverment, 1812–23' in Vaughan, *New Hist. Ire.*, v, pp .61–2.

75 *SR*, 4, 18, Jan. 1816.

76 Collins, *Evidence, 1825, pp.* 93–4.

77 Fenning, H., 'Typhus epidemic in Ireland, 1817–18: Priests, ministers and doctors', *Collectanea Hibernica*, no. 41 (1999), pp. 124–5.

78 Collins, *Evidence 1825*, pp. 93–4.

79 Robinson to Gregory, 9 Mar. 1817; SOC, 1835/6.

80 Coombes, J., 'Sea trade in potatoes in south-west Cork (1730–1850)', *Seanchas Chairbre*, no. 3, 1993, pp. 3–16.

81 Crotty, R. D., *Irish agricultural production: its volume and structure*, Cork, 1966, p. 284.

82 Newenham, T., *A view of the natural, political and commercial circumstances of Ireland*, London, 1809, p. 26.

83 Barrow, G. L., *The emergence of the Irish banking system*, Dublin, 1975, pp. 17–8.

84 O'Kelly, E., *The old private banks and bankers of Munster*, Cork, 1959, p. 42.

85 Cathedral files in Cork Archives Council.

86 Tuckey, *Rembrancer*, p. 268.

87 *Census of Ireland for the year, 1851*, pt i, ii, HC, 1852–3, xci, pp. 238.

88 Carleton, W., *The Black Prophet*, New York and London, 1979 ed., pp. iv, 149.

89 *Census Ire.*, *1851*, pt. i, ii, xci, p. 239.

90 *Abstract of answers and return, pursuant to Act 55 Geo. 3 for taking account of the population of Ireland in 1821* [577], HC, 1824, xxii, pp. 152–5, 411.

91 Carbery to Wellesley, 16 Apr. 1822; Goulburn papers, pp. 10, 11.

92 *Freeman's Journal*, 30 Apr.; 5, 9, May 1822.

93 O'Neill, T. P., 'The famine of 1822', MA, NUI, 1966, p. 10.

94 He was the father of the Clerke sisters, Bruck, M. T., 'Ellen and Agnes Clerke, scholars, writers', *Seanchas Chairbe*, no. 3 (1993), pp. 22–43.

95 *SR*, 21 May 1822.

96 O'Neill, 'The famine of 1822', p. 14.

97 *Report of the proceedings of the committee of management for the relief of distressed districts in Ireland appointed at a general meeting held in the Mansion House, Dublin on the 16 May 1822*, Dublin, 1822, p. 2.

98 *SR*, 28 May 1822.

99 Cathedral files, *op. cit.*

100 Jagoe to Committee, 17 Jun. 1822, Guildhall Library, London, Ms 7476, Bundle 1.

101 *ibid.*

102 McCarthy, C. J. F., 'A man of war – Jeremiah Coghlan', *Seanchas Chairbre*, no. 8, 1993, pp. 5–21.

103 *ibid.*

104 *SR*, 1 Jun. 1822.

105 Murphy to Wellesley, 4 Jun. 1822, HO, pp. 205, 27.

106 *CC*,14 Jun. 1822.

107 *Report of the committee for the relief of distressed districts in Ireland, appointed at a general meeting held at the City of London Tavern, on the 7th May 1822; with an appendix*, London, 1823, p. 43.

108 *SR*, 8 Jun. 1822.

109 Jagoe to Traill, 14 Jun. 1822; Jagoe to London Committee, 14, 17 June 1822; London Guildhall Mss 7476, Bundle 1.

110 *CC*, 21 Jun. 1822.

111 *Report Lon. Tav. Comm.*, p. 3.

112 *CC*, 19, 21 Jun. 1822.

113 *A return of vessels with provisions, which landed at the southern and western parts of Ireland*, HO 100, 204, pp. 292–5.

114 Morrit to Committee, 10 June 1822, Guildhall MSS, 7476, Bundle 1.

115 Dore to Committee, 4 June 1822, *ibid.*

116 Murphy, I., *The diocese of Killaloe*, Dublin, 1992, pp. 24–5.

117 *CC*, 26 July 1822.

118 Guildhall MSS, Bundle 5.

119 *ibid.*

120 *Report Lon. Tav. Comm.*, 117–120.

121 O'Neill, T. P., 'Minor famines and relief in County Galway, 1815–1925', in *Galway: history and society*, edited by Moran, G., & Gillespie, G., Dublin, 1996, p. 449.

122 *Report Lon. Tav. Comm.*, p. 326.

123 O'Neill, 'Famine of 1822', p. 80.

124 Collins, *Evidence*, 1825. p. 95.

125 *CC*, 19 Jun. 1822.

126 See Chapter X.

127 *CC*, 11 Sept. 1822.

128 *Report Dub. Comm.*, pp. 8–10.

129 Murphy MSS, Maynooth, M97, p. 244.

130 Guildhall MSS, Bundle 5.

131 *CC*, 8 Jan. 1823.

132 Parish records, Schull.

133 Coombes, J., *Utopia in Glandore*, Butlerstown, 1970, pp. 13–15.

134 *Report Lon. Tav. Comm.*, pp. 203–4.

135 *Report of the deputation of the National Fishing Company on the subject of fishing on the south and west coasts of Ireland*, 1825; Halliday Collection.

136 *ibid.*, pp. 348.

137 *Freeman's Journal*, 13 May 1822 (hereinafter cited as *FJ*).

138 *Report. Lon. Tav. Comm.*, pp. 43, 150, 163.

139 Collins, *Evidence*, 1825, p. 57.

140 O'Rourke, J., *The history of the great Irish famine of 1847, with notices of earlier Irish famines* (Dublin), 1875, p. 32.

141 *Report Lon. Tav. Comm.*, p. 79.

142 Collins, *Evidence*, 1825, p. 54.

143 *Report Lon. Tav. Comm.*, p. 148.

144 *SR*, 25 May 1825.

145 Chapter IV.

146 Bowen, D., *The Protesant Crusade in Ireland, 1800–70*, Dublin, 1978, pp. 211–8.

147 *Report on the roads made at public expense in the southern districts by Richard Griffith*, 2; HC, 1831 (119), xii, p. 61.

148 *Report to the Irish Government on the employment of the poor; No. 1, Report on the southern districts by Richard Griffith*, 6 [249], HC, 1823, x, p. 41.

149 O'Donnell, R., *Aftermath post-Rebellion insurgency in Wicklow, 1799–1803*, Dublin, 2000, p. 62.

150 Young, A., *Arthur Young's tour in Ireland (1776–1779)*, edited by Hutton, A. W., pp. i, 77.

151 Trevelyan, *British History*, p. 24.

152 *DNB*, xii, pp. 395–6.

153 *Memorial*, B. 4054, Registered Papers, CSO, 1822.

154 Ó Lúing, S., 'Richard Griffith and the roads in Kerry', *Journal of the Kerry Archaeological and Historical Society*, no. 8, 1975, pp. 89–113.

155 Griffith to Gregory, 10 July 1823; same to same, 19 July 1823; Griffith Report, 1823, pp. 21, 23.

156 Griffith Report, 1823, pp. 9–10.

157 *Report on the southern districts in Ireland containing a statement of the progress made during the year 1823, in the several roads carried out at public expense in that district: under the order of his excellency, the lord lieutenant*, 4–5 [352], HC, 1824, xxi, p. 352.

158 Griffith Report, 1823, p. 29; Griffith Report, 1824, p. 9.

159 *First Report of his Majesty's Commissioners for inquiring into the condition of the poorer classes, with appendix and supplement*; Appendix (A) [36], HC, 1835, xxxii, p. 12.

160 Cox, R. C., 'The engineering career of Richard Griffith', in *Richard Griffith, 1784–1878*, edited by Davies, G. L., & Mollan, R. C., Dublin, 1980, p. 44.

161 Griffith Report, 1831, 5, 15; he built 5 miles of road in Caheragh between Skibbereen and Bantry and also Aughaville bridge, £52.

162 O'Keefe, P. J., 'Richard Griffith, planner and builder of roads', in *Richard Griffith, 1784–1878*, edited by Davies, G. L. & Mollan, R. C., Dublin, 1980, pp. 57, 75.

163 Griffith Report, 1831, pp. 13–19.

164 *Report on Roads carried out at public expense under the order of his excellency, the lord lieutenant*, 62–5 [389], HC, 1829, xxii, p. 120.

165 Harris, R. A., 'Searching for missing friends in the *Boston Pilot* newspaper', in *The Irish diaspora*, edited by A. Bielenberg, Harlow, 2000, pp. 170, 175.

166 Chapter VI.

167 Griffith Report, 1823, p. 21.

168 *Final report of the Board of Works in relation to measures adopted for the relief of distress in July and August 1847*, Irish University Press series of Parliamentary Papers on the Famine, Shannon, 1970, viii, *379–85* (hereinafter cited as P.P. *Famine*).

169 *FJ*, 11 Feb. 1847.

170 Hull to Gregory, 2 July 1822; SOC, 2346/2.

171 Donnelly, J. S., Jr, 'Pastorini and Captain Rock: millenarianism and sectarianism in the Rockite movement of 1821–4', in *Irish peasants and social unrest, 1780–1914*, edited by Clarke, S. & Donnelly, Jr., J. S., Manchester, 1987, p. 118.

172 Collins, *Evidence*, 1825, p. 116.

173 Coghlan to Charles Grant, 27 Oct. 1822: SOC 2347/20.

174 *CC*, 16 Mar. 24.

175 Grand Jury to Wellesley, 21 Apr. 1823; HO 100, 208, 130.

176 *Minutes of evidence taken before the select committee of the House of Lords appointed to inquire into the nature and extent of disturbances …* [20], HC, 1825, vii, p. 37.

177 Audley to Gregory, 22 Apr. 1823; SOC, 2512/30.

178 Note by Wellesley on above letter.

179 *SR*, 21 Mar. 1824, 1 Apr. 1824.

180 *ibid.*, 21 Mar. 1824.

181 *SR*, 21 July 1825.

182 Broeker, *Rural disorder*, p. 225.

183 Lowe W. J. & Malcolm, F. L., 'The domestication of the Royal Irish Constabulary', *Ir. Econ. & Soc. Hist.*, xix, 1992, p. 35.

184 *The Freeholder*, 3 Mar. 1823.

185 *SR*, 12 July 1823.

186 Collins to Mahony, 26 July 1823, Goulburn Papers, II, p. 14.

187 Peel to Goulburn, 16 Aug. 1823; *ibid.*

188 Brady, *Clerical records*, ii, pp. 480.

189 *The Freeholder,* 14 Mar. 1824.

190 Goulburn to Hobhouse, 1 Feb. 1822, HO 100, box 203.

191 Ó Gráda, C., *An Drochshaol: béaloideas agus amhráin,* Baile Átha Cliath, 1994, pp. 86–7.

192 Trevor to Peel, HO 100, Box 205.

193 Broeker, *Rural Disorder*, pp. 150–5.

194 Burke, *Priests in penal times*, p. 207.

195 Collins, *Evidence*, 1825, pp. 61, 71, 49.

196 Chapter IV.

197 *Cork Mercantile Chronicle*, 5 Dec. 1825.

198 *SR*, 22 Mar. 1827.

199 Inscription at court-house; Coombes, J., *Timoleague and Barryroe,* n.p., 1969, p. 49; Coombes, 'Smuggling', p. 65.

200 Donnelly, 'Pastorini', pp. 136–7; Ó Tuathaigh, G., *Ireland before Ireland the famine*, Dublin, 1972, p. 67.

CHAPTER III: RELIGION AND EDUCATION

1 Brady, *Clerical records*, pp. i, 174–6, 247–8.

2 O'Donoghue, D. J., *History of Bandon*, Cork, 1970, pp. 94–95.

3 Cullen, W. E., *Bi-centenary Souvenir*, Skibbereen, 1938, p. 67.

4 Crookshank, C. H., *History of Methodism in Ireland*, 2 vols, Dublin, 1886, pp. ii, 152.

5 Stewart A. & Rivington, G., *Memoirs of the life and labours of Rev. A. Averell*, Dublin, 1858, pp. 179, 249–51.

6 Cullen, *op. cit.,* pp. 10–11.

7 de Breffny, B. & Mott, G.,*The Churches and Abbeys of Ireland*, London, 1976, p. 145.

8 Cullen, *op. cit.,* pp. 15, 24–5.

9 Akenson, D. H., *The Church of Ireland, Ecclesiastical reform and revolution 1800–1895*, New Haven and London, 1971, p. 79.

10 Brady, *Clerical Records*, i, p. 248.

11 The First Fruits were the first year's revenue of a benefice. The Board of First Fruits was established in Ireland in 1711; this revenue was used for the building of churches and glebe houses.

12 Breffny & Mott, *op. cit*, p. 145.

13 Brady, *op. cit.* pp. 457–9, 496.

14 Cited, ffolliot, R., *The Pooles of Mayfield and other Irish families*, Dublin, 1958, p. 251.

15 Fisher, *Irish Intelligence*, v (1852), p. 17.

16 Fisher, April 1880, quoted in his biography, Carson, J. B., *Forty Years in the Church of Ireland: or the pastor, the parish and its people*, London, 1882, p. 15.

17 Notes of Isaac Notter of Goleen.

18 Bowen, D., *The Protestant Crusade in Ireland*, 1800–70, Dublin, 1978, p. 89.

19 Bowen, D., *Souperism: myth or reality*, Cork, 1970, pp. 89, 83–85.

20 Jermyn, N., *My Parish*, n.p., 2000, no pagination.

21 *CE*, 4 Sept. 1846.

22 Cited in Carson, *Pastor*, p. 6; *Irish Intelligence*, v, pp. 16–17.

23 Foley, D., *Missionary tour through the south of Ireland undertaken for the Irish Society*, Dublin, 1849, p. 20.

24 Carson, *Pastor*, p. 6.

25 Ó Riain, P., 'Séamus Ó Súilleabháin, *bíoblóir*', *Archiv. Hib.*, no. 8, 1968, pp. 96–105.

26 Carson, *Pastor*, p. 10.

27 See Chapter I.

28 Grosch, H. J., 'How Fr Harte became a priest', *The Month*, 131, no. 648, Jan. – Jun. 1918, p. 475.

29 *Faulkner's Dublin Journal*, 30 Dec. 1774; Brady, *Clerical Records*, pp. ii, 55. For other conversions, see, Finegan, F., 'The Irish Catholic convert rolls', *Studies*, xxxviii, no. 149, Mar. 1948, pp. 73–82.

30 *Dublin Chronicle*, 12 May 1787.

31 Bolster, *Cork, Penal era to famine*, p. 258.

32 Collins, *Evidence*, 1825, pp. 91–102.

33 O'Donovan, M., 'Ballinskea church', *Mizen Journal*, no. 4, 1996, p. 66.

34 *SR*, 6 May 1825.

35 Fr Prior was one of those priests who were incardinated into the diocese of Cork from Cashel. Others were Dore of Caheragh, Quin of Muintir Bháire, and Doheny of Dunmanway.

36 *SR*, 23 Nov. 1825.

37 *SR*, 12 Dec. 1825.

38 *SR*, 21 June 1826.

39 *Evidence taken before her Majesty's Commissioners of inquiry into the state of law and practice in respect to the occupation of land in Ireland*, pt. ii, 949 (616), HC, 1845, xx, p. 1.

40 Brady J. & Corish, P. J., *The Church under the Penal Code*; Corish, P. J., *Irish Catholicism*, pp. iv, 65; Coombes, J., 'Catholic Churches in the nineteenth century: some newspaper sources', *JCHAS*, lxxxi, no 223, Jan.–Jun. 1975, pp. 6, 11.

41 *SR*, 29 Sept. 1825.

42 *SR*, 26 Jan. 1826.

43 Drury, W. B. & Walsh, F. W. (eds), *Reports of cases argues and determined in the High Court of Chancery during the time of Lord Chancellor Plunket*, 2 vols (1838–9–40), ii, p. 122.

44 *ibid.*

45 *SR*, 5 Mar. 1840.

46 Parish records.

47 *SR*, 10 Nov. 1836.

48 Murphy, I.,'Some attitudes to religious freedom and ecumenism in Pre-Emancipation Ireland', *The Irish Ecclesiastical Record*, no. 1178, Fifth series, cv, no. 2, Feb 1966, pp. 93–104.

49 Whelan, K., 'The Catholic parish, the Catholic chapel and village development in Ireland', *Irish Geography*, xvi, 1983, passim.

50 Collins, *Evidence*, 1825, p. 112.

51 *First report of the commissioners of public instruction, Ireland*, 1835, xxxiii, pp. 131–151.

52 Miller, D.W. 'Mass attendance in Ireland in 1834' in *Piety and power in Ireland: essays in honour of Emmet Larkin*, edited by Browne, S. J. and Miller, D. W., Belfast, 2000, p. 158–175; Corish, P., *The Irish experience: a historical survey*, Dublin, 1985, p. 167.

53 Collins, *Evidence*, 1825, 92; *Minutes of evidence taken before the select committee appointed to inquire into the disturbances in Ireland*, HC, vii, p. 359.

54 *Abstract of answers and returns ... Population of Ireland Act 1821*, 152; *Abstract of answers ... Population Acts, Ireland, 1836*, p. 144.

55 Keenan, D. J., *The Catholic Church in nineteenth-century Ireland – a sociological study*, Dublin, 1983, pp. 97–99.

56 Kerr, D. A., *Peel, priests and politics: Sir Robert Peel's administration and the Roman Catholic Church in Ireland, 1841–1848*, Oxford, 1982, pp. 46–48.

57 Ó Laoire, D., 'Local hedge schools and education', *Tousist 6000* (Tousist, 1999), p. 142.

58 Akenson, Donald H., *The Irish educational experiment*, London and Toronto 1970, pp. 84–91.

59 Dowling, P. J., *The hedge schools of Ireland*, Cork, 1968.

60 This fund was set up in 1819 following an appeal on behalf of Catholics by William Parnell, MP, for Wicklow. Up to 1825, only £12 out of £481, went to Catholics, Akenson, *The Irish education experiment, the National System of education in the nineteenth*

century, pp. 83–85.

61 *Second report of the commissioners of Irish education inquiry*, HC, 1826–7 (12), 1, Appendix, no. 22, Parochial returns, pp. 911–31.

62 Otway, C., *Sketches in the south of Ireland*, Dublin, 1829, pp. 126–7.

63 Collins, *Evidence*, 1825, pp. 106–7.

64 Bolster, *Cork, Penal era to famine*, p. 272.

65 Akenson, *Educational experiment*, p. 97.

66 *CC*, 27 Mar. 1832.

67 *National Board Applications* (1832–1844), Application no. 101 (hereinafter cited as *NBA* (1832–44)).

68 *County Register Books*, vol. ii, folio 141 (hereinafter cited as *CRB*).

69 *NBA* (1832), no. 164.

70 *CRB*, Vol. i, folio 168; vol. ii folio 85, vol. iii, folio 6.

71 Akenson, *Educational experiment*, p. 151.

72 *NBA* (1832–4), no. 192.

73 *CRB*, Vol. i, folio 169: Vol. ii, folio 86; Vol. iii, folio 7.

74 *NBA* (1832–44), no. 161.

75 *CRB*, vol. i, folios 74, 198.

76 *NBA* (1832–44), no. 188: *CRB*, vol. ii, folio 7; vol. iii, folio 8.

77 *NBA* (1832–44), no. 253.

78 *NBA* (1845–7), no. 12.

79 *NBA* (1845–7), no. 323.

80 *CRB*, vol. ii, folios 202, 210.

81 Sullivan, A. M., *New Ireland*, London, 1877, p. 13.

82 Daly, M., 'The development of the national school system, 1831–40' in *Studies in Irish history presented to R. Dudley Edwards*, edited by Cosgrove, A. & McCartney, D., Dublin, 1978, p.163.

83 Thackeray, W. M., *The Irish sketch-book 1842*, London, 1843, pp. 56–7.

84 Akenson, *Educational experiment*, p. 197.

85 *Third annual report of the Church Education Society for Ireland*, Dublin, 1842, pp. 46–7.

86 *Fourth annual report of the Church Education Society for Ireland*, Dublin, 1843, p. 41.

87 *Seventh annual report of the Church Education Society for Ireland*, Dublin, 1846, p. 51.

88 *Twelfth report of the commissioners of national education in Ireland for the year 1845*, p. 32.

89 *Seventh annual report of the Church Education Society*, p. 7.

90 *Twelfth report of the commissioners … for the year 1845*, [711], HC, 1846, xxii, p. 47.

91 Akenson, *Education Experiment*, pp. 225–74.

92 *Thirteenth report of the commissioners … for the year 1846*, p. 74.

93 *Report of the Commissioners appointed to take the census for Ireland for the year 1841*, 1843, [504] xxiv, plate 3, General Table, p. 177.

94 *Twelfth report of the commissioners … for 1845.*, p. 18, (711), HC, 1846, xxii, p. 47.

95 Kane, R., *The Industrial resources of Ireland*, Dublin, 1945, pp. 406–7.

96 Larkin, E., 'The devotional revolution in Ireland in Ireland, 1850–75', *The historical dimension of Irish Catholicism*, Dublin, 1997, p. 70.

97 Cullen, *Vincentian Foundations*, pp. 20–9.

98 Bolster, *Cork, Penal era to famine*, p. 310.

CHAPTER IV: MINING FOR COPPER AND BARYTES

1 Hall, *Ireland*, i, 140–1; Crofton Croker, T., *Researches in the south of Ireland*, London, 1824, p. 312.

2 *Memoirs of the Geological Survey of Great Britain*, London, 1850, ii, pt ii, p. 713, Table 2, *Sales in Swansea from Irish mines*, compiled by Hunt, R.

3 *Mining Journal*, xxx, 1860, 565; xiv, 1875, p. 876 (hereinafter cited *MJ*).

4 Harrington, S., *MJ*, xxxvi, 1866, p. 103.

5 Captain Thomas, 'Mining in the south of Ireland', *MJ*, xxiii, 1853, p. 52. Perrier A., 'Report on Mizen Head copper mining company', *ibid.*, p. 58.

6 Griffith to Audley, 10 Feb. 1819, Drury & Walsh, *Reports*, ii, pp. 94–6; see T. Reilly and D. Cowman, 'Cappagh mine, an endangered heritage site', *MJ*, no 6, 1999, pp. 163–174.

7 Griffith to Audley, 28 Dec. 1821, Drury & Walsh, *Reports*, p. 78.

8 Drury & Walsh, *Reports*, p. 78.

9 Hunt, *Memoirs*, Table 2.

10 Lewis, S., *A topographical dictionary of Ireland* … 1837, London, ii, p. 561.

11 *MJ*, x, 1840, p. 20.

12 Clarke, C. & Finnelly, W., *Reports of cases decided in the House of Lords on the appeals and writs of error, during the sessions 1841 and 1842*, London, 1843, viii, p. 564.

13 Clarke & Finnelly, *Cases in House of Lords*, p. 222.

14 *Mining Company of Ireland*, Reports etc., 1824–40, Dublin, 1841; report for 1 July – 1 Dec. 1824, p. 4.

15 *Company Reports*, 5 July 1825, 5 Jan. 1826; Purdy to Moore, 28 July 1825; Drury & Walsh, *Reports*, pp. 108–10.

16 Drury & Walsh, *Reports*, pp. 186–92

17 *Company Reports*, 5 July 1826, 1 Dec. 1826.

18 Hunt, *Memoirs*, Table 2.

19 *Company Reports*, *op. cit.*, p. 8.

20 Lewis, S., *A topographical dictionary of Ireland* … 1837, London, ii, p. 561.

21 *Company Reports*, 1 June – 1 Dec. 1827, p. 6.

22 *Company Reports*, 1 June – 1 Dec. 1828, p. 3.

23 *Company Reports*, 1 June – 1 Dec. 1829, p. 3; Hunt, *Memoirs*, Table 2.

24 Kane, *Industrial Resources*, p. 193.

25 Clarke & Finnelly, *Cases in the House of Lords*, p. 222.

26 Drury & Walsh, *Reports*, pp. 186–192.

27 Williams, R. A., *The Berehaven copper mines*, Sheffield, 1991, p. 36.

28 *ibid.*, pp. 121–4.

29 Clarke & Finnelly, *Cases in House of Lords*, p. 570.

30 *MJ*, x, 1840, p. 206.

31 *MJ*, ix, 1842, p. 69.

32 *MJ*, 16 Sept. 1843. p. 61.

33 Hall, *Ireland*, i, p. 141.

34 Keane, *op. cit.*, p. 192; O'Reilly, T. A., 'Richard Griffith and the Cappagh copper mine fraud', Davies & Mollan, *Griffith*, pp. 197–210.

35 Hunt, *Memoirs*, Table 2.

36 *MJ*, xii, 1842, p. 68.

37 Kane, *op., cit.*, pp. 193–4.

38 John and Charles Wesley used to stay in his father's house; Charles Thomas, Cornwall, private correspondence.

39 See Chapter VI.

40 *MJ*, xii, 1843, p. 386.

41 *Evidence taken before her majesty's commissioners of inquiry into the state of law and practice in respect to the occupation of land in Ireland*, pt ii [616], HC, 1845, xx, pp. 157–9, 213.

42 *First Report of the Commissioners of Inquiry into the employment and conditions of children in mines and manufacturers* [380], HC, 1842, xv, p. 46.

43 Kane, *Industrial Resources*, p. 194.

44 *MJ*, xvi, 1846, p. 117.

45 *MJ*, xiv, 1843, p. 400.

46 *MJ*, xiii, 1842, 403; *MJ*, xix, 1849, p. 199.

47 *MJ*, xvi, 1846, p. 158.

48 *MJ*, xvi, 1846, p. 21.

49 For plan see Geological Survey, Kildare St., Dublin, R. 10, 1863. One shaft was called after Dr Traill.

50 Hunt, *Memoirs*, Table 2.

51 Foley, Pierre, 'Mineral resources of Ireland', *MJ*, no. 16, 1846, p. 58. A complete list of the mines and more trials was provided by Griffith, 'On the copper beds of the south coast of the County Cork', *Journal of the Geological Society of Dublin*, vi, 1855, pp. 204–5.

52 Hallissey, T., *Memoirs of the Geological Survey of Ireland, mineral resources, barytes in Ireland*, Dublin, 1923, ii, p. 36.

53 *MJ*, xv, 1845, p. 799.

54 Cole, G. A. T., *Memoir of the geological survey of Ireland: mineral resources. Memoir and map of localities of minerals of economic importance in Ireland*, Dublin, 1922, p. 20.

55 *CC*, 28 Oct. 1845.

56 O'Brien, W. F., 'Mining at Derrycarhoon, County Cork', *JCHAS*, xciv, no. 35, 1989, pp. 1–18.

57 Cowman, D., 'The mining community in Avoca' in *Wicklow: history and society*, edited by Hannigan, K. and Nolan, W., Dublin, 1994, pp. 649–692.

58 O'Mahony, C., 'Copper-mining at Allihies, Co. Cork', *JCHAS*, xcii, no. 251, 1987, p. 74.

59 Cowman, D., 'Life and labour in three Irish mining counties c. 1840', *Saothar*, no. 9, 1983, p. 10.

60 *SR*, 26 Jan. 1847.

CHAPTER V: TITHES; POVERTY

1 Akenson, *Church of Ireland*, p. 108.

2 Tithe Applotment Books, Schull.

3 Tithe Applotment Books, Kilmoe.

4 Tithe Applotment Books, Aughadown.

5 Tithe Applotment Books, Kilcoe.

6 Brady, *Clerical Records*, i, pp. 195, 284, 464, 495.

7 Tithe Applotment Books, Kilcoe.

8 Akenson, *Church of Ireland*, p. 110.

9 Bolster, *Cork: Penal era to famine*, p. 276.

10 Casey, D., *Cork Lyrics*, Cork, 1857, pp. 131–2.

11 *CC*, 24 Nov. 1829.

12 *CC*, 28 Nov. 1829.

13 Bowen, D., *The Protestant Crusade in Ireland, 1800–70*, 1978, pp. 161–2.

14 MacDonagh, O., *O'Connell: the life of Daniel O'Connell, 1775–1847*, London, 1991, p. 348.

15 *The Cork Mercantile Chronicle*, 24 June 1832.

16 *ibid.*, 11 July 1832.

17 *Dublin Evening Mail*, 31 Oct. 1832.

18 Skelton, R., *J. M. Synge and his world*, London, 1971, p. 9.

19 Synge Harbord, R., *The diary of reverend Robert Traill (1793–1847)*, privately published, p. 5.

20 Ó Donnchadha, L., 'The murder of Rev. C. Ferguson, 1832', *Bandon Journal*, no. 6, 1990, p. 6.

21 Bowen, D., *Souperism: Myth or Reality?*, Cork, 1970, p. 39.

22 *Third Report of the Commissioners for inquiring into the condition of the poorer classes in Ireland*, Appendix E., 178, [37] HC, 1836, xxxii, p. 238.

23 *SR*, 16 Jan. 1834.

24 *SR*, 24 Apr. 1838.

25 *SR*, 8 Mar. 1838.

26 Akenson, *Church of Ireland*, pp. 192–3.

27 Trevelyan, *British history in the nineteenth century*, pp. 278–9.

28 Akenson, *Church of Ireland*, p. 147.

29 *Cork Evening Herald*, 24 Aug. 1834.

30 *Christian Advocate*, 1 Sept. 1887.

31 Traill, *Diary*, pp. 29–31; Hickey, 'Four peninsular parishes', pp. 197–9.

32 *First report of his Majesty's Commissioners for inquiring into the condition of the poorer classes in Ireland, with Appendix (A) and supplement*, 27, [369] HC, 1835 (369), p. xxxii.

33 Connell, K. H., 'Illegitimacy before the Famine', *Irish peasant society*, Oxford, 1968, pp. 52–86.

34 Power, Canon, 'Place-names and antiquities of S.E. Cork', RIA *Proc.*, xxxiv (1918), sect. C, no. 9, p. 203.

35 Nolan, R., *Within the Mullet*, Galway, 1998, p. 89.

36 Poor Inquiry, *First report, Appendix (A)*, pp. 339– 66.

37 *CC*, 21 Dec. 1848.

38 Cummins, N. M., *Some chapters of Cork Medical history*, Cork, 1957, p. 83.

39 Traill, *Diary*, pp. 6, 9.

40 Poor Inquiry, *op. cit.*

41 *ibid.*, pp. 350–5.

42 Ó Ciosáin, N., 'Boccoughs and God's poor: deserving and undeserving poor in Irish popular culture', in *Ideology*, edited by Foley and Ryder, p. 98; Ó Ciosáin, N. (introduction), *Poverty before the Famine: County Clare 1835*, Ennis, 1996, p. 62.

43 Poor Inquiry, *First Report, Appendix* (A), 443–8.

44 Ó Gráda, C., 'Poverty, population and agriculture' in Vaughan, *New Hist. Ire.*, v, p. 117.

45 Poor Inquiry, *op. cit.*, p. 459.

46 Poor Inquiry, *First Report, Supplement to Appendix (A)*, p. 194.

47 Townsend H. & Fleming, May, cited in ffolliott, R., *The Pooles of Mayfield*, pp. 251–8.

48 *Supplement to Appendix (E), 115.* Poor Inquiry (Ireland) Appendix (E) – containing baronial examinations relative to food, cottages and cabins ... drinking, and supplement containing answers to questions ... circulated by the commissioners [37], HC, 1836, xxii, p. 1.

49 Coombes, J., 'Europe's first temperance society', *JCHAS*, lxxii, 1967, p. 51.

50 *SR*, 11 July 1838.

51 Kerrigan, C., 'The social impact of the Irish temperance movement', *Ir. Econ. Soc. Hist.*, xiv, 1987, p. 24.

52 Traill, *Diary*, p. 22.

53 Hall, *Ireland*, ii, pp. 426–7.

54 O'Brien, R. B., *Thomas Drummond, Life and Letters*, London, 1899, p. 246. O'Donnell, P., *The Irish faction fighters in the nineteenth century*, Dublin, 1975, pp. 41–2.

55 *SR*, 10 Aug. 1844.

56 O'Neill, T. P., 'The Irish workhouse during the great Famine', *Christus Rex*, xii, no. 1, 1958, p. 15.

57 *CC*, 5 Mar. 1839.

58 *CE*, 26 Jan. 1842.

59 Burke, H., *The people and the Poor Law in 19th century Ireland*, n. p., 1987, pp. 47–50.

60 *Parliamentary Gazetteer for Ireland 1844–45*, 240; for plan see Irish Architectural Archives, 73 Merrion Square, Dublin 2; 85 - 138 - 69

61 Thackeray, *Irish sketch book 1842*, p. 99.

62 *CE*, 21 Nov. 1842.

63 *CE*, 21 Dec. 1842.

64 *CE*, 21 Nov. 1842.

65 Inglis, B., 'O'Connell and the Irish press 1800–45,' *IHS*, viii, no. 29, March 1952, pp. 6–7.

66 Coombes, J., 'An historical memorial in Skibbereen', *Seanchas Chairbre*, No. 1, Dec. 1982, p. 39.

67 *CE*, 19 June 1843.

68 *CE*, 14 June 1843.

69 *CC*, 1 June 1843.

70 Lecky, W. E. H., *Leaders of public opinion in Ireland*, cited in MacDonagh, O., *The life of Daniel O'Connell, 1775–1847*, London, 1991, p. 406.

71 *ibid.*, p. 516.

72 *CE*, 23 Jun. 1843.

73 *Appendix (C)*, 65; Poor Inquiry, *Ireland*; [35] HC, 1836, xxx, p. 35.

74 *Topog. Dict. Ire*, ii, p. 560.

75 White, J. W., 'The age of O'Connell', in *The course of Irish history*, edited by Moody, T. W. & Martin, F. X., Cork, 1967, p. 260.

76 Ó Muirithe, D., 'O'Connell in Irish folk tradition' in *Daniel O'Connell*, edited by Nolan, K. B. & O'Connell, M. R., Dublin, 1984, p. 55.

77 MacDonagh, *O'Connell*, p. 598.

CHAPTER VI: AGRICULTURE, FISHERIES, AND POPULATION

1 O'Donovan, J., *The economic history of livestock in Ireland*, Cork, 1940, pp. 177–82.

2 Seebohm, M. E., *The evolution of the English Farm*, London, 1927, p. 278.

3 Whitlock, R., *A short history of the English farm*, London, 1965, p. 114.

4 Evans, E. E., *Irish folk ways*, London, 1957, p. 129.

5 Young, A., *Arthur Young's Tour in Ireland (1776–1779)*, edited by Hutton, A. W., 2 vols London and New York, 1892, ii, p. 131.

6 *Evidence taken before her Majesty's Commissioners of Inquiry in to the state of law and practice in respect to the occupation of land in Ireland*, pt. ii [616], HC, 1845, xx, pp. 955–6.

7 Poor Inquiry *(Ireland); App. (A.), supp.*, pp. 683–5.

8 Poor Inquiry, *App. (D.), supp.*, pp. 190–2.

9 Collins, *Evidence*, 1825, p. 96.

10 *SR*, 8 Jan. 1827.

11 Grace, D., *The Great Famine in Nenagh Poor Law Union, Co. Tipperary*, Nenagh, 2000, p. 184.

12 O'Brien, G., *Economic history of Ireland from the Union to the Famine*, pp. 54–56.

13 Coombes, J., 'Goleen parish', *Fold*, xv, no. 6, Dec. 1967, p. 14.

14 Fisher to central relief committee of Society of Friends, 12 Dec. 1846, *Extracts from correspondence*, i, Society of Friends Library, Dublin.

15 *CC*, 24 Oct. 1843.

16 *SR*, 28 Feb. 1839.

17 Hancock, W. N., *On the causes of the distress at Schull and Skibbereen during the famine in Ireland: a paper read before the statistical section of the British Association at Edinburgh, 2 August 1850*, Dublin, 1850.

18 *Cork Mercantile Chronicle*, 15, 17, 19, 21, Aug. 1838.

19 Langford, É., *Cape Clear Island: its people and landscape*, Cape Clear, 1999, p. 27.

20 *Evidence taken before her Majesty's commissioners of inquiry into the state of the law and practice in respect to the occupation of land in Ireland*, pt ii, appendix no. 32.

21 Hill, G., *Facts from Gweedore*, Dublin, 1853 ed., p. 6.

22 *Devon Comm., Evid.*, ii, pp. 947–65.

23 *CE*, 24 Feb., 1845.

24 Crotty, *Agricultural production*, pp. 51–5.

25 Evans, *Irish Folk ways*, pp. 233–240.

26 O'Brien, G., *The Economic History of Ireland from the union to the famine* (1972 ed.), p. 289.

27 Went, A. E. J., 'Pilchards in the south of Ireland', *JCHAS*, li, 1946, pp. 144–6.

28 Coombes, *Timoleague and Barryroe*, p. 54.

29 *First Annual report of the Commissioners of fisheries (Ireland)* [224], HC, 1843, xxviii, p. 17.

30 *CC*, 16 Jan. 1830.

31 Blake, J. A., *The sea fisheries of Ireland*, Waterford, 1868, pp. 32–6.

32 *First report of the commissioners of Irish fishery Inquiry* [77], HC, 1837, xxii, pp. 30–6.

33 *First annual report of the Commissioners of fisheries*, pp. 17–19.

34 *Second annual report of the Commissioners of fisheries (Ireland)* [502], HC, 1844, xxx, pp.

31–9.

35 *Fourth annual report of the Commissioners of fisheries, (Ireland)* [713], HC, 1846, xxii, pp. 61–2.

36 *Devon comm. evid.*, ii, 958.

37 Foster, T. C., *Letters on the condition of the people of Ireland*, London, 1847, pp. 432–5.

38 *Report of the committee for the relief of the distressed districts in Ireland*, [203], HC, 1823, xxi, p. 9.

39 Rogers, P., *Jonathan Swift*, New Haven and London, Appendix I.

40 Cadogan & O'Mahony, 'Shipwrecks', *Mizen Journal*, no. 7, 1999, pp. 76–84; for Callanan, see, *Gems of the Cork Poets: comprising the complete works of Callanan, Condon, Casey, Fitzgerald, and Cody*, n.p., n. d.

41 Webb, *H.M. Coast-guard*, p. 33.

42 Lewis, *Topog. Dict. Ire.*, ii, 311.

43 *Parliamentary Gazetteer for Ireland*, 2 vols, i, p. 546.

44 Hamilton, A. K., *Cornwall and its people*, London, 1988, p. 66.

45 Ó Criomhthain, T., *An t-Oiléanach*, Baile Átha Cliath, 1969, p. 224.

46 *Census Ire., 1821*, pp. 152–5; *Return of the population of the several counties of Ireland, as enumerated in 1831* [254], HC, 1833, xxxix, pp. 101–3; *Return of the Commissioners appointed to take up the census of Ireland for the year 1841* [504], HC, 1843, xxiv, pp. 176–7.

47 Parish records.

48 Poor Inquiry, appendix (A), pp. 441–2.

49 Drake, M., 'Population Growth and the Irish economy' in *The formation of the Irish economy*, edited by Cullen, L. M., Cork, 1969, 67.

50 Lee, J., 'Marriage and population in Pre-famine Ireland', *Economic History Review*, ser. 2, xxi, no. 2, Aug. 1968, p. 294.

51 Kennedy, Ell, Crawford & Clarkson (eds), *Mapping the Great Irish Famine : A Survey of the Famine Decades*, Dublin, 1999, p. 50.

52 Malthus, T. R., *An Essay on the principles of population*, London, 1973, pp. 44–5.

53 *Census Ire., 1841*, pp. lii–liii.

54 Connell, K. H., *The Population of Ireland, 1750–1845*, Oxford, 1950, p. 29.

55 Lee, J., 'Marriage and population', p. 294.

56 *CC*, 1 Jan. 1846.

57 Ó Gráda, C., 'Poverty, population and agriculture' in Vaughan, *New Hist. Ire.*, v, pp. 120–1.

58 Corkery, D., *The Hidden Ireland*, Dublin, 1975, ed., p. 23.

59 Miller, K. A., *Emigrants and exiles*, New York and Oxford, 1985, p. 29.

60 Kenny, K., *The American Irish: a history*, New York, 2000, p. 45.

61 Lower, A. R. M., *Great Britain's woodyard*, Montreal, 1973, pp. 242–3.

62 Adams, W. F., *Ireland and Irish emigration to the new world; from 1815 to the famine*, New Haven, 1932, p. 214.

63 King, J. A., *The Irish lumberman-farmers*, California, 1982, p. 50.

64 King, J. A., *The uncounted Irish in Canada and the United States*, Ontario, 1990, p. 69.

65 Poor Inquiry, *appendix (F) [supp.]*, pp. 720–21.

66 Fitzgerald & King, *Uncounted Irish*, pp. 60–1, 90, 292; King, *Lumberman-farmer*, p. 127. (The authors are descendants of the Harrigans/Fitzgeralds); Hamilton, W. D., *Old North Esk on the Miramichi*, Fredericton, 1979, pp. 191–2. The Harrigans changed their name from 'Horgan' when they arrived in Canada.

67 See Chapter XIII.

68 *Ford in Ireland, 1917–77*, n.d, n.p., pp. 4–5.

69 *Census Ire., 1841*, p. iv.

70 *Census Ire., 1851*, pt vi, General report, p. iv.

71 *Devon. comm. evid.*, p. 959.

72 *SR*, 20 May 1847.

73 'Castle and cabin: housing the people' in *Mapping the Great Irish Famine*, edited by Kennedy, Ell, Crawford & Clarkson, p. 76.

74 *Census Ire., 1841*, Munster, xvii; General Table, pp. 175–9.

75 Poor Inquiry, App. (E.), p. 182.

76 *Census. op. cit.*

77 Lewis, *Topog. Dict. Ire.*, ii, pp. 560–1; i, p. 132.

78 Woodham-Smith, C., *The Great hunger, Ireland 1845–49*, London, 1962, pp. 15–37.

79 Ó Tuathaigh, G., *Ireland before the famine*, Dublin, 1972, pp. 114–6.

80 Ó Gráda, C., *Black '47 and beyond: the great Irish famine in history, economy and memory*, New Jersey, 1999, p. 58.

81 Thomson, D., *England in the nineteenth century (1815–1914)*, London, 1971, p. 135.

82 McDowell, R. B., 'Ireland on the eve of the famine' in *The Great Famine: studies in Irish history*, edited by Edwards, R. D. & Williams, T. D., Dublin, 1956, p. 33.

83 Batterby, W. J., *The Complete Catholic Directory*, 1845, p. 34.

84 Froggatt, P., 'The response of the medical profession to the Great Famine' in *Famine: the Irish experience, 900–1900*, edited by Crawford, E. M., Edinburgh, 1989, p. 135.

85 Corish, P., *Maynooth College*, Dublin, 1995, p. 445.

86 Ordnance Survey, six inch map; Aughadown sheet no. 141; Ballydehob, 140; Schull, 139; Goleen, p. 147; Original edition, 1845.

87 *Names of places in Great Britain and Ireland in which a penny post is established*, 5 [86], HC, 1837, i, p. 507.

88 Strauss, E., *Irish Nationalism and British Democracy*, London, 1951, p. 79.

89 Kane, *Industrial resources*, pp. 406–7.

CHAPTER VII: ROTTING POTATOES AND ROAD-MAKING

1 Gray, P., *Famine, Land and Politics: British government and Irish society, 1843–1850*, Dublin, 1999, p. 109.

2 Woodham-Smith, *Hunger*, pp. 44–7.

3 O'Neill, T. P., 'The scientific investigation of the potato crop in Ireland, 1845–6', *IHS*, v, no. 18, Sept. 1946, pp. 123–7; Bourke, P. A., 'The scientific investigation of the potato blight, 1845–6' in *The visitation of God: the potato and the great Irish famine*, edited by Hill, J. & Ó Gráda, C., Dublin, 1993, pp. 129–140.

4 *CC*, 1 Nov. 1845.

5 MSS LS 3 C 7: 364, RIA; *SR*, 11 Dec. 1845; *CE*, 10 Dec. 1845.

6 Buttimer, C. G., 'Cloch sa leacht – an Gorta Mór i lámhscríbhinní déanacha na Gaeilge', in *Gnéithe den Ghorta* edited by Póirtéir, C., Baile Átha Cliath, 1995, pp. 89–90.

7 Relief Commission Papers 2/441/13, Z16066, Z15966 (hereinafter cited as RC).

8 *CC*, 1 Nov. 1845.

9 *CC*, 1 Nov. 1845.

10 *SR*, 28 Oct. 1845; *SR*, 12 Nov. 1845.

11 *CE*, 1 Dec. 1845.

12 *SR*, 11 Dec. 1845; *CE*, 10 Dec. 1845.

13 *SR*, 11 Dec. 1845.

14 Woodham-Smith, *Hunger*, pp. 57–62.

15 Distress Papers 1846, D 2671; Chief Secretary's Office (Distress Papers hereinafter cited as D).

16 A. McCabe to chief secretary, Lord Lincoln, 3 June 1846, D 1839.

17 Fisher to W. Stanley, 27 May 1846, D 2671.

18 9 Vic., C. 1–4.

19 D 2964.

20 *CE*, 31 Aug., 1846.

21 Thomas to Beamish, 21, 22 Aug.; Beamish to Trevelyan, 24 Aug. 1846; *Correspondence from July 1846 to January 1847 relating to measures adopted for the relief of distress in Ireland*, in

Irish University Press series of Parliamentary Papers on the Famine, Shannon, 1970, v, *p. 45* (hereinafter cited as P.P. *Famine*).

22 Trevelyan to Beamish, 28 Aug. 1846; *ibid.*

23 *CE,* 19 Aug. 1846; *SR,* 20 Aug. 1846.

24 Woodham-Smith, *Hunger,* pp. 106–113.

25 *SR,* 27 Aug. 1846.

26 *SR,* 8 Sept. 1846.

27 *CE,* 10 Aug. 1846.

28 Barrett to Bessborough, 5 Sept. 1846, D 4744.

29 Redington to Barrett, 14 Sept. 1846, D 4744.

30 Same to Same, 18 Sept. 1846, D 4748.

31 *SR,* 27 Sept. 1846.

32 Notter and Fisher to Routh, 7 Oct. 1846, D 6226.

33 Notter and Fisher to Bandon, 19 Oct. 1846, D 7096.

34 Bandon to Labouchere, 22 Oct. 1846, D 7098.

35 Labouchere to Bandon, 29 Oct. 1846, D 8036.

36 Notter and Fisher to Routh, 4 Nov. 1846, D 7144; *CC,* 7 Nov. 1846; *CE,* 8 Nov. 1846; *Dublin Evening Mail,* 8 Nov. 1846; *The Times,* 11 Nov. 1846.

37 *CE,* 20 Nov. 1846.

38 *SR,* 17 Sept. 1846; *CC,* 17 Sept. 1846.

39 *CC,* 17 Sept. 1846; *SR,* 17 Sept. 1846; *CE,* 19 Sept 1846.

40 *CE,* 28 Sept. 1846.

41 Donovan, 'Memoir of his experience during the Famine … ' in O'Rourke, J., *Irish famine of 1847,* Dublin, 1875, pp. 233–5; *Tablet,* 17 Oct. 1846.

42 P.P., *Famine,* v, p. 593.

43 Sen, A., *Poverty and famines; An essay on entitlement and deprivation,* Oxford, 1981, p. 49.

44 *SR,* 22 Oct. 1846.

45 *SR,* 22 Oct. 1846; *SR,* 5 Dec. 1846.

46 T. 64/364.

47 P.P., *Famine,* v, p. 286.

48 *CE,* 28 Oct. 1846.

49 Jones to Trevelyan, 14 Nov. 1846; Woodham-Smith, *Hunger,* p. 112.

50 D 7391.

51 D 10517, D 2195, D 2284, D 2195, 2284, D 2632.

52 *SR,* 24 Nov. 1846.

53 *CE,* 30 Nov. 1846.

54 *CE,* 28 Oct. 1846.

55 *SR,* 1 Dec. 1846.

56 *CE,* 7 August 1846.

57 P.P., *Famine,* vi, p. 139.

58 *SR,* 1 Dec. 1846.

59 D 7259, 1846.

60 Traill and Limrick to Hughes, 13 Sept. 1846, P.P., *Famine,* v, pp. 508–10.

61 O'Neill, T. P., 'The organisation and administration of relief' in Edwards & Williams, *Famine,* pp. 230–1.

62 Board of Works to T. Redington, 8 Dec. 1846; D 9478.

63 *SR,* 3 Dec. 1846.

64 *SR,* 24 Dec. 1846.

65 For map see Hickey, P., 'Four peninsular parishes', ii, map 8.

66 *CC,* 2 Jan. 1847.

67 *CC,* 17 Dec. 1846.

68 Ó Gráda, C., *Black '47 and beyond: the great Irish famine in history, economy, and memory,* New Jersey, 1999, p. 36.

CHAPTER VIII: SWIFT FAMINE AND TARDY RELIEF

1 *CC*, 29 Dec. 1846.

2 *Transactions of the central relief committee of the Society of Friends during the famine in Ireland in 1846 and 1847*, Dublin, 1852, pp. 33, 37.

3 Harrison, R. S., *Cork City Quakers: a brief history*, n. p., 1991.

4 Central Committee of the Society of Friends, *Correspondence*, i, 21.

5 *CC*, 29 Dec. 1846.

6 Inglis to Routh, 23 December, P.P., *Famine*, v, 843.

7 *CC*, 2 Jan. 1847.

8 *CC*, 9 Jan. 1847.

9 Ó Gráda, C., *An Drochshaol, Béaloideas agus amhráin*, Dublin, 1994, p. 44.

10 Cummins, Nicholas, 'Incidence of famine in Cork and county', *Mizen Journal*, no. 4, 1996, pp. 78–9.

11 *CC*, 29 Dec. 1846.

12 P.P., *Famine*, v, pp. 842–3.

13 Woodham-Smith, *Hunger*, p. 161.

14 P.P., *Famine*, v, p. 783.

15 *ibid.*, pp. 622, 875.

16 Parker to Jones, 31 Dec. 1846; *Correspondence relative to measures adopted for the relief of distress in Ireland* (Commissariat series), fourth part, 1847, P.P., *Famine*, v, pp. 876–7.

17 *ibid.*

18 *ibid.;* Trevelyan to Routh, 5 Jan. 1847.

19 Hewetson to Trevelyan, 30 Dec. 1846; Woodham-Smith, *Hunger*, p. 167.

20 O'Brien, J. B., 'Agricultural prices and living costs in Pre-famine Cork', *JCHAS*, lxxxii, no. 235, Jan.–Jun., 1977, p. 9.

21 O'Mahony, C., *The Maritime gateway to Cork*, Cork, 1986, p. 38.

22 Routh to Trevelyan, 7 Jan. 1847; Treasury minute, 8 Jan. 1847; P.P., *Famine*, v, pp 880–1.

23 Woodham-Smith, *Hunger*, p. 164.

24 Swanton to Routh, 6 Jan. 1847; *RC 9021*.

25 *SR*, 29 Dec. 1846.

26 Noble to Routh, 2 Feb. 1847; *RC 10151*.

27 Cummins, *op. cit.*, p. 79.

28 *Report of the British Relief Association for the relief of distress in the remote parishes in Ireland and Scotland*, London, 1849, pp. 15–18.

29 *SR*, 21 Jan. 1847.

30 *Report Brit. Rel. Assoc.*, p. 17.

31 *CC*, 13 Jan 1847.

32 *SR*, 12 Jan 1847.

33 Notter and Fisher to Bishop, 9 Jan. 1847; *RC 9026*.

34 Notter to Routh, 19 Jan. 1847; *RC 9413*.

35 Notter to Routh, 23 Jan. 1847; *RC 9757*.

36 *CC*, 28 Jan. 1847.

37 For such coffins see Hickey, P., 'Coffin is a reminder of famine times', *CE*, 24 Mar. 1987.

38 *CC*, 7 Jan. 1847.

39 Sweetnam to Limrick, 19 Jan. 1847, enclosed in Limrick to Routh 19 Jan. 1847; *RC 9360.*

40 *CE*, 6 Jan. 1847.

41 *CC*, 17 Dec. 1846.

42 *CE*, 13 Jan. 1847.

43 *Tablet*, 13 Feb. 1847

44 *SR*, 12 Jan. 1847.

45 *CE*, 18 Jan. 1847.

46 *SR*, 14 Jan. 1847.

47 Limrick to Routh, 9 Jan. 1847; *RC 8975*.

48 Limrick to Routh, 19 Jan. 1847; *RC* 9360
49 Bishop to Routh, 10 Jan. 1847; P.P., *Famine*, v. p. 920.
50 *CC*, 26 Jan. 1847. Anna Maria Lee was an aunt of the Protestant curate of Aughadown, J. Lee. *CC* 4 Feb. 1847.
51 Limrick to Routh, 17 Jan. 1847; *RC*, 9010.
52 *SR*, 14 Jan. 1847.
53 *SR*, 28 Jan. 1847.
54 *SR*, 14 Jan. 1847.
55 Bishop to Routh, 7 Jan. 1847; P.P., *Famine*, vii, p. 397.
56 *CE*, 3 Feb. 1847.
57 *Tablet,* 30 Jan. 1847.
58 *CE*, 20 Jan. 1847; *SR*, 24 Jan. 1847.
59 Nowlan, K. B., 'The political background' in Edwards & Williams, *Famine*, pp. 154–9.
60 *SR*, 19 Jan. 1847.
61 *Tablet*, 20 Feb. 1847; *CE*, 17 Feb. 1847.
62 Kinealy, C., *This great calamity; the Irish famine*, Dublin, 1994, p. 136.
63 *CC*, 6 Feb. 1847.
64 *CE*, 8 Feb. 1847.
65 Ó Faoláin, S., *King of the Beggars*, Dublin, 1970, p. 326.
66 Nowlan, *op. cit.*, pp. 159–61.
67 P.P. *Famine*, vii, p. 483.
68 Swanton to Relief Commission, 9 Feb. 1847; *RC*, 18786.
69 Swanton to Routh, 18 Feb. 1847; R. C., 11618.
70 Swanton to Relief Commission, 9 Feb. 1847; *RC*, 18786.
71 Triphook to Relief Commission, 14 Feb. 1847; *RC*, 11684.
72 Resolution of Committee, 15 Feb. 1847; R.C. 11618.
73 *Statement of the condition of the Skibbereen Poor Law union … 1 Feb. 1847; RC*, 15 Feb. 1847, no. 13014.
74 *Tablet*, 13 Feb. 1847
75 *CC*, 7 Feb. 1847.
76 *Report of Brit. Rel. Assoc.*, pp. 59–60.
77 Bishop to Routh, 7 Feb. 1847; Pigot to Routh, 10 Feb. 1847; P.P., *Famine*, vii, p. 483.
78 P.P. *Famine*, vii, p. 388.
79 *CC*, 9 Feb. 1847.
80 *SR*, 13 Feb. 1847.
81 *CC*, 21 Feb. 1847.
82 MacArthur W. P., 'Medical history of the Famine' in Edwards & Williams, *Famine*, pp. 263–315.
83 *CC*, 25 Feb. 1845.
84 Bishop to Trevelyan, 19 Feb. 1847, P.P., *Famine*, vii, p. 522; *CC*, 18 Feb. 1847.
85 P.P., *Famine*, vii, pp. 485–6.
86 O'Rourke, J., *The history of the great Irish famine of 1847 with notices of earlier famines*, Dublin, 1875, p. 408.
87 James Mahoney (1810–1879) was born in Cork, studied in Rome and settled in London; *Strictland's Dictionary of Irish Artists* (Dublin, 1978), pp. 88–90; Hickey, P., 'The visit of the artist, James Mahoney, to West Cork in 1847', *The O'Mahony Journal*, xx (1992), pp. 26–32.
88 Skelton, *Synge and his world*, 9; Hickey, P., 'J. M. Synge and his roots in West Cork', *CE*, 9 Feb. 1989.
89 *Illustrated London News*, 13, 20 Feb. 1847.
90 Crawford, M., 'The great Irish famine 1845–9; image versus reality', *Ireland: art into history*, Dublin, 1994, pp. 75–88.
91 *SR*, 21 Jan. 1847; *Transactions of central relief committee*, p. 58.

92 Caffin to Hamilton, 15 Feb. 1847; P.P., *Famine*, vii, p. 518.

93 *CC*, 18 Feb. 1847; *CE*, 24 Feb. 1847; 19 Feb. 1847; *The Times*, 26 Feb. 1847.

94 *FJ*, 19 Feb. 1847.

95 *Daily News*, 20 Feb. 1847.

96 *CC*, 18 Mar. 1847.

97 Kinealy, C. & Parkhill, T. (eds) *The famine in Ulster; the regional impact*, Belfast, 1997, p. 81.

98 P.P., *Famine*, vii, pp. 520–3.

99 Nicholls, George, *A history of the Irish Poor Law*, London, 1856, pp. 300, 306; McArthur, P., 'Medical History' in Edwards & Williams, *Famine*, p. 299.

100 *CC*, 18 Feb. 1847.

101 *SR*, 2 Mar. 1847.

102 *SR*, 6 Mar. 1847.

103 *Report Brit. Rel. Assoc.*, pp. 63–4.

104 *SR*, 6 Mar. 1847

105 P.P., *Famine*, vii, p. 180.

106 *CC*, 11 Mar. 1847

107 Burritt, E., *A Journal of a visit of three days to Skibbereen and its neighbourhood*, London, 1847, p. 10.

108 *CE*, 3 Mar. 1847.

109 *Nation*, 13 Mar. 1847.

CHAPTER IX: BRINGING FOOD AND PEOPLE TOGETHER

1 *SR*, 4 Mar. 1847

2 Traill, R., *The Jewish War of F. Josephus, a new translation*, London,1847.

3 *CC*, 5 Mar. 1847.

4 *Report Brit. Rel. Assoc.*, pp. 17, 63.

5 Ladd to Trevelyan, 19 Mar. 1847, T. 64/362A.

6 Limrick to Routh, 26 Mar. 1847, *RC*, 16006.

7 Swanton to Relief Commission, 17 Mar. 1847, *RC*, 17289

8 Freke to Routh, 26 Mar. 1847, *RC*, 16593.

9 Lord Dufferin and the Hon. G. F. Boyle, *Narrative of a journey from Oxford to Skibbereen during the Irish famine*, Oxford, 1847, p. 6.

10 Parker to Trevelyan, 1 Mar. 1847, T. 64/36213.

11 Trevelyan to Routh, 6 Mar. 1847, T. 64/3638.

12 Trevelyan to Jones, 4 Mar. 1847, Trevelyan, Private Letter Book, xii.

13 Trevelyan, C., *The Irish crisis*, London, 1848, pp. 45–7.

14 Grace, *Famine in Nenagh*, pp. 29, 97, 163.

15 P.P. *Famine* v, p. 460

16 CC, 1 Apr., 1847

17 *Illustrated London News*, 27 Feb. 1847.

18 F. F. Trench, 22 Mar. 1847, Trench, W. S., *Realities of Irish Life*, London, 1868, pp. 108, 396–7.

19 *CC*, 27 Apr. 1847; *SR*, 29 Apr. 1847.

20 Trench, 2 Apr. 1847, *Realities*, p. 403.

21 *CC*, 2 Mar. 1847.

22 *CC*, 27 Apr. 1847.

23 Trench, R. C., *Letters and memorials ed. by the author of Charles Lowder*, 2 vols, London, 1886, i, p. 289.

24 Trench, *Realities*, pp. 404–7.

25 Trench, *Letters*, p. 290.

26 Trevelyan to Hughes, 28 Apr. 1847, Private Letter Book, xii.

27 *CC*, 6 Apr. 1847.

28 *CC*, 20 Apr. 1847; *FJ*, 23 Apr. 1847.

29 *CC*, 22 Apr. 1847.

30 Morash, C., *The hungry voice: the poetry of the Irish famine*, Dublin, 1989, p. 245; also Hickey, P., 'Some famine letters of Dr Traill', *Mizen Journal*, no. 3, 1995, pp. 11–19.
31 *SR*, 6 Apr. 1847.
32 MacArthur, W. P., 'Medical history of the famine', Edwards & Williams, *Famine*, p. 296.
33 *Return of the number of paupers in the workhouses in each of the years 1844, 1845, 1846*, P.P., *Famine*, i, pp. 63–110.
34 Workhouse minute books.
35 Dufferin & Boyle, *Narrative*, pp. 14–15.
36 O'Donovan Rossa, D., *Rossa's recollections, 1838–1998*, New York, 1898, p. 167.
37 Póirtéir, C., *Famine echoes*, Dublin, 1995, p. 120.
38 *Census Ire., 1851*, pt. v; *Table of Deaths*, ii, *Containing the tables and index*, 32 (2087–II), HC, 1856, xxx, p. 67; *Appendix to the third report of the relief commissioners*, P.P., *Famine*, vii, p. 124
39 Woodham-Smith, *Hunger*, p. 243.
40 *CE*, 26 Apr. 1847; *CC*, 27 Apr. 1847.
41 *CE*, Apr. 1847
42 Kinealy, *Calamity*, pp. 139–40
43 Trevelyan MSS, films 1187, p. 8.
44 *CC*, 5 Oct. 1847.
45 *Second report of the relief commissioners …* , p. 3; P.P., *Famine*, vii, p. 83.
46 Donnelly, J. S., Jr, 'The soup-kitchens' in Vaughan, *New Hist. Ire.*, v, p. 309.
47 *SR*, 12 Apr. 1847
48 Gibbons to Jones, 19 Apr. 1847, enclosure, Jones to Trevelyan, 24 Apr. 1847, T. 64/363B.
49 *CE*, 12 May 1847.
50 Trevelyan 5 Apr. 1847, Private Letter Book, xiii.
51 *CE*, 12 May 1847.
52 *SR*, 8 May 1847.
53 *SR*, 20 May 1847.
54 *SR*, 22 May 1847.
55 *SR*, 20 May 1847.
56 *SR*, 5 June 1847.
57 Cíll Thiomáin NS, Mss 288.
58 *Report, Brit. Relief Assoc.*, p. 14.
59 *Census Ire., 1851*, pt v, i, p. 287.
60 *CC*, 23 Sept. 1847.
61 *SR*, 20 May 1847
62 *SR*, 22 May 1847.
63 *SR*, 10 June 1847; *CE*, 2 Aug. 1847.
64 Thomas to N. Ludlow Beamish, 22 Apr. 1847, *SR*, 1 May 1847.
65 *Tablet*, 19 Jun. 1847.
66 *CC*, 22 June 1847.
67 *SR*, 5 Oct. 1847.
68 O'Neill, 'The Administration of relief' in Edwards & Williams, *Famine*, p. 241.
69 O'Neill, *ibid.*, p. 240.
70 *SR*, 17 July 1847.
71 *CC*, 5 Oct. 1847.
72 O'Neill, *op. cit.*, p. 243.
73 Kineally, *Calamity*, pp. 368–9.
74 *Third report of the commissioners …* , P.P., *Famine*, viii, p. 113.
75 Woodham-Smith, *Hunger*, pp. 299–301.
76 Coombes, J., 'The Swanton's of Ballydehob', *Southern Star*, 12 Nov. 1978.
77 *CE*, 30 June 1847.
78 *CE*, 5 July 1847.

79 *SR*, 19 Aug. 1847.

80 Woodham-Smith, *Hunger*, p. 303.

81 *SR*, 2 Sept. 1847

82 O'Donovan, M. R., 'Goleen (Kilmoe) in famine times', *Mizen Journal*, no. 6, 1998, p. 63.

83 *Third report of relief commissioners*, P.P., *Famine*, viii, p. 351.

84 *CC*, 5 Oct. 1847.

85 *Final report of the Relief Commissioners* … , P.P., *Famine*, viii, p. 297.

86 Trevelyan, *Irish Crisis*, p. 64.

CHAPTER X: VOYAGE TO THE NEXT WORLD OR NEW WORLD

1 Sen, A., *Poverty and famines: an essay on entitlement and deprivation*, Oxford, 1981, pp. 78, 202.

2 Cited, O'Rourke, *Famine*, pp. 333–4.

3 *CC*, 29 July 1847.

4 Donovan, D., 'Observations on the peculiar disease to which the famine of last year gave origin and on the morbid effects of insufficient nourishment', *Dublin Medical Press*, xix, 1848, p. 69.

5 Trench, *Realities*, p. 110.

6 *Nation*, cited, *CC*, 1 June 1847; *Nation*, 29 Apr. 1847.

7 Mitchel, J., *Jail Journal*, Dublin, n.d., p. xxxviii.

8 O'Rourke, *Famine*, p. 252.

9 Cousens, S. H., 'Regional death rates in Ireland during the great famine, from 1846 to 1851', *Population Studies*, xiv, no. 1, July 1960, pp. 55–74.

10 Daly, M. E., *Social and economic history of Ireland since 1800*, Dublin, 1981, pp. 20–1.

11 Mokyr, J., *Why Ireland starved; a quantitative and analytical history of the Irish economy, 1800–45*, London, 1985, pp. 263–66.

12 Boyle, P. P., & Ó Gráda, C., 'Fertility trends, excess mortality, and the great Irish famine', *Demography*, xxiii, 1986, p. 555.

13 *Census 1851*, pt v, i, *General report*, li, p. 243.

14 *Nation*, 15 May; 3, 9, 19 Jun. 1847; for a death census see Grace, *Famine in Nenagh*, pp. 164–5.

15 *CC*, 5 Oct. 1847; *SR*, 5 Oct. 1847.

16 Donovan, 'Observations', p. 131.

17 *Papers relating to the relief of distress in Ireland, 1847–48*, P.P., *Famine*, ii, p. 22.

18 *CE*, 12 May 1847.

19 *CC*, 20 Mar. 1847.

20 The eastern part is in Dunmanway Union.

21 *CC*, 7 Jan. 1847.

22 Lee, J., 'On the accuracy of pre-Famine censuses' in *Irish population economy and society: essays in honour of the late K.H. Connell*, edited by Goldstrom, J. M. & Clarkson, L.A., Oxford, 1981, p. 54.

23 *Statement of the condition of the Skibbereen Union to the Relief Commissioners, February 1 1847*, pp. 2–3, RC 13014.

24 *CC*, 7 Jan. 1847; Bishop's report, P.P., v, *Famine*, p. 900.

25 *CC*, 15 Feb. 1847.

26 *CC*, 7 Feb. 1847.

27 *CC*, Mar. 22 1847.

28 Cousens, S. H., 'The regional variations in mortality during the great famine', *Proceedings of the RIA*, lxii, section c, no 3, 1963, p. 131.

29 Mokyr, *Why Ireland Starved*, p. 267.

30 *SR*, 17 July 1847.

31 Jaouen, J., *La Salette?: un signe, une grace*, Corps, n.d., p. 755.

32 *Census, 1851*, pt v, i. pp. 247, 253.

33 Fitzpatrick, D., 'Women and the great famine' in *Gender perspectives in nineteenth-century Ireland: Public and private spheres*, edited by Kelleher, M. & Murphy, J. H., Dublin, 1997, p. 55.

34 Boyle & Ó Gráda, 'Fertility trends', p. 555

35 *Census, 1851*, pt v, ii, 35; Hickey, P., 'Famine, mortality and emigration: a profile of six parishes in the Poor Law Union of Skibbereen, 1846–7' in *Cork: history and society*, edited by Flanagan, P. & Buttimer, C. G., Dublin, 1993, pp. 894–5.

36 Private correspondence.

37 Daly, M. E., *The famine in Ireland*, Dublin, 1986, pp. 100–1.

38 *CC*, 7 Feb. 1847.

39 Treuherz, F., *Homoeopathy in the Irish potato famine*, London, 1995, p. 102.

40 'Report on the epidemic fever in Ireland', *Dublin Quarterly Journal of Medical Science*, viii, 1849, p. 287.

41 *Irish Examiner*, 16 Oct. 2000.

42 RC, no. 24587, parish of Drimoleague.

43 *CC*, 27 Apr. 1847.

44 *Census, 1851*, pt v, ii, p. 240.

45 *ibid.*, pt v, ii, p. 470.

46 Donovan, 'Observations', p. 131

47 McCormick's letter, *Dublin Medical Press*, 17 Nov. 1847, p. 322.

48 Crawford, M., 'Scurvy in Ireland during the Great Famine', *Social history of medicine*, i, no. 3, 1988, p. 299.

49 P.P. *Famine*, vii, p. 397.

50 Dr Lamprey, 'Report on the epidemic fever in Ireland', *Dublin Journal of Medical Science*, vii, 1849, pp. 103–4.

51 Geary, L. M., 'Famine, fever and the bloody flux', in Póirtéir, *Famine*, p. 76.

52 Donovan, *op. cit.*, p. 276.

53 For deaths from diseases and starvation see, Kennedy, Ell, Crawford & Clarkson, *Mapping the great Irish famine*, pp. 104–124.

54 Murray Papers, Dublin Diocesan Archives.

55 *SR*, 20 May 1847.

56 *SR*, 24 Oct. 1847.

57 P.P., *Famine*, vii, p. 488.

58 Donovan, 'Observations'. p. 131.

59 *CE*, 30 July 1849.

60 *Illustrated London News*, 20 Feb. 1847.

61 *CC*, 16 Nov. 1848.

62 *Papers relative to emigration to British North American provinces, 1847–48*, 58–9, [50], HC, 1849, xlvii, pp. 254–56.

63 MacDonagh, O., 'Irish emigration to the United States of America and the British Colonies during the famine', in Edwards & Williams, *Famine*, pp. 366.

64 *Papers relative to emigration to British North American provinces, 1847–48*, pp. 58–9, [50], HC, 1849, xlvii, pp. 254–256.

65 Woodham-Smith, *Hunger*, p. 239.

66 Cushing, J. E., Casey, T. & Robinson, M., *A chronicle of Irish emigration to Saint John, New Brunswick 1847*, St John, 1979, p. 22.

67 Davin, N. F., *The Irishman in Canada*, Toronto, 1877, p. 541.

68 MacDonagh, 'Emigration', p. 488.

69 Whalen, J. M. , '"Allmost as Bad as Ireland": the experience of the Irish famine immigrant in Canada, St John, 1847', in *The untold story: the Irish in Canada*, edited by O'Driscoll, R. & Reynolds, L., Ontario, 1988, i, p. 163.

70 MacDonagh, *op. cit.*, p. 488

71 *SR*, 20 May 1847.

72 MacDonagh, *op. cit.* p. 321.

73 *FJ*, 12 Mar. 1847.

74 *CC*, 3 Apr. 1847.

75 Gibbons to Jones, 19 Apr. 1847, in Jones to Trevelyan; Treasury 64/363B.

76 Fitzpatrick, D., 'Emigration 1801–70' in Vaughan, *New Hist. Ire.*, v, p. 577.

77 Glazier, I. A. & Tepper, M., *The famine immigrants: lists arriving at the port of New York 1846–1851*, Baltimore, 1983.

78 *Papers emigration BNA*, p. 256.

79 Coombes, J., 'The cruise of the *Margaret Hughes*', *Cork Holly Bough*, 1974, p. 6.

80 *CC*, 21 Aug. 1847.

81 Fitzgerald & King, *Uncounted Irish*, p. 60.

82 Whalen, J. M., *op. cit*, p. 162.

83 *Tablet*, 3 July 1847.

84 MacDonagh, *op. cit.*, p. 371.

85 Whalen, *op. cit.*, p. 162.

86 Donovan, 'Observations', p. 130.

87 Cushing, Casey & Robinson, *Chronicle*, pp. 22–37.

88 *CC*, 4 Sept. 1847.

89 *CC*, 21 Sept. 1847.

90 MacDonagh, *op. cit.*, p. 366.

91 Daly, *Famine*, p. 107; O'Gallaghar, M., *Grosse Ile; gateway to Canada*, Quebec, 1984, p. 88; Whalen, *op. cit.*, p. 154.

92 O'Gallagher, *Grosse Ile*, p. 117.

93 Popham, J., 'Report on the endemic fevers … ', *Dublin Medical Press*, viii, 1849, p. 279.

94 *Quebec Mercury*, 18 Feb. 1847;

95 *ibid.*, 8 Apr. 1847.

96 *ibid.*, 23 Feb. 1847

97 *ibid.*, 2 Apr. 1847; 4 May 1847.

98 *ibid.*, 25 Mar. 1847.

99 *ibid.*, 2 Nov. 1847.

100 Donnelly, J. S., Jr, 'Excess mortality and emigration' in Vaughan, *New Hist. Ire.*, v, pp. 351, 355; see also, Donnelly, J. S., *The great Irish potato famine*, Gloustershire, 2001, pp. 169–186.

101 Cousens, S. H., 'The regional pattern of emigration during the great famine, 1846–1851, *Transactions and papers of the Institute of British Geographers*, xxviii, 1981, p. 87.

CHAPTER XI: POT OF SOUP OR WORD OF GOD?

1 Cited, Fanning, R., 'The great enchantment': uses and abuses of modern Irish history' in *Interpreting Irish history*, edited by Brady, C., Dublin, 1994, p. 146.

2 See passim, Branach, N. R., 'Edward Nangle and the Achill Island mission', *History Ireland*, viii, no. 3, Autumn 2000, pp. 35–8.

3 *CE*, 4 Sept. 1846; *CC*, 1 Sept. 1846; for controversy between O'Grady and Fr Enright see Murray Papers, Dublin Diocesan Archives.

4 Thompson, D. P., *A brief account of the change in religious opinion now taking place in Dingle and the west of County Kerry*, Dublin, 1846, p. 28.

5 Whelan, I., 'The stigma of souperism', in Póirtéir, *Famine* , p. 135.

6 P.P. *Famine*, vii, p. 482.

7 St Vincent's Seminary was where the Mercy Hospital now is. It moved to Farranferris in 1887.

8 *CE*, 8 Feb. 1847; *Nation*, 13 Feb. 1847; *Tablet*, 13 Feb. 1847.

9 Limrick to Routh, 26 March 1847; *RC* 16006.

10 Somerville-Large, Peter, *The coast of West Cork*, London, 1974, p. 128.

11 Bowen, D., *The Protestant Crusade in Ireland, 1800–70*, Dublin, 1978, p. 186.

12 *Sunday Tribune*, 29 Sept. 1985; Also Gus Smith, *Sunday Independent*, 29 Sept. 1985; for my objections to this representation of Laurence O'Sullivan and Harris' reply see, the *Sunday Tribune*, 13, 27 Oct., 3 Nov. 1985 ; Hickey, P., 'Laurence O'Sullivan P.P. Goleen (1828–48) and *Souper Sullivan* by Eoghan Harris', *Fold*, Apr. 1986; *Sunday Times*, 23 July 1995.

13 Whelan, 'Souperism', in Póirtéir, *Famine* , p. 135.

14 *CC*, 18 Feb. 1847.

15 *Illustrated London News*, 22 Feb. 1847.

16 *Tablet*, 20 Feb. 1847.

17 Whelan, J. A., 'Where Reagan's grandparents married', *Evening Echo*, 25 Nov. 1980; Fr Cotter donated the land to found the Convent of Mercy, Bantry.

18 *Tablet*, 6 Mar. 1847

19 *Tablet,* 13 Mar. 1847.

20 Corish, P. J., *Maynooth College, 1795–1995*, Dublin, 1995, pp. 441–485.

21 *CE*, 26 Feb. 1847.

22 *CE*, 21 May 1847.

23 Kerr, D. A.,'*A Nation of Beggars'?: Priests, people, and politics in famine Ireland, 1846–1852*, Oxford, 1994, p. 171.

24 *CE*, 20 Sept. 1847.

25 *Tablet*, 19 Jun., 3 July 1847.

26 [Carson, J. B.] *Forty years in the church of Ireland or the pastor, the parish, and its people, from 1840 to 1880*, London, n.d., p. 7.

27 Fisher, 'A memorial of the Irish famine of 1845–7' cited, Carson, *Parson*, p. 58.

28 Brady, *Clerical records*, i, p. 176.

29 A list of these has been lost recently; Canon Hilliard, a former rector, told me that he read it.

30 O'Casaide papers; MS 10692, NLI.

31 Mackey, M., 'An account of local famine relief in the Parish of Kilmoe 1847–1848 from the John Coursey manuscript', *Mizen Journal*, no. 7, 1999, p. 67.

32 Table 23, p. 252.

33 *Census Ire. 1851*, pt i, ii, pp. 187, 429, 499.

34 *Fifteenth report of the commissioners of national education in Ireland*, 1848 [1066] HC, 1849 xxiii, p. 71, Appendix, xx.

35 *Annual report of the Church Education Society for 1848*, Dublin, 1849, p. 48.

36 Foley, D., *Missionary tour through the south of Ireland undertaken for the Irish Society*, Dublin, 1849, p. 61.

37 *CE*, 2 Feb. 1848.

38 Island and Coastal Society; Minute Book, 1846–93; MSS Library, Trinity College.

39 Ó Mainín, M., 'Bíoblóireacht agus gorta' in *An gorta mór*, edited by Ó Fiannachta, P., An Daingean, 1997, p. 61.

40 *CC*, 20 Oct. 1849: Lankford, *Cape Clear*, pp. 85–6.

41 *Irish Intelligence*, iv, p. 4.

42 *ibid.*

43 Troy, B., *Famine industry in Ballycotton: Four reports on progress*, privately published.

44 Bolster, E., *A history of the diocese of Cork; the episcopate of William Delany, 1847–1886* Cork, 1993, p.8–9, 16.

45 *CE*, 12 Mar. 1883.

46 Reilly, A. J., *Fr John Murphy, Famine priest*, Dublin, 1963, p. 73.

47 Davitt, Thomas, 'Saint Vincent's Seminary, Cork I', *Colloque*, no. 10, Autumn 1984, pp. 294–5.

48 Minutes of Provincial Council, 1848, Provincial Archives, 4 Cabra Rd, Dublin.

49 From Mullinahone, County Tipperary; Roger's father had been a convert from Protestantism; Comerford, R. V., *Charles J. Kickham*, Dublin, 1979, p. 14.

50 Cullen, *Vincentian foundations*, p. 48.

51 Correspondence Books, 1848, Provincial Archives, *op. cit.*, p. 18.

52 Minutes of Provincial Council, *op. cit.*

53 *Bulletin de Saint Vincent de Paul, 1848–49*, Paris, 1849, p. 157.

54 Dowley to Etienne, 4 Oct. 1848; Congregation of the Mission Archives, Rome.

55 Hickey, 'Four peninsular parishes', p. 515–6

56 Larkin, E., 'The devotional revolution in Ireland, 1850–1875', *The historical dimensions of Irish Catholicism*, Dublin, 1997.

57 *Bulletin, 1848–49*, p. 158.

58 *Fourth Report of the Society of St Vincent de Paul (Ireland) 1848*, p. 21.

59 *Thirty-first report of the Irish Society, 1849*; 16, Halliday Pamphlets, no. 2060.

60 *Fifth report of the Society of St Vincent de Paul (Ireland) 1849*, 18, Halliday Pamphlets, no. 2161.

61 *ibid.*, p. 19.

62 *CC*, 30 Nov. 1848.

63 *ibid.*, 12 Oct. 1848.

64 NBR 2/8, folio 202; Parish records, Goleen, Kilmurry, Douglas. O'Sullivan probably came to Goleen in 1821 when St Mary's Seminary, Cork, where he had been teaching was closed.

65 Ó Mainín, '*Bíoblóireacht agus Gorta*', 61; Murphy, J. H., 'The role of Vincentian parish missions', *Irish Historical Studies*, xxiv, no. 94, Nov. 1984, p. 60.

66 Foley, *Missionary tour*, p. 63.

67 *Irish Intelligence*, v, p. 198.

68 A. B., 'Fragments of a tour in Ireland in the autumn of 1849', *Irish Intelligence*, iii, pp. 51–5.

69 Carson, *Parson*, p. 15.

70 Ó Mainín, M., 'Achrann creidimh in Iarthar Dhuibhneach', Ó Cíosáin, M., *Céad bliain, 1871–1971*, Baile an Fheirtéaraigh, 1973, p. 44.

71 Bowen, *Protestant crusade*, p. 69.

72 *Irish Intelligence*, iv, pp. 90–1.

73 Barry, P. C., 'The legislation of the Synod of Thurles 1850', *Studies*, xxvi, No. 2, Apr. 1959, pp. 33–5.

74 *CC*, 14 May 1850.

75 *CC*, 29 Apr. 1851.

76 *CC*, 6 May 1851.

77 *CC*, 20 May 1851.

78 Parish records, Coachford.

79 *CE*, 10 Jan. 1849.

80 *CE*, 1 July 1850.

81 *ibid.*

82 *ibid.*

83 *CC*, 11 Oct. 1851.

84 *CC*, 22 May 1852.

85 National School folklore returns, Dunmanus NS, 440–3; McCarthy, B. G., 'Black Eagle of the North, the story of Archdeacon John Murphy', *Studies*, xxxviii, no. 1, Mar. 1949, p. 55.

86 Ó Mainin, M., 'Achrann creidimh', Ó Cíosáin, *Céad bliain*, p. 44.

87 Lankford, *Cape Clear Island*, pp. 82–3.

88 *Seventh annual report of the Church Education Society for Ireland*, Dublin, 1846, pp. 51–52. *Eighth annual report of the Church Education Society for Ireland*, Dublin, 1848, pp. 62–63. *Ninth annual report of the Church Education Society for Ireland*, Dublin, 1849, pp. 47–48. *Tenth annual report of the Church Education Society for Ireland*, Dublin, 1850, pp. 58–60. *Eleventh annual report of the Church Education Society for Ireland*, Dublin, 1851, pp. 54–56. *Twelfth annual report of the Church Education Society for Ireland*, Dublin, 1852, pp. 53–54. *Thirteenth annual report of the Church Education Society for Ireland*, Dublin, 1853,

pp. 51–52.

89 *Tenth annual report*, p. 10.

90 *Eleventh annual report*, pp. 11–12.

91 Akenson, *Irish educational experiment*, pp. 290–1.

92 *CC*, 7 June 1851.

93 Preachers's Book, Ballydehob church.

94 Ó Beolain, A., 'Rev. Canon James Goodman 1826–1896, *Séamus Goodman: A Shaol agus a Shaothar*', Ó Fiannachta, P., *An Canonach Goodman*, Baile an Fheirtéaraigh, pp. 48–50.

95 *Irish Intelligence*, v, 215, p. 179.

96 Ó Beoláin, 'Goodman', pp. 58–62.

97 Preacher's Book, *op. cit.*

98 Ó Mainín, '*Is mairg do thréig an t-aon chreideamh cóir'*, Ó Ciosáin, *Céad Bliain*, pp. 63–5; Ó Mainín, '*Bíoblóireacht agus an Gorta'*, p. 68; Goodman's poem is Ms 5345B, National Library of Wales.

99 Kerr, '*Nation of Beggars'?* pp. 308–9.

100 *CE*, 8 Mar. 1852.

101 *CE*, 17, 31, 1852.

102 One of these handbills survives in the parish records of Kilmurry to which parish Fr. Foley was transferred in 1867.

103 *The Fold*, xiv, no. 4, October 1966, p. 30.

104 *Irish Intelligence*, v, p. 17.

105 Brady, *Clerical Records*, i, pp. 176–7.

106 *Census of Ireland for the year 1861, pt iv: Reports and tables relating to the religious professions, education, and occupations of the people*, vol. iv, 190, 198, [3204–111], HC, 1863, p. lx.

107 *ibid.*, p. 9.

108 Ó Mainín, 'Achrann creidimh in Iarthar Dhuibhneach', Ó Cíosáin, *Céad bliain*, pp. 53–56.

109 Ó Mainín, *Bíoblóireacht agus Gorta*, p. 61; also private correspondence.

110 Whelan, I., 'Edward Nangle and the Achill Mission, 1834–1852' in '*A various county'*, *Essays in Mayo history, 1500–1900*, edited by Gillespie, R. & Moran, G., Westport, 1987, pp. 132–3.

111 Lankford, Cape Clear, p. 87.

112 Copy of application in my possession.

113 *Irish Intelligence*, i, p. 91.

114 MacSuibhne, M., *Famine in Muskerry: an Drochshaol*, Midleton, 1997, p. 60.

115 Cullen to Cardinal Fransoni, Sept. 1851, quoted, Mac Suibhne, P., *Paul Cullen and his contemporaries*, 4 vols, Naas, 1965, iii, pp. 90–1.

116 See Chapter III.

117 Bowen, *Protestant Crusade*, p. 271.

118 Brady, *Clerical Records*, i, pp. 175, 284, 495, 461.

119 Larkin, *op. cit.*, p. 651.

120 Brady, *Clerical records*, i, pp. 175, 284, 495, 461.

121 See Chapter III.

122 Quigley, E. J., 'Grace abounding, a chapter in Irish History', *Irish Ecclesiastical Record*, xx, July–Dec. 1922, p. 561.

123 Bowen, *Protestant crusade*, pp. 249–50.

124 Bowen, D., *Souperism: myth or reality: a study in souperism*, Cork, 1970, p. 234.

125 Quoted by Trench, W. S., *Realities of Irish Life*, pp. 400–1.

126 *SR*, 17 July 1847.

127 *CE*, 4 Sept. 1848.

128 *Tablet*, 27 Mar. 1847.

129 O'Neill, T. P., 'Sidelights on souperism, *Irish ecclesiastic record*, fifth series, lxxxi, Jan.–Jun. 1949, p. 50.

130 Bowen, *Protestant crusade*, pp. 188–9

131 Kerr, 'Nation of beggars?', p. 214.

132 Trench, *Realities of Irish life*, p. 402.

133 Daly, *Famine*, p. 68.

134 Carson, *Parson*, pp. 31, 36.

135 Galvin, *Black blight*, p. 228.

Chapter XII: Towards Local 'Pauper Home Rule'

1 Woodham-Smith, *Hunger*, p. 308; Kinealy, *Calamity*, pp. 177, 181.

2 This William Gregory was a son of William Gregory, under-secretary (1821–31).

3 O'Rourke, *Famine*, p. 332.

4 *CC*, 23 Mar. 1875; he was a classmate of Bishop Delany in Maynooth and then studied in the Irish College in Rome.

5 *Final report of the Board of Works*, P.P., *Famine*, viii, pp. 379–85.

6 Griffiths, A. R. G., 'The Irish Board of Works in the Famine Years', *Historical Journal*, xiii, no. 4, Dec. 1970, p. 652.

7 O'Regan, L., 'Anna Parnell in West Cork', *Southern Star*, 23 Nov. 1991.

8 O'Donovan Rossa, *Recollections*, p. 118.

9 Field Books, 1850, West Carbery, Valuation Office; Collins, J. F., 'Influence of local circumstances on Land Valuation in South-West Cork in the mid 19th century', *Mizen Journal*, no. 7, 1999, p.139; for map see Hickey, 'Four peninsular parishes', p. 330.

10 *Return of agriculture produce in Ireland in the year 1847*, pt i; *Crops* [923], HC, 1847–8, pp. lvii, vi.

11 *Return of agriculture produce 1849* [1245], HC, 1850, pp. li, vi.

12 *CE*, 10 Sept. 1847; *Nation*, 18 Sept. 1847.

13 *Nation*, 25 Sept. 1847.

14 Russell/Anstey; *Nation*, 5 Oct. 1847; *Tablet*, 9 Oct. 1847; *CE*, 4 Oct. 1847; see passim, Donnelly, J. S., Jr, ''Irish property must pay for Irish poverty': British public opinion and the Great Irish Famine' in *Fearful realities: New perspectives on the Famine*, edited by Morash C. & Hayes, R., Dublin, 1996.

15 MacDonagh, O., 'The economy and society', in Vaughan, *New Hist. Ire.*, v, p. 219.

16 Woodham-Smith, *Hunger*, pp. 302–6.

17 Mitchel, J., *The last conquest of Ireland (perhaps)*, Glasgow, Manchester, Liverpool, n.d., p. 123.

18 *CE*, 4 Feb. 1848.

19 Cited, Kerr, 'Nation of beggars?', preliminaries.

20 There was a severe shortage of food in Trujillo, Peru, in 1991 and the priests and nuns of the Cork and Ross mission fed almost 30,000 people by means of soup-kitchens. Yet they received a death-threat from the Maoist organisation, *Sendero Luminoso*, *Muerte a los imperalistas Irlandeses*, 'Death to the Irish imperialists'. The *Sendero* held that if food and the means of its production were distributed justly there would not have been any hunger in the first instance. In the eyes of these revolutionaries the Irish were only collaborating with, and propping up the internationalist capitalist system which was robbing the country in the same way as Mitchel and the *Nation* maintained that England was robbing Ireland. Source: conversations with Murphy J., Brophy, R. and Crowley, E. on the mission.

21 *CE*, 2 Feb., 1847.

22 *CE*, 26 Mar. 1847.

23 Fogarty, L., *James Fintan Lalor*, Dublin 1918, pp. 8–10, 17.

24 'To create and to foster public opinion in Ireland and to make it racy of the soil'.

25 Nowlan, K. B., 'The political background', Edwards & Williams, *Famine*, pp. 170–1.

26 *SR*, 30 Nov. 1847.

27 *CE*, 4 Nov. 1847.

28 *SR*, 30 Nov. 1847.

29 *CE*, 17 Nov. 47.

30 *Tipperary Vindicator*, 16 May 1849.

31 Woodham-Smith, *Hunger*, 409.

32 Blacker, W., *Prize essay, addressed to the agricultural committee of the Royal Dublin Society, on the management of landed property in Ireland*, Dublin, 1834.

33 *SR*, 29 Nov. 1847.

34 *SR*, 16 Sept. 1847.

35 *SR*, 4 Mar. 1847; *SR*, 23 Sept.; 29 Nov. 1847.

36 Donovan, 'Observations', 129.

37 *CE*, 20 Aug. 1847; *CC*, 24 Aug. 1847.

38 *CC*, 24 Aug. 1847.

39 *CE*, 10 Sept. 1847.

40 *SR*, 23 Sept. 1847.

41 *CC*, 25 Sept. 1847.

42 *SR*, 23 Sept. 1847.

43 *CE*, 10 Sept. 1847.

44 *CC*, 16, 17 Nov. 1847.

45 *CC*, 23 Dec 1847.

46 *Sixteenth report of the Commissioners of Public Works in Ireland*, 24 [983] HC, 1847–8, xxxvii, p. 213.

47 *CE*, 11 Mar. 1847; 5 May 1848; Lankford, *Cape Clear*, p. 64.

48 Ó Gráda, C., *Ireland before and after the famine,* Manchester, 1988, p. 119.

49 Lankford, *Cape Clear*, p. 40.

50 Report of J. R. Barry and W. J. Ffennell to Commissioners of Public Works, 7 Feb. 1848, *Sixteenth report of the Commissioners of Public Works in Ireland*, pp. 47–8.

51 *Appendix to the sixteenth report of the Commissioners of Public Works*, pp. 58–9.

52 *CE*, 14 Feb. 1848.

53 O'Neill, T. P., 'The Society of Friends and the Great Famine', *Studies*, xxxiv, no. 154, 1950, p. 206.

54 *Transactions of the central relief committee of the Society of Friends*, pp. 406–15.

55 *CC*, 22 Aug. 1848.

56 Marshall to the Poor Law Commissioners, 4 Nov. 1847, *Papers relating to proceedings for the relief of distress, and state of the unions and workhouses in Ireland*, P.P., *Famine*, ii, p. 224.

57 Commissioners to Marshall, *State of Unions*, P.P., *Famine*, ii, p. 225.

58 Woodham-Smith, *Hunger*, pp. 314, 318.

59 Marshall to Commissioners, 30 Nov. 1847, P.P., *Famine*, iii, pp. 378.

60 *State of Unions*, P.P., *Famine*, ii, p. 925.

61 Ó Gráda, *Black '47*, p. 75.

62 Marshall to Commissioners, 2 Dec. 1847; P.P., *Famine*, ii, pp. 926–31.

63 *Report of British Relief Association*, p. 31.

64 Marshall to Commissioners, 2 Dec. 1847, P.P, *Famine*, ii, p. 929.

65 Haly, secretary of British Relief Association, *ibid.*

66 Marshall to Commissioners, 22 Dec. 1847, P.P., *Famine*, ii, p. 931.

67 *CE*, 5, 9 Feb. 1848.

68 *CE*, 19 Feb. 1847.

69 Marshall to Commissioners, 17 Feb. 1848, P.P., *Famine*, iii, p. 530.

70 O'Connor, J., *The workhouses of Ireland*, Dublin, 1995, p. 177.

71 Marshall to Commissioners, 17 Mar. 1848, P.P., *Famine*, iii, p. 535.

72 *State of the Unions*, P.P. *Famine*, iii, pp. 538–40.

73 *CE*, 4 Feb. 1848.

74 Marshall to Commissioners, 4 Feb., 30 Mar. 1848, *State of unions*, P.P. *Famine*, iii, p. 537.

75 *Census Ire., 1851*, pt v, ii, p. 32.

76 Marshall to Commissioners, 30 March 1848; *State of Unions*, P. P. *Famine*, iii, p. 537.

77 *CC*, 28 Mar. 1848.

78 *CE*, 3 May 1848.

79 CE, 22 May 1848.

80 *CE*, 26 Jun. 1848.

81 *State of the workhouses*, P.P., *Famine*, iii, p. 532.

82 O'Neill, 'Administration of relief', Edwards & Williams, *Famine*, p. 252.

83 CE, 21 Oct. 1846, 14 Dec. 1847; *SR*, 11 Dec. 1847.

84 O'Neill, *op. cit.*

85 *CE*,18 Dec. 1848.

86 Kinealy, *Calamity*, p. 263.

87 *CE*, 22 May 1848.

88 *CE*, 14 May 1848.

89 *CE*, 23 Feb. 1848.

90 Mitchel, J., *Jail Journal*, p. xxxix.

91 *CE*, 9 Feb. 1848.

92 *CE*, 22 Mar. 1847.

93 Ó Gráda, C., *Ireland: a new economic history, 1780–1939*, Oxford, 1994, p. 204.

94 *ibid.*; *Census Ire. 1851*, pt vi, General report, p. 243.

95 *CE*, 21 Oct. 1846; 14 Dec. 1847.

96 O'Neill, *op. cit.*

97 Donovan, 'Observations', p. 67.

98 *Census Ire. 1851*, pt vi, General report, p. 243.

99 O'Day, A. & Stevenson, J. (eds) *Irish historical documents*, Dublin, 1992, p. 64.

100 Lowe, W. J., 'Policing famine Ireland', *Eire Ireland*, xxix, no. 4, 1994, p. 51.

101 Bishop to Marshall, 21 Jan. 1848; Bishop to Admiral, 27 Feb., 2, 23, 27 Apr.; War Office, 63/103.

102 Mitchel, J., *Jail Journal,* Dublin, n.d., pp. 3, 14, 16.

103 *CC*, 22 Mar. 1848.

104 Rossa, *Recollections*, p. 309.

105 Duffy, C. G., *My life in two hemispheres*, London, 1903, ii, p. 243.

106 A. M. Sullivan, a native of Bantry and brother of T. D. Sullivan, was editor and proprietor of the *Nation* 1857–76.

107 Ó Maidín, P., 'Patriot and Benefactor in West Cork' [McCarthy Downing], *CE,* 11 Jan. 1977.

108 Rossa, *Recollections*, p. 251.

109 *CE*, 29 May 1848.

110 Woodham-Smith, *Hunger,* p. 318.

111 *CE,* 4 Sept. 1848.

112 *CC*, 27 March 1847.

113 Kerr, *'Nation of beggars'?* p. 336.

114 *Nation*, cited *CC*, 1 Jun. 1847.

115 Mitchel, *Last conquest*, 112; see *passim*, Ó Ciosáin, N., *'Dia, bia agus Sasana: an Mistéalach agus* íomhá *an ghorta*, Pórtéir, C. (eag.), *Gnéithe den nGorta*, Dublin, 1995, pp. 151–163.

116 O'Neill, T. P., 'Food problems during the great famine', *The journal of the Royal Society of Antiquaries of Ireland*, lxxxii, 1952, p. 108.

117 Bourke, 'Grain Trade', in *The visitation of God*, Hill & Ó Gráda, p. 168.

118 *SR*, 20 May 1847.

119 Solar, P., 'The great famine was no ordinary famine' in Crawford, *Famine*, p. 123–5.

120 Bourke, *op. cit.*, p. 165.

121 Donnelly, J. S., Jr, 'The administration of relief, 1846–7' in Vaughan, *New Hist. Ire.*, v, p. 297–8.

122 *CC*, 28 Oct. 1848; *Tablet*, 25 Nov. 1848 citing *SR*, For exports from Cork 1846–7 see *SR*, 9 Dec. 1848.

123 Bourke, 'Grain Trade', in *The visitation of God*, Hill & Ó Gráda, p. 168.

124 Dufferin & Boyle, *Narrative*, p. 5.

125 Bourke, *op. cit.*, p. 165.

126 Kineally, *Calamity*, p. 354.

127 Mac Suibhne, P., *Paul Cullen and his contemporaries*, Naas, 1971, i, p. 291.

128 Ó Murchadha, C., 'The onset of Famine: Co. Clare, 1845–46', *The other Clare*, xviv, 1997, p. 50.

129 Ó Murchadha, C., *Sable wings over the land; Ennis, County Clare and its wider community during the Great Famine*, Ennis, 1998, p. 78.

130 Coakley, D., *The Irish school of medicine: outstanding practitioners*, Dublin, 1988, p. 92.

131 McDowell, 'Ireland on the eve of the famine', Edwards & Williams, *Famine*, p. 34.

132 Ní Úrdail, M., *The scribe in eighteenth- and nineteenth-century Ireland: motivations and milieu*, Münster, 1997, p. 122.

133 Woodham-Smith, *Hunger*, p. 377.

134 Ó Gráda, *Ireland before/after famine*, p. 85; O'Connor, *Workhouses*, p. 177; Bourke, 'Grain Trade', p. 165.

135 Murphy, I., 'Kilkee and its neighbourhood during the second year of the great famine', *North Munster Antiquarian Journal*, xxiii, 1981, p. 87.

136 *Second annual report of the commissioners for the administration of the laws for the poor in Ireland*, Dublin, 1849, p. 14.

137 *SR*, 17 May 1849.

138 *CE*, 24 May 1849.

139 *CE*, 4 July 1849

140 *Report of the commissioners of health, Ireland, on the epidemics of 1846 to 1852*, P.P. *Famine*, vii, p. 37.

141 *First report of the commissioners appointed to enquire into the numbers and boundaries of the poor law unions in Ireland*, 7–8 [1015], HC, 1849, xxiii, p. 26.

142 *CE*, 13 Nov. 1849.

143 *Report of the Irish Poor Law Commissioners on the measures for the carrying into effect of the recommendations of the Boundary Commissioners* [1162] HC, 1850, xxvi, p. 2.

144 *CC*, 28 Oct. 1849.

145 *Third annual report of the Commissioners for administrating the laws for the relief of the poor in Ireland* [984], HC, 1850, xxvii, p. 136; *Fourth annual report of the Commissioners for administrating the laws for the relief of the poor in Ireland* [498], HC, 1851, xxii, 100, p. 147.

146 Mackey, M., 'Schull Workhouse', *Mizen Journal*, no. 8, 2000, p. 45.

147 O'Connor, *op. cit.*, p. 178.

148 Trevelyan, *Crisis*, cited Ó Cathaoir, *Famine Diary*, Dublin, 1999, p. 163.

CHAPTER XIII: EMERGENCE OF POST-FAMINE SOCIETY

1 Fogerty, L., *James Fintan Lalor: patriot and political essayist, 1807–1849*, Dublin and London, 1918, p. 10.

2 Table 5; *Thirteenth report of the Commissioners of national education in the year 1846*, pp. 69–74 [832], HC, 1847–8, xxix, p. 219; *Fifteenth report … for the year 1848*, pp. 66–73 [1066], HC1849, xxxiii, p. 101. *Sixteenth report … for the year 1849*, pp. 50–54 [1231–11], HC, 1850, xxv, p. 141. *Seventeenth report … for the year 1850*, pp. 165–78 [1405], HC, 1851, xxxiv; *Eighteenth report … for the year 1851*, pp. 133–50 [1582], HC, 1852, xxxiii. *Nineteenth report … for the year 1852*, 158–167 [1688], xliii, pt i, p. 1.

3 *CC*, 25 Feb. 1847.

4 *Fourteenth report … for the year 1847*, p. 85.

5 County Register Books, vol. i, folio 141.

6 *Sixteenth report … for the year 1849*, p. 76.

7 Table 23, p. 252.

8 *National Board Applications* (1845–49), numbers 110, 121, 122, 120 and 109 respectively (hereinafter cited as *NBA* (1845–49)).

9 *ibid.*, numbers 138, 115.

10 *NBA* (1849–55), numbers 185, 229, 178, 181.

11 *CRB*, ii, folio 201. It was here that Dean Sheehan, founder of the Cork Historical and Archaeological Society, went to school; *NBA*, no. 109.

12 *NBA* (1845–49), numbers, 110, 119.

13 *NBA* (1845–49), no. 109.

14 *CRB*, vol. iii, folio 146.

15 Akenson, *Irish educational experiment*, pp. 258–9, 299–301; Ó Heideain, E., *National school inspection in Ireland: the beginnings*, Dublin 1967, pp. 55–118.

16 *CRB*, iii, folio 146.

17 *CRB*, ii, folio 5.

18 *CRB*, iv, folio 200

19 Table 23, p. 252.

20 See Tables 23 and 29.

21 Diary of Nassau Senior cited, Mac Suibhne, P., *Paul Cullen and his contemporaries*, iii, p. 376.

22 Akenson., D. H., *A Protestant in purgatory: Richard Whately, Archbishop of Dublin*, Hamden, 1981, passim.

23 Akenson, D. H., 'Pre-university education, 1782–1870' in Vaughan, *New Hist. Ire.*, v, pp. 534–536.

24 *SR*, 1 Jan. 1850, quoting the *Dublin Evening Mail*.

25 *CE*, 28 Dec. 1849.

26 *CE*, 4 Jan. 1850; *CC*, 3 Jan. 1850.

27 12 and 13 Vict., c. 77 (28 July 1849)

28 Lane, P. G., 'The Encumbered Estates Court, Ireland, 1948–49', *Economic and Social Review*, 3, no. 3, Apr. 1972, pp. 31–32.

29 Donnelly, *Land and people*, pp. 71–72.

30 *CE*, 10 Jan. 1849.

31 Stark, A., *The South of Ireland in 1850, being the journal of a tour in Leinster and Munster*, Dublin, 1850, 180; *CE*, 18 Dec. 1848.

32 *CE*, 15 May 1849.

33 The particulars of sale are in O'Brien's rentals, vol. ii, Sept–Oct 1851, No. 6.

34 *CE*, 18 Dec. 1851.

35 Particulars of sale.

36 *CE*, 13 Oct. 1851.

37 See Chapter IV.

38 Hancock, *Causes of distress at Skull and Skibbereen*, pp. 5–8.

39 Encumbered Estates Court, index to conveyances, vol. iii, Aug. 1852 – July 1853, no. 3828; See also particulars of sale.

40 *CE*, 9 Nov. 1852.

41 Lane, P. J., 'The encumbered estates court and Galway land ownership, 1849' in *Galway: history and society*, edited by Moran, G. & Gillespie, R., Dublin, 1996, p. 417.

42 *Mining Companies of Ireland, reports, 1842–64*, Dublin 1864, p. 5.

43 *CC*, 9 May 1854.

44 See map, Hickey, 'Four peninsular parishes', p. 577.

45 Lee, J., *The modernisation of Irish society, 1848–1918*, Dublin 1973, p. 37.

46 Mokyr, *Why*, p. 92.

47 Sullivan, *New Ireland*, p. 142.

48 Donnelly, J. S., Jr, 'Landlords and tenants' in Vaughan, *New Hist. Ire.*, v, p. 348.

49 de Burgh, U. H. H., *The landowners of Ireland: an alphabetical list of owners of estates of 500*

acres or £500 *valuation and upwards in Ireland, with acreage and valuation in each county* ... Dublin, 1878, p. 135.

50 Ó Gráda, 'New perspectives on the Irish famine', *Bullán*, iii, no. 2, 1997–98, p. 18.

51 Gray, P., *Famine, land and politics and Irish society 1843–1850*, Dublin, 1999, pp. 190–1.

52 *Return of all notices served upon relieving officers for poor law districts in Ireland, under the act of last session, 11 and 12 vict., c. 47 intituled 'an act for the protection and relief of destitute poor evicted from their dwellings'*, p. 32 [45], HC, 1849, xlix, p. 279.

53 Donnelly, *Land and people*, p. 118.

54 Stark, *South of Ireland'*, p. 176.

55 Donnelly, J. S., Jr, 'Mass eviction and the great famine' in Póirtéir, *Famine*, pp. 147–156

56 *SR*, 9 Apr. 1849.

57 Póirtéir, C., 'Folk memory and the famine' in Póirtéir, *Famine*, p. 230.

58 *CC*, 16 Feb. 1852.

59 O'Day, J. & Stevenson, J., *Irish historical documents since 1800*, Dublin, 1992, p. 73.

60 *SR*, 2 Mar. 1852.

61 Whyte, J. H., 'The influence of the Catholic clergy in elections in nineteenth century Ireland', *English Historical Review*, lxxv, 1970, pp. 239–59.

62 *CE*, 26 March 1852.

63 *CE*, 5 Apr. 1852.

64 *CE*, 24 Mar. 1852.

65 *CE*, 22 Mar. 1852.

66 *CE*, 22 Mar. 1852.

67 *CE*, 12 Apr. 1852; 21 Apr. 1852.

68 O'Donovan Rossa, *Recollections*, pp. 149–50, 166, 189.

69 Walker, B. M., (ed.), *Parliamentary election results in Ireland, 1801–1922*, Dublin, 1978, p. 83.

70 White, J. H., *The independent Irish party,1850–9*, Oxford, 1958, p. 81.

71 Field book for Schull, p. 6.

72 Field book for Kilcoe, p. 12.

73 Donnelly, *Land and people*, p. 135.

74 *Twentieth report of the Board of Works (Ireland) with appendices, appendix (G)*, 135 [1569] HC, 1852–3, xii, p. 407.

75 *Mapping the great Irish famine*, p. 163.

76 *Census Ire., 1851, Return of Agricultural produce* [1589], HC, 1852–3, xciii, p. 541.

77 Tithe Applotment Books, Kilcoe.

78 Field Book for Kilcoe, pp. 12–13.

79 *Census Ire., 1851*, pt. i, ii, p. 143.

80 *Eighteenth report of the Commissioners of Public Works (Ireland)*, appendix J, 198 [1235], HC, 1850, xxv, p. 509.

81 *CE*, 28 Dec. 1848.

82 *CE*, 9 Mar. 1849.

83 *Report on the memorials presented to the Lords of the Admiralty, with reference to the harbours and lighthouses of the coast of County Cork*, 3 [97] HC, 1849, xiix, p. 35.

84 *CE*, 2 May 1849.

85 *SR*, 4 Aug. 1849; Kissane, N., *The Irish famine: a documentary history*, Dublin, 1995, p. 65.

86 *SR*, Apr. 25 1849.

87 *CE*, 4 Mar. 1849.

88 Maguire, J. F., *The industrial movement in Ireland as illustrated by the National Exhibition of 1852*, Cork, 1852.

89 Scott, C. W., *History of the Fastnet lighthouses*, Schull, 1993 ed., p. 3; this was replaced by the present granite structure at the end of the century.

90 *Census Ire., 1851*, pt vi, *General report*, xlvii.

91 Ó Conchúir, B., 'Thomas Swanton, *Réamhchonraitheoir in Iar-Chairbre, JCHAS*, vol. 98, 1993, pp. 50–3.

92 Windele Ms 4. B. 8.

93 Townsend, H., *A general and statistical survey of the County of Cork*, 2 vols, I, Cork, 1815, p. 343.

94 Windele correspondence, 4B, 6, 697.

95 *Minutes of evidence taken before the select committee … to examine the nature and extent of disturbances …* [20], HC, 1825, vii, p. 230.

96 *Appendix to Seventeenth Report of Commissioners of National Education in Ireland*, Dublin, 1851, p. 188.

97 Ó Cúiv, B., 'Irish language and literature 1691–1845' in *A New History of Ireland* iv, edited by Moody, T. W. & Vaughan, W. E., p. 380.

98 Fitzgerald, G., 'Estimates for the baronies of minimum level of Irish-speaking amongst successive decennial cohorts: 1771–1781 to 1861–1871', *Proceedings of the Royal Irish Academy*, vol 84, C, no. 3, Dublin, 1984, pp. 128, 132.

99 Ó Conchúir, 'Thomas Swanton', p. 55.

100 Nic Craith, M., *Malartú Teanga: an Ghaeilge i gCorcaigh sa naoú hAois déag*, Bremen, 1994, p. 61.

101 Woodham-Smith, *Hunger*, p. 379

102 *CC*, 4 May 1849.

103 Kinealy, *Calamity*, p. 263; Woodham-Smith, *Hunger*, p. 380.

104 Chapter VI.

105 *SR*, 17 May 1849.

106 Kinealy, *Calamity*, p. 258.

107 Galvin, *Black blight*, p. 265.

108 *CE*, 25 Jan. 1850.

109 *Census Ire., 1851*, pt v, ii, *Table of Deaths*, p. 375.

110 *ibid.*, pt v, i, p. 248.

111 *CE*, 2 Jan. 1850.

112 *CE*, 30 Apr. 1850.

113 *CE*, 10 Jun. 1850.

114 *CE*, 11 Aug. 1850.

115 *CE*, 8 Oct. 1850.

116 *CE*, 11 Sept. 1850.

117 *CE*, 16 May 1851.

118 *CE*, 10 Sept. 1852.

119 *CE*, 18 Mar. 1848.

120 Robins, J. A., 'Irish orphans emigration to Australia 1848–1850', *Studies*, lvii, 1968, p. 376.

121 Kinealy, *Calamity*, pp. 315–8.

122 *CC*, 22 Apr. 1849.

123 McClaughlin, T., 'Lost children? Irish famine orphans in Australia', *History Ireland*, Winter 2000, p. 32.

124 Kinealy, *op. cit.*, pp. 224–6; Robins, *op. cit.*, p. 287.

125 *Fourth report of the Poor Law Commissioners*, p. 193.

126 *ibid.*, p. 193; Burke, H., 'The break up of the Poor Laws: the impact on Schull and its neighbourhood 1851–1872', *Mizen Journal*, no. 8, 2000, p. 89.

127 Ó Cathaoir, B., *Famine Diary*, Dublin, 1999, p. 78.

128 *CE*, 4 Sept. 1850.

129 *ibid.*

130 *SR*, 10 April 1851.

131 Kinsella, A., *County Wexford in Famine years*, Enniscorthy, 1997, pp. 78–94.

132 Donnelly, J. S., Jr, 'Production, prices, and exports', 1846–51' in Vaughan, *New Hist. Ire.*, v, p. 293.

133 *Return of agricultural produce in Ireland in the year 1847*, pt i: *Crops* [923], HC, 1847–8, lvii,

vi, pp. 4–5; *Return of the agricultural produce in Ireland in the year 1847*, pt ii: *Stock* [1000], HC, 1847–8, lvii,pp. 4–5; *Census Ire.*,1851, pt ii: *Returns of Agricultural produce in 1851* [1589], HC, 1852–3, xciii, pp. 541, 637; *Census Ire., 1851*, pt., General report, p. 242. Suggestions regarding cattle and pig numbers have been accepted from Bourke, P. A., 'The agricultural statistics of the 1841 Census of Ireland: a critical review', in *The visitation of God*, Hill & Ó Gráda, pp. 74–89.

134 *SR*, 14 Apr. 1851.

135 Thompson, D., *England in the nineteenth century*, Middlesex, 1971, p. 100.

136 Comerford, R. V., 'Ireland 1850–70: post-famine and mid-Victorian' in Vaughan, *New Hist. Ire.*, v, p. 372.

137 All data are taken from *Census Ire., 1851*, pt i, *showing the area, population and number of houses by townlands and electoral divisions*, vol ii, *province of Munster, County of Cork* [1550, 1551], HC, 1852–3, xii–xiv, pp. 521–9; also Table 28, p. 294.

138 *Census Ire., 1851*, P.P. Famine, xii, p. 449; *Census Ire., 1851*, pt v, ii, Table of Deaths, p. 32; *CC*, 31 Dec. 1846.

139 *Census Ire.*,1851, i, pt v, ii, p. 245.

140 Chapter VIII.

141 Dudley Edwards, R. M., *An atlas of Irish history*, London, p. 219; *Census Ire., 1851*, pt v, i, p. 247.

142 O'Malley, P. T., 'Surviving the famine: one townland's experience on the Mizen Peninsula', *Mizen Journal*, no. 8, 2000, pp. 60–7.

143 Griffith Valuation, 1851, Barony of W. Carbery, W. Div., p. 8.

144 Rossa, *Recollections*, p. 142.

145 O'Regan, L., 'O'Donovan Rossa and his brief marriage with Ellen Buckley', *Mizen Journal*, no. 7, 1999, p. 128.

146 Fitzgeralds & King, *Uncounted Irish*, pp. 55, 293.

147 Private correspondence from Grant Maxwell, a relative of the Fields.

148 Driscoll, C. B., *Kansas Irish*, New York, 1943, p. 3.

149 Parish records, Rosscarbery.

150 Marriage cert. of Margaret Field and James Hickey, 23 Nov. 1887; Death cert. of Mary Agusta Kennedy (née Hickey), 20 May 1923, Health Dept, Registry Division, City of Boston; Brennan, J. F., *The evolution of Everyman* (Ancestral lineage of John F. Kennedy), Dundalk, 1968, p. 198.

151 Cambell, M., 'Immigrants on the land: a comparative study of Irish rural settlements in nineteenth-century Minnesota and New South Wales' in *Irish diaspora*, edited by Bielenberg, p. 188.

152 Harris R.-A. M. & Jacobs, D. M., *The search for missing friends, 1831–1850*, i, Boston, 1989, p. 285.

153 *ibid.*, p. 285.

154 Ó Gráda, C., *Ireland, a new economic history, 1780–1939*, Oxford, 1994, p. 225.

155 *ibid.*, p. 541.

156 Harris R.-A. & O'Keeffe, B. E., *The search for missing friends*, ii, Boston, 1991, p. 314.

157 *ibid.*, pp. 208, 287.

158 Harris R.-A. M. & Jacobs, D. M., *The search for missing friends, 1831–1850*, i, Boston, 1989, p. 337.

159 Harris R.-A. & O'Keeffe, B. E., *The search for missing friends*, ii, Boston, 1991, p. 39.

160 O' Donnell, E., 'The scattered debris of the Irish Nation: The Famine Irish in New York city, 1845–55' in *The hungry stream: essays on emigration and famine*, edited by E. M. Crawford, Belfast, 1997, p. 53.

161 Fitzpatrick, D., *Irish emigration 1801–1921*, n.p., 1990, p. 33.

162 Ó Gráda, *Black '47*, p. 120.

163 Maguire, J. F., *The Irish in America*, New York, 1869, p. 233.

164 Ó Cathaoir, *Famine diary*, pp. 177–8.

165 Rossa, *Recollections*, p. 143.

166 MacDonagh, O., 'Irish Catholic clergy and emigration during the great famine', *Irish Historical Studies*, v, no. 17, Mar. 1946, pp. 287–342.

167 Kerr, *'Nation of beggars'?*, pp. 299, 333.

168 Miller, K. A., *Emigrants and exiles: Ireland and the Irish exodus to North America*, New York & Oxford, 1985.

169 Ó Gráda, *Black '47*, p. 107.

170 *CE*, 22 Dec. 1851.

171 Macleod, *Highlanders*, p. 288.

172 Ó Gráda, *Ireland 1780–1939*, p. 234.

173 Galvin, *Black blight*, p. 312.

174 Jordan, D., 'The famine and its aftermath in County Mayo' in *'Fearful realities': new perspectives on the Famine*, edited by C. Morash & R. Hayes, 1996, p. 37

175 *Census Ire., 1851*, pt v, iii, pp. 28–9, 77.

176 O'Connor, *Workhouses*, p. 177.

177 *Census, 1851*, pt v, ii, Table of Deaths, p. 95.

178 O'Donovan, *Celtic Miscellany*, p. 397.

179 *Census Ire., 1851*, pt vi, i, xiii, xiv.

180 *Census Ire., 1851*, pt vi, General report, xxiii

181 *Illus. Lond. News*, 13 Feb. 1847.

182 Data on housing is *Census Ire., 1851*, pt vi, General report, p. 250; Table 10, p.136 .

183 *Census, 1851*, pt v, i, p. 254.

184 *Census Ire., 1851*, pt vi, General report, p. xxxviii.

185 *Census, ibid.*, p. 346.

186 Parish Records.

187 Pophan, J., 'Report on epidemic fevers … ' *Dublin Medical Press*, viii, 1849, p. 279.

188 Donovan, 'Observations', p. 130.

189 Ó Gráda, *Black '47*, pp. 90, 171, 227.

190 Ó Gráda, *An Drochshaol: béaloideas agus amhráin*, p. 47; Ó Mainín, P., 'Amhrán an Ghorta' in *Céad Bliain*, edited by Ó Ciosáin, p. 192.

191 O'Neill, T. P., 'The famine in Offaly' in *Offaly: history and society*, edited by Nolan, W. & O'Neill, T. P., Dublin, 1998, p. 702; Ó Gráda, *Black '47*, p. 86; McAtasney, G., 'The Famine in County Armagh' in *The Famine in Ulster: the regional impact*, edited by Kinealy, C. & Parkhill, T., Belfast, 1997, pp. 45–6.

192 Church of Ireland Parish Records, NLI

193 Lee, J., *Modernisation of Irish society, 1848–1918*, Dublin, 1973, p. 5.

194 Connell, K. H., *Irish peasant society*, p. 121.

195 Parish records.

196 Galvin, *Black blight*, pp. 335–42.

197 Marnane, D. G., 'The famine in South Tipperary – part five', *Tipperary Historical Journal 2000*, pp. 109–111.

198 O'Neill, 'The famine in Offaly' in *Offaly: history and society*, edited by Nolan & O'Neill, pp. 703.

199 *Census Ire., 1851*, pt v, i, p. 254.

200 Duby & Wallon, *France rurale*, pp. 97–130.

201 Lyons, F. S. L., *Ireland since the famine*, London 1971, p. 47.

202 HO, R. 58, map and survey.

203 Charles Bart to J. Culvert, 10 May 1857 (uncatalogued), Hewett Papers in Archives Council, Cork.

204 Williams, *Berehaven copper mines*, p. 16.

205 Donnelly, *Land and people*, pp. 145–6.

206 Chapter VI.

207 Hill, *Facts from Gweedore*, p. 13.

208 Hourihan, K., 'Rural settlement and change near Bantry 1600–1845', *Bantry Historical and Archaeological Society Journal*, i, p. 52.

209 Whelan, K., 'Pre and post-famine landscape change' in Póirtéir, *Famine*, p. 31.

210 Evans, E. E., *The personality of Ireland: habitat, heritage and history*, Dublin, 1992 ed., p. 60.

211 Ó Gráda, *Black '47*, p. 156.

212 Geary, 'Famine fever and the bloody flux', in Póitéir, *Famine*, p. 85.

213 *CE*, 23 Apr. 1855.

214 Lee, *Modernisation of Irish society*, p. 5.

215 Ó Gráda, *Ireland before/after famine*, p. 163.

216 Ó Gráda, *Ireland, 1780–1939*, p. 215.

EPILOGUE

1 Miller, K., *Emigration, ideology, and identity in post-famine Ireland*, *Studies*, vol. 75, no. 300, Winter 1986, p. 6.

2 Crowley, P. J., *A rebel with many causes: Fr Jeremiah J. Crowley*, privately printed.

3 O'Regan, L., 'Anna Parnell ', *Southern Star*, 23 Nov. 1991.

4 O'Regan, L., 'The Castle Island evictions', *Mizen Journal*, no. 6, 1998, pp. 116–129.

5 Synge, J., *Collected works*, ii, p. 326.

6 Ó Cathaoir, E., 'The Poor Law in County Wicklow' in *Wicklow: history and society*, edited by Hannigan, K. & Nolan, W., Dublin, 1994, p. 553.

7 Mackey, M., 'Schull workhouse', *Mizen Journal*, no. 4, 1996, p. 49.

8 Dufferin & Boyle, *Narrative of a journey from Oxford to Skibbereen*, p. 3.

9 Whelan, K., 'Pre and post-Famine landscape change' in Póirtéir, *Famine*, p. 32.

10 Sullivan, *New Ireland*, i, p. 142.

11 Crawford, E. M., 'William Wilde's table of Irish famines, 900–1850' in Crawford, *Famine*, p. 7.

12 Whelan, *op. cit.*, p. 32.

13 McL. Côté, J., *Fanny and Anna Parnell*, Dublin, 1991, p. 45.

14 Carbery, Mary, *The Farm by Lough Gur*, London, 1937, p. 58.

15 Ó Gráda, *Ireland before/after famine*, p. 78.

16 Cited in Ó Gráda, p. 116.

17 Rossa, *Recollections*, p. 148.

18 *Nation*, 29 Apr. 1847.

19 Donnelly, J. S., Jr, 'The administration of relief' in Vaughan, *New Hist. Ire.*, v, p. 331; 'The soup-kitchens', *ibid.*, p. 315; 'Mass eviction and the Great Famine' in Póirtéir, *Famine*, p. 173.

20 Lecky, W. E. H., *A history of Ireland in the eighteenth century*, Dublin, 1892, i, p. 186. See also, Donnelly, *Potato famine*, pp. 24, 209.

21 Dickson, *Arctic Ireland*, pp. 72, 50, 41.

22 Cited in Ó Gráda, *Black '47*, p. 94.

23 Fitzpatrick, D., 'The disappearance of the Irish agricultural labourer, 1841–1921', *Irish economic and social history*, vii (1980), pp. 66–92.

24 *CC*, 4 Mar. 1847.

25 *CC*, 12 Jan. 1847.

26 *CC*, 3 Apr. 1847.

27 *Nation*, 8 Jan. 1848.

28 Bourke, P. A., 'Apologia for a dead civil servant' in *The visitation of God*, edited by Hill & Ó Gráda, p. 173.

29 Boylan T. A. & Foley, T. P., 'A nation perishing of political economy' in *Fearful realities*, edited by Morash & Hayes, p. 144.

30 Sullivan, *New Ireland*, i, p. 142.

31 Connell, K. H., 'Peasant marriage in Ireland after the Great Famine', *Past and Present*, no. 12, 1957, pp. 76–91.

32 Guinnane, T. W., *The vanishing Irish: households, migration, and the rural economy in Ireland, 1850–1914*, New Jersey, 1997, p. 14.

33 P.P., *Famine*, v, p. 928.

34 Dear, I. C. B. & Foot, M. R. D. (eds), *The Oxford companion to the Second World War*, Oxford, 1995, p. 558.

35 *CC*, 24 Nov. 46.

36 *ibid.*, 17 Sept. 1846.

37 *CC*, 29 July 1847.

38 Ryder, S., 'Famine and the *Nation*' in *Fearful realities*, edited by Morash & Hayes, p.1 58.

39 Cited, *CC*, 1 Jun. 1847.

40 See in general, Miller, K. A., 'Revenge for Skibbereen': Irish Emigration and the meaning of the Great Famine' in *The Great Famine and the Irish diaspora in America*, edited by Gribben, A., Boston, 1995, pp. 180–195.

41 Cooney, D. A. L., 'Methodists in the great Irish famine', in *Bulletin of the Wesley Historical Society*, iii, pt i, Autumn 1996, p. 14.

42 *CC*, 4 Feb. 1847.

43 Whelan, K., 'Pre- and post-famine landscape change' in Póirtéir, *Famine*, p. 27.

44 Sullivan *op. cit.*, p. 45.

45 Rossa, *Recollections*, 166.

46 Fleming, L. S., *Head or Harp*, London, 1965, p. 13.

47 *SR*, 30 Nov. 1847.

48 Kerr, D., *The Catholic Church and the famine*, Dublin, 1996, pp. 52–63.

49 O'Rourke, *Famine*, p. 522.

50 Sullivan, *op. cit.*, p. 63.

51 Walsh, T. J., *In the tradition of St Finbarr*, Cork, 1951, p. 25; Ní Úrdail, *The scribe*, p. 87.

52 *CC*, 27 Mar. 1847.

53 *CE*, 2 Apr. 1847.

54 *CE*, 7 Jun. 1847.

55 *CE*, 14 Jun. 1847; Galvin, *Black blight*, p. 246.

56 *CE*, 18 Jun. 1847.

57 *CE*, 13 Aug. 1949.

58 Data from inscriptions.

59 Lankford, *Cape Clear*, p. 151.

60 *CE*, 12 Mar. 1853.

61 Troy, B., P.P., Private correspondence; O'Shea, K., 'In the line of duty': priests who ministered to the Famine victims' in *The famine in Kerry*, edited by Costello, M., Tralee, 1997, pp. 28–31: Murphy, *Killaloe*, p. 222.

62 *Batterby's registry … or Catholic dictionary … for 1848*, p. 341; Ó Fiannachta, P., *An gorta mór*, An Daingean, 1997, p. 107; Grace, D., 'Priests who died in the great famine', *Tipperary Historical Journal*, 1997, pp. 178–9.

63 O'Shea, K., 'The nuns in Kerry; the unsung heroines of the Famine' in *The famine in Kerry*, edited by Costello, M., Tralee, 1997, p. 57.

64 Bolster, *Cork, Penal era to famine*, p. 314.

65 O Mahony, C., *In the shadows: life in Cork, 1750–1930*, Cork, 1997, p. 159.

66 O'Gallagher, *Gateway to Canada*, pp. 86–89; Quigley, M., 'Grosse Île: The most important and evocative Great Famine site outside of Ireland' in *Hungry stream*, edited by Crawford, p. 33.

67 Daly, *Famine*, p. 68.

68 Brady, *Clerical records*, i, p. 127; *CC*, 6 Apr. 1847.

69 *CC*, 14 May 1850.

70 Crookshank, *Methodism*, vi, p. 65.

71 *Transact. of the comm. of Soc. Friends*, p. 108.

72 *CC, CE*, 23 Aug. 1847.

73 Relief Commission Papers, parish of Schull, NA.

74 *Transactions of the Central Committee of the Society of Friends*, p. xvi.

75 Froggatt, P., 'The response of the medical profession to the great famine' in *Famine*, edited by Crawford, p. 149.

76 *CC*, Aug. 20 1847.

77 *CE*, 19 May 1847.

78 *CC*, 31 July 1847; 1 Apr. 1847; see also *Cork Evening Echo*, 10 Nov. 1954.

79 Nicholls, G., *A history of the Irish Poor Law*, London, 1856, p. 140.

80 Marnane, D. J., 'The famine in South Tipperary – part 2', *Tipperary Historical Journal*, 1997, p.1 34.

81 Lowe, 'Policing famine Ireland', p. 67.

82 Bourke, in *The visitation of God*, Hill & Ó Gráda, p. 184.

83 Kerr, *'Nation of beggars'?* p. 339.

84 Cole, J. H., *Church and parish records of the united dioceses of Cork, Cloyne and Ross*, Cork, 1903, p. 72.

85 *CC*, 4 Aug. 1911.

86 Information given to me by Mrs O'Mahony of Seafort, Schull.

87 *CE*, 1 July 1893.

88 Hickey, P., 'Cross is a reminder of famine times', *CE*, 24 Mar. 1987

89 Obituary, *CE*, 12 Mar. 1883; Reilly, *Famine priest*, p. 98.

90 Dunne, S., 'A famine journey', *Cork Review; Sean Dunne, 1956–1995*, Cork, 1996, p. 56.

91 Cited, Cleary, P. & O'Regan, P., *Dear Old Skibbereen*, Skibbereen, 1995, p. 2, from S. & D. Ó Cróinin, *Seanachas Ó Chairbre*, Baile Átha Cliath, 1885.

92 Ormsby , F. (ed.), *The collected poems of John Hewitt*, Belfast, 1991, p. 177.

93 Dunne, 'A famine journey', p. 57.

BIBLIOGRAPHY

MANUSCRIPT SOURCES
IRELAND

DUBLIN

NATIONAL ARCHIVES
Rebellion Papers, 1796–8
Outrage Papers, 1810–33
Distress Papers, 1822, 1845–8
Official Papers, 1840–8
Relief Commission Papers, 1845–8
National Board Records, 1832–52
Tithe Applotment Books
Office of Public Works Record
O'Brien Rentals

NATIONAL LIBRARY
Peel Papers (microfilm)
Church of Ireland records (microfilm)
O'Casaide MSS
Mss 15B (34–6)

ROYAL IRISH ACADEMY
Windele Correspondence

TRINITY COLLEGE
Records of Irish Islands and Coastal Society

UNIVERSITY COLLEGE, DUBLIN, DEPT. OF FOLKLORE
National School accounts of the Famine.

VALUATION OFFICE, Ely Place
Griffith Valuation; Field Books, House Books.

VINCENTIANS (CM), Phibsboro
Minute Books, 1848.

DUBLIN DIOCESAN ARCHIVES
Murray Papers

COUNTY CORK

DIOCESAN ARCHIVES, CORK

GOLEEN
Parish records
Catholic

SCHULL
Parish records
Catholic
Church of Ireland

AUGHADOWN
Parish records
Catholic

SKIBBEREEN
Parish records
Catholic

CORK
Cork Archives Council
Hewitt Papers
Dunmanway and Bantry Workhouses, Minute Books.

ENGLAND

LONDON

PUBLIC RECORD OFFICE
Home Office Papers, 1811–22
Treasury Papers 1846–7
War Office Records, 1847–8

GUILDHALL LIBRARY
Records of London Tavern Committee, 1822

SURREY PUBLIC RECORD OFFICE
Goulburn Papers, 1822

OXFORD
Bodlean Library
Trevelyan's Private Letter Book, 1847–8
Trevelyan MSS, 1847–8

ROME

VINCENTIANS (CM)
Dowley/Etienne correspondence, 1848

NEWSPAPERS AND PERIODICALS

Cork Constitution, 1822–52
Cork Evening Herald, 1833–41
Cork Examiner, 1841–52
Cork Mercantile Chronicle, 1802–35
Freeholder, 1823
Freeman's Journal, 1846–8
Illustrated London News, 1847
Mining Journal, 1840–52
Quebec Mercury, 1847–8
Southern Reporter, 1822–52
Southern Star, 1991
Tablet, 1847–8

Bulletin de Saint Vincent de Paul, 1848–9
Dublin Medical Press, 1847–9.
Dublin Journal of Medical Science, 1847–9
Irish Intelligence, 1848–52

BRITISH PARLIAMENTARY PAPERS

Abstract of answers and return, pursuant to Act 55 Geo. 3 for taking account of the population of Ireland in 1821 [577], HC, 1824, xxii.
Report to the Irish government on the employment of the poor. No. i, Report on the southern districts by Richard Griffith [249], HC, 1823, x.
Report on the southern districts in Ireland containing a statement of the progress made during the year 1823, in the several roads carried out at public expense in that district: under the order of his excellency, the lord lieutenant 1824 [352], xxi.
Evidence taken before the select of the Lords and commons ... to inquire into the state of Ireland (London, 1825).
Minutes of evidence taken before the select committee appointed to inquire into the disturbances in Ireland, HC, 1825, vii.
Return of the population of several counties of Ireland, as enumerated in 1831 [254] 1833, xxxix.
Report on the roads made at public expense in the southern districts by Richard Griffith, pt i [119], 831, xii.
Report on roads carried out at public expense under the order of his excellency, the lord lieutenant [389], HC, 1829, xxii, p. 20.
Second report of the commissioners of Irish education inquiry, 1826–7 [12], xxx.
First report of his Majesty's Commissioners for inquiring into the condition of the poorer classes, with appendix and supplement: Appendix (A.) [369] HC, 1835, xxxii, pt i.
Poor Inquiry (Ireland): *Appendix (D.) containing baronial examinations relative to earnings of labourers, cottier tenants, employment of women and children, expenditure; and supplement containing answers to questions 1 to 12 circulated by the commissioners* [36], HC, 1836, xxxi.

———— Appendix (E.) containing baronial examinations relative to food, cottages and cabins, clothing and furniture ... drinking; and supplement containing answers to questions 13 to 22 circulated by the commissioners [37], HC, 1836, xxxii.

———— Appendix (F.), containing baronial examinations relative to con-acre ... emigration ... landlord and tenant, nature and state of agriculture ... [38], HC, 1836, xxxiii.

Names of places in Great Britain and Ireland in which a penny post is established [86], 1837, x.

First annual report of the commissioners of fisheries (Ireland) [224], 1843, xviii.

Second annual report of the commissioners of fisheries (Ireland) [502], 1844, xxx.

Fourth annual report of the commissioners of fisheries (Ireland) [713], xxii.

Report of the commissioners appointed to take the census of Ireland for the year 1841 [504], 1843, xxiv.

First Report of the Commissioners of Inquiry into the employment and conditions of children in mines and manufactures [93], HC, 1842, xv.

Evidence taken before her Majesty's commissioners of inquiry into the state of law and practice in respect to the occupation of land in Ireland, pt ii [616], HC, 1845, xx.

Correspondence explanatory of the measures adopted by her majesty's government for the relief of distress arising from the failure of the potato crop in Ireland in Ireland [735], HC, 1846, xxxvi.

Correspondence from July 1846 to January 1847 relating to the measures adopted for the relief of distress in Ireland, Board of Works series [764], HC, 1847, l.

Correspondence from July 1846 to January 1847, relating to the measures adopted for the relief of distress in Ireland and Scotland, commissariat series [761], HC, 1847, li.

Correspondence from January to March 1847, relating to the measures adopted for the relief of distress in Ireland, Board of Works series, pt ii [796], HC, 1847, lii.

Correspondence from January to March 1847, relating to the measures adopted for the relief of distress in Ireland in Ireland, commissariat series, pt ii [796], HC, 1847, lii.

Return of agricultural produce in Ireland in the year 1847, pt i : Crops [923], HC, 1847–8, lvii.

Return of agricultural produce in Ireland in the year 1847, pt ii: Stock [1000], HC, 1847, lvii.

Sixteenth annual report of the Commissioners of Public Work in Ireland 1847–8 [983], xxxvii.

Final report of the Board of Works (Ireland) relating to measures adopted for the relief of distress in July and August 1847 [1047], 1849, xxiii.

First report of the commissioners appointed to enquire into the numbers and boundaries of the poor law unions in Ireland [1015], HC, 1849, xxiii.

Papers relative to emigration to British North American Provinces, 1847–48 [50], HC, 1849, xlvii.

Second report of the commissioners for the administration of the laws for the relief of the poor in Ireland, Dublin, 1849.

Return of all notices served upon relieving officers for poor law districts in Ireland, under the act of last session, 11 and 12 vict., c. 47 intituled 'an act for the protection and relief of destitute poor evicted from their dwellings' [48], HC, 1849, xlix.

Report on the memorials presented to the Lords of the Admiralty, with reference to the harbours and lighthouses of the coast of County Cork [97], HC, 1849, xiix.

Eighteenth report of the Commissioners of Public Works (Ireland) [1235], HC, 1850, xxv.

Third annual report of the commissioners for administrating the laws for the relief of the poor in Ireland [23], xxvii, 1850.

Fourth annual report of the commissioners for administrating the laws for the relief of the poor in Ireland [68], xxii, 1851.

Twentieth report of the Commissioners of Public Works (Ireland) [1569], 1852, xii.

The census of Ireland for the year 1851, pt i: showing the area, population, and number of houses by townlands and electoral divisions, vol ii, province of Munster, County of Cork (1550), 1852–3, xci.

―――― pt v, Table of Deaths, vol i, containing the report, tables of pestilences, and analysis of the tables of deaths (20871–I), 1856, xxix.

―――― pt vi, General report (2134), 1856, xxix.

OTHER CONTEMPORARY RECORDS

Report of the deputation of the National Fishing Company on the subject of the fisheries on the South and West coasts of Ireland, 1825 (Halliday Collection).

Report of the proceedings of the committee of management for the relief of distressed districts in Ireland appointed at a general meeting held in the Mansion House, Dublin, on 16 May 1822, Dublin, 1822.

Report of the committee for the relief of the distressed districts in Ireland, appointed at a general meeting held at the City of London Tavern, on 7 May 1822; with an appendix, London, 1823.

Transactions of the central relief committee of the Society of Friends during the famine in Ireland in 1846 and 1847, Dublin, 1852.

Drury, W. B. & Walsh F. W. (eds), Reports of cases argued and determined in the High Court of Chancery during the time of Lord Chancellor Plunkett, 2 vols, Dublin, 1842.

Hunt, R., Memoirs of the Geological Survey of Great Britain, London, 1850

Clarke C., & Finnelly W., Reports of cases decided in the House of Lords on the appeals and writs of error, during the sessions 1841 and 1842, London, 1843.

Mining Company of Ireland, Reports, etc., Dublin, 1841.

Third annual report of the Church Education Society for Ireland, Dublin, 1842.

Fourth annual report ... Dublin, 1843.

Fifth annual report ... Dublin, 1844.

Sixth annual report ... Dublin, 1845.

Seventh annual report ... Dublin, 1846.

Eight annual report ... Dublin, 1847.

Ninth annual report ... Dublin, 1848.

Tenth annual report ...Dublin, 1848.

Eleventh annual report ... Dublin, 1849.

Twelfth annual report ... Dublin, 1850.

Thirteenth annual report ... Dublin, 1851.

Fourteenth annual report ... Dublin, 1852.

Fifth report of the Society of St Vincent de Paul, 1849.

Report of the British Relief Association for the relief of distress in the remote parishes in Ireland and Scotland, London, 1849.

Hancock, W. N., On the causes of distress at Schull and Skibbereen during the famine in Ireland: a paper read before the statistical section of the British Association at Edinburgh, August, 1850, Dublin, 1850.

Griffith, R., 'On the copper beds of the south-west coast of County Cork', Journal of Geological Society of Dublin, vi (1855), pp. 201–6.

CONTEMPORARY WORKS; memoirs, travellers' accounts, etc.

Burrit, E., *A journal of a visit of three days to Skibbereen and its neighbourhood*, London, 1847.

Crofton Croker, T., *Researches in the south of Ireland*, London, 1824.

Donovan, D., 'Observations on the peculiar diseases to which the famine of last year gave origin, and on the morbid effects of insufficient nourishment', *Dublin Medical Press*, xix, 1848, pp. 67–68, 130–32, 275–78.

Dufferin & Ava, marquis of, & Boyle, G.F., *Narrative of a journey from Oxford to Skibbereen during the Irish famine*, London, 1847.

Foley, D., *Missionary tour through the south of Ireland undertaken for the Irish Society*, Dublin, 1849.

Foster, T. C., *Letters on the condition of the people of Ireland*, London, 1847.

Hall, S. C. & A. M., *Ireland: its scenery, character* ... 3 vols, London, 1841–3.

Harbord, R. Synge, *The diary of Rev. Robert Traill (1793–1847)*, privately published.

Kane, R., *The industrial resources of Ireland*, Dublin, 1845.

Lamprey, Dr, 'Report on the epidemic fever in Ireland', *Dublin Journal of Medical Science*, vii (1849), pp. 103–5.

Maguire, J. F. *The Irish in America*, New York, 1969 ed.

Malthus, T. R., *An essay on the principle of population*, London, 1973 ed.

Mitchel, J., *Jail Journal*, Dublin, n.d.

Mitchel, J., *The last conquest of Ireland (perhaps)*, Glasgow, Manchester, Liverpool, n. d.

Newenham, *A view of the natural, political and commercial circumstances of Ireland*, London, 1809.

Nicholls, G., *A history of the Irish Poor Law*, London, 1856.

O'Donovan, J., *Miscellany of the Celtic Society*, Dublin, 1849.

O'Donovan Rossa, J., *Rossa's Recollections, 1838–1898*, Shannon, 1972.

Popham J., 'Report on the endemic fevers ... ', *Dublin Medical Press*, viii (1849), pp. 277–83.

Steward, A. & Rivington, G., *Memoirs of the life and labours of Rev. A. Averell*, Dublin, 1858.

Sullivan, A. M., *New Ireland*, 2 vols, London, 1877.

Thompson, D. P., *A brief account of the change in religious opinion now taking place in Dingle and the west of County Kerry*, Dublin, 1846.

Townsend, H., *A general and statistical survey of the County of Cork*, 2 vols, Cork, 1815.

Traill, R., *The Jewish War of F. Josephus, a new translation*, London, 1847.

Trench, R. C., *Letters and memorials ed. By the author of Charles Lowder*, 2 vols, London, 1886.

Trench, W. S. *Realities of Irish life*, London, 1868.

Trevelyan, C. E., *The Irish Crisis*, London, 1848.

Young, A., *Arthur Young's tour of Ireland (1776–1779)*, edited by A. W. Hutton, 2 vols, London and New York, 1892.

LATER WORKS

Adams, W. F., *Ireland and Irish emigration to the new world: from 1815 to the famine*, New Haven, 1932.

Akenson, D. H., *The Church of Ireland, ecclesiastic reform and revolution 1800–1895*, New Haven and London, 1971.

Akenson, D. H., 'Pre-university education, 1782–1870' in *A New History of Ireland*, v,

Ireland under the Union, i, *1801–70*, edited by Vaughan, W. E., Oxford, 1989, pp. 523–537.

Akenson, D. H., *The Irish educational experiment*, London and Toronto, 1970.

Appleby, J. C., 'Settlers and pirates in early seventeenth century Ireland', *Studia Hibernica*, no 25, (1989–90), pp. 12–17.

Barry, P. C., 'The legislation of the Synod of Thurles', *Studies*, xxvi, no. 2, April 1959, pp. 133–5.

Bielenberg, A. (ed.), *The Irish diaspora*, London, 2000.

Blake, J. A., *The sea fisheries of Ireland*, Waterford, 1868.

Bolster, A., *A history of the diocese of Cork from the penal era to the famine*, Cork, 1989.

Bolster, A., *A history of the diocese of Cork: the episcopate of William Delany, 1847–1886*, Cork, 1993.

Bourke, P. A., in *The visitation of God: the potato and the Irish famine*, edited by Hill, J. & Ó Gráda, C., Dublin, 1993.

Bowen, D., *Souperism, myth or reality?*, Cork, 1970.

Bowen, D., *The Protestant crusade in Ireland, 1800–70*, Dublin, 1978.

Boyle P. P. & Ó Gráda, C., 'Fertility trends, excess mortality, and the great famine', *Demography*, xxiii, 1989.

Brady, J., & Corish P. J., The Church under the Penal Code, *Irish Catholicism*, iv, p. 65.

Burke, H., *The people and the Poor Law in nineteenth century Ireland*, n.p., 1997.

Burke, H., 'The break up of the Poor Laws: the impact on Schull and its neighbourhood 1851–1872', *Mizen Journal*, no. 8, 2000, pp. 83–95.

Cadogan, T. 'James O'Sullivan of Roaring Water', *Seanchas Chairbre*, no. 3, pp. 17–22.

Campbell, M., 'Immigrants on the Land: a comparative study of Irish rural settlement in nineteenth-century Minnesota and New South Wales', *Irish diaspora*, edited by Bielenberg, pp. 176–194.

Carbery M., *The Farm by Lough Gur*, London, 1937.

Carson, J. B., *Forty years in the Church of Ireland or the pastor, the parish, and its people, from 1840 to 1800*, London, n.d.

Clarke, S. & Donnelly, J. S., Jr. (eds), 'Pastorini and Captain Rock: Millenarianism and Sectarianism in the Rockite movement of 1821–4', in *Irish peasants, violence and political unrest, 1780–1914*, Manchester, 1983, pp. 103–143.

Cleary, P, & Regan, P., *Dear Old Skibbereen*, Skibbereen, 1995.

Cole, G. A. T., *Memoir of the geological survey of Ireland: mineral resources. Memoir and map of localities of minerals of economic importance in Ireland*, Dublin, 1922.

Collins, J. F., 'Influence of local circumstances on land valuation in south-west Cork in the mid-nineteenth century', *Mizen Journal*, no 7, 1999, pp. 134–161.

Connell, K. H., 'The history of the potato', *Economic History Review*, ser. 2, iii, no. 3 (1951), pp. 388–95.

Connell, K. H., *The population of Ireland, 1750–1845*, London, 1973.

Connolly, S. J., 'Union Government, 1812–23' in *A New History of Ireland*, v, *Ireland under the Union*, i, *1801–70*, edited by Vaughan, W. E., Oxford, 1989, pp. 61–2.

Coombes, J., 'Catholic churches in the nineteenth century: some newspaper sources', *JCHAS*, lxxxi, no. 2231 (Jan.–Jun. 1975), pp. 6–11.

Coombes, J., 'Goleen parish', *Fold*, xv, no. 6 (Dec. 1967), pp. 12–17.

Coombes, J., 'Europe's first temperance society', *JCHAS*, lxxii, 1967, pp. 49–51.

Coombes, J., 'The cruise of the *Margaret Hughes*, *Cork Holly Bough*, 1974.

Coombes, J., 'The Swantons of Ballydehob', *Southern Star*, 12 Feb. 1977.

Coombes, J., 'The Swantons of Ballydehob', *Southern Star*, 12 Nov. 1978.

Coombes, J., *A history of Timoleague and Barryroe*, n. p., 1969.

Coombes, J., 'An historical memorial in Skibbereen', *Seanchas Chairbre*, no. 1, Dec. 1982, pp. 38–9.

Coombes. J., 'Sea trade in potatoes in south-west Cork (1730–1850)', *Seanchas Chairbre*, no. 3, 1993, pp. 3–16.

Cooney, D. A. L., 'Methodists in the Great Irish Famine', *Bulletin of the Wesley Historical Association (Irish Branch)*, iii, pt i, Autumn 1996, pp. 12–18.

Corish, P. J., *Maynooth College*, Dublin, 1995.

Corkery, D., *The hidden Ireland*, Dublin, 1975 ed.

Cousins, S. H., 'Regional death rates in Ireland during the great famine, from 1846 to 1851', *Population Studies*, xiv, no. 1, July 1960, pp. 55–74.

Cousins, S. H., 'The regional variations in mortality during the famine', *Proceedings of the RIA*, lxii, section c, no. 3, 1963, pp. 129–34.

Cowman, D., 'Life and labour in three mining counties, c. 1840', *Saothar*, no. 9, 1983, p. 6–24.

Cowman, D., 'The mining community at Avoca' in *Wicklow: history and society*, edited by Hannigan & Nolan, Dublin, 1994, pp. 761–788.

Cox, R. C., 'The engineering career of Richard Griffith' in *Richard Griffith, 1784–1878*, edited by Davies, G. L. & Mollan, R. C., Dublin 1980, pp. 40–46.

Crawford, E. M., 'Scurvy in Ireland during the Great Famine', *Social history of Medicine*, i, no. 3, 1988, pp. 297–203.

Crawford, E. M., 'William Wilde's table of Irish famines, 900–1850' in *Famine: the Irish experience*, edited by Crawford, E. M., Edinburgh, 1989, pp. 1–30.

Crawford, M., 'The great Irish famine: image versus reality', *Ireland: art into history*, Dublin, 1994, pp. 75–88.

Crawford, M., (ed.) *The hungry stream: essays on emigration and famine*, Belfast, 1997.

Crookshank, C. H., *History of Methodism in Ireland*, Dublin, 1886.

Crotty, R. D., *Irish agricultural production: its volume and structure*, Cork, 1966.

Cullen, E. J., *The origin and development of the Irish Vincentian Foundations, 1833–1933*, Dublin, 1933.

Cullen, L. M. 'Irish history without the potato', *Past and Present*, no 40, July 1968, pp. 72–82.

Cummins, N., 'Incidence of famine in Cork and county; *Mizen Journal*, no. 4, 1996, pp. 78–9.

Cushing, J. E., Casey, T., & Robinson, M., *A chronicle of Irish emigration to St John, New Brunswick, 1847*, St John, 1979.

Daly, M. E., *Social and economic history of Ireland since 1800*, Dublin, 1981.

Daly, M. E., *The famine in Ireland*, Dublin, 1986.

Davies, G. L. and Mollan, R. C. (eds), *Griffith*, Dublin, 1980.

Davin, N. F., *The Irishman in Canada*, Toronto, 1877.

Davitt, T., 'Saint Vincent's Seminary', Cork i, *Colloque*, no. 10, Autumn 1984, pp. 42–5.

De Breffny B., & Mott G., *The churches and abbeys of Ireland*, London, 1976.

Dickson, D., *Arctic Ireland: the extraordinary story of the Great Frost and the Forgotten Famine of 1740–41*, Belfast, 1997.

Dickson, D., 'The other great Irish famine' in *The Great Irish Famine*, edited by Póirtéir, C., Cork, 1995, p. 55.

Donnelly, J. S., Jr, 'Production, prices, and exports, 1846–51' in *A New History of Ireland*, v, *Ireland under the Union*, i, *1801–70*, edited by Vaughan, W. E., Oxford, 1989, pp. 286–293.

Donnelly, J. S., Jr, 'The soup-kitchens' in *A New History of Ireland*, v, *Ireland under the Union*, i, *1801–70*, edited by Vaughan, W. E., Oxford, 1989, p. 309.

Donnelly, J. S., Jr, *The land and people of nineteenth-century Cork*, London and Boston, 1975.

Donnelly, J. S., Jr., 'Mass eviction and the Great Famine' in *The Great Irish Famine*, edited by C. Póirtéir, Cork, 1995, pp. 155–173.

Donnelly, J. S., Jr, 'Irish property must pay for Irish poverty' in *'Fearful realities': new perspectives on the Famine*, edited by Morash, C. & Hayes, R., Dublin, 1996.

Donnelly, J. S., Jr., *The great Irish potato famine*, Gloucestershire, 2000

Dowling, P. J., *The hedge schools of Ireland*, Cork, 1968.

Drake, M., 'Marriage and population growth in Ireland, 1750–1845', *Economic History Review*, ser. 2, xvi, no 2, Dec. 1963, pp. 301–3.

Drake, M., 'Population growth and the Irish economy' in *The formation of the Irish economy*, edited by Cullen, L. M., Cork, 1969.

Driscoll, B., *Kansas Irish*, New York, 1943.

Duby, G. & Wallon A., *Histoire de la France rurale: 3. De l789 à 1914*, Paris, 1976.

Edwards, R. D., and Williams, T. D. (eds), *The great Irish famine: studies in Irish History, 1845–52*, Dublin, 1956

Elliot, M., *Partners in revolution, the United Irishmen and France*, London, 1989.

Elliot, M., *Wolf Tone, prophet of Irish independence*, London, 1989.

Evans, E. E., *Irish Folk Ways*, London, 1957.

Evans, E. E., *The personality of Ireland, habitat, heritage and history*, Dublin, 1992 ed.

Fenning, H., 'Typhus epidemic in Ireland: priests, ministers and doctors', *Collectanea Hibernica*, no. 41, 1999, pp. 117–152.

Fetherstonhaugh, A. J., 'The true story of the two chiefs of Dunboy: an episode in Irish history', *The Journal of the Royal Society of Antiquaries of Ireland*, xxiv, 1894, pp. 35–43.

ffolliott, R., *The Pooles of Mayfield and other Irish families*, Dublin, 1958.

Finegan, F., 'The Irish Catholic convert rolls', *Studies*, xxxviii, no. 149, Mar. 1948, pp. 73–82.

Fitzgerald, G., 'Estimates for the baronies of minimum level of Irish speaking amongst successive decennial cohorts: 1771–1781 to 1861–1871', *Proceedings of the Royal Irish Academy*, vol. 84, C, no. 3, pp. 3–153.

Fitzgerald, M. E., & King J. A., *The uncounted Irish in Canada and the United States*, Toronto, 1990.

Fitzpatrick, D., *Irish emigration, 1801–1921*, n.p., 1990.

Fitzpatrick, D., 'Emigration 1801–70' in *A New History of Ireland, v, Ireland under the Union, i, 1801–70*, edited by Vaughan, W. E., Oxford, 1989, p. 577.

Fleming, L. S., *Head or Harp*, London, 1965.

Fogarty, L., *James Fintan Lawlor: patriot and political essayist, 1807–1849*, Dublin and London, 1918.

Foley, T. and Ryder, S. (eds), *Idealogy and Ireland in the nineteenth century*, Dublin, 1998.

Freeman, T. W., 'Land and people, c. 1841' in *A New History of Ireland, v, Ireland under the Union, i, 1801–70*, edited by Vaughan, W. E., Oxford, 1989, pp. 242–265.

Froggatt, P., 'The response of the medical profession to the great famine' in *Famine*, edited by Crawford, pp. 134–56.

Geary, L., 'Famine, fever and the bloody flux' in *Famine*, edited by Póirtéir, C., pp. 74–85.

Glazier I. A., & Tepper, M. (eds) *The famine immigrants; lists of Irish Immigrants arriving at the Port of New York, 1846–1851*, Baltimore, 1983, vols i– iv.

Grace, D., 'Priests who died in the Great Famine', *Tipperary Historical Journal*, 1997, pp. 176–200.

Grace, D., *The Great Famine in the Nenagh Poor Law Union Co. Tipperary*, Nenagh, 2000.

Gray, P., *Famine, Land and politics: British government and Irish society, 1843–1850*, Dublin, 1999.

Griffiths, A. R. G., 'The Irish Board of Works in the famine years', *Historical Journal*, xiii, no. 4, Dec. 1970, pp. 646–53.

Grosh, J.,'How Fr Harte became a priest', *The Month*, 131, no 6, Jan. – Jun. 1918, p. 20.

Guinnane, T. W., *The vanishing Irish: households, migration, and the rural economy in Ireland, 1850–1914*, New Jersey, 1997.

Gwynn, D., *A hundred years of Catholic Emancipation (1829–1929)*, London, 1929.

Hallissey, T., *Memoir of the Geological Survey of Ireland: mineral resources, barytes in Ireland*, 2 vols, Dublin, 1923.

Harris, R.-A. M. & Jacobs, D. M., *The search for missing friends, 1831–1850*, i, Boston, 1989.

Harris, R.-A. M. & O'Keeffe, B. E., *The search for missing friends, 1851–53*, ii, Boston, 1991.

Harris, R.-A. M., 'Searching for Missing Friends in the Boston *Pilot* Newspaper, 1831–1863', in *The Irish diaspora*, edited by A. Bielenberg, London, 2000.

Hickey, P., 'Invasion' and 'Rebellion': Mizen Peninsula 1796–98', *Mizen Journal*, 1998, pp. 18–20.

Hickey, P., 'Famine, mortality and emigration: a profile of six parishes in the Poor Law Union of Skibbereen, 1846–7' in *Cork: history and society*, edited by O'Flanagan, P. & Buttimer, C. G., Dublin, 1993, pp. 873–918.

Hickey, P., 'Laurence O'Sullivan P.P., Goleen and Souper Sullivan by E. Harris', *Fold*, April 1986.

Hickey, P., 'J. M. Synge and his roots in West Cork', *CE*, 9 Feb. 1989.

Hickey, P., 'The visit of the artist, James Mahoney, to West Cork in 1847', *The O'Mahony Journal*, xx, 1992, pp. 26–32.

Hourihan, K., 'Rural settlement near Bantry', *Journal of the Bantry Historical Society*, no i, 1991, pp. 44–54.

Keenan, D. J., *The Catholic Church in the nineteenth-century – a sociological study*, Dublin, 1983.

Kennedy, L., Ell, P. S., Crawford, E. M. & Clarkson, L. A., *Mapping the Great Irish Famine*, Dublin, 1999.

Kenny, K., *The American Irish: a history*, Harlow, 2000.

Kerr, D. A., *'A nation of beggars?': priests, people and politics in famine Ireland*, Oxford, 1994.

Kerr, D. A., *The Catholic Church and the Famine*, Dublin, 1996.

Kinealy, C. & Parkhill, T. (eds), *The famine in Ulster*, Belfast, 1997.

Kinealy, C., *This great calamity: the Irish famine*, Dublin, 1994.

King, J. A., *The lumberman-farmers*, California, 1982.

Kingston, D., 'Tadhg an Asna and the Battle of the Big Goss', *Mizen Journal*, No. 7, 1999, pp. 87–92

Kinsella, A., *County Wexford in the famine years 1845–1849*, Enniscorthy, 1995.

Kissane, N., *The Irish Famine: a documentary history*, Dublin, 1995.

Lane, P. J., 'The Encumbered Estates Court, Ireland, 1948–49', *Economic and Social Review*, no. 3, Apr. 1972, pp. 30–5.

Larkin, E., 'The devotional revolution in Ireland, 1850–75', *The historical dimension of Irish Catholicism*, Dublin, 1997.

Lee, J., 'Marriage and population in Pre-famine Ireland', *Economic History Review*, ser. 2, xxi, no. 2, Aug. 1968, pp. 283–95.

Lee, J., 'On the accuracy of pre-Famine censuses' in *Irish population economy and society:*

essays in honour of the late K. H. Connell, edited by Goldstrom, J. M. & Clarkson, L. A., Oxford, 1981.

Lowe, W. J., 'Policing famine Ireland', *Eire Ireland*, xxix, no. 4, 1994, pp. 60–65.

MacArthur, W. P., 'Medical history of the famine' in *The Great Famine: studies in Irish history,* edited by Edwards, R. D., & Williams, T. D., New York, 1957, pp. 263–315.

MacDonagh, 'The catholic clergy and emigration during the famine', *Irish Historical Studies,* v, no. 17, Mar. 1956, pp. 287–342.

MacDonagh, O., *O'Connell: the life of Daniel O'Connell, 1775–1847,* London, 1991.

Mackey, M., 'An account of local famine relief in the parish of Kilmoe 1847–1848', *Mizen Journal,* no. 7, 1999, pp. 50–73.

Mackey, M., 'Schull workhouse', *Mizen Journal,* no. 4, 1996, pp. 43–55.

MacSuibhne, M., *Famine in Muskerry: an Drochshaol,* Midleton, 1997.

MacSuibhne, P. (ed.), *Paul Cullen and his contemporaries,* 5 vols, Naas, 1961–77.

Marnane D. G., 'The famine in South Tipperary – part five', *Tipperary Historical Journal 2000,* pp. 73–119.

Maurice, J. F., (ed.) *Sir John Moore, Diary,* London, 1904.

McCarthy, B.G., 'Black Eagle of the North; the story of Archdeacon John Murphy', *Studies,* xxxviii, no. 1, Mar. 1949, pp. 53–8.

McCarthy, P. & Hawkes, R., *Northside of the Mizen,* Dublin, 1999.

McClaughin, T., 'Lost children? Irish Famine orphans in Australia', *History Ireland,* viii, no. 4, 2000, pp. 30–4.

Miller, D. W. 'Mass attendance in Ireland' in *Piety and power in Ireland 1760–1960: essays in honour of Emmet Larkin,* edited by Browne, S. J. & Miller, D. W., Belfast, 2000.

Miller, K. A., 'Revenge for Skibbereen': Irish emigration and the meaning of the Great Famine' in *The Famine and the Irish diaspora in America,* edited by A. Gribben, Boston, 1999.

Miller, K. A., *Emigrants and exiles: Ireland and the Irish exodus to North America,* New York and Oxford, 1985.

Mokyr, J., *Why Ireland starved: a quantitative and analytical history of the Irish economy, 1800–50,* London, 1985.

Murphy, I., 'Children in the Kilrush Union during the famine', *North Munster Antiquarian Journal,* xxiv, 1982, p.80.

Murphy, I., 'Kilkee and its neighbourhood during the second year of the great famine', *North Munster Antiquarian Journal,* xxiii, 1981, p. 87.

Murphy, I., 'Some attitudes to religious freedom and ecumenism in Pre-Emancipation Ireland', *Irish Ecclesiastical Record,* no. 1178, fifth series, cv, no. 2, Feb. 1966, p. 93.

Murphy, I., *A people starved: life and death in west Clare, 1845–1851,* Dublin, 1996.

Murphy, J. H., 'The role of Vincentian parish missions', *Irish Historical Studies,* xxiv, no. 94, November 1984, pp. 154–60.

Nic Craith, M., *Malartú teanga: An Gaeilge i gCorcaigh sa naoú haois déag,* Bremen, 1994.

Nolan, K. B., 'The political background' in *The great famine: studies in Irish history,* edited by Edwards, R. D. & Williams, T. D., New York, 1957.

Ó Beoláin, A., 'Rev. Canon James Goodman 1826–1896, Séamus Goodman: a shaol agus a shaothar' in *An Canónach Goodman,* edited by Ó Fiannachta, P., Baile an Fhirtéaraigh, 1990, pp. 45–69.

Ó Cathaoir, B., *Famine Diary,* Dublin, 1999.

Ó Cathaoir, E., 'The Poor Law in County Wicklow' in *Wicklow: history and society,* edited by Hannigan, K. & Nolan,W., Dublin, 1994, pp. 503–8.

Ó Ciosáin, N., 'Dia, bia agus Sasana: An Mistéalach agus íomhá an Ghorta' in *Gnéithe den nGorta*, edited by Póirtéir, C., Dublin, 1995, pp. 151–163.

Ó Ciosáin, N. (introd.), *Poverty before the Famine: County Clare 1835*, Ennis, 1996.

Ó Coindealbháin, S., 'The United Irishmen in County Cork', *JCHAS*, lvi, 1951, pp. 17–25.

Ó Conchúir, B., 'Thomas Swanton, *Réamhchonraitheoir in Iar-Chairbre*', *JCHAS*, vol. 98, 1993, pp. 50–60.

Ó Cróinín S. & D., *Seanchas Ó Chairbre*, Dublin, 1885.

Ó Cúiv, B., 'Irish language and literature 1691–1845' in *A New History of Ireland*, iv, edited by Moody, T. W. & Vaughan, W. E., Oxford, pp. 360–381.

Ó Dalaigh, M., 'Tadhg na Samhna Mac Cáraigh', *Seanchas Chairbhe*, Dec., 1982, pp. 1–5.

Ó Fiannachta, P. (eag.), *An gorta mór*, An Daingean, 1997.

Ó Fiannachta, P., 'Corca Dhuibhne le linn Shéamais Goodman' in *An Canónach Goodman*, edited by Ó Fiannachta, P., Baile an Fhirtéaraigh, 1990, pp. 13–36.

Ó Gráda, C., 'Poverty, population and agriculture' in *A New History of Ireland*, v, *Ireland under the Union*, i, *1801–70*, edited by Vaughan, W. E., Oxford, 1989, pp. 108–136.

Ó Gráda, C., *Ireland before and after the famine*, Manchester, 1988.

Ó Gráda, C., *Ireland: a new economic history, 1780–1939*, Oxford, 1994.

Ó Gráda, C., *An Drochshaol: Béaloideas agus Amhráin*, Dublin, 1994.

Ó Gráda, C., 'New perspectives on the Irish famine', *Bullán*, iii, no. 2 (1997–98), pp. 15–19.

Ó Gráda, C., *Black '47 and beyond: the great Irish famine in history, economy, and memory*, New Jersey, 1999.

Ó Lúing, 'Richard Griffith and the roads in Kerry', *Journal of the Kerry Archaeological and Historical Society*, no. 8, 1975, pp. 89–113.

Ó Maidín, P., 'Patriot and benefactor in West Cork' [Timothy McCarthy Downing], *Cork Examiner*, 11 Jan. 1977.

Ó Maidín, P., 'Pococke's tour of the south and south-east Ireland in 1757', *JCHAS*, lxxviii, 1958, pp. 70–81.

Ó Mainín, M. '*Bíoblóireacht agus gorta*' in *An gorta mór*, edited by Ó Fiannachta, P., An Daingean, 1997.

Ó Mainín, M., 'Achrann chreidimn in Iarthar Dhuibhneach' in *Céad bliain*, edited by Ó Ciosáin, Baile an Fheirtéaraig, 1970.

Ó Murchada, C., *Sable wings over the land: Ennis, Co. Clare, and its wider community during the Great Famine*, Ennis, 1998.

Ó Riain, P., Séamus Ó Súilleabháin, bíoblóir, *Studia Hibernica*, no 8, 1968, pp. 96–105.

Ó hÚrdail, R. 'An Pleantéir agus an Gael Díshealbhaithe: Seán Pocslí agus Mortí Óg Ó Súilleabháin, etc.' in *Saoi na hÉigse: Aistí in ómós do Sheán Ó Tuama, Féilscríbhinn Sheáin Uí Thuama*, 2000, pp. 105–151.

O'Brien, G., *The economic history of Ireland from the union to the famine*, London, 1921.

O'Brien, J., 'Agricultural prices and living costs in pre-famine Cork', *JCHAS*, lxxxii, no. 235, Jan.–Jun., 1977, pp. 1–10.

O'Brien, W., ' A primative mining complex at Derrycarhoon, Co. Cork, *JCHAS*, xciv, no. 253, 1998, pp. 1–18.

O'Brien, W., *Mount Gabriel: Bronze Age mining in Ireland*, Cork, 1994.

O'Connor, J., *The workhouses of Ireland*, Dublin, 1995.

O'Donovan, J., *The economic history of livestock in Ireland*, Cork, 1940.

O'Donovan, M., 'Goleen (Kilmoe) parish in famine times', *Mizen Journal*, no. 6, 1998, pp. 56–70.

O'Donovan, M., 'Ballinskea Church', *Mizen Journal*, no. 4, 1996, p. 64–8.

O'Flanagan, P., 'Three hundred years of urban life: villages and towns in County Cork c. 1600–1901', O'Flanagan & Buttimer, *Cork: history and society*, pp. 391–468.

O'Gallagher, M., *Grosse Île: gateway to Canada*, Quebec, 1984.

O'Keefe, P. J., 'Richard Griffith, planner and builder of roads' in *Griffith*, edited by Davies, G. L. & Mollan, R. C., Dublin, 1980.

O'Kelly, E., *The old private banks and bankers of Munster*, part one, *Bankers of Cork and Limerick cities*, Cork, 1959.

O'Mahony, J., 'The O'Mahonys of Kinelmeky and Ivagh', *JCHAS*, xvi, 1910, pp. 9–39.

O'Mahony, J., *West Cork and its story*, Cork, 1975.

O'Mahony, P. T., 'Surviving the Famine: one townland's experience on the Mizen Peninsula', *Mizen Journal*, no. 8, 2000, pp. 60–67.

O'Neill, F., *Irish minstrels and musicians*, Chicago, 1913.

O'Neill, T. P., 'Food problems during the great Irish famine', *Journal of the Royal Society of Antiquaries of Ireland*, lxxxii, 1952, pp. 99–108.

O'Neill, T. P., 'Sidelights on souperism', *Irish ecclesiastical record*, lxxxi, Jan.–Jun., 1949, pp. 46–51.

O'Neill, T. P., 'The organisation and administration of relief' in *The Great Irish Famine*, edited by Edwards, R. D. & Williams, T. D., Dublin 1956, p. 209–54.

O'Neill, T. P., 'The famine in Offaly' in *Offaly history and society*, edited by Nolan, W. & O'Neill, T. P., Dublin, 1998.

O'Neill, T. P., 'The Society of Friends and the Great Famine', *Studies*, xxxiv, no. 154, 1951, pp. 203–213.

O'Neill, T. P., 'Minor famines and relief in County Galway, 1815–1925' in *Galway: history and society*, edited by Moran, G. & Gillespie, R., Dublin, 1996, pp. 444–481.

O'Regan, L., 'Anna Parnell in West Cork', *Southern Star*, 23 Nov. 1991.

O'Regan, L., 'The Castle Island evictions', *Mizen Journal*, no. 6, 1998, pp. 121–128.

O'Regan, L., 'O'Donovan Rossa and his brief marriage with Ellen Buckley', *Mizen Journal*, no. 7, 1999, pp. 124–132.

O'Reilly, T. A., 'Richard Griffith and the Cappagh mining fraud' in *Griffith*, edited by Davies, G. L. & Mollan, R. C., Dublin, 1980, pp. 197–210.

O'Rourke, J. *History of the great Irish famine of 1847 with notice of earlier famines*, Dublin, 1875.

O'Shea, K., 'In the line of duty: priests who ministered to the Famine victims' in *The Famine in Kerry*, edited by Costello, M., Tralee, 1997, pp. 8–31.

O'Shea, K., 'The nuns in Kerry: the unsung heroines of the Famine' in *The Famine in Kerry*, edited by Costello, M., Tralee, 1997, pp. 55–57.

Pike, W. P., (ed.), *Contemporary biographies, R. J. Hodges, Cork and county in the twentieth century*, Brighton, 1911.

Póirtéir, C., *Famine echoes*, Dublin, 1995.

Póirtéir, C., *Glórtha ón nGorta*, Dublin, 1995.

Póirtéir, C., *Gnéithe den nGorta*, Dublin, 1995.

Póirtéir, C. (ed.), *The Great Irish Famine*, Mercier Press, Cork, 1995.

Quigley, E. J., 'Grace abounding, a chapter in Irish history', *Irish ecclesiastical record*, xx, July–Dec. 1922, pp. 561–6.

Reilly, A. J., *Fr John Murphy, famine priest*, Dublin, 1963.

Reilly, T. & Cowman, D., 'Cappagh Mine, an endangered heritage site', *Mizen Journal*, no. 6, 1998, pp. 163–176.

Robins, J. A., *Irish orphan emigration to Australia, 1848–1850*, *Studies*, lvii, 1968, 374–9.

Scott, C. W., *History of the Fastnet lighthouses*, Schull, 1993 ed.

Somerville-Large, *The coast of West Cork*, London, 1974.

Stark, A. G., '*The south of Ireland in 1850, being the journal of a tour in Leinster and Munster*, Dublin, 1850.

Trevelyan, G. M., *British history in the nineteenth century and after: 1782–1919*, London, 1965.

Vaughan, W. E. (ed.), *A New History of Ireland*, v, pt 1, *Ireland under the Union, i, 1801–70*, Oxford, 1989.

Went, A. E. J., 'Pilchards in the south of Ireland', *JCHAS*, i, 1946, pp. 144–6.

Went, A. E. J., 'Sir William Hull's losses in 1641', *JCHAS*, iii, 1947, pp. 55–68.

Whalen, J. M., 'Allmost as Bad as Ireland': the experience of the Irish famine immigrant in Canada, St John, 1847' in *The untold story: the Irish in Canada*, edited by O'Driscoll, R. & Reynolds, L., Ontario, 1988.

Whelan, I., 'Edward Nangle and the Achill Mission, 1834–52' in '*A various country': Essays in Mayo history, 1500–1900*, edited by Gillespie, R. & Moran, G., Westport, 1987, pp. 113–134.

Whelan, I., 'The stigma of souperism' in Póirtéir, C., *The Great Irish Famine*, Cork, 1995, pp. 135–154.

Whelan, K., 'Pre- and post-Famine landscape change' in Póirtéir, C., *The Great Irish Famine*, Cork, 1995, pp. 19–33.

Whelan, K., 'The Catholic parish, the Catholic chapel and village development in Ireland', *Irish Geography*, xvi, 1983, pp. 1–15.

White, J. H., 'Political problems, 1850–60' in *A history of Irish Catholicism*, edited by P. J. Corish, Dublin and Melbourne, 1969.

Whyte, J. H., 'The influence of the Catholic clergy in elections in nineteenth century Ireland', *English Historical Review*, lxxv, 1970, pp. 239–59.

Whyte, J. H., *The independent Irish Party, 1850–59*, Oxford, 1958.

Williams, R. A., *The Berehaven Copper mines*, Sheffield, 1991.

Woodham-Smith, *The great hunger, Ireland 1845–49*, London, 1962.

UNPUBLISHED DISSERTATIONS

Hickey, P., 'A study of four peninsular parishes in West Cork, 1796–1855' (MA, UCC, 1980).

O'Neill, T. P., 'The Famine of 1822' (MA, NUI/UCD, 1965).

REFERENCE

Battersby, W. J., *The complete Catholic directory* … , Dublin, 1836–52.

Brady, W. M., *Clerical and parochial records of Cork, Cloyne and Ross*, 3 vols, Dublin, 1863.

Burke, J. & J. B., *A genealogical and heraldic dictionary of the landed gentry of Great Britain and Ireland*, 3 vols, London, 1843–9.

Cole, J. H., *Church and parish records of the united dioceses of Cork, Cloyne and Ross*, Cork, 1903.

Lewis, S., *Topographical dictionary of Ireland*, 2 vols with atlas, London, 1837.

Parliamentary Gazetter for Ireland, 1843–44, The, vols i–iii.

411

Kilmeen, 50

Kilmichael, 40, 337–8

Kilmoe, parish: 13, faction fights, 35; rents high in 41; population, 42; 1822 famine in, 43–5; parish and hedge schools, 76; Great Famine road-making, 159, 161; famine and fever, 168–9

Kilmurry, 337–8

Kilrush, 45

Kinealy, Christine, 206

King, John and Ellen, 236

King, Mr, 188

King, William, 238

Kingsley, Charles, 197

Kingsmill, Admiral, 21

Kinmare, 45, 329

Kinsale, 14, 18, 313

Koch, Robert, 220

Kyle, J. T., 346

Kyle, Samuel, Bishop of Cork, Cloyne and Ross, 67, 250

Labouchere Letter, 157

Labour Rate Act, 148, 154, 157, 176, 200, 208

Labourers, emigrated after 1822 disturbances, 61; and sickness, 103–104; unemployed, 105; migrant, 105–6; evicted farmers became, 116; pre-famine, 96, 121–2; farmers harder on than landlords on the farmers, 148; wages of, 166; extermination of, 169, 172, 173; protest at Skibbereen, 144, 153, Goleen, 153, Ballydehob, 156, Crookhaven, 188; numbers employed on roads, 154; discharged, 162, 200; reduced in numbers, 192; very poor in Drimoleague and Drinagh, outrage against farmer, 218–9

Ladd, Captain, 191

Ladies' Association, Ballydehob, secretary, Jane Noble, 167; aided pregnant women, 170; complimented by Bishop, 171; given food and clothes by Harston, 179, 191; meets Trench, 193

Ladies' Association, British, 167

Ladies' Association, Schull, 191

Ladies' Relief Association, Cork, 167, 170

Ladies' Society, Cork, 48

Lady Charlotte, 127

Lady Harriett, 127

Laharn, 189

Lake, General, 24, 26

Lalor O'Shea, John, 111, 112, 174

Lalor Sheil, Richard, 61

Lalor, James Fintan, 272–3, 296

Lamphier, Joseph, Rev., 254

Lamprey, Dr, 195, 197, 199

Landlords (*see also* evictions), improvement, 115–8, 122–3; Traill refuses to expose, 146; little hope of subscriptions from, 148; defaulting, Barry and Traill on, 146; 'niggardly subscription' from, 148; on road-making, 151; blamed for death of labourer, 156; receive little rent, 168; absentees, 161; of Schull, denounced by Kelliher, 283; blamed for pauperism, 294; accused of murder by Russell, 305; intimidation at election, 308

Lane, P. J., 304

Lang, Capt., 292

Langford, Francis, 57, 97

Larcom, Thomas, 148, 293, 318

Larkin, Emmet, 243

Lavelle, Patrick, Fr, 232

Lawton, Hugh, 51

Leader, Nicholas, 207

League, Gaelic, 308, 313

Leamcon, 13, 15, 30, 39, 267

Leap, 157, 286

Lecky, William, 112

Lee, Ann Marie, 48, 167, 170

Lee, Eliza, 238

Lee, J., Rev., 349

Lee, Joseph, 130, 131, 337, 340

Leicesters, 115

Letter, 159

Leviathan, 225, 226

Liebig, Justin, 115

Lighthouses and Signal Towers, 30

Limerick (City), 41

Limerick (County), 34, 37, 42, 57, 141

Limrick, John, praises Traill's potato pit, 143; obtains food supplies, 154; on cattle stealing, 161; on food imports, 162; thanks Society of Friends, 163; efforts only drop in ocean, 169; food supplies delayed by wind, 170; complimented by Barry, 189; supplies boilers, 191; meets Trench, 194; accepts Marshall's Return, 211; accused of seizing cattle, 274; buys some Audley mines, 305; on responsibility for famine, 349–50

Limrick, Paul, 17

Lindley, John, 141

Lisburn (Co. Antrim), 43

Lisgould, 199

Lisheen, 72, 80

Lissacaha, 65, 76, 158

Lissigriffin, 39, 76, 159

Lissydonnell, 308

Listowel Bridge, 54

Liverpool, 44, 226

London Metropolitan Police, 37

London Tavern Committee, relieves 1822 famine, 43, 44; sends potatoes, 45; supports road-making, 46; visitors from 46–47; success of relief measures, 46–47; supplies clothes, 48–49; promotes fishing, 48

Long Island, seized by Normans 13; pirates on 14; ship shelters at, 21; ship plundered at, 31; arms taken from ship at, 34; cargo of precious metals wrecked on, 127; famine-relief ship near, 176, 179; Driscoll emigrated from, 322

Long, Michael, 31

Longhorns, 115

Longueville, Lord, 21

Looshtauk, 226

Loughlinstown, Co. Dublin, 343

Loughtrasna, 127

Love, Mr, 46

Love, Robin, 238

Lovell, John, 351

Lowe, W. J., 351–2

Lower, Arthur, 132

Lowertown (bridges), 54

Lucas, Frederick, 234, 306, 308

Luke, Matthew, 87